PCs All-in-One Desk Reference For Dummies, 3rd Edition

D0764880

Windows XP Window Key Shortcuts

Key	Function
Win	Displays (or hides) the Start menu
Win+D	Displays the XP desktop
Win+E	Opens a Windows Explorer window
Win+F	Displays the Search window for files and folders
Win+Ctrl+F	Displays the Search window for computers
Win+L	Displays the Welcome/Logon screen
Win+M	Minimizes all open windows
Win+Shift+M	Restores all windows minimized with Win+M
Win+R	Opens the Run dialog box
Win+U	Displays the Utility Manager
Win+F1	Displays Windows XP Help
Win+Break	Displays the System dialog box

Mark's Windows XP Maintenance Checklist

Task	Schedule
Check for updates with Windows Update	Once a day/automatically
Check all hard drives for errors	Once a week
Run Disk Cleanup Wizard	Once a week
Defragment all hard drives	Once a month
Manually scan for viruses (Norton AntiVirus)	Once a month
Back up your hard drives	Once a month (at a minimum)
Check for latest video and sound card drivers	Once a month
Check Device Manager for hardware problems	Once a month

For Dummies: Bestselling Book Series for Beginners

PCs All-in-One Desk Reference For Dummies, 3rd Edition

Cheat Sheet

Favorite PC Power User Web Sites

Name	Address	Description
Tom's Hardware Guide	www.tomshardware.com	PC hardware news and reviews
Pricewatch	www.pricewatch.com	Compare hardware prices
Microsoft Download Center	www.microsoft.com/downloads	Latest Office/Works downloads
WindowsXP-Drivers.com	www.windowsxp-drivers.com	XP driver archive for all hardware
Windows XP Expert Zone	www.microsoft.com/windowsxp/expertzone	XP tips and tricks from Microsoft
PC World Online	www.pcworld.com	Online edition of PC World
Dilbert.com	www.dilbert.com	Computer humor at its best

Mark's Common Format Guide

Name or Extension	Type of File	Good For
AAC	Audio	Playing music from Apple's iTunes Music Store
AVI	Video	Playing video clips on any PC with Windows 98/Me/2000/XP
BMP	Image	Archival storage of images on CD or DVD
JPEG	Image	Sending photos through e-mail or displaying on the Web
MOV	Video	Playing video clips on PCs and Macs
MP3	Audio	Playing music on your hard drive or MP3 player
MPEG	Video	Playing video clips on PCs, Macs, and Linux computers
PDF	Document	Sharing and printing high-quality documents online
PNG	Image	Best format for displaying images on a Web page
RAR	Archive	Archiving and compressing multiple files into one file
TIFF	Image	Sharing files between PCs, Macs, and Linux computers
WAV	Audio	Sound effects within Windows XP
ZIP	Archive	Archiving and compressing multiple files into one file

For Dummies: Bestselling Book Series for Beginners

PCs
ALL-IN-ONE DESK REFERENCE
FOR
DUMMIES®
3RD EDITION

PCs
ALL-IN-ONE DESK REFERENCE
FOR
DUMMIES®
3RD EDITION

by Mark L. Chambers

WILEY

Wiley Publishing, Inc.

PCs All-in-One Desk Reference For Dummies, 3rd Edition

Published by
Wiley Publishing, Inc.
111 River Street
Hoboken, NJ 07030-5774

www.wiley.com

For general information on our other products and services, please contact our Customer Care Department within the U.S. at 800-762-2974, outside the U.S. at 317-572-3993, or fax 317-572-4002.

For technical support, please visit www.wiley.com/techsupport.

Wiley also publishes its books in a variety of electronic formats. Some content that appears in print may not be available in electronic books.

Library of Congress Control Number: 2005936634

ISBN-13: 978-0-471-77082-4

ISBN-10: 0-471-77082-5

Manufactured in the United States of America

10   9   8   7   6   5   4   3   2   1

3B/RT/QR/QW/IN

WILEY

About the Author

Mark L. Chambers has been an author, computer consultant, BBS sysop, programmer, and hardware technician for more than 20 years — pushing computers and their uses far beyond "normal" performance limits for decades now. His first love affair with a computer peripheral blossomed in 1984 when he bought his lightning-fast 300 BPS modem for his Atari 400. Now he spends entirely too much time on the Internet and drinks far too much caffeine-laden soda.

With a degree in journalism and creative writing from Louisiana State University, Mark took the logical career choice: programming computers. However, after five years as a COBOL programmer for a hospital system, he decided there must be a better way to earn a living, and he became the Documentation Manager for Datastorm Technologies, a well-known communications software developer. Somewhere in between writing software manuals, Mark began writing computer how-to books. His first book, *Running a Perfect BBS*, was published in 1994 — and after a short decade or so of fun (disguised as hard work), Mark is one of the most productive and best-selling technology authors on the planet.

Along with writing several books a year and editing whatever his publishers throw at him, Mark has also branched out into Web-based education, designing and teaching a number of online classes — called *WebClinics* — for Hewlett-Packard.

His favorite pastimes include collecting gargoyles, watching St. Louis Cardinals baseball, playing his three pinball machines and the latest computer games, supercharging computers, and rendering 3-D flights of fancy with TrueSpace — and during all that, he listens to just about every type of music imaginable. Mark's popular world-wide Internet radio station, *MLC Radio* (at www.mlcbooks.com), plays only CD-quality classics from 1970 to 1979, including everything from Rush to Billy Joel to the *Rocky Horror Picture Show*.

Mark's rapidly expanding list of books includes *iMac For Dummies,* Fourth Edition; *Mac OS X Tiger All-In-One Desk Reference For Dummies; Building a PC For Dummies,* Fifth Edition; *Scanners For Dummies,* Second Edition; *CD & DVD Recording For Dummies,* Second Edition; *PCs All-In-One Desk Reference For Dummies,* Second Edition; *Mac OS X Tiger: Top 100 Simplified Tips & Tricks; Microsoft Office v. X Power User's Guide; BURN IT! Creating Your Own Great DVDs and CDs; The Hewlett-Packard Official Printer Handbook; The Hewlett-Packard Official Recordable CD Handbook; The Hewlett-Packard Official Digital Photography Handbook; Computer Gamer's Bible; Recordable CD Bible; Teach Yourself the iMac Visually; Running a Perfect BBS; Official Netscape Guide to Web Animation;* and the *Windows 98 Troubleshooting and Optimizing Little Black Book.*

His books have been translated into 14 different languages so far — his favorites are German, Polish, Dutch, and French. Although he can't read them, he enjoys the pictures a great deal.

Mark welcomes all comments and questions about his books. You can reach him at mark@mlcbooks.com, or visit MLC Books Online, his Web site, at www.mlcbooks.com.

Dedication

This book is dedicated to my daughter in-between, Chelsea Chambers — fashion designer, mathematician, and audiophile — with all my love.

Author's Acknowledgments

Books don't produce themselves — and no book that I've written is complete without a round of sincere thanks (and applause) that's due to everyone involved!

First, my appreciation to my technical editor, Vinay Veeramachaneni, who spent weeks checking every fact and verifying every menu choice in this book. I do a lot of technical editing myself, and I can tell you that it's no simple task to wade through this many chapters . . . it takes a combination of long nights and lots of soda.

This is my fourth All-in-One Desk Reference For Dummies volume, and again, the Wiley Composition Services team has outdone itself in designing and preparing the material. All the beautiful formatting in this book (including every single figure and screen shot, all the step-by-step procedures, and the regular appearances of Mark's Maxims) is a testament to this team's hard work.

As with all my books, I'd like to thank my wife, Anne, and my children, Erin, Chelsea, and Rose, for their support and love — and for letting me follow my dream!

And I won't forget the support, the patience, and the guidance of Tiffany Franklin, my Acquisitions Editor, and Mark Enochs, my Project Editor. Tiffany, I hope I kept any headaches to a minimum, even with a tome this size. And Mark, you deserve a parade for helping me deliver two monster books in a row! My heartfelt thanks to you both.

Publisher's Acknowledgments

We're proud of this book; please send us your comments through our online registration form located at www.dummies.com/register/.

Some of the people who helped bring this book to market include the following:

Acquisitions, Editorial, and Media Development

Project Editor: Mark Enochs

(Previous Edition: Rebecca Huehls)

Acquisitions Editors: Terri Varveris, Tiffany Franklin

Copy Editor: Heidi Unger

Technical Editor: Vinay Veeramachaneni

Editorial Managers: Leah Cameron, Kevin Kirschner

Media Development Manager: Laura VanWinkle

Editorial Assistant: Amanda Foxworth

Cartoons: Rich Tennant (www.the5thwave.com)

Composition Services

Coordinator: Adrienne Martinez

Layout and Graphics: Andrea Dahl, Stephanie D. Jumper, Barbara Moore, Heather Ryan, Melanee Prendergast, Julie Trippetti

Proofreaders: Mildred Rosenzweig, Leeann Harney, Joe Niesen

Indexer: Broccoli Information Management

Special Help: Jean Rogers, Andy Hollandbeck, Teresa Artman

Publishing and Editorial for Technology Dummies

Richard Swadley, Vice President and Executive Group Publisher

Andy Cummings, Vice President and Publisher

Mary Bednarek, Executive Acquisitions Director

Mary C. Corder, Editorial Director

Publishing for Consumer Dummies

Diane Graves Steele, Vice President and Publisher

Joyce Pepple, Acquisitions Director

Composition Services

Gerry Fahey, Vice President of Production Services

Debbie Stailey, Director of Composition Services

Contents at a Glance

Table of Contents

Introduction

What's the definition of a reference book? Well, I like to think of this book as a snapshot. Sure, it's a very *heavy* photograph, weighing in at over 700 pages — but nevertheless, it captures the current state of today's PCs, including hardware, the most popular applications, and of course, the latest and greatest incarnation of the Windows operating system that we all cherish (in this case, Windows XP Home and Professional).

That covers a lot of ground, especially when you consider how the PC has branched out into all sorts of new directions in the last few years. What used to be primarily a simple word processing platform in the early days of DOS has now become a hub for digital video and CD-quality audio, an optical recording center, an Internet communications system, a digital darkroom, a 3-D gaming console, an office productivity center . . . the list goes on and on. Therefore, fitting the features and functionality of today's PCs into a single volume was a challenge for me — and it proved singularly rewarding as well because PCs are both my career and my favorite hobby!

With that comprehensive approach in mind, this book still holds true to the *For Dummies* format: step-by-step instructions on each major feature within Windows XP, Microsoft Office 2003, and other popular PC applications, with a little personal opinion, my recommendations, and my attempts at humor mixed in to add spice. I take the time to explain each topic for those who have just entered the PC universe, but you'll uncover plenty of advanced information as well. With this book in hand, you can set up a wireless network, navigate an Excel spreadsheet, diagnose hardware problems, and even work magic with your digital camera.

I sincerely hope that you enjoy this book and that it will help open up the countless possibilities offered by your PC. Thanks to the efforts of all those software developers, engineers, and hardware manufacturers, you and I get to play!

What's Really Required

Here's a short section for you — you need a PC, preferably running Windows XP.

(I told you it was short.)

What's Not Required

If you've read any of my earlier books, you already know the score. But just in case you haven't (hint, hint), here's the list of what you *won't* be needing:

✦ **A degree in computer science:** Computers are *supposed* to be *easy*. I like 'em that way, and I get very testy when faced with anyone who tries to make a PC artificially complex. 'Nuff said.

✦ **All sorts of expensive software:** Because Microsoft Office 2003 is so doggone popular, I cover it here — but virtually everything else is either included in Windows XP or is cheap to get.

✦ **An Internet connection:** Some folks should be reminded that PCs are quite productive by themselves. Naturally, you need an Internet connection to use Internet Explorer and Outlook Express, but you **don't have to be online** to enjoy your computer.

About This Book

Each of the eight mini-books in this Desk Reference squarely addresses a specific topic, and there's no need to read this whole book in a linear fashion. You certainly can, if you like, but it's not necessary. Instead, each mini-book (and on a lower level, each individual chapter) has been designed to be self contained. You can jump from chapter to chapter, pursuing information on what you're working on right now — and happy in the knowledge that when you *do* decide to invest in a digital camera (or a scanner or a memory upgrade), it's covered!

Conventions Used in This Book

Like other *For Dummies* books, this volume uses a helpful set of conventions to indicate what needs to be done or what you'll see onscreen.

Stuff that you type

When I ask you to type something, like a command or an entry in a text box, the text appears like this:

Type me

Press the Return key to process the entry.

Menu commands

When I give you a specific set of menu commands to use, they appear in the following format:

    Edit⇨Copy

In this example, you should click the Edit menu and then choose the Copy menu item.

Display messages

If I mention a specific message that you see on your screen, it looks like this on the page:

`This is a message displayed by an application.`

How This Book Is Organized

Time for a quick summary of what's included in those eight mini-books (with cross-references where appropriate, included at great expense).

Book 1: PC Hardware

It's not a PC without the hardware. In this mini-book, I discuss both the standard equipment (like your monitor, keyboard, and mouse) and optional things that you can attach (like a scanner or a game controller). I also cover the different ports on your PC and the proper methods of maintaining your PC hardware.

Book 11: Windows XP

A mini-book for the XP generation — with everything that you need to know about today's most popular PC operating system, including the basics, advanced customizing topics, the included applications, maintenance, and (insert ominous chord here) . . . *troubleshooting*.

Book 111: The Internet

The obligatory Internet stuff fills this mini-book. Discover how to navigate the Web, block that infernal spam from your e-mail, fritter away countless hours with instant messaging, and — most important — keep yourself secure while you're online.

Book IV: Microsoft Works

Most people call Works 8 "the programs I got with my PC." But as you discover in this mini-book, there's no shortage of features or functionality within Works (even though it's usually overshadowed by the behemoth that is Microsoft Office 2003). You'll find out how to use each of the Works applications and how to use them in tandem to accomplish tasks.

Book V: Office 2003

Okay, so I decided to cover the behemoth as well. The major components of Microsoft Office 2003 comprise Word, Excel, PowerPoint, Access, and Outlook — and the gang's all here, with each application covered in a separate chapter. If you use Office 2003, you'll treasure this mini-book — if not, you'll still enjoy it as a spellbinding work of nonfiction. (Sure, Mark.)

Book VI: Fun with Movies, Music, and Photos

Your PC is now a digital, multimedia production center — and a great combination for watching video and listening to music, to boot. In this mini-book, I show you the latest cutting-edge fun that you can have with your DV camcorder, your MP3 player, and your digital camera . . . wait until you show your home movies on DVD!

Book VII: Upgrading and Supercharging

The gloves come off in this mini-book: If you're hankering to turn the corner and become a PC power user, use these chapters to help you upgrade your PC's hardware, including your system RAM, your CPU and motherboard, your graphics card, and even external connections like USB 2.0 and FireWire. "To the Batcave!"

Book VIII: Home Networking

The final mini-book is devoted to one of the fastest-growing segments of the PC population — those folks who are adding a home (or small office) network. In these chapters, I demonstrate how to install your own wired network as well as how to expand with the latest wireless technology. Then I turn your attention to security so that you can use your network without fear of intrusion.

Icons Used in This Book

In a book stuffed to the gills with icons, my editors have decided to use — you guessed it — *more icons*. Luckily, however, the book's icon set acts as visual signposts for specific stuff that you don't want to miss.

Okay, so Mark's Maxims aren't marked with an icon, per se. However, they represent way-important stuff, so I call your attention to these nuggets in bold, like this:

> **These are My Favorite Recommendations — in fact, I'll bet just about any PC power user would tell you the same. Follow my Maxims, and you'll avoid the quicksand and pitfalls that I've encountered with all sorts of PCs!™**

A Tip icon points to a sentence or two that might save you time, trouble, and quite possibly cash as well.

Consider these tidbits completely optional, but if you're captivated by things technical — as I am — you'll find trivia of interest here. (A good feature for those who enjoy cutaway drawings of the Titanic and those who actually know what JPEG means.)

Speaking of the Titanic, *always* read the information next to this icon first! Your PC is usually a very safe harbor, but icebergs can appear from time to time if you're not careful.

These icons mark the latest and greatest in PC hardware — you'll usually pay a bit more, but you'll also enjoy faster performance!

As you might expect from its name, this icon highlights stuff that you might want to, well, remember.

Book I

PC Hardware

"I think the cursor's not moving, Mr. Dunt, because you've got your hand on the chalk board eraser and not the mouse."

Contents at a Glance

Chapter 1: Starting with the Basics

In This Chapter

- Defining hardware, software, and peripherals
- Identifying the common components of all PCs
- Comparing desktop and laptop PCs
- Understanding RAM and your PC's CPU
- Defining the operating system

If your name is Hemingway or Faulkner or King, the first chapter is always the toughest to write. For me, however, this chapter will be fun to write because it tackles the basic questions, such as what components make up your PC and why you need an operating system. You'll discover more about the specific parts of your PC that determine how fast it is, and I also discuss the pros and cons of choosing a laptop over a desktop PC.

If you're a hardware technician or a PC power user, you might decide to eschew these basic concepts and move on . . . and that's okay. But if you're new to the world of IBM personal computers or you're going to buy your first PC, this chapter is a great place to start. In fact, you'd be amazed by how many folks I talk to who have owned a PC for a year or two and still don't know some of the terms that you'll read here!

Here's the first Mark's Maxim for this book:

> **It takes a solid foundation to build a power user.**™

So read on!

Defining Basic Terms

My high school chemistry teacher, a learned man whom I have always admired (even then), always told us, "Never jump into anything before defining your terms." (Thanks, Mr. Owen. Because of you, I succeeded in not blowing myself to pieces!)

Before you venture farther, commit these terms to memory, and you'll have taken a giant first step toward becoming a PC power user.

There's no reason to walk around with this stuff tattooed on your arm; you certainly don't need to know these technicalities just to check your e-mail or use Microsoft Word. However, when you grow more knowledgeable about Windows and your PC, you'll find that these terms crop up in your computer conversations more and more often.

Hardware

In the PC world, *hardware* is any piece of circuitry or any component of your computer that has a physical structure. For example, your computer's monitor is a piece of hardware, as is your PC's keyboard. Even those components that you normally can't see or touch — the ones that are buried inside your case — are considered hardware, too, like your PC's motherboard and power supply. (And yes, your computer's case is technically a piece of hardware as well, although it's not electrical.)

Figure 1-1 illustrates a common piece of hardware — in this case, a video card with an Accelerated Graphics Port (AGP) connector.

Figure 1-1: Hardware like this AGP video card is, well, hard.

Software

The other side of the PC coin is the software that you use. *Software* refers to any program that you run, whether it resides on your hard drive, a floppy disk, a CD or DVD disc, or somewhere on a network.

When you hear folks discussing a software *upgrade, patch,* or *update,* they're talking about (you guessed it) yet another piece of software! However, the upgrade/patch/update program isn't designed to be run more than once; rather, its job is to apply the latest features, bug fixes, and data files to a piece of software that's already installed and running on your PC, updating it to a new *version.* (Virtually all software developers refer to successive versions of their software, such as *Version 1.5* or *Version 3;* the later the version, the more features that the software includes.)

Typically, think of software as an application that you buy or download, such as Microsoft Works or Windows Media Player (see Figure 1-2). However, the term *software* actually applies to any program, including Windows itself and the driver programs that accompany the hardware that you buy. Unfortunately, computer viruses are software as well.

Figure 1-2:
You can listen to your MP3 music collection with software from Microsoft.

And software might be cheap!

You'll probably encounter two other types of "ware": freeware and shareware. *Freeware* is a program that's either been released into the public domain — in which case the author generally releases the programming code needed to modify it or maintains the rights to it — but you can still use it for free.

Shareware, on the other hand, is not free: You get to try it before you buy it; if you like it, you send your payment directly to the author. Because there's no middleperson (you won't

catch me using a sexist term) and you're not paying for an expensive box or advertising, shareware is usually far cheaper than a similar commercial program.

Before using freeware or shareware, check to make sure that the author offers regular updates. When you work for peanuts, you're not going to be able to afford a Quality Assurance Department or comprehensive beta testing!

From time to time, you might see the word *firmware* in a magazine or on a hardware manufacturer's Web site. This sounds like a strange beast, but I can explain: *Firmware* is the software instructions that you find stored in the internal memory or the internal brain of a piece of hardware, so it's not quite software, and it's not quite hardware. For example, your CD or DVD recorder has a firmware chip inside that controls the mundane tasks required to burn a disc — likewise, your video card's firmware contains instructions for all sorts of 3-D magic that can be turned on and off by those games you play. Generally, you won't have to fool with firmware, but a manufacturer might release a firmware upgrade to fix bugs that have cropped up with a piece of hardware (or even add new features). To upgrade firmware, you run a software utility program supplied by the manufacturer.

Peripherals

Peripherals comprise things that reside outside your PC's case, which can include all sorts of optional hardware. Examples include

- ✦ Printers
- ✦ External CD and DVD recorders (such as the model shown in Figure 1-3) and hard drives
- ✦ Web cams
- ✦ Graphics tablets
- ✦ Joysticks and other game controllers
- ✦ Network hardware such as Internet-sharing devices
- ✦ Scanners and digital cameras

Figure 1-3:
This external CD recorder peripheral enjoys sunshine and clean air.

TIP

I should point out that three pieces of external hardware that are found on every PC — your monitor, keyboard, and your mouse (or trackball or touchpad) — are generally *not* considered peripherals because they're required to operate your PC. Call 'em hardware instead.

Peripherals connect to your computer via the ports that are built into the back (and often the front) of your PC. I go into more detail on ports in Chapter 3 of this mini-book; any PC power user worthy of the name will be able to identify any common port on a computer on sight. (If you're a hardware technician, you can identify them in the dark, like how a soldier knows his weapon. Don't ask me why — I'm not at liberty to discuss it.)

The Common Components of a Desktop PC

"Aw, crikey . . . look what we have here, mates! This little beaut is a PC — step back now, mind ya, for if one of these digital guys goes bonkers, it'll spread itself all over yer bloomin' desktop!"

Although a PC is hardly a crocodile, your system can grow like one — and it can become just as unwieldy and tough to move. Turn your attention to the components that you'll find equipped on just about any PC that you buy (or assemble) these days.

The computer

The computer itself is housed in a case, which protects all the internal parts from damage. (Unfortunately, dust will still find its way inside, which is why I recommend that you remove the case at least once a year and blow all that dust out by using a can of compressed air.)

Techs refer to your PC by any of the following names:

✦ Box.

✦ CPU. (You'll meet your PC's actual *CPU* — which is a single integrated chip — later in this chapter.)

✦ Chassis.

✦ $*Q(#*$*!%. (Reserved for special occasions.)

Consider thy form factor

Not all PCs are created equal; several different form factors are available. (Geez, yet another two-dollar word for a fifty-cent concept.) A *form factor* determines the height and "spread" of your computer, depending on the case. (In the original days of the IBM PC, all computer cases were designed to straddle your desk, parallel to the floor; however, folks soon realized that a PC takes up far less room if it stands vertically.)

Your desktop PC's case can look like any of the following:

✦ **The standard tower machine:** Because a tower case (see one in Figure 1-4) gives you the largest number of expansion bays and room for multiple fans, it's the case favored by PC power users and network administrators. Tower cases are often placed on the floor because they are sometimes too tall for your computer desk.

✦ **The mini-tower machine:** The standard case offered with most PCs, the mini-tower is simply a shorter version of a tower case. The mini-tower is suitable for home and standard office workstation use — however, don't expect it to have as many expansion (or *card*) slots, or as many empty drive bays waiting for you to fill with additional hard drives and another DVD recorder.

✦ **The lunchbox and pizza box machines:** These are the smallest PC cases of all, built for those areas where space is at a premium (or you know ahead of time that expansion won't be required in the future). These machines are often used in larger corporate offices, hospitals, banks, and the like. Figure 1-5 shows a pizza box case, which sits flat on your desktop rather than standing upright.

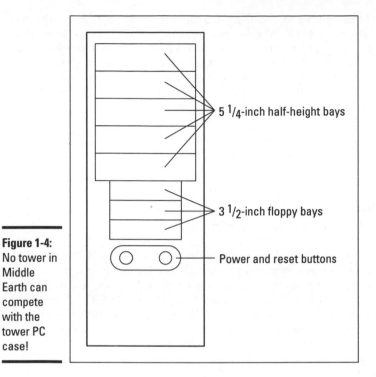

Figure 1-4: No tower in Middle Earth can compete with the tower PC case!

5 1/4-inch half-height bays

3 1/2-inch floppy bays

Power and reset buttons

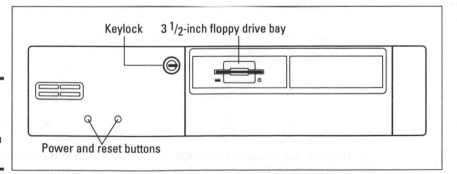

Figure 1-5: An example of a lean, mean "pizza box" PC.

Keylock   3 1/2-inch floppy drive bay

Power and reset buttons

Custom colors are great (for a while, anyway)

You might be interested in buying a PC with a special color scheme. Typically, these machines are black or brushed aluminum, but I've seen them in every color of the rainbow as well. (I particularly fancy the neon green and Florida orange.)

Personally, I think these works of art are fun, but I will caution you up front: Finding a neon green CD-ROM drive in any store — online or otherwise — is more difficult than getting a teenage girl off the telephone. Therefore, you might find it difficult to maintain that exotic color scheme when you start upgrading your hardware because most of the civilized world uses PCs that are off-white or beige. Black computers are the next easiest to match because black is the second-most popular color for PCs.

Of course, if you're a Macintosh owner, all bets are off . . . but that's another book entirely. (Specifically, *iMacs For Dummies*, Fourth Edition, published by Wiley, which I also wrote.)

The monitor

Today's monitors come in two different varieties:

✦ **The traditional CRT monitor:** The cathode ray tube (CRT) monitor is big, brassy, and less expensive to buy than a liquid crystal display (LCD) monitor, but it uses more electricity, gets hot while you use it, and emits all sorts of radiation. (Nothing harmful, mind you, but it's there all the same.) Because CRT monitors use older technology that's similar to a TV set, they're bulky, but they're also significantly cheaper than an LCD monitor, especially at larger screen sizes such as 19" and 21". Most CRT monitors are flat-screen models; older designs with curved screens tended to distort the image that you see.

✦ **The LCD monitor:** LCD monitors — also called flat-panel monitors — share the same technology as laptop computer screens, so they're very thin and use much, much less electricity than a CRT monitor. (Many are even designed to hang on the wall.) LCD screens emit neither heat nor radiation. In fact, the only downside to an LCD monitor is the (slightly higher) price, and LCD monitors are rapidly replacing CRT monitors in "package" deals from big-name PC manufacturers.

Either type of monitor is fine for a home or office environment, but (naturally) I recommend an LCD monitor if you can afford one. The larger the monitor size, the easier it's likely to be on your eyes, and the more windows and documents that you can stuff on your desktop at once.

The keyboard and mouse

Keyboards are rather mundane. Virtually all today's models have the Windows-specific keys that will help any PC power user — but I still have a suggestion or two:

✦ **Consider an ergonomic keyboard.** That cool, curved appearance that makes ergonomic keyboards such as the Microsoft Natural Keyboard Elite stand out in a crowd isn't just for looks. You'll find that you can type longer, faster, and with less strain on your wrists if you use an ergonomic keyboard, as shown in Figure 1-6.

Figure 1-6:
Ergonomic keyboards are user-friendly on your wrists.

✦ **Keyboard tasks are easier with one-touch buttons.** Many keyboards on the market today — and most that ship with today's systems — feature one-touch keys that you press to automatically display your e-mail program or Web browser, print a document, or mute your computer's audio. Even if you don't use the standard functions for these keys, they can generally be reprogrammed to work with other applications. For example, I've reprogrammed the Print key on my server's keyboard (which isn't connected to a printer) to run my network management application instead.

On the other side of the coin, most PC power users will eventually find themselves looking for a different mouse or pointing device; the standard equipment mouse rarely gets the job done unless you're buying a more expensive system that comes with a premium mouse. Mouse-y features to consider include the following:

✦ **Cordless mice:** These mice are sans tails: Instead, they use a built-in infrared (IR) emitter or Bluetooth wireless connection to communicate with a separate base station, which in turn connects to your PC. The base station often acts as a battery charger for the mouse when you're not using your PC. Many folks find these mice liberating because there's no tail to drag around and because you can place the mouse farther away from the computer.

✦ **Optical operation:** Optical mice advantages include no mouse ball to clean, far fewer moving parts, and better control — no wonder that optical pointing devices are so popular! If you're still using an old mouse with a ball, jettison it and pick up an optical mouse.

✦ **Multiple buttons:** Of course, any self-respecting PC mouse has two buttons, but most of the new offerings include a programmable third button and a scroll wheel, which you use to scroll the contents of a page just by turning the wheel with your fingertip. (For example, I have the middle button programmed as a double-click.)

✦ **Trackballs and touchpads:** Many tech types swear by these alternatives to the traditional mouse. To use a *trackball,* which is kind of like a giant stationary mouse turned on its back, you move the ball with your thumb or the tips of your fingers. With a touchpad (like what's found on many laptops), you move the tip of your finger across a pressure-sensitive pad.

Speakers

Today's multimedia PCs are just as attractive to an audiophile as a traditional stereo system. If you think that you're limited to two desktop speakers and a chintzy volume knob, I invite you to contemplate the latest in PC speaker technology:

✦ **Flat-panel speakers:** Like LCD screens are to CRT monitors, so are flat-panel speakers to older PC speakers. Most flat-panel speakers are less than half of an inch thick yet provide the same power and punch as their older brethren.

✦ **Dolby Surround sound:** I get into more detail about high-fidelity PC audio in Book VII, Chapter 6. For now, suffice it to say that with the right sound card and multiple speakers, your PC can equal the clarity and realism of a home theater system. And consider this: What home theater system will let you play the latest 3-D games?

✦ **Universal Serial Bus (USB) digital connections:** For the ultimate in sound quality, today's best digital speakers connect to your system through the USB port — you can say goodbye to old-fashioned analog forever.

Desktop PCs versus Laptop PCs

"So should I buy a desktop or a laptop PC?" Naturally, if the portability of a laptop PC is a requirement for you — if your job or your lifestyle demands plenty of travel every year — you really have no choice but a laptop computer. Luckily, today's laptops are virtually as powerful as desktop PCs, so you no longer have to feel like a second-class citizen, even when it comes to features such as high-resolution graphics, larger hard drives, and CD/DVD recording, which used to be very expensive options in the laptop world.

However, if you're sitting on the fence and portability is a lesser requirement, I generally recommend a desktop system for the following three reasons:

✦ **Laptops aren't as expandable as desktops.** Although you can hang plenty of peripherals off a modern laptop (using USB and FireWire ports), desktops are just plain easier to expand and upgrade (especially the processor and your graphics card, which are practically impossible to swap on a laptop).

✦ **Laptops are more expensive than desktops.** My friend, you'll pay dearly for that portability. So if you don't need it, jump to the desktop side of the fence. It's as simple as that.

✦ **Laptops cost much more to repair.** If the sound card fails in your desktop, you can replace it yourself with a new, relatively inexpensive adapter card. However, if the sound hardware fails in your laptop, it's time to pull out your wallet because you can't fix it yourself, and the entire motherboard inside the unit will probably need to be replaced. (Remember, part of that portability stems from the fact that laptop manufacturers tend to put all the graphics and video hardware on the motherboard to save space.)

Luckily, most of this book will still be valuable to laptop owners. Just ignore the parts about upgrading the components that you can't reach.

RAM and Processors: The Keys to Performance

When you hear PC owners talking about the speed and performance of their computers, they're typically talking about one of three different components (or all of these components together, as a group):

✦ **Your system memory, or random access memory (RAM):** The more memory that your PC has and the faster that memory is, the better your PC will perform — especially Windows, which enjoys memory like the proverbial hog. I tell you more about slops — sorry, I mean memory — in Book VII, Chapter 2.

✦ **The central processing unit (CPU):** Most of today's PCs use either an Intel Pentium 4 or its cheaper and slower cousin, the Celeron. The other popular processor is the AMD Athlon 64, along with its cheaper and slower cousin, the Sempron. The speed of your processor is measured in either megahertz (MHz) or gigahertz (GHz), with 1 GHz equaling 1000 MHz. The faster the speed of your processor, the faster your PC will perform. (I go into this big-time in Book VII, Chapter 3.)

✦ **The graphics processing unit (GPU):** This is the chipset used on your video card. The better the chipset, the faster and the more realistic 3-D graphics that your PC can produce. For the skinny on graphics cards, visit Book VII, Chapter 6.

To display what type of processor your PC uses, its speed, and how much RAM your PC has, right-click My Computer in Windows 2000/XP and then choose Properties from the pop-up menu that appears. You should see a dialog box appear like the one in Figure 1-7 with these interesting facts.

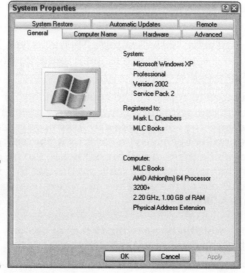

Figure 1-7:
Display your
System
Properties
in Windows
XP.

Your Friend, Your Operating System

Windows, which is your PC's *operating system,* is the program that you run in order to

✦ Navigate through the files on your hard drive.

✦ Run other programs.

✦ Listen to music, view pictures, or watch movies.

✦ Copy, move, and delete things, and much more.

Actually, Windows is composed of hundreds of smaller programs, but you'll rarely notice anything else running. Instead, Windows presents a cohesive and relatively easy-to-use interface to the world. (The tech word *interface* simply means the design of the screen and the controls that you see when you're using software.)

In this book, when I refer to Windows, I'm talking about Windows XP. In my opinion, XP is the easiest-to-use and most stable version of Windows that I've ever used, and I heartily recommend that you upgrade to it if your PC meets the minimum requirements. To see the requirements for the Home, Professional, 64-bit, Tablet PC and Media Center versions of Windows XP, visit Microsoft online at www.microsoft.com/windowsxp/evaluation/default.asp. (Book II is completely dedicated to Windows XP — there's another reason to upgrade!)

I should mention, however, that Windows isn't the only operating system that runs on a PC. For example, you can run UNIX, Linux, Windows 2000, or even good old-fashioned DOS. To be honest, your PC's hardware couldn't care less — but it's a good bet that the programs that you want to run are designed for Windows, and much of the hardware in your PC either won't work or will be harder to configure if you use another operating system. Therefore, I heartily suggest that you stick with Windows XP: The various flavors of Windows are the choice of the vast majority of PC owners.

Chapter 2: Additional Toys Your PC Will Enjoy

In This Chapter

✓ Comparing printers

✓ Adding a scanner to your system

✓ Upgrading your input devices

✓ Adding a game controller

✓ Introducing digital cameras and digital video (DV) camcorders

✓ Adding new storage to your system

✓ Protecting your PC with a surge protector or an uninterruptible power supply (UPS)

You've bought your PC — congratulations! — or you've decided to finally turn on that totem pole of a desktop computer that you've been looking at for the last six months. Here's a friendly warning for you in the form of a Mark's Maxim:

> **Serious computing requires serious peripherals.™**

In other words, those PC owners who are hoping to get the maximum return and explore the maximum power of their computers will need additional stuff (*peripherals*, as you can read in Book I, Chapter 1) that connect to your PC to take care of a specific job. Printers are a good example; a PC certainly won't produce hard copy by itself.

In Chapter 1 of this mini-book, I discuss hardware and software. This chapter is designed as both a showcase and an introduction to PC peripherals that will familiarize you with the most popular additional toys for your computer. Some of these devices are covered in great detail later on — for example, scanners have all of Book VI, Chapter 1 to themselves — and others are covered primarily right here.

One warning: This chapter can be hazardous to your wallet or purse.

Printers

The first stop in the world of peripherals is the most common (and most folks would say the most useful) device of all: the system *printer,* which allows your PC to produce hard copies of documents, artwork, and photographs.

Inkjet versus laser printers

In the digital days of yore — in other words, more than ten years ago — making a choice between an inkjet and a laser printer was ridiculously easy. After all, laser printers were prohibitively expensive, and they couldn't print in color. Therefore, every home PC owner picked up an inkjet printer and got on with his or her life. These days, however, the line between inkjet and laser printers has blurred, so here's a list of the advantages of each so that you can shop with the right type of printer in mind.

Laser printer advantages

Today's monochrome laser printers start at around $100–$300 U.S., which is still mind-bendingly weird for an old hardware hacker like me who still remembers the days when the *absolute* cheapest (and likely refurbished) laser printer that you could find would set you back $1,500–$2,000 U.S. Advantages of the laser printer include

+ **Speed:** A laser printer can turn out pages more quickly than an inkjet printer.

+ **Low cost:** Over time, toner costs for a laser printer will total far less per page than refilling/replacing inkjet printer cartridges.

+ **Quiet operation:** A laser printer is generally quieter than low-cost inkjet printers — which is a big deal in a quiet office, where the printer usually occupies a central location.

+ **Best quality text:** No inkjet printer — no matter how much you pay for it — will ever turn out black text and line graphics as crisp as a laser printer.

Also, if you can afford the $400 U.S. or so for a color laser printer, you'll find that it offers better quality color output than most low-cost inkjet printers. With these advantages in mind, pick a monochrome laser printer if most of the pages that you'll print will be text and if color isn't a requirement. You'll be glad that you chose that laser model after you've gone three months without changing a single toner cartridge!

The monochrome laser printer shown in Figure 2-1 can produce 12 pages per minute without blinking an eye. (If it had one.)

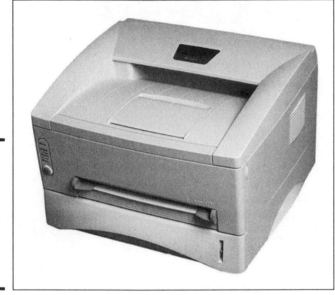

Figure 2-1:
Invest in a
low-cost
mono-
chrome
laser
printer for
document
printing.

Inkjet printer advantages

Inkjet printers are still cheaper than laser printers. You can find an acceptable color inkjet printer for under $100 U.S. anywhere on the planet, and they're still the color printing solution for the home PC owner. Other advantages include

✦ **Versatility:** A color inkjet can print on many types of media, including craft paper, T-shirt transfers, and even printable CD/DVD discs.

✦ **Smaller size:** This saves you space on your desktop.

✦ **Larger paper sizes:** If you spend more, you can add a large-format inkjet printer to your system that can print 11 x 17-inch or larger items.

The inkjet printer in Figure 2-2 costs less than $200 U.S. yet includes both Ethernet and Universal Serial Bus (USB) connections. It can print near laser-quality black text at seven pages per minute and photo-quality color images at five pages per minute. You can even set this model to print on both sides of the paper.

Figure 2-2:
This inkjet printer produces stunning photo-quality color.

Photo printers

Photo printers are specifically designed to create photographs that rival any 35mm film print. They either use the best quality inkjet technology, or they rely on dye-sublimation (dye-sub) technology (also called *thermal wax* printing). A *dye-sub printer* transfers heated solid dye from a ribbon to specially coated paper, producing the same continuous tones that you see in a photograph produced from a negative. Photo printers can often accept memory cards from digital cameras directly, so you don't need a PC to print your digital photographs.

Although a number of different sizes of photo printers are on the market, most are smaller than typical inkjet printers. (They can't use standard 8.5 x 11-inch paper, and they're lousy at printing black text, which makes an inkjet printer far more versatile.) Both photo and inkjet printers can produce borderless images (just like a film print), but a true dye-sublimation photo printer is far slower than an inkjet, and the special paper and dye ribbon that it requires make it much more expensive over the long haul.

If you're a serious amateur or professional digital photographer, a photo printer is worth the expense. For a typical home PC owner, however, a standard color inkjet printer is the better path to take.

Label printers

Before I move on, I'd like to discuss a popular new class of printers — the personal *label printer,* like the DYMO LabelWriter that I use (www.dymo.com). These printers might look a little like toys — they're not much bigger than the label tape that they use — but I've found that a label printer is worth twice its weight in gold (see Figure 2-3).

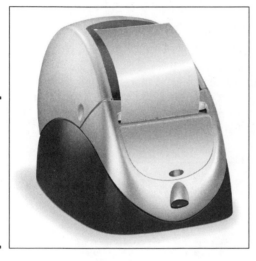

Figure 2-3:
A personal label printer is a convenient tool for printing all types of labels.

For example, the LabelWriter 400 Turbo can produce all these materials with aplomb:

✦ **Address and shipping labels**, complete with your logo

✦ **ID badges**

✦ **CD and DVD labels**

✦ **Bar codes and U.S. mail codes**

✦ **File folder labels**

✦ **Floppy disk labels** (for those who still use floppy disks, anyway)

✦ **VHS tape and cassette labels**

When you design your labels, the software that ships with the LabelWriter gives you control over fonts, time and date stamping, line drawings, and even thumbnail photographs. You can rotate and mirror text or set up bar coding with ease. Plus, you get the capability to print labels directly from applications such as Outlook, Word, ACT!, and QuickBooks.

Just as valuable as the output, however, is the sheer convenience that you get from one of these printers! A label printer frees you from the hassle of designing and preparing labels on your inkjet or laser printer, and you don't have to hunt for your label sheets every time that you need to print a new batch. (Anyone who's fought tooth and nail to align and print a bar code or address labels on a standard laser printer knows just what I mean.)

The LabelWriter 400 Turbo uses a USB connection and sells for about $150 U.S. online.

Scanners

Scanners are interesting beasts — and man, you get a lot of bang for your buck! In fact, a perfectly serviceable USB scanner (as shown in Figure 2-4) is waiting for you at your local Maze O' Wires store for under $100 U.S., and it can do all of the following:

Figure 2-4:
This scanner can bring all sorts of printed material to your PC monitor.

✦ **Produce digital images from magazine and book pages, photographs, and just about any other printed material.** These images can later be edited to your heart's content, sent as an e-mail attachment, or recorded to CD or DVD.

✦ **Read text from a printed document into your word processor.** This trick is called *Optical Character Recognition* (OCR) and can save you hours of typing.

✦ **Produce images that you can fax with your PC's fax/modem.**

✦ **Produce images from transparencies or slides (with the right attachment).**

✦ **Create copies of a document (in concert with your printer).**

The scanner shown in Figure 2-4 features seven one-touch buttons on its front. You can e-mail, copy, or even create PDFs from the original — or even run your OCR software with a single punch of a button. *Sassy!*

Specialized scanners are designed especially for things such as bar codes and business cards. A unique favorite of mine is a digital, hand-held pen scanner (see one in Figure 2-5) with which you can re-create what you draw or write on special sheets of paper in the included notebook and a special type of self-adhesive notes. I use the Logitech io (www.logitech.com). No more stuffing napkins with scribbles all over them into your jacket pocket after lunch! You can also use the io to enter appointments and To Do data into Microsoft Outlook or Lotus Notes and also flag information that should be automatically entered into an e-mail message when you connect the pen to your PC. (It uses a USB connection.) If you're like me — constantly moving back and forth between old-fashioned pen and paper one minute and a mouse and Adobe Illustrator the next — you'll find that the newest model, the io2, is worth every penny of the $175 U.S. that you'll pay for it.

I go into more detail on scanners in Book VI, Chapter 1. For now, just remember that they are the very definition of the cat's pajamas.

Figure 2-5:
A digital
pen is a
specialized
scanner.

Keyboards, Tablets, and Pointing Things

Gotta have 'em. Using a PC without an input device is . . . well, I guess it's like playing Ping-Pong without paddles. In this section, I discuss the upgrades that you can make to your PC's existing keyboard and mouse. (Although they're technically not peripherals, as I mention in Book I, Chapter 1, some of these hardware devices are too cool not to cover.)

Tickling keys wirelessly

As I discuss in the previous chapter of this mini-book — and as you can read in Book II, Chapter 1, when I start talking Windows XP — Mr. Bill has remodeled the hoary PC keyboard in his own fashion, adding extra keys that make it easier to control Windows. If you're using a PC built in the last few years, you'll already have these keys handy. I mention a few keyboard features to look for in the previous chapter of this mini-book, such as ergonomic keyboards that can help reduce the strain of typing on your wrists. But what if you want to relax in a better chair several feet away from that big-screen monitor?

Enter the wireless keyboard, which is the perfect complement to a wireless mouse or trackball. The wireless keyboard shown in Figure 2-6 is a combination of both a wireless keyboard and wireless mouse that use the Bluetooth short-range wireless network technology I cover in Book VIII, Chapter 3. This keyboard is festooned with no less than 11 one-button hotkeys and even includes a set of audio CD player controls for listening to your music.

Figure 2-6: This wireless keyboard/ mouse combo is the nomad's dream.

Putting a tablet to work

If you're a graphic artist, a professional photographer, or someone who wants to paint or draw freehand, consider a *graphics tablet* (shown in Figure 2-7), which allows you to draw or make notes with a stylus in the familiar old-fashioned method. Like an ergonomic keyboard, a tablet can also help ease the strain on your wrist.

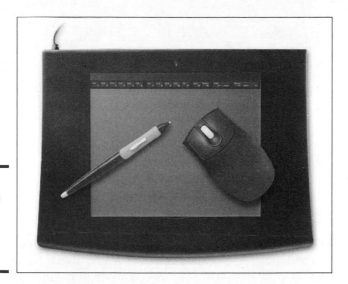

Figure 2-7:
A graphics
tablet
makes
drawing
a breeze.

"But what about the fine control I get with paper or canvas?" No problem! Today's tablets can recognize thousands of different levels of pressure. Some can even detect the angle of the stylus, allowing you to tilt your virtual brush in graphics applications like Photoshop CS2 and Painter for special effects with watercolor, chalk, and pencil filters.

A typical tablet like the Intuos3 from Wacom (www.wacom.com) has no batteries or cords on the stylus, and it even comes with its own mouse. The tablet uses a USB connection to your PC, and it sells for about $330 on the Web — that's the 6 x 8-inch model. (The 9 x 12-inch model is about $100 more.)

Repeat after me: Buy a trackball!

I can't work with a traditional mouse any longer — I'm now firmly set in the trackball camp. A trackball offers a number of benefits:

✦ **Compact:** Trackballs require far less space on your desktop because just the trackball moves (instead of the entire device).

✦ **Control:** Many folks find that using a trackball provides a finer level of cursor control.

✦ **Cleanliness:** A trackball stays cleaner than a mouse. (Even optical mice get dirtier than trackballs.)

Figure 2-8 illustrates a trackball mouse that you control with your thumb; other trackballs use the first finger to control the ball. This particular model uses either a USB or PS/2 connection to your PC and sells for about $35 U.S. online.

Figure 2-8: A trackball is much more efficient than the traditional mouse.

Big-Time Game Controllers

Ah, do you remember the old Atari joysticks that ushered in the age of the video game (and the Atari personal computers after that)? A plastic tube, a base with a single red button, and a cord . . . what more could you possibly want, right?

Because modern game players want a lot more than one button, witness the arrival of the game controller (which I think has a much grander sound than just *a joystick*). For example, check out the controller shown in Figure 2-9 — does that look like an old-fashioned joystick to you? In fact, this model is more like a combination of a mini-keyboard and a gamepad (reflecting the current complexity of PC games, which rely as much on the keyboard as the pointing device that you're using). Your entire hand fits on top of the controller, much like a trackball, and your fingers use the keys while your thumb operates the gamepad directional control. (You can also use this controller along with your regular mouse or trackball.) This model, which sells for about $30 U.S. online, can even be programmed to fit your preferences for each individual game that you play. Sweet!

Figure 2-9: It's a bird, it's a plane . . . no, it's the latest in PC game controllers!

Another popular feature of today's game controllers is *force feedback,* where the controller actually rumbles or provides resistance to your hand that matches the action onscreen, such as a steering wheel that gets tougher to turn in curves or a joystick that shakes each time that your WWII fighter is hit by enemy fire.

Consider the Logitech MOMO steering wheel, which has the same optical tracking mechanism as today's optical mice and trackballs. It even has its own onboard processor, which keeps track of what's happening within the game and activates the wheel's internal motors to provide the matching feedback. (Naturally, it also has programmable buttons. What a surprise.) Anyway, you get the steering wheel and a set of pedals to boot for about $100 U.S., making you the hit of your NASCAR crowd!

Video and Digital Cameras

Images and full-motion video have traditionally been based on film (which retains an image when exposed to light) or magnetic tape. That whole approach, however, is now strictly '90s . . . and very early '90s to boot. Today's digital cameras and digital video camcorders have heavy-duty advantages over film cameras and tape camcorders:

✦ **No processing** at Wal-Mart is required. Your digital images can be downloaded directly to your PC.

✦ **Editing is easy,** using programs like Adobe Photoshop CS and Paint Shop Pro (for digital images) and Adobe Premiere (for video).

✦ **No film rolls to buy.** Instead, you simply delete images from your digital camera after they're downloaded.

✦ **Your images and videos can be saved to a CD or DVD for permanent storage.**

✦ **Images can be sent via e-mail or displayed on your Web page.**

✦ **You can create your own DVD movies from your video clips.**

A specialized model of DV camcorder (about the size of a baseball) is designed especially to sit atop your desktop PC: a Web cam. Folks use them to send digital video over the Internet, to add a video signal to their Web pages, or to record simple movies from their chair. Web cams have been in use as Internet videoconferencing tools for years now; most cost less than $100; and they use either a FireWire or USB cable connection to your PC.

Figure 2-10 illustrates a typical digital camera, which looks and operates much like its film counterpart. Figure 2-11 shows a camcorder, ready to record straight to digital video, which you can transfer over a FireWire connection to your PC.

Figure 2-10: The image maker of the new millennium: the digital camera.

Figure 2-11: With a digital camcorder, you can record your footage on a DVD.

For the skinny on digital cameras, see Book VI, Chapter 5. And for a look at how the video clips that you take with your DV camcorder can be turned into movies, see Book VI, Chapter 3.

External Drives

Next, consider how simple it is to add fast storage — or the ability to record your own CDs and DVDs — to today's PCs. If you're the least bit nervous about digging inside your PC's innards in order to add more hard drive space, you'll be pleased to know that it's easy to connect a fast external hard drive to your system . . . providing that you have the FireWire or USB 2.0 ports available on your PC. (If you're not familiar with these high-speed connections, fear not: I launch into a complete discussion of both of these in Book VII, Chapter 5.)

In fact, not every form of external storage even needs a cable. Read on to see what I mean.

Portable hard drives and CD/DVD recorders

Forget the huge external hard drives of just five years ago. Those doorstops have been replaced by slim, trim models (see Figure 2-12) that run faster and are more reliable and yet are no bigger than a pack of playing cards. At current prices, you can pick up an external 80GB hard drive for about $150 U.S. that is a mere one inch thick and shock resistant yet can connect effortlessly to PCs with either FireWire or USB 2.0 ports.

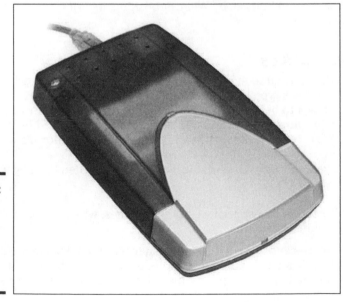

Figure 2-12:
This external 80GB drive means mobile storage.

On the CD and DVD recording scene, you'll find five major types of drives:

✦ **CD-R/CD-RW drives:** Can store around 700MB on a CD

✦ **DVD-R/DVD-RW drives:** Can store 4.7GB on a DVD

✦ **DVD-RAM drives:** Can store 9.4GB on a double-sided DVD

✦ **DVD+R/DVD+RW drives:** Can store 4.7GB on a DVD

✦ **Dual Layer (DL) DVD+R drives:** Can store 8.5GB on a DVD

The *RW* in the drive moniker stands for *rewriteable,* meaning that you can reuse a CD-RW, DVD-RW, or DVD+RW over and over. All these recorders can produce audio CDs and standard data CD/DVDs, but only the drives that can record the DVD-R and DVD+R formats are likely to create a DVD movie that can be played in your standalone DVD player. Unfortunately, the rewriteable DVD-RW and DVD+RW standards aren't compatible with each other, and they're not compatible with older standalone DVD players, either; you'll have to watch your discs on your PC. (Insert sound of palm slapping forehead here.)

The current morass that is the DVD standards battle is too complex to go into in this chapter. If you'd like the full story about what works with what and how to record any type of disc under the sun (audio, video, data, and even a mix), I can heartily recommend my book *CD and DVD Recording For Dummies,* Second Edition, by Wiley Publishing, Inc. (It'll keep your library consistent, too.)

Backup drives

Backup drives used to mean inexpensive, slow-running tape drives — however, today's typical 60GB and 80GB drives are simply too humongous for such tapes to be worth much anymore. Heck, I remember when everyone backed up to floppy disks, and now even the highest-priced digital audio tape (DAT) drives are losing ground fast in the backup storage world.

Instead, you now have three choices to pick from when backing up your system:

✦ **DVD recorders,** especially DVD-RAM drives, which can store over 9GB per double-sided disc.

✦ **Online backups,** using a commercial Internet backup service. (This is really only a viable solution if you're using a broadband connection to the Internet; backing up a big hard drive takes too long over a pokey 56KB modem.)

✦ **External FireWire and USB 2.0 backup hard drives** like the 300GB Maxtor One-Touch II (www.maxtor.com), which allows you to start a full, automated backup of your system by pressing the button on the front of the drive.

The Maxtor unit isn't cheap at $250 U.S., but how much are your documents and files worth? No matter what backup method you use, I strongly urge you to do your duty as your PC's guardian and *back up your system!*

USB flash drives

The final storage toy is a little something different: the *USB flash drive,* which is a keychain-sized unit that needs no batteries and has no moving parts! Instead, it uses the same method that digital cameras use to store images. Your files are stored on memory cards (either removable cards or built-in memory inside the unit). Most USB drives now range anywhere from 64MB to 2GB of storage, and after you plug them into your PC's USB port, they look just like any external hard drive (or a whomping huge floppy disk), but they can be unplugged and carried with you in your pocket. These drives don't need any extra software — Windows 2000 and XP recognize them instantly — so they make a great "digital wallet."

Figure 2-13 illustrates a 1GB flash drive that sells for about $50 U.S. online. It even includes a write-protect switch so that you can safeguard your data from being accidentally erased.

Figure 2-13: Carry 1GB in your pocket with a USB flash drive.

Surge Protectors and UPS Units

You know, one clear sign of a PC power user is at the end of the PC's power cord. True power users will use either a surge protector or a UPS to safeguard their system. However, I always make sure that I stress the following fact when I'm talking about surge protectors and UPS units: Neither will be able to protect your PC from a direct lightning hit on your home or office wiring! (That's just too much current for any commercial surge device to handle.)

Otherwise, using both a surge protector and a UPS will help guard against less serious power surges, and both will provide additional AC sockets for your rapidly growing system. If you can afford to spend $200–$300, the UPS is the better choice because of the following reasons:

✦ **Safety nets:** A UPS provides a number of extra minutes of AC power if your home or office experiences a power failure — generally enough so that you can close any documents that you're working on (like that Great American Novel that you've been slaving over for 20 years) and then shut down your PC normally.

✦ **Auto shutdowns:** More expensive UPS models can actually shut down your PC automatically in case of a power failure.

✦ **Current cleaners:** Most UPS units filter the AC current to smooth out brownouts and noise interference from other electronic devices.

✦ **Audible alerts:** Some UPS units sound an alarm whenever a power failure or significant brownout occurs.

The number of minutes that your UPS will last during a power failure depends on the power rating of the battery. Don't forget, however, that a honking big cathode ray tube (CRT) monitor will use much more power than the PC itself, so you should allow for it when deciding on which UPS to buy.

If you're using a dialup, cable or digital subscriber line (DSL) modem connection, make sure that you get a surge protector or UPS that will also protect your modem from electrical surges — that juice can travel just as easily across a phone line as across your power line.

Chapter 3: Connectors, Ports, and Sundry Openings

In This Chapter

✔ Connecting USB devices

✔ Connecting FireWire devices

✔ Putting the antique serial port to rest

✔ Recognizing the PC parallel port

✔ Connecting your monitors

✔ Locating the jacks and ports on your sound card

✔ Connecting your mouse and keyboard

In the beginning (okay, last century), there was the serial port and the parallel port — who would have needed anything else? If you could afford a printer back then, it was connected to the parallel port, and your modem (or perhaps your mouse) was hooked to your serial port. End of story.

Today's typical PC sprouts only one of those original two ports — the serial port is all but extinct, although most modern motherboards still provide a parallel port. Modern PCs rely on a number of relatively new connectors that greatly expand the range of peripherals that you can add to your system. In this chapter, I help you make sense of the various ports and sundry openings that you'll find on the back of your PC.

Using USB Stuff

The first port on the tour is the most important standard PC connector on the planet these days. A Universal Serial Bus (USB) port (see Figure 3-1) allows you to connect all sorts of peripherals, and it's even becoming popular for connecting keyboards and mice. Intel is responsible for this most versatile of ports.

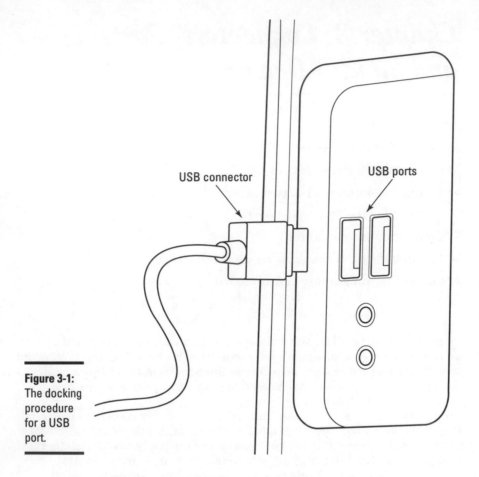

USB connector

USB ports

Figure 3-1:
The docking
procedure
for a USB
port.

A USB connection is the cat's pajamas because

+ **It's plug and play.** You don't even need to reboot your PC after you connect a USB device because Windows automatically recognizes the connection, and you can start using your USB peripheral immediately.

+ **One port supports dozens of devices.** A single USB port can support up
  to 127 different devices, either connected in a daisy-chain configuration
  or by using a USB hub. I doubt that you have that many connections to
  handle. (But if you do, please take a photo of your system with your digital camera and send the picture to mark@mlcbooks.com because I can
  hardly wait to see it.)

+ **It's relatively fast.** USB devices come in two flavors: the older USB 1.1
  standard (which still delivers data transfer speeds that are many times
  that of a traditional serial port) and the USB 2.0 standard (which is one
  of the fastest external connections currently available for the PC).

I discuss USB connections in greater detail in Book VII, Chapter 5; for now, just remember that any device with a USB port connection is a better choice over the same device with a serial port or parallel port connection.

Riding in the Fast Lane with FireWire

Until recently, the FireWire port (often referred to by its more official name, IEEE 1394) was the fastest port on any personal computer and has therefore become the standard for digital video (DV) camcorders and high-resolution scanners — both of which produce honking big files that need to be transferred to your computer as quickly as possible. Believe it or not, Apple Computer is the proud parent of FireWire.

The original FireWire standard has now been overtaken in raw speed by USB 2.0, but because FireWire has been around far longer, it's in no danger of disappearing any time soon. In fact, I personally would pick FireWire over USB 2.0 every time for my digital video equipment because many older pieces of my digital movie gear will never recognize USB 2.0.

Unlike USB ports — which are included with every PC today — FireWire ports are generally available as optional equipment, so make certain that you have a FireWire port before spending the big bucks on that new DV camcorder. (Of course, you can always buy an adapter card to add FireWire ports to your computer.) Like USB, FireWire is also a plug-and-play connection; a FireWire port can support 63 devices (using a daisy-chaining technique).

Find more information about FireWire in Book VII, Chapter 5, where I introduce the FireWire 800 standard, which ups the ante in the port speed race, churning an incredible 800 Mbps (or twice as fast as original FireWire)!

Back off, SCSI!

Many hardware technicians and techno-wizards are familiar with Small Computer System Interface (SCSI) connectors. *SCSI* was the original high-speed, daisy-chaining technology that allowed you to add a string of multiple devices *(a SCSI chain)* both inside and outside your PC's case. Even today, SCSI internal hard drives are some of the fastest on the market.

However, external SCSI devices are somewhat scary: A SCSI chain is much harder than USB 2.0 or FireWire to configure. In fact, I've devoted entire chapters to it in some of my older books. External SCSI devices aren't plug and play, and an external SCSI peripheral is much slower when it comes to transferring data than the newer USB/FireWire technologies.

For these reasons, I advise even PC power users to give SCSI the cold shoulder when considering an external device unless your PC already has SCSI hardware, and you're experienced with configuring SCSI hardware. Take my word for it; you'll be glad you did.

Your Antique Serial Port

Okay, perhaps the serial port isn't *antique,* but it is one-half of the original Dynamic Duo that first appeared with the premiere of the IBM PC.

Today, most peripherals have jumped the serial ship and joined the USB bunch. However, you can still find the following serial devices from time to time (usually used, and probably on eBay):

✦ Modems

✦ Game controllers (especially the more complex joysticks)

✦ Digital cameras

✦ Personal digital assistant (PDA) docks for Palm and Pocket PC units

Serial devices aren't plug and play, so you'll have to reboot your PC before Windows will recognize a serial device. Also, serial devices — especially modems — might require additional manual configuration inside Windows, such as editing files with Notepad and turning off certain port features.

All in all, go USB. Everyone else is, and it's a good thing.

The Once-Renowned Parallel Port

Ah, I remember those days . . . the early 1980s, when the parallel port was truly the Queen of the PC Connections. Printers were hideously expensive peripherals that only a doctor, lawyer, or Supreme Court Justice could afford. And if you did have a printer, it was connected to your PC's parallel port with all the pomp, grace, and grandeur of the RMS Queen Elizabeth II. (Perhaps I need more Diet Coke.)

Figure 3-2 illustrates a standard PC parallel port. Unlike the serial port, the parallel port is still somewhat useful today; a large number of parallel port printers are still manufactured, and the parallel port is also used with other peripherals such as Zip drives and scanners (usually with older PCs without USB support).

I'm sorry to report, however, that the parallel port's days are numbered. The popularity of the USB port as a printer connection has doomed the parallel port to obsolescence, and we can wave goodbye to her with a wistful smile. Again, like the serial port, Mark's Maxim prevails:

Buy USB. You'll be happier.™

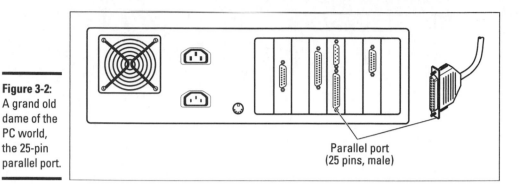

Figure 3-2:
A grand old dame of the PC world, the 25-pin parallel port.

Parallel port
(25 pins, male)

Many laptops feature an infrared port (commonly called an *IrDA* port, short for *Infrared Data Association*) that can be used to communicate with devices such as PDAs and other laptops. Windows provides full support for an infrared connection. However, these ports don't do diddly-squat if the external peripheral that you're trying to communicate with doesn't have its own IrDA port — and not many do, so you won't be able to use this whiz-bang technology with many devices.

Meet Your Video Port

At last, a port that's been around for many years and still rocks! Yes, friends and neighbors, today's video cards still use the same 15-pin, D-SUB video port that originally appeared with the IBM Video Graphics Array (VGA) specification. However, another new face is on the block: the 29-pin, *DVI-I port,* which is used to connect digital flat-panel (also called liquid crystal display or LCD) monitors. Figure 3-3 shows the business end of a typical video card that offers both ports onboard.

If you're wondering, virtually every card that has both of these video ports can actually use two monitors at once (either showing an *expanded* desktop, where your mouse moves seamlessly from one monitor to the other, or two separate and discrete desktops).

In a pinch, a DVI-VGA adapter allows you to use the DVI-I port to connect a standard cathode ray tube (CRT) monitor, so you can use two analog monitors instead.

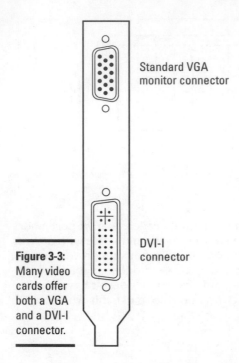

Standard VGA
monitor connector

DVI-I
connector

Figure 3-3:
Many video
cards offer
both a VGA
and a DVI-I
connector.

Audio Connectors You'll Likely Need

Today's speakers connect to your PC's sound card in one of four ways:

+ **Through standard analog Line-Out/Speaker jacks on the card:** These are the familiar audio jacks that you'll find on the card itself, just like the headphone jacks on your MP3 player or boom box. Most PC speakers use these jacks, shown in Figure 3-4.

+ **Through standard analog RCA jacks on the card:** Some cards also include the RCA jacks that most folks associate with a stereo system or a VCR. These jacks are more convenient than the Line-Out/Speaker jacks because you don't need a miniplug-to-RCA adapter to use your stereo system with your PC's audio output.

+ **Through standard optical and coaxial digital (SPIDF) connectors:** Audiophiles who truly want the best sound reproduction are willing to spend the extra dollars on an all-digital connection betwixt card and speakers (or card and a high-end stereo system). These connectors are also standard equipment on most Dolby Surround sound systems.

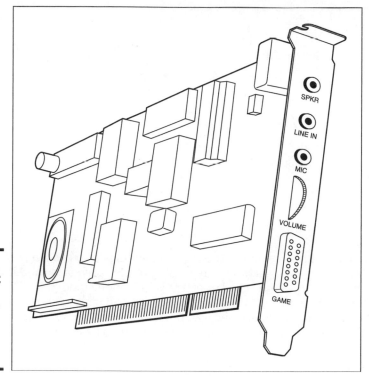

Figure 3-4:
A typical PC
sound card
showing off
its speaker
jack and
game port.

✦ **Through the USB port:** Surprise! It's our new-old-friend making another appearance. This time, your speakers can use any USB port on your system for a digital audio connection — analog gets tossed out the door, and audiophiles can wax enthusiastic about their pristine digital sound.

You'll also find a PC game port on most audio cards, allowing you to connect a joystick or other game controller. The game port is going the way of the dodo (thanks once again, as you can guess, to USB game controllers), but they're still quite common on today's sound cards.

Keyboard and Mouse Ports on Parade

The final stop on the port tour is the ubiquitous PS/2 keyboard/joystick port. Figure 3-5 illustrates the plug that fits in these ports. Each port is typically color coded and marked with an icon to indicate which piece of hardware gets connected where.

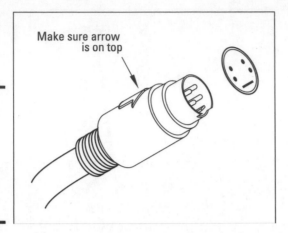

Make sure arrow
is on top

Figure 3-5:
A PS/2
keyboard/
mouse
connector.
Awesome
sight,
isn't it?

I hate to bring it up, but at the risk of sounding like a broken record, many PC hardware manufacturers are turning to USB keyboards and USB mice. (See why I stress just how important USB is to the modern PC?) In this case, however, I see no real advantage to using a USB keyboard or mouse over a PS/2 keyboard or mouse because the latter really don't require any configuration, and they're not constantly being unplugged and reconnected.

Chapter 4: Maintaining Your Hardware

In This Chapter

✔ **Moving your PC the right way**

✔ **Dusting your PC**

✔ **Keeping cables under control**

✔ **Cleaning your monitor and scanner**

✔ **Freshening your mouse and keyboard**

✔ **Practicing printer maintenance**

With the right credit card balance, anyone can buy a supercharged $2,500 U.S. PC — but maintaining that expensive equipment is another kettle of fish altogether. Although your PC's case might appear to be a closed environment, those fans draw in dust while they're cooling things down . . . and what about peripherals such as your printer and scanner, which are always more exposed to dust, dirt, and contaminants? The only PC that I've encountered that doesn't need regular maintenance is the model that you can buy in The Sims.

In this chapter, I cover the basic cleaning and maintenance necessary to keep your hardware in top shape — long enough for it to become a seriously outdated antique! (And that's coming from the proud owner of two antique RadioShack computers and three antique Atari computers.)

When Should I Move My PC?

Counter to popular myth, even a desktop PC can go mobile whenever it wants. Of course, you won't be stowing it with your other carry-on items on a plane, but if you've been challenged to a LAN game at someone's apartment or you're moving to a new home, you'll find that your PC actually enjoys chaperoned trips. (Rather like a dog, without the tongue out the window.)

Ready for one of my Maxims? (Get your highlighter out, if you like.) When you're ready, consider these guidelines that you should follow when moving your PC:

✦ **Never move your PC until it's completely powered down.** In this case, *move* means any movement whatsoever (even nudging your PC's case a few inches across your desktop). Harken to this particularly important Mark's Maxim:

> **Never move your desktop PC if it is running.**™

(Even laptop computers shouldn't be jolted or jerked around while they're running.) Many PCs have only a handful of moving parts, such as fans, CD/DVD recorders, and hard drives — but brother, any movement while the latter two are still spinning carries the possibility that you can shorten the drive's operational life. Always give your PC at least ten seconds after it shuts down before you pick it up.

✦ **Never set your PC upright in a seat or the floor of your car.** We've all seen the videos of crash test dummies . . . and your beloved digital friend doesn't have a car seat in case you come to a sudden stop. You can actually use seatbelts to secure your PC in a vehicle, but I think it's just easier to lay your PC's case down flat on the floor of your vehicle. The same also goes for your monitor, which is also dangerous (for itself and your head) when airborne for short distances.

✦ **Use your towel.** If your PC has to ride on top of a surface that might scratch your case, wrap your PC in a towel or blanket to protect its finish. (Fans of the *Hitchhiker's Guide to the Galaxy* series know what I'm on about.)

Avoiding Dust Bunnies

Think I'm kidding? Dust bunnies are **real** — and they seem to reproduce as fast as their namesake, too. Thanks to your trusty can of techno-nerd compressed air, however, you can banish that dust from your PC and get back to work or play.

Here's a checklist of what to do:

✦ **Open and dust your PC at least once a year.** Consider it a birthday present for your computer. Unscrew or unlatch your PC's case and use your compressed air (available at any office supply store) to blow any accumulated dust from the motherboard, adapter cards, and cables. If allowed to accumulate, that dust can act as a comfy heat-retaining blanket over your PC's circuitry, and overheated components have a significantly shorter lifespan. (For proof, check out the fans at the back of your PC's case and the fan on top of the processor. Heat is the enemy.)

✦ **Remove dust that's settled on the fan blades.** Speaking of fans, use your compressed air to get rid of any additional dust on fan blades and within air intake holes. In order to properly ventilate and cool your PC, these openings need to be free of dust bunnies.

+ **Wipe down your PC's case and your monitor with a clean, dry cloth every few months.** You should never use any household solvents to clean your PC's case, but antistatic cleaning solutions and cloths are made just for cleaning computer hardware. You can find antistatic solutions and cloths at your local computer shop or office supply store.

Are you facing a stain that won't come off your PC's case, even when you use an antistatic cleaning cloth? Then try my secret weapon: Armor All protectant (which you've probably been using on your car's rubber and vinyl for years!). Apply a small amount of Armor All directly on the stain and try again.

+ **Avoid eating around your PC.** I know; it's difficult not to snack while you're on the Internet, but at least be diligent about cleaning up afterwards and **never** park anything liquid anywhere near your computer!

+ **Keep your workspace clean and open.** Surrounding your PC with papers and knickknacks might optimize your desktop space (or at least help you feel more human around an inhuman boss), but you'll be contributing to the accumulation of dust inside your computer. And, in the worst case, you'll actually be blocking the flow of air. I try to leave at least six inches of free space around the base of my PC at all times.

If your PC must be located in a dusty environment, consider an air cleaner and ionizer unit. I use one in my office, and I find significantly less dust to clean from my PC every year.

Watching Your Cables

With the popularity of external Universal Serial Bus (USB) and FireWire peripherals these days, the forest of cables sprouting from the back of your PC can look like Medusa on a bad hair day. Normally, this isn't a problem . . . until you decide to move your PC, or you want to repair or upgrade an internal component. Talk about the Gordian knot!

Here's a list of tips for keeping your cables under control:

+ **Use ties to combine and route cables.** I'm a big fan of the reusable Velcro cable tie strips that you can find at your local office supply store. With these ties, you can easily combine cables that are heading in the same direction into a more manageable group. You can also fasten these cable ties to the underside of your desk or behind furniture to keep network and power cables hidden and out of danger.

+ **Label your cables!** Sure, you can tell the source and destination of some cables at a glance — for example, network cables are pretty easy to spot — but what about your USB printer and scanner, which both use the same type of cable? If you must move your PC or unplug cables regularly, avoid the ritual of tracking each cable to its source by doing what techs and computer shops do: Use a label machine to identify the tip of each cable with the peripheral name.

✦ **Tighten those connectors.** "Gee, my monitor was working last night. What gives?" If you didn't use the knobs on either side of the video cable connector to tighten things down, small shifts in position over time could make cables work loose.

✦ **Check your cables for damage periodically.** I have two cats — or, should I say, they have me. Does a cat have you? How about a dog? If so, don't be surprised to find a chewed cable one morning . . . and pray that it isn't a power cable. (I keep all animals away from my office for this reason — not to mention the mess that a shedding dog can leave around your PC.) Of course, cables can also be damaged by bending or stretching them, so I recommend checking each cable at least once a year; I combine this ritual with my PC's yearly cleaning.

Cleaning Monitors and Scanners

Most PC owners are aware that they should keep the glass surfaces of their monitor and scanner clean — but beware, because you can do more harm than good if you don't know what you're doing. Here are the guidelines that I recommend you follow when working with monitor and scanner glass:

✦ **Abrasives are taboo!** Even some household glass cleaners — which you might think could be trusted — can scratch the glass in your monitor or flatbed scanner when used with a rag or paper towel. With a scanner, small scratches can mean real trouble because a scratch can easily show up in your images at higher resolutions. Therefore, I recommend that you use only a dry, soft photographer's lens cloth (which won't scratch) or lens cloths with alcohol that are made specifically for monitors and scanners.

✦ **Never spray liquids onto a flatbed scanner.** If liquid gets under the glass and into the body of the scanner, you could end up with condensation on the inside of the scanner when you use it. Again, a dry, photographer's lens cloth is a good choice . . . or pre-moistened lens cloths, which don't carry enough alcohol to do any harm. (I launch into scanners full-scale in Book VI, Chapter 1.)

✦ **Monitors should never be opened.** Never take the cover off any type of monitor, even if it needs cleaning. Why? Well, your PC's monitor is one of the two components of your system that carry enough voltage to seriously hurt you (the other being your PC's power supply). If your monitor needs to be serviced or cleaned on the inside, take it to your local computer shop. (Find more about monitors in the first chapter of this mini-book.)

✦ **Use a cover for your scanner.** Scanners are somewhat different from most external peripherals. They don't generate any heat while they're on (unlike an external hard drive), and most of us only use a scanner once or twice a week. Therefore, your scanner is a perfect candidate for a cover that will keep it clean . . . and, by no small coincidence, you'll find such covers at your local office supply store.

Cleaning Your Mouse and Keyboard

"Natasha, why we must clean Moose and Squirrel?" (Sorry, I couldn't help it.) Mice and keyboards get *grimy* — *fast* — because your PC's keyboard and pointing device are constantly in use, and they get pawed by human hands. (Of course, you could always wear surgical gloves, but what about your kids?)

Never fear. Here's a list of guidelines that will help you keep your pointing device and keyboard clean and working:

✦ **Buy an optical mouse or trackball. (You'll thank me.)** If you're still using an old-style mouse with a ball — how very '80s — clean it once a month as well. Unscrew the retaining ring on the bottom, remove the mouse ball, and use a cotton-tipped swab dipped in tape-cleaning alcohol (which is 90+ proof and will leave no residue) to clean the rollers inside. Also, make sure that your mousepad is clean and dust-free, and you'll prolong the life of your rodent. (Chapter 1 of this mini-book talks trackball.)

An optical mouse or trackball doesn't need to be cleaned anywhere near as often (if ever) — that's why I keep crowing about them.

✦ **Do the Keyboard Shake!** No, it's not a new dance craze, but it is the best method of cleaning accumulated gunk from your keyboard, and I recommend doing this at least once a month. Turn your keyboard upside down and shake it vigorously back and forth; prepare to be amazed (or grossed out, especially if the whole family uses your PC).

✦ **Find yet another use for your compressed air.** Your keyboard can collect debris that can't be shaken free. If so, using compressed air will likely blow it free (unless it's alive and well dug-in, but I haven't encountered anything like that in my travels so far).

Cleaning and Maintaining Your Printer

Time to consider a peripheral that not only needs cleaning but can also contribute mightily to its own mess. If you've ever had to clean up spilled laser printer toner, I think you know what I mean. Printers have all the necessary features that make them prime targets for regular maintenance:

+ They're open to the outside world.

+ They're stuffed full of complex moving parts.

+ They're constantly running out of ink or toner.

+ They act as a magnet for dust.

In this section, I show you how to clean and maintain yon printing instrument.

Cleaning laser printers

Your laser printer contains a mortal enemy — *toner,* that insidious stuff that seems to have a diabolical mind of its own. Luckily, most cartridges are at least partially sealed, and only older models of laser printers can produce a really nasty Three Mile Island-level spill. If any toner escapes, however, you'll quickly find that it's a very fine powder that's sensitive to static charges and that immediately heads to every corner of your printer. Those nooks and crannies can be a real pain to clean. And because toner can permanently stain clothing and carpet — *and* it's harmful to pets and kids — you should be doubly careful to keep toner inside the cartridge where it belongs.

Therefore, please take the time to completely read the instructions for your specific laser printer before you install that first toner cartridge. Also avoid shaking the cartridge unless the manufacturer recommends a particular motion to help distribute the toner evenly.

If you do spill toner, head to your local office supply store for toner clean-up cloths. These handy wipes contain a chemical that attracts toner and keeps it on the cloth. Oh, and don't use warm or hot water to wash toner off your hands — toner can literally melt and adhere to your skin!

Never attempt to clean the interior of your laser printer while it's on! Laser technology uses very high temperatures to bond toner to paper, so you could be subject to serious burns if you're not careful. I always make sure that a laser printer has been off for at least 30 minutes before I clean or service it.

Although you should follow the specific instructions for your brand and model of laser printer while cleaning the interior, here's a list of the parts that are generally covered in a good cleaning:

+ **Corona wires:** These wires (see Figure 4-1) transfer a static charge to the paper to attract toner, but if they get dusty, you'll immediately see spotting and degraded print quality in your printed documents. Most manufacturers advise that you use a clean, dry cotton swab to gently wipe the wires. You should find the wires close to the paper rollers inside your printer. (Look for labels added by the manufacturer that point to them and also check your printer's manual if necessary.)

✦ **Toner guard:** These felt pads trap excess toner before it gets on your documents. You might receive a new toner guard set with each cartridge, but in a pinch, you can probably remove the pads from your printer and rub them on a clean cloth to remove that built-up toner.

✦ **Paper feed rollers:** Use a cotton swab soaked in alcohol to clean the buildup from your paper rollers, as shown so artistically in Figure 4-2.

✦ **Fan vent:** Yep, your laser printer has its own fan — remember the intense heat that I mention a few paragraphs ago? And just like the fan cleaning that I recommended for your PC, it's a good idea to use compressed air to blow any dust from the fan and the ventilation grill.

I highly recommend using the laser printer cleaning sheets that you can find at your local office supply store. These papers are treated to remove dust and excess toner from the printer's paper path, which you normally wouldn't be able to clean. Plus, they're very easy to use: You just run them through the printer as if they were regular sheets of paper. If your printer resides in a dusty or smoky room, these sheets are worth their weight in gold.

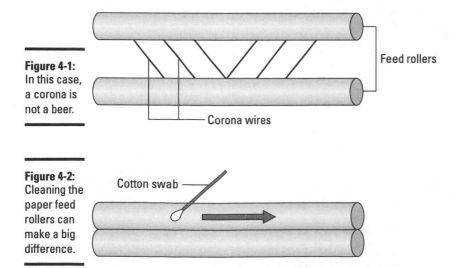

Figure 4-1: In this case, a corona is not a beer.

Feed rollers

Corona wires

Figure 4-2: Cleaning the paper feed rollers can make a big difference.

Cotton swab

Changing inkjet cartridges

Here are two methods of determining when you need to change the cartridges in your inkjet printer:

✦ **The automatic route:** Most inkjet printers on the market today have onscreen alerts that appear when the ink level of the cartridge is low. Or, like you see in Figure 4-3, your printer might actually be able to display the amount of ink remaining in a cartridge. (A very valuable trick, indeed, especially for students with term papers looming in the near future.)

✦ **The "Man, I can barely read this page!" method:** If you have an older inkjet printer, you might not receive any warning at all about the ink levels in your cartridges — but when they're empty, pardner, you'll know.

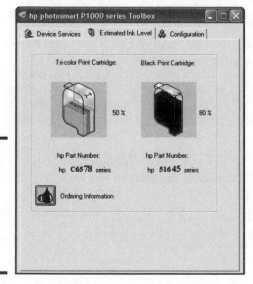

Figure 4-3: Checking the ink levels on late-model inkjet printers is a cinch.

After you know that you need to change your cartridges, however, the general procedure is the same for virtually every inkjet printer that I've ever encountered:

1. **Open the top of your printer.**

   This will cause most printer models to politely center the carriage to provide you with access to the cartridges.

2. **After you have access to the cartridges, turn your printer off.**

   Never try to change the cartridges in a printer that's still powered on! (Your fingers will thank me.)

3. **Lift or turn the latches holding the ink cartridge in place.**

   Most inkjet printers have at least two cartridges — one for black and one for color — so make sure that you're working with the right cartridge before you remove it.

4. **Remove the used cartridge and consider refilling it.**

   I discuss the pros and cons of refilling cartridges later in this chapter.

5. **Load the new cartridge and fasten the latch to hold it down.**

6. **Turn your printer back on and close the lid.**

**Book I
Chapter 4**

Maintaining Your
Hardware

Calibrating your printer

This maintenance task is reserved only for inkjet printer owners. (My, aren't we lucky?) *Calibration* refers to the proper alignment of the inkjet cartridge nozzles to both the paper and each other; without a properly calibrated printer, your print quality will degrade over time. This is usually the problem when folks complain that lines appear fuzzy in artwork or when colored areas in printed images start or stop before they should.

If you hear a professional photographer or graphic artist talk about *color calibration,* that's something completely different; color calibration is the process of color matching between the colors that appear on your monitor and the colors produced by your printer. Most of us will never need that level of precise color, and most inkjet printers now allow you to make changes to the hue and saturation of your prints by simply dragging a slider in a printer's Properties dialog box. But if you need to perform a full color calibration, check your printer's manual for more information about using Windows color profiles.

Your printer will automatically calibrate itself when you first load a new cartridge, so I recommend that you calibrate either three months after installing a new cartridge or when you notice that your print quality is suffering . . . whichever comes first. (Of course, the time period will vary according to how often you use your printer and the length of your average printed document.)

Although each brand (and sometimes each model) of printer has different onscreen controls for calibrating output, you should be able to access them from the printer's Properties dialog box. Follow these steps in Windows XP:

1. **Choose Start⇨Printers and Faxes (or Start⇨Settings⇨Printers and Faxes, depending on how your Start menu is configured).**

   You see the available printers on your system (see Figure 4-4).

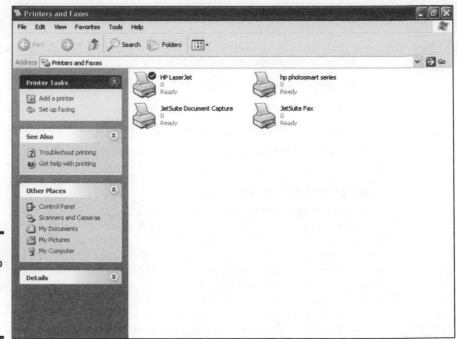

Figure 4-4:
Preparing to
calibrate a
printer in
Windows
XP.

2. **Right-click the printer that you want to calibrate and then choose Properties from the pop-up menu that appears.**

A dialog box somewhat similar to Figure 4-5 appears.

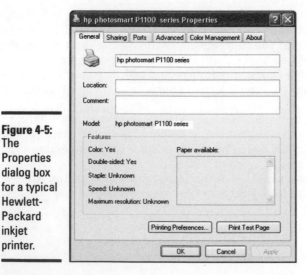

Figure 4-5:
The
Properties
dialog box
for a typical
Hewlett-
Packard
inkjet
printer.

3. **If the printer's calibration function isn't visible from the General tab, you might have to search for it on the Advanced tab. You can try clicking the Printing Preferences button as well — in my case, I have to do that and also click the Services tab.**

If it still fails to appear, check your printer manual for the location of the calibration controls; some printer manufacturers provide a separate application that you can run to display your maintenance toolbox.

Figure 4-6 illustrates the calibration dialog box for my HP printer.

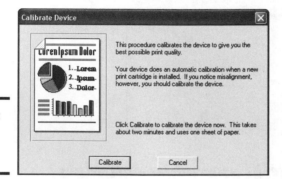

Figure 4-6:
Ready to
calibrate,
Captain!

4. **Run the calibration. (In my case, I click the Calibrate button.)**

The process takes under a minute and uses a single sheet of paper.

Cleaning inkjet cartridges

Here's yet another fun task limited to just inkjet owners. I usually clean my inkjet cartridge nozzles about once every three months or whenever the output from my printer suddenly starts showing streaks of horizontal white lines. (As you've probably guessed, the nozzles control the placement and amount of each droplet of ink.) The good news is that you won't need a bucket and a scrub brush for this chore; instead, your printer can take care of cleaning its own cartridges (with your approval, of course).

A new inkjet cartridge provides your printer with a brand-new set of nozzles, so you should restart that three-month period when you change cartridges. However, if you refill an inkjet cartridge — which I discuss in the next section — you should clean the cartridge nozzles immediately after the refilled cartridge has been reinstalled.

Like the calibration controls that I discuss in the preceding section, the location of your printer's cartridge cleaning controls is very likely buried somewhere within its Properties dialog box, or it's available when you run the maintenance program supplied by your printer manufacturer. To display the Properties dialog box for your printer, follow the procedure that I cover earlier.

Figure 4-7 illustrates the cleaning controls for my HP inkjet printer. I just click the Clean button, wait about a minute, and I'm done.

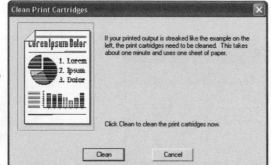

Figure 4-7: Preparing to clean my inkjet printer nozzles.

Should you refill used inkjet cartridges?

I'll be honest with you: I don't refill inkjet cartridges, and I don't recommend that you do, either. The only real advantage to refilling cartridges is the money that you save over buying a new cartridge. As a fellow inkjet owner myself, I feel your pain when you're standing in the checkout line at Wal-Mart with a $40 U.S. cartridge in your hand.

However, here are the reasons why I buy new cartridges — consider these the facts that you *won't* see when that refill kit TV commercial appears for the umpteenth time:

✦ **You'll probably get messy.** Even if you're experienced at refilling an ink cartridge, there's a good chance that you'll end up with a toxic spill. Make sure that you cover your work surface with a plastic sheet and don't wear anything formal.

✦ **You get substandard ink.** One of the reasons why ink refills are cheaper is that the quality of the ink used in the refill kits is usually never as good as the ink in a new cartridge. That second-rate ink can cause color changes or uneven coverage and might also end up taking longer to dry (resulting in Smear City).

✦ **You're reusing the nozzles.** I mention cleaning cartridge nozzles in the previous section. Unfortunately, those nozzles are not meant to be reused, and refilling a cartridge can result in clogs. You'll have to clean your cartridges far more often, and the quality of your printer's output might drop appreciably over time when you use a refilled cartridge.

Thus my decision and my recommendation — let someone else suffer below-par print quality by refilling their used cartridges.

Book II

Windows XP

The 5th Wave   By Rich Tennant

"It's a ten step word processing program. It comes with a spell—checker, grammar—checker, cliche—checker, whine—checker, passive/aggressive—checker, politically correct—checker, hissy—fit—checker, pretentious pontificating—checker, boring anecdote—checker and a Freudian reference—checker."

Contents at a Glance

Chapter 1: Shake Hands with Windows XP

In This Chapter

✔ **Celebrating the advantages of Windows XP**

✔ **Starting and shutting down Windows XP**

✔ **Introducing Windows controls**

✔ **Using the keyboard**

✔ **Searching for help**

✔ **Contacting Microsoft for support**

Of all the many Windows flavors that I've seen over the last decade — everything from mixed berry to plain vanilla — Windows XP Home and Professional are the best versions that I've ever used. The XP operating system offers the top appearance, performance, and functionality available for your PC today . . . as long as you're using an Intel Pentium or Advanced Micro Devices (AMD) Athlon processor. (If you're using an older Pentium III machine, I'd consider sticking with Windows 98SE because your PC doesn't have the necessary horsepower to provide real performance in Windows XP.)

Note: There are actually five different editions of Windows XP: Home and XP Professional are by far the best sellers, whilst XP Professional x64 Edition, XP Tablet PC and XP Media Edition fill more specialized needs. (You can tell which version you have when you start your PC because Windows XP displays an identifying welcome screen while it's loading.) The Home Edition is the best-selling version of Windows XP, although it omits a handful of networking and security features found in XP Professional (the most glaring being the lack of the Backup Wizard). For a typical home PC owner or small office PC user, the Home and Professional Editions are just about identical in look, taste, and smell — therefore, everything that you find in this chapter applies to both the Home and Professional versions of XP. (When disparities occur later in this mini-book, I'll send up a flare.)

In this chapter, I present you with the beginning of your Windows XP manual — the invaluable, indispensable paper volume that you *didn't* get when you bought XP or bought your PC. (Can you tell that I used to write software user manuals?) This book assumes no prior experience with XP, so I start with shutting down your PC and the most important controls and keys that you'll use in the following chapters.

Why Windows XP, Anyway?

If you're wondering why I consider Windows XP to be the pick of Microsoft's litter — and why you shouldn't run an older version, such as Windows 2000, Millennium (Me), or 98SE — allow me to point out its advantages as well as the occasional downside.

✦ **It's attractive:** Microsoft has gone to a lot of work to make XP a graphics jewel — menus fade in and out, 3-D effects abound, and even your mouse has a fashionable shadow under it. (This graphics banquet has its cost: You'll need a Pentium 4, Pentium Extreme Edition, Athlon XP or Athlon 64 processor, at least 512MB of random access memory [RAM], and a graphics card of recent manufacture to enjoy these visual perks without slowing down your PC.)

✦ **It's fast:** With a PC built within the last year or so, XP will perform better than older versions of Windows — and that includes Windows 2000, which was used as the foundation for XP.

✦ **It's customizable:** You can tweak, remove and re-engineer things like toolbars, menus, and your desktop within Windows XP. (In this chapter, however, I stick with the defaults to avoid confusing you with my crazy personal preferences!)

✦ **It's easier to use:** No downside here! Older versions of Windows made it harder to take care of chores such as creating an Internet connection and adding a printer to your system. The folks in Redmond have been working overtime to help automate these processes.

✦ **It supports the latest standards:** Again, this is nothing but the very definition of Good. XP can handle all the acronyms that you want (but might not yet know): MP3, MPEG, JPEG, USB, Wi-Fi, DSL, and many more. (All those cryptic escapees from a bowl of alphabet soup get explained in this book.) Unlike older versions of Windows — which either don't support the latest technology at all or do require additional software to use — XP has built-in support for today's neatest toys.

✦ **It's harder to crash:** Windows XP is descended from Windows 2000, which in turn dates back to Windows NT — and all three are more crash resistant and reliable than the Windows 95/98/Me crowd. XP also includes better protection for system files; for example, you can set a restore point that can be used as a backup if your system files are corrupted. Fewer crashes and better reliability mean that you can actually get up from your PC for lunch without worrying whether it will still be running when you return.

How much space does Windows XP need?

On my desk is an original copy of Microsoft Windows/286 — version 2.1 of Windows, which dates back to the late '80s and was designed for 80286-powered PCs. I keep it as a conversation piece. The entire installation took a whopping seven, low-density floppy disks, and only one actually holds the operating system! (The other six disks store applications, fonts, printer drivers, and such.)

Over the years, Windows has inflated like a Macy's Parade balloon on Thanksgiving Day. Installing Windows XP Home will cost you at least 1.5GB in hard drive space; if you choose XP Professional, you need at least 2GB. (And you can forget the floppies — Windows is only available on CD-ROM now.)

Remember, however, that those figures don't include the extra hard drive territory that XP will demand for things such as temporary files and virtual memory, so it's best to add another 500MB (or even 1GB) to those totals. With today's hard drives, a spare gigabyte of space is easy to come by, so there's no reason to feel claustrophobic.

Book II
Chapter 1

Shake Hands
with Windows XP

Shutting Things Down

After you install Windows XP, starting (or, as techno-types continue to call it, *booting*) your PC is as easy as pressing the power switch. Some diagnostic and troubleshooting options are available during the startup process, but I cover those in detail in Chapter 5 of this mini-book. For now, just remember the power switch.

There's more to consider, however, when you're ready to shut down Windows XP. In this section, I discuss the five methods that you can use to shut down XP partially or completely.

Shutting down completely

The first option is the full deal: turning off your PC completely. Choose Start⇨ Turn Off Computer, and XP displays the Turn Off Computer dialog box that you see in Figure 1-1. Click the Turn Off button, and your PC will (eventually) turn itself off.

Figure 1-1: What'll it be — Stand By, Turn Off, or Restart?

Windows XP tries to be a friend by automatically closing any applications that you're currently running before it shuts down. However, if a program has an open document or file that hasn't been saved, the application is *supposed* to prompt you to save your changes first. Note that I said *supposed* there: Some misbehaving or badly written programs *won't* prompt you before they zap themselves out of existence, so don't use the Turn Off or Restart options unless you've manually saved all open documents (or you trust any application that's open, such as Microsoft Word).

Restarting your PC

Restarting your PC comprises shutting down Windows XP and then immediately turning it back on again. (*Restarting* is also called *rebooting.*) To restart your computer, choose Start⇨Turn Off Computer; from the Turn Off Computer dialog box that appears, click the Restart button. You don't need to actually press the power button to turn your PC back on again. Dame Windows, she can do it all.

You might need to restart when you install new software or upgrade existing software. (You'll typically see a dialog box that displays a Restart button.) I also recommend rebooting if your PC starts acting flaky — like when error messages keep appearing, programs refuse to close, or strange graphics appear on your desktop.

Using standby mode

Standby mode immediately puts your PC in a low-power mode: The monitor goes black, and XP appears to shut down. However, you can return to your work just as you left it by pressing one of the arrow keys on the keyboard or moving the mouse. It's rather like your monitor waking up from a screen-saver snooze; it saves electricity and makes it easier to return to your work "already in progress." To go into standby mode, choose Start⇨Turn Off Computer; from the Turn Off Computer dialog box that appears, click the Stand By button.

Not all PCs support standby mode. Check your PC or motherboard manual to see whether you can use this feature. If you can use XP's standby mode, you can also set your PC's power switch to activate standby mode rather than turning off the computer. Or your PC can go into standby mode automatically after a certain amount of inactivity. For more information, see Chapter 6 in this mini-book.

Manually save your documents before putting your PC in standby mode because putting your machine into standby mode does *not* save the files that you're working with to your hard drive. You'll lose everything if your PC is hit with a power failure and you haven't saved your documents.

Yes, your PC can hibernate

Hibernation is a variation of standby mode that's popular with laptop owners. It takes longer for your PC to switch to hibernation mode or to return from hibernation, but that's because a snapshot of XP (including all open applications and files) is saved to your hard drive. Unlike standby mode, a power failure while your PC is hibernating won't result in lost files!

Like standby mode, your PC's motherboard must support XP's hibernation mode. First enable hibernation mode: Open the Windows XP Control Panel, choose Power Options, click the Hibernate tab in the dialog box that appears, and then mark the Enable Hibernation Support check box. Click OK to save your changes. When you want to put your machine in hibernation mode, choose Start⇨Turn Off Computer; then click the Hibernate button in the Turn Off Computer dialog box that appears. (You can also set your PC to automatically hibernate when a certain period of inactivity has passed, and most laptops can be set to hibernate automatically when you close them. More on the thrills of hibernation in Chapter 6 of this mini-book.)

Logging off

Your final choice when leaving your PC is to log off. This leaves your PC running, but others can log on to the PC if they enter a valid username and password. Like a true shutdown, logging off an XP machine automatically closes most applications and any open documents.

Windows XP keeps track of each different user's account data and documents, so you can be assured that everything that you don't want seen by others remains private. Yet, if you want to share a document with other users on your system, you can make use of shared folders that allow others to open and edit your files. I go over multi-user operation in Chapters 4 and 6 of this mini-book, so don't worry . . . all will become clear there.

To pass the computing torch to someone else, choose Start⇨Log Off to display the Log Off dialog box and then click Log Off again.

Your Windows XP Controls

After you become an expert in starting and shutting down your PC, survey the landscape of Windows XP. Here I show you the various graphical WUDs (short for *Wondrous User Devices*) represented on your desktop and how you can use them to exercise your will within.

Icons

The first stop on your journey is the lowly icon . . . often jeered and often the target of a string of impassioned and unprintable words. Yet, icons are still the building blocks of today's graphical user interfaces (GUIs; that's a 10-cent synonym for operating systems such as Windows, Mac OS X, and Linux, which all use a mouse). Believe me, icons will be around long after you and I are no longer worried about PCs.

Icons look like a picture, and that's no accident because they are simple representations of different locations and items on your computer. For example, Windows XP displays different types of icons to represent things such as the following:

- ✦ **Files and folders**
- ✦ **Programs** that you can run
- ✦ **Hardware** such as hard drives, CD/DVD drives, and printers
- ✦ **Internet connections**
- ✦ **Other computers** on your home or office network

Figure 1-2 shows a gaggle of different types of icons in their natural environment. I go into much more detail about what you can do with icons in the next two chapters of this mini-book. For now, just remember their versatility and that they represent something else on your system besides a thumbnail-sized picture.

That constantly changing cursor

Within Windows XP, your mouse cursor is more than just a focus for your clicking finger — although that *is* its main use. When it's not pointing the way (depending on the desktop action that you're performing or the application that you're running), your cursor can also

- ✦ **Show status:** Indicate that your PC is busy doing something, such as loading a file or applying your last command.
- ✦ **Show selection:** Specify the text or graphics that you want to select (in order to do something nefarious, I'm sure).
- ✦ **Show location:** Indicate a position in a document where you can move.
- ✦ **Show file movement:** Show that you're copying or moving files between locations on your system.

Figure 1-2:
I have
always
depended
upon the
kindness
of icons.

By the way, you can also click your right mouse button *(right-click)* when your mouse cursor is resting atop something to display a pop-up menu that includes commands that are specific to the item that you're hovering over. (To techno-nerds, the term for this pop-up is a *contextual menu*. Geez.) For example, if you right-click a digital photograph that you've saved to your hard drive, you can choose to preview it, edit it, or print it. Personally, I'm a big fan of contextual menus because they usually contain everything that applies to a particular file. Some programs, such as Paint Shop Pro, actually add their own commands to the contextual menu.

If you encounter a strange cursor shape or animation within a program that you're running, you can usually refer to the program's manual to determine what the heck your little friend is trying to tell you.

For even more interesting things that you can do with your mouse cursor, check out Chapter 6 of this mini-book.

The Start menu

Another familiar face that you'll see often in Windows XP is the Start menu, as shown in Figure 1-3. Someone at Microsoft should get a steak dinner for this one. The name actually fits the purpose because you can start virtually every activity and task that your PC can perform from this one menu.

Figure 1-3:
The
invaluable
Start menu.

To use the Start menu, move your mouse cursor to the bottom of your desktop until the Start button appears at the lower-left corner. Click the Start button to display the Start menu, move your cursor to the desired icon or command, and then click.

Highlights of the Start menu include

✦ The **All Programs** pop-up menu, where you can choose to run any program that you've installed on your PC.

✦ The **Recent Applications** list on the left, which makes it easy to run a program that you've used . . . well . . . recently.

✦ The **My Documents** menu, where you can load all sorts of documents that you've created yourself or saved to your hard drive (such as photos, videos, and music).

✦ The **Control Panel**, where you configure Windows XP to your preferences. (Chapter 6 of this mini-book centers on the Control Panel.)

✦ The **Search** command, which can help you track down specific files, folders, or locations within your system.

✦ The **Run** command, which allows you to run a program by actually (gasp!) typing its name.

✦ Access to your system **printers** and **fax/modem.**

✦ Access to your network locations, such as your **Internet connection** and any home or office **network** that your PC can use.

I discuss all these controls in later chapters of this mini-book — but you've got to admit that it's really *sassy* to have all of 'em together in one place! (Note, however, that your Start menu will look different from mine because I customized mine to fit the way that I work, and I've also been running my own set of programs.)

The taskbar

The next stop on the XP Express — no pun intended, but I'll take it, anyway — is the *taskbar,* which is that little strip of buttons and miniature icons that runs along the bottom of the screen. Like the Start menu, the taskbar is another great control that you can use to accomplish all sorts of things, and it remains out of sight until you need it. (Depending on the settings that you choose for your taskbar, it might remain hidden until you move your mouse cursor to the bottom of the screen, see Figure 1-4.) I talk more about configuring the taskbar in Chapter 3 of this mini-book.

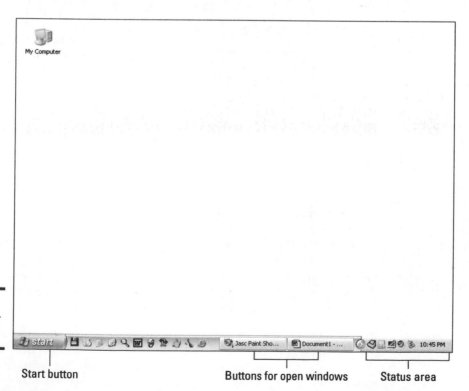

Figure 1-4:
The taskbar
revealed.

Start button   Buttons for open windows   Status area

Don't worry if your taskbar doesn't look like mine in the figure. The appearance of the taskbar varies according to the programs that you're running and the custom controls that you've added to it. In other words, the taskbar is another of those controls that quickly becomes personalized to your needs, depending on the programs that you install and the programs that are currently running. The taskbar allows you to

✦ **Switch quickly between applications** that are running.

✦ **Run the programs** that you specify with a single mouse click.

✦ **Control background programs** that normally run hidden, such as Norton AntiVirus.

✦ **Control hardware** such as your printer and modem.

✦ **Connect and disconnect Universal Serial Bus (USB) and FireWire peripherals** such as a digital camera and an external DVD recorder.

✦ **View the time and date.**

✦ **Access the Start menu.**

You'll find the full scoop on the taskbar in Chapter 3 of this mini-book.

Menus and toolbars

Here's one more set of Windows XP common controls, which are found in just about any program that you run because they're part of Microsoft's grand user interface design standard. (Thus making all Windows programs easier to understand and use, often without the need to refer to that ridiculous Web-based user manual.) Both of these common controls — menus and toolbars — are shown in the multipurpose Figure 1-5.

The miracle of menus

Menus are the drop-down secret to life itself. Each menu contains either a group of similar commands or a group of commands that fall under the same category. To use a menu, you can either

✦ **Go mousing:** Click the menu name and then click the command from the list that appears.

✦ **Go digital:** Hold down the Alt key, press the underlined letter in the menu name *(a hot key),* use your cursor keys to choose a command, and then press Enter to use it.

For example, to open a file in virtually any Windows application, click the File menu at the top of the window and then click Open from the drop-down list that appears. Alternatively, while holding down the Alt key, press F (the hot key for the File menu) and then press O (the hot key for the Open menu).

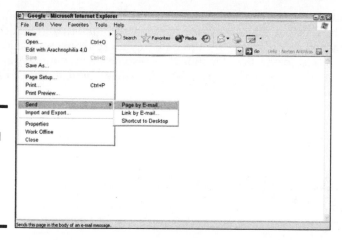

Figure 1-5:
Menus and
toolbars
abound
in the
Windows
world.

Those tremendous toolbars

A *toolbar* is a collection of buttons that allows you to use the most common menu commands in a program with a single click. Typically, toolbars appear at the top of a program window, but many applications (such as Adobe Photoshop, for example) either have floating toolbars that exist as separate windows or have toolbars that can be resized and relocated anywhere in the application window. Some applications will let you go even further. For example, the toolbars in Microsoft Word can be customized with buttons for the menu commands that you use the most.

To illustrate how easy it is to use a toolbar, consider opening a file. If the application that you're using has a File Open button on the toolbar, click it. End of story. (The moral is: Toolbars rule!)

To display the name of a toolbar (which is usually all you need to identify it or to jog your memory), leave your mouse pointer motionless on top of the toolbar button for a moment or two. Such motionless conduct is called *hovering* among techno-types.

Using Bill's Funky Keys

Not all Windows-specific controls are meant for your mouse. Thanks to the Power of Bill, today's PC keyboards come complete with additional keys that are tied directly to Windows, so you can use your keyboard for navigation instead of your mouse. As any PC power user will tell you, the mouse that can move faster and more efficiently than your fingertips hasn't been (and likely never will be) invented. Just wait until Bill gets those new letters that he wants in the alphabet!

Most of the keys on your computer keyboard work like they do on standard typewriters. For instance, pressing Shift in combination with another alphabetic key still creates a capital letter. PC keyboards, however, also sport nifty special keys for navigation, functions, and (sometimes) Windows-specific commands. For your reference, Figure 1-6 illustrates a typical modern 104-key PC keyboard.

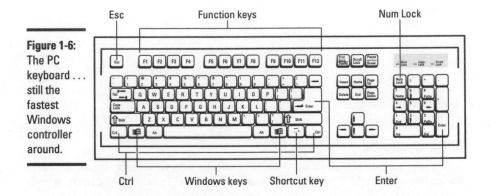

Esc   Function keys   Num Lock

Figure 1-6: The PC keyboard ... still the fastest Windows controller around.

Ctrl   Windows keys   Shortcut key   Enter

The Windows keys

Ah, the Windows keys — they rest snugly between the Alt and Ctrl keys on both sides of the spacebar on your keyboard. You can press either of these keys at any time to display the Start menu. Additionally, a number of other keys can be used in combination with a Windows key. Just hold a Windows (Win) key down and try one of the keys listed in Table 1-1.

Table 1-1	Windows Key Combinations
Sequence	*Action*
Win+D	Displays the Windows desktop (even with other programs running)
Win+E	Runs Windows Explorer, where you can manage your files
Win+F	Opens the Search/Find Files dialog box from which you can locate a file or folder
Win+R	Opens the Run dialog box from which you can run a program by typing its name

The Shortcut key

Remember how enamored I am of contextual menus? A quick poke at the Shortcut key — which is located on the right side of the keyboard between the Windows and Ctrl keys — will act as a right-click (displays a contextual menu) when you've selected an icon anywhere in Windows. After the pop-up menu appears, you can use your cursor keys and the Enter key to choose a command.

Other PC-specific keys

These old friends have been around since the days of Genghis Khan — or at least the beginnings of the IBM PC, whichever came first. Anyway, these keys still come in quite handy in the Windows world.

✦ **Enter:** PC keyboards have two of these beauties: one above the Shift key on the right side of the alphabetic keys and the other at the lower right of the numeric keypad. Within your word processor, of course, pressing Enter creates a new paragraph. But elsewhere within Windows, pressing Enter almost always starts a command or selects an item. (A friend of mine still calls this the *Submit key*. He's great fun at parties.)

✦ **Escape (Esc):** Press Esc (far upper-left on your keyboard), and you're jetted off to your favorite vacation spot with a ton of cash to spend and your favorite movie star. (No, not really — although Bill is rumored to be working on the new enhanced Escape key for Windows Vista.) Actually, you use Esc to back out of things. Pressing Esc can cancel many commands, close some windows, and exit dialog boxes.

✦ **Num Lock:** Press this key (upper-left of the numeric keypad) to toggle those keys between the numbers (great for spreadsheets and data entry) and navigational keys (note the cursor arrow symbols on the 2, 4, 6, and 8 keys).

✦ **Control (Ctrl) keys:** These two keys (either side of the spacebar) are used in conjunction with other keys for editing and keyboard commands within many applications. For example, pressing the combination Ctrl+B within Microsoft Word makes selected text bold.

✦ **Alternate (Alt) keys:** Like the Ctrl keys, your Alt keys are used in league with other keys, typically for invoking menus and special features within your applications.

✦ **Function keys:** These 12 sentinels across the top of your keyboard are used for different purposes throughout Windows — and in many cases, even within specific applications (hence the generic name). They're usually abbreviated as *F1* through *F12*.

Other keys on your keyboard — like Home, End, Page Up and Page Down — will also have specific uses within every application. To become a power user of a certain application, consult that program's Help system for the special keystrokes that it uses. You'll zip through documents while others plod along!

Using the Windows XP Help System

Speaking of help, I'm happy to say that Windows XP comes with the best Help system that's ever shipped with any version of Windows. It even has online components that you can refer to for the latest information on features (and the *occasional* bug). With the Help system, you can

✦ **Locate specific help** on nearly any topic.

✦ **Follow task tutorials** that guide you step by step through all sorts of procedures (such as printing, troubleshooting, and updating Windows with the latest patches).

✦ **Search the Microsoft Windows XP newsgroups** (with an Internet connection).

✦ **Scan tips and tricks** from Windows experts (with an Internet connection).

✦ **View the latest headlines** on new XP features (with an Internet connection).

Displaying Help

The two methods of displaying Help within Windows itself are

✦ **Press F1 while on your desktop.** Click anywhere on your desktop and then press the F1 key to load the top-level Windows Help system window that you see in Figure 1-7. (Check out that spiffy toolbar at the top of that window!) *Note:* If you're currently using a program, pressing F1 will display the Help system for that program.

✦ **Click Help from the Start menu.** This is yet another neat function of the Start menu.

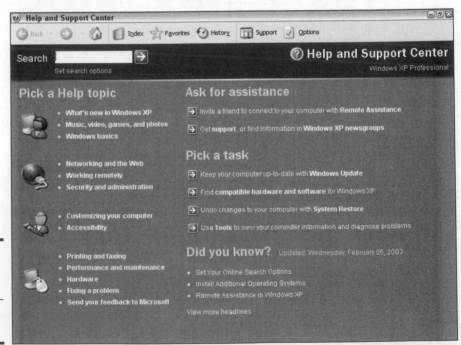

Figure 1-7: The oracle of all things Windows — the XP Help system.

Searching for specific help

After the XP Help window is displayed, feel free to click any of the *links* (the bolded words) to display the corresponding topic. However, you'll usually visit the Help system to search for specific help on a Windows feature or command. To search for a word or phrase within Help, follow these steps:

1. **Click within the Search box at the top of the Help window.**

2. **Type the word or phrase that you want to search for and then press Enter.**

   The fewer words that you enter, the better the chance of getting a match that will address your topic.

   The Help system hums happily to itself for a few seconds and then displays the results page that you see in Figure 1-8. (I searched for the phrase *burning a cd* in this example.)

3. **To display the information in a topic, click the topic name (found in the Search Results area).**

   Windows displays the information in a separate pane, as shown in Figure 1-9, with all occurrences of your word or phrase highlighted so that they're easier to spot.

**Book II
Chapter 1**

**Shake Hands
with Windows XP**

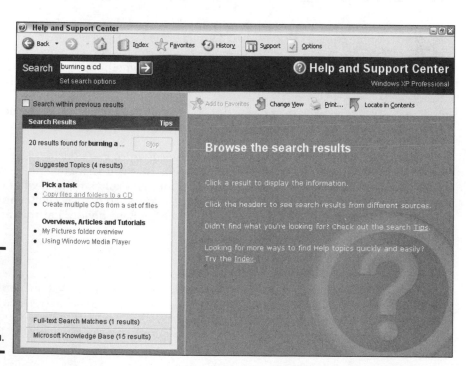

Figure 1-8:
The results
of a typical
search
through the
Help system.

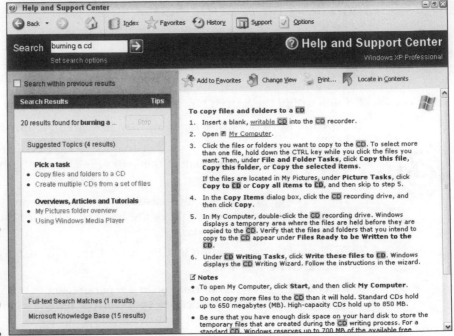

Figure 1-9:
Your search
may provide
you with a
step-by-step
Help topic.

Some steps have *links* (look for underlined text), which you can click to open the dialog box or window in question or run the program mentioned in the Help text. (This really makes it easy to fix something, especially when you don't quite know where that one particular setting is within the XP behemoth.)

To move backward through Help topics to where you started, click the Back button on the toolbar at the top left of the Help window.

Some search results will return *technical articles* — consider them *Tips for Techno-nerds* — that relate to the topic that you've found. Technical articles can include bug fixes, workarounds, or just explanations of what precisely is happening when you use a Windows feature. To display the technical articles for a topic, click the Microsoft Knowledge Base divider bar that appears in the Search Results pane.

Yelling for assistance

If you can't find what you're looking for within the Help system, you can turn to Microsoft for direct support. From the top-level Help menu (refer to Figure 1-7), click the Get Support link (under the Ask for Assistance heading) to display the Support window that you see in Figure 1-10. (You can also click the Support button in the toolbar.)

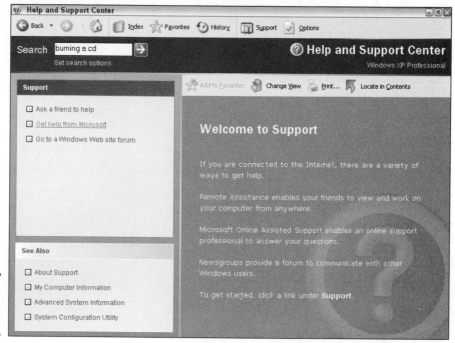

Figure 1-10:
Go to the top
for support.

Unless you have a very knowledgeable friend who has already mastered the Remote Assistance feature of Windows XP, I *strongly* urge you to avoid using the Ask a Friend for Help option. This involves your friend connecting to your PC over the Internet and gaining control of XP . . . with all the possible nastiness that entails. Personally, I recommend that you turn to Microsoft support instead.

In the Support window, click the <u>Get Help from Microsoft</u> link — you'll need an Internet connection, of course, like any undertaking in the civilized world these days — and then click the product that's giving you trouble. Most products offer both e-mail and phone support; some are free services (at least for the first request), while additional support requests are currently $35 per incident). Depending on the option that you choose, you might get a Web-based e-mail form or a real-time chat with a support representative.

If you lost your Internet connection or you don't have an e-mail address, naturally, you can also contact Microsoft for support by telephone . . . at least for now. (Insert ominous chord here.) If you opt for phone support, you'll get one support request for free, but after that, Microsoft will charge you $35 for each successive incident.

Chapter 2: The Many Windows of Windows

In This Chapter

✔ Managing windows

✔ Recognizing icons

✔ Selecting one (or many) icons

✔ Using toolbars in Windows XP

Doing things graphically is what Windows XP is all about. The idea of visual control is at the heart of today's graphical user interfaces (GUIs), like Windows and Mac OS X (and Linux, when it's wearing the right makeup).

In this chapter, I introduce you to the graphical building blocks of Windows XP. Plus, I show you the "antique" keyboard combinations that are even faster than a speeding mouse. (Hey, any power user will tell you that pressing a sequence of two or three keys is often faster than clicking!)

Managing Windows Means Productivity

What's that on the horizon? Oh boy, it looks like another of those weighty Mark's Maxims:

Learn the Zen of the window and become a power user. ™

In this section, you do just that — and your efficiency and speed in XP will amaze your friends and family. (And that's what it's all really about, right?)

Windows XP has a helpful feature that displays a short pop-up description of the controls in a window. If this book isn't handy, you can find out the function of a button or widget by leaving your mouse pointer sitting motionless on top of the control in question. (Interesting trivia fact: This mouse action is *hovering*.)

Opening and closing windows

You rarely need to manually open a new window in XP, which is a trademark of good design from the Redmond troop. XP will automatically open a window when you

✦ **Run Explorer** (as shown in Figure 2-1). Just double-click the My Computer icon on your desktop.

✦ **Run most Windows applications.** Some programs, however, run in the background or don't automatically create new document windows.

✦ **Create a new document in a Windows application.**

By default, the left portion of the Explorer window contains common tasks and locations within XP. Personally, I prefer the older-style navigation tree that you see in Figure 2-2, which dates back to previous versions of Windows. To display this view, click the Folders button in the toolbar at the top of the window . . . more on toolbars later in this chapter.

The Close button

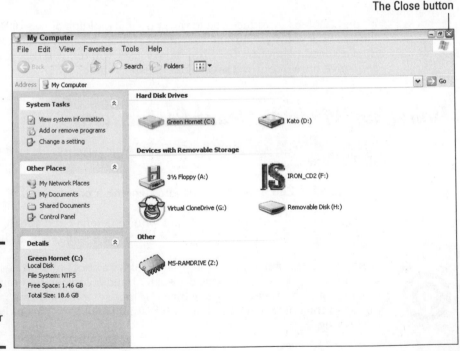

Figure 2-1: The most common XP window is the Explorer window.

The Folders button

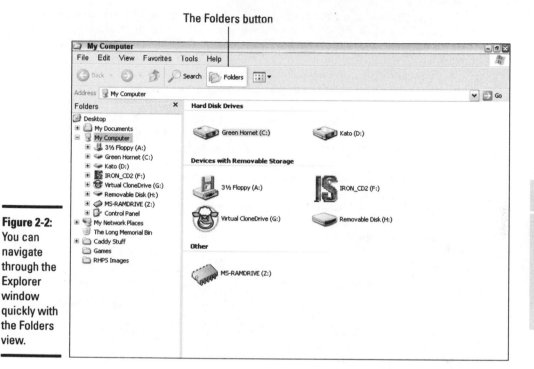

Figure 2-2:
You can
navigate
through the
Explorer
window
quickly with
the Folders
view.

You will, however, need to close windows often to keep your desktop tidy
and to free up system resources for other things. To close a window, move
your mouse pointer over the *Close button* — the red button with an X at the
top-right corner of the window, as shown in Figure 2-1 — and then click the
left mouse button. Alternatively, you can usually choose File⇨Close from
the window's menu.

"But what if I have an open document in a window?" There's a safety net
in place within any well-behaved Windows application (such as Word or
Photoshop, for example): The program will first ask you for confirmation
before it closes a window containing an unsaved document.

Scrolling windows

Suppose that you're reading page one of a six-page document, and you
decide to jump ahead to page five — unfortunately, page five is nowhere in
view. (In the same vein, you could be using Explorer to navigate a hard drive

with dozens of folders, and the folder that you want is farther down within that gaggle of folders.) How do you get to the item or the information that you want to see?

That's the job of those unsung heroes, your *scroll bars* (as shown in Figure 2-3). To move through the contents of the window, just click in the area above or below the scroll button or click the up and down buttons at the top and bottom of the scroll bar. (*Note:* If your document is wider than the application window, you'll get a horizontal scroll bar as well. It works the same way, just moving the contents of the window to the left or to the right.)

To really move like the wind within a window (bad pun that I won't repeat), you can even click the scroll button and drag it. When you drag something, you first click it — in this case, the scroll button — and then hold down the mouse button while you move the mouse in the desired direction. You'll find more uses for dragging later in this chapter.

Up and down buttons

Scroll button

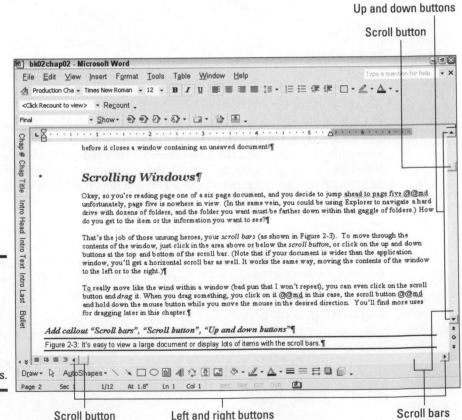

Figure 2-3:
Use scroll bars to easily view a large document or display lots of items.

Scroll button   Left and right buttons   Scroll bars

Many applications allow you to scroll through the contents of a window with your keyboard arrow (navigation) keys. And pressing the Page Up and Page Down keys should move you an entire page at a time through the contents of a window.

Minimizing and restoring windows

Sometimes you want to keep a window open, but you don't want it on your desktop. For example, you might be checking a Web site in Internet Explorer, and you need to copy a picture into a Word document. How do you get the Internet Explorer window out of your way temporarily without closing it? This is a job for the Minimize button, as shown in Figure 2-4.

Minimizing a window hides it. Well, more accurately, the window is stored as a button in your taskbar at the bottom of the screen. To return the window to its original glory, simply click the button in the taskbar. If you have a large number of windows open, the taskbar might sprout its own set of scroll buttons so that you can actually scroll through the minimized windows within the taskbar.

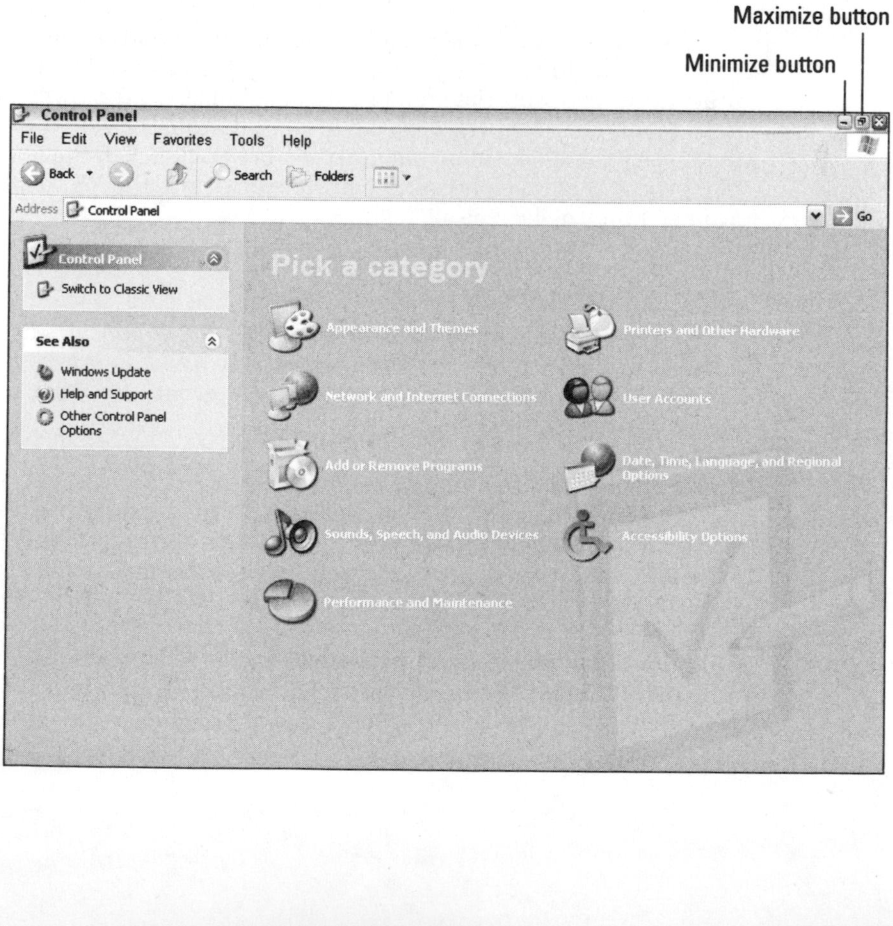

**Book II
Chapter 2**

The Many Windows
of Windows

Maximize button

Minimize button

Figure 2-4:
The window
control
buttons are
old friends
of any
power user.

The XP taskbar also uses another trick if you have a large number of windows open. Separate windows within a single application are grouped together as a single taskbar button, but a number appears on the button label to indicate that multiple windows are minimized from that program. You can *click and hold* — place the mouse pointer atop the taskbar button and then press and hold the mouse button — to display a pop-up menu of the different windows, and then you can select the right window from the menu.

"So does a program continue to run when it's minimized?" Good question. Most do, but some applications will pause when minimized (such as games or video players) and then restart when the window returns to the desktop.

Maximizing and restoring windows

If you've already guessed that maximizing a window is the opposite of minimizing it, pour yourself another soda as a reward! *Maximizing* a window expands it to fill the entire screen, giving you plenty of elbowroom to work with. In fact, applications such as Microsoft Word will take advantage of a maximized window by displaying as much of your document as possible, using automatic word wrap.

If the window isn't maximized, click the Maximize button once — it's the middle button in the group at the upper right, as shown in Figure 2-4. After the window expands, the multitalented Maximize button turns into the Restore button. When you click the Restore button, the window returns to the original dimensions that it had before you clicked the Maximize button, and that doggone button morphs back into the Maximize button again. ("Ethel, make it stop!")

Moving windows

When you need to move a window from one area of your desktop to another, Windows XP is there for you. On a typical day, I end up juggling multiple windows like the world's worst circus clown. (Alternatively, you can buy a larger monitor. Yeah, right.)

To move a window to another piece of desktop real estate, click and drag the window's *title bar* — that colored strip at the top of the window that displays the application or document name — and the entire window will follow. When the window is in the right place, release the mouse button to drop it. (Of course, you can't do this when the window is maximized. Go figure.)

To arrange multiple document windows within an application, choose Window⇨Arrange All, and the document windows line up in an orderly fashion so that you can choose one.

Resizing windows

A window can be resized to different dimensions as necessary — sorry, no triangles, though. Simply move your mouse pointer over the lower-right corner of the window or to one of the sides of the window until the mouse cursor changes to an arrow icon. Then click and drag to move that window in the indicated direction.

Switching windows

Although you can easily open 10 or 15 windows within your XP desktop, keep in mind that only one window is actually *active* at once. And the active window takes precedence, appearing on top of other windows, because it's the window that you're currently viewing, editing, or using. Windows that are currently open on your desktop — and not minimized — are *inactive* windows. They're dimmed (or shaded) to indicate that they're currently offline. (Note, however, that you can still copy or move files to an inactive window, which I demonstrate in the next chapter of this mini-book.) You can see both the active and several inactive windows in Figure 2-5; in this case, Internet Explorer owns the lucky active window.

**Book II
Chapter 2**

**The Many Windows
of Windows**

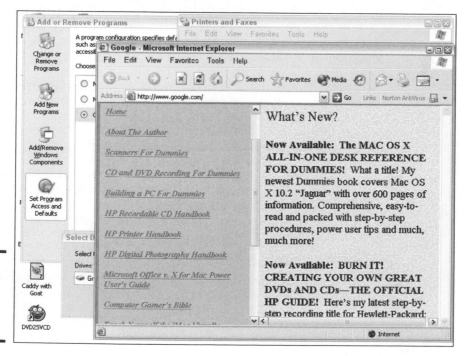

Figure 2-5:
The active
window is
the belle of
the XP ball.

To switch to a different window, you can

✦ Click anywhere within the desired inactive window.

✦ Move your mouse cursor to the taskbar and click the desired application or window button.

✦ Cycle through the open applications by holding down the Alt key and repeatedly pressing Tab until the window that you want becomes active.

Note that you can still use a window's Minimize, Maximize/Restore, and Close buttons even when it's inactive. Also, an application might continue to run while its window is inactive.

A Field Guide to Icons

Here I begin my discussion of icons with a classic Greek comedy. (Those readers familiar with my books will already know about my propensity for vignettes.)

XP and *The Iliad*
(with apologies to Homer)

As the play opens, Hector is tussling with his new installation of XP. He's knee deep in an Explorer window that's filled to the brim with icons.

Hector: "I want to run Microsoft Word! Which of these furshlugginer little pictures stands for the program, and which of these are my documents? What do I double-click? **Help!**"

[Enter proud Odysseus, hero of the Trojan War and experienced XP power user.]

Odysseus: "Do not panic, good Hector. You see, Microsoft Word has its own *program icon,* and each Word document that you create uses the Word *document icon.* The same is true for everything from Excel to Adobe Acrobat."

Hector: "So how do I learn which is which?"

Odysseus: "Read the manual that you got with the application or open an Explorer window and look in the folder where you saved a document from the application. Each software developer creates a unique program and document icon combination, but most of them are pretty self explanatory."

Hector: "Or I could eschew icons completely by running Word from the Start menu, and then I can load the document that I want from Word's File menu, right?"

Odysseus: "That's right, or you can even double-click the document icon itself within that Explorer window, and it will automatically load Word with that document."

Hector: "Hey, bud, that's in the next chapter. And where's that Trojan horse you promised me?"

Odysseus: "Whoops . . . busted again. I'm out of here!"

Fin

In this section, I help Hector (and you) out by identifying each type of icon and showing some common examples.

 Don't be afraid to right-click an icon to see its properties. Just put your mouse pointer over the icon in question and press the right mouse button once, which displays a pop-up contextual menu. Click Properties, and you can see what application created a document — or, as XP calls it, *opens with* — as well as other nifty stuff that I discuss at several points in later parts of this book.

Hardware icons

Only a select few hardware devices have their own icons in XP, but you'll be surprised at what does, including rather nebulous things such as network and Internet connections. These hardware icons tend to hang out on your desktop or in a top-level Explorer window.

Here's a representative list of hardware that's represented by XP as icons, many of which are shown in Figure 2-6:

+ **Hard drives**

+ **CD and DVD-ROM drives**

+ **Printers**

+ **Removable storage** such as floppy drives, Zip drives, and portable Universal Serial Bus (USB) flash drives

+ **External devices** such as MP3 players and digital cameras

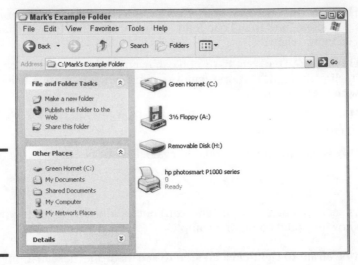

Figure 2-6:
A well-ordered passel of hardware icons.

In general, you can open, activate, or control a hardware device by double-clicking its icon (depending on what type of hardware device it is). Find more on this in appropriate spots later in this book.

Program icons

Because you already know about program icons (thanks to Hector and Odysseus), I won't go into much detail here. Double-clicking a program icon runs the application from an Explorer window or your desktop, and a single click will suffice from the Start menu.

Figure 2-7 illustrates a number of well-known program icons.

File icons

Technically, document icons are actually a subspecies of *file icons,* which can represent any type of data file on the planet. Windows XP actually has a couple of generic icons that it uses to represent files that it doesn't recognize, so every file on your system — and I mean *every* file — can be represented by some kind of an icon.

Like a document icon, XP will attempt to open any data file that you double-click. If XP knows the application that created the file, the program runs automatically to display the file. On the other hand, if XP doesn't recognize the file type, you get a dialog box that looks like Figure 2-8, where you can choose to

✦ Instruct Windows XP to look for an updated file type list by using the Web service (which requires an Internet connection).

✦ Select the program (from a list) that you want to use to load the file.

Book II
Chapter 2

The Many Windows of Windows

Figure 2-7:
A number of program icons caught on camera.

Figure 2-8:
Time to specify how Windows XP should handle unrecognized files.

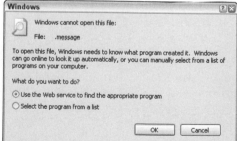

Figure 2-9 parades a selection of common file icons.

Figure 2-9:
File icons
that you
might meet
in Windows
XP.

Folder icon

All folders use the same icon, as shown in Figure 2-10. And as you already
know, a *folder* holds (and organizes) other items, which can include both
icons and subfolders.

Figure 2-10:
The unsung
hero — the
common
folder icon.

Shortcut icons

A *shortcut* is represented by a unique icon. Although it looks much like a regular icon, a thorough examination will reveal a curved arrow at the bottom of the image. (The phrase `Shortcut to` might also appear at the beginning of the icon label.)

Think of a shortcut as a signpost or a link to another item within your XP system. For instance, you can set up a shortcut to Norton Disk Doctor that will run the program just as if you had clicked directly on the program icon in the Start menu or had double-clicked the program icon in the Explorer window.

However, because shortcuts only take up a few bytes of hard drive real estate, they come in handy when you're customizing your desktop or organizing a folder. This allows you to set up a program to be run from any folder (without requiring that you dig down with Explorer). Too, a shortcut can be easily tossed into the Recycle Bin after you're finished with it because it's actually not a part of the original application.

In fact, many games and applications now offer to add a shortcut to your desktop during installation, and I usually take 'em up on the offer. A desktop shortcut is very convenient, and the software developer knows that you can delete it quickly and easily if necessary. You can also move a shortcut to the taskbar, which I cover later in this mini-book.

Because a shortcut is only a link to a program (or folder, or even a hardware device), you can create multiple copies for different locations in your system and still not waste a tremendous amount of hard drive territory. (A friend of mine always creates a folder on his desktop with shortcuts to all the documents and files relating to his latest project. That way, he can immediately work on anything relating to that project and just delete the folder with the shortcuts after the job is done.)

"But Mark, can't I just take matters into my own hands and just move the application?" Let me put out this potential fire with a well-placed Maxim:

Never try to simply copy or move an application that you've installed in XP from one folder to another.™

Not only is the application not likely to work (because it can't find any of its support files), but you also won't be able to use the Add and Remove Programs feature to uninstall the application later! (More on uninstalling software the *right* way later in the book.) Instead, create a shortcut — which I demonstrate in Chapter 4 of this mini-book — and move that shortcut to the desired location.

Figure 2-11 shows off a number of shortcut icons, along with their original source icons.

Shortcut icons

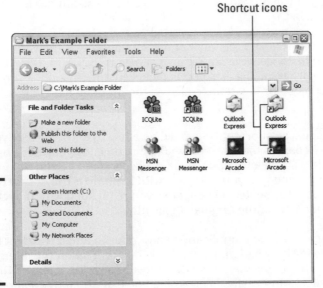

Figure 2-11: Shortcut icons are a great way to organize your stuff.

System icons

The final type of icons represents a system function or a system location in Windows XP, such as My Computer, the Recycle Bin, or My Documents. Most of these important icons can't be moved or relocated — XP wants them left where they are, thank you very much — but you can use them or right-click them to display a context-sensitive pop-up menu. For example, right-clicking the Recycle Bin displays a menu with a number of choices that directly apply to deleted files.

I discuss these icons and what they represent in various spots throughout the book (especially in Chapter 4 of this mini-book).

Selecting Icons

After you become familiar with icons, you might be wondering how you can manipulate them. I go into more detail in the next two chapters of this mini-book, but for now, you need to know how to select one or more icons: that is, how to highlight the icon(s) that you want to use when performing the next action (such as copying, moving, or deleting the selected icons).

I should note at this point that XP offers different ways to view the contents of a folder, which I discuss later in this mini-book. For example, you can display icons in a list format as well. The methods of selecting icons, however, do not change.

Selecting a single icon

To select a single icon, click it once — you'll notice that XP has highlighted it to indicate that it has been selected. Figure 2-12 shows a highlighted single icon in a window, along with other icons for comparison.

A selected icon

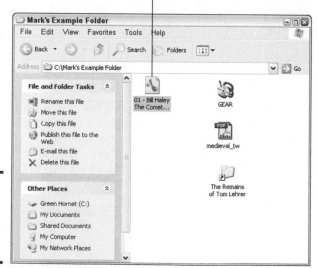

Figure 2-12:
One
selected
icon within
a window.

Selecting multiple contiguous icons by dragging

To select a group of icons that are next to each other, click your mouse in a part of the window above and to the left of the first icon, and then drag the mouse down to a spot below and to the right of the last icon that you want to select. Figure 2-13 illustrates the selection box that Windows XP draws; any icons within the box are selected and highlighted.

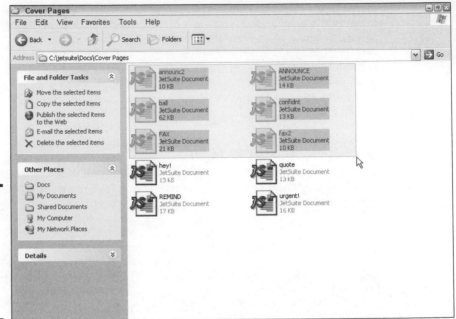

Figure 2-13:
Drag a box
around
multiple
contiguous
icons
to select
them all.

Selecting multiple contiguous icons by clicking

Another method of selecting a group of contiguous icons is to select the first
icon in the group by clicking it, holding down the Shift key, and then clicking
the last icon that you want to select. This method is especially handy when
viewing files in list mode, as you see in Figure 2-14.

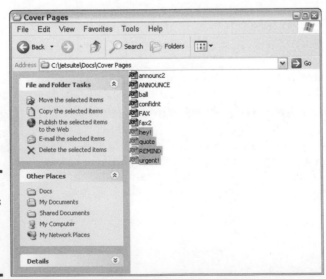

Figure 2-14:
Select icons
in list view
with the
mouse and
keyboard.

Selecting multiple separated icons by clicking

Whoops, Figure 2-15 shows a number of selected icons that aren't contiguous. How do you select them? In this case, click the first icon that you want to select, hold down the Ctrl key — don't stop holding it down — and then click each additional icon that you want to select. After you select everything that you need, release the Ctrl key.

To deselect an icon that you pick by mistake, click it again. ***Remember:*** You must continue holding down the Ctrl key until you've finished selecting (and deselecting) what you want.

Book II
Chapter 2

The Many Windows of Windows

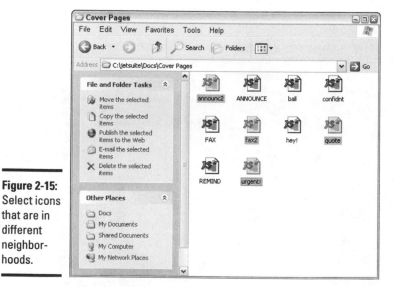

Figure 2-15:
Select icons
that are in
different
neighbor-
hoods.

Using the Toolbar

The final stop in the graphical Windows world — at least in this chapter — is the toolbar. Most Windows applications now use toolbars; you can see in Figure 2-1 that the Explorer window has its own toolbar. Each button typically replicates one of the application's popular menu commands and performs the same function as if you had selected the menu command.

If you already know how to click a button in Windows, you know how to use a toolbar: Just move your mouse pointer on top of the desired button and click the left button once. Whoosh!

However, not all toolbars are stuck at the top of a window. For example, check out Figure 2-16, which illustrates a favorite image editing application of mine: Paint Shop Pro. Note that this application has toolbars across the top and both sides of the screen, along with — gasp! — floating toolbars that you can click and drag to wherever you like!

Where am I going with this? Well, I'm suggesting that you read the manual for an application thoroughly because often you'll find that you can customize that application's toolbars with just the commands that you want. Why take up valuable space on that toolbar with a Print button if you don't have a printer? I show you how to customize toolbars in several spots throughout the book, but for now, just enjoy using toolbars because they can save you all kinds of time.

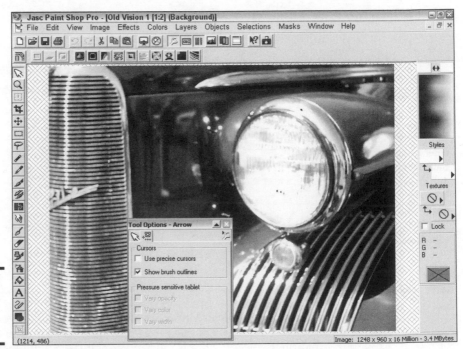

Figure 2-16: Man, dig those crazy toolbars!

Chapter 3: Windows XP Basics

In This Chapter

✔ **Starting an application**

✔ **Exiting an application**

✔ **Moving, copying, and deleting items**

✔ **Creating new folders and renaming items**

✔ **Recovering valuable stuff from the Recycle Bin**

✔ **Using and configuring the Start menu**

✔ **Working with printers**

✔ **Using and configuring the taskbar**

✔ **Terminating a misbehaving program**

*B*oot camp is over — now it's time to discover some of the more advanced tasks within Windows XP.

For example, no PC owner can ever hope to become a power user without becoming good friends with both the Windows XP Start menu and the XP taskbar. You need to know how to run programs, whether they've been installed and appear on the Start menu, or whether you have to track 'em down and run them from your hard drive or CD-ROM drive.

Files and folders need to be copied, moved, or removed; deleted files need to be permanently erased (or recovered, in case of an accident); and new folders need to be created while you're using your PC. You might need to change printer settings, shut down a program that's no longer responding, or locate another computer on your local network with the shared file that you have to copy to your hard drive. All these tasks are basic, yet a surprising number of PC owners are in the dark about these basics — they still know only one way to exit a program, or they aren't aware that you can change the characteristics of a printer by just right-clicking it and choosing Printer Preferences!

That's what this chapter is all about — delving into the different methods of taking care of basic tasks within Windows XP. Here you find how to handle all these tasks and more!

I even show you how to format a floppy disk — because of contractual obligations.

Running Applications from the Start Menu

First things first: XP becomes a lonely place indeed if you can't run any applications. To run a program from the Start menu, follow these steps:

1. **Move your mouse pointer to the bottom-left of the screen and click the Start button on the taskbar.**

   Or, if you have a keyboard with Windows keys, press one of them to display the Start menu. (Your keyboard probably has two of these critters. Just look on either side of the Alt keys, which are on either side of the spacebar. The Windows keys look like the fluttering Windows flag.)

   Figure 3-1 illustrates the Start menu and taskbar. Any applications that you've recently used will probably appear in the Recent Applications list on the left side of the Start menu.

2. **To run a recently used application again, click the application name, and dance around the room because you were able to do things The Convenient Way.**

3. **If the program doesn't appear on the Recent Applications list, click All Programs.**

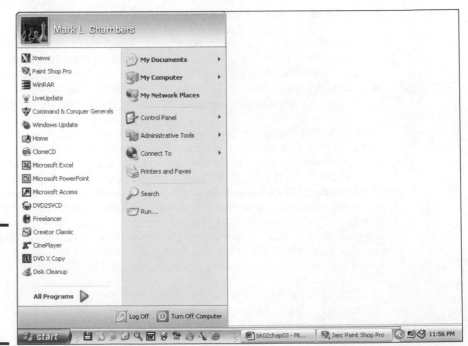

Figure 3-1:
The Start menu and taskbar — truly a Dynamic Duo!

Whomp! XP displays all the applications that you've installed on your PC in a *cascading* (another term for "rather hard to manage sometimes") list. Program groups (think of them as subfolders) are displayed as menu items with arrows at the end of their names, whereas individual applications are stuck at the end.

If you've recently installed a number of programs, they might appear loitering at the end of the All Programs menu. You can arrange everything in alphabetized order again by right-clicking anywhere in the All Programs menu and then choosing Sort by Name from the pop-up menu that appears.

4. **Move your mouse pointer carefully to the program group that contains the application you want to run — it will display yet another pop-up menu.**

   Sooner or later, you're going to track down the doggone program that you want, so be patient. (I've actually seen program groups that have two or three subfolders!) If the program appears by itself at the end of the All Programs menu, you can rejoice.

5. **Click the application name to run it.**

Many software developers include supplementary programs with the actual application, such as utilities, game editors, and the like. That's nice of them — but unfortunately, those additional application icons can get kind of confusing, so make sure that you're clicking the Real Deal to avoid embarrassment (and the hassle of exiting a program that you didn't want to run in the first place).

Running Applications from Your Hard Drive

Often you'll want to run a program from the forested undergrowth that is your hard drive. Perhaps you've downloaded a program from the Web, or you're running a shareware application that doesn't install itself in the All Programs menu. Follow these steps:

1. **Double-click the My Computer icon on your desktop to open the Explorer window (behold it in Figure 3-2).**

2. **Double-click the hard drive that contains the program that you want to run.**

   If necessary, continue clicking folders and subfolders until you see the desired application. This, good reader, is *navigating,* and I do a lot of navigating in this book!

3. **Double-click the application icon to run it.**

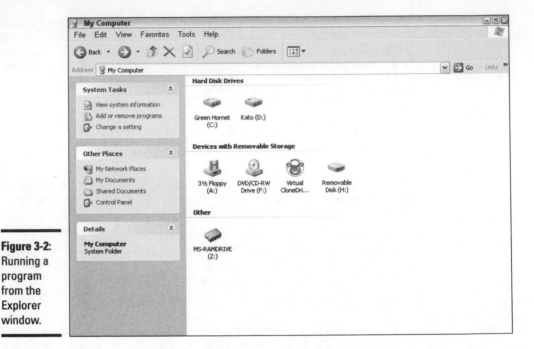

Figure 3-2:
Running a program from the Explorer window.

Running Applications from a CD-ROM or DVD-ROM

By default, Windows XP loves to be helpful. So usually when you load an application's CD-ROM into your drive to install the program, XP automatically runs the installation program for you. However, from time to time, you might need to venture onto Planet Optical and run a program directly from a CD-ROM or DVD-ROM. Follow these steps:

1. **Press the button on your CD-ROM/DVD-ROM drive to eject the tray; load the disc (shiny side down) and press the button again to retract the tray.**

   If the application's installation menu appears, just click the Close button or click Exit/Quit to shoo it away.

2. **Double-click the My Computer icon on your desktop to open the Explorer window.**

3. **Double-click the CD-ROM or DVD-ROM drive that contains the desired application.**

   If necessary, navigate to the location of the program by double-clicking any folders and subfolders. (See? I told you that you'll be navigating XP all the time!)

4. **Double-click the application icon to run it.**

Running Applications from a Network Drive

If your PC is connected to a LAN (engineer-speak for a wired or wireless network), you *may* have access to programs located on other network computers. As my grandfather used to exclaim, "Zounds!" (It's really not magic, though.) Follow these steps:

1. **Click the Start menu.**

2. **Click the My Network Places item in the Start menu.**

   Windows XP obligingly displays a My Network Places window, displaying all of the shared folders and hard drives on your network.

3. **Double-click the network folder/hard drive that contains the program that you want to run.**

4. **Double-click the application icon to run it.**

Before you imagine a wonderland where anyone on your network can run any program on your PC, there are two caveats to running an application over a network:

✦ **You need the proper user access.** The person using the "host" PC must give you proper access to run the program.

✦ **The program must support networking.** Not only does the application need to support network operation, but you may also need a separate user serial number to run it from another PC on the network.

For more information on the ins and outs of networking, visit Chapters 1 and 2 in Book VIII, which covers home networking (and tell 'em I sent you).

Exiting a Program

After you perform whatever magic you need within an application, I recommend exiting the program. Of course, you can leave it running, like a Web browser, but most of the time, you'll avoid slowing down your PC's performance by closing applications you're not using. (Even when you're not directly using a program, Windows XP spends processor time and memory keeping it ready for you.)

To shut down a program, use one of the following methods:

✦ **Click the Close button (the big X) at the top-right corner of the window.**

✦ **Choose File➪Exit.**

✦ **Press Alt+F4.** This doesn't work on all programs, but many still honor the old Exit keyboard shortcut.

Where the @#&! is the @#&! Alt+F4 key?

If you're scanning your PC's keyboard in vain for the Alt+F4 key, you should stop now: There is no single key named that on any keyboard. Instead, Alt+F4 stands for a key *sequence* — it's actually two keys pressed together. When you see two keys conjoined by a plus sign, press the first key and hold it while pressing the second key. For example, if I tell you to press the sequence Ctrl+C (which copies a selection), I'm asking you to hold down the Ctrl key while you press the C key. After you press the C key, you can release the Ctrl key.

Most Windows XP shortcut key sequences use one of three keys as the first key: Alt, Shift, or Ctrl.

You can press the specified key on either side of the keyboard, so lefties might press the Shift key that's under the Enter key. It's all gravy to XP. In fact, most PC owners are familiar with the Ctrl+C (copy), Ctrl+X (cut), and Ctrl+V (paste) sequences.

Some rare key sequences involve three keys: The first two keys are held down while you press the third one. The most famous three-key sequence, of course, is the infamous Three Finger Salute — the legendary Alt+Ctrl+Delete sequence that would reboot a PC running DOS. In Windows XP, applying the Three Finger Salute displays the Windows Task Manager, which I discuss a bit more later in this chapter.

If you haven't saved any open documents and you try to exit an application, most Windows programs will prompt you for confirmation so you won't lose your stuff by accident — as shown in Figure 3-3, where I'm trying to exit Word without saving this chapter. No, Mark, don't do it!

Figure 3-3:
Word won't
allow you to
exit without
considering
open files.

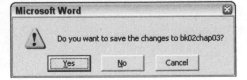

Putting Your Files in Order

Next, consider how you'll manage files in Windows XP. You can use the Explorer window to take care of your chores, as you'll see in this section.

You can find file management alternatives to Windows Explorer. One of my favorites is Total Commander (shown in Figure 3-4), which has been a popular $34 U.S. shareware favorite for many years now. Total Commander is list based, so you see and select more than the traditional icon view in Explorer. (I show you how to switch views in the next chapter of this mini-book.) You can download a copy to try out from www.ghisler.com.

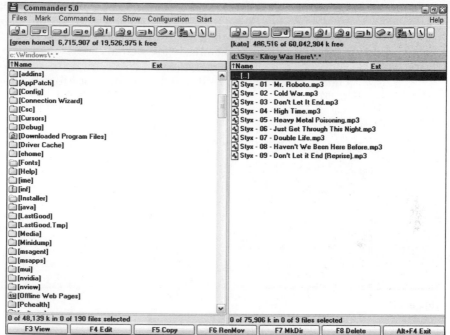

Figure 3-4:
Total
Commander
is a great
alternative
to Explorer.

Copying and moving stuff

To copy selected files and folders from one Explorer window to another —
or to the desktop or to a drive — you can use one of these methods:

✦ **Click the selected items and drag them from one Explorer window to
the destination Explorer window.** Of course, this requires you to open
two Explorer windows, but that's life in the big XP. Also, note that in order
to copy from one location on a drive to another location *on the same drive,*
you must hold down Ctrl while you drag. Otherwise, Windows XP assumes
that you want to *move* the items instead. (If you're copying something
from Drive C to a location on Drive D, you don't have to hold down the
Ctrl key.) You can always tell when you're copying something with the
mouse because XP adds a small plus sign (+) to the items while you drag.

✦ **Right-click the selected items and drag them to their destination.**
IMHO (short for *In My Humble Opinion* on the Internet), this is always
the better choice than copying with the left mouse button. Why? Well,
you don't have to hold down Ctrl — Windows XP pops up a menu when
you release the mouse button and asks whether you want to copy or
move the file. Much more civilized, don't you think?

✦ **Choose Edit⇨Copy from the Explorer menu, click in the destination
Explorer window, and then choose Edit⇨Paste.** From the keyboard,
you can press Ctrl+C to copy or Ctrl+V to paste.

✦ **Click Copy This File/Folder from the Explorer Task pane.** XP displays the Copy Items dialog box that you see in Figure 3-5; navigate to the destination and then click the Copy button. If you like, you can create a new folder first. Remember, click the plus signs (+) to expand drives and folders or click the minus signs (–) to contract them. From the menu, choose Edit➪Copy to Folder to display the Copy Items dialog box.

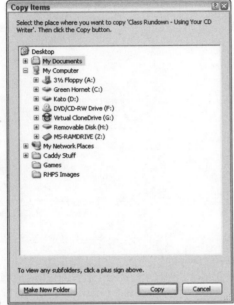

Figure 3-5:
Preparing to copy a file via the Explorer window Task pane method.

To move selected items, use one of these methods:

✦ **Right-click the selected items and drag them to their destination.** Again, my favorite — release the mouse button and choose Move from the pop-up menu that appears.

✦ **Choose Edit➪Move from the Explorer menu, click in the destination Explorer window, and then choose Edit➪Paste.** From the keyboard, you can press Ctrl+X to cut or Ctrl+V to paste.

✦ **Click Move This File/Folder from the Explorer Task pane.** The Move Items dialog box looks just like the Copy Items dialog box that I mention earlier, and it works the same way.

If you attempt to copy or move files that already exist in the target folder or drive, Windows XP will prompt you for confirmation before overwriting anything.

If you need to reverse direction when navigating — for example, if you click one subfolder too many and now you need to return to the previous folder — don't forget about the Back button on the Explorer toolbar, which functions just like the Back button in Internet Explorer. (The Back button resides in the upper-left corner of the Explorer window.)

Creating a new folder

Creating new folders is the cornerstone to good organization in Windows XP. Dumping everything in your My Documents folder is a bad idea because it will rapidly resemble a sold-out rock concert (complete with additional files struggling to get in).

To create a new folder within the current location in Windows Explorer, use one of the following methods:

+ **Choose File⇨New⇨Folder.** Explorer adds the new folder icon and also opens a text box underneath it in which you can type a name for the new folder.

+ **Right-click any open spot in the Explorer window and then choose New⇨Folder from the pop-up menu that appears.** Note that I said *open spot* — if you happen to right-click an icon or control, you'll get a completely different pop-up menu, so pick an unoccupied parcel of territory.

+ **Click Make a New Folder from the Explorer Task pane.**

Deleting stuff with mouse and keyboard

Kinda sounds like "Deleting Stuff with Moose and Squirrel," don't you think? (Boy, howdy, sometimes I turn into a real laugh riot. Usually when I've had very little sleep.) Anyway, if you need to delete unnecessary files or folders from your system, Windows Explorer can handle that as well.

Use your mouse to select the items that you want to trash and then choose File⇨Delete. Alternatively, you can right-click the selected items and then choose Delete from the pop-up menu that appears. If you're into dragging things, you can drag an item from the desktop or an Explorer window and drop it on top of the Recycle Bin.

From the keyboard, just select the unwanted items and press Delete. It doesn't get any easier than this, folks.

Deleted stuff gets whisked away to the Recycle Bin — but that stuff may not be permanently deleted quite yet. (More on your Recycle Bin later in the chapter.)

Displaying properties

You might want to display an item's Properties dialog box for an item for a number of reasons:

✦ If it's a shortcut, you might want to find the location of the original file.

✦ If it's a folder, you can see how much total space the folder uses and how many files it contains.

✦ If you're displaying a drive's properties, you can see how much free space the drive has left, or you can scan it for errors and then defragment it. (More on scanning and defragmenting in Chapter 5 of this mini-book.)

Here's the point: Every item on your XP desktop and in an Explorer window has a Properties panel, and the contents change depending on what the item is. Throughout the rest of the book, I show you how to use the Properties settings for all sorts of items.

To display the properties for an item, right-click it and then choose Properties from the pop-up menu that appears. For example, Figure 3-6 illustrates the properties for my drive C.

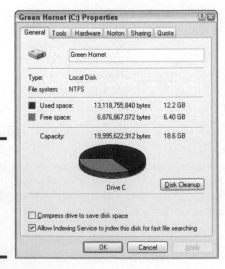

Figure 3-6: Displaying the Properties dialog box for a hard drive.

Renaming items

You have four ways to rename an item in an Explorer window. Here's the first half of the process (telling XP what it is that you want to rename).

- ✦ **Click the item once, pause a second or two, and then click again.** Unfortunately, this takes a bit of experience to do reliably.

- ✦ **Click the item to select it and then press F2.**

- ✦ **Right-click the item and then choose Rename from the pop-up menu that appears.**

- ✦ **Click the item to select it and then click Rename This Item from the Task pane.**

Regardless of which method you use, XP opens a text entry box with the current name. To delete the current name completely, just type the new name. To use a portion of the original name, click in the text box and use your cursor keys and the Delete key to remove the unwanted characters.

Emptying the Recycle Bin

"Mom, where do we empty the recycled files?" Techno-nerds still chuckle about "recycled" ones and zeroes, but the XP Recycle Bin is a popular spot on your desktop, and you'll eventually have to empty it. (You can tell whether it's holding deleted items because the icon shows a discarded document in the bin.)

To delete the contents of the Recycle Bin, right-click it and then choose Empty Recycle Bin from the pop-up menu that appears.

Windows will eventually delete older items from the Recycle Bin automatically — or when you use the Disk Cleanup Wizard. However, you'll free up space every time that you empty the Recycle Bin, and sometimes that extra space can come in very handy on a drive that's filled to the brim.

By default, Windows will prompt you for confirmation before deleting your trash. If you feel that such clucking is overdoing things and you want to banish this file deletion confirmation, right-click the Recycle Bin and choose Properties to display the settings that you see in Figure 3-7. (If you're wondering how my Recycle Bin got its name, I use Symantec's Norton Utilities, which includes the Norton Protected Recycle Bin — and it allows you to name your Recycle Bin whatever you like.) Click the Global tab and then clear the Display Delete Confirmation Dialog check box to disable it.

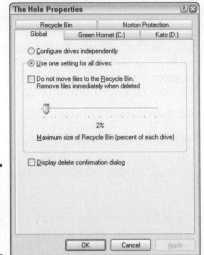

Figure 3-7:
Turning off
that darned
file deletion
dialog box.

Recovering Items from the Recycle Bin

Here's a feeling that we've all shared from time to time: You suddenly realize that you just dropped your Great American Novel into the XP Recycle Bin by mistake. (**Hint:** If you back up your files on a regular basis, you won't panic nearly as much as the poor PC owner who has never backed up.)

However, there's still a chance that you can recover from your mistake and recover that orphaned Word document from the Recycle Bin! (The quicker that you try a rescue after you realize the error, the better; read on to discover why.) Follow these steps:

1. **Double-click the Recycle Bin to display its contents.**

2. **Select the item(s) that you want to restore.**

3. **Click Restore the Selected Items from the Recycle Bin window Task pane. Alternatively, you can right-click a single item and then choose Restore from the pop-up menu that appears.**

The Recycle Bin is great, but it's not a perfect solution because Windows XP might use the space taken up on your hard drive by a deleted item to store new data, which will make restoration impossible. That's why I recommend that you restore a deleted item *as soon as possible* — I try to do it immediately after I catch my mistake.

Putting the Start Menu through Its Paces

Ready to disassemble the Start menu? That's what this section is all about: helping you gain control of the ungainly (yet extremely useful) Start menu and customizing it for your specific needs. (I won't be discussing the My Documents folder here because I cover that in the next chapter of this mini-book.)

Tossing the Recent Applications list

You can read how to use the Recent Applications list at the beginning of this chapter, but if security is an issue, you might want to disable it. After all, does your boss *really* need to know that you recently played Tetris, Dungeon Siege II, and DOOM 3? I think not.

**Book II
Chapter 3**

Windows XP Basics

To disable the list, follow these steps:

1. **Right-click the Start button and then choose Properties from the pop-up menu that appears.**

   This displays the Task Bar and Start Menu Properties dialog box that you see in Figure 3-8.

2. **Click the Customize button to display the dialog box that you see in Figure 3-9.**

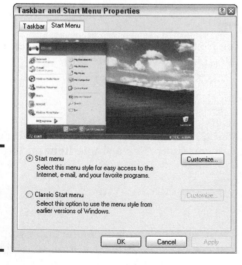

Figure 3-8:
Yep, the Start button has its own Properties dialog box.

Figure 3-9:
Customizing
the Start
menu
begins here.

3. **Click in the Number of Programs on Start Menu box and type a zero.**

   While you're here, you can specify large or small icons for the Start menu and also toggle the display of Internet and e-mail items on the Start menu. (If you do decide to enable the Internet and/or E-mail check boxes, you can click their respective drop-down list boxes to choose the applications that will run when you click the menu items.)

4. **Click OK and then click OK again.**

Using the Run item

You can run any application from the Run item on the Start menu. Just click Run, and you'll see the dialog box shown in Figure 3-10.

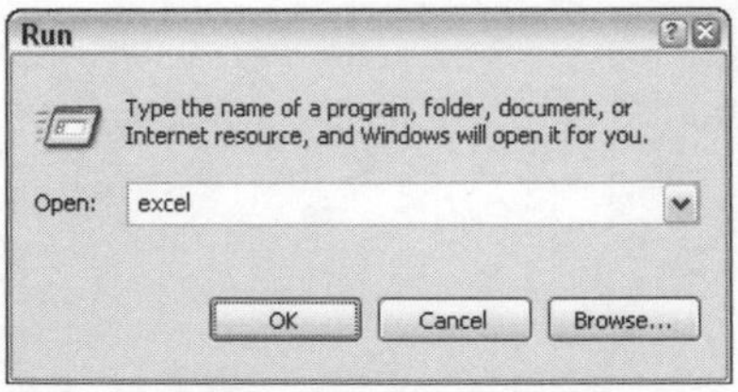

Figure 3-10:
Run
programs
from here.

Click in the Open text box and type the actual filename of the application that you want to run; or, you can click the Browse button to navigate to the application. If you've recently used the Run dialog box to start the same application, click the arrow at the right side of the Open drop-down list box and choose that application from the list.

When the filename appears in the Open box, click OK to run it.

When you're using the Run dialog box, remember that the name of the program you want to run might *not* be the same as the actual application filename — and you must enter that actual application filename! For example, you can run Microsoft Word from the Run dialog box, but entering **word** or **word.exe** will result in an error. In fact, the filename that you need to enter is **winword.exe**.

Accessing printers and faxes

To add a printer or install fax support, choose the Printers and Faxes item from the Start menu. Your Printers and Faxes window will likely contain different printers than mine does in Figure 3-11, but the items in the window's Task pane will be the same. (Read more about installing fax support in the next chapter of this mini-book.)

This is also the place for changing the settings provided by your printer manufacturer's XP driver. For example, you can likely change the print quality, and perhaps you can clean your inkjet's print nozzles or check on your ink levels. Right-click the desired printer icon and then choose Printing Preferences to see what you can change. What you see depends on your printer manufacturer. In Figure 3-12, which illustrates the Printing Preferences dialog box for my HP PhotoSmart inkjet printer, is an example of what you might see.

Book II
Chapter 3

Windows XP Basics

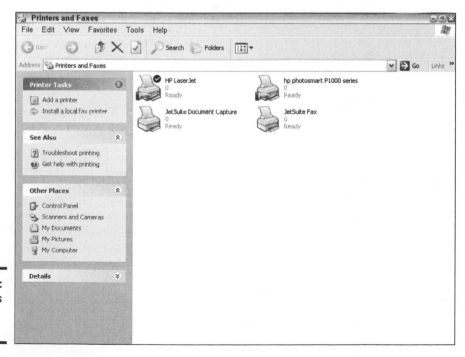

Figure 3-11:
My Printers
and Faxes
window.

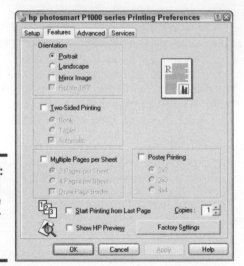

Figure 3-12:
Display the
Preference
settings for
your inkjet
printer.

To choose your default printer throughout XP, right-click the desired printer and then choose Set as Default Printer. Windows XP adds a check mark symbol to the printer's icon to indicate that it is the default printer.

Note that XP also displays several advanced printer settings on a printer's Properties dialog box, including printer sharing (which I cover in Book VIII) and color management for color printers.

Windows applications are likely to use one of three different methods to print:

✦ **Choose File➪Print.**

✦ **Click the Print icon on the program's toolbar.**

✦ **Press Ctrl+P.**

To display (and control) pending printing jobs, click a printer to select it and then click the See What's Printing item (assuming that you're printing something) of the Printers and Faxes window Task pane. This displays the dialog box that you see in Figure 3-13, which lists details about the pending printer jobs. You can pause all your print jobs on the selected printer by choosing Printer➪Pause Printing; to restart the printer, click the Pause Printing menu item again. (If your printer is on a network, you need Administrator rights to pause all print jobs.)

Figure 3-13:
View, pause, and cancel print jobs here.

To pause a single print job, click the desired job in the list and then choose Document⇨Pause. To resume printing, click the desired job in the list and then choose Document⇨Restart.

Working with your network

Click My Network Places (on your desktop) to open shared folders on other networks (including File Transfer Protocol [FTP] servers on the Internet). From here, you can

+ **Open a network place for moving, copying, or opening documents.** Just double-click the network icon to open it.

+ **Open a network place for running an application.** Again, double-click the network icon to open it.

+ **Add a new network place.** Click this item in the window's Task pane to run the Add a Network Place Wizard, which will walk you through the short process of creating a new icon in the My Network Places window.

+ **View network connections.** This item displays all the available network connections recognized by Windows XP (as shown in Figure 3-14); note that all these connections might not be active at this moment. (For example, I have two FireWire IEEE 1394 ports on my main Windows XP machine, but I'm not using either of them on a FireWire network. XP doesn't care — it displays them anyway.) You can also display the properties of a network connection from this window by right-clicking the connection icon.

+ **Set up a network.** XP actually makes setting up a network as easy as possible. I explain the entire procedure in Book VIII, Chapter 2.

+ **View workgroup computers.** Click this Task pane item to see the other computers assigned to the same workgroup as your computer on your local network.

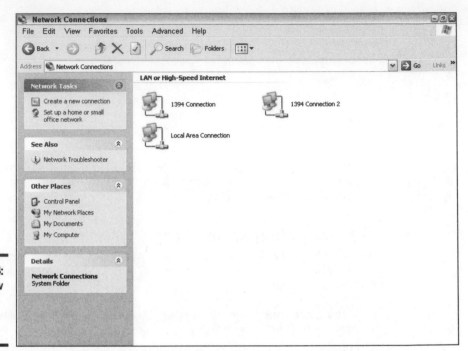

Figure 3-14:
Hey, I know those network connections!

I refer to many of these network Task pane items throughout later chapters of the book, so remember how you got here.

Configuring the Start menu

I'm not quite ready to leave the Start menu yet — at least, not until I discuss the Advanced panel of the Customize Start Menu dialog box. (Remember from earlier in the chapter?) Right-click the Start button, choose Properties, choose Customize, and then — finally! — click the Advanced tab to display the settings that you see in Figure 3-15.

From here, you can modify a number of features of the Start menu:

✦ **Open submenus:** If you'd rather click a submenu in the All Programs list instead of watching them pop up and down like crazed frogs, disable this check box.

✦ **Highlight Newly Installed Programs:** This feature displays programs that you've just installed with a highlighted band in the All Programs list. If you have a huge number of installed programs, enable this check box, and you'll be able to locate that new application much more easily.

✦ **Start Menu Items:** This scrolling list allows you to specify what you want shown on the Start menu and whether certain items should be shown as a link (which opens a separate window) or as a menu.

✦ **Recent Documents:** Remember the Recent Applications list? The Recent Documents list works the same way, only it contains recently opened documents rather than recently used programs. Again, if you're worried about your security (or your reputation) and you don't want others to know what you're doing, you can disable the list entirely.

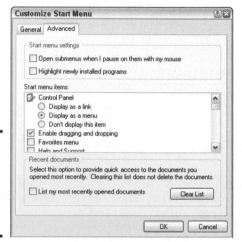

Figure 3-15: Putting the whammy to the Start menu settings.

Handling the Taskbar

Yep, it's yet another XP control. This time, I'm talking about the *taskbar,* which is that loyal strip of screen real estate that appears at the bottom of the screen — or at the side, or the top. (More on this in a second.) In this section, I tell you more about the often-neglected taskbar.

Switching programs

The primary use of the taskbar — and one that's been around since Windows 95 — is to allow you to easily switch between the windows of the programs that you're running. You can switch between programs by clicking your mouse pointer on the taskbar button for the program that you want to use.

Shhh . . . there's also another method of switching programs that doesn't use the taskbar — and since we're on the topic, I'll tell you about it here. You can press Alt+Tab to move between the programs that you're running. To step through the programs, hold down Alt while you press Tab repeatedly, and you'll advance through your programs like Tiny Tim tiptoeing through the tulips.

Controlling the notification area

Next on the Taskbar Hit Parade is the *notification* area — that's the far right end of the taskbar, as shown in Figure 3-16. Most of these icons represent a program that's running. In the figure, for example, you can see the tiny Norton AntiVirus computer icon and my PowerStrip icon (which looks like a tiny monitor), which indicate that these programs are running. However, you can also see the Volume icon (which you can click to set your PC's volume or mute sound altogether) as well as my laser printer icon.

Quick Launch icons   Program buttons

Figure 3-16:
Your taskbar, your friend.

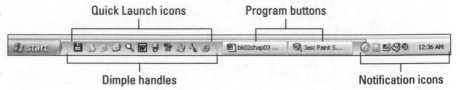

Dimple handles   Notification icons

So what did you glean here? ("Bueller? Bueller? Anyone?") Not everything in the notification area is a program; rather, the icons that appear there indicate (or notify you about) things that are available and things that are currently happening on your PC. You can, however, right-click most notification icons to display pop-up menus. Typically, the menu allows you to control whatever program or feature the notification icon represents (including the ability to close or exit, if the icon represents a program that's running).

The Service Pack 2 (or SP2) update to Windows XP introduced a new icon to the notification area — if you see a tiny yellow or red medieval-looking shield appear, right-click on it immediately to display the Windows Security Center, which will display the reasons why you're seeing a warning icon. Typically, Windows XP is shooting a flare to warn you that your firewall or virus protection has been limited or disabled; in addition, if you disable automatic updates, you'll also receive the warning icon. When you have set things right, the Security Center shield icon will disappear from the notification area.

If you see an arrow pointing to the left at the end of your notification icons, XP is hiding the icons that you haven't used recently to make more room for program buttons. To see these hidden icons, click the arrow.

Don't need the clock in the notification area? Then right-click in any open space on the taskbar, choose Properties, and clear the Show the Clock check box (as shown in Figure 3-17) to disable it.

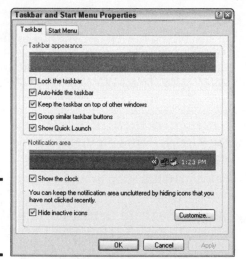

Figure 3-17:
Displaying
the Taskbar
properties.

Adding Quick Launch icons

At the left end of the taskbar — next to the Start button — you'll find the
Quick Launch icons, which are probably the least-appreciated icons within
Windows XP. You can right-click and drag any program icon, file icon, or
folder icon down to the Quick Launch area, release the mouse button, and
then choose Create Shortcut. From that point on, clicking the icon in the
taskbar runs the application, opens the document, or opens the folder.

Naturally, your space on the Quick Launch portion of the taskbar is limited,
so I recommend that you add only the programs, folders, and items that you
use the most. I even added the Add/Remove Programs Control Panel icon to
my Quick Launch buttons. It's easy to right-click and drag any Control Panel
icon to the taskbar when you configure the Control Panel as a menu, as I
show you in Chapter 6 of this mini-book.

"Hey, I can't put anything on the Quick Launch area!" That's probably because
the taskbar is currently *locked,* which prevents anyone (including you) from
inadvertently dragging a Quick Launch icon off to the desktop or from making
any changes to the dimensions or location of the taskbar. Right-click anywhere on the taskbar itself (and not on an icon or control), choose Lock the
Taskbar to unlock things, and then try again. After you're done arranging the
taskbar as you like it, it's a good idea to lock it again.

If you don't need the Quick Launch area of the taskbar, you can reclaim that
space from the Taskbar and Start Menu Properties dialog box. Right-click
any open part of the taskbar, choose Properties, and then clear the Show
Quick Launch check box to disable it.

Configuring the taskbar

Would you rather have your taskbar on the left or right side of the XP desktop? How about at the top of the desktop? No problem. First, make sure that the taskbar is unlocked; then click in the center of the bar and drag it to any other side of the screen. (Check out Figure 3-18.)

While the taskbar is unlocked, you can also

✦ **Expand it** by clicking the edge closest to the desktop (where the thin strip appears) and dragging it up.

✦ **Resize the Quick Launch and notification areas** by clicking the dimpled handles on the taskbar and dragging them.

✦ **Swap the default locations of the Quick Launch and program buttons** by dragging the dimpled area to the left of the Quick Launch area to the right of the second dimpled line.

Now that you see how easy it is to alter the taskbar, you'll understand the necessity of locking it! Don't forget to batten down the hatches after you have things just as you want them. When the taskbar is locked, the dimpled handles disappear, and the strip along the desktop edge of the taskbar disappears as well.

Figure 3-18: Zounds! For those who gravitate to the right . . .

Terminating a Program with Prejudice

Sometimes a program just decides to misbehave. At least things are better in Windows XP than they were in Windows 98 or Me, where one locked program was likely to lock the entire machine. In XP, you should be able to force a nonresponsive program to quit without losing any open files or having to restart your PC — although I always save my files in the other applications, just in case!

To force a locked program to terminate, follow these steps:

1. **Press Alt+Ctrl+Delete to display the Task Manager and then click the Applications tab, as shown in Figure 3-19.**

Figure 3-19:
Control
the Task
Manager,
and you
control
Windows
XP.

2. **Click the name of the application that's causing the problems.**

   It will usually be marked Not Responding in the Status column.

3. **Click the End Task button to initiate the terminate sequence.**

   Note: It might take several seconds for the terminated program to disappear, or you might need to repeat this step two or three times to force termination.

   XP displays a dialog box saying that the program will not shut down properly.

4. **Click the End Now button.**

   The program will disappear from the Applications list.

5. **Click the Close button to close the Task Manager.**

By the way, you can also restart and shut down Windows XP from the Task Manager. Click the Shut Down menu to see these choices. To see who's logged in to your machine — either locally or remotely — click the Users tab, where you can also disconnect or log off any undesirables.

Formatting a Floppy Disk

I'd rather you not. Honestly. Let me tell you my story.

Years ago, I lost an irreplaceable document that was very near and dear to my heart. The floppy that it was stored on gave up the ghost, and I was left a broken man (for at least half a day). It was then that I embarked upon a sacred mission to banish the floppy disk from my PC . . . and from the PCs of all those who would heed my call:

✦ Those who have also lost valuable data to the vagaries of the Plastic Pretender, where data can be readable one second and unreadable the next

✦ Or those who have realized that practically nothing fits within 1.44MB of space any longer

✦ Or those who have encountered the recalcitrant floppy that will read perfectly well on one PC and stubbornly refuse to be read on another

✦ Or those who need compatibility between PCs and Macs

✦ Or those who are sick and tired of that grinding sound and the slow transfer rate of that prehistoric magnetic media

For an entire decade, I have carried on this fight in every book that I've written. Here's your chance to join me. Just repeat the following chant:

> **"Begone, floppy!** Leave my sight! I banish you forever to the Land of Obsolete Technology. *As it is written, so shall it be done."*

Instead, I offer you the USB flash drive, which works perfectly on any PC with a Universal Serial Bus (USB) port. And if the PC is running at least Windows 98SE, you shouldn't need any installation software or drivers. Most of these drives are so small that they fit on your keychain, and they even work with Macintosh and Linux computers. They're sturdy, with no moving parts to wear out. And because a USB flash drive is Plug and Play, you can connect and disconnect it without having to reboot your PC.

Even older USB 1.1 flash drives are fast, with transfer rates up to 12 Mbps. USB 2.0 flash drives really rock, offering transfer rates of up to 480 Mbps! My USB 2.0 flash drive has 512MB of storage space and cost $30 U.S., but you can get a drive with up to 2GB of storage for a mere $200 U.S. or so. All hail the new King of Personal Storage!

To sum up, a classic Mark's Maxim:

With a flash drive, you'll never lose a document to a floppy again.™

Aw, geez, my editors say I have to tell you how to format a floppy. Something about a contract that I purportedly signed. Okay, it's your data's funeral, not mine. Floppy disks (like Zip disks and hard drives) must be formatted before they can (unreliably) store any data; this prepares the magnetic surface of the disk to hold stuff.

Load the floppy that you want to format. Just locate the goofy drive bay that looks like it could eat a graham cracker and push the disk into it until you hear a satisfying click that sounds like you stepped on a June bug. Double-click My Computer (on your desktop) to display the drives on your system. Right-click the floppy drive (probably named *A* for *Abysmal*) and then choose Format to display the dialog box that you see in Figure 3-20. If you need to create a floppy that will boot a PC into DOS, mark the Create an MS-DOS Startup Disk check box to enable it. Click Start . . . and good luck.

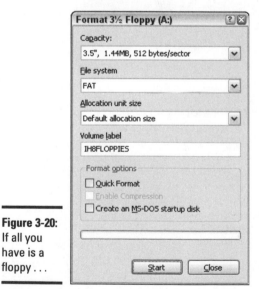

Figure 3-20:
If all you
have is a
floppy . . .

Chapter 4: Customizing Windows XP

In This Chapter

- ✔ Customizing your desktop background
- ✔ Fine-tuning the toolbars
- ✔ Using Explorer bars
- ✔ Understanding the My Documents folder
- ✔ Working with Favorites
- ✔ Understanding multi-user computing
- ✔ Sending and receiving faxes in Windows XP
- ✔ Playing MP3 files in Media Player
- ✔ Viewing and downloading digital photographs
- ✔ Recording your own data CDs in XP

If you've followed along so far in this mini-book, you've been a slave to the Microsoft defaults. That might be status quo for novice XP users, but if you want to mold Windows XP into *your* operating system (and thus become a PC power user), you must master the customization features within XP. Just say "No!" to Icons view, or the Explorer window Task pane, or that too-familiar desktop background — add your favorite sound effects from *The Rocky Horror Picture Show* to your XP experience. (I boot up every morning to the lilting sounds of "The Time Warp," much to the consternation of our family cats.)

This chapter ties what you need to transform your PC from a personal computer into a *personal tool* — which, I might add, should be the end goal of every hardware manufacturer and software developer, including the Microsoft crowd. In these pages, I do my part: You discover how to optimize your toolbars for productivity, share your computer with others in a multi-user environment, visit your favorite Web sites directly from the Explorer window, and send and receive faxes with your PC's fax modem. I also introduce you to Windows Media Player, which you can use to enjoy all sorts of digital multimedia. And stick around for a brief look at viewing/downloading digital photographs. I even show you how to burn a CD-R with data files from your hard drive . . . *without* buying an expensive CD recording application!

So, good reader, prepare yourself — turn that cookie-cutter machine with its vanilla Windows XP into your personal, custom-made *muscle PC,* and take it up a notch!

Personalizing Your Desktop

Don't get me wrong — I like the soothing blue sky and calm green hills of the typical Windows desktop. After a few weeks, though, you'll say to yourself, "Self, you spent two grand on this system. Why not jazz it up a little bit?" In this section, I show you how to take care of spicing up the look and sound of Windows XP.

Changing the background

First up on the makeover tour is the most popular trick — changing your desktop background to something more palatable. Windows XP prefers JPEG and bitmap images for your background.

Follow these steps to select a new background:

1. **Right-click anywhere on the open space of your current desktop and then choose Properties from the menu that appears.**

   (In other words, don't click an icon or Windows XP control, like the Start menu.) The Display Properties dialog box appears.

2. **Click the Desktop tab to display the settings that you see in Figure 4-1.**

Figure 4-1: The Desktop tab of the Display Properties dialog box.

3. **To choose a desktop image from your Windows folder, click it in the Background list.**

   To rebel completely against background images, click None. Alternatively, you can load your own image by clicking the Browse button and navigating to the location of the image; then just double-click the image file to load it.

4. **You can choose to stretch an image that doesn't quite fit across your entire desktop by selecting Stretch from the Position drop-down list box. If the image is too small to stretch, pick Center to put it in the middle of the desktop; or if the image is a repeating pattern, choose Tile.**

5. **To set the desktop to a solid color — or to change the color of the desktop that surrounds a centered image — click the Color drop-down list box and then click the desired color.**

Any changes you make are reflected in the Preview window. After the preview looks good, click Apply to try out the background; if you like what you see, click OK. If the result would make Andy Warhol cringe, try again.

Using themes

A Windows XP *theme* is a package deal: Selecting a theme gives you a background, a color scheme, an icon set, and sound effects. Themes are available from Microsoft, or you can download themes (of varying quality) from sites all over the Web. To choose a theme, follow these steps:

1. **Right-click anywhere on the open space of your desktop and then choose Properties from the pop-up menu that appears to display the Themes settings of the Display Properties dialog box (see Figure 4-2).**

Figure 4-2:
You've got
themes
to meet
every need.

2. **Click the Theme drop-down list box and click a theme to view it in the Sample window.**

3. **To create a theme of your own based on the current desktop settings, click the Save As button.**

   Yup, you get the standard Save As dialog box, in which you name your custom theme.

4. **When you're satisfied with the theme, click the Apply button to check it out on your desktop; or click OK to close the Display Properties dialog box.**

Changing system sounds

Windows XP offers a number of events that can be heralded by system sound files in WAV format. Follow these steps to assign sounds:

1. **Choose Start⇨Control Panel⇨Sounds and Audio Devices and then click the Sounds tab to display the settings that you see in Figure 4-3.**

   If you've switched to the classic Start menu, you should choose Start⇨ Settings⇨Control Panel⇨Sounds and Audio Devices instead.

2. **To choose an existing sound scheme, click the Sound Scheme drop-down list and then click the scheme that you want.**

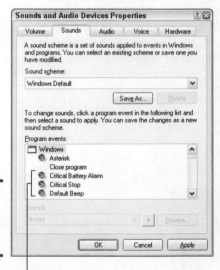

Figure 4-3: The sounds of Windows XP.

Speaker icons indicate that a sound has been assigned to an event.

3. **To assign sounds individually to events, click the desired event within the Program Events list box and then click the Sounds drop-down list box to display all the sounds that have been installed within XP.**

To hear a sound, click the right-arrow Play button. (When you assign a sound to an event, XP marks that event with a tiny speaker icon.)

4. **You can also use WAV format sound files from another folder on your hard drive; click the Browse button, navigate to that folder, and then double-click the file to load it.**

If you create your own custom sound scheme, don't forget to click Save As to save it under a unique name so that you can load it in a flash in the future.

5. **When you're ready to rock, click OK to close the Sounds and Audio Devices Properties dialog box.**

Switching Views and Sorting Items

Next, allow me to discuss the different views within Windows XP Explorer — and how you can switch between 'em in a flash.

To switch between views in the Explorer window, open the Views menu from the toolbar (in Figure 4-4, see how the menu drops down). Your choices are

✦ **Thumbnails:** This view displays images and video clips as *thumbnails* (tiny pictures), but be warned: It can take XP a significant amount of time to process a folder containing a lot of images, especially on an older machine with less than 256MB of RAM. In this view, folders contain pictures that are displayed as tiny thumbnails of the images that they contain . . . *sassy* indeed!

✦ **Tiles:** Choose this view to make items appear as icons on well-spaced tiles at regular intervals, thus making it easy to click an item without running something else by accident.

✦ **Icons:** This view is a traditional favorite, where each item appears as an icon. However, spacing is much tighter than the Tiles view, so longer filenames are often abbreviated (and you must be more careful when clicking).

✦ **List:** Another long-standing favorite, List view features each item arranged in list format — one entry per line.

✦ **Details:** If you like the List view but wish you had more information on each item, choose the Details view. Again, the Details view takes a little more time to display, so expect a delay before you see the statistics — the larger the folder, the longer it takes.

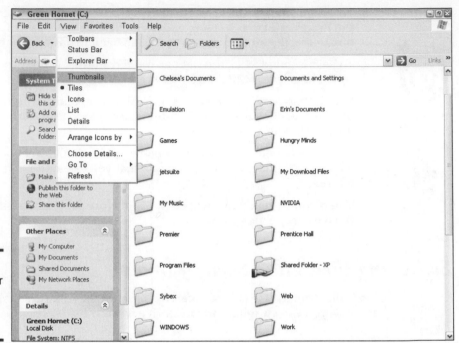

Figure 4-4:
Choose your
view in the
Explorer
window.

To sort the items in the Explorer view to your particular fancy, choose View➪ Arrange Icons By and then choose the sorting criteria that you want to use. (I find that Name, Type, and Total Size are the most useful.)

Note that you can also elect to group items together — choose View➪ Arrange Icons By➪Show in Groups.

To keep your icons from straying all over creation, choose View➪Arrange Icons By➪Auto Arrange. With the Auto Arrange feature turned on, Windows XP arranges everything in orderly rows for you. (Note that this option is only available in Thumbnails, Tiles, and Icons views.)

Adjusting toolbars

Toolbars used to be static controls but not any more. With Windows XP, you can add and remove buttons to create The Perfect Explorer Toolbar! Follow these steps:

1. **Right-click the toolbar in the Explorer window and then choose Customize from the menu that appears.**

This displays the Customize Toolbar dialog box that you see in Figure 4-5.

Figure 4-5:
Why settle
for the
default
toolbar?

You can also choose View⇨Toolbars⇨Customize if you're averse to right-clicking.

2. **From the list on the left, click the button that you want to add and then click the Add button to include it on the toolbar; to remove an existing toolbar button, click the button name in the list on the right and then click the Remove button.**

3. **To fit more icons on the toolbar, click the Icon Options drop-down list and then choose Small Icons.**

4. **To choose the placement of button labels — or to remove them altogether — click the Text Options drop-down list box.**

5. **Need to modify the placement of a toolbar icon? Click it in the Current Toolbar Buttons list and then click either the Move Up or the Move Down button to redistribute it just so.**

6. **Click Close to save your changes.**

To toggle the display of individual toolbars within the Explorer window, right-click the Explorer bar and then click the toolbar that you want to hide or display.

Using the Explorer bar

The default Explorer window displays the Task pane, which is a multipurpose "control thing" on the left side of the Explorer window (the hoopla is a-happenin' in Figure 4-6). It provides you with a number of commands that apply to whatever you're viewing. For example, you can make a new folder or share the current folder on your network. You can also display the details on the currently selected item.

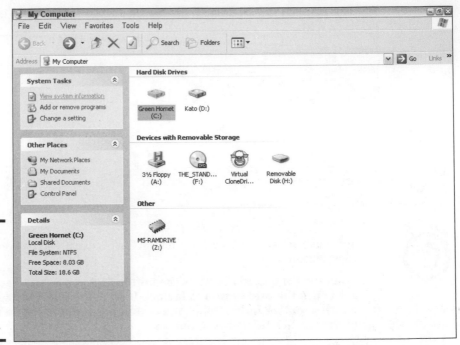

Figure 4-6:
The Task pane is a useful conglomeration of commands.

However, that's not the only set of controls vying for the left side of the screen: Enter the Explorer bar. Besides looking rather suave, it can help you with

✦ **Searching for all sorts of things:** Choose View➪Explorer Bar➪Search (or press Ctrl+E) to display the Search Explorer bar, as shown in Figure 4-7. (Actually, it *feels* more like a wizard than a plain toolbar.) Click the item, person, computer, or piece of information that you want to search for, and the Search Explorer Bar leads you through a series of questions to help you fine-tune your search.

✦ **Jumping to Favorites:** Choose View➪Explorer Bar➪Favorites (or press Ctrl+I), and you'll see your Favorites collection listed in the Explorer bar. A single click of any Favorite jumps directly to it. (More on Favorites later in this chapter.) You can also click the Favorites menu (within the Explorer window) and click a Favorite from there.

✦ **Watching and listening to multimedia:** Choose View➪Explorer Bar➪Media to see and hear the latest multimedia files from WindowsMedia.com (see the left side of Figure 4-8) or to listen to Internet radio. (Note that at least a 56 Kbps dialup connection is recommended for listening to Internet radio stations.) Media Player controls are included at the bottom of the Media Explorer bar, so you can take care of mundane chores like adjusting volume, switching tracks, or stopping and starting playback.

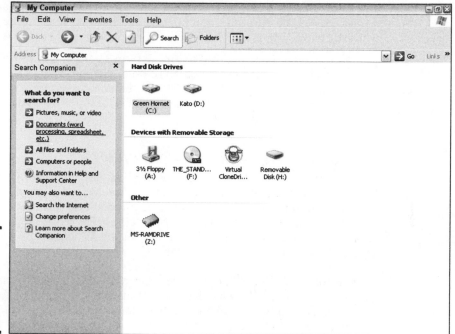

Figure 4-7:
Locating
things is
easy from
the Search
Explorer bar.

Book II
Chapter 4

Customizing
Windows XP

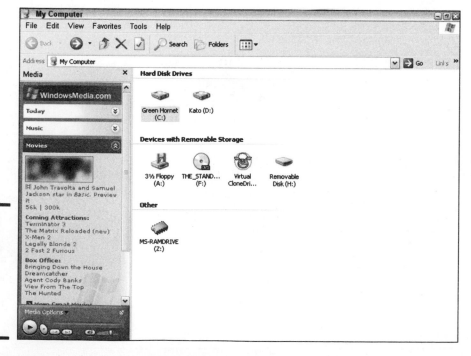

Figure 4-8:
Invite
Hollywood
and
Nashville
to your
Explorer
window.

✦ **Returning to where you've been:** Choose View➪Explorer Bar➪History to display the Web sites and documents that you've used recently — to return to a Web site or load a recent document, just click the name.

As you might imagine, the History Explorer bar can get rather crowded after a long day at the keyboard. To help sort the chaos, click the View button at the upper-left of the History Explorer bar, and you can sort by date or site visited or by the total number of times that you've visited each site or document.

And don't forget the Folders view!

Probably the most familiar of the Explorer bars is the Folders Explorer bar, as shown in Figure 4-9. It's the old standby "tree" display (from Windows 3.1 and 95/98) of the folders on your system. You don't even have to use the View menu to display the Folders Explorer bar, either. It's remained so popular (and so convenient and fast and useful) that the XP Explorer window contains a Folders button on the toolbar.

From within the Folders Explorer bar, click a drive or folder to expand it and display its contents. You can also click a plus sign (+) to expand an item or click a minus sign (–) next to an item to collapse it again. The Explorer window is updated automatically with the contents of the drive or folder that you're viewing.

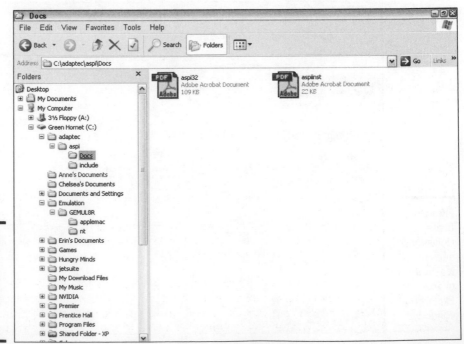

Figure 4-9:
The mighty
Folders
view is as
everlasting
as a
redwood.

What's This Stuff in the My Documents Folder?

Windows XP gives each user a separate My Documents folder, which you can reach in a number of different ways:

✦ From the Windows XP desktop

✦ From the Start menu

✦ From the Other Places section of the Explorer Task pane

✦ From the My Documents button in Save (As) and Open dialog boxes

If you're in a hurry, you can get to your My Documents folder from anywhere in a flash: Press the Win+D key sequence (using either of the Windows keys on your keyboard) to display your desktop, press the Home key (which highlights the upper-left icon, which in this case is the My Documents icon on the desktop), and then press Enter (to open it).

As you can see in Figure 4-10, the My Documents folder is a regular repository of everything that's yours, including stuff like

✦ Your images, video clips, and music

✦ Your games

✦ Your downloaded files

✦ Your personal Web sites that you've created

You'll also find many subfolders created by different applications in the My Documents folder, as well as things like theme files, background images, and Office XP documents. That's because the Redmond Gang wants you to use the My Documents folder as your center of operations, and most software developers respect the Microsoft standard. Thus, most programs will default to installing themselves there and saving their documents there as well (or to one of the standard subfolders within My Documents, like My Pictures).

If you're using Microsoft Backup, you should definitely use the My Documents folder because that's what Backup uses for source files as a default.

You can create as many subfolders in the My Documents folder as you like, and it's a logical place to keep your stuff (at least on your C drive, where Windows XP is usually installed).

Remember, there's actually a separate My Documents folder for each user that you've created in Windows XP, so the stuff that you see in your My Documents folder *won't* be the same as what Brother Elroy sees in his My Documents folder. What Windows XP displays is keyed to the active user account.

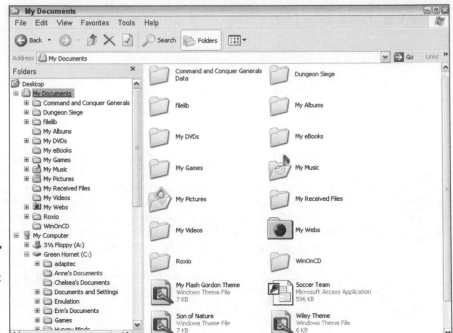

Figure 4-10:
Your XP pad:
the My
Documents
folder.

Share the Documents

By the way, the contents of the My Documents folder are also hidden from other users, so you can't put a document there and expect other users of your PC to be able to reach it. Instead, use the Shared Documents folder, which you can reach from the Windows Explorer Task pane. When you copy a file or folder to the Shared Documents folder, anyone using another account on your PC can open and copy the file.

By default, the Shared Documents folder is *not* shared amongst the other PCs on your network — it's only used with files shared locally among users of the same PC.

Using Favorites

Yep, you also have access to your favorite Web sites from within the Explorer window. Earlier in this chapter, I talk about the Favorites Explorer bar, and you might already know how to use Favorites within Internet Explorer (which I explain in Book III, Chapter 4). But how does one add Favorites *without* using Internet Explorer? That's what this section is all about.

Ever wonder why the XP Explorer window and the Internet Explorer window look so similar — or why it takes so little time to jump to a favorite Web site inside the Explorer window? Well, bunkie, it's because Microsoft made a decision some time back to merge its Windows operating system with its Web browser. After missing the early Internet boat, His Gateness decided to embrace the Internet with open arms, so now the traditional Explorer window is actually generated with the same code that runs Internet Explorer.

Adding a favorite

You can add a Favorite from the currently displayed Web page or folder in the Explorer window in two ways. First, however, bring up the Favorites Explorer bar by choosing View➪Explorer Bar➪Favorites (or press Ctrl+I).

Book II
Chapter 4

Customizing
Windows XP

+ **From the Favorites Explorer bar:** Click the Add button, and Windows XP displays the dialog box that you see in Figure 4-11. Type a new name (if you like) and click the Create In button to select the Favorites folder where you want to store the entry. Then click OK to save the Favorite.

+ **From the Favorites menu:** Choose Favorites➪Add to Favorite to display the same dialog box. Type a new name (if you like) and click the Create In button to select the Favorites folder where you want to store the entry. Then click OK to save the Favorite.

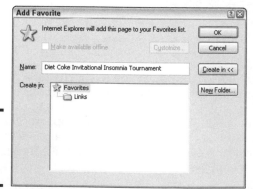

Figure 4-11:
My favorite
way to add
a Favorite.

Organizing favorites

To organize your Favorites, either click the Organize button on the Favorites Explorer bar or choose Favorites➪Organize Favorites. XP displays the dialog box that you see in Figure 4-12.

✦ **To add a new Favorite folder:** Click the Create Folder button to add a new folder (which appears in all Favorites locations near you).

✦ **To move a Favorite into a folder:** Click the desired Favorite, click the Move to Folder button, click the destination folder, and then click OK.

✦ **To rename a Favorite:** Click the desired Favorite, click the Rename button, type the new name, and then press Enter.

When you're done organizing your Favorites, click Close to return to the Explorer window.

Figure 4-12: Now do you really want disorganized Favorites? I think not!

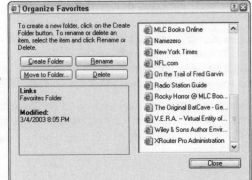

Creating a Shortcut

In Chapter 2 of this mini-book, I introduce you to shortcuts — now it's time to create them. Here are two methods of creating a shortcut:

✦ **Right-click an icon:** From the pop-up menu that appears, choose Create Shortcut, and XP does just that — a new shortcut appears in the same folder as the original icon. You can then copy or move the shortcut to another location on your system.

✦ **Drag an icon:** Right-click the icon and drag it to the location where you want to place the shortcut. When you release the mouse button, choose Create Shortcuts Here from the pop-up menu that appears.

Ever wonder where the shortcut's original file is located? To find out, right-click the shortcut, choose Properties from the resulting pop-up menu, and then click the Shortcut tab to display the Target field (see Figure 4-13). The target path points to the original file.

Figure 4-13:
Clearing a
path to a
shortcut's
target (so
to speak).

Multi-user Operation

Earlier in this chapter, I mention the Shared Documents folder: where the local users on your PC can share files and folders. That's an example of *multi-user* operation. Unlike a network environment — where multiple computers are connected — a multi-user PC need not be part of a network. Instead, different people use the same PC; each person has their own user account; and Windows XP keeps track of everyone's Control Panel preferences, Explorer views, desktop backgrounds, Favorites files, and all the other sundry things that I show you how to customize XP in this mini-book.

In this section, I discuss how multiple folks can share a single workhorse PC.

Windows XP offers three different user account levels:

+ **Administrator:** In this level, the user has full access to the Control Panel, can manage other user accounts, and can install programs and hardware. If you're the only person who will be using your PC, Windows XP sets you up with an Administrator account — as it should.

+ **Limited:** In this level, the user can only change the account password, can't install hardware or software, and has full control over only those files that he or she creates. If you're setting up accounts for others and you're less than impressed with their computing skills, by all means give them Limited accounts!

+ **Guest:** I tell you more about the Guest account in a tad in the upcoming section, "Be my guest."

Logging in

Your first chore when you sit down to a multi-user PC is to log in. This step identifies you to XP and allows the operating system to load and apply all your custom settings. You can log in to Windows XP in a number of ways:

✦ **Boot your PC with multiple users active:** If you start Windows XP with more than one user account, you'll either get the Welcome screen or the Logon screen (more on the difference between the two in a moment).

✦ **Log off from the Start menu:** Click the Start menu, click Log Off, and XP displays either the Welcome screen or the Logon screen. If you're using Fast User Switching (which I explain in a second), you'll see the dialog box in Figure 4-14; otherwise, you'll simply be prompted for confirmation before the logoff actually takes place.

✦ **Switch users:** If you've enabled Fast User Switching, you can allow another person to log on without actually closing any of your programs. Just make doggone sure that the other user knows not to turn off the PC completely! (XP helps prevent any tragedies by displaying the number of programs that the original user is running on the Welcome or Logon screen.) After the switched user completes his session, he should simply log off so that your programs remain running. Click the Start menu, click Log Off, and then click Switch Users.

Figure 4-14:
Which will it be — log off or switch?

So what's the difference between the Welcome screen and the Logon screen? A big one: the password prompt! You see, if you've configured XP to use the Welcome screen, a user logs on by simply clicking her username on the screen, and whoosh! She's logged in. On the other hand, if you've disabled the Welcome screen, a user has to

✦ Type the correct username — and it had better be spelled correctly.

✦ Type the correct password — ditto.

The logon method that you use depends on your security needs. If you live with a trusted roommate or spouse and you can be reasonably sure of who's sitting at the keyboard, by all means, bypass thc unnecessary security and use the Welcome screen. (It'll save you countless fruitless logon attempts because you missed a letter of your password.)

To choose between the Welcome screen and the Logon screen — or to enable Fast User Switching — you need to visit the Control Panel and open the User Accounts Wizard (see Figure 4-15). I demonstrate how to use the Control Panel and how to reach the User Accounts Wizard in Chapter 6 of this mini-book.

Be my guest

Before I cast off from Multi-user Land, I should elaborate on the third type of user account: the Guest account is perfect for someone who needs to use your PC right this moment but isn't going to need an account in the future. The Guest account

+ Doesn't require a password.

+ Can't be duplicated or deleted — there is only one Guest account.

+ Can be turned on or off. Again, this is done from the User Accounts Wizard accessed from the Control Panel.

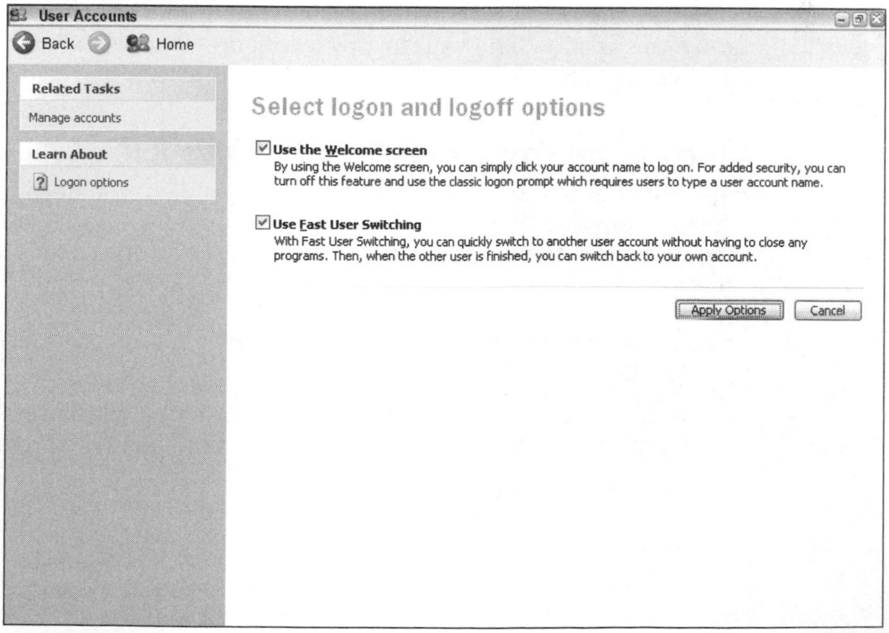

Book II
Chapter 4

Customizing
Windows XP

User Accounts

Back   Home

> **Related Tasks**
> Manage accounts
>
> **Learn About**
> ? Logon options

Select logon and logoff options

☑ **Use the Welcome screen**
By using the Welcome screen, you can simply click your account name to log on. For added security, you can turn off this feature and use the classic logon prompt which requires users to type a user account name.

☑ **Use Fast User Switching**
With Fast User Switching, you can quickly switch to another user account without having to close any programs. Then, when the other user is finished, you can switch back to your own account.

[Apply Options]   [Cancel]

Figure 4-15:
You can create, modify, and delete user accounts from the Control Panel.

So what exactly can a Guest do? Basically, the Guest account has the same abilities as a Limited user account: The Guest can use your PC, but Windows XP prevents that person from abusing your PC.

Fax Me, Please

Yep, I know that many readers are exclaiming, "Hey! I didn't know that Windows XP could act as a fax machine! That is positively *trick!*" And indeed it is — all you need is a fax modem, a telephone line, and the instructions in this chapter.

There are actually four separate programs that you use to handle faxing in XP:

✦ The Fax Configuration Wizard

✦ The Send Fax Wizard

✦ The Fax Cover Page Editor

✦ The Fax Console

Unfortunately, Microsoft — for some unknown reason — doesn't install these fax programs during a default installation of Windows XP. (Sound of hand slapping forehead *twice*.) Here's the drill. Stick your XP installation disc in your CD-ROM drive. Click Start, click Printers and Faxes, and then click Set Up Faxing in the window's toolbar. XP whirrs busily to itself and copies a number of files from your XP installation disc. You're returned to the Printers and Faxes window, and you can now configure Windows XP to send and receive faxes. Sigh.

Setting up faxing under Windows XP

Sigh Part 2. After you get the fax programs installed, you need to configure the fax support within Windows XP before you tell folks that you're ready to accept calls from their fax machine. Follow these steps to set up your fax service:

1. **Choose Start⇨All Programs⇨Accessories⇨Communications⇨Fax⇨ Fax Console.**

   (Whew. Way to bury this thing, Redmond.) After all that work, XP obligingly displays the first screen of the Fax Configuration Wizard.

2. **Click Next to continue.**

The wizard displays the rather frightening screen that you see in Figure 4-16.

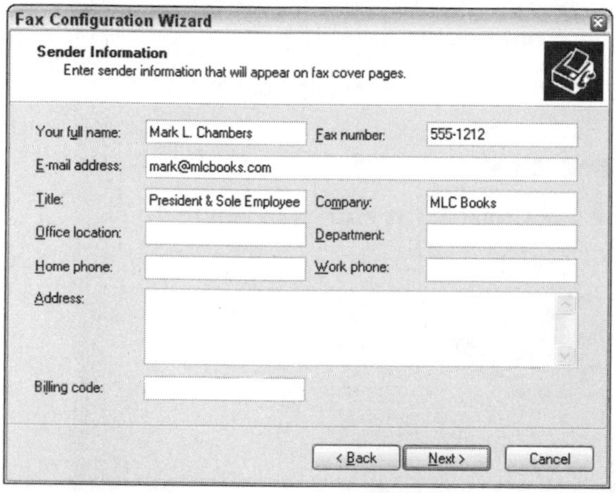

Figure 4-16: Man, that is one boatload of text boxes.

Book II Chapter 4

Customizing Windows XP

3. **Yep, by law, you've got to type at least your full name, fax number, and company name — but put the rest in, too, because it'll come in handy. Then click Next to continue.**

4. **In the screen that appears, select the device that will be used to send faxes from the drop-down list box. Also specify here whether**

   • You want the fax modem to pick up automatically (after a certain number of rings).

   • You should manually answer incoming fax calls.

   Then click Next to continue.

5. **Time to enter your TSID, or Transmitting Subscriber Identification.**

   You can use up to 20 characters, so you have enough space to identify you or your business. This is the string sent when you call another fax machine to send a fax; it identifies your name or company in the recipient's fax transmission report. Click Next to continue.

6. **Type another 20 characters for your CSID, or Called Subscriber Identification.**

   Most folks use the same string as the one entered for the TSID. This string appears on the fax machine that's calling you. Click Next to continue.

7. **You must specify where received faxes are to be routed:**

   - Print it on the printer that you select in the drop-down list box.

   - Save a copy in the folder that you specify.

   - Choose both options.

   All incoming faxes are also stored in the Fax Console Inbox. Click Next to continue.

8. **All done! Click Finish.**

   XP opens the Fax Console (as shown in Figure 4-17).

Figure 4-17: A first glimpse of the Fax Console.

Sending and receiving faxes

If you've followed along the previous two sections, you are now XP-fax-sending-empowered. To send a fax, follow these steps:

1. **In its native application, open (or create) the document that you want to fax.**

   For example, fax a Word document from within Word.

2. **Press Ctrl+P to display the Print dialog box.**

3. **Click the Printer drop-down list box and then choose the fax device.**

   Click the Preferences button to switch between Normal (200 x 200 DPI) and Draft (200 x 100 DPI) quality. Draft is quicker, but it's, well, draft quality.

4. **Click Print.**

5. **After the Send Fax Wizard launches, click Next to continue.**

6. **Type the name of the recipient and the person's fax number. Or, if he's in your Address Book, click the Address Book button and choose the contact from there.**

   (Optional) If you like, you can enter multiple recipients and click Add to include them in the list.

   When you're done, click Next.

7. **(Optional) Adding a cover page is optional but highly recommended.**

   a. **Choose a cover page template from the drop-down list.**

   b. **Type a subject line. (If you like, you can also add notes.)**

   c. **Click Next to continue.**

8. **Choose the transmission priority and a scheduled time to send the fax (any time from immediately until 24 hours from now) and then click Next to continue.**

9. **Verify the settings on the final wizard screen.**

   • If they check out okay, click Finish.

   • To back up and fix something that's wrong, click Back and, um, fix it.

If you configure XP for automatic reception of incoming faxes after a specified number of rings, you really don't have to do anything to receive faxes other than keep your PC running and stay off that telephone line. (See Step 4 in the previous section for the lowdown on how you want the fax call answered.) However, if you specify manual answering for incoming faxes, you have to follow these steps for each incoming fax:

1. **Choose Start➪All Programs➪Accessories➪Communications➪Fax➪ Fax Console to run the program.**

2. **When you hear the phone ring, choose File➪Receive a Fax Now.**

3. **Verify that the incoming fax has been properly detected by watching the Fax Monitor; the Fax Console also displays a Reception Complete dialog when the fax has been received.**

Doing the Multimedia Thing

The final stop on this customization trip concerns multimedia. Windows XP can be dead boring without liberal doses of digital audio, digital photographs, and DVD movies! In this section, I show you how to enjoy all sorts of digital entertainment as well as how you can record your own CDs from within Windows XP.

Playing your MP3 files

MP3 files are the modern solution to crystal-clear, high-quality music that's

✦ **Standardized and compatible:** MP3 files are supported within every computer operating system these days, along with countless personal music devices, hand-held personal digital assistants (PDAs), and palm PCs.

✦ **Easy to create, copy, and share:** Okay, perhaps *too* easily created, copied, and shared . . . but I'm just reporting on what you *can* do, not involving myself in the ongoing copyright debate over MP3 distribution. (And, like the bumper sticker on the back of my Jeep reads, "MP3 is not a Crime.")

✦ **Easy to record on CD-Rs:** Same copyright argument, same excuse on my part — but it is currently legal to make "compilation discs" of MP3 songs as long as you own the original audio CDs.

To play MP3 files within Windows XP, you can double-click an MP3 file within the Explorer window. Unless you've installed an alternate MP3 player, XP cranks up Windows Media Player, as shown in Figure 4-18, and begins playing the music immediately.

If you're wondering what the heck all the dancing lights mean, they're what Microsoft calls a *visualization* — essentially, a fun "optical oscilloscope" that constantly changes. To switch to the next visualization, click the small, right-arrow button at the bottom left of the visualization window. To turn visualizations off completely, just choose View⇨Visualizations⇨ No Visualizations.

The familiar controls at the bottom of the Media Player window are shown in Figure 4-18 as well. You can click and drag the progress slider to change your current point in the song or to mute or pause the playback.

For a complete discussion of MP3 files — including how you can "rip" your own digital music from existing audio CDs — see Book VI, Chapter 2.

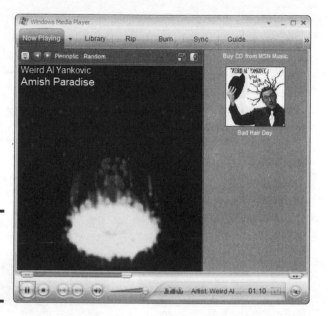

Book II
Chapter 4

Customizing
Windows XP

Figure 4-18:
Weird Al
sounds
just fine in
digital form!

Viewing and downloading digital photographs

If you've got a digital camera, Windows XP has three features that you'll
want to try:

+ **Thumbnails view:** I discuss the Thumbnails view within the Explorer
  window at the beginning of this chapter. As I mention there, it's slower
  than List or Icons view, but if you're sifting through a folder full of digital
  images and you want to move, copy, or delete some, Thumbnails view is
  the row to hoe. Figure 4-19 illustrates a folder from my digital photograph
  collection as seen in Thumbnails view.

+ **Preview:** If you haven't installed an image editor like Photoshop or
  Paint Shop Pro, you can still view a picture on your hard drive by
  double-clicking it. Windows XP runs the Viewer program, as shown in
  Figure 4-20. (Viewer also displays received faxes.) The toolbar at the
  bottom of the Viewer window lets you zoom in or out, rotate the image,
  annotate it, print it, or copy it to another location.

+ **The Camera and Scanner Wizard:** This wizard kicks in automatically
  when you connect your Universal Serial Bus (USB) digital camera to
  your PC, allowing you to view images and choose which will be downloaded to your PC.

Figure 4-19: View thumbnails of your digital photo folders.

Figure 4-20: Previewing a digital photograph.

The disk cognoscenti

Want to avoid looking like an idiot when talking with a PC power user? Then listen up. The round, shiny object that you load into your CD-ROM or DVD-ROM drive is a *disc,* ending with a *c* — and **not** a *disk,* ending with a *k.* The latter word more accurately describes your hard disk or a Zip disk, or even one of those irritating floppy disks. (Think Latin, think Greek, think *disc*us, think *disc*ography — it's just plain round.) Anyone who pretends to be a PC power user and talks oh-so-knowingly about a *CD-ROM disk* or *DVD disk* is a dweeb. Shun them like you would dandruff.

You'll find much more information on digital cameras and these features in Book VI, Chapter 5.

Recording your own CDs

Most CD and DVD recorders are accompanied by their own recording programs — like Roxio Easy Media Creator (see Figure 4-21), from Sonic Solutions (www.sonic.com).

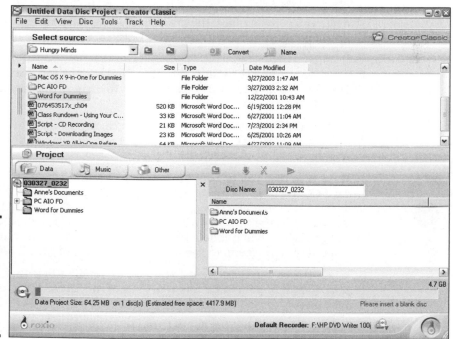

Figure 4-21: The Cadillac of CD recording software — Easy Media Creator.

For complete coverage of today's popular CD and DVD recording software, pick up a copy of my book *CD and DVD Recording For Dummies*, Second Edition, published by the good folks at Wiley Publishing, Inc.

However, you can record a data disc within Windows XP without a separate commercial CD-recording application. Grab a blank CD-R and follow these steps:

1. **Load the blank disc into your CD recorder.**

   Windows XP displays a dialog box asking what the heck you want to do with the disc.

2. **Click Open Writable CD Folder Using Windows Explorer from the list and then click OK.**

   If you're not planning on installing a CD-recording application any time soon, mark the Always Do the Selected Action check box to enable it before you click OK.

3. **Double-click My Computer (on your desktop) to open the Explorer window and then select the files that you want to record to the CD folder window by choosing the File⇨Send To⇨CD Drive menu command. Or, just right-click the file(s) that you want to copy and then choose Send To⇨CD Drive from the pop-up menu that appears.**

   While you copy the files, they're actually magically transported to a special folder on your hard drive. *Note:* Nothing has actually been recorded yet, as XP continues to remind you!

4. **When you're ready to burn the disc, double-click My Computer and then double-click the CD recorder icon to display the files in the storage folder.**

   Note that each ghostly file or folder icon carries a funky down-arrow, which indicates that it's been stored and is now awaiting the Great Writing.

   Make sure that you're copying less than a total of 650MB for a standard CD-R! For some furshlugginer reason, Windows XP doesn't check to make sure that you have enough room on the disc before the recording begins. Therefore, take a moment and select all the files that you're going to burn; then right-click them and choose Properties from the resulting pop-up menu to see how much space that they'll need.

5. **When you're ready to record and you've verified that there's less than 650MB of data to be burned, click Write These Files to CD in the Task pane.**

6. **Type a volume label for the disc (up to 16 characters long) and then click Next.**

7. **Sit back and relax — this can take some time (anywhere from 5 to 20 minutes, depending on the speed of your drive).**

Watching a DVD movie

I've got to be completely honest with you — I don't like the Windows XP Media Player as a DVD player. That's because it doesn't have many of the features of a commercial software DVD player like PowerDVD or Sonic's CinePlayer (see Figure 4-22). However, it's free . . . and it doesn't crash (two of the characteristics of truly fine software).

Book II
Chapter 4

Customizing
Windows XP

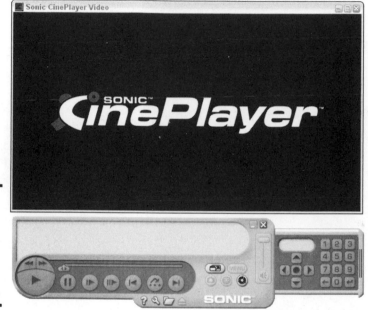

Figure 4-22: Sonic's CinePlayer is a full-featured DVD software player.

To watch a DVD movie disc within Windows XP, run Media Player by choosing Start➪All Programs➪Windows Media Player. Click Play; click DVD, VCD, or CD Audio; and then select the movie from the pop-up window. You can switch between the window display and a full-screen display by pressing Alt+Enter. To capture a still image from the film, press Ctrl+I.

Plus, you get the same familiar set of control buttons that appear at the bottom of the Media Player window. They work for everything from MP3 files to digital video clips to DVDs. Oh, joy . . . rapture.

Chapter 5: Maintaining the XP Beast

In This Chapter

✔ Scanning your hard drives for errors

✔ Defragmenting to speed up your PC

✔ Backing up your files in XP

✔ Using System Restore

✔ Using boot and recovery options in XP

✔ Taking Windows Update for a ride

Maintenance. It's important, and you've got to do it — so why not make it *exciting?* Instead of dull preventive care, think of the pit crew around an Indy car, and . . . well, on second thought, that might be a stretch. Anyway, you've gotta do it.

You might not find this chapter overly exciting, but if you follow on a regular basis the procedures that you find here, I guarantee that you'll be happy with the performance and stability of your PC running Windows XP. And who knows? Maybe that Indy pit crew job will materialize someday. (Even if it doesn't, you'll have the smoothest-running PC on the block, and that counts for a lot.)

Device Manager: The Hardware Tool

The first stop on your maintenance tour is the Windows XP Device Manager, which I recommend that you check at least once a month. *Device Manager* is essentially a status window that displays the operating status of each of the hardware devices in your PC as well as the peripherals connected to it. With one glance, you can see any hardware device that Windows has marked as a troublemaker, and locating trouble is the first step in solving it.

Now, don't panic at the idea of rooting around in your hardware. In fact, the idea of a hardware conflict is easy to understand. Just about every hardware device in your PC needs a unique pathway to be able to communicate with the CPU and other devices. For instance, your modem must be able to send and receive data to and from the Internet without getting spurious stuff that's actually meant for your printer. (Imagine the fun that you'd have if your hard drive and your CD or DVD-ROM drive kept exchanging data by accident . . . harrumph.)

To keep things straight, Windows XP assigns two values that identify devices: a direct memory address (DMA) and an interrupt request (IRQ). Because each device in your PC needs a unique data path — think of your e-mail or your home address — devices need unique settings for DMA and IRQ as well. If a value is shared between two devices, Windows XP might lock up because the operating system has no idea whom it's talking to and where the data is coming from.

Luckily, Windows XP does a great job allocating these hardware resources, especially if you're using Universal Serial Bus (USB) and FireWire peripherals. However, sharing problems do still crop up from time to time with older hardware that might not have an up-to-date driver. (A *driver* is a program that tells Windows XP how to communicate with and use a specific hardware device.) Not only can Device Manager display what devices are causing trouble, but it can also help you update the drivers for that device.

Follow these steps to use Device Manager in Windows XP:

1. **Right-click the My Computer icon on your desktop and choose Properties from the pop-up menu that appears to display the System Properties dialog box; then click the Hardware tab.**

2. **Click the Device Manager button to open the Device Manager window that you see in Figure 5-1.**

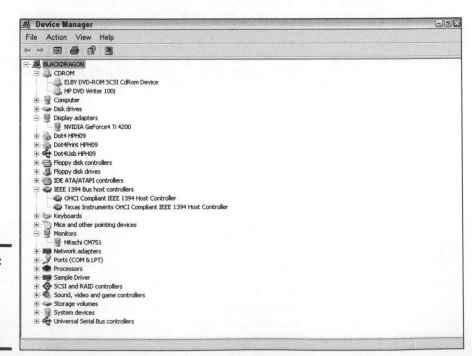

Figure 5-1: Check for possible problems in Device Manager.

If a device in the Device Manager window is marked with a yellow exclamation point or a red check mark, it might be in conflict with another device, which, in turn, might also be marked by a yellow exclamation point.

3. **To check for possible conflicts with a particular piece of hardware, right-click the marked device and then choose Properties from the pop-up menu that appears to display its settings (as shown in Figure 5-2).**

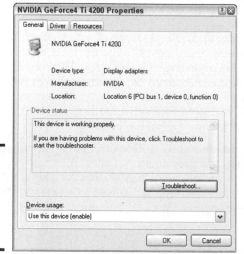

Figure 5-2:
Display the
settings for
a specific
hardware
device.

If nothing is flagged, skip to Step 5 — Windows XP has given your hardware the all-clear! You might also find helpful information in the Device Status display.

- If a Driver tab appears in the device's Properties dialog box, you can try updating your system with the latest driver for the device. (Go to Step 4.) This often fixes things right away.

- If no Driver tab exists, scurry on to Step 5.

4. **Click the Driver tab and then click the Update Driver button to run the Hardware <u>Update</u> Wizard.**

The wizard will lead you through the process of checking for a new driver online or from a floppy disk or CD-ROM supplied by the manufacturer.

Don't forget to check the manufacturer's Web site for drivers as well.

5. **Click OK to return to the Device Manager dialog box and then choose File⇨Exit to close the Device Manager window.**

If you made changes, Windows XP will prompt you for confirmation before rebooting your PC.

If updating the driver doesn't do the trick, display Device Manager again and click the Troubleshoot button on the General tab to run the Troubleshooter. (That's Microsoft's fancy name for the Help system, which will lead you through possible solutions to the problem.)

Checking Your Hard Drives in Windows XP

Here are two very common misconceptions concerning hard drives I think that I should clear up right here:

+ **Hard drives do malfunction.** Oh, yes. Even if you've never had a hard drive crash, you've likely heard about them. Even so, today's hard drives are generally so reliable and so long lasting that folks often forget. Hard drive errors can be *physical* (caused by a malfunction in the drive's hardware) or *logical* (where the error is in the format or the data stored on the drive). If your PC is caught by a power failure and file corruption occurs, you're the victim of a logical file error.

+ **Errors might not be immediately noticeable.** Most logical errors won't cause your PC to crash, and they might not affect files that you're currently using, so they often go unnoticed. (They share this trait with computer viruses, which use stealth to hide themselves.) Over time, logical errors can cause real damage to your files and documents, so catching them quickly is vital.

For these reasons, scanning your PC's hard drives often (both internal and external) for potential problems is important. Microsoft makes this easy in Windows XP by providing an error-checking feature that you can reach from a hard drive's Properties panel (for you crotchety Windows old-timers, think *ScanDisk*). Follow these steps to scan a hard drive for errors:

1. **Double-click the My Computer icon on your desktop to display the hard drives on your system.**

2. **Right-click the hard drive that you want to scan, choose Properties from the pop-up menu that appears, and then click the Tools tab to display the buttons that you see in Figure 5-3.**

3. **Click the Check Now button to display the Check dialog box, which has the settings shown in Figure 5-4.**

   Always enable the Automatically Fix File System Errors check box.

4. **To check the drive's hardware for physical errors, select the Scan for and Attempt Recovery of Bad Sectors check box and then click Start.**

   Note: This can take a very long time (as in two or three hours) on larger drives (60GB or larger). I recommend that you use this feature once every three or six months because today's drives rarely exhibit bad sectors until the entire drive crashes.

Figure 5-3:
Microsoft
hides these
programs
away, but
power users
know where
they are.

Figure 5-4:
Preparing
to check a
hard drive
for errors in
Windows
XP.

When the scanning program finishes, you'll see one of two windows:

- *The scan completed without you needing to reboot.*

  Just click OK to close the scan and return to the desktop.

- *The scan completed, and you do need to reboot.*

  If the scanning program determines that you need to reboot
  Windows XP to finish the error checking, click OK to close the scan.
  You'll need to reboot manually (the scan is actually scheduled to
  run the next time that you boot XP). Shut down any other programs
  that might be running, choose Start⇨Turn Off Computer, and then
  click Restart.

  Shut down any open applications that you're running and then
  reboot your PC.

  Windows XP automatically completes the check-up during the boot
  process.

TIP

I prefer (and highly recommend) using *New Technology File System* (NTFS), which is the hard drive format first introduced with Windows NT. A hard drive formatted as an NTFS volume is much more reliable than the old FAT16/FAT32 formatting used in Windows 95, 98, and Me — and it's much harder for logical errors to crop up under NTFS.

Commercial utilities are also on the market that can check your hard drive for errors; the most popular and best-known is Symantec's Norton Utilities (www. symantec.com), which includes Norton Disk Doctor (shown in Figure 5-5). I usually recommend the Norton line of programs, but in this case, Disk Doctor really doesn't do much more than XP's built-in, error-checking feature.

Figure 5-5: Norton Disk Doctor can also scan your drives for errors.

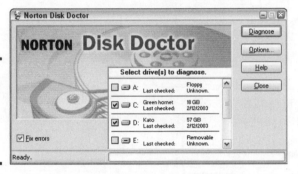

Defragmenting Just Plain Rocks

Another program that you can reach from any hard drive's Properties dialog box is the Disk Defragmenter. I admit that it's a strange name, but returning file fragments to their proper place can significantly increase your hard drive's performance. (Techno-nerds call this *running a defrag.* Très nerd.)

So what the heck are fragmented files? Here's the straight skinny: Each time that you delete or move files from one spot on your PC to the other, you open up sections of your hard drive so that new files can be stored there. When you're ready to save a file, however, it might not fit into any one of the open areas on your hard drive, so Windows XP saves the file in pieces, or *segments,* across several open sections.

As an example, suppose that you're downloading a 300MB game demo, but your hard drive doesn't have 300MB of contiguous open space handy. Windows XP decides to save 50MB in one spot, 120MB in another, and the rest in a third open space. When you decide to install the demo and run the file, Windows XP automatically pulls the right data from these different spots on your hard drive and assembles the pieces back into the original file. (I bet you didn't know all that was happening when that little green light blinks on and off, but then, XP can be a mysterious beast.)

Of course, this assembly process takes more time if the file has been broken in more pieces. And when your drive is really fragmented with little segments of thousands of files that Windows XP has to keep track of, your hard drive performance really starts to suffer. Fragmentation slows everything down, and Windows XP has to work harder every time that you open or save a file.

The XP Disk Defragmenter restores the files on your drive to smooth, unbroken data storage territory. (Think the *Bonanza* spread, but with ones and zeroes instead of cattle.) Figure 5-6 illustrates your drive before you run Disk Defragmenter, and Figure 5-7 shows your drive afterwards. The program reads fragmented files, combines those nomadic segments, and then saves the defragmented file back to the disk. Outstanding!

Book II
Chapter 5

Maintaining
the XP Beast

I recommend defragmenting your hard drives when you're not using your PC because the process takes much less time to finish that way. Most PC owners defragment at nights or on weekends. Shutting down programs that are running in the background also helps. Just display the taskbar; in the notification area at the right, right-click each icon for programs that you don't need, and then click Exit or Close to shut them down.

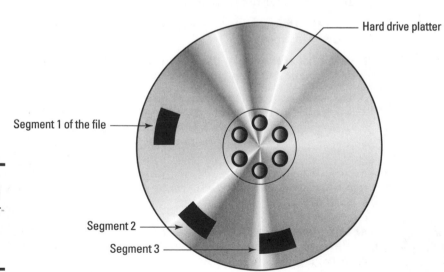

Figure 5-6:
Fragmented
files sap per-
formance
from your
hard drive.

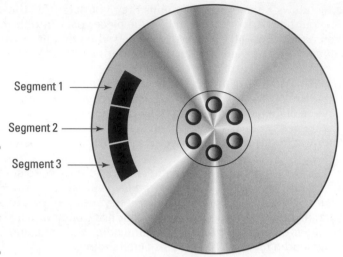

Segment 1

Segment 2

Figure 5-7:
Wow! Check
out the
contiguous
sectors on
that platter!

Segment 3

To run Disk Defragmenter, follow these steps:

1. **Double-click the My Computer icon on your desktop.**

2. **Right-click the hard drive that you want to defragment, choose Properties from the pop-up menu that appears, and then click the Tools tab (refer to Figure 5-3).**

3. **Click the Defragment Now button to open Disk Defragmenter, which you see in Figure 5-8.**

4. **In the list at the top of the window, click the drive that you want to defragment and then click the Analyze button.**

   This shows you a display of just how badly defragmented your drive really is. (The more red that you see in the Estimated Disk Usage before Defragmentation bar, the worse the fragmentation.)

   Disk Defragmenter displays a dialog box with its recommendation (view the analysis, run the defrag, or simply close the application).

5. **If warranted, click the Defragment button to start cleaning up that hard drive.**

Disk Defragmenter requires that the drive have at least 15 percent of its total space free, so you'll have to delete files and programs that you don't need if your drive is full.

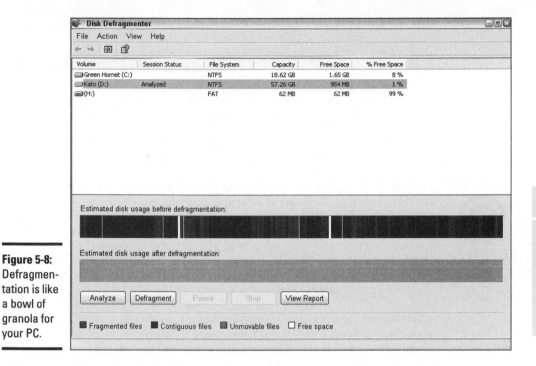

Figure 5-8:
Defragmen-
tation is like
a bowl of
granola for
your PC.

Be Smart: Back Up Your Stuff

In this third part of your hard drive triple-header, I talk about how you can back up your hard drive to safeguard your data against future calamity. I'm not going to lecture you here — oh, what the heck, yes I *will* — **DO IT.** All smart PC owners take the trouble to save their stuff. Back up on a regular basis, and someday (it might be years from now) you'll send me an e-mail message at mark@mlcbooks.com with the subject "Thanks, Mark, My Backup Saved My Tail!" Then we can both celebrate that you did the smart thing. **SO DO IT.**

By default, the XP Backup or Restore Wizard is included only with Windows XP Professional, but with a little harmless hacking, you can install it from the XP Home installation disc. Double-click the My Computer icon from your desktop, right-click your CD-ROM drive icon, and then click Explore. Locate the \valueadd\msft\ntbackup folder and then double-click the NTBACKUP.MSI icon, which will install Backup for you.

How often is often enough when it comes to backing up your data? That depends completely on how often your data changes. The idea is to back up often enough so that you always have a recent copy of your important files close by. If you wait too long to freshen your backup, you'll find that you'll spend far too much time restoring the changes that you made between back-ups. For example, a small business or home office with a large, constantly changing database might back up anywhere from every night to every three days. (If you decide that you have to back up every night, you might want to consider a commercial backup solution that can be automated.) On the other hand, a typical home PC might require a backup only once a month.

If you'd rather not use the XP Backup or Restore Wizard, either buy a commercial backup application or consider copying your most important files to a CD-RW or DVD-RW disc on a regular basis — including the contents of your My Documents folder. You'll still have to reinstall Windows XP and your major applications if you have a crash or your computer is stolen, but at least the irreplaceable stuff is safe. **Do not use a floppy disk** for this important job because floppy disks are unreliable and might not be readable on another PC. (I hate floppies, really I do. Have you noticed?)

Unfortunately, the Backup or Restore Wizard doesn't support CD or DVD backups, but most commercial backup applications, such as Retrospect from Dantz (www.dantz.com), do allow disc backup. If you use Retrospect or another commercial backup program, I recommend that you use rewrite-able DVDs as your backup media — alternatively, you can always use CD-RWs, but you'll need several more discs.

Although you can't use CDs or DVDs to back up with the XP wizard, you can back up to

✦ **A tape drive supported by Windows XP.**

✦ **Zip disks.** (I recommend the latest high-capacity 750MB Zip disks to make things easier.)

✦ **A network folder.** (This uses space on your network's file server or another PC's hard drive.)

✦ **A USB 2.0 or FireWire external hard drive that's especially made for backups.** (Nothing works as fast as another hard drive!)

✦ **Floppy disks.** (Oh . . . yes, you *can* use floppies. But please don't. It'll take a lifetime to back up anything, and those floppies will last as long as a snowman in Miami.)

To back up your files with the XP Backup or Restore Wizard, follow these steps:

1. **Double-click the My Computer icon on your desktop to display the hard drives on your system.**

2. **Right-click the hard drive that contains the files that you want to back up, choose Properties from the pop-up menu that appears, and then click the Tools tab.**

3. **Click the Backup Now button to run the Backup or Restore Wizard and then click Next to continue.**

4. **Select the Click Back Up Files and Settings radio button and then click Next to continue.**

   The wizard displays the options that you see in Figure 5-9. Decisions, decisions.

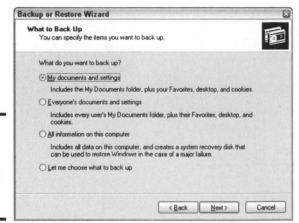

Figure 5-9:
Select
options for
the Backup
or Restore
Wizard.

- *If you're the only one using the PC and you want a fast backup of the most important things on your system, select the My Documents and Settings radio button.*

   You should only use the My Documents and Settings option if you've used the default My Documents folder to keep all your personal files and documents. (Because I have, I save media and time by choosing the My Documents and Settings option.)

- *If others also have separate accounts on your system, you can back up their stuff as well by selecting the Everyone's Documents and Settings radio button.*

- *Or, you can select individual files and folders by selecting the Let Me Choose What to Back Up radio button.*

If you put your documents and files in folders that you create yourself (as opposed to using the default My Documents folder), you should use the Let Me Choose What to Back Up option.

You'll notice that you can also go the whole route and back up the entire drive — but *only* if you're using XP Professional — by selecting the All Information on This Computer. This option uses *Automated System Recovery* (ASR), which I describe later in this chapter, and ASR is not included in XP Home. Remember, Microsoft thinks that XP Home users won't have installed the Backup or Restore Wizard. Sorry about that.

5. Click Next to continue.

If you select the Let Me Choose What to Back Up radio button in Step 4, you'll see the Items to Back Up page of the Backup or Restore Wizard that you see in Figure 5-10.

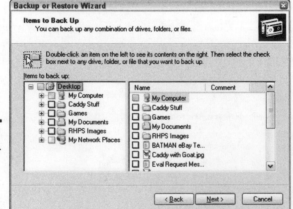

Figure 5-10: Specify your own files and folders to back up.

   a. Enable the check boxes for the files and folders that you want to back up.

   To expand a folder, click the plus sign next to it.

   b. When you've marked the items you want to back up, click Next to continue.

   The wizard prompts you for the location where you want to save the backup data, as well as its name, as shown in Figure 5-11.

6. To choose a destination drive, click the Choose a Place To Save Your Backup drop-down list box; to choose a specific folder, click the Browse button.

Figure 5-11:
Select a
backup
target
location
and then —
thrills! —
name it.

7. **Type a descriptive name in the Type a Name for This Backup text box
   and then click Next.**

   I recommend that you use today's date as part of the name as well as the
   name of the source drive.

   The wizard displays a summary screen like the one that you see in
   Figure 5-12.

8. **If you approve of the settings, click Finish, and the backup process
   begins.**

Figure 5-12:
Check the
backup
summary
before the
fun begins.

To restore from a backup that you've made, load the backup media, follow the preceding Steps 1 through 3, and then mark the Restore Files and Settings radio button. The wizard will display the backups that you've made and allow you to select the files and folders that you want to restore (using the same file selection boxes that I describe in Step 5). Click Finish and breathe a sigh of relief.

Safeguarding Your System with System Restore

Remember when you were a kid, and you held your fingers crossed behind your back when you made a promise? A "take-back" was a big deal back then. And even though you're all grown now, XP gives you the chance to say, "I take it back!" if an installation goes awry.

This great feature is *System Restore,* which allows you to set *restore points* (think of them as snapshots of your important system files) that you can return to whenever XP experiences problems. Most folks turn to System Restore if the installation of new hardware or software causes instability in XP; I've also used it when a system file has accidentally been erased or altered. Note that System Restore can recover only your XP *system* files, so if you accidentally trash Aunt Harriet's prized family brownie recipe, you're still out of luck. (Symantec's Norton Utilities includes Norton Protection for your Recycle Bin, which *can* help you recover Aunt Harriet's treasure from accidental deletion.)

XP automatically saves restore points on a regular basis (at least once every day), but you can follow these steps to manually create a restore point as a safety net — for example, if you're about to install a new device.

After you apply a restore point, XP must reboot. Therefore, I recommend closing down any applications that you have running with open documents *before* you run the System Restore wizard.

Follow these steps to create a new restore point:

1. **Choose Start➪All Programs➪Accessories➪System Tools➪System Restore to run the System Restore wizard (see Figure 5-13).**

2. **Select the Create a Restore Point radio button and then click Next.**

3. **In the following wizard window, type a descriptive name in the Restore Point Description box — something like XP before adding new video card — and then click the Create button.**

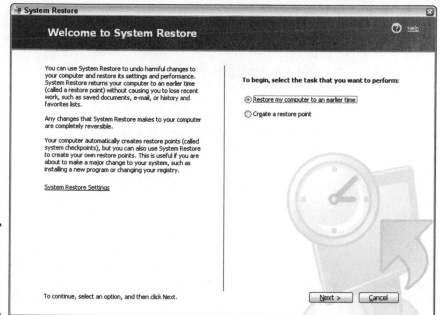

Figure 5-13:
Preparing to
save a new
restore
point.

XP displays a confirmation message indicating that the restore point has been successfully saved.

4. Click Close to return to your desktop.

If you need to use a restore point to recover from a calamity, follow these steps:

1. Choose Start⇨All Programs⇨Accessories⇨System Tools⇨System Restore to run the System Restore wizard.

2. Select the Restore My Computer to an Earlier Time radio button and then click Next.

The wizard displays the calendar view that you see in Figure 5-14.

3. Click a date (when you created the restore point) to display the points that you can use for that date in the list box on the right, click the desired point to highlight it, and then click Next to continue.

XP displays a confirmation message with information about the point that you chose.

4. Click Next to apply the restore point.

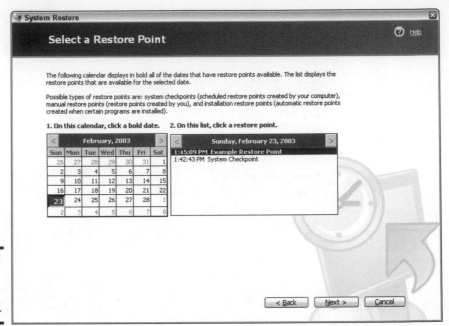

Figure 5-14:
Choose
a restore
point to use.

Have At Thee, Foul Virus!

One of the first book chapters that I ever wrote concerned viruses — that was way back in 1992. I recommended a number of antivirus applications (only one has survived to this day: McAfee VirusScan) and a number of guidelines to help readers avoid viral infection. Unfortunately, many folks ignored viruses back then and paid the price later.

Viruses are much harder to ignore these days. The number of viruses circulating today has jumped dramatically, and you read about viral attacks constantly in your newspaper and your favorite news Web sites. What's more incredible, Microsoft doesn't include any antivirus protection in Windows XP! Luckily, antivirus software has stayed current with "infection technology." In fact, the good guys are now out in front, and I'm happy to report that it's now child's play to surround Windows XP with a protective antiviral wall.

How easy? Just install either the latest version of Norton AntiVirus ($40 U.S.; www.symantec.com), shown in Figure 5-15, or McAfee VirusScan 7 ($40; www.mcafee.com), and sit back and watch the viruses (and nasty spyware programs) beat themselves to deletion trying to get to your system. Unlike the antivirus software of 1992, when you had to scan for viruses from the DOS command line once a day, everything now works in real time. Although you can (and should) still scan your entire system manually once every 6 months or so, your antivirus program will monitor every document that you open and every program that you run in the interim. It's actually fun to open your e-mail and see viral-laden spam identified and killed *before* you even open the message.

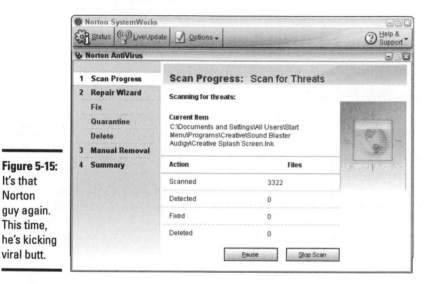

**Book II
Chapter 5**

Maintaining the XP Beast

Figure 5-15:
It's that
Norton
guy again.
This time,
he's kicking
viral butt.

These packages will cover the entry points used by viruses to reach your PC, including

✦ Your **e-mail**

✦ **Programs** that you download or receive on disk or CD from others

✦ **Office documents** that might contain dangerous macros

However, here is one important task that you must never take for granted, and it's definitely a Mark's Maxim:

> **Keep your antivirus data files up to date, or you're toast.™**

This step is so important that today's antivirus programs can automatically update their data files without your help! (As long as your PC can connect to the Internet, anyway.) Why? Well, without the latest data files, your antivirus software is out of date, and the latest viruses can attack your system undetected.

Windows XP Boot and Recovery Options

Ninety-nine percent of the time when you boot Windows XP, you'll be talking on the phone, or pouring another Diet Coke, or perhaps looking through your (paper) junk mail. That's because XP requires no help when it's running normally. You just press your PC's power button and wait.

However, if your PC isn't working correctly, you might need one of the options available during XP's boot process. In this section, I take you on a tour of what you can do in Windows XP *before* your attractive desktop appears.

Using Safe mode

Think of Safe mode as generic Windows XP. If a hardware device conflict is locking up your PC, or if a driver that you recently installed or updated is causing Windows to crash, you can use Safe mode to run XP in a stripped-down mode.

In Safe mode, external devices can't be used, and much of the functionality available with your internal hardware will also be disabled. For example, you'll immediately notice that your fancy video card is using the lowest resolution possible at 640 x 480 . . . but at least you can move or delete files and use Windows Explorer.

To use Safe mode, reboot your PC and press the F8 key when you see the scrolling-line display (before the Windows banner screen appears, so you only have a second or two). Then choose Safe Mode from the Advanced Options menu and press Enter.

You'll also notice two other specialized forms of Safe mode:

✦ **Safe mode with networking** (where XP loads network drivers and services so that you can log on to your network). If you need to copy files from a network server or copy your latest documents to a network drive for safekeeping (just in case), this is the Safe mode to use.

✦ **Safe mode with command prompt** (where Windows XP loads in Safe mode but reverts to that cryptic DOS-like command prompt). This option should be used only at the request of a tech support person.

Using the Last Good Configuration

Here's another boot option that's a favorite with anyone who's facing severe problems with Windows. XP automatically stores the last-known, working system configuration — including drivers that were loaded successfully and system settings that worked — and offers that as a choice on the Advanced Options menu. By choosing this option, you effectively reset your XP configuration to how it was before your problem cropped up. It doesn't work every time — for example, it won't restore missing system files — but it's a much better choice than reinstalling Windows, using ASR (see the following section), or the hassle of restoring from your backup (see the earlier section "Safeguarding Your System with System Restore").

To use this feature, reboot your PC and press the F8 key when you see the scrolling-line display. From the Advanced Options menu, choose Last Known Good Configuration and then press Enter.

Using ASR

Automated System Recovery (ASR) is a feature of the Backup or Restore Wizard that I cover earlier in the chapter. With ASR, you XP Professional users can restore your Windows XP configuration in case you have a massive meltdown, and your Windows system files have been damaged so badly that using a restore point won't work. Note that I'm just talking to XP Professional owners now because ASR isn't included in XP Home.

To create an ASR image, follow the backup procedure that I provide in the earlier section "Be Smart: Back Up Your Stuff." In Step 4, select the All Information on This Computer radio button. This launches the ASR portion of the wizard, which will lead you through the rest of the process. (It's actually just like the regular backup process except that the wizard prompts you to load a floppy disk to store partition information; you'll need this floppy disk in a second.)

However — listen up here — **an ASR recovery does not restore your documents and other data!** The ASR security blanket only includes your system files and XP system configuration, which Windows XP will use to recover itself. You have to back up your personal files, data, and documents with the process that I describe earlier.

When the dreaded moment arrives, and Windows is dead in the water — hopefully, never — you can restore using ASR by following these steps:

1. **Load your XP Professional installation disc into your CD or DVD drive.**

2. **Close any open applications and reboot your PC.**

   You might have to press a specific key to boot your PC with the XP Professional installation disc.

3. **Look for the prompt that tells you to press F2 to use ASR and then pounce on that key like a fierce jungle cat.**

4. **Load the floppy disk created by the Backup or Restore Wizard.**

5. **Load the backup file that you created during the ASR process and follow the instructions that appear.**

In effect, Windows XP actually reinstalls itself by using the configuration data and system files from your ASR backup . . . pretty neat, I think. (I just hope that I never have to use it.)

Using Windows Update

Windows Update is a gas. It automatically searches for XP patches and upgrades from Microsoft and then applies them while you relax. This is a good thing because any piece of software as complex and powerful as Windows XP is going to need frequent patching (especially since every hacker on the planet wants a piece of His Billness). The two methods of using Update are that you can either leave it completely to XP or that you can run Windows Update manually.

The fully automatic way

XP can take care of virtually all the update process in the background, so you're not bothered with it. To configure Update to run automatically, you must be logged in as an Administrator user. Follow these steps:

1. **Right-click the My Computer icon on your desktop; from the pop-up menu that appears, choose Properties.**

2. **From the System Properties dialog box that appears, click the Automatic Updates tab, which displays the settings that you see in Figure 5-16.**

Figure 5-16:
Set
Windows
Update for
automatic
operation.

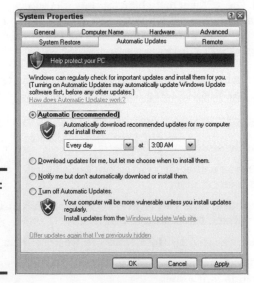

3. **Select the Automatic (recommended) radio button to enable it.**

4. **Click the first drop-down list box to select the day for updating and then click the second drop-down list box to choose the time.**

5. **Click OK to return to your desktop.**

Note that there are also three other Windows Update settings. You can set XP to:

✦ Notify you when updates have been downloaded, allowing you to install them whenever you like. (A notify icon appears in your System Tray.) To install the updates that XP has downloaded, right-click on the notify icon.

✦ Notify you when updates are available, without automatically downloading or installing them. (Again, XP displays a notify icon in the System Tray.) To download and install the updates, right-click on the notify icon.

✦ Turn off Automatic Updating completely.

Naturally, I recommend setting XP to Automatic — however, if you're running an older PC and you'd rather not slow it down with all that hidden background activity (or if you're using a dialup connection), you can follow The Manual Path.

The (somewhat) manual way

You can also run Windows Update at any time. Perhaps you've heard of an important patch that Microsoft has just released, or you just want to impress your spouse. For whatever reason, follow these steps:

1. **Open Internet Explorer (just click its icon on your desktop).**

   Yep, that's one of the easiest ways to get to Windows Update — at least, I find it the easiest. (Plus, the manual version of Windows Update actually runs inside Internet Explorer, so it makes sense.)

   For the lowdown on Internet Explorer, skip ahead to Book III, Chapter 4.

2. **Choose Tools⇨Windows Update to display the page that you see in Figure 5-17.**

3. **Click Express.**

   After a bit of thrashing and churning, Internet Explorer updates the panel on the left of the screen with any updates it finds, and the number of updates in each category is displayed.

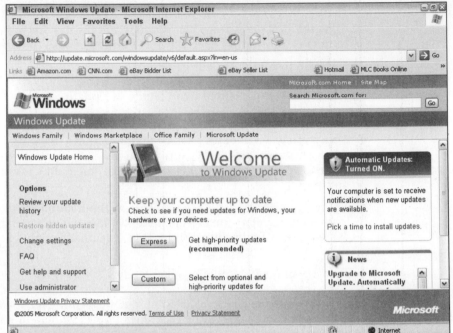

Figure 5-17:
The
Windows
Update wel-
come page.

4. **Click the desired type to view its updates.**

   A short description of each update is given, and you can click the plus sign button to display more information.

5. **To add an update item to the download list, click the check button next to the item's description to mark it.**

   Note: Items in the High Priority category are automatically added for you, but some items must be downloaded and installed separately from other items. Update will take care of this for you.

6. **After you mark all the update items that you want to apply, click Review and Install Updates.**

   This displays the summary page that you see in Figure 5-18, where all the updates to be downloaded and applied are listed for you.

7. **Click the Install Now button to begin the update process, following any onscreen instructions.**

Note that if XP must reboot to install a critical update or Service Pack, you'll have to rerun Windows Update to install any other update items.

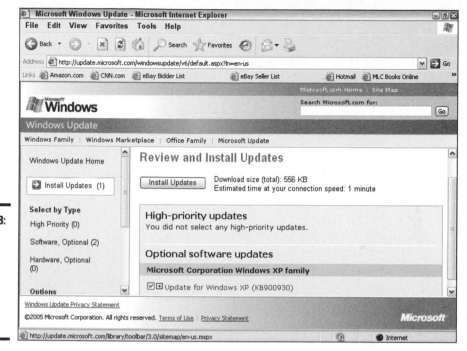

Figure 5-18:
Make one
last check
of the
proposed
updates
before
you go.

Chapter 6: Taking Control of the Control Panel

In This Chapter

✔ Configuring the Control Panel the right way

✔ Setting your PC's date and time

✔ Tweaking your display settings

✔ Adding scheduled tasks

✔ Fine-tuning power options

✔ Adjusting your keyboard

✔ Changing mouse settings

✔ Setting Internet options

✔ Removing programs the right way

✔ Configuring user accounts

✔ Setting your phone and modem options

*P*icture this: You're the engineer on the bridge of the starship Enterprise — the first one, the *real* Enterprise — and Captain James T. Kirk suddenly bellows, "I need more power!" in your direction. Where do you turn? What panel has the right randomly blinking lights and the right fake switches?

In the Windows XP galaxy, my friend, you (and Scotty) need go no farther than the XP Control Panel (where all the switches are real). Just about all the check boxes, drop-down list boxes, and buttons that determine how Windows XP acts are available from this one menu item. And in this chapter, I show you how to poke a tiny flashlight into the most commonly used Control Panel dialog boxes to fix your starship's shields. (Whoops. I mean, customize Windows XP for your needs.)

Sorry — like most other first-generation techno-nerds, I *really* enjoy my *Star Trek*.

But First, Put the Control Panel on the Start Menu!

To open the Windows XP Control Panel the *right* way, it should be configured as a pop-up menu on the Start menu. The default Windows XP category view is about as convenient as a car wash in a monsoon: You *can* use it, but why? A true PC power user will jettison the default Control Panel in a heartbeat.

Follow these steps to configure the Control Panel as a Start menu pop-up:

1. **Right-click the Start button and then choose Properties from the menu that appears.**

2. **In the Properties dialog box that appears, click the Customize button and then click the Advanced tab to display the settings that you see in Figure 6-1.**

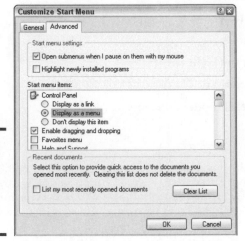

Figure 6-1: Configure the Control Panel as a Start menu pop-up.

3. **In the Start Menu Items list, find the Control Panel section and then select the Display as a Menu radio button.**

4. **Click OK to exit the Advanced settings and then click OK again to save the change to the Start menu.**

Voilà! Now click Start, move your mouse pointer over the Control Panel menu item, and revel in all that pop-up goodness, as shown in Figure 6-2! Now you can access any of the Control Panel dialog boxes that I cover in the rest of this chapter with just two mouse clicks.

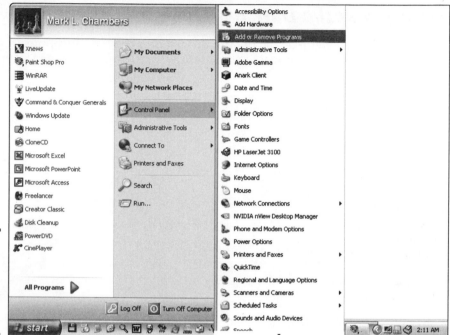

Book II
Chapter 6

Taking Control of
the Control Panel

Figure 6-2:
That, sir and
madam, is a
power user
Control
Panel.

You'll note that each Control Panel dialog box sports two spiffy buttons: Apply and OK. These actually do the same thing — any changes that you've made get saved — but here are two important differences:

✦ **OK:** When you click OK, the dialog box closes, and you can make no more changes to that dialog box. Because many Control Panel dialog boxes have multiple panels (each of which might have a setting that you want to change), it makes sense to click Apply if you need to hang around.

✦ **Apply:** When you click Apply, Windows XP makes the setting change immediately. Usually, a setting change won't do anything obvious right off the bat, but if you're working in the Display Control Panel dialog box, you'll usually be able to see what changed (like your background or your screen resolution). If you don't like the effect that you've just wrought, you can easily choose another setting without the hassle of opening the dialog box again.

Configuring the Date and Time

The first stop on the Control Panel tour is the Date and Time Properties dialog box. Check out its first tab, Date & Time, as shown in Figure 6-3.

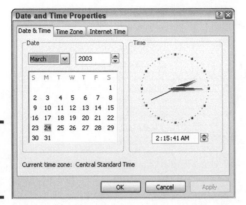

Figure 6-3:
Configuring
the Date
and Time.

Settings on this tab include

✦ **The month and year boxes:** Click the month drop-down list box to choose the current month. Then use the up- and down-arrow buttons to set the year, or you can just click directly in the year box and type the year.

✦ **The calendar display:** To select the current day, click it in the calendar display.

✦ **The Time clock:** You can either click the hours:minutes:seconds display and then click the up- and down-arrows to set the time, or you can — I love this — click and drag the hands of the clock. (Gotta love that Microsoft, eh? An analog anachronism in a digital world.)

The Time Zone tab

Click the Time Zone tab to set your current time zone via the drop-down list box. You can also set Windows XP to automatically adjust for daylight savings time.

The Internet Time tab

The last tab of this Properties dialog box is my favorite: Click Internet Time to display the settings that you see in Figure 6-4. If you've got an Internet connection that you use every day — either a dialup or an always-on digital subscriber line (DSL)/cable modem connection — you can set XP to automatically set its own clock by using an Internet time server! Forget setting the clock manually.

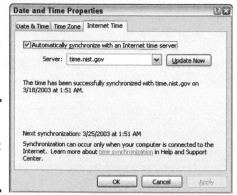

Figure 6-4:
Yet another
use for "that
Internet
thing."

Select the Automatically Synchronize with an Internet Time Server check
box to enable it and then click the Server drop-down list to select a time
server. I personally prefer the `time.nist.gov` server because the idea of
handing over my PC's time to the Redmond Empire is somewhat unsettling.
(Sure, Mark — like they don't already control your waking hours through
Windows XP?)

Changing Display Settings

Most PC owners have seen the Display settings shown in Figure 6-5. You can
also get to them by right-clicking any open space on your XP desktop and
then choosing Properties from the pop-up menu that appears.

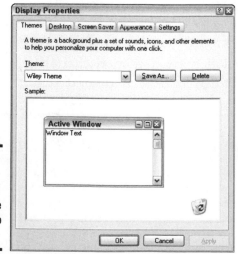

Figure 6-5:
Display
properties
are available
on a desktop
near you.

The Themes tab

On the Themes tab, you can click the Theme drop-down list and choose a Microsoft desktop theme. Or, you can save your own theme with your current desktop background, color scheme, icons, and sounds by clicking the Save As button and then typing a new name in the File name box. Then click Save to seal the deal.

The Desktop tab

Click the Desktop tab to choose a background from the list there. If you want to load your own picture, click the Browse button and then navigate to the location of the image. (XP automatically updates the Preview image in the middle of the dialog box.) Although an image with a lower resolution can be stretched to fit across your entire desktop from the Position drop-down list box, don't be surprised if it loses quality. Instead, pick Center to put it in the middle of the desktop — or if the image is a repeating pattern, choose Tile.

To use a plain-color background, choose None in the Background list, click the Color drop-down list, and then pick your favorite shade.

Click Customize Desktop on the Desktop tab to specify which icons you want to appear on your desktop or to choose different icons.

The Screen Saver tab

Click the Screen Saver tab to configure these settings:

✦ **The screen saver:** Click this drop-down list to choose a Microsoft screen saver or a screen saver that you've installed yourself.

✦ **Settings:** If the screen saver has any configuration options (like toggling sound effects on or off, or increasing the number of flying small appliances on the screen at once), you can set them by clicking the Settings button.

✦ **Preview:** Click this button to see how the selected screen saver will look. To return to the Display dialog box, move your mouse.

Beware some screen savers

It's very easy to write a "bad" screen saver — by that, I mean a screen saver that can slow down or even hang your PC. (Because of their popularity, screen savers are also prime targets for spreading viruses.) Therefore, take care when adding a new screen saver to your system that's not from Microsoft. Your antivirus program should be running, and you should watch your PC's performance carefully after the screen saver has been running to make sure that it hasn't caused any problems.

Click the up- and down-arrows to choose the delay period before the screen saver will kick in. You can optionally require your user password to be entered before the screen saver will return you to Windows XP.

Click the Power button to display the Power Options tab, which I describe later in this chapter.

The Appearance tab

This tab is home to these settings:

✦ **The windows and buttons style:** Click this drop-down list box to switch between the flashy, oh-so-modern Windows XP appearance and the ho-hum, mundane classic Windows appearance.

✦ **Color scheme:** You can select a color scheme that applies throughout Windows XP from this drop-down list box.

✦ **Font size:** If you're having trouble reading smaller text on your desktop — like icon labels, for example, or menu titles — click this drop-down list box and then choose Large or Extra-Large fonts.

To select or disable the animated transition effects for menus — or to switch between large and regular icons — click the Effects button.

 If you're running Windows XP on an older Pentium III PC (or you're using a video card made before the turn of the century), I recommend disabling the Transition Effects and the Show Window Contents While Dragging check boxes of the Effects dialog box.

Click the Advanced button to set the color and text formatting attributes for desktop screen elements such as title bars, menus, and scrollbars.

The Settings tab

From the Settings tab (as shown in Figure 6-6), you have the following smorgasbord to choose from:

✦ **Screen Resolution:** Click this slider and drag it to set a new screen resolution.

✦ **Color Quality:** Whenever possible, leave this value set to 24-bit or 32-bit color. However, if you have an older video card, you might not be able to display higher resolutions at these color-quality levels.

Click the Troubleshoot button to display the Windows XP Video Trouble-shooter. Clicking the Advanced button displays a number of video card and monitor-specific settings; generally, unless you're told by a technical support person to change these, leave these alone.

Figure 6-6:
A familiar
sight for XP
power users
(especially
those gamer
types).

Scheduling Tasks

If you need Windows XP to automatically run a program at a certain time every day (or at a regular period), you can schedule that task from the Control Panel. For example, you might like to run a network-monitoring program on your office PC each night after you're gone. (Or, in my case, I like to run the great freeware utility Ad-Aware SE Personal Edition from Lavasoft (www.lavasoft.com), which helps remove "ad-ware" surreptitiously installed by many shareware applications and online Web stores; I've set it up as a regular, daily scheduled task. (Many anti-virus applications now include ad-ware protection as well.) Some ad-ware programs monitor the Web sites that you visit or send information back to the developer about your system . . . actions that I label as JPI, or *Just Plain Intolerable*.

Follow these steps to add a scheduled task:

1. **From the Control Panel menu, choose Scheduled Tasks↔Add Scheduled Task.**

   Windows XP runs the Scheduled Task Wizard, which displays its welcome screen.

2. **Click Next to continue.**

   The wizard displays a list of suggested applications (see Figure 6-7).

3. **If the program that you want to run is in the list, click it. If the program isn't in the list, click the Browse button, navigate to the location of the application, and double-click it. Then click Next to continue.**

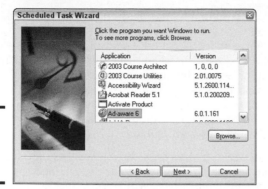

Figure 6-7:
Select a
program to
schedule.

Book II
Chapter 6

Taking Control of
the Control Panel

4. **The next wizard screen prompts you to type a descriptive title for your new task and choose the schedule period (schedule choices include One Time Only, When My Computer Starts, and When I Log On). Then click Next to continue.**

The contents of the next wizard screen depend on the schedule period that you pick. For example, Figure 6-8 shows the settings for the daily schedule.

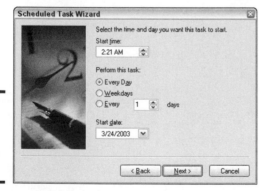

Figure 6-8:
Daily set-
tings for a
scheduled
task.

5. **Select the settings that you need and then click Next to continue.**

The next wizard screen prompts you for your XP account information. Why? Well, because by default, the task is scheduled to run in your name.

6. **Click in the Enter the Password box, type your XP user account password, press Tab, and type it again to confirm it. Then click Next to continue.**

If you change your XP user account password, you should also update your password on your tasks. Otherwise, a task with an improper password might prevent you from logging on later! To update the password for a specific task, choose Start➪Control Panel➪Scheduled Tasks, right-click each task in the pop-up menu that appears, and then click Properties to display the Properties dialog box for the selected task. Click the Set Password button on the Task pane, type the new password in the Password box, and then type it again in the Confirm Password box. Click OK to save your password change.

By the way, you can also temporarily disable a scheduled task from the same Task Properties dialog box. Just clear the Enabled (Scheduled Task Runs at Specified Time) check box. When you want the task to run again, return to this pane and enable the check box.

7. **The final wizard screen (as shown in Figure 6-9) summarizes the task schedule that you've created.**

   Click Finish to close the wizard.

Figure 6-9: Begone, adware and spyware — my scheduled task will take you out!

Adjusting the Power Options

Open the Control Panel menu and choose Power Options to display the dialog box that you see in Figure 6-10.

The Power Schemes tab

The Power Schemes tab allows you to choose a default power scheme, which controls the steps that your PC takes to conserve power. Power conservation is a handy trick for laptop PC owners but still important for desktop PC owners as well. The settings include

✦ **Power Schemes:** Click this drop-down list to specify a power scheme (either one of the default schemes or one that you've saved by using the Save As button).

✦ **Turn Off Monitor:** Here, select the amount of inactivity that Windows XP will wait through before switching your monitor to *standby* mode (where the screen goes blank, and the power light usually flashes or turns a different color). The monitor is automatically turned back on when you move your mouse or press a key.

Today's liquid crystal display (LCD) monitors use less power than traditional cathode ray tube (CRT) models, but you'll save a surprising amount of money when *any* monitor is switched to standby. In fact, your monitor probably uses more electricity than your PC! Therefore, I always set this value to the smallest amount of time that I can (without the feature becoming a hassle or inconvenience, where I'm constantly having to awaken my screen). For me, this is typically the After 30 Mins setting.

✦ **Turn Off Hard Disks:** Click this drop-down list to determine how long of a period of inactivity Windows XP will wait through before powering down your hard drive. I know that sounds dangerous, but it's actually a harmless feature that will save you energy because your hard drives will no longer be kept spinning unnecessarily. Like your monitor in standby mode, a mouse movement or a key press will return your hard drives to active duty.

✦ **System Standby:** Most PCs made in the last several years support *standby mode,* in which the entire PC (instead of just your monitor and hard drives) switches to low-power mode. Click this drop-down list box to select the period of inactivity required to activate standby mode. Again, mouse activity or the press of a key on your keyboard should return your PC to life, with all programs and files intact. However, some older PCs might require you to press a button on the PC's case to return to full power.

After you choose your power scheme settings, you can click the Save As button to save the scheme under a new name.

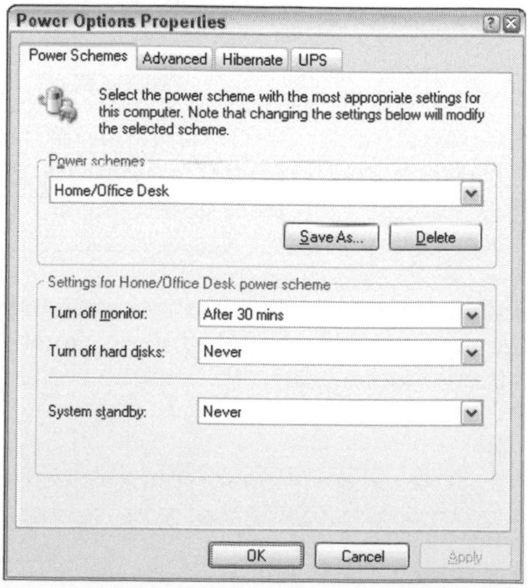

**Book II
Chapter 6**

**Taking Control of
the Control Panel**

Figure 6-10:
Select a
power
scheme
here.

Power Options Properties

Power Schemes | Advanced | Hibernate | UPS

Select the power scheme with the most appropriate settings for this computer. Note that changing the settings below will modify the selected scheme.

Power schemes

Home/Office Desk

[Save As...] [Delete]

Settings for Home/Office Desk power scheme

Turn off monitor: After 30 mins

Turn off hard disks: Never

System standby: Never

[OK] [Cancel] [Apply]

The Advanced tab

If you need to tweak the operation of your PC's power button or configure the taskbar icon, click the Advanced tab. The settings on this tab include

✦ **Always Show Icon on the Taskbar:** If you're using a laptop PC, the power taskbar icon shows you an approximate estimate of your remaining battery power (as a tiny battery, no less, which slowly drains of color). When your laptop is plugged into an AC outlet, the icon also displays when your battery is charging. (Of course, desktop PC owners can disable this check box and regain room in the taskbar.)

✦ **Prompt for Password:** This is a similar security feature to the screen saver password check box. You can require XP to prompt for your user password before you're allowed to return from standby mode.

✦ **When I Press the Power Button:** PCs made in the last two or three years allow you to actually specify what action Windows XP should take when you press the power button on your computer: You can opt to shut down the PC, do nothing (think the wandering fingers of a three year old), prompt for the action to take, or switch immediately to standby mode.

The Hibernate tab

As I explain earlier, your PC can hibernate instead of enter standby mode. The difference is one of security for your data. In *hibernation mode,* the contents of your PC's memory are saved to your hard drive; thus, if a power failure occurs, you won't lose any work. "Waking up" from standby mode is quicker than hibernating because the data doesn't have to be reloaded from disk, but you run the risk of losing your files.

Select the Enable Hibernation check box to use hibernation mode. Note that some PCs won't be able to use hibernation because their motherboards lack this feature — in such cases, the Enable Hibernation check box is grayed out.

The UPS tab

If your PC's uninterruptible power supply (UPS) unit supports Windows XP's status mode, this tab will display both an estimate of how long the UPS will run in case of a power failure and the condition of the battery. (You'll find more about UPS units in Book I, Chapter 2.)

Most UPS manufacturers come with an install CD that configures the manufacturer and model settings on this dialog box, but if you must set things manually, click Select and then choose your UPS and the serial (or COM) port that it's using.

Tweaking the Keyboard

Choose the Control Panel menu and choose Keyboard to display the Keyboard Properties dialog box, as shown in Figure 6-11.

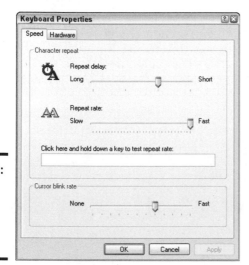

Figure 6-11: Customize your keyboard settings here.

The Speed tab

You can use the settings on this tab to customize your keyboard to fit your preferences:

✦ **Repeat Delay:** Drag this slider to specify how long Windows XP will wait before repeating a character when you hold down a key. (If you're a slower typist and your keys keep repeating, set this slider closer to Long.)

✦ **Repeat Rate:** Drag this slider to set the rate at which characters are repeated when you hold down a key.

To test the repeat delay and repeat rate, click in the test box and hold down a key.

The Hardware tab

If you have multiple keyboards (or an input device configured as keyboard, like some specialized game controllers), you can display the properties of that device (including information about any driver software that it requires) or troubleshoot it from this tab.

If you're having problems with your keyboard, click the Troubleshoot button to display the *Windows XP Keyboard Troubleshooter,* which is a wizard that leads you through the keyboard troubleshooting process.

Adjusting Thy Mouse

The settings that you see when you choose Control Panel⇨Mouse will vary according to the manufacturer of your mouse. For example, my Logitech trackball displays a completely different Mouse Properties dialog box (see mine in Figure 6-12) than does a Microsoft mouse because Logitech supplies its own mouse driver.

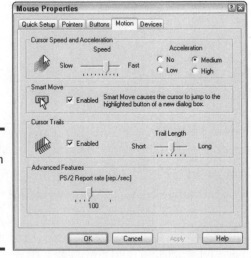

Figure 6-12: My Logitech trackball has these Control Panel settings.

No matter which pointing device you own, however, you're likely to find the following settings. They might be named slightly differently, but they should be there, nonetheless.

✦ **Middle button function:** You can specify what action is produced when you click the middle button on a three-button pointing device. Possibilities might include a double-click, cutting or copying, maximizing or minimizing the active window, or even running a program that you specify. (Personally, I have mine set as a double-click because it prevents accidental double-clicking with the left button, which sometimes happens when you only wanted to click the left button once.)

✦ **Pointers:** You can usually choose either a Windows XP pointer scheme or assign your own pointer symbols.

✦ **Mouse trails:** This feature adds a number of trailing pointers when you move your mouse. This is a very helpful trick when you're using a laptop because the mouse pointer is often hard to find on a laptop screen. Visually impaired PC owners might also find this helpful.

✦ **Acceleration:** If you enable acceleration, your mouse pointer moves faster the farther you move it. This is a good idea for those running their desktops at a whopping 1600 x 1200 resolution, where the mouse can seem to take forever to get anywhere!

Configuring Internet Properties

Next on the Control Panel hit parade is the always-fascinating world of Internet Properties. (Figure 6-13 bears all.) Sit back for the ride, folks, 'cuz this is gonna be a big 'un. (And that's partly because many of the settings that should be tucked away in Internet Explorer are instead dumped here.)

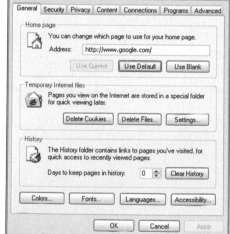

Figure 6-13:
My heavens,
what a
dialog box!
The Internet
is a Complex
Thing.

The General tab
This tab allows you to set

✦ **Your Home Page:** In the interests of brevity, you'll find a complete discussion of this setting in Book III, Chapter 4.

✦ **Temporary Internet Files:** Internet Explorer (IE) uses these cache files to speed up the display of pages that you've already seen, but after a while, they can become true hard drive hogs. You can elect to delete all the temporary files in one fell swoop by clicking the Delete Files button, or you can simply click the Settings button and drag the file folder disk space slider to 3 or 4MB. (That will prevent too much waste, and you won't have to use the Delete Files button any longer.)

You might be wondering what cookies are doing in this dialog box. The name actually has nothing to do with baked goods in this context. Instead, *Web cookies* are small files that are saved to your hard drive by your Web browser to allow Web sites to automatically determine who you are. (Ever wonder how Amazon.com always knows that it's you who is visiting? That's because of a cookie.) Most cookies are innocuous (and some sites even require them), but they can be used to store information about you, the sites that you visit, and the type of Web browser that you use. So, if you like, you can click the Delete Cookies button and wipe 'em out. Also, many Internet security programs — such as Symantec's Norton Personal Firewall (www.symantec.com) — will take care of cookies as well by either blocking them or by prompting you to determine whether you want to accept them.

✦ **Your History:** Again, a lot of this stuff applies only to IE. I discuss the History file in detail in Book III, Chapter 4.

✦ **Colors:** Click this button to specify the colors that you want to use for links (both visited and new), the default text color on Web pages, and the default background color on Web pages.

✦ **Fonts:** A click here specifies which fonts are used when a Web page doesn't include its own font definition.

✦ **Languages:** Internet Explorer can display multiple languages. Click here to select which languages you need or to add extra language packs that you've downloaded.

✦ **Accessibility:** To force IE to use your font style, font color, and font size — no matter what the page is designed to do — click this button. (These features help folks with limited eyesight who have customized their browser font settings.)

The Security tab

You'll see the settings shown in Figure 6-14 on the Security tab:

✦ **The Web content zone:** Betcha didn't know that you could specify different security sites for the Internet as a whole, your local company intranet, and the Web sites that you trust (*and* those that you'd like to restrict), did you? Click the desired icon to set the security level for that zone. To add sites to the zone that you've selected, click the sites button.

✦ **The security level:** Drag the slider here to specify a security level, and Windows XP displays the actions that it will take based upon the security level that you choose. You can build your own custom security level by clicking the Custom Level button, or you can return this zone to what Microsoft feels is appropriate by clicking the Default Level button.

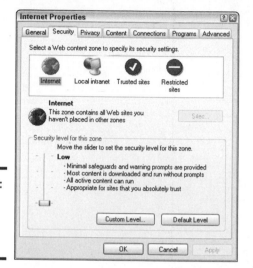

Figure 6-14:
Set your
browser
security
level.

The Privacy tab

The Privacy tab is another "slider" tab, as you see in Figure 6-15. However, the settings that you find here affect only the Internet zone:

✦ **The privacy level:** Drag the slider to choose an overall privacy setting for the Web sites that you visit. *Note:* This also controls the cookies that I mention a bit earlier in this section. Each privacy level is described next to the slider. To import an existing IE privacy preferences file — something that your company might ask you to do — click the Import button. Click the Advanced button to override the cookie handling at the privacy level that you've chosen; you can specify your own cookie handling here.

✦ **Web site privacy:** Heck, if you're *really* interested in security, you can even click the Sites button to specify the cookie handling for individual Web sites! This might be just the ticket if a site that you like to visit requires you to use its cookies, but you eschew cookies otherwise. (Man, that is one ridiculous sentence. Who named these things, anyway? Pee Wee Herman?)

✦ **The pop-up blocker:** I hate pop-ups — any red-blooded PC user hates 'em, too. Pop-up banners and advertisements litter the Web like the fair streets of New Orleans on the day after Mardi Gras; if you enable the Block Pop-ups check box, however, Windows XP does a commendable job of blocking these pop-up pests. (Instead, you can choose to display the Information Bar in Internet Explorer. From the Information Bar, you can choose to selectively allow pop-ups you actually want — some Web sites use pop-ups to display honest-to-goodness information.) To view your list of sites where pop-ups are allowed (and to change the notification and filter settings), click the Settings button.

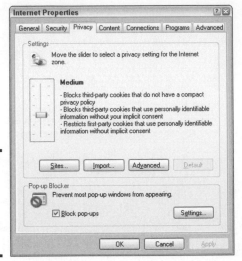

Figure 6-15:
Privacy is
easy to
set — or
override, as
necessary.

The Content tab

Here's a tab that will interest every parent who's concerned about kids surfing the Web (hang ten on Figure 6-16). The Content tab settings here include

✦ **The Content Advisor:** You can enable the Content Advisor to protect your kids, but be aware that it's nowhere near perfect. Although to be honest, no Web content filter really is, including the expensive commercial programs. Why? Well, some sites rate themselves incorrectly. And other sites include valuable medical and artistic information that might inadvertently trigger alarms — for example, if you're searching for information on the human body for a science project. Anyway, to choose a level of content safety, just click the Enable button and drag the "offensive" slider.

My recommendation is that you enable this feature only if you feel that it's absolutely necessary — and that you *don't* rely on it as a foolproof solution. (Instead, many parents simply limit Internet access to one computer and keep a close eye on what's being seen. This isn't a foolproof idea, either, but in my opinion, it's better than relying on imperfect software.)

✦ **Certificates:** These controls allow you to verify your identity to a Web site; many companies use certificates to ensure the privacy of their intranet data. Certificates can get pretty complex, which is why most normal human beings don't bother with 'em.

✦ **AutoComplete:** With AutoComplete enabled, IE automatically fills out online forms, Web addresses, and username/password combinations that you've previously entered on a site. Click the AutoComplete button to specify which types of data you want filled out. You can also clear your AutoComplete history or clear the passwords in the history.

✦ **My Profile:** Click this button to select an Address Book entry that IE should use as your Personal Profile. This is typically used only when sending an e-mail message from a link on a site or when a site requests your personal information. (Naturally, I get edgy about this one, so be careful what you enter in your profile.)

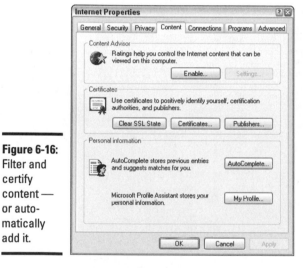

Figure 6-16: Filter and certify content — or auto-matically add it.

The Connections tab

The settings on this tab can be used to set up a dialup Internet connection, a virtual private networking (VPN) connection, or a special proxy server configuration; you can also modify your local area network (LAN) Internet connection. Again, this ground is covered in other chapters, so I won't repeat myself here. To wit:

✦ Setting up a dialup connection is covered in Book III, Chapter 2.

✦ Setting up a VPN connection is covered in Book VIII, Chapter 4.

✦ Setting up a LAN connection to the Internet is covered in Book VIII, Chapter 2.

To set up a proxy configuration, you'll need several pieces of information from your network system administrator or your Internet service provider's (ISP) technical support department. And you should only set up and use a proxy server at their specific request because configuring or using one incorrectly can seriously mess around with your dialup and VPN connections. Therefore, leave any proxy settings alone unless you're told to change 'em. (I do the same thing, so don't feel bad.)

The Programs tab

Figure 6-17 illustrates the Programs tab; from here, you can choose which programs handle your Internet functions, including

Figure 6-17:
So, like, what program does what?

+ The program that runs when you edit a Web page.
+ The default e-mail application within Windows XP.
+ The default program that Windows XP uses when you read and post Usenet newsgroup messages.
+ The program used for your Internet voice communications.
+ The Internet calendar application used within Internet Explorer.
+ The default contact list or Address Book used while you're on the Internet.

Note that a program that you install might overwrite these settings.

Click the Manage Add-ons button to display, manage, and update the add-on programs that add extra functionality to Internet Explorer. Most add-ons are offered by third-party companies (such as Symantec's AntiVirus "helper" add-on that appears in the Internet Explorer window), but some add-ons are even bestowed upon us by Microsoft itself. You can selectively enable and disable add-ons, or you can update them from the Manage Add-ons dialog box.

You can also choose to reset Internet Explorer to its default home and search pages from the Programs tab by clicking the Reset Web Settings button.

If you use both IE and another browser (such as Netscape or Firefox), you've probably been nagged about whether Internet Explorer should be rightfully returned to its spot as the default browser. To get rid of this irritating dialog box, mark the Internet Explorer Should Check to See Whether It Is the Default Browser check box.

The Advanced tab

The final tab on the Internet Properties dialog box is chock-full of dozens of individual features that you can enable and disable. These settings affect both Internet Explorer and many other Internet applications, so they're often mentioned in program manuals (and in hushed tones around late-night campfires). The options are divided into seven rather nebulous categories; some are a little more self-explanatory than others — like those in the Browsing and Multimedia categories — but most are pretty cryptic.

Because it would take an entire chapter just to explain each setting — and you won't use 90 percent of them unless you're asked to by your ISP, network administrator, or clergy — I'll recommend that you right-click any field and then click the What's This? pop-up to display the individual help text for that option.

Click OK to save your settings.

Adding or Removing Programs

Every Windows XP user should be familiar with the Control Panel window shown in Figure 6-18 because the Add or Remove Programs window is the one truly safe method of uninstalling applications from your system. (Alternatively, some programs add an uninstall menu item in their All Programs folder; this is fine, too, because it's basically just a different way of starting the same procedure.)

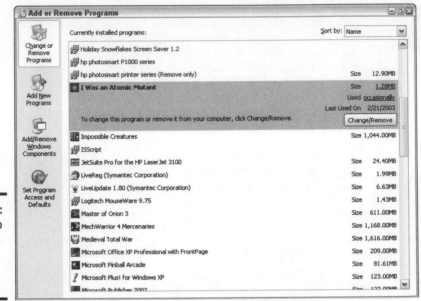

Figure 6-18:
You want to
uninstall a
program?
You talk
to me.

Let me reiterate: **Never uninstall an application by simply deleting the program and its folder!** This can raise all sorts of havoc within XP — your XP Registry file will eventually end up looking like Bourbon Street after a particularly long night of Mardi Gras revelry. (And that's A Bad Thing.) In the worst-case scenario, deleting a program folder willy-nilly can even lead to lockups and affect other programs that you didn't even know were distant cousins to the original application.

Follow these steps to remove a program safely:

1. **Click Control Panel from the Start menu and then choose Add or Remove Programs.**

   After a few seconds, the Add or Remove Programs window appears. You'll see a list of the programs that you've installed within Windows XP.

2. **Click the application entry in the list.**

   The entry expands to display more information, including a Change/Remove button.

   If you're having problems locating a program, you can click the Sort By box at the upper-right of the dialog box to sort by Name, Size, Frequency of Use, and Date Last Used.

Sorting by size is a great way to see which applications are taking up the most space on your crowded hard drive. Removing a program at the top of the list that you don't need will free up a surprising amount of territory.

3. Click the Change/Remove button.

This will launch the application's uninstall procedure, which varies according to application and manufacturer.

4. Follow the onscreen instructions to complete the uninstall process.

Unfortunately, some uninstall procedures don't remove all the files associated with a program. Games, for example, are famous for leaving orphan folders with Save files. Also, if you've relocated a shortcut that was placed on your desktop, that shortcut won't be deleted because it's in a different place. Therefore, I always take a moment to check to make sure that a program folder has been completely dusted after running the uninstall procedure. After you've officially uninstalled the application, you can indeed delete any orphan folders left on your drive without fear of toasting your system.

To help keep your drive cleaner and fresher smelling, you can also use a commercial uninstall program like CleanSweep from Norton (`www.symantec.com`). It can remove orphans for you as well as duplicate files and all sorts of temporary files that would otherwise take up space. In fact, CleanSweep (see Figure 6-19) can actually monitor the programs that you install and make doggone sure that they're completely uninstalled when you no longer need them.

To close the Add or Remove Programs window, click the Close button at the upper-right corner.

**Book II
Chapter 6**

**Taking Control of
the Control Panel**

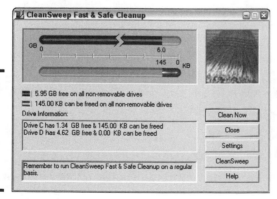

Figure 6-19: Hey, that's Norton Clean Sweep! A tidy app indeed.

Fine-Tuning User Accounts

The User Accounts Control Panel dialog box isn't really a dialog box. As you can see in Figure 6-20, it's actually a classy and helpful wizard that features full onscreen instructions for everything you do. (Way to go, Big M!) Therefore, I won't go into step-by-step detail concerning each function, but I would like to take a moment to list what can be done from the wizard because everyone who shares a machine with others will likely need to perform some type of magic with a user account.

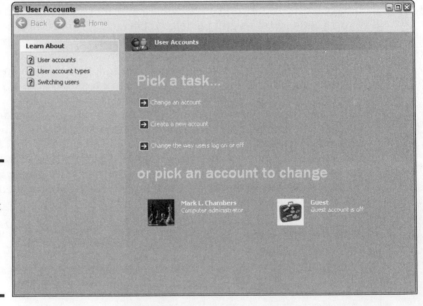

Figure 6-20:
The truly magnificent User Accounts Control Panel wizard.

From the wizard, you can

+ Create a new account.

+ Change your account name.

+ Change a pesky password.

+ Change the picture associated with an account.

+ Change the type of account. (You can choose either Administrator or Limited.)

+ Turn the Guest account on or off.

+ Specify whether your users see the Welcome screen or a login prompt.

+ Turn on fast user switching (where one user doesn't have to fully log off to allow another user to log on).

Configuring Phone and Modem Options

The last commonly used Control Panel dialog box is the Phone and Modem Options dialog box, as shown in Figure 6-21.

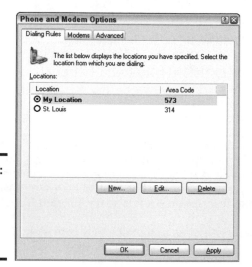

Figure 6-21: Setting up locations is easy in Windows XP.

The Dialing Rules tab

From this tab, you can create or switch locations. Whoops, you haven't been properly introduced: A *location* holds a single dialing configuration for your PC's modem. This includes

✦ The local area code

✦ Any dialing prefixes or numbers necessary to access an outside line

✦ Any codes required by your long distance or international carrier

✦ The ability to disable call waiting

✦ Whether the PC should use tone or pulse dialing

Of course, locations are a great feature for those who travel extensively with a laptop PC because you can set up a different location for each town that you visit often. In old Madrid one day and Berlin the next? No problem, just change locations and — bam! — you can make a call or connect to a local dialup provider without any fuss. Click the New button to set up a new location, or click the Edit button to change the rules for the selected location.

To switch to a new location, just click it in the list.

The Modems tab

If you have more than one modem connected to your PC — or if you're using a laptop and a Personal Computer Memory Card International Association (PCMCIA) modem — you can add or remove the modem from your system from this tab or modify its properties (like turning down or turning off that doggone speaker).

Click Add to run the Add Hardware wizard, which will help you install a new modem. Click a modem to select it from the list and then click Remove; you can then unplug an external modem safely (or shut down your PC and remove an internal modem).

The Advanced tab

This is definitely not a tab to mess around with unless you have specific instructions from your ISP or modem manufacturer's technical support department. These telephony providers are actually software drivers and sundry pieces of your operating system that control how Windows XP handles your modem. (If that description sounds scary, I meant it that way.)

However, if you do have instructions to install a new provider, click Add to select it from the Add Provider list. To delete a provider, select it from the Provider list and then click Remove. Select a provider from the Provider list and click Configure to change its properties.

Chapter 7: Easy XP Troubleshooting

In This Chapter

✔ Taking a moment to relax

✔ Troubleshooting your hardware and software

✔ Using Automated System Recovery (ASR)

✔ Re-installing Windows XP

✔ Locating troubleshooting help

I *hate* my Rubik's Cube. I've never been able to solve the silly thing, and it just sits on my desk taunting me, driving me to distraction until I grab it and make yet another futile attempt to match up all those squares. (Perhaps I'm in need of cube therapy.) What really gets me, though, is how a 10-year-old kid can pick up that same cube, spend 45 seconds turning it in some wizard way, and then drop the solved puzzle and move on to something different. Geez! Why is such a difficult thing so easy for some people to do?

Troubleshooting Windows XP has the same frustrating effect on most PC owners. You sit, staring at the keyboard, wondering why your operating system no longer works right and how you can fix it. Often, the solution is to call a friend or family member who can help — or, in the worst case, pack the entire heap up and take it to a computer shop where techno-types smile that mysterious little smile and fix your problem in 45 seconds. And then charge you an arm and a leg.

This chapter is here to help you tackle your XP troubleshooting puzzle. It might take more than 45 seconds, but you'll feel an enormous sense of accomplishment. Plus, you might avoid lightening your wallet.

Relax and Breathe Easy

Here's the first step in Mark's Troubleshooting Procedure: When the going gets tough, the techs relax. That's right, I said *relax*. Even though Windows XP — or your PC in general — is acting crazy, keep these important points in mind:

✦ **Never blame yourself.** Even the most nimble-fingered computer pro-grammer or hardware technician can make a mistake. (Heck, I've heard that even His Billness makes them every so often.) Accidents eventually happen — and, as with poorly written software or viruses, the fault might not even be yours, anyway. Don't treat yourself to a guilt trip.

✦ **Remember your backup.** As long as you take my advice throughout this book (ahem! *back up your data!*), you won't lose your life's work.

✦ **This, too, shall pass.** Even when hardware and software fail, you *can* find the problem. And remember that it's only temporary . . . certainly not unsolvable. (Not even my Rubik's Cube is impossible to solve.) You *will* be able to get your PC back.

✦ **Help is available.** Besides friends and family, PC user group members, and resources that you can find on the Internet, you can always turn to the tech experts at your local computer store for professional help at a price. (But wouldn't it feel great if you could fix it yourself?)

And one final tip while you're preparing to troubleshoot:

✦ **Your PC is *not* against you.** The troubleshooting process is not a battle between you, your hardware, and your software. Many folks tell me that they find it very easy to personalize the anger they feel and direct it towards that inanimate hunk of metal, plastic, and silicon. Stay calm, and remember this important Mark's Maxim:

> **Don't take out your frustration on your PC (no matter how uncooperative it seems).**™

To illustrate this last point, here's an honest-to-goodness true story that I love to tell. In the days of DOS, before Plug and Play or automatic configurations within Windows, adding a Small Computer System Interface (SCSI) adapter card and even just one SCSI device to your PC was a feat on the order of Hercules cleaning the Augean Stables. An old friend of mine — who was actually quite handy with a screwdriver and normally very well versed in PC hardware — spent over six continuous hours attempting to install a standard SCSI card and a SCSI hard drive in his 386 PC. He didn't curse, and he didn't scream. I'll never forget the look of utter peace on his face when he good-naturedly clamped the recalcitrant card in his metal vise and proceeded to melt that SCSI adapter with his portable torch.

He uses Windows XP these days — but he never has forgiven the SCSI interface standard.

The Troubleshooting Process, Step by Step

Time for the star of our show: Mark's Step-by-Step XP Troubleshooting Procedure! You'll note that this process doesn't center completely on software because it's often hard to tell at the beginning whether the problem at hand is caused by Windows XP or by your PC's hardware.

1. **Simply shut down Windows XP.**

   Many folks often don't have to move past this first step. Believe it or not, a simple shut down will solve a good 25 percent of the temporary glitches that you might encounter, such as a frozen mouse or a locked-up PC resulting from a power failure. Shutting down works because it resets all your PC's hardware (and XP itself), returning everything to normal. (By the way, if you can't reach the Start menu because your PC is locked up tight or the mouse doesn't move anymore, you have the right to simply press and hold your power button until your PC turns itself off.)

   Always check for hard drive errors after you've been forced to shut down XP by simply turning off your PC. For instructions on how to scan your drives for errors, see Chapter 5 of this mini-book.

2. **If you've reset your PC and the problem continues, double-check all the cables leading to your PC.**

   Yes, I know this sounds ridiculous, but I'll bet you your next paycheck that they do this on nuclear submarines, too. You might not have problems with your AC power cord, for example, but it's very easy to accidentally unplug other connectors from your PC — like your keyboard, network, or external devices such as your modem and printer. If you've recently moved or bumped against your PC, loose connections are prime suspects for all sorts of mischief.

   If you've just replaced a cable, and a peripheral is now an expensive doorstop (or your network suddenly no longer recognizes your PC), try a spare cable that you know works. Although bad cables are rare, they do happen. (Bad Ethernet cables have been known to cause insomnia.)

3. **If all your cables are shipshape, your next mission is to sit — and *think*.**

   Take a moment to consider any software or hardware that you've recently installed that might be causing (or contributing to) the problem. This is why I always install new hardware or software one piece at a time: It's very easy to tell which new addition is wreaking havoc. A PC that was originally chugging along nicely can suddenly turn rogue with one seemingly innocent change. (Note that this also includes any program or operating system updates, patches, or upgrades that you might have just applied.)

   I also use System Restore points liberally when installing new stuff. Find more on the System Restore utility in Chapter 5 of this mini-book.

4. **Still no go? Time to shut down and remove any offending external devices — such as an external hard drive that's dead in the water — to see whether your PC suddenly returns to normal.**

   If so, that peripheral is your prime suspect, so try it on another PC to determine whether the device is still working. Also try using another cable. If the peripheral works fine on another PC, your problem lies in either the device driver or the device configuration that you've set up in XP. Check the manual for the device, re-install the device driver, and — if all else fails — contact the manufacturer's technical support.

5. **Uninstall any programs that are misbehaving or locking up XP and then re-install them.**

   Before you apply a patch or upgrade, try using the application to see whether it still exhibits the problem. If not, the software developer has (as Desi so eloquently put it) "some 'splainin' to do." Visit the developer's Web site and check for information about compatibility, especially with Windows XP Service Pack patches, which often wreak havoc on unprepared software.

6. **If you've recently made changes in the Control Panel, the System Properties dialog box, or your networking dialog box, take a moment to revisit those settings and verify that they're still correct.**

   Unfortunately, anyone can easily and accidentally change a setting within one of the Control Panel applets. To make sure that you don't disturb something, just click Cancel if everything looks okay.

7. **If you're still having problems, check your hard drives (see Figure 7-1).**

Figure 7-1:
Check your hard drive often for errors.

Use the procedure that I demonstrate in Chapter 5 of this mini-book to verify that your drives are free from disk errors.

8. **Scan your hard drives and removable disks.**

   I talk about antivirus software throughout the book; I use Norton AntiVirus from Symantec (www.symantec.com), as shown in Figure 7-2.

   Each time that you run a scan, take a second to make sure that you're using the latest antivirus signature data file from the developer's Web site. Or, if you're using Norton AntiVirus, you can schedule LiveUpdate to automatically check for updated virus data files.

9. **Verify that you're still connected to and receiving packets from your home or office network — or, if you're using a broadband connection, your cable modem or digital subscriber line (DSL).**

   a. **Display your network connections (as shown in Figure 7-3) by choosing Start⇨Connect To⇨Show All Connections.**

   b. **Check to make sure that each connection reads** Enabled.

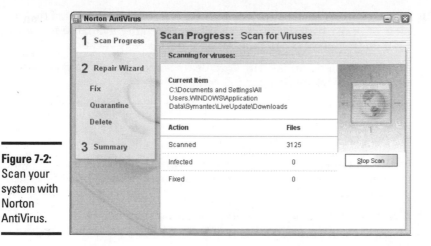

Figure 7-2:
Scan your
system with
Norton
AntiVirus.

If your network is down, XP has a nasty habit of slowing down to a crawl
when you open files or use Windows Explorer . . . and many applications
that expect a network connection as their divine right can lock up tighter
than Fort Knox. Don't forget to berate your network administrator or tech
staff — boy, they just *love* it when you do that!

Check network connections

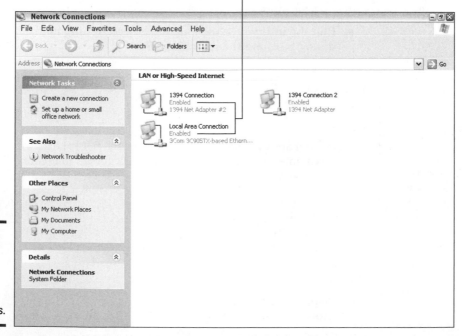

Figure 7-3:
Check the
status
of your
network
connections.

10. **If you're using a shareware or freeware screensaver, realize that a slew of really badly written screensavers readily available for download on the Internet can take XP on a permanent vacation.**

    To test whether your favorite Care Bears screensaver is causing those intermittent lockups, use the following steps.

    a. **Right-click your desktop, choose Properties, and then click the Screen Saver tab.**

    b. **Choose None and then click OK.**

    c. **Reboot and use your PC for a day without any screensaver — or choose one of the XP screensavers provided by Microsoft, which are proven stable.**

11. **Check whether another user with Administrator access might have changed the write-protect status of your applications or your documents.**

    This step is for those who share a PC with other users by taking advantage of XP's multi-user features.

    This is usually the case when Word complains that it doesn't have the rights to open a document that you were working on yesterday. Have a user with an Administrator account log in and verify the permissions on your applications and document files (more on this in Chapter 4 of this mini-book).

12. **Even if you can boot in Safe mode, first try the XP System Configuration Utility (see Figure 7-4), which can help you diagnose where the trouble lies in your boot process.**

    a. **Run the utility by choosing Start➪Run, typing** msconfig **in the Run dialog box, and then clicking OK.**

Figure 7-4:
Try a selective startup with the System Configuration Utility.

Note that you can try a *Diagnostic Startup* (which offers more functionality than Safe mode), or you can choose a *Selective Startup* and specify which boot steps to enable.

b. **After you choose your boot options, click OK and then reboot Windows XP.**

To disable just one startup program, click the Startup tab and clear the check box alongside the offending application. This makes it a breeze to troubleshoot problems that you encounter when installing new software that loads automatically during the boot process. You can repeat this process to disable more than one startup item. If Windows XP suddenly boots correctly and your problem appears to be solved, immediately uninstall the program that you last disabled and contact the software developer's technical support.

13. **If you're still with me, it's time to get serious with your hardware and display Device Manager (see Figure 7-5), as I describe in Chapter 5 of this mini-book.**

Make sure that XP hasn't flagged any of your hardware devices as either disabled or not working; if a component is flagged with an exclamation point, a little investigation might very well turn up the solution to the problem.

At this point, you've exhausted most of the easier troubleshooting chores and fixes that you can perform. It's time to get drastic.

Figure 7-5:
Device
Manager is
a handy
hardware
diagnostic
tool.

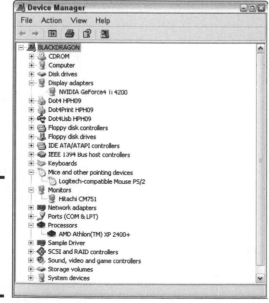

Safe mode to the rescue

If your PC is locking up before you even get a chance to click the Start button (or freezes before your desktop icons even appear), it becomes nearly impossible to get far enough to fix anything. Although you can boot from the Windows XP install disc, your choices are severely limited. Even when you know what needs to be done (like a specific driver file that needs to be deleted or a device that needs removed in Device Manager), the old witticism remains true: "You can't get there from here."

Luckily, Windows XP maintains an old friend from the days of Windows 95 and Windows 98:

Safe mode, which is the alternate boot-up mode where device drivers are disabled (generally a very good thing if your PC is experiencing bad karma) and you once again have access to Windows Explorer and basic XP functionality. Although Safe mode isn't always available — sometimes Windows XP is so badly obfuscated that even Safe mode won't work — it's a valuable addition to your troubleshooting toolbox.

If your PC is in the midst of a breakdown and you can't reach Windows, you'll find in-depth Safe mode coverage in Chapter 5 of this mini-book.

Drastic Things That You Won't Do Often

As I say at the beginning of this mini-book, Windows XP is much harder to crash than previous versions of Windows. In fact, it even attempts to automatically fix system files that are corrupted by other programs by using the *Windows File Protection* feature. However, the folks in Redmond can only do so much to armor-plate their favorite son. You might end up with a PC that makes even the most dedicated PC technicians shake their heads in defeat . . . and if that happens, it's time to read this section.

Using Automated System Recovery

As I mention earlier, I take full advantage of XP's System Recovery utility. But if your PC is in truly bad shape and you can't run the System Recovery program, your next step will likely be to run the XP *Automated System Recovery* (ASR) feature, which you can activate during the boot cycle.

I cover ASR in detail in Chapter 5 of this mini-book, so I won't go into specifics here. Just remember that ASR is only available with Windows XP *Professional,* so if you're running Windows XP *Home,* you can forget that I even brought up the idea. (Sorry.)

Re-installing Windows XP

If your entire operating system is in serious jeopardy — that is, it won't boot, or it locks up every single time you use it as soon as your mouse cursor appears — you can re-install Windows. (Microsoft also calls this remedy a *repair installation* or an *in-place upgrade.* I find the latter rather humorous.)

So-called learned people in the world will swear up and down that you should never, **never** re-install Windows XP. Mention such a drastic step to these self-appointed experts, and they'll immediately start whooping, "There's no reason to do it, and you might possibly launch a thermonuclear warhead at Nepal if you diddle with a single setting. Just suffer! After all, it's Windows."

Well, good reader, I'm here to tell you the honest truth. You certainly *won't* be re-installing Windows XP every weekend but only as a last resort after you've tried ASR and consulted with the techs at your local computer repair shop. However, there are situations (like the two I just mentioned) where re-installing your operating system might solve your problem.

Back up whatever personal files you can from your system before re-installing Windows XP. (Perhaps use Safe mode, which I mention earlier in this chapter.) Also, if you'd like to try to keep the personal files that are on the drive, **do not choose a clean install,** which basically wipes out the existing Windows installation.

If your PC came equipped with a system restore CD-ROM, note that using a system restore disc is not the same thing as re-installing just Windows XP! When you use the manufacturer's system restore disc, your hard drive will probably be completely erased and reformatted, and the hard drive will be restored to the exact condition that it was in the first time when you booted your PC. **All your files, applications, and settings will be gone,** and you'll have to set up all your multi-user accounts as well! If there's no other way, and you can't re-install Windows XP from an actual Windows XP installation CD-ROM, please make certain that every file you want to save has been safely stored on a Zip disk or CD-R disc before you use the system restore disc. (Oh, and don't trust floppy disks with the backup job. They're far too unreliable.)

If you did receive (or buy) a bona fide Windows XP installation CD-ROM, follow the instructions that accompanied the CD-ROM to install Windows XP. Make sure that you choose to *Upgrade* on the Welcome to Windows Setup page when prompted for the installation type. However, here are a few tricks that I want to mention first:

✦ **You might have to re-install some applications.** Although the information that most programs place in the Registry (and in their own .ini files) won't be affected by a re-install, some applications might no longer work after you re-install Windows XP. (If you're re-installing Windows XP, you're dangling from the end of your rope anyway, so you might as well go for the gusto and take the chance of having to re-install a few applications.)

✦ **You need the same product key.** If Windows XP came pre-installed on your PC, you should find the product key on an official-looking sticker somewhere on the PC's case.

✦ **You have to reactivate Windows XP.** Remember how you had to activate Windows XP when you first installed it or first started your new PC? *Activation* is Microsoft's anti-piracy protection scheme; luckily, the folks

**Book II
Chapter 7**

Easy XP
Troubleshooting

in Redmond have made allowances for catastrophe and will allow you to reactivate a legitimate copy of Windows XP.

✦ **You can back up the Windows XP Product Activation file.** It's named `wpa.dbl`, and you'll find it in your `C:\Windows\System32\` folder. This file can be copied back into the same folder after you've re-installed XP, if necessary (as long as you haven't made any drastic changes to your hardware in the interim).

✦ **You'll lose all your System Restore points.** Of course, if you can't get to 'em, they don't do that much good . . . but I wanted to mention the loss, anyway.

Once again, the best-laid plans of mice and trackballs (sorry about that) can go awry, but as long as you've backed up your personal files and important documents, you *will* persevere! (Even if you do have to perform that clean install and manually reload your files and applications.)

HELP! Additional Troubleshooting Resources

If you have an XP troubleshooting question, you might be able to make a phone call to your local computer shop for a quick answer — even after the warranty expires — but most folks I know turn more often to the source. After all, Microsoft built the doggone thing.

In this final section, I discuss the three troubleshooting resources offered by Mother Bill. (And there's even an option that doesn't require the Internet.)

The Windows XP Help system

I show you how to use the Help system in the very first chapter of this mini-book. (See, I told you I like to plan ahead.) But I'd also like to point out that the Microsoft Knowledge Base entries that you'll find in Help (which, to no one's surprise, are pulled directly from Microsoft's Knowledge Base Web site) are particularly valuable when you're troubleshooting problems with XP.

I also like to use the Search within Previous Results feature when digging for troubleshooting information in the Help system. For example, if I'm trying to diagnose a problem with a video card, I can search for *video card troubleshooting* and then search within just those results for *media player*. You'll find the Search within Previous Results check box when you display the results of a top-level search, as shown in Figure 7-6.

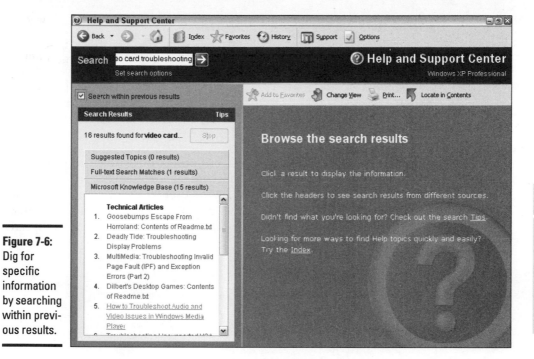

Book II
Chapter 7

Easy XP
Troubleshooting

Figure 7-6:
Dig for
specific
information
by searching
within previ-
ous results.

Microsoft tech support

Microsoft offers both online and telephone technical support, using real
human beings. This is probably the most valuable, free troubleshooting
resource around, along with the technical support that you receive from the
manufacturer when you buy your PC. Because all Microsoft products have
different support telephone numbers, check your XP documentation for the
proper number to call.

The Microsoft Web site

Of course, you can also always find Microsoft online (if you can still get
online with the trouble that you're encountering) at www.microsoft.com.
The Microsoft Web site is stuffed full of information, and each product
typically has its own home page. For example, you can visit the XP site
at www.microsoft.com/windowsxp/default.asp and download that
seasonal screensaver that you wanted so badly. (Yeah, right.)

Those unsupported newsgroups

Called *Windows newsgroups* within Windows Help, don't be fooled into thinking that these Usenet newsgroup discussions are moderated or monitored by Microsoft in any way. Therefore, you'll get plenty of opinions (and what passes for wit on the newsgroups) if you post a troubleshooting question here, but there is a chance that someone else will recognize the trouble that you're having and volunteer a solution. Take any solution you're handed, however, with a whopping big grain of salt.

Don't provide anyone with any personal information within these newsgroups because the individuals with whom you're talking *do not* work for Microsoft. (This is a common sense Internet thing.)

Book III

The Internet

By Rich Tennant

©RICHTENNANT

"Ronnie made the body from what he learned in Metal Shop, Sissy and Darlene's Home Ec. class helped them in fixing up the inside, and then all that anti-gravity stuff we picked up off the Web."

Contents at a Glance

Chapter 1: Making Sense of the Internet

In This Chapter

✓ Defining the Internet

✓ Exploring Internet technologies

✓ Comparing Internet connection methods

✓ Checking your PC's minimum hardware and software requirements

*W*hile the Internet continues to grow and change before our eyes, it seems to be getting more complex instead of simpler to use. The search tools once used to locate stuff before the arrival of the new millennium (such as ARCHIE and GOPHER) are practically extinct now, and more everyday uses for the Internet become less exotic seemingly every month . . . instant messaging, Web cams, streaming Internet radio stations, blogs. I know some folks who have told me they're ready to throw their modems out the window and return to the blissfully ignorant days when we all wrote letters with (gasp) paper stamps affixed.

If you're somewhat wary of the Internet, however, don't give up hope. In this chapter, I explain what's available online, using actual English words of fewer than five letters. (Usually. I might have to hyphenate some of the techno-nerd terms, however.) If all you currently do online is visit sites on the Web and communicate through e-mail, you're missing out on a ton of cool activities, and you're likely a year or two behind the latest Internet technologies. Hey, I live for this stuff.

So stick with me here to gain a good grasp of what you can do via the Internet and what types of Internet connections are, well, hip and happening. You can then jump to the other chapters within this mini-book for in-depth coverage of major Internet applications such as your Web browser and e-mail program.

Exactly What Is the Internet, Anyway?

Many of the PC owners whom I talk to are convinced that the Internet is a real substance. They're not quite sure whether it's animal, vegetable, or mineral, but they're sure that they've either *got it* or *want it* inside their computer. (It's probably a tiny, glowing ball: a cross between Tinkerbell and St. Elmo's fire.)

Seriously, though, you don't need to know what the Internet is in order to use it. From a PC owner's standpoint, you'd actually be correct (in a way) if you said that the Internet begins at the phone connection or the cable modem coaxial cable. Therefore, if you'd like to skip to the next section and avoid a glance underneath the hood (or if you've already read my description of the Internet in another book), be my guest.

Still here? Good. To find out a little more about how your PC connects to the online world, Figure 1-1 illustrates the process.

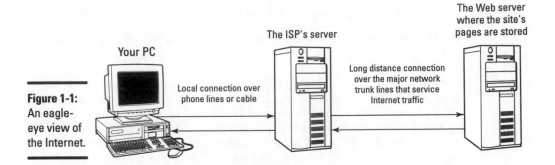

Figure 1-1: An eagle-eye view of the Internet.

When you connect to the Internet, here's a brief description of what's actually happening when you visit a Web site via a Web browser:

✦ **Your PC connects to an ISP.** *ISP* is the techie slang for *Internet service provider,* which allows you access to the Internet proper. Your ISP account will usually include reserved space on its computers for your own Web site as well as one or two e-mail addresses. This is analogous to you dialing the telephone for a voice call, using a specific number that will connect you to the other party.

✦ **Your ISP locates the Web site across the Internet.** You might hear techie types talk about *pipelines* when they discuss the Internet. Although no physical pipes are involved, the term makes a certain warped sense. In this case, your ISP uses the desired Web site's name (its Universal Resource Locator, URL) that you request to locate the computer that it resides on (a *Web server*) and then creates a pipeline between your PC and the server. (For example, the URL www.mlcbooks.com leads to my Web site, which runs on my coal-driven Pentium III server in my office.)

✦ **Your computer communicates directly with the Web server.** After you make a connection with a Web site, a Web page displays in which you can click links and images to send commands to the Web server, which loads other pages or even sends your PC packing to other Web servers. (How rude!) This is much like the end result of a voice telephone call: You're conversing with the other party, using a language that you both understand.

This is the essence of everything that you do on the Internet: computers connecting with other computers (no matter where on the planet they might be) and exchanging information of various types (e-mail messages, Web pages, or a real-time video signal).

So how does your ISP know where that particular Web server is on the network? I won't go into any crush-depth detail here, but here's the quick version. Every computer on the Internet is assigned an address — *Internet Protocol address,* or IP address for short — that identifies it to other computers. (This address is technically a Transmission Control Protocol/Internet Protocol [TCP/IP] address. No glazing over of the eyes yet.) This IP address takes the form of four groups of numbers separated by periods, like this example: 192.168.1.100. (Sophisticated computers keep track of who has what IP address and also what English-language Web address, like Microsoft.com, is tied to what IP address.)

See? Like I said, it's beautifully organized chaos, and I'm proud to say that my Web server adds three or four additional Web sites to the billions on the planet!

Exploring the Possibilities of Your Internet Connection

Whew! Now that the egghead description is complete (for those who gave a hoot), here's what you can actually do when your PC is connected to the Internet. You've got the Web to explore; you can host your own site and keep journals online; you can keep in touch with e-mail, and more.

Exploring the potential of the Web

Start with the familiar. When it comes to the wonders of the modern Internet, you just can't get any more mundane and humdrum than the World Wide Web. Heck, my kids actually don't remember the days when a TV commercial didn't list a company's Web site or when schoolwork didn't involve an online search. (The endless cycle continues: What did we do before the Web? Or microwave ovens? Or air conditioning? Or the telephone? Or a sharpened stick?)

Surfing the Web

Visiting Web sites is as simple as starting your browser (in this case, Internet Explorer, as shown in Figure 1-2), typing in a Web site address in the Address field, and pressing Enter. Boom. (That's my company Web site, MLC Books Online, which you're welcome to visit at www.mlcbooks.com.) Folks will surf for all sorts of reasons, including online shopping, research, banking, and various types of fun.

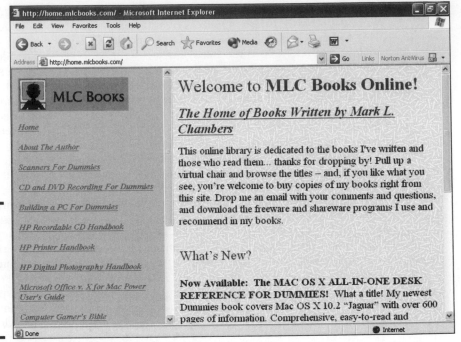

Figure 1-2:
Web browsing is as easy as typing an address or clicking a link.

I discuss Internet Explorer (IE) in all its exquisite design in Chapter 4 of this mini-book.

A Web site's *extension* (the three-character suffix behind the period) can help you keep track of the major categories of sites. Some common ones are

✦ `.com`: A commercial or business site

✦ `.org`: Usually a club, organization, or nonprofit group

✦ `.gov`: A federal or state government Web site

Building a Web site

Aha, here are more interesting waters. Despite the somewhat magical techno-wizard reputation of Web masters and Web designers, you can run your own Web site to support your needs whether it concerns your hobby, your business, or your grandchildren. You need

✦ **A little creative work**

✦ **The proper type of Internet connection**, whether an always-on connection such as cable, a digital subscriber line (DSL), or a network

✦ **The right software**, such as the Windows XP Web Publishing Wizard or Microsoft's FrontPage

Unfortunately, all the intricacies of designing and building Web pages and running a Web site are beyond the scope of this mini-book, but a short stroll through the shelves of your local bookstore will provide you with dozens of books devoted completely to the subjects of Web design and Web server setup. I can personally recommend the great books *Building a Web Site For Dummies,* 2nd Edition, and *Creating Web Pages All-in-One Desk Reference For Dummies*, 2nd Edition, both from Wiley Publishing, Inc.

Blogging along on the Web

Until a few years ago, I would have thought that blogging was a bread pudding that's gone bad or a B-movie monster. However, now that I run my own Web log, or *blog* for short, I'm much more sophisticated. (Can't you tell?)

Blogs, the latest cutting-edge Internet technology in writing a diary, are Web sites that are updated on a fairly constant basis by an individual, crammed full of daily entries like a journal. Instead of keeping your journal private, however, the idea behind a blog is to share your thoughts with anyone who's interested — family members, co-workers, or fellow hobbyists. Blogs usually include the books and music that the person is currently enjoying as well as links to other sites that the person favors.

If you're interested in blogging, try the blog creation program I use: Blog, by Fahim A. Farook, which is available on his Web site at `www.farook.org`. Figure 1-3 illustrates the server side of the program, where you type or paste your entries. If you'd rather create a site directly on the Web (without using your PC as a server), try Blogger at `www.blogger.com`.

You're welcome to immerse yourself in my random thoughts on my blog, On the Trail of Fred Garvin, at `http://theblog.mlcbooks.com`. *War and Peace* it ain't, but I certainly do have my opinions.

Communicating via e-mail

Long before the arrival of the Web, the Internet provided a number of truly valuable services — and today, Internet e-mail is still the most important thing that I do online. Avoiding spam like a bull fighter, I can converse with folks planet-wide and send them all sorts of stuff: Microsoft Office documents, programs, Web links, and even photos of my 1964 Cadillac two-door hardtop (lovingly named Princess Grace), as you can see in Figure 1-4.

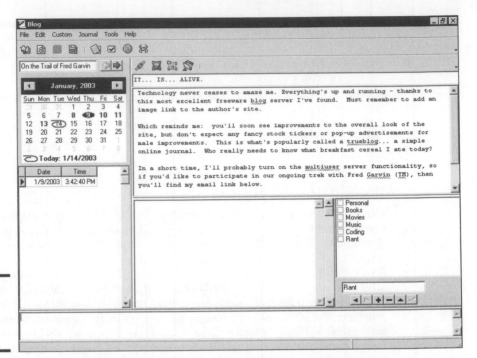

Figure 1-3:
Blogging
can be
good fun.

Figure 1-4:
Now *that,*
ladies and
gentlemen,
is a car . . .
even in
e-mail!

Anyone running Windows XP can use Outlook Express to send, receive, and manage e-mail. I think that Outlook Express is one of the best free programs that Microsoft has ever produced . . . and to that end, Chapter 5 of this mini-book is dedicated to Outlook Express.

If you travel often or you need to check your e-mail on any computer with a Web browser, you can use a Web-based e-mail account like those offered by Microsoft's Hotmail (www.hotmail.com) and Yahoo! (www.yahoo.com). Most Web-based e-mail services are free, but in order to get the really choice features — like spam filtering or additional space for attachments — you must subscribe for a monthly or yearly fee.

You can also use applications that will allow you to run your own *mailing list,* which is an automated e-mail discussion group, usually concentrating on a specific topic or supporting a specific company/product. Check out the Arrow Mailing List Server at www.jadebox.com/arrow for a good example of a shareware mailing list server.

File transferring via FTP

File Transfer Protocol (FTP) is one of the bona fide dinosaurs of the Internet; unlike other antique Internet applications, however, FTP is still alive and doing very well, thank you. You can use FTP to transfer files to and from remote computers; the computer that you connect to runs (you guessed it!) an *FTP server.*

Internet Explorer provides built-in support for FTP transfers, but IE is definitely on the Spartan side when it comes to features. If you're planning on using FTP often, I recommend that you use a separate application to transfer files. Figure 1-5 illustrates AceFTP Pro, my FTP program of choice. It's a shareware bargain at only $30 U.S. when you download your copy; you can register at the Visicom Media Web site, www.visicommedia.com.

Communicating with instant messaging

E-mail is great, but what if you want to share that gossip *now?* With Windows XP and Microsoft Messenger, you can chat with others by typing your messages in real-time — as long as your family and friends are online and available, you can now communicate with them in seconds.

For the full details on Messenger (and other instant messaging programs from folks other than Microsoft), check out Chapter 6 of this mini-book.

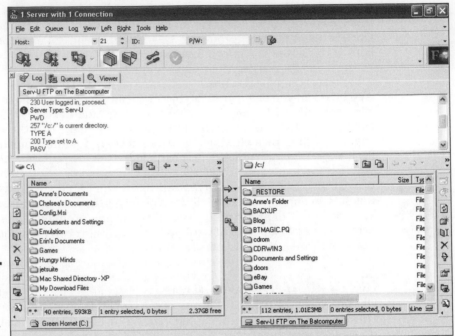

Figure 1-5:
Do the FTP
thing with
AceFTP Pro.

Reading newsgroups

Think of *newsgroups* as huge discussion boards. Most aren't moderated, and virtually all participants choose to remain anonymous, so opinions and arguments abound . . . and often escalate into the dreaded *flame war,* where dozens of messages get heaped on some poor defenseless, unsuspecting new member (called a *newbie* in newsgroup vernacular). Remember, there's no sheriff in town, so most newsgroups are wild, lawless territories.

With that understood, I absolutely *adore* newsgroups! Each newsgroup is dedicated to a certain topic, be it Elvis, WWII fighter planes, *The Simpsons,* or something in-between. Thanks to the specific nature of newsgroups, *subscribing* (joining) to only those newsgroups with information that you find of interest is relatively easy. Your ISP will usually provide you with access to its newsgroup server when you sign up.

And newsgroups offer more than just the chance to discuss a topic: Many groups are dedicated to certain types of file downloads, so you can share images, sounds, movies, and even programs with others. I've also found newsgroups to be invaluable sources of free tips and advice — always taken with a grain of salt, naturally.

As a first stop before you join the group scene, pick up a copy of my favorite freeware newsreader: Xnews, written by Luu Tran, and available on his Web site at `http://Xnews.newsguy.com`. Figure 1-6 shows Xnews in action. As a free alternative, try Google Groups at `http://groups.google.com` — it's all Web based, so no additional software is necessary.

Using Web cams and Web videoconferencing

I shouldn't forget one of the cornerstones of Web technology that's been "right around the corner" now for several years: the ability to send video from one computer to another by using a special type of minimal digital video (DV) camera: a *Web cam.* For some time now, early adopters have been trumpeting the idea of Web *videoconferencing* (where several folks can get together over the Net for a real-time video meeting).

Is the widespread use of video on the Web still so far away? Large corporations that have nationwide or global offices have been using Web videoconferencing for some time, but they have the super-fast T1 connections to the Internet that can easily handle video data. Regular folks with dialup modem connections, however, simply don't have the bandwidth for decent video streaming.

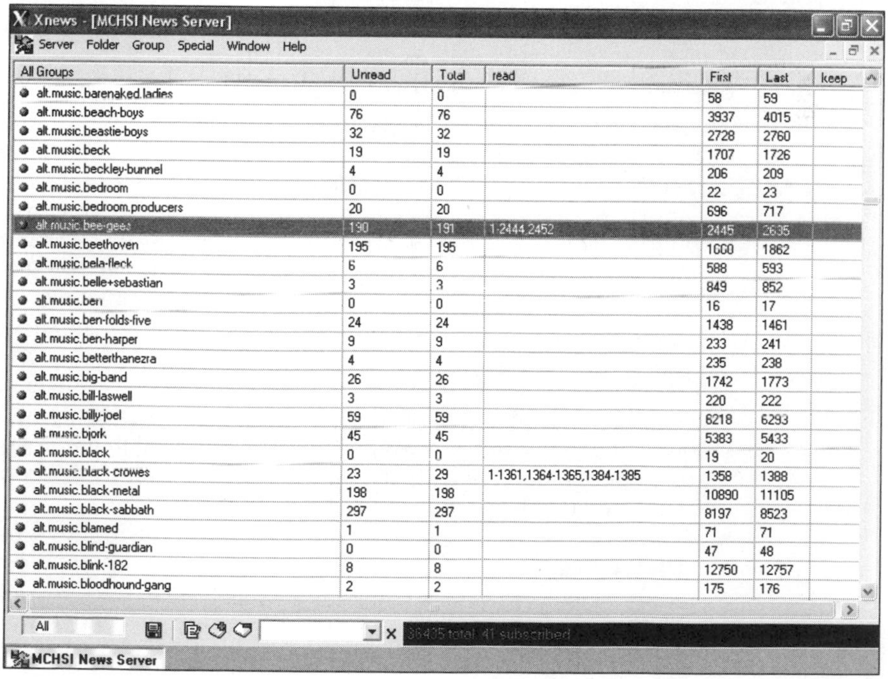

Figure 1-6: Share a piece of your mind with Xnews.

The recent popularity of high-speed broadband connections such as DSL and cable make it much more likely that you'll be able to offer a video feed that's larger than a postage stamp. So who knows? Maybe the large-scale acceptance of Web videoconferencing really *is* just over the next technological hill.

Listening to music over the Internet

If you enjoy music as much as I do, this is really exciting stuff — streaming Internet radio offers FM-quality (or even CD-quality) stereo music broadcasts that you can tune into with your Web browser or MP3 software.

Although you can't capture the music as separate MP3 files, I find Internet radio to be a wonderful resource that I can tune into wherever an Internet connection is handy. Like video feeds, a high-speed Internet connection is a must if you're interested in listening to the higher-quality stations.

In fact, I've been running my own station for years now! It's called *MLC Radio*, specializing in music from The Era That Will Never Come Again: the 1970s! With a broadband connection, you'll hear hundreds of classic '70s hits in 128 Kbps CD-quality stereo; to tune into MLC Radio, visit my Web site at `www.mlcbooks.com` and click the MLC Radio link.

If you're interested in listening to streaming Internet radio — or you want to start a station of your own — visit the good people at SHOUTcast, at `www.shoutcast.com`. It's even free . . . talk about *sassy!*

Understanding Internet Connections

If you're wondering what *DSL* stands for or how the speed of a cable modem connection stacks up against your old phone modem, here I discuss each of the common connection types as well as their pros and cons.

Dialup connections

Still the single most common type of Internet connection, the hoary dialup modem dates back to the days of the early '80s. Dialup connections use standard telephone lines. In fact, you can consider a dialup connection to be a telephone call between two computers.

Dialup pros

✦ **Simple equipment:** A dialup connection requires only a standard voice telephone line and an inexpensive modem.

✦ **Easy access:** Dialup Internet access is available anywhere that telephone service exists.

✦ **Less cost:** ISPs charge a minimal amount for dialup access ($10–$25 U.S. per month, as long as you're calling a local access number).

Dialup cons

✦ **Busy signals:** A dialup connection might leave your telephone line busy (depending on the feature set offered by your modem).

✦ **Slow speed:** A dialup connection is much, much slower than all other forms of Internet access.

✦ **Reconnection hassles:** Your PC must dial your ISP each time to make a connection before you have online access.

Dialup access still has its merits, but I wouldn't recommend a dialup connection unless your Internet needs are limited to e-mail and five minutes' worth of browsing a day.

ISDN connections

I'll be brutally honest: Avoid ISDN at all costs. (ISDN stands for *Integrated Services Digital Network* — or, as witty hardware types call it, *It Still Does Nothing*.) Heck, I'm not even going to recommend it in place of a dialup connection. ISDN was the first broadband connection method that used regular phone lines, and all the techno-wizard pundits predicted that ISDN would be the cornerstone of civilization as we know it.

Unfortunately, ISDN hardware is more expensive and complex than any other high-speed connection technology, and you still have to dial up. That's right, it's not always on like the better broadband technologies that I discuss next. Plus, the least expensive ISDN connection is only a little more than twice as fast as a dialup connection, yet DSL and cable are much faster.

For these reasons, ISDN never had a chance and has been completely obscured by DSL and cable. Don't touch ISDN with the proverbial ten-foot pole.

DSL connections

DSL, which turns out to be what ISDN was *supposed* to be, is one of the two most common high-speed connections. As long as you're within the DSL service area of your telephone provider and your ISP, you can move to DSL.

DSL pros

✦ **Always-on connection:** No dialing is necessary before you surf.

✦ **Fast:** These are true broadband access speeds.

✦ **Basic equipment:** DSL uses standard telephone wiring.

Book III
Chapter 1

Making Sense of the Internet

DSL cons

✦ **Cost:** ISPs usually charge at least double the cost of a dialup Internet account for a DSL account.

✦ **More cost:** You must either rent or buy a DSL modem, which is more expensive than a familiar dialup modem.

✦ **Limited access:** DSL access might not be available in your area.

I recommend DSL for anyone who spends more than an hour a night online or who specifically needs faster data transfer.

Cable modem connections

Cable Internet access just plain rocks; it's the other popular broadband connection technology on your block.

Cable pros

✦ **Always-on:** No dialing is necessary.

✦ **Very fast:** These are true broadband access speeds (in some areas, faster than DSL).

✦ **Simple equipment:** The service uses your cable TV coaxial cabling to connect.

Cable cons

✦ **Cost:** Cable access is about twice as expensive as a dialup account.

✦ **More cost:** You must either rent or buy a cable modem.

✦ **ISP limitations:** A limited number of ISP choices accompany cable access (generally, it's one ISP or none at all).

Cable access speeds vary according to how many fellow users are connecting to the Internet in your neighborhood: The more people who are connected, the slower your access will be. (Keep that in mind if you're renting an apartment.) Mind you, the difference might not be significant. I have cable modem access, for example, and because my average connection speed is about one-third faster than the DSL in my area, I still end up with faster surfing and download speeds. Therefore, a bit of checking and speed comparison is in order before you choose between cable and DSL in your area.

I recommend cable for folks who spend more than an hour a night online or who specifically need faster transfers.

Satellite connections

A satellite Internet connection provides the fastest transfer speeds of all, but (as you might have guessed) satellite technology is also usually the most expensive. You usually rent your equipment (an internal adapter card) from your ISP, and the account is typically more expensive as well. Bad weather or heavy cloud cover can also slow your connection. However, if you're living in the middle of Alaska and can't get anything else but long distance access to an ISP, the satellite route will likely be the way to go.

Here is one possible caveat about satellite service (depending on what type of satellite equipment you install): Don't throw away your dialup modem quite yet! You see, your Internet data is beamed to your home or office from a satellite overhead — hence the speed — but the data that *you* send back to your ISP might actually be transferred over a standard dialup modem connection.

Normally, this isn't a big deal because you'll probably be sending a very small amount of data compared with what you receive: Web page addresses, e-mail, and the like. On the other hand, if you must upload large files to an FTP server or you want to host a Web site, the slow crawl of your dialup connection will likely drive you batty.

The latest satellite service uses the satellite antenna to both send and receive data, so a dialup connection is no longer necessary. Check with your satellite ISP for information about what type of connection is offered and how much it will cost before you sign on the dotted line.

So What Exactly Do 1 Need?

Here's the list of minimum requirements to achieve an Internet connection from your PC:

✦ **Your PC:** Natch. Windows XP is preferred in my little chunk of the universe.

✦ **An Internet account from a local ISP:** Most larger ISPs will offer at least dialup and DSL. If you choose cable or satellite access, your ISP is actually the company providing the connection.

✦ **A modem of one sort or another:** Whether a telephone modem, a DSL or cable modem, or a satellite adapter, you just can't connect a cable to your PC and expect it to work.

✦ **A service call (for cable or DSL access):** You can connect a telephone modem by yourself, and most satellite systems are do-it-yourself, but a service technician will have to perform a number of magic tricks if you choose cable or DSL access.

Chapter 2: Adding a Dialup Connection to Windows XP

In This Chapter

✔ Obtaining the right account data

✔ Checking your physical connection

✔ Adding a dialup connection to Windows XP

✔ Troubleshooting a faulty Internet connection

Albert Einstein once said, "Imagination is more important than knowledge." When it comes to adding an Internet connection, however, our friend Albert is just plain wrong. (No disrespect intended — Albert was truly a genius.)

You'll find that this chapter is definitely a work of nonfiction — and for good reason, too. For most PC owners, the process of "installing the Internet" (as I've heard it called) seems to be one of the most daunting tasks possible. And that's a shame because adding an online connection is really a simple process . . . it's just full of all sorts of strange and weird numbers and snippets of data.

This chapter removes the mystery so that you can get — and stay — online!

Gathering the Incantations

Unfortunately, setting up an Internet account is still not a plug-and-play operation, but that's not the fault of Windows XP. Rather, blame it on how the Internet works (which I discuss in the previous chapter of this minibook) and the information that other computers need to know before they can communicate with your PC. Without the proper setup, you can have the fastest network connection to the Internet on the planet, and plugging in your PC will provide you with absolutely zip — or, as my dad used to say, "The big diddly-squat."

But don't lose hope! Before you get waist-deep in the Sea of Nervous Tension, let me reassure you that there are only a few MIVs that you need to gather (that's my own abbreviation, short for *Mysterious Internet Value*). Plus, they should all be given to you (for free) by your Internet service provider (ISP) when you sign up for an Internet account!

Here's a list of the required information that you'll need to set up your Internet access in Windows XP via a dialup modem:

✦ **Your ISP account name and password:** *Note that this is often different from your e-mail account username and password.* This is the first troubleshooting question that I ask when folks tell me that they can't connect.

✦ **The local access number provided by your ISP:** Note that many ISPs offer more than one local access number.

✦ **The name of your ISP:** If you have multiple accounts from the same ISP, you'll want to use more descriptive names, such as *Business account* and *Personal account.*

Now, of course, that's not all the gobbledygook that you'll get from your ISP, but that's all that you need to know to handle the steps in this chapter. The rest of the arcane knowledge is required later in this mini-book, when I cover Outlook Express in Chapter 5 . . . but by that time, you'll be a certified techno-nerd.

Making the Physical Connection

First, make sure that you're plugged in. You've likely heard the horror stories about recalcitrant PCs that stubbornly fail to accept an Internet connection only to find later that the doggone thing simply wasn't hooked up correctly.

Before you delve into the next section, here's a list of the physical connections necessary for each type of Internet access:

✦ **If you're using a dialup connection,** your modem needs to be connected to the telephone wall jack. If you're using an external modem, make sure that it's connected to either your Universal Serial Bus (USB) or serial port. (See Book I, Chapter 3 for more on ports.)

✦ **If you're using a digital subscriber line (DSL) or cable connection,** your modem needs to be connected to the telephone wall jack (for a DSL connection) or your cable TV coax connection (if you're using cable access), and your PC's network card should be connected to the modem with an Ethernet cable. As I mention in the previous chapter, both of these Internet technologies are typically installed by a professional, so you shouldn't have to worry about your physical connections. (In fact, if you have a DSL or cable connection, you might not need anything in this chapter, either, because most install techs are very nice individuals and usually set up the entire shootin' match for you.)

✦ **If you're using a satellite connection,** your PC's network card should be connected to the satellite dish's signal box with an Ethernet network cable.

If you need to transfer an Internet connection that was working on a previous computer, use the File and Settings Transfer Wizard. You'll find it by choosing Start⇨All Programs⇨Accessories⇨System Tools⇨Files and Settings Transfer Wizard. (Why Microsoft continues to call these programs *Accessories,* I will never know . . . it sounds like this wizard is a vanity mirror in a new BMW.)

Creating a New Connection in Windows XP

Of course, your ISP might also have provided you with complete instructions for setting up your account in XP — in fact, I'd look sideways at the ISP if it didn't — so feel free to follow those instructions instead of the steps in this section. Of course, if you didn't get any instructions, you're still covered.

This procedure covers the most common scenario, where

✦ You've already signed up for an account with a local ISP.

✦ Your ISP didn't provide a set of detailed instructions — thanks a heap.

✦ You're using a dialup modem.

As I mention earlier, it's very likely that a DSL or cable modem installation will either be performed for you, or the equipment will be accompanied by a very detailed set of instructions. Don't forget this:

> **If the manufacturer or your ISP gives you more specific instructions than the generic steps that you see here, use those instead!**™

(It's what I would do . . . you won't hurt my feelings.)

With that said, take a deep breath and follow these steps:

1. **Choose Start⇨Control Panel (or Start⇨Settings⇨Control Panel, depending on how your XP Start menu is set up) and then double-click the Network Connections icon.**

2. **Click Create a New Connection in the Task pane to the left (which displays the New Connection Wizard that you see in Figure 2-1), and then click Next.**

3. **Click Connect to the Internet and then click Next.**

   So far, so good, but the screen in Figure 2-2 is where some people go astray.

Figure 2-1:
The friendly
face of
the New
Connection
Wizard.

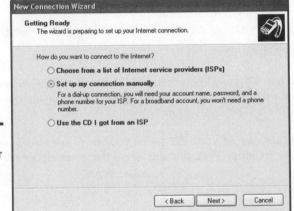

Figure 2-2:
Repeat after
me: "I'll do
this
manually."

4. **Because you'll be using the settings supplied by your ISP, select the Set Up My Connection Manually radio button and then click Next.**

   If you jumped into this process without first signing up with an ISP, Microsoft actually does a creditable job of helping you choose an ISP:

   a. **Select the Choose from a List of Internet Service Providers (ISPs) radio button and then click Next.**

   b. **In the next screen that appears, mark the Select from a List of Other ISPs radio button and click Finish.**

   You'll be provided with a list, and the wizard leads you through an alternate path to righteousness.

5. **Type the name of the ISP (or an identifying name that you can remember) into the ISP Name box and then click Next.**

6. **Type the local access number provided by your ISP and then click Next.**

If the number is a toll-free call, don't forget to add the *1-* prefix. On the other hand, if your ISP doesn't provide a local access number and you have to call long-distance to connect, run (do not walk!) to your telephone and cancel that account! (These days, no one should have to incur long distance charges on top of Internet access! Look for a local ISP instead.)

The resulting wizard page (shown in Figure 2-3) looks like a real bear, but it's a teddy when you know the drill.

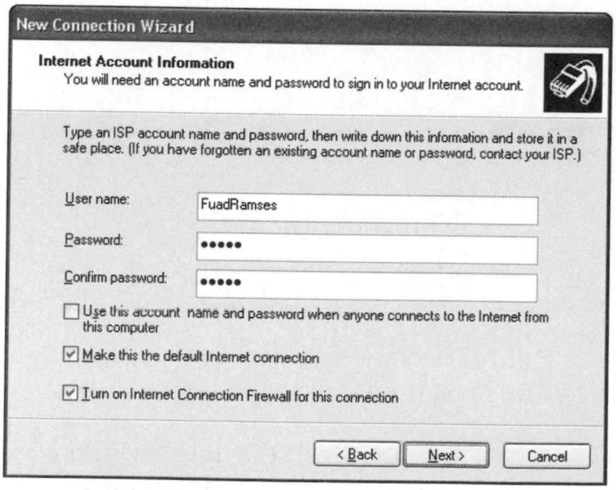

Figure 2-3:
Set up your
ISP account
name and
password
here.

> **New Connection Wizard**
>
> **Internet Account Information**
> You will need an account name and password to sign in to your Internet account.
>
> Type an ISP account name and password, then write down this information and store it in a safe place. (If you have forgotten an existing account name or password, contact your ISP.)
>
> User name: FuadRamses
>
> Password: •••••
>
> Confirm password: •••••
>
> ☐ Use this account name and password when anyone connects to the Internet from this computer
>
> ☑ Make this the default Internet connection
>
> ☑ Turn on Internet Connection Firewall for this connection
>
> < Back   Next >   Cancel

**Book III
Chapter 2**

**Adding a Dialup
Connection to
Windows XP**

7. **Type your username and password provided by your ISP into the corresponding boxes and then type your password again into the Confirm Password box to make sure that it's correct.**

For security, the wizard displays round bullet characters instead of the actual letters and numbers that you type.

If this is your primary Internet account:

a. **Enable the Make This the Default Internet Connection check box.**

b. **Always — always — enable the Turn on Internet Connection Firewall for This Connection check box.**

Security is a good thing, as you'll find out in the next chapter.

TIP

If you're sharing your computer with another person and you don't want them to be able to use your account, disable the Use This Account Name and Password When Anyone Connects to the Internet from This Computer check box.

8. **Click Next to continue.**

The final wizard screen shown in Figure 2-4 sums up what you've done and the settings that you chose.

Figure 2-4:
Huzzah!
You're a
bona fide
Internet
Connection
Specialist.

That's it! See — I told you it was (practically) painless.

TIP

In the final wizard window, I recommend selecting the Add a Shortcut to This Connection to my Desktop check box. Although Windows XP automatically connects to the Internet when a program requests it (such as Outlook Express), the desktop shortcut makes it easy to connect whenever you want with a simple double-click.

Is My Connection Alive?

The final step in your odyssey is the testing: Have you successfully connected your PC to the Internet? The easiest way to test your work is to run Internet Explorer and try loading a popular site, such as CNN.com or Amazon.com. After you type the site name in the Address box and press Enter, your PC should automatically dial out. (You might not hear the dial tones, but Windows XP should display a progress dialog box to let you know what's going on.)

If your browser displays the site, you're online! Or, as pilots say, "You're in the pipe, five by five." (I don't know why.)

My Connection Appears to Be Dead

If you don't end up clapping your hands in celebration, here are the common troubleshooting tips that I always offer to my consulting customers:

+ **Check your physical cable connections.** It's always possible that your external modem simply isn't plugged in, connected to your PC, or connected to the phone jack. An internal modem needs only a cable from the correct port on the PC to the wall phone jack.

Speaking of correct ports, remember that most modems have two ports on the back: one is for the cable running to your wall jack, and the other allows you to plug in a regular telephone to the back of the modem so that you can use your telephone line in the old-fashioned, human-powered manner. Make sure that you plug your phone line from the wall socket into the right port, which is usually decorated with an icon showing a wall jack.

+ **Verify the telephone number provided by your ISP.** Pick up your phone and dial the old-fashioned way using the exact sequence of numbers that you entered for the ISP's phone number in Step 6 of the previous section. If you hear the familiar screeching banshee wail of a modem on the other side, you know that the number is correct.

+ **Double-check the account name and password.** If Windows XP displays a dialog box saying that your account name or password isn't correct, make sure that you typed your ISP account username and password and *not* your e-mail account username and password. If all appears okay, a call to your ISP's technical support is in order.

Chapter 3: Protecting Your Internet Privacy

In This Chapter

✔ **Understanding the risks of the Internet**

✔ **Using your common sense online**

✔ **Using Windows XP's built-in firewall**

✔ **Using a commercial firewall program**

✔ **Protecting your PC against viruses**

A m I really taking any risks with my computer or my privacy when I'm online?

That is one of the most common questions that I receive from my readers. I wish that I could assure you that security accompanies the once-unimagined freedom of the Internet — but unfortunately, the opposite is true. For once, the popular media's perception of computer crime is quite accurate: With your Internet connection comes the possibility of exposure to hackers and con artists.

But just what *can* happen online? How much is hype, and how much is reality? With the right precautions and a little additional hardware and software, you can be reasonably sure that you're well insulated from the bad guys on the Internet! In this chapter, I provide you with everything that you need to know — the same recommendations that I've made to my friends and family for over a decade now — to protect your privacy online.

So What Can Really Happen?

Before I present you with the worst that the Internet can offer, please keep these two important points in mind:

✦ **Are you a target?** The very likely answer is "no" — I'm glad to say that's my answer as well. Virtually all private citizens really don't draw the attention of the serious hackers and other bad guys on the Internet. Hackers would rather attack someone famous, the government, or a corporation instead of spending their time trying to get a copy of your

Word documents, your e-mail, and your Quicken data. (Of course, hackers are getting younger and younger these days, so it's possible that you might be targeted as a practical joke or a juvenile prank. To me, there's nothing remotely humorous about attacking someone else's online personal life . . . the effect is the same.)

✦ **Are you a tough nut to crack?** Yes! (Or at least you will be after you institute the safeguards in this chapter.) Plenty of "open PCs" are on the Internet, whose owners haven't protected themselves, so (like any car thief) a hacker will focus on the easy mark — or in this case, the "unlocked PC." In fact, with the right protection, it's virtually impossible for a hacker to even detect your presence on the Internet, much less try to invade your privacy, thereby preventing most of the nasty scenarios that I'm about to describe.

Okay, now take a deep breath and relax. Here's what can *actually* happen to you with an Internet connection or a network with a shared Internet connection:

✦ **Others might try to contact you or other members of your family.** Believe me, there are some truly unpleasant and sleazy individuals who can use all the great communications features of the Internet for the wrong reasons. They can use Microsoft Messenger, Web discussion boards, e-mail, or newsgroups. With common sense and diligence, you can stop these people from communicating with you.

✦ **You could be the target of identity theft.** The con game is alive and well and thriving on the Internet, where your credit card number, address, and personal information should be guarded like the jewels that they are.

✦ **Hackers can turn your PC into an Internet weapon.** If a hacker can gain access to your PC, your PC can be fooled into participating in attacks against public Web servers and File Transfer Protocol (FTP) servers. Remember the denial-of-service attacks that occurred a couple of years ago? Such attacks can actually shut down Web sites like eBay, Amazon.com, and Yahoo!. In simple English, the hackers manipulate PCs that they have "appropriated" over the Internet to flood these Web sites with millions of simultaneous connections, causing the Web server to simply freak out.

✦ **The files on your network could be read or erased.** Woe unto those who run an unprotected network — especially a wireless network, which can be accessed from outside your home or office.

✦ **Your system could be hit with a virus or harmful macro.** Most of us have already heard of the havoc that a virus infection can wreak on your system — deleted files or even empty hard drives.

I told you that it was a grim list . . . but if all these bad things actually happened to the majority of people who go online, the Internet wouldn't be anywhere as popular and important today as it is. Most of us use our common sense — a most valuable commodity that can help safeguard your Internet presence.

Common Sense Goes a Long Way

And with it comes one of the best of Mark's Maxims, which I hope you'll immediately commit to memory:

If something seems like a bad idea online, it probably is.™

You see it happen all the time on the Internet. People give out sensitive (personal and financial) information and communicate with others on a level that they would never do over the telephone or through the mail. Chalk it up to the siren song of the online world and the charms of technology, I guess.

Take a second to review a number of common sense guidelines that should govern your time online.

Passwords

First, consider the password: It's not an elegant solution to the problem of security, but it's been around since the early days of the online bulletin board systems (or BBSes, for short) in the late '80s and early '90s. No one has found an easier way to protect your identity on the Internet — unless, of course, you want to install fingerprint sensors on everyone's keyboard. (Such sensors actually exist right now, but don't hold your breath waiting to see them in common use.)

Here are the guidelines that I recommend following when using passwords:

✦ **Use random passwords.** I know that using random passwords is a hassle, but they work. Even adding a single number to the end of a word can mean the difference between someone guessing your password and your identity remaining pristine. Some operating systems and online sites recognize the difference between uppercase and lowercase characters, and you can also mix cases to make your passwords even better. *Remember:* Never use something that's easily guessed, such as the names of family or friends, or your birth date.

✦ **Use a different password for each site and server.** If you connect to a dozen systems and need a dozen passwords each night when you're online, this will probably not be feasible — I understand that. However, for the majority of the PC owners online, only three or four passwords are used on a daily basis; in that case, using multiple passwords helps keep things as secure as possible.

✦ **Do not write down your passwords.** If you store that sheet of paper or Post-It note in a safe, you're okay. A desk drawer, on the other hand, makes that crib sheet a bad idea.

✦ **Don't share passwords.** Or why use them at all? 'Nuff said.

✦ **Use Internet Explorer's AutoComplete feature sparingly.** Most Web browsers can automatically store many passwords for you, but I don't recommend using this feature. I show you how to turn off this feature within Internet Explorer later in this mini-book (in Chapter 4).

Of course, your lifestyle might make it easier to skirt some of these recommendations. For example, if you live by yourself, you're already considerably more secure than an office worker surrounded by fellow employees. Just evaluate your own need for security and follow as many of these guidelines as possible. (See there? I can be reasonable.)

Risky behavior

Next, consider a number of online practices that are sadly lacking in (you guessed it) plain, common sense. Although you might find it hard to believe, each of these mistakes is committed countless times every day by intelligent individuals (who should really know better):

✦ **Divulging personal information to strangers during a chat.** Chatting is great fun unless the total stranger whom you're chatting with asks for personal information. (Is the person on the other end of this conversation *really* a 17-year-old cheerleader from Omaha?)

✦ **Offering personal information in Internet newsgroups.** This is especially bad. These newsgroups are public discussion areas, and posting anything personal is asking for trouble. (It's no accident that virtually everyone who participates in a newsgroup uses an alias and a fake e-mail address.) Also, these messages remain on newsgroup servers for years, so a single telephone number or e-mail address that you've divulged can come back to haunt you in years to come. After something has been posted on a newsgroup, it's there to stay in the great pile of searchable data that is the Internet.

✦ **Replying to spam.** Just ignore those irritating junk e-mail messages in your Inbox, even if they claim that by replying, you'll remove your name from their list. (Yeah, right, and I've got some great oceanfront property in Kansas for you, too.) By replying to spam, you're actually verifying that your e-mail address is correct, and you'll get double or triple the messages overnight.

✦ **Avoid phishing expeditions.** If you're not familiar with the relatively new Internet term *phishing,* it refers to an attempt to gain your personal information through a combination of an e-mail message tied to a bogus (but official-looking) Web site. Unfortunately, these criminals are good at creating the impression that you're receiving mail from eBay or Amazon, requesting that you "verify your account information" or "update your user ID and password" by clicking on the accompanying link (which will take you to a page that even looks like the company's actual Web site). It's important to remember that *no self-respecting company will ever request personal information from you through e-mail!* If you're unsure, visit the company's Web page (by typing in the bona fide address or using a bookmark) and contact their customer support staff. You may just be able to report an intended crime, and help put the bad guys out of the phishing business.

✦ **Allowing just anyone to access your PC remotely.** Windows XP includes a remote control feature that allows someone on the Internet to use your PC as if they were sitting at the keyboard. *Do not use this feature unless you're absolutely sure of the person who'll be controlling your PC* — such as a technical support representative or your Aunt Harriet. Remember, the person controlling your PC can delete files and open your personal documents at will. (Sobering thought, ain't it?)

✦ **Downloading files from a site that you don't trust.** It's up to you to decide which sites are trustworthy. But if you do download anything, at least make sure that your computer is protected by a good antivirus scanning program when you run the downloaded program.

✦ **Buying something from an online store without a secure connection.** Reputable online stores will establish a secure connection between their Web server and your browser. Information is encrypted, so it can't be easily intercepted. (Of course, this is especially important when you're entering your credit card information.) If a small padlock icon appears in the status bar at the bottom of your browser window — as shown in Figure 3-1 — you've got a secure connection. If the connection isn't secure, *don't enter any personal information and don't provide your credit card number* — just find another store that does offer a secure connection!

✦ **Opening e-mail attachments without a good antivirus program.** These include executable (or .exe) files and Word documents. E-mail attachments are becoming the prime method of distributing viruses. And because the virus uses the victim's e-mail program to replicate itself, those horrid e-mail booby-traps can actually originate from your "e-friends and e-family"!

Book III
Chapter 3

Protecting Your
Internet Privacy

Dodging those personal questions

I generally don't provide my real name, age, address, or phone number on most Web sites, either. If a Web site demands such personal information and I don't trust the company or organization, I use false information. (And coincidentally, I receive very little spam on my private e-mail accounts. Go figure.) I know that sounds dishonest — and it's going to burn any Web master who might be reading this — but why do I have to enter my personal information just to download a demo or use a free service? I'm a Web master myself, and I don't need that information from casual visitors to my sites. Naturally, if you're registering a piece of hardware or software — or if you're contacting technical support — you should provide the required information.

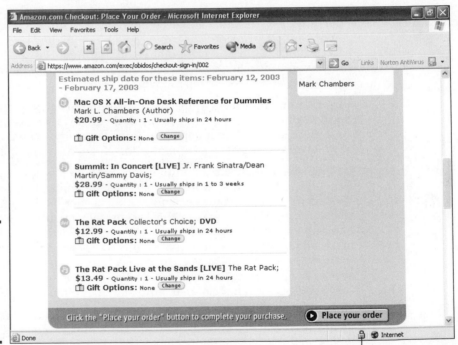

Figure 3-1:
When buying online, a padlock icon is A Good Thing.

The padlock icon indicates a secure connection.

E-mail

I mention spam in the previous section. You *can* fight back, you know. Most e-mail applications have their own built-in armor plates, called *filters* or *rules,* which allow you to automatically move junk mail to a separate folder, where it can be quickly perused and tossed at your leisure. I show you how to enable spam protection in Outlook Express in Chapter 5 of this mini-book.

TIP

By the way, get in the habit of at least reading the subject lines for probable spam; that way, you can verify that an honest-to-goodness valuable message didn't get accidentally tagged as junk.

Personally, however, I've ramped things up a notch. Because my public e-mail address, `mark@mlcbooks.com`, is readily available in my books and on my Web sites, I needed an anti-spam application with more power and flexibility than Microsoft Outlook had to offer. I invested in McAfee's SpamKiller, shown in Figure 3-2, which works with any e-mail program. It provides advanced features such as

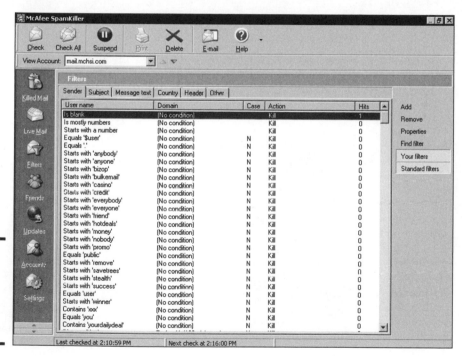

Figure 3-2:
McAfee's
SpamKiller
is a great
junk mail
manager.

- ✦ Customized filters for all sorts of criteria (things such as *text contains, subject contains,* and *starts with*)

- ✦ Automatic updates with the latest filters from McAfee

- ✦ Configurable Friends List with verified e-mail addresses

- ✦ The ability to send complaints about spam messages to the sender's Internet service provider (ISP)

You can purchase and immediately download SpamKiller from the company's Web site at www.mcafee.com for about $40 U.S.

Your Friend, the Firewall

Believe me, good people, your firewall *will* be your best friend if, for some reason, a serious hacker does indeed become interested in accessing your PC or your network. A *firewall* is a software application or a separate hardware device (or both) that performs a number of duties:

- ✦ It masks your PC or network from others on the Internet, making it practically impossible for a hacker to locate your PC (much less attack it).

- ✦ It prevents incoming Internet traffic for the services that you specify (such as Web and FTP services), as illustrated so very well by Figure 3-3.

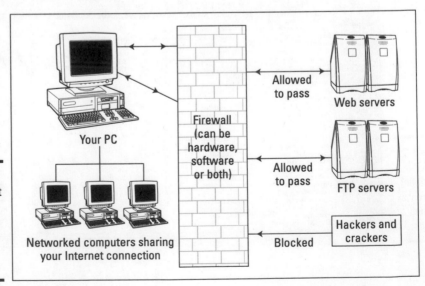

Figure 3-3: The Internet traffic that you want gets in through a firewall.

✦ It monitors outgoing traffic and blocks any activity that you've specified (for example, visits to particular Web sites or any Microsoft Messenger communications).

So which is better? A hardware or software firewall? That depends on the number of PCs on your network — if you have one — and the level of security that you need:

✦ For a single PC (or a shared Internet connection through Windows XP) with typical home/home office security, the built-in Windows XP firewall will be all that you need.

✦ For a network of several PCs — or for any environment where you demand the best security — turn to a hardware firewall device. For example, Figure 3-4 illustrates some of the port protection features that are built into my Internet router.

If you're using an Internet-sharing device — such as an Internet router, switch, or hub — that includes NAT, then celebrate! NAT stands for *Network Address Translator,* which performs the masking that I mention earlier. Most devices with NAT support also include a hardware firewall. Check the device's manual to be sure.

Figure 3-4:
My Internet
router
can be
configured
to block just
about
anything.

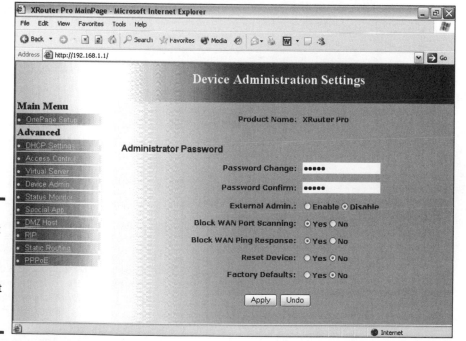

Using the built-in XP firewall

If you've perused Chapter 2 of this mini-book, you'll know that I recommend that you enable the built-in firewall in Windows XP when you create your Internet connection.

It's easy to enable the Windows Firewall, but you'll need a user account with administrator access to do the job. Follow these steps:

1. **Choose Start⇨Control Panel⇨Network Connections and then click your Internet connection to display the Status dialog box.**

2. **Click Properties and then click the Advanced tab.**

3. **Click the Settings button to display the Windows Firewall dialog you see in Figure 3-5.**

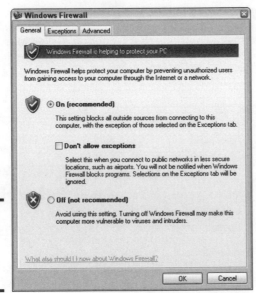

Figure 3-5:
Watch your firewall there, friend.

4. **Click the desired radio button to enable (or disable) the firewall as necessary and then click OK.**

Windows Firewall is a smart puppy; it shouldn't interfere with any of the Internet activities that a typical home PC owner is likely to try. However, many multiplayer games have trouble sharing your PC with a firewall, and you may not be able to use your firewall if you're also using XP's Virtual Private Networking (VPN) feature, which I chew on in Book VIII, Chapter 4. If a specific program has problems with the Windows Firewall, check the program's manual to see whether you need to make changes to accommodate a firewall.

TIP

Of course, you can easily disable a software firewall for an hour or so while you use an incompatible Internet application, and the chance that someone would pick that very moment to hack your system is quite small. I've done this before, but believe me — I don't do it very often.

Commercial firewall alternatives

Okay, suppose that you have a number of programs that just won't work with Windows Firewall, and you need those doggone applications to survive on planet Earth. Perhaps you'd rather spend a little cash (say $50 U.S.) for more features and power than Windows Firewall can offer. No problem: Enter commercial firewall programs such as Norton Personal Firewall, from Symantec, www.symantec.com (shown in Figure 3-6).

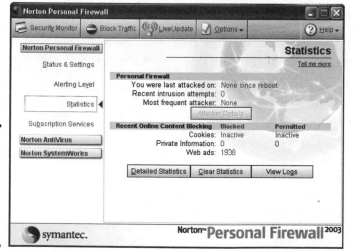

Figure 3-6: My favorite Internet suit of armor — Norton Personal Firewall.

Book III Chapter 3

Protecting Your Internet Privacy

I use Norton Personal Firewall instead of Windows Firewall because I need many of its enhanced features:

✦ **Web ad and pop-up blocking,** which prevents me from losing my temper over the spread of wanton commercialism while I'm using Internet Explorer

✦ **Automatic security** updates from Symantec

✦ **The ability to control the access** of individual applications to the Internet

✦ **Control over what specific personal data** that I want to allow to be sent over the Internet

✦ **Adjustable security alerts,** which tell me when a program is attempting to access the Internet

I can heartily recommend Norton Personal Firewall — it works, and it's highly configurable for those who need flexibility so that everything that needs to run works right (and everything that you're guarding against still hits that brick wall).

Hey, how about a free test of your new firewall? No, pardner, I'm not offering to hack into your system. Instead, I'm inviting you to visit Gibson Research Corporation at www.grc.com where you can try out ShieldsUP!! This great *free* online utility checks your Internet connection for a number of entrance-ways popular with hackers and even gives you advice on how to fine-tune your firewall to close 'em up.

Using Antivirus Software

The last stop on the Internet security tour is a good antivirus program. Windows XP contains no built-in, robust virus protection. Instead, look to McAfee for VirusScan or Symantec for Norton AntiVirus; either program will do a great job protecting your computer from viral attack.

As I see it, the two most important points about any antivirus program are

✦ **Real-time scanning:** Whatever you run or load, your antivirus program should check it before your PC is exposed. I also appreciate the fact that Norton AntiVirus checks all my Word and Excel documents for danger-ous macro viruses. With real-time scanning, the need to check your entire hard drive for viruses is reduced to once every three months or so instead of once every week.

✦ **Automatic and frequent updates:** The best antivirus protection in the known universe isn't worth a plug nickel the moment you stop applying updates. Without updates that contain the latest virus signatures, your antivirus program becomes vulnerable to the newest strain. (A *signature* is a set of characteristics that your antivirus program can use to spot a particular virus.) Therefore, make sure that the antivirus program that you choose is updated often and automatically — both McAfee and Symantec excel in providing at least one or two updates a month.

Figure 3-7 illustrates Norton AntiVirus at work.

By the way, Norton AntiVirus also works inside Outlook and Outlook Express, checking both the incoming file attachments that you receive and the outgo-ing files that you send . . . just in case.

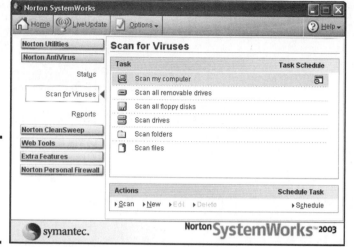

Figure 3-7:
I don't fear viruses with Norton AntiVirus on the job.

Chapter 4: Cruising the Web with Internet Explorer

In This Chapter

✔ Starting Internet Explorer

✔ Introducing the browser window and controls

✔ Adding and using Favorites

✔ Searching for Web sites

✔ Downloading files

✔ Using the History file

✔ Printing and saving Web pages

And the answer to that unspoken question is, "Yes, you *still* need this chapter, even if you've been using Internet Explorer now for the last several years."

You see, Internet Explorer (and any Web browser in general) is one of the simplest applications on the planet to use, requiring only three or four buttons on the toolbar to operate most of the absolutely necessary functions. Many PC owners that I've met don't even know that Internet Explorer (IE) offers a ton of additional features to help you organize sites, print pages just-so, and search for the Web content that you need.

In this chapter, I show you the power user side of Internet Explorer — it's time to supercharge your surfing!

Running Internet Explorer

Here are a number of methods that you can use to start IE. (After all, the Web has its tentacles in practically everything, right?)

✦ Double-click the IE icon on your desktop.

✦ Choose Start⇨Internet Explorer.

✦ Click the IE button on the Quick Launch portion of the taskbar.

✦ Click an embedded link (a HyperText Transfer Protocol/HyperText Markup Language [HTTP/HTML] hyperlink in many applications and documents, such as Word and Excel documents).

✦ Run Windows Update (weird, but you can surf after you update XP).

Don't forget that you can choose Start➪Run to display the Run dialog box, where you can use your fingers for something other than clicking. Type **iexplore** in the Open box and then press Enter (or click OK, if you absolutely have to click something). This runs Internet Explorer, but you can get even fancier: Type **iexplore**, followed by a Web site address (like **iexplore mlcbooks.com**), and then press Enter or click OK. The program runs and automatically loads my Web site.

The Explorer Window and Basic Controls

After Internet Explorer unveils itself in all its stately grandeur — as you can see in Figure 4-1 — note the following major controls and important spots, in order of appearance from top to bottom:

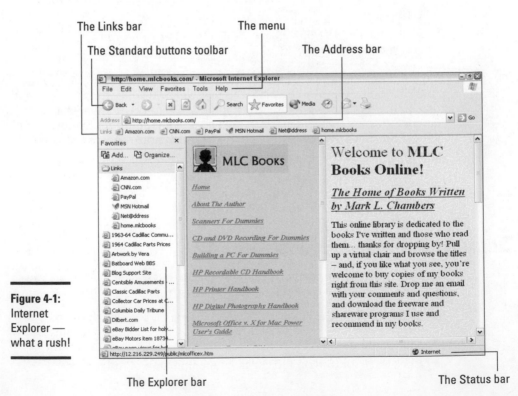

Figure 4-1:
Internet
Explorer —
what a rush!

The Links bar

The Standard buttons toolbar

The menu

The Address bar

The Explorer bar

The Status bar

✦ **The menu:** You knew that was coming, right? Note the standard Windows application menu, containing commands that I discuss for the rest of this chapter. At the far upper-right, you'll see an animated Windows flag, which waves brilliantly in the cyber-breeze whenever IE is busy loading content from a Web site or searching for a page.

✦ **The Standard toolbar:** Again, no big surprise here. The Standard buttons toolbar display can be toggled on and off from the View⇨Toolbars menu (as can the rest of the bar family, whom you're about to meet).

✦ **The Address bar:** Here's where you'll type (or paste) the URLs for Web sites. You can click the drop-down list box to see those addresses that you've recently visited. Click a site in the list to return to it with a minimum of fuss.

✦ **The Links bar:** Home of the Web sites that you visit most often, you can add sites to the Links bar and jump to them with a single click. (More on how you can add and remove sites from your Links bar in a bit.)

✦ **The Explorer bar:** I don't know why Microsoft calls this huge panel a *bar* — but then again, who gives a flip? Anyway, no matter what you call it, you'll find this configurable panel very convenient. It can be toggled between displaying all sorts of information, including your Favorites, your surfing History, and the Internet Explorer Search box. To display the Explorer bar, you can choose View⇨Explorer Bar and then choose the panel that you want to see, or you can press the shortcut key combinations that I provide later (see the following section, "More buttons for your buck"). To banish the Explorer bar from your Internet Explorer window, click the Close button at the top-right corner of the bar.

You can resize the width of the Explorer bar by hovering your mouse pointer over the right edge of the bar until it turns into a double-arrow cursor. Then click and drag the separator to the desired spot.

✦ **Content window:** Believe it or not, the IE window actually shows you Web content, too (amongst all the bar family). Clicking an underlined or graphic link in the Content window whisks you somewhere else (either within the same site or on a completely different Web site). The Content window often contains underlined text and graphical icons that transport you to other pages when you click them. Other Windows-style controls — such as drop-down list boxes and text entry boxes — can also be displayed and used as part of your surfing. It all depends on the Web master who designed the page that you're viewing . . . or the Web mistress, as the case may be.

One of my favorite IE keyboard shortcuts is Ctrl+N, which opens a new Internet Explorer window with the current page loaded. Opening a new window comes in handy when you suddenly need to compare the contents of two Web pages because you can navigate to the second page without disturbing the first.

**Book III
Chapter 4**

Cruising the Web with Internet Explorer

✦ **Status bar:** Last and smallest — but certainly not the least — the Internet Explorer Status bar displays important information about the page that you're viewing, including the all-important Secure Sockets Layer (SSL) encryption icon. If you do a lot of online shopping, you've seen this tiny lock icon when you're entering your personal data or credit card number; it indicates that the site you're visiting is *secure,* which means that the encrypted information you're typing can't be intercepted by hackers. If you rest your mouse pointer on a link or a photo on a Web page, the status bar also displays information about that item.

More buttons for your buck

Just in case you've never been properly introduced to the default buttons on the toolbar, they include

✦ **Back:** With a click of the Back button, Internet Explorer returns to the last page you visited, and each subsequent click of the Back button takes you a page farther back. You can also press the Backspace key on your keyboard to move backward.

✦ **Forward:** If you've clicked Back, you need a way to return, right? Click the Forward button to take you to the next page (or pages) where you originally were, in forward order. From the keyboard, you can press Alt+→ (right-arrow navigation key) to move forward.

If you notice that the Back button is disabled (grayed out), you haven't visited at least two sites yet. If the Forward button is disabled, you haven't used the Back button yet. (Little did we all know that the Internet Explorer toolbar had a PhD in quantum physics.)

✦ **Stop:** Refreshingly self-explanatory. Click Stop to cancel a page from loading. Pressing Esc does the job from the keyboard.

✦ **Refresh:** Clicking the Refresh button reloads the contents of the current Web page, which allows the Web server to update the page with any new information. (Good for connections to news sites like CNN.com.) You can press Ctrl+R or F5 to refresh as well.

✦ **Home:** Click this button to immediately jump to your home page. Mine is Google.com, for example, which makes a Google search always one click away. From the keyboard, press Alt+Home.

✦ **Search:** Clicking this button displays the Search pane in the Explorer bar, which I cover later in the chapter (see the "Navigating the Web" section). Pressing Ctrl+E does the same thing.

✦ **Favorites:** Click this button to display the Favorites pane in the Explorer bar. (Again, more on this later in this chapter.) Press Ctrl+I from the keyboard.

✦ **Media:** Click this button to display the Media pane in the Explorer bar. The Media pane allows you access to the latest in multimedia content from WindowsMedia.com, such as video, music, and Internet radio stations.

✦ **History:** Click the History button to display the History pane in the Explorer bar or press Ctrl+H. I discuss History later in this chapter (see "Keeping Track of Where You've Been").

✦ **Mail and News:** Clicking this button launches Outlook Express, which allows you to read and send e-mail and participate in Usenet newsgroups. The next chapter in this mini-book provides all the details on Outlook Express.

✦ **Print:** A click of this button (or pressing the Ctrl+P shortcut) prints the contents of the current page.

To display a short one- or two-word description of a toolbar button, just leave your mouse pointer motionless over the button for a second or two.

You can customize the toolbar with a number of different functions — choose View➪Toolbars➪Customize to display the dialog box shown in Figure 4-2.

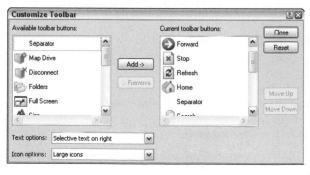

Figure 4-2:
Customize
the Internet
Explorer
toolbar from
here.

**Book III
Chapter 4**

Cruising the Web
with Internet
Explorer

From the left column, click the button that you want to add and then click Add to place it on the toolbar. To remove a toolbar button that you don't use, click the offending button (in the right column) and then click Remove. To change the sequence of buttons in the right column, click the button that you want to move and then click either the Move Up or the Move Down button to change its position on the toolbar. Click the Text Options dropdown list box to determine where the button label text should appear or to ban button labels entirely. Also, you can click the Icon Options drop-down list to toggle between large and small toolbar icons.

"The Story of Little URL"

Every Web-touring saga begins with the URL — short for *Uniform Resource Locator* — that identifies every Web site on the planet. It's commonly called a *Web address* because the URL is as unique as a traditional mailing address.

Most URLs begin with the now-oh-so-darn-ubiquitous `www.` prefix. However, Internet Explorer doesn't actually require that you type the triple-w when you're entering a new Web address to visit. For example, if you just type **cnn.com** into the Address bar and then press Enter, IE automatically adds the `www.` prefix for

you. You get to visit CNN.com and save four characters of typing to boot. Also, you need never type the `http://` portion of the URL because IE always tries to load an address as a Web site unless you specifically indicate that you're trying to connect to a File Transfer Protocol (FTP) site by using the `ftp://` prefix.

Also, you might have noticed recently that a number of sites no longer use the triple-w at all. Therefore, don't assume that an URL starts with `www.`, or you might not be able to load the page. Instead, always enter the URL exactly as it's given to you.

After you're satisfied with your new creation, click the Close button to save your changes. Click the Reset button at any time to return to the toolbar configuration that you originally had.

Finding a home page

I always encourage everyone on the planet to choose your own home page. If you're constantly returning to the same spot on the Web, you'll find that your home page can greatly speed up your surfing, which is why I use Google as my home page. From within Internet Explorer, follow these steps:

1. **Navigate to the desired page.**

2. **Choose Tools⇨Internet Options to display the dialog box that you see in Figure 4-3.**

3. **On the General tab, click the Use Current button to set the home page to your current page.**

   Alternatively, if you just want Internet Explorer to start very quickly each time that you run it, click the Use Blank button instead. (Using a blank home page is a great way to prevent Windows XP from dialing out each and every doggone time you start Internet Explorer.)

4. **Click OK to save your changes and return to the browser window.**

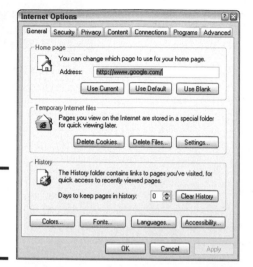

Figure 4-3:
There's no
place like
home
(page).

Navigating the Web

Earlier in this chapter, I talk about how you can visit a site by typing or pasting a URL directly into the Address bar and pressing Enter. Internet Explorer will automatically show you any sites with a matching address while you type the URL. And if you've visited the site before, just press Enter when you see the proper address appear.

However, here are other methods of navigating to a new site:

✦ **Click a link** within another Web page.

✦ **Click the Home button,** which takes you to your home page.

✦ **Click a Web link** in a document, e-mail message, or an application.

✦ **Click an HTML file** from Windows Explorer.

✦ **Click a Favorite** within the Explorer bar or from the Favorites menu.

✦ **Use the Search panel** in the Explorer bar.

In this section, I tell you more about the last two options: Favorites and the Search panel.

Simplifying surfing with Favorites

After you select a Web page as a Favorite, you can easily reach that site quickly (and without a forest of sticky notes appearing all over your monitor). To add a Favorite, display the page that you want within IE and use one of these methods:

✦ **Choose Favorites➪Add to Favorites**, which displays the dialog box that you see in Figure 4-4. Type a new name (if necessary), click the Create In button to select the Favorites folder where you want to store the entry, and then click OK.

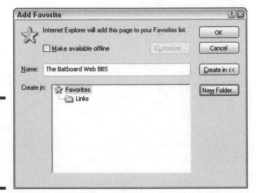

Figure 4-4:
Add a Web
page as a
Favorite
here.

✦ **Press the Ctrl+D keyboard shortcut,** which adds the site as a Favorite without any prompting.

✦ **Click the Add button in the Favorites panel.**

To add a Favorite to the Links bar, display the Favorites panel and click and drag the desired Favorite to the Links folder. You can also add the current site to the Links bar by dragging the icon at the left of the URL in the Address bar directly to the Links bar.

After you set up your Favorites, using them is simplicity itself:

✦ From the Favorites menu, click the desired Favorite.

✦ Click the Favorite itself on the Favorites bar — if it's not displayed, click the Favorites button in the toolbar. (To show the contents of a folder in the Favorites panel, give it a click.)

✦ Click the desired Favorite on the Links bar.

When you add Favorites, you'll find them easier to use if you spend a moment to organize things. Follow these steps:

1. **Choose Favorites➪Organize Favorites to display the Organize Favorites dialog box that you see in Figure 4-5.**

   Alternatively, click the Organize button on the Favorites bar.

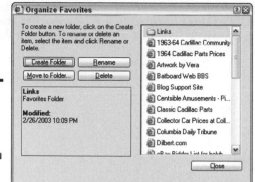

Figure 4-5:
Organize
your
Favorites
any way you
like.

2. **Click the Create Folder button to add a new folder, which appears in both the Favorites menu and the Favorites bar.**

3. **To move a Favorite into a folder, click the desired Favorite, click the Move to Folder button, click the destination folder, and then click OK.**

4. **To rename a Favorite, click the desired Favorite, click the Rename button, type the new name, and then press Enter.**

5. **When you're done organizing your Favorites, click the Close button to return to the browser window.**

To change the order of the Favorites from the Organize Favorites dialog box, just click and drag a Favorite to its new spot and release the mouse button to drop it.

To modify the URL that's connected to a Favorite, right-click the Favorite and then choose Properties (from the contextual menu that appears) to display the Properties dialog box that you see in Figure 4-6. Click the Web Document tab, type (or paste) the new address into the URL text box, and then click OK to return to the Web.

Searching for the hay in the needlestack

To search for a specific Web site amongst the billions on the planet, use the Search bar. Follow these steps:

1. **Press Ctrl+E to display the Search bar, as shown in Figure 4-7.**

2. **Type a complete sentence — but as short and lucid as possible — into the What Are You Looking For? text box and then press Enter.**

    If Internet Explorer finds any matches, they appear in the content window.

3. **Click a page link to view that page.**

**Book III
Chapter 4**

**Cruising the Web
with Internet
Explorer**

As a shortcut, you can also search by typing **Find** *whatever* (*whatever* is what you're looking for, like **Find popcorn**) in the Address bar and then pressing Enter. I use this one a lot. Figure 4-8 shows the result of my attempt to find Elvis.

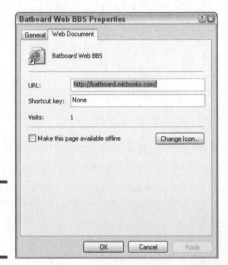

Figure 4-6:
Change a
Favorite's
URL here.

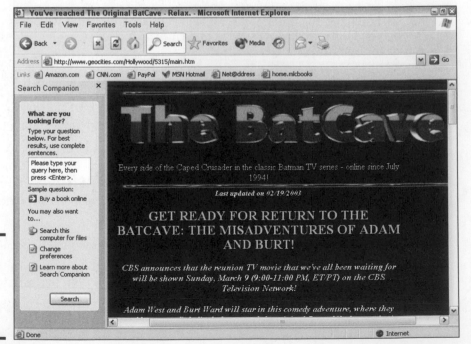

Figure 4-7:
See Dick
search —
use the
Search bar,
Dick.

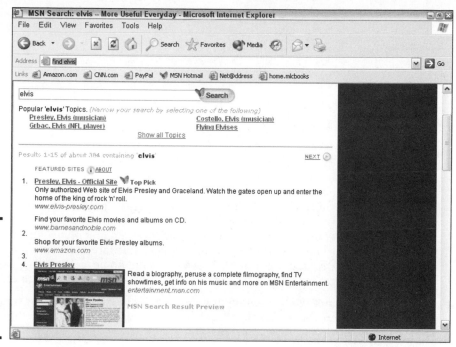

Figure 4-8:
You can
search for
The King
from the
Address bar
as well.

Although using the Search bar is good, it's still somewhat primitive compared with using either *Google* or *Yahoo!,* which are dedicated search sites. Therefore, don't forget that you can make your favorite search engine site your home page, or you can add a Favorite with your search engine site to your Links bar.

Downloading Files

Downloading files is a simple operation, indeed. When you click a download link within a Web page, Internet Explorer automatically downloads the file to your hard drive.

However, note this catch: Unless you're running an antivirus program that will check your downloaded files, you might be receiving a malignant virus instead of a bona fide treasure. That's why Internet Explorer displays the dialog box that you see in Figure 4-9 when you click a download link that includes an executable program.

So how best to handle this situation? Here are my recommendations:

✦ **If you're using an antivirus program** such as Norton AntiVirus or McAfee VirusScan, go ahead and click Save — these programs can check the file when you run it.

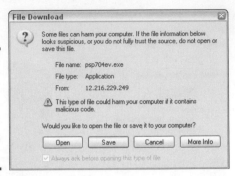

Figure 4-9: IE warns you of possible problems when downloading.

+ **If you're not using an antivirus program**, click Save. After you've saved the file to disk, don't run it until you close any open applications and disconnect from the Internet. However, I'd much, *much* rather that you proceed *immediately* to your closest software store and buy a copy of Norton AntiVirus or McAfee VirusScan! An unprotected PC is a perfect target for viruses from downloaded files or e-mail attachments.

+ **Do not click Open** unless you're downloading a patch or update from Microsoft's Web site. It's always a better idea to execute the download from your drive instead of on the fly.

When you click Save, IE prompts you for the location where you want to store the file, as shown in Figure 4-10. You can choose to use the original file name, or you can type a new name. Click Save to begin the download.

Here's a pickle. You see an image that you'd like to download from a Web site, but it's actually not a file that's set up for downloading — instead, it's part of the Web page itself. No problem: Just right-click the image that you want and then choose Save Picture As from the menu that appears. Internet Explorer prompts you for the location where you want to save the file. You can also choose Print Picture, or you can instantly make the picture become your Windows desktop background by choosing Set as Background. (Unfortunately, Internet Explorer can't make a small picture look good across your entire desktop — or a low-resolution shot into a better-quality background — so use this feature only with larger, high-resolution pictures.) Keep in mind that displaying an image as your background is different from using it in your documents: "Copyrights, people, copyrights!"

Not all downloaded files can be run immediately. Many sites *compress,* or archive, their download files by using the *Zip standard,* which saves time when downloading (because the compression reduces the file size) and saves hassle (because multiple files are archived into a single file). Zip archives end (predictably enough) with the extension .zip. To *restore* the archive, or decompress it, you need a Zip file utility, and there's none better than WinZip, from WinZip Computing (www.winzip.com). I've been a loyal customer of this great shareware program (shown in Figure 4-11) for many years now.

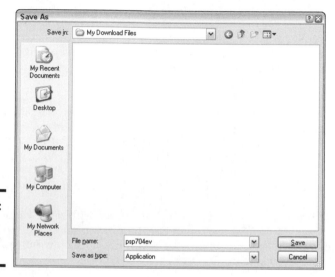

Figure 4-10:
Where do you want it, Mac?

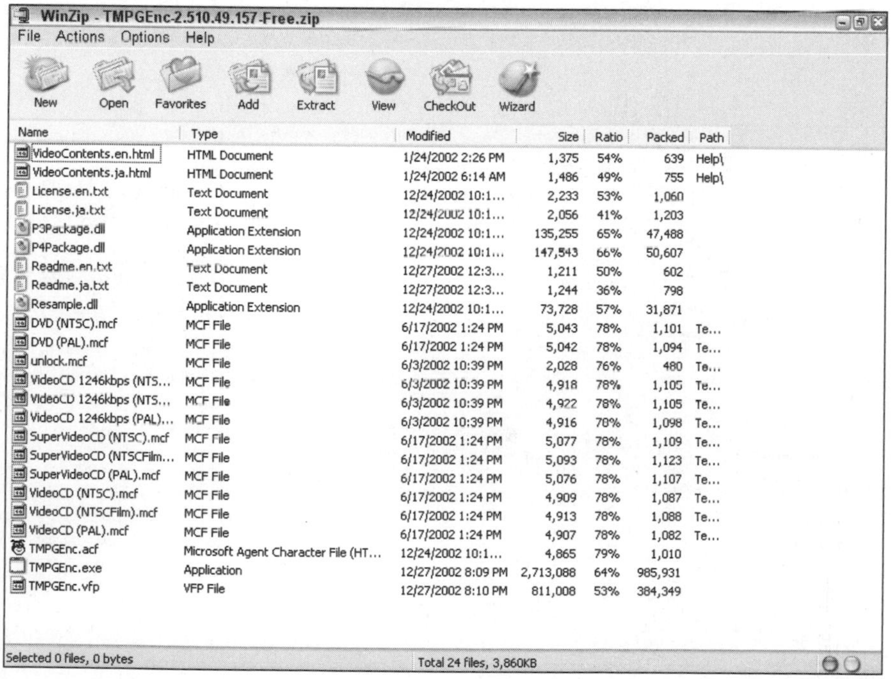

Figure 4-11:
Preparing to unzip the contents of a Zip archive.

Keeping Track of Where You've Been

Bet you didn't know that you were building a history when you tour the Web. But what happens if you need to return to a site that you visited an hour ago, and you don't remember the URL or how you got there?

Don't worry. The History list (see Figure 4-12) makes it easy to retrace your virtual steps. To display the History list, click the History button in the toolbar or press Ctrl+H. You can immediately return to any page in the list by clicking it.

Note that Internet Explorer keeps track of your history on a site-by-site basis, with all the pages on each site grouped together in a single folder. However, you can also display the History list by using other sort criteria. Just click the View drop-down list box at the top of the History bar, and you can specify a sort order based on the date visited, the sites that you visited most often, and the sites in the order that you visited them today.

You can also search for a specific word or phrase within the History list. Click the Search button at the top of the History bar and then type that word or phrase in the Search For text box. Click the Search Now button to display any sites that contain matching text in the page title.

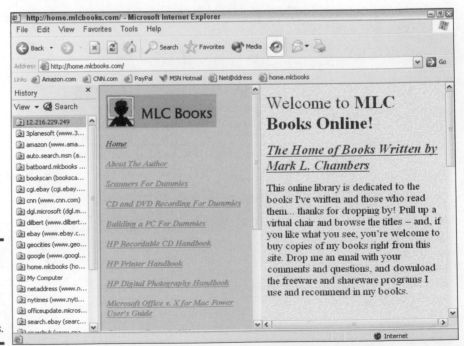

Figure 4-12: Display the history of your recent Web explorations.

If you're somewhat leery of keeping a History file at all, choose Tools⇨ Internet Options. From the General tab of the Internet Options dialog box, you can specify how many days that IE should keep the History list. Set the Days to Keep Pages in History to zero, and Internet Explorer will disable the History list altogether. You can also click the Clear History button to immediately delete the current contents of the History list.

Printing and Saving Web Pages

From time to time, you'll want a printed copy of the content on a Web page. Or you might want to actually save the page itself, complete with all its content, graphics, and links, to a set of files on your hard drive. In this section, I serve you these two palatable options.

Putting the Web in print

I *could* say that printing a Web page is as simple as clicking the Print button in the toolbar (or pressing Ctrl+P) — and technically, I'd be right. But there's really more to it than that . . . specifically, the Options tab in the Print dialog box, as shown in Figure 4-13.

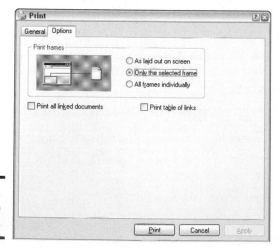

Figure 4-13: Print a Web site from IE.

If the page that you're printing uses *frames* — a method of putting different panels on a Web page, each with its own content — you can choose to print the page in three different ways:

✦ **As laid out onscreen,** which prints the entire Web page.

✦ **Only the selected frame,** which prints only the contents of the active frame on the page. You can usually activate a frame by clicking within it or by using a scroll bar within the desired frame.

✦ **All frames individually,** which prints out the contents of each frame separately.

By default, IE prints only the current page. However, you can print out the current page and any documents that it links to by enabling the Print All Linked Documents check box. This is a good choice if you want to print the contents of a Web site with multiple pages.

You can also choose to print an index of links that appear on the page that you're printing. This index is a handy tool when the printed page has a large number of links that lead to other documents that you might need. Select the Print Table of Links check box to enable it.

Saving the best (for last)

Occasionally I run across a page that I want to save in its entirety. Sometimes because I need to view it offline, while I'm traveling, or if a large number of images accompanies the page. Internet Explorer makes it easy to save the currently displayed Web page as a set of files on your hard drive. Simply follow these steps:

1. **Choose File➪Save As, which displays the special Save Web Page dialog box that you see in Figure 4-14.**

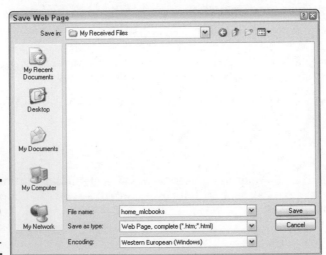

Figure 4-14: Preparing to save a Web page to disk.

2. **Type a name for the saved page in the File Name text box and then navigate to the desired location on your PC.**

3. **Click the Save as Type drop-down list box and choose Web Page, Complete.**

   This is my favorite, where the program stores the entire kit and caboodle so that you can display the page from the file just as it appeared online.

   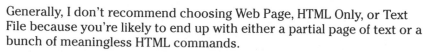

   Generally, I don't recommend choosing Web Page, HTML Only, or Text File because you're likely to end up with either a partial page of text or a bunch of meaningless HTML commands.

4. **Click Save to begin the download process.**

IE creates an HTML file that you can double-click to display the page, which links to a separate folder that contains all the images and documents from the original page.

"Yo, Adrian! Who typed that?"

If Internet Explorer suddenly starts completing Web site addresses and fields within online forms — like your name, your address, or even your password — don't panic. There's no reason to call Ghostbusters. You're seeing Internet Explorer's *AutoComplete* feature, which automatically fills out online forms, Web addresses, and username/password combinations that you've previously entered on a site.

This is all friendly and downright convenient, but what if you're more interested in privacy or security? No problem. You can toggle AutoComplete off for certain types of data, or you can turn it off completely. Choose Tools⇨ Internet Options to display the Internet Options Control Panel dialog box and then click the Content tab. Click the AutoComplete button to specify which types of data that you want filled out; if you're already nervous, click the Clear Forms and Clear Passwords buttons to wipe any AutoComplete data for online forms and passwords.

For a detailed discussion of these Internet Options — many of which affect Internet Explorer — check out Book II, Chapter 6.

Chapter 5: Harnessing Your E-Mail

In This Chapter

✔ Touring the Outlook Express window

✔ Configuring your e-mail account

✔ Receiving and reading your incoming mail

✔ Replying to a message

✔ Composing and sending a new message

✔ Sending and receiving e-mail attachments

✔ Blocking that dastardly spam

✔ Using the Address Book

✔ Working with identities in Outlook Express

E-mail rules the Internet roost. Sure, the Web gets a lot of attention, but what one single service provided by the Internet would cause the most chaos if it were interrupted? That's right . . . the lowly Internet e-mail message that invites you to lunch or informs you of a new baby (or brings you junk advertising that promises to refinance your home at 2%). Without e-mail, most of today's business world would be left stricken — and you wouldn't get those blonde jokes in your Inbox every morning. The mind reels — the soul cries out for more Diet Coke at the very thought.

Because of this mind-boggling importance of e-mail, Microsoft put a lot of work into designing a truly first-class e-mail application for Windows XP. And it's free (believe it or not)! You don't get some of the really powerful features of Outlook 2003, but as an e-mail application, Outlook Express can stand proudly on its own.

In this chapter, I describe how you can keep track of your e-mail messages, your contacts, and your identities in Outlook Express. You'll discover how to ward off junk mail messages as well as how to attach Aunt Gertrude's Big Bang Brownie recipe to the next e-mail that you send. (For the brownie lover on your Contacts list.)

Introducing the Outlook Express Window

Before you venture into the world of Internet communications, get familiar with the controls that you'll be using in the Outlook Express window (catch the hoopla in Figure 5-1). They include

✦ **The menu:** Your standard Windows XP application menu: Click a menu family to display the menu items. You can then click a menu item to perform that action.

✦ **The toolbar:** Click a toolbar button to perform the same function as the corresponding menu item. You can customize the toolbar by adding and removing buttons. Just choose View➪Layout and then click the Customize Toolbar button to display the dialog box that you see in Figure 5-2. (You can also right-click the toolbar and then click Customize to display the same dialog box.) Click the button that you want to add from the list on the left and then click Add to include it on the toolbar; to remove an existing toolbar button, click the button name in the list on the right and then click the Remove button. You can also specify large or small toolbar icons and whether the toolbar buttons have labels.

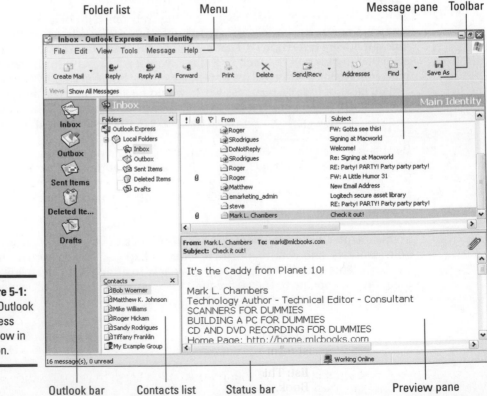

Figure 5-1:
The Outlook Express window in action.

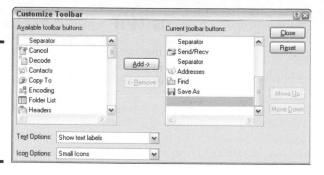

Figure 5-2:
Make
changes to
the Outlook
Express
toolbar
here.

+ **The Outlook bar:** Those folks who have used Outlook 2002 are already familiar with this unique toolbar. You can use it to immediately switch between different views, like contents of your Inbox, Drafts folder, and Sent Items folder.

+ **The Folders list:** Click any folder icon in this tree display to display the contents of that folder.

To add a new folder to the Folders list, right-click any folder in the list and then click New Folder from the pop-up menu that appears. Outlook Express displays the Create Folder dialog box that you see in Figure 5-3, where you can type a name for your new folder and select the existing folder that will act as its "parent." Click OK, and the new folder appears in the Folders list.

Figure 5-3:
Add a new
folder to the
Folders list
here.

+ **The Message pane:** The messages in the currently selected folder are displayed in list form in the Message pane.

+ **The Contacts list:** This window contains a list of the e-mail addresses in your Address Book.

✦ **The Preview pane:** Clicking a message in the Message pane displays it in the Preview pane (without the hassle of actually opening the message in a separate window). After all, we are a people interested in convenience, are we not?

The Preview pane is a highly configurable little beastie. Choose View⇨ Layout to display the Window Layout settings that you see in Figure 5-4. The Preview pane can be hidden, or you can display it below or next to the Message pane. You can also toggle the display of the header in the Preview pane, which displays the To, From, and Subject fields from the message being previewed. (If you've got a ton of mail, losing the header can help conserve screen space.) You can also mark the check boxes to display or hide various pieces 'n' parts of the Outlook Express window.

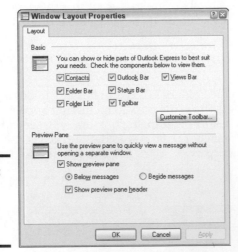

Figure 5-4:
Fix your window layout "just so."

✦ **The Status bar:** Last — and actually pretty much least — is our old friend, the status bar. You can get basic totals on the number of read and unread messages in this bar as well as your Online/Offline status. (The program is typically offline if you're not connected to the Internet.) It also shows you when Outlook Express is sending and receiving mail.

You can easily adjust the size of any pane in the Outlook Express window: Move your mouse pointer over the divider bar that you want to move until it turns into opposing arrows and then drag to relocate the bar.

Setting Up Your Mailbox

Even the mightiest barrage of e-mail begins with a single step. Well, actually two steps, because you have to start Outlook Express for the first time . . . but then, mind you, you're down to a single step! I'm talking about adding at least one e-mail mailbox account to your Outlook Express configuration; without a mailbox account, you get diddly-squat.

To create a mailbox account, follow these steps:

1. **Choose Tools➪Accounts to display the Internet Accounts dialog box that you see in Figure 5-5.**

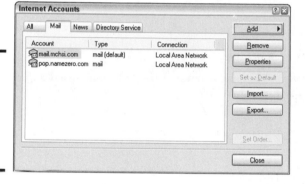

Figure 5-5: Creating a new account with zest and panache.

2. **Click the Add button and then click the Mail item from the pop-up menu that appears to display . . . tah-dah! a wizard!**

   No, not that Gandalf guy. Even the Dark Lord Gates himself couldn't afford that kind of talent.

3. **Type your name as you'd like it to be displayed when you send messages and then click Next to continue.**

4. **Type the e-mail address that your Internet service provider (ISP) gave you and then click Next to continue.**

   Figure 5-6 illustrates the next screen, which prompts you to enter your incoming (POP3) server and outgoing (SMTP) server addresses. If that's as coherent to you as the scribbling on the blackboard in a particle physics class, refer to the documentation or instructions provided by your ISP. That stuff has to be there somewhere because your ISP has to supply it, and you can't just make it up.

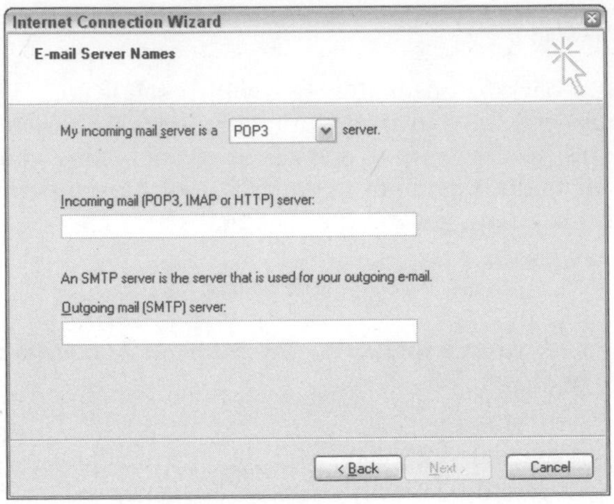

Figure 5-6:
Time to
enter some
of that
Internet
gibberish.

5. **Click Next to continue.**

6. **Enter the e-mail account name and e-mail password supplied by your ISP, as shown in Figure 5-7.**

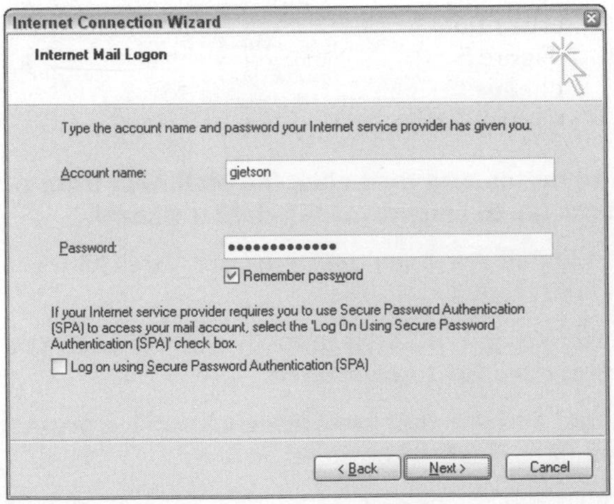

Figure 5-7:
Enter your
e-mail
account
name and
password
here.

See why those ISP folks get paid the big bucks? They have to supply you with a lot of stuff.

7. **Make sure that you're entering your e-mail name and password — a combination that's typically different from your account logon name and password that you use to connect to the Internet — and then click Next to continue.**

Did your ISP's documentation and instructions tell you to select the Log on Using Secure Password Authentication (SPA) check box? If not, you're going to throw a brick to your e-mail server instead of a password . . . or, in layman's language, you won't be supplying the right type of password, and you'll never be allowed to retrieve your mail. You should only enable SPA when you've been specifically told to do so by your ISP. (Harrumph.)

If your PC is located in a secure spot — nestled in your family's game room, for example, or bolted down in the back of your 1972 Ford LTD station wagon — it's okay to leave the Remember Password check box marked. Outlook Express won't bug you for a password each time that you connect to send and receive mail. However, if your PC is sitting on your side table in your dorm room — the room with the door that anyone can open with a paper clip — I highly recommend that you clear this check box to disable it and thus avoid the embarrassment of someone sending messages that purport to come from you.

8. **That's it! Talk about painless! Click Finish.**

   Your new e-mail account appears in the Internet Accounts dialog box.

9. **Click Close to return to Outlook Express.**

Note that you can return to the Internet Accounts dialog box at any time to change the settings on your e-mail account. Click the account in the list and then click the Properties button, which displays the Mail Properties dialog box that you see in Figure 5-8. Most of this stuff will never change, but occasionally an ISP will change the name of an e-mail server or set up new security measures that require a change on your end.

**Book III
Chapter 5**

**Harnessing
Your E-Mail**

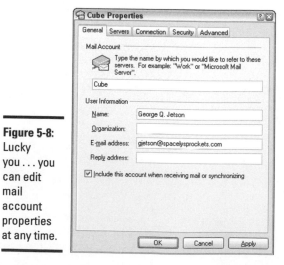

Figure 5-8:
Lucky
you . . . you
can edit
mail
account
properties
at any time.

The Three R's: Receiving, Reading, and Replying

Time to check your e-mail? Click the Send/Recv button on the toolbar. That's it.

Okay, okay — you can press Ctrl+M as well. Whoops, I'm being secretive. Here's the chop: Outlook Express will connect to the Internet (if necessary), and new messages will show up as bolded entries in the Message pane. You can double-click a message to open it; Outlook Express displays the message in its own separate window (as in Figure 5-9).

If the Preview pane is visible, you can scan a message by clicking it once (or by using the up- and down-arrow keys to move through the list). As soon as you've scanned or read a message, it's marked as read, and the bolding disappears.

If you encounter a message from someone who's not in your Address Book and you want to add that sender, right-click the message in the Message pane and then choose Add Sender to Address Book from the pop-up menu that appears. The e-mail address appears in the person's e-mail address in the Contacts list.

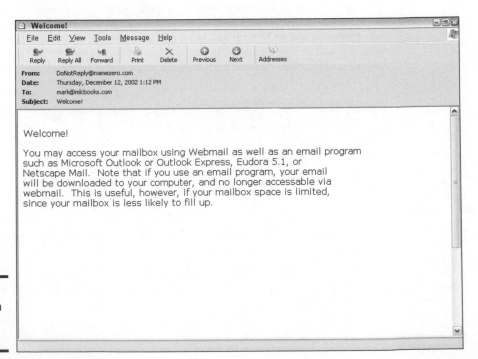

Figure 5-9: Reading an incoming message.

"There is Another . . ."

One look at the new message or reply windows, and it's apparent that Outlook Express only supports regular carbon copies. But wait . . . is that *really* true?

You can also send a *blind carbon copy (Bcc)*, which is a carbon copy message to recipients in which the e-mail addresses of the other recipients are hidden. (If you send standard carbon copies of your message, each recipient can see who else received the message — and even add the e-mail addresses of the other folks to his or her Address Book.) In some cases, sending regular carbon copies can be a serious breach of privacy.

To expose the Bcc Easter egg within a new message or reply window, choose View⇨All Headers. Boing! There it is! Other than the extra privacy, Bcc addresses are handled in the same manner as Cc addresses.

To reply to an incoming message, follow these steps:

1. **Click the desired message in the Message pane list to select it and then click the Reply button on the toolbar.**

   If you're reading the message in its own window, click the Reply button within the window. You can also click the Reply All button to send your reply to others who also received the message (including those who received carbon copies).

   You can also choose to *forward* a message, allowing you to add a comment to the body of the original message before you send it to the new recipient(s). To forward a message, click the Forward button instead of the Reply/Reply All button.

   A Reply window appears (feast on Figure 5-10) with the insertion cursor at the top of the message box. The text of the original message is included under the `Original Message` header, and Outlook Express has already filled in the `To` field with the name of the person who sent the original e-mail.

2. **Although Outlook Express has already inserted the prefix `Re` in front of the original subject line, you can click in the Subject box and type a new subject if necessary.**

3. **If you want to send the reply to more than one person, click in the Cc (carbon copy) box and type the addresses manually (separated by semicolons).**

   Alternatively, click the Cc button to choose names from your Address Book (as shown in Figure 5-11).

Book III
Chapter 5

Harnessing
Your E-Mail

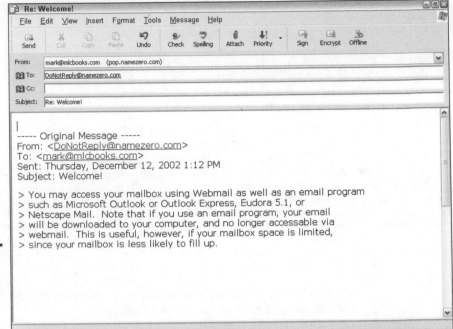

Figure 5-10:
Let's just
reply to that
message,
shall we?

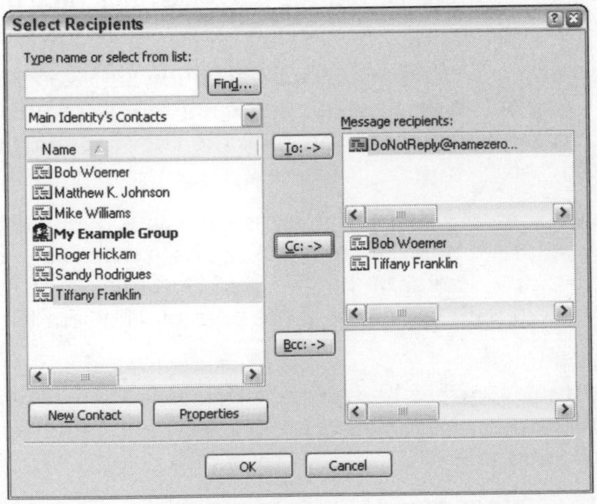

Figure 5-11:
Extract
addresses
from your
Address
Book.

4. **Click in the message box — if necessary — and type the contents of your message.**

You can select text that you want to spice up by clicking and dragging across it and then applying formatting to it from the Formatting toolbar. You can also add attachments (use the procedure that I outline in the upcoming section "Sending and Receiving File Attachments").

If the Formatting toolbar isn't present in the reply window — or if the Formatting menu is disabled — you're writing your e-mail message in plain text. Choose Format➪Rich Text (HTML), and all your formatting controls will be available. However, I'm personally not a big fan of Rich Text (HTML) messages for two reasons. One: Not all e-mail programs handle HyperText Markup Language (HTML) messages properly (especially older e-mail applications running on Linux or Windows 98). Two: Rich text messages are much larger than plain text messages and can take longer to send and receive.

5. **When you're ready to send your message, click the Send button to usher it on its way immediately (or press Alt+S from the keyboard).**

   You can save the message in draft form and delay sending it until later (choose File➪Save and then close the window); the message appears in your Drafts folder.

6. **(Optional) To send a draft message, double-click the Drafts folder to open it, double-click the message to open it, and then click Send.**

   You can also move a draft message to your Outbox, and it will be sent the next time that Outlook Express connects to the Internet to send and receive mail; to move a draft message to your Outbox, choose File➪Send Later.

Messages that you've sent are deposited in your Sent Items folder. You can peruse them at any time if your memory needs refreshing.

Book III
Chapter 5

To delete a message that you no longer need from any folder, click the message in the Message pane list and then press Delete or click the Delete button on the toolbar. The messages are deposited in your Deleted Items folder and can be retrieved if necessary.

Harnessing Your E-Mail

Sending E-Mail to Friends and Enemies

If you need to send a message to one of your contacts in your Address Book, nothing could be simpler. Just right-click the person's name in your Contacts list and then choose Send Email from the pop-up menu that appears. However, sometimes you have to send a message to a person who's not listed in your Contacts list: Click the Create Mail button on the toolbar or choose File➪New➪Mail Message.

Either way, Outlook Express opens the New Message window that you see in Figure 5-12. Here's the rest of the story:

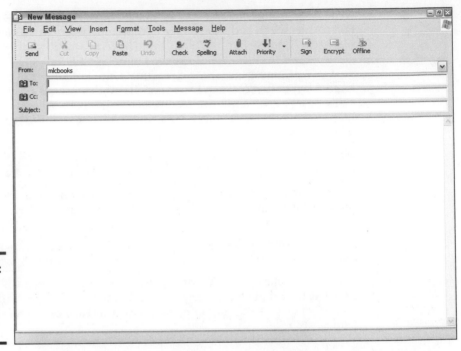

Figure 5-12:
Say, isn't
that a New
Message
window?

1. **If the recipient isn't in your Contacts list, click in the To box and then type the e-mail address.**

   Of course, you can also add carbon copies and blind carbon copies by clicking in the Cc and Bcc boxes, respectively.

2. **Click in the Subject field, type the subject for this message, and then press Tab to move to the message editing box.**

3. **Type the text of your message; if it's set as an HTML message, apply any desired formatting to the text.**

4. **Add attachments to your message, if necessary.**

   Find more on this later in this chapter.

5. **If you'd like to check the spelling in your message, click the Spelling button on the toolbar.**

   If Outlook Express encounters a word with — shall we say, "question-able" spelling — you'll see the dialog box shown in Figure 5-13. To substitute the word in the Change To box, click the Change button; to substitute a word in the Suggestions list, click it and then click the Change button. (If you've mangled the word several times in the same message, click the Change All button instead.)

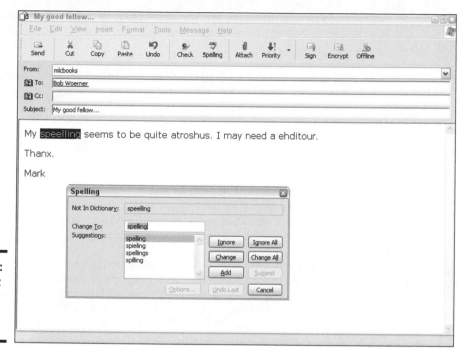

Figure 5-13:
Speelling iz
ophten
sumwatt
importunt.

Did you spell *thakamology* correctly? If so, you can choose to ignore this occurrence (click the Ignore button) or ignore all occurrences (click Ignore All) to avoid further unnecessary nagging during a spell check. If you use *thakamology* quite a bit in your messages, click Add to add the word to the Outlook Express dictionary, and the program shan't bother you again.

6. **Does this message deserve immediate attention? "Help, Mom, I'm stuck in Vienna with no cash!" If so, click the Priority button on the toolbar and then choose High Priority from the drop-down list box.**

This doesn't actually send the message any faster, nor does it travel with any extra gusto. However, it will show up with a priority flag in the recipient's e-mail application.

7. **If you'd like to verify that a message has been read, choose Tools⇨ Request Read Receipt.**

Note: This *will not guarantee* that you'll receive notice when the message has been read. The recipient is prompted for confirmation beforehand, so a read receipt can be canceled.

**Book III
Chapter 5**

**Harnessing
Your E-Mail**

8. **Ready to ship it? You have the same options available as you have when replying to a message:**

   - Click Send to send it immediately.

   - Choose File⇨Save (or press Ctrl+S) to save it in your Drafts folder.

   - Move the message to your Outbox by choosing File⇨Send Later.

Sending and Receiving File Attachments

Why limit your messages to that silly message box? Break out of the box with file attachments! Just about any type of file can be attached to a message, and you can save that file to your hard drive from within the read message window. (And yes, that includes most files sent to you by your friends with those funky Macintosh and Linux computers!)

Unfortunately, some file attachments that you might receive should be *immediately* cast out. I'm speaking, naturally, about e-mail viruses and macros with a homicidal bent, which are becoming as common these days as the generic junk mail messages that you receive every day. Luckily, you can use an antivirus program like Norton AntiVirus (from Symantec, at www. symantec.com) that will automatically scan attachments for any dangerous programs before you use them. **Never open an attachment without proper antivirus protection!** And that includes attached files that you've received from folks whom you know and trust! (They could unknowingly be hosting a virus themselves — some of these bugs are smart enough to actually replicate themselves by enclosing copies of themselves in innocuous-looking messages!)

With that stern admonishment in mind, here's how you can add an attachment to your outgoing message:

1. **Reply to a message or compose a new message.**

2. **Click the Attach button on the toolbar to display the Insert File dialog box.**

3. **Navigate to the location of the file(s) you want to attach; then click the first filename to select it.**

   To add more than one file, hold down Ctrl while you click.

4. **Click the Attachment button to add the files to the message.**

   Outlook Express displays attached files in the Attach box within the header area of the message dialog box (as shown in Figure 5-14).

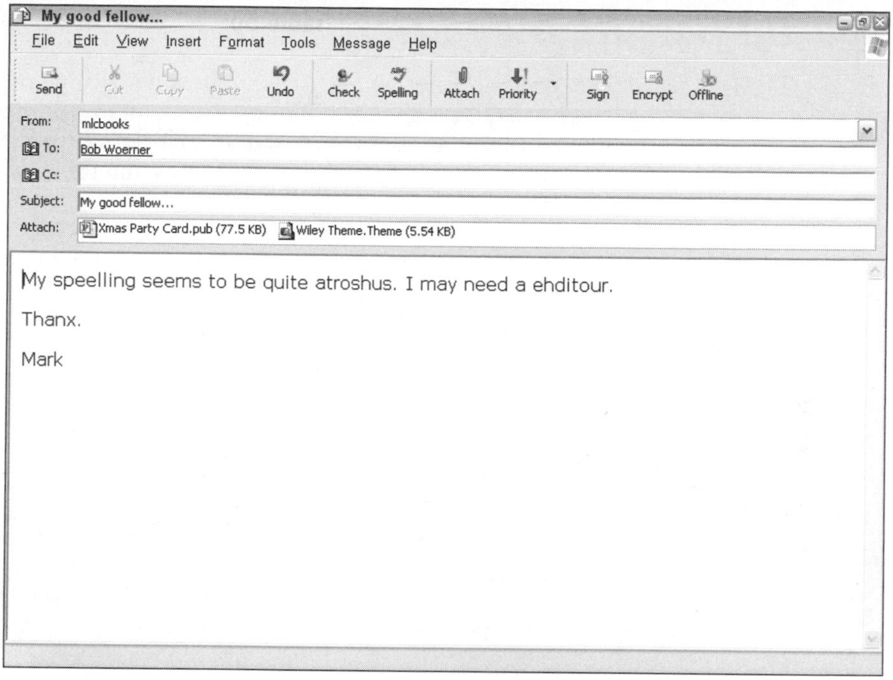

My good fellow...

| File | Edit | View | Insert | Format | Tools | Message | Help |

Send | Cut | Copy | Paste | Undo | Check | Spelling | Attach | Priority | Sign | Encrypt | Offline

From: mlcbooks
To: Bob Woerner
Cc:
Subject: My good fellow...
Attach: Xmas Party Card.pub (77.5 KB)   Wiley Theme.Theme (5.54 KB)

My speelling seems to be quite atroshus. I may need a ehditour.

Thanx.

Mark

Figure 5-14:
An attached
file is
displayed
in the
message
header.

When you receive an e-mail message with an attachment, a paper clip icon is displayed next to the message entry in the Message pane. To download an attachment from an incoming message, right-click the file attachment in the header and then choose Save As to select a spot on your system where the file will be stored. (From within the Message window, right-click the attachment in the Attach box and then choose Save As from the pop-up menu that appears.)

You might be wondering why folks don't use file attachments for everything instead of resorting to those silly CD-ROMs for big file transfers. Well, it takes a very long time to download a big file over a dialup connection, so all ISPs put a limit on the size of an individual message and all its attachments. This limit usually rejects any message over 1 or 2MB in total size. (The exact limit is determined by both your Internet e-mail server and the recipient's e-mail server.) Therefore, I recommend limiting your total attachment size to 1MB or less. It's easy to tell when your attachments are too doggone big: Either your ISP's mail server or the recipient's mail server will send you an error message that your original e-mail is undeliverable.

Spam: 1 Hate It! Truly 1 Do!

Is there anyone on the planet who'll actually *open* a message promising instant hair regrowth? Or a once-in-a-lifetime investment opportunity? Or some sort of illicit physical offer that you neither want nor need? Why does junk mail exist? Aren't these spam-slingers just wasting their time?

Good questions, all . . . but for some reason, junk mail continues to accumulate on your Internet doorstep. Not even the government can stop it — something about that pesky Bill of Rights — but you can sure doggone reduce the flow of spam to a trickle by using the mail-blocking feature within Outlook Express.

When you receive a junk mail message from someone, click it in the Message pane list and then choose Message⇨Block Sender. Outlook Express displays the confirmation dialog box that you see in Figure 5-15. If you want to sweep the active folder clean of every trace of the sender, click Yes; to leave this message and any others in the active folder, click No.

Figure 5-15: We won't be getting any more mail from this "entrepreneur."

Use this method to block all messages from a specific e-mail address. Any mail that you receive from that source will now be dumped directly into your Deleted Items folder. (You can still look at it there, of course, just to verify that the proper trash was picked up.)

However, nefarious junk mail villains can still get around a blocked sender list by changing their sending address: For example, `imajerk@justan example.com` suddenly becomes `hahastillhere@justanexample.com` or something similar. Does this mean that you have to continue to suffer?

Not in the least, good Internet citizen! You can also block an entire *domain name,* which is the part of an e-mail address that follows the @ sign, like `bonehead@spamtwit.com`. That way, no matter what silly username they try to use, Outlook Express will still throw anything that they send straight into the trash. To block an entire domain name, first add a sender to the blocked sender list by using the process that I outline above and then follow these steps to knock them out completely:

1. **Choose Tools⇨Message Rules and then click Blocked Senders List.**

   Outlook Express displays the Message Rules dialog box that you see in Figure 5-16.

Book III
Chapter 5

**Harnessing
Your E-Mail**

Figure 5-16:
We're
comin'
for you,
spammer . . .

2. **Click the address of the offending twit whom you want to completely can.**

   Boy howdy, do I hate spammers, or what? *Yes, indeed I do.*

3. **Click the Modify button.**

   You'll see the Edit Sender dialog box, as shown in Figure 5-17.

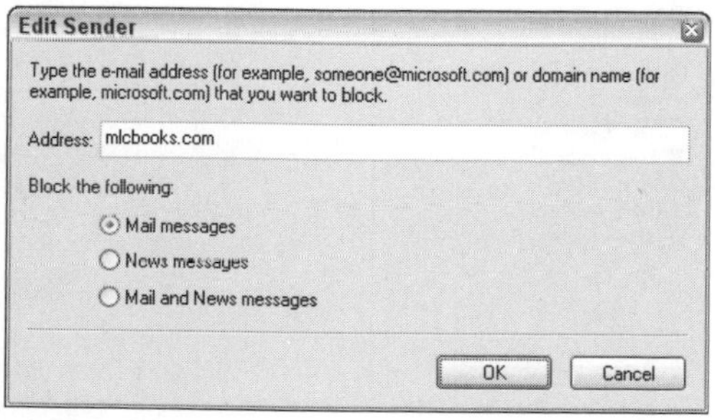

Figure 5-17:
Edit a
blocked
address to
wipe out
anything
from an
entire
domain.

4. **Click in the Address field and delete everything in front of and including the @ sign so that the only thing left is the domain name (such as** `mlcbooks.com`**).**

By the way, please don't *really* block `mlcbooks.com`. You can be sure that I'll never distribute unsolicited mail to *anyone*.

5. **Click OK and then click OK again to return to the Outlook Express window.**

You can add an address or an entire domain to your blocked list by accident. To return that address or domain to good standing, display the Message Rules dialog box again, click the address in the blocked list, and then click Remove.

If you get a message from an obvious spam tycoon who includes a line about how you can oh-so-conveniently "unsubscribe" from his mailing list, don't do it! This is a scam that's designed to verify that your e-mail address is valid; if you unsubscribe, you'll end up with a regular tidal wave of junk mail.

Working with the Address Book

The Contacts list in Outlook Express is usually all most folks will need for 99 percent of their workday. I explain earlier in this chapter how you can add contacts simply by right-clicking the author's e-mail address in a message; that's the most common action that you'll take.

However, you can reach the Address Book proper from within Outlook Express. Just click the Addresses button on the toolbar, and the Address Book window appears (behold Figure 5-18).

Figure 5-18:
Open the Address Book from within Outlook Express.

From this window, you can

✦ **Create a new contact:** Click the New button on the toolbar and then choose New Contact (or just press Ctrl+N); the Address Book displays that contact's Properties dialog box, like you see in Figure 5-19. Click in each field that you need to complete to add the contact's information. To save your new contact, click OK.

✦ **Edit an existing contact:** Click the contact that you want to edit. Then click Properties from the toolbar to display that contact's Properties dialog box, which includes all the fields that you originally saw when you created the contact. You can click in any field to either change existing data or add new information. To save your changes, click OK.

✦ **Send an e-mail message:** Select a contact, click the Action button on the toolbar, and then click Send Mail. You'll be returned to the Outlook Express window, where you'll find a brand-new New Message window (already addressed to the contact, naturally).

✦ **Make a voice phone call:** If your modem has a telephone connected to it, you can use your modem as an auto-dialer to place a call to the contact. (After you hear the phone ringing, pick up the handset on the phone, and you're in business.) Select a contact, click the Action button, and then click Dial. The Address Book displays the New Call dialog box that you see in Figure 5-20, where you can tweak any dialing properties or select from multiple telephone numbers stored for the contact. When you're ready to dial, click the Call button.

**Book III
Chapter 5**

**Harnessing
Your E-Mail**

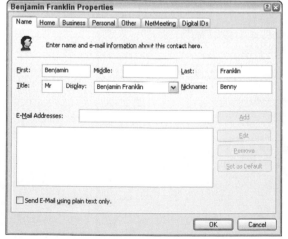

Figure 5-19:
Adding a
new contact
from the
Address
Book.

✦ **Create groups:** A *group* is a collection of individual e-mail addresses that you can refer to as a category, like your bridge club or your department within your company. After you create a group, you can address e-mail messages to all group members easily without messing with carbon copies. Press Ctrl+G or choose New⇨Group from the toolbar to display the Group Properties dialog box shown in Figure 5-21. Type a name for the group and then click the Select Members button to add members from your Address Book. Click Close, and you'll see that the group entry appears in the folder tree at the left of the Address Book window.

✦ **Import contact data:** You can import vCard information from others. A *vCard* is a small text file that contains all the contact information for one or more people in a standard format that you can pass around to others like a *v*irtual business *Card*. (Cute, eh?) Address Book can also import contacts stored in another Address Book file (which end in the .wab extension). To import, choose File⇨Import and then choose the file type that you want to read from the pop-up menu. Address Book will prompt you for the location of the import file.

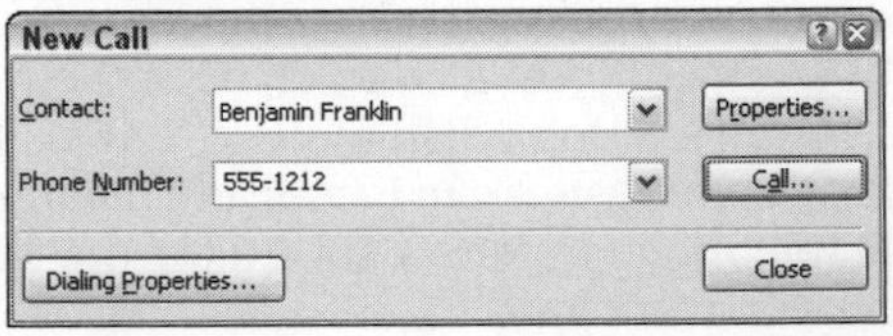

Figure 5-20: Preparing to use my modem as an auto-dialer.

Figure 5-21: Creating an Address Book group.

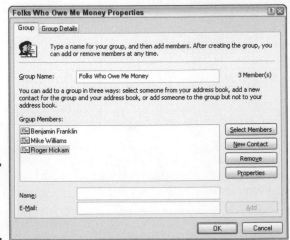

✦ **Export a vCard file:** To export a single contact in vCard format, first select the contact record that you want to export and then choose File➪Export. From the pop-up menu that appears, choose Business Card (vCard), type a filename, and then navigate to the spot where you want to save the file. Click Save to create the vCard file, which you can then send as an attachment to an e-mail message or place on your Web site for others to download.

"Hey, Who Are You Now?"

From time to time, you might find that you need to be someone else on the Internet — at least, in your e-mail. For example, you might use your real name for personal e-mail that you send from the office, but you might also represent your company (as a technical support representative, for example). Microsoft calls these different manifestations *identities*.

Luckily, Outlook Express can help you with your multiple personality needs — rather frightening, I admit, but Microsoft has always been thorough in designing applications! To create an alternate identity within Outlook Express, follow these steps:

1. **Choose File➪Identities and then click Add New Identity, which opens the dialog box that you see in Figure 5-22.**

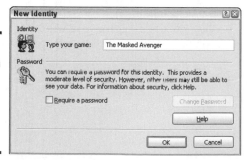

Figure 5-22: Yes, you can become the Masked Avenger . . . in e-mail, anyway.

2. **Type a descriptive name for this identity and decide whether you want to password-protect it. If you do need the protection, enable the Require a Password check box and then click the Change Password button to set the password. Finally, click OK to continue.**

3. **Outlook Express prompts you to determine whether you want to switch to your new identity immediately. Click Yes to switch or click No to keep your current identity.**

No matter whether you click Yes or No, you're deposited at the Manage Identities dialog box (yup, in Figure 5-23).

**Book III
Chapter 5**

**Harnessing
Your E-Mail**

Figure 5-23:
Hey, wait a
second; *I'm*
the Masked
Avenger.

4. **From this dialog box, you can add more identities, modify an existing identity, and delete an identity.**

   If you work quite a bit with multiple identities — I won't ask — you can specify which identity to use throughout Windows XP when you run an application (and which identity to use as your default).

5. **Click Close to return to Outlook Express.**

After you establish your new identity, you can switch to it at any time within Outlook Express. Choose File⇨Switch Identities to display the dialog box that you see in Figure 5-24. Click the identity that you want to assume (and enter the password if necessary) and then click OK to become — well — someone else, I guess.

Figure 5-24:
Switching to
another
identity in
Outlook
Express.

Chapter 6: Instant Messaging Done Right

In This Chapter

✔ Comparing Messenger with the competition

✔ Running Windows Messenger

✔ Setting your Messenger configuration

✔ Building a Messenger contact list

✔ Chatting with others

✔ Changing your Messenger status

✔ Blocking unwanted communications

The ability to communicate with someone else halfway across the globe is nothing new. Just ask Benjamin Franklin, who would tell you that the U.S. Postal Service was a civilized and modern convenience. And the ability to communicate by typing to someone via your computer? Heck, any SYSOP (System Operator) like myself who was worth the title offered real-time chatting between users on the Bulletin Board Systems (BBSes) that were so popular in the '80s and '90s before the arrival of the Internet.

Ah, but *combine* the two — real-time chatting over the Internet among an entire group of people — and you have something really amazing. In this chapter, I show you how to use Windows Messenger to communicate in style (as long as you have an Internet connection, that is).

Selecting a Chat Client

Although Windows Messenger is included in Windows XP, you have other choices for your instant messaging application. And before I jump into Messenger, I'd like to mention the competition (just in case you like choices).

Like Windows Messenger, both of these programs display chat messages on your screen within a few seconds after they're sent, which is the definition of instant messaging. You'll also find universal support for transferring files and images while you're chatting, adding icons and symbols (called *emoticons* or *smileys*), text formatting, and a list of your favorite people that you can use to check who's online. However, note this downside: At the time of this writing, each different application has a completely separate membership group, so if you're using AOL Instant Messenger (AIM), you can't communicate with someone using Windows Messenger or I Seek You (ICQ). Such is the Tower of Babel (or is that *Babble?*) that results from proprietary software developers. (Sigh.)

AIM

AOL Instant Messenger (or AIM, as it's popularly known) is the free messaging application distributed by America Online. And, to debunk a popular myth, you don't have to be a member of America Online to use AIM.

AIM works fine in all popular flavors of Windows. Its features include

✦ **Skins** that you can apply to customize the appearance of your AIM window

✦ **Integration with Outlook Express**, where you can display your Buddy List and send messages from within Outlook Express

✦ **Voice support** for honest-to-goodness verbal communication (among AIM members with the right hardware)

✦ **A typing indicator** that appears to show you that someone else is preparing a message to you (a great boon for those One-Finger Wonder [OFW] typists)

✦ **A commercial enterprise system** that allows offices to use AIM (along with providing network administrators a method of controlling it)

In order to use AIM, you have to set up a screen name — think *register* — but it's a simple process, and AOL won't hound you to join. (At least AOL hasn't hounded me.) You can download the program from www.aim.com.

ICQ

The other well-known alternative to Messenger is ICQ — short for *I Seek You* (which I've always felt is stretching the mechanics of an acronym about as far as possible). You can download the free version from www.icq.com. ICQ 5 (which doesn't offer the advanced features of ICQ Pro, like e-mail checking and file transfers) runs fine in Windows 98 or later.

You'll find that ICQ, one of the first instant messaging programs to reach the public, offers a number of very powerful options as well:

✦ **The ability to send messages** to cell phones and wireless pagers

✦ **Internet (or IP) telephony,** where ICQ members can talk from their PC to an honest-to-goodness standard telephone

✦ **Peer-to-peer applications** such as games

✦ **A chat history feature** that saves all that important dialog for later perusal

✦ **Multilingual support** so that you can type to friends in any language supported within Windows

ICQ assigns you a unique user number when you join; the number acts as your ID number (much like your unique e-mail address), and others can connect to you by using your user number.

Running Windows Messenger

If you decide to follow The Gates Way and use Windows Messenger, you can also use MSN Messenger, which offers improved functionality and is tied closely to Microsoft's MSN Web site. Depending on your installation of Windows XP, you'll either be using Windows Messenger version 4.7 (which comes with Windows XP, as shown in Figure 6-1) or version 7.0 of MSN Messenger (which you can download and install separately from www. msn.com). Since I'm a big believer in covering defaults when it comes to Microsoft software, this chapter will focus on Windows Messenger — luckily, however, most of the material you'll find here also applies to MSN Messenger. (Hurrah!)

If you're already using Microsoft's Hotmail service for Web-based e-mail, Messenger not only automatically uses your Hotmail ID, but it also keeps you updated in the Messenger window with the number of unread Hotmail messages. To open Internet Explorer and read any unread mail, just click the New E-Mail Message(s) link in the Messenger window.

Here are two ways to access the Messenger window:

✦ **From the Start menu:** Choose Start➪All Programs➪Windows Messenger.

✦ **From the taskbar icon:** If you see a Messenger icon in the notification area of the taskbar (which looks like a little round-headed person), double-click it. (Clicking the Messenger icon once displays a menu with common Messenger commands, so it's not really necessary to double-click to send a message.)

If you haven't set up a Microsoft .NET Passport yet, you'll have to do so before you can use Messenger. Click the Click Here to Sign In link to run the Passport Wizard, which will lead you through the sign-in process. The *.NET Passport* is a sort of common "universal" username and password that can act as your logon for all sorts of Microsoft Web sites and online services.

Book III
Chapter 6

Instant Messaging
Done Right

Figure 6-1:
The
Windows
Messenger
window.

Configuring Windows Messenger

The default configuration settings for Messenger will fly straight for just about everyone, but here are a handful that I'd like to specifically cover just in case you'd like to fine-tune how the program works. From the Windows Messenger 4.7 window, choose Tools⇨Options to display the Options dialog box that you see in Figure 6-2.

On the Personal tab:

✦ **My Display Name:** Here you can change the name that Messenger displays when you chat.

✦ **My Public Profile:** Click the Edit Profile button to change your MSN user profile that others can display or match when using the Member search feature.

Figure 6-2:
Set your
preferences
within
Messenger.

✦ **My Status:** If you don't type a message or use the Messenger window for a specified number of minutes, your account is listed as Away within the Messenger system, and your friends will know that you're not immediately available. However, you can alter the inactivity delay period or even disable the check box altogether and always be listed with the Online status. Personally, I like the five-minute default value for the Away feature.

From this tab, you can also format message text by selecting the font to use in your messages and enabling or disabling emoticons/smileys.

On the Privacy tab:

Here you can determine who has access to you online by using the Allow and Block Lists (which I cover later in this chapter). You can also view which Messenger members have added you to their contact lists and also force Messenger to prompt you for your password when you check your Hotmail messages.

On the Preferences tab:

✦ **Sign In:** Use these options to configure whether Messenger starts automatically when Windows XP boots and whether the program should sign in automatically whenever your PC is connected to the Internet.

✦ **Alerts:** From here, you can specify when you want Messenger to alert you of specific events, like when a person on your contact list comes online or if you receive e-mail on your Hotmail account. I recommend leaving the Display Alerts When a Message Is Received check box enabled so you'll know that you have a new message even when you're knee-deep in an Excel worksheet or a Word document.

Feel free to modify any of the configuration settings as you like, but remember that you can exit without saving any changes to the Messenger options by clicking the Cancel button (just in case you decide that you'd rather back out).

Keeping Track of Friends and Family

Windows Messenger allows you to keep a *contact list,* which is essentially a simple address book that you can use to display the online/inactive/not online status of your friends and family. The contact list appears within the Messenger window, grouped by the current status of its members.

To add a contact to Messenger by using the person's e-mail address or a Microsoft Passport sign-in name, follow these steps:

1. **Click the Add a Contact button in the Messenger window, which displays the Add a Contact Wizard that you see in Figure 6-3.**

Figure 6-3:
Add a
contact via
a sign-in
name or
e-mail
address.

2. **Select the By E-Mail Address or Sign-in Name radio button and then click Next.**

3. **In the following wizard window, type the person's e-mail address into the text box and then click Next.**

   If Messenger can't locate that MSN member's account, you can send a message to the person telling them you'd like them to join MSN so that you can jaw with them.

4. **If the person's account is found, Messenger adds the person to your contact list.**

5. **Click Finish to exit the wizard.**

To add a contact by using your Address Book, follow these steps:

1. **Click the Add a Contact button in the Messenger window.**

2. **Select the Search For a Contact radio button and then click Next.**

   The wizard displays the search criteria shown in Figure 6-4.

Figure 6-4:
Search for a
contact
from your
Address
Book.

**Book III
Chapter 6**

Instant Messaging
Done Right

3. **Click the Search For This Person At drop-down list box and click Address Book On This Computer.**

4. **Type the person's first name and last name into the appropriate boxes and then click Next.**

5. **Click (highlight) the name that you want to add and then click Next.**

6. **Click (highlight) the name that you want to add and then click Next.**

   On this last wizard screen, you can choose to send an e-mail message to the person stating that you want to chat with this person via Messenger, offering information on how to install it.

7. **Click Finish to exit the wizard.**

To remove a person from your contact list, click the entry once to highlight it in your list and then press Delete. Messenger will prompt you for confirmation before removing the contact.

To share your contact list with others — or to copy your work contact list to Messenger on your home PC — choose File➪Save Contact List. After you save the file to disk and transfer it to the other PC, choose File➪Import Contacts from a Saved File.

Even though you add someone to your contact list, you're still not quite home free. The person whom you added sees a dialog box prompting for permission to allow you to chat — and this new contact can also block you from seeing and contacting him/her. This precaution makes it tough for lounge lizards (and worse) to cruise through Messenger looking for new victims.

To make more room for a longer contact list, choose Tools➪Show Actions Pane to toggle it off. Remember that you can still reach all the same actions from either the Actions menu or by right-clicking a name in the contact list.

Chatting with Your Brethren

After you successfully add folks to your contact list, you're ready to party! Follow these steps to initiate a chat session:

1. **Double-click any name that appears in the Online section of the contact list.**

   Double-clicking a name in the Not Online section automatically creates a new e-mail message because you're obviously not going to be able to chat with that person in real-time if they aren't online at the moment.

   Messenger displays the Conversation window that you see in Figure 6-5.

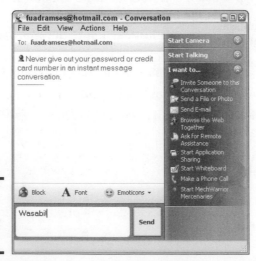

Figure 6-5: Begin a Messenger chat here.

To send a message from the menu system, choose Actions⇨Send an Instant Message. You can also right-click any name in your contact list and choose the same actions from the pop-up menu that appears.

2. **Click in the bottom text box and type your message.**

3. **To insert an emoticon at the current cursor position in the text box, click the Emoticons drop-down list (see Figure 6-6) and then click the desired symbol.**

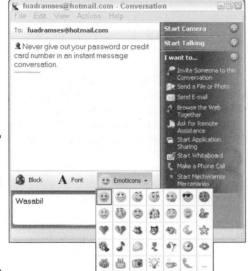

Figure 6-6: You need just the right emoticon (technically referred to as a smiley face).

Book III
Chapter 6

Instant Messaging
Done Right

4. **To change your message font attributes, click the Font button to display the dialog box shown in Figure 6-7.**

From here, you can choose a different font, change the size and color of your text, or add italic and bold attributes. Click OK to return to the Messenger window.

5. **When your message is ready to send, press Enter or click the Send button.**

You can also send a message to the selected name in your contact list by clicking the Send an Instant Message button at the bottom of the Messenger window.

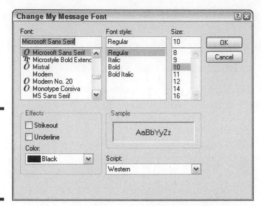

Figure 6-7:
Change the
font used in
your text
messages.

You're not limited to a single person when you chat. Click the Invite Someone to This Conversation button (under the I Want To heading), and Messenger prompts you for the name of the contact whom you want to invite into your current conversation. Click OK to send the invitation. Again, the other party will have the chance to decline if he/she doesn't like the crowd that you're seeing.

Like ICQ, Messenger also provides support for the following (either as buttons under the I Want To heading, or as commands on the Actions menu):

✦ **Video:** Click the Start Camera button to use your Web camera to send video to the other person. (Naturally, this works best over a broadband connection.)

✦ **Audio:** If you and the other person have microphones (or, preferably, headsets) set up within Windows XP, you can actually talk to one another directly. Click the Start Talking button, and Messenger will attempt to set up an audio conversation.

✦ **Sending files:** To send a file or image to the other person, click the Send a File or Photo button. Messenger displays the familiar Open dialog box, where you can select the desired file. *Note:* The person on the receiving end must approve the transfer before it will begin.

✦ **Linked browsing:** This is a really neat feature. Click the Browse the Web Together button, and you both simultaneously see the same Web pages! Either of you can click links, making it a neat way to demonstrate things or even virtually shop together. (Unfortunately, both parties must be subscribing MSN 8 members, or this feature won't work.)

✦ **Interacting using applications:** You can run the Microsoft Whiteboard application to draw on a shared virtual whiteboard.

✦ **Phone calls:** If you've signed up with an Internet telephony provider, click the Make a Phone Call button. This service allows you to use a headset connected to your PC to make a call to anyone over his telephone. (Again, this isn't a free service.)

✦ **Launching multiplayer games:** If Messenger recognizes a Microsoft game with multiplayer support on your hard drive, you can start a multiplayer game. For example, I use this feature to start a multiplayer game of MechWarrior Mercenaries.

Before you decide to use the Ask for Remote Assistance feature, make doggone sure that you're talking to a reliable person whom you know and trust — not someone who happens to be sitting at his keyboard — and *definitely not a party that you've just met!* Remember, Remote Assistance allows the other person to directly manipulate your copy of Windows XP, and nasty (I mean *truly* nasty) things can happen at the hands of an ill-meaning (or just inexperienced) person.

If you want to view the profile information associated with a Messenger member, right-click her name within your contact list and then click View Profile; this can include the person's e-mail address and any personal information that she's specified as visible.

To leave a chat, you simply close the Conversation window.

**Book III
Chapter 6**

**Instant Messaging
Done Right**

Selecting a Status

As I mention earlier in this chapter, Windows Messenger will automatically change your status to Away if you don't use Messenger for five minutes.

However, you can change your status at any time, which is a good idea if you step away from your PC for a soda. When you change your status, Messenger instantly updates your icon in other's contact lists.

To change your status, click the My Status drop-down list box at the top of the Messenger window and then choose the desired status (as shown in Figure 6-8). Alternatively, you can choose File⇨My Status and then click the status that you want from the pop-up menu that appears.

To change your status so that you look like you're completely offline, you can choose Appear Offline, which actually moves you to the Not Online section of the contact list.

Figure 6-8:
Changing
your status
is a cinch.

Squelching the Unwelcome Few

From time to time, you'll encounter folks whom you simply would rather not communicate with at all. Sorry, but even Microsoft can't produce a program that can turn away the common Internet Turkey. Luckily, you can manually take care of turkeys in Messenger (when you recognize 'em for what they are, anyway).

✦ **From the contact list:** If you're mad at an ill-mannered individual — who also happens to be in your contact list — you can block any further communication with them by right-clicking that name in your list and then choosing Block from the pop-up menu that appears.

✦ **From the Conversation window:** Click the Block button from within the Conversation window. If you're chatting with multiple folks, you can click the name of the offending person and then click Block to screen out just that person. To unblock the person, click the blocked name again to select it and then click the Unblock button (which toggles between Block and Unblock.)

A blocked name appears with a red slash mark in your contact list. However, you can unblock the person if you have a change of heart by right-clicking the blocked name and then choosing Unblock from the pop-up menu that appears.

Book IV

Microsoft Works

The 5th Wave   By Rich Tennant

"It's a free starter disk for AOL."

Contents at a Glance

Chapter 1: An Overview of Works

1 like Microsoft Works.

It's a guilty feeling — a little like kicking back with a marathon of *Gilligan's Island, Petticoat Junction,* or *The Love Boat.* We all know that Microsoft Office 2003 is the most popular and powerful application suite on the planet — but deep down inside, doesn't everyone like the underdog, like its little brother, Works 8? For many PC owners who don't need complex and expensive features (like all those weird Excel formulas and 500 different PowerPoint business templates), Works fits the bill quite nicely, thank you!

In this chapter, I introduce you to the surprising stuff in "that program I got free with my PC," as well as how to get help throughout the program. After you're done here, you'll have an overview of what Works 8 can do, and you'll be ready to delve into the following chapters in this mini-book — each takes an in-depth look at one of the major applications in Works. (Online, you'll find the headquarters for Works at `www.microsoft.com/products/works/default.asp`.)

Oh, and forget about the guilt. Works is a classic, just like *The Beverly Hillbillies.*

What Can 1 Do with Works?

Works 8 is a *productivity suite* — in other words, a number of discrete applications that share data and use the same general commands and much of the same menu system. With Works, you can take care of all these tasks in a single sitting:

✦ Edit and print your résumé in the Word Processor

✦ Pare those unnecessary expenses from your home budget with the Spreadsheet

◆ Create a list of chores that need doing around the house with the Organizer

Hopefully, you can avoid this last particular set of tasks. Anyway, in this section, I provide a description of each of the applications that are packed into Works.

Word processing

Figure 1-1 illustrates the Microsoft Works Word Processor, which can handle your text documents with aplomb.

The high points of the Word Processor include these features:

◆ Embedded Web hyperlinks, database fields, and watermarks

◆ Mail Merge and label printing support with the Works Database

◆ Linked images, spreadsheets, charts, and tables that can be automatically updated

◆ Templates and projects for all sorts of printing projects, such as brochures, greeting cards, newsletters, and flyers

◆ Mail Merge support with the Works Database (for more on this, see the section entitled "Databases" later in this chapter)

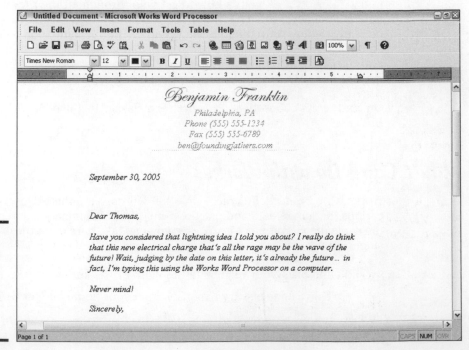

Figure 1-1:
The Works Word Processor and a typical project.

✦ A thesaurus, a spell checker, and a grammar checker

✦ The same AutoCorrect feature found in Word, which corrects the words that you commonly misspell or omit

✦ Graphics produced by the WordArt font editor and a clip art library

If you happen to have any Word documents lying around your hard drive that need to be opened, the Works Word Processor can use them. (As Microsoft reminds us, however, Word contains advanced features that Works doesn't, so some features that appear in your Word document won't work in Works.)

Spreadsheets

Spreadsheets don't rank up there with pizza and computer games in popularity with home PC owners, but when you need to view figures and relationships between numbers in an easy-to-comprehend fashion, you'll be glad that Works includes the Spreadsheet application, as shown in Figure 1-2. Works Spreadsheet can open documents created with Excel without batting an eyelash.

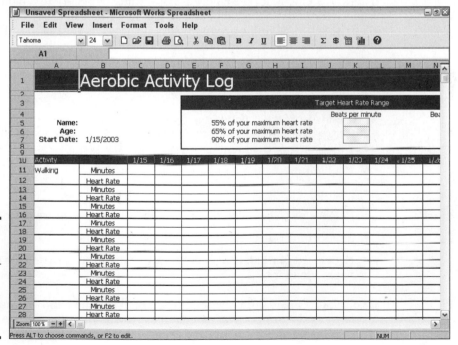

Figure 1-2: It looks like Excel Lite — boy, now isn't *that* a disturbing thought?!

Outstanding features of the Works Spreadsheet include

✦ Automatic wizards to help you create lists and charts

✦ AutoFormat, which can apply a preset formatting template to a selected area

✦ Functions and formulas for complex calculations

✦ The Easy Calc Formula Creation Wizard

✦ The ability to manipulate named cells and groups

✦ Header and footer support

✦ Borders and shading for professional-looking printed spreadsheets

Everyone knows that spreadsheets make great tools for budgeting and income forecasting, but I can vouch for the ability of a spreadsheet to help organize a soccer team as well.

Calendar

The Works Calendar (see Figure 1-3) is a thing of beauty to anyone who wants to organize a busy digital lifestyle. Just think, actually being able to plan the rest of your life around board meetings, golf games, and those endless socialite parties. (Yeah, right — try band practice, 30-minute lunch [cough] "hours," and Recycle Pickup Day.) Regardless of your high-society standing, Calendar will likely become an indispensable application for you within a few weeks.

The best features in Calendar include

✦ Event and appointment scheduling

✦ Configurable reminders for upcoming events

✦ Multiple calendar views

✦ Categories to help you organize your events and information

✦ Support for repeating events and appointments

✦ HyperText Markup Language (HTML) calendar exporting for posting your calendar to a Web site

If you share calendar data with others, you'll also be happy to know that Works Calendar supports *vCalendar* files (the standard import/export format for exchanging appointments and events between calendar programs) — trade and swap your calendar with your friends. What fun!

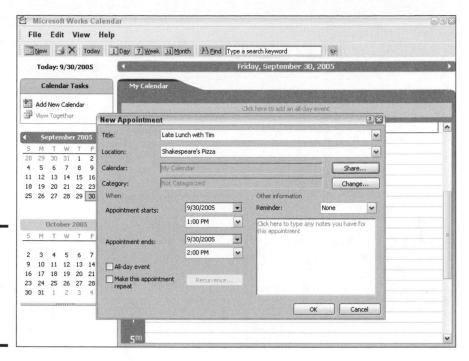

Figure 1-3:
Works
Calendar
is no-
nonsense
and easy
to use.

To Dos

Whoa, Nellie, that almost looks like *To DOS* — nope, I'm not trying to drive
you back to the days before Windows! Figure 1-4 captures the essence of the
To Do list. On this screen, everything is organized by project — what you're
working on and when everything is due. Again, this is classic stuff — suitable
for business or personal use, too.

In fact, Works can automatically generate a To Do list according to the type
of project or event that you're planning. For example, the Plan a Party project automatically includes tasks and templates such as invitations, maps, a
guest list, and even thank-you cards. (Too bad your PC can't help you clean
up afterwards.)

After you complete your To Do list, you can associate different types of documents with it — perhaps you've got a great invitation already prepared —
and you can "connect" that document on your hard drive with the Invitation
To Do item. (When the invitation needs printing, click that To Do item to
open the invitation document and print it; then mark the To Do item as completed.) You can print your task list, import appointments into Calendar,
or even generate a Web page with your schedule! Microsoft got it right with
this one.

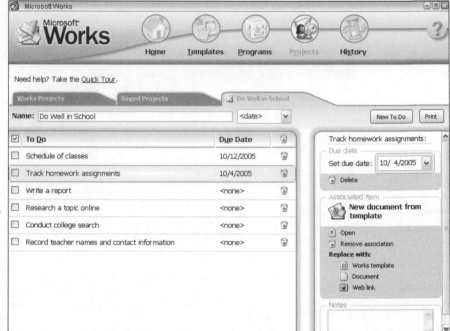

Figure 1-4:
Keep everything on schedule with the Project screen.

Databases

Last (but certainly never, never least) is the Works Database, which is the repository for all your information — everything from the folks on your Christmas list to the ingredients in your fudge brownie recipe. Figure 1-5 illustrates the Works Database.

Works Database includes all sorts of fun features:

✦ An automated ReportCreator for building custom reports based on the data that you specify

✦ A form view and form designer

✦ A list view for fast data entry and editing

✦ Data security through a write-protect mode

✦ Field formatting with automatic default values for each field

✦ Filters that you can create to display only certain records

Naturally, the Database application works in league with all the other Works programs to share your data seamlessly wherever it's needed. In plain English, that means that you'll never type your address again (no matter whether you're writing a letter, creating a bill planner, or creating an appointment with your dentist).

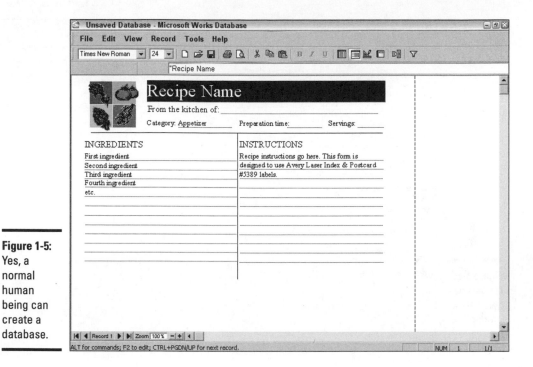

Figure 1-5:
Yes, a normal human being can create a database.

Introducing the Task Launcher

"Mark, these combined applications and this seamless cooperation are just plain *sassy* — but what holds all this stuff together? Where do I start?"

The answer, good reader, is the Works Task Launcher, as shown in Figure 1-6. Consider this your combination Works entryway/desktop alternative/project launching pad. From the Task Launcher, you can

+ Open projects that you've already created

+ Create a new blank project or open a pre-designed project supplied with Works (which opens the corresponding To Do list)

+ Check or edit today's (or any day's) appointments

+ Launch any of the separate applications that I discuss in earlier sections of this chapter

+ Load a specific task document, such as a financial worksheet or a photo frame

+ Synchronize a Palm Pilot or a Pocket PC with data from Works

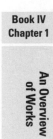

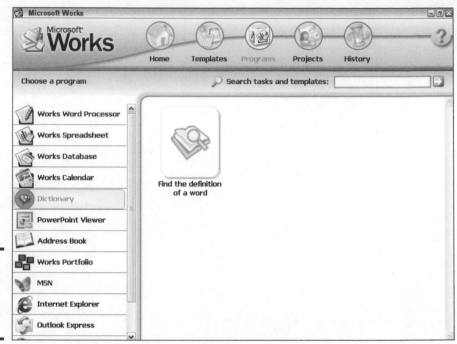

Figure 1-6:
It all starts
here — the
Works Task
Launcher.

✦ Run Outlook Express or Internet Explorer

✦ Display a history of the documents that you've worked on

After you're comfortable with Works, I recommend leaving the Task
Launcher running the entire day. Believe me; you'll be using it constantly.

Displaying Help within Works

To take full advantage of Works, you need to know about its comprehensive
Help system. A program this size and with this many features can rapidly
turn into a headache without the right information and guidance. Luckily,
Microsoft has provided Works with a great context-sensitive Help system
(see Figure 1-7).

To activate help in Works, use one of the following methods:

✦ **Click the question mark icon,** which appears in various places throughout Works (such as the menu bar and the Help pane)

✦ **Press F1**

✦ **Click any of the Quick Tours hyperlinks** anywhere in Works

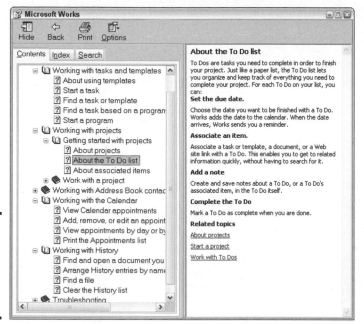

Figure 1-7:
Discover
how to look
for help in
all the right
places.

If you're displaying the Help system using a task pane within an application, you can ask the Help system a specific question by typing it into the Answer Wizard text box and then clicking the Search button. In order for this feature to work, keep your questions as short and as specific as possible.

If you're displaying the Help system within the Works Task Launcher, you can search for a specific topic by clicking the Search tab and entering at least one keyword — click the List Topics button to display the matching topics. You can also search through Works Help using an index view, or simply display the top-level Table of Contents to locate a topic.

If the Help pane displays an underlined hyperlink that you'd like to see, click it just like you'd click an underlined Web link in Internet Explorer. Click Print from the Help system button bar to print the current Help topic.

**Book IV
Chapter 1**

**An Overview
of Works**

Chapter 2: Word Processing in Works

In This Chapter

✔ Running the Works Word Processor

✔ Introducing the word processing window

✔ Selecting and editing text

✔ Finding and replacing text

✔ Formatting text and paragraphs

✔ Formatting bulleted and numbered lists

✔ Inserting graphics

✔ Checking your spelling

✔ Printing your documents

The Works Word Processor is a faithful companion — not quite as fast or as functional as that thoroughbred of word processing, Microsoft Word 2003, but it does come from the same lineage, and you'll find lite versions of many of the same features hanging out under the Word Processor's menu system. Because Works is often shipped as standard equipment with Windows XP Home Edition, you might have had it installed on your PC for months, tucked away in a corner.

Let this chapter be your guide to the basics of the Word Processor. Discover here how to type, select, and edit text; how to format your document; add graphics; search for and replace text; and much more. Oh, and don't forget the projects that you can open from the Works Task Launcher. They can provide you with a foundation for many a common document, so you can get right to work composing your prose.

Running the Word Processor

First things first — you can run the Works Word Processor in the following ways:

✦ Double-click the Works shortcut on your desktop to run the Task Launcher and then click the Word Processor in the Quick Launch bar.

(You can also click the Programs toolbar button to display all of the Works applications.)

✦ Double-click a Works Word Processor document within Windows Explorer or on your desktop.

✦ Choose Start (or press a Windows key, if your keyboard is so equipped) and then choose Programs➪Microsoft Works➪Microsoft Works Word Processor.

Your Word Processing Tools

The Works Word Processor main window appears in Figure 2-1. Naturally, it has many similarities to its elder brother Microsoft Word, but you'll notice a number of important differences as well.

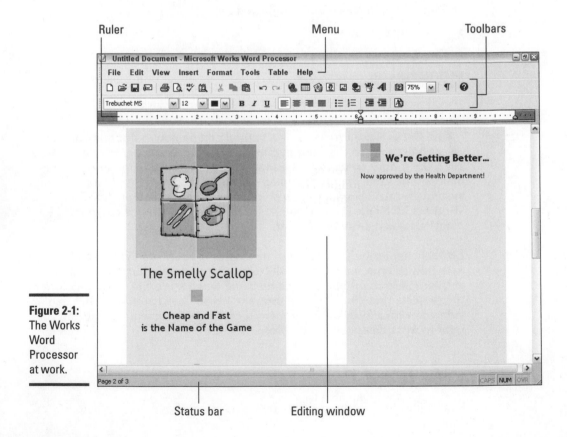

Figure 2-1:
The Works
Word
Processor
at work.

The major controls include

✦ **The menu:** Familiar and functional, the menu system sports the usual suspects.

✦ **The toolbars:** Far simpler than the system in Word, the Works Word Processor has only two toolbars (Standard and Formatting). Click a toolbar button to perform the same task as the corresponding command on the menu system. Unlike in Word, however, these buttons can't be added or removed, and these toolbars can't be relocated. You can, however, toggle the display of large toolbar icons by choosing View➪Toolbars➪ Large Icons. (If the window is too small to display all the toolbar icons, click the small, double-arrow icon pointing to the right at the end of a toolbar to choose from the buttons that didn't fit.)

To make more room in the editing window, you can toggle the display of the Standard or Formatting toolbars. Just choose View➪Toolbars and then click a specific toolbar in the menu to toggle it off or on.

Each menu item that's replicated on the toolbars carries the icon next to it, so you can quickly locate the toolbar button that performs the same action as a particular menu command.

✦ **The editing window:** This section of the window represents your virtual page, in which you type your text and add graphics and tables.

✦ **The ruler:** A very versatile control, the ruler can be used to set tabs, margins, and indents . . . or you can use it to gauge page dimensions. (Go figure.)

✦ **The status bar:** You can use the Word Processor status bar to track your current page number as well as to immediately tell the status of your Caps Lock key, Num Lock key, and insert/overwrite mode.

Typing Text

In this program — as with any word processor — the *insertion cursor* (which looks like a blinking bar) indicates where new text and graphics will appear. You can relocate the insertion cursor by clicking the I-beam-shaped mouse pointer in the desired spot; from the keyboard, use the movement keys provided in Table 2-1.

By default, the Works Word Processor enters text in Insert mode, in which new characters are inserted at the cursor point, pushing existing characters to the right. You can also toggle into Overwrite mode by pressing the Insert key; in *Overwrite mode,* new characters that you type overwrite any existing characters.

Table 2-1	Movement Shortcut Keys in the Word Processor
Key	*Movement*
Left arrow (←)	Moves the cursor one character to the left
Right arrow (→)	Moves the cursor one character to the right
Up arrow (↑)	Moves the cursor to the preceding line
Down arrow (↓)	Moves the cursor to the next line
Ctrl+←	Moves the cursor one word to the left
Ctrl+→	Moves the cursor one word to the right
Ctrl+↑	Moves the cursor one paragraph up
Ctrl+↓	Moves the cursor one paragraph down
Page Up	Moves the cursor up one screen
Page Down	Moves the cursor down one screen
End	Moves the cursor to the end of the current line
Home	Moves the cursor to the beginning of the current line
Ctrl+Page Up	Moves the cursor to the top of the previous page
Ctrl+Page Down	Moves the cursor to the bottom of the current page
Ctrl+Home	Moves the cursor to the beginning of the document
Ctrl+End	Moves the cursor to the end of the document

Selecting and Editing Text

You can use both the mouse and the keyboard to select text and graphics in the Works Word Processor. With the mouse, click and drag the I-beam cursor across the text (or graphics) to be edited or formatted. (You can also automatically select a word under the I-beam cursor by double-clicking.) Table 2-2 illustrates the keyboard commands for selecting text and graphics.

Table 2-2	Selection Shortcut Keys in the Word Processor
Key	*Selection*
Shift+←	Selects one character to the left of the cursor
Shift+→	Selects one character to the right of the cursor
Shift+↑	Selects characters to the previous line
Shift+↓	Selects characters to the next line
Shift+End	Selects characters to the end of the current line
Shift+Home	Selects characters to the beginning of the current line
Shift+Page Down	Selects characters to the next screen
Shift+Page Up	Selects characters to the previous screen

Key	Selection
Ctrl+Shift+←	Selects characters to the beginning of the word
Ctrl+Shift+→	Selects characters to the end of the word
Ctrl+Shift+↑	Selects characters to the beginning of the current paragraph
Ctrl+Shift+↓	Selects characters to the end of the current paragraph
Ctrl+Shift+Home	Selects characters to the beginning of the document
Ctrl+Shift+End	Selects characters to the end of the document

To select a line of text, click anywhere to the left of the line outside the margin. You can also select a large amount of text and graphics by using the mouse and keyboard in unison. Click to place the insertion cursor at the start of the material that you want to highlight and then hold down Shift while clicking at the end of the material. The Word Processor selects everything in between.

To select the contents of the entire document from the menu system, choose Edit⇨Select All — but be careful of your next action because whatever you do affects the whole shootin' match! (And don't forget Ctrl+Z, which is the Undo command; using this command reverses the last action that you took.)

The editing keys shown in Table 2-3 are available after you select text or graphics in the Word Processor editing window. Also, you can perform actions from the toolbars or the menu system that will affect only the selected text.

Table 2-3	Editing Shortcut Keys in the Word Processor
Key	Function
Any character	Replaces the selected text
Delete	Deletes the selected text and graphics
Ctrl+X	Cuts the selection and places it on the Clipboard
Ctrl+C	Copies the selection to the Clipboard
Ctrl+V	Replaces the selection with the contents of the Clipboard

Finding and Replacing Stuff

Need to locate the only occurrence of *unseen* in a 20-page school report? Then it's time to put Find and Replace to work — and I show you how you can quickly jump to any page in your document.

Follow these steps to use Find or Replace:

1. **Choose Edit⇨Replace or press Ctrl+H.**

   This displays the Find and Replace dialog box as shown in Figure 2-2, with the Replace tab selected. (The Find dialog box has the same fields but no Replace With text box.)

Figure 2-2:
The Find
and Replace
dialog
box — an
unsung
work of art.

2. **In the Find What field, type the word or phrase that you need to locate or change.**

   If you've searched for the same string earlier in this writing session, just click the down-arrow next to the box and select that string from the drop-down list.

3. **Type the word or phrase that you want to substitute in the Replace With field (or click the down-arrow and choose a Replace With value that you've used earlier in this session).**

   If you need to search for a formatting character — such as a tab or paragraph mark — click the Special button and then click the desired special character from the menu that appears.

4. **Need to look further? Click the Find Next button to find the next occurrence or click the Replace button to replace the next occurrence.**

   Alternatively, you can throw caution to the wind and click the Replace All button to locate and replace all occurrences of the word or phrase. (Just be careful and remember to use the Undo command from the Edit menu to recover from a Find and Replace disaster!)

5. **When you're done, click the Cancel button.**

To jump directly to a specific page in your document, click the Go To tab, type the desired page number in the Enter Page Number field, and then click the Go To button. You can also jump to different tables in your document as well.

Formatting Fonts and Paragraphs

Like most other Windows applications, the Works Word Processor includes the Big Three of text-formatting attributes:

+ **Bold:** Press Ctrl+B or click the Bold button (**B**) on the Formatting toolbar to add emphasis to the selected text.

+ *Italic:* Press Ctrl+I or click the Italic (*I*) button on the Formatting toolbar to italicize the selected text.

+ <u>Underline:</u> Press Ctrl+U or click the Underline (<u>U</u>) button on the Formatting toolbar to underline the selected text.

To display the other text formatting options, select one or more characters and then choose Format⇨Font, which displays the settings that you see in Figure 2-3:

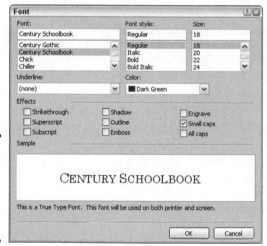

Figure 2-3:
Need to
make a font
change?
You're in the
right place.

+ **Font:** Click the font name that you want to use or click the Font drop-down list box on the Formatting toolbar.

+ **Size:** This box lists the size of the selected characters (in points); select a size from the list or type a specific size directly into the Size box.

+ **Color:** Click the font Color drop-down list to choose a color. (Automatic, which is the default, selects the best font color according to the background color of the printed page. Black is usually the best choice with white, no?)

+ **Effects:** Select any of the Effects check boxes to enable or disable that attribute — the application displays the results in the Sample window.

To use paragraph formatting, click anywhere in a paragraph (or select the entire paragraph) and then choose Format⇨Paragraph to display the settings that you see in Figure 2-4:

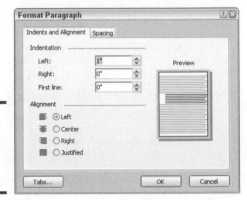

Figure 2-4:
Paragraph
formatting
is our
specialty.

✦ **The indentation:** You can use these settings to create custom indented paragraphs — but there's no need to use them to create bulleted or numbered lists because you can create those automatically from the toolbar. (More on this in a moment.)

✦ **The alignment:** Paragraphs can align to the left or right margin, or you can choose to center them in the page. A paragraph can also be *justified,* which stretches each full line in the paragraph from the left to the right margin.

✦ **The spacing:** Click the Spacing tab to specify double spacing or to choose a custom line spacing amount.

You don't have to select text first in order to use these formatting features in the Works Word Processor. If no text or no paragraph is currently selected, the Word Processor applies your font and paragraph changes to any new text that you type at the current location of the insertion cursor.

The Works Word Processor also includes the Format Gallery (see Figure 2-5), which you can display from the Formatting toolbar; alternatively, you can choose Format⇨Format Gallery. From the Gallery, you can

✦ Click the Format All tab to set the font formatting for your entire document. Click and drag the Font Set slider to choose a font family, and click and drag the Color Set slider to choose a balanced color scheme.

✦ Click the Format Item tab to set the font formatting for the currently selected text. Click the Font Set drop-down list button to choose a font family; then click the font size from the list. Click the Color Set drop-down list button to select a color scheme.

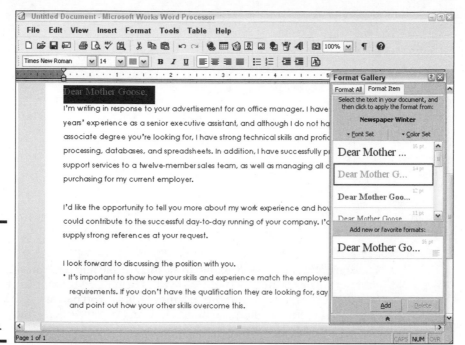

Figure 2-5:
Use the
Format
Gallery to
gussy up
your
documents.

Formatting Bullets and Numbered Lists

You can instantly format bulleted and numbered lists within the Word
Processor with a single click on the Formatting bar. But first, the more
lengthy (and customizable) method . . . just follow these steps:

1. **Click anywhere within the desired paragraph.**

2. **Choose Format⇨Bullets and Numbering to display the Bullets and
   Numbering dialog box that you see in Figure 2-6.**

3. **Choose the list format that you want:**

   - **Bulleted list:** On the Bulleted tab, click the type of bullet graphic that
     you want to use. You can also change the default bullet indent and
     specify a different indent for the bullet text.

   - **Numbered list:** For a numbered list, click the Numbered tab; you can
     specify what type of numbering to use, the starting number, and the
     indent values.

4. **Click OK to apply the formatting.**

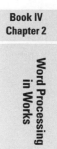

**Book IV
Chapter 2**

**Word Processing
in Works**

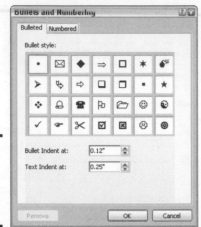

Figure 2-6:
Create a
custom
bulleted list
from here.

These niceties are also available from the Formatting toolbar. Just click the Numbering or the Bullets buttons on the Formatting toolbar to create numbered or bulleted lists with the default settings. You can also click the Decrease Indent and Increase Indent buttons to alter the position of the text by a tab stop.

Adding Graphics

What's a document without graphics? *Boring!* To insert a picture or a clip art image, click in the desired spot to move the insertion cursor to that point and then use one of the following methods:

✦ **Paste it from the Clipboard.** Press Ctrl+V to paste a graphic from your Windows Clipboard (check it out in Figure 2-7). *Remember:* You can only paste items from the Clipboard after you've copied them to the Clipboard by pressing Ctrl+C.

✦ **Insert it from a file.** If the graphic is stored on your hard drive, choose Insert⇨Picture⇨From File. Word displays the Insert Picture dialog box, complete with a Preview window (so that you can see what the file *1991pickup.jpg* really is instead of guessing). Navigate to the location of the image and click the filename once to preview it. When you've found the perfect picture, click the Insert button.

✦ **Insert a clip art image.** Choose Insert⇨Picture⇨Clip Art to display the Insert Clip Art dialog box shown in Figure 2-8. To locate clip art by a keyword, type a search word into the Type a Keyword text box (on the Find tab) and then click the desired type of graphic in the Select a Media Type list box. Click the Search button to display thumbnail images of any matching clip art or photographs. To browse through the Works clip art collection by category and subcategory, click the Browse tab. Again, you can specify what type of media that you want to browse. When you've located the artwork that you want to use, click the thumbnail and then click the Insert button.

If a thumbnail for a clip art image has a tiny CD-ROM icon in the corner, you'll have to load your Microsoft Works CD-ROM in your PC's drive to insert that image.

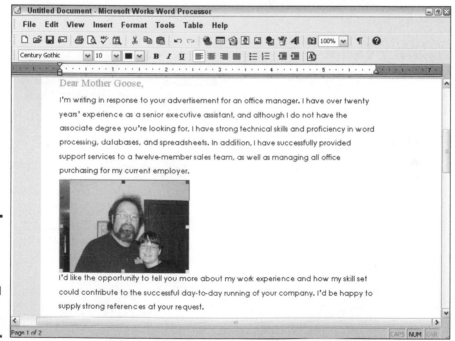

Figure 2-7:
A pasted graphic inhabits a Works Word Processing document.

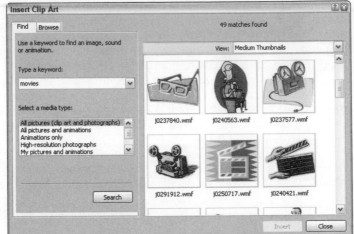

Figure 2-8:
Need clip
art? It's right
here!

Adding Tables

If you're faced with the task of adding text in column format to your Works
document, consider using a table. The Works Word Processor includes a
number of predesigned table formats.

To add a table, follow these steps:

1. **Click in the desired spot within your document.**

2. **Choose Table⇨Insert Table to display the dialog box shown in
   Figure 2-9.**

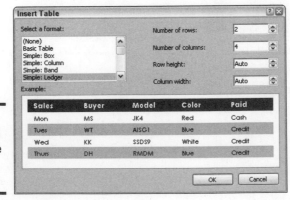

Figure 2-9:
Construct a
sturdy table
for your
document.

3. **Click within the Number of Rows and the Number of Columns text boxes and then type the number of rows and columns, respectively, that you need for your table.**

4. **If you need to specify a particular row height and column width, click the up- and down-arrows next to the corresponding boxes to set the dimensions in inches.**

5. **In the Select a Format list box, click the formatting that you'd like to apply.**

   The program automatically updates the Example window to show you how the finished table will appear.

6. **Click OK to insert the table.**

7. **Click in each table cell and type the information for that cell.**

Having trouble determining where to begin typing in a table cell? Click the Show All button (looks like a big backward *P*) in the Standard toolbar or choose View⇨All Characters to toggle the display of paragraph and placeholder marks. Then click in front of the placeholder within each cell. (This is also a good method of keeping track of those pesky paragraph marks, which determine where a paragraph format begins and ends.)

Checking Your Spelling

I've yet to meet a person who can nail down every spelling monstrosity without flinching. (For example, consider the word *anaerobic* — and yes, I had to check that.) Luckily, you can use the built-in spell checker within the Works Word Processor to fix those embarrassing literary flubs before you print.

By default, the Word Processor underlines misspelled words with a wavy red line while you type. Unfortunately, sometimes it just doesn't recognize a valid word because that word isn't in the program's dictionary. You can fix the spelling of these words on the spot. Just right-click the wavy-red-underlined word, and the Word Processor displays a pop-up menu of likely spellings from its dictionary, as shown in Figure 2-10. Click the correct spelling, and the Word Processor automatically replaces it. (If the word is spelled correctly, you can add it to the program's dictionary so that you won't have to correct it again; just click Add from the menu instead.)

Every good writer turns to a thesaurus from time to time to revive a stagnant word. If you need a synonym for a word, select it and then press Shift+F7 to display the Thesaurus dialog box that you see in Figure 2-11. If you find the word that you need, click it in the list on the right and then click the Replace button to automatically replace the selected word.

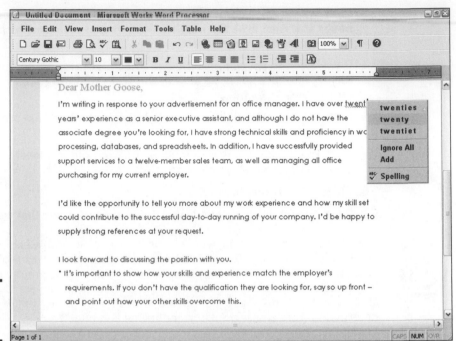

Figure 2-10: Fix a broken word here.

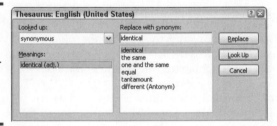

Figure 2-11: What's a good synonym for *synony-mous,* anyway?

You can also correct your spelling in one fell swoop. If you have any under-lined potential spelling errors, press F7 and you can view each potential problem as well as any suggested spellings. (You can also add valid words to the dictionary from here, too.)

Printing Your Documents

Before I bid adieu to the warm shores of the Works Word Processor, I should discuss how to print your documents . . . unless, of course, you plan to only admire them onscreen. (Not very likely.)

As a first step, choose File⇨Print Preview; see how this looks in Figure 2-12. This will show you how the document will appear when printed, giving you the opportunity to correct any problems before you spend time, paper, and toner (or ink). Click the Close button to exit Print Preview mode.

When you're satisfied with the appearance of your document, you can print by using any of these methods:

✦ **Click the Print toolbar button on the Standard toolbar.** Why wait? A click of this toolbar button immediately prints the entire document with the current settings.

✦ **Click the Print button in the Print Preview window.** Talk about convenient! This prints the document immediately with the current settings.

✦ **Choose File⇨Print.** If you need to specify additional copies or limit the print job to only certain pages, use this method (which displays the Print dialog box). Here, you can also choose a target printer if you have multiple printers available or display the printer-specific options supported by the printer's software driver (click the Properties button).

✦ **Press Ctrl+P.** This keyboard shortcut is an alternate method of displaying the Print dialog box.

You can also choose File⇨Send (or click the Send button on the Standard toolbar) to automatically create an e-mail message with the Works Word Processor document attached. Neat!

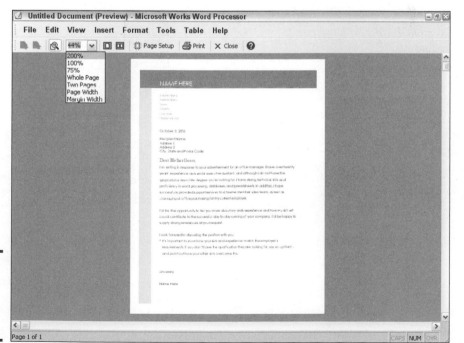

Figure 2-12:
Check your document before you print.

Chapter 3: Working with Spreadsheets

In This Chapter

✔ Starting the Works Spreadsheet

✔ Touring the Spreadsheet window

✔ Selecting and editing text

✔ Formatting cells, rows, and columns

✔ Inserting and deleting rows and columns

✔ Using Easy Calc

✔ Adding a chart

✔ Printing your spreadsheet

*O*h, heavens, it's a spreadsheet! That immediately means that it's complex, right? For once, you've met a spreadsheet application that breaks the mold: The Works Spreadsheet is the easiest application that I've ever used for such things as arranging numbers, forecasting important numeric trends, and taking care of a household budget. And unlike Excel 2003 — which many folks find just too doggone powerful and confusing — the Works Spreadsheet application is specifically designed with the home PC owner in mind.

In this chapter, I provide you with the explanations and procedures that you need to begin using the Spreadsheet program. You discover how to enter, select, and edit data; how to format that data to fit your needs; and how to create formulas the easy way. You also see how to create a chart as well as how to print your Spreadsheet documents. When you combine these building blocks with the task-oriented Spreadsheet templates and projects found in the Works Task Launcher, you can proudly proclaim to all, "I'm the master of my spreadsheet!"

Running the Spreadsheet

To begin using the Works Spreadsheet application, use one of these methods to start the program:

✦ Double-click the Works shortcut on your desktop to run the Task Launcher and then click the Spreadsheet button in the Quick Launch bar.

✦ Double-click a Works Spreadsheet document in Windows Explorer or on your desktop.

✦ Choose Start (or press a Windows key) and then choose Programs➪ Microsoft Works➪Microsoft Works Spreadsheet. (The Windows keys bear the waving Windows flag and are located on either side of your spacebar if your keyboard is so equipped.)

Introducing the Spreadsheet Window

Figure 3-1 illustrates the Spreadsheet window, which will be familiar territory to you if you've used Microsoft Excel.

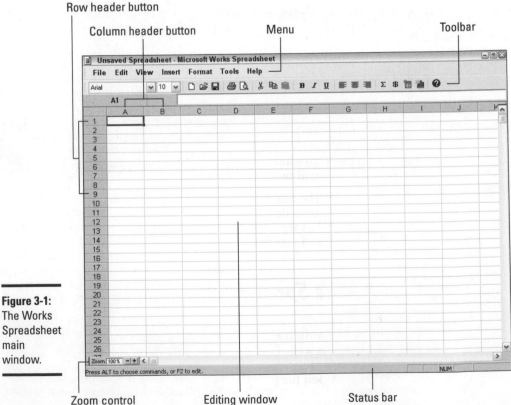

Figure 3-1:
The Works
Spreadsheet
main
window.

The highlights of the window include

✦ **The menu:** The Spreadsheet program sports the standard commands that you know (and I explain many in this chapter).

✦ **The toolbar:** Only one toolbar is necessary in this Works application. A click of a toolbar button works the same as selecting the corresponding item from the menu system. (To make more room for cells in the editing window, you can choose View➪Toolbar➪Show Toolbar to hide the toolbar.) The Spreadsheet toolbar is static and can't be customized or removed, but you can display a larger set of toolbar icons by choosing View➪Toolbars➪Large Icons. (If the program displays a small double-arrow icon at the end of the toolbar, the window is too small to display all the buttons — just click the double-arrow icon to select one of the extra buttons.)

To display a pop-up description of a toolbar button, hover your mouse pointer over it for a second, and its name will pop up.

✦ **The editing window:** The Spreadsheet editing window contains the cells that are familiar to anyone who's ever worked with a spreadsheet application. You type numbers, text, and formulas and insert charts into these cells.

✦ **The row and column header buttons:** You can click these buttons to select an entire row or column; they come in handy when you need to adjust the formatting of a row or column. (I mention more about the buttons later in the chapter.)

✦ **The Zoom control:** Click the plus or minus buttons next to the Zoom box (located in the far lower-left of the window) to magnify or shrink the view in the editing window. (Zooming out is a great way to see more of your spreadsheet at once.)

✦ **The status bar:** The Spreadsheet status bar contains information about the possible commands that you can choose (depending on what's selected) as well as the status of your Caps Lock key, Num Lock key, and insert/overwrite mode.

A Word about Works Spreadsheets

Although the Works Spreadsheet loads and saves files in its own Works 8 format (which ends with the `.xlr` extension), Microsoft has included support for Excel files as well. To load an Excel file, follow these steps:

1. **Choose File➪Open (or press Ctrl+O) to display a standard Open dialog box.**

2. **Click the Files of Type drop-down list and choose Excel SS (*.xl*).**

3. **Navigate to the location of the Excel file and double-click it to open it.**

Because Excel is a much more powerful program, however, the Works Spreadsheet isn't able to support a number of Excel features. The list of unsupported features includes

✦ **Cell comments**

✦ **Data validation**

✦ **PivotTables:** They're converted to simple data.

✦ **Charts:** They must be re-created by using the Works Spreadsheet charting commands.

✦ **Images and pictures:** Works Spreadsheet doesn't support images or pictures.

Works also cannot handle more than 16,384 rows in a spreadsheet or more than 2,047 characters in a cell.

If you've protected any cells in a worksheet — or the entire worksheet itself — that protection must be removed in Excel before you can open the file in the Works Spreadsheet. (For more information on Excel worksheets, visit Book V, Chapter 3.)

Navigating the Spreadsheet and Entering Data

You can use the scroll bars to move around in your spreadsheet, but when you're entering data into cells, moving your fingers from the keyboard is a hassle. (The same is true of just about any program that uses the keyboard to enter data, including the Works Word Processor and the Works Database.) For this reason, the Spreadsheet has a number of movement shortcut keys that you can use to navigate, and I provide them in Table 3-1. If you commit these to memory, your productivity will shoot straight to the top.

Table 3-1	Movement Shortcut Keys in the Works Spreadsheet
Key	*Movement*
Left arrow (←)	Moves the cursor one cell to the left
Right arrow (→)	Moves the cursor one cell to the right
Up arrow (↑)	Moves the cursor one cell up
Down arrow (↓)	Moves the cursor one cell down
Home	Moves the cursor to the beginning of the current row
Ctrl+Home	Moves the cursor to the beginning of the active worksheet

Key	Movement
Ctrl+End	Moves the cursor to the last cell in the worksheet with a value
Page Down	Moves down one screen
Page Up	Moves up one screen
Enter	Moves the cursor one cell down (also works within a selection)
Tab	Moves the cursor one cell to the right (also works within a selection)
Shift+Enter	Moves the cursor one cell up (also works within a selection)
Shift+Tab	Moves the cursor one cell to the left (also works within a selection)
Ctrl+arrow key	Moves the cursor to the corresponding edge of any range containing data

After you navigate to the right cell and you want to enter data, either click it with the mouse, press the spacebar, or press F2 and then begin typing. When you're ready to move on, press Enter (to save the data and move one cell down) or press Tab (to save the data and move one cell to the right).

Selecting and Editing Cells

Often, you want to perform a function on more than one cell at a time — for example, if you're formatting the contents with the Bold attribute. In this section, I show you how to select multiple cells and how to edit the contents of a cell.

You can use the mouse to select cells in the Works Spreadsheet:

✦ To select a *single* cell, click it.

✦ To select a *range* of multiple adjacent cells, click a cell at any corner of the desired range and then drag the mouse in the desired direction.

✦ To select a *column* of cells, click the alphabetic heading button at the top of the column.

✦ To select a *row* of cells, click the numeric heading button at the far left of the row.

✦ To select cells from the keyboard, employ the shortcuts in Table 3-2.

**Book IV
Chapter 3**

**Working with
Spreadsheets**

Table 3-2	Cell Selection Shortcut Keys In the Works Spreadsheet
Key	**Selection**
Ctrl+A	Selects all cells in a worksheet
Shift+←	Selects one cell or column to the left (depending on the current selection)
Shift+→	Selects one cell or column to the right (depending on the current selection)
Shift+↑	Selects one cell or row above (depending on the current selection)
Shift+↓	Selects one cell or row below (depending on the current selection)

Finally, let me discuss editing the existing contents of a cell. By using the mouse, you can double-click a cell to edit it and then click and drag to select characters. From the keyboard, select the cell, press F2, and then use the shortcuts shown in Table 3-3 to select and edit the contents.

Table 3-3	Cell Selection and Editing Shortcut Keys in the Works Spreadsheet
Key	**Selection**
Shift+←	Selects one character to the left of the cursor
Shift+→	Selects one character to the right of the cursor
Shift+End	Selects characters to the end of the text
Shift+Home	Selects characters to the beginning of the text
Any character	Replaces the selected text
Alt+Enter	Starts a new line within the same cell
Delete	Deletes the selected text or the character to the right of the insertion cursor
Ctrl+X	Cuts the selection and places it in the Clipboard
Ctrl+C	Copies the selection to the Clipboard
Ctrl+V	Replaces the selection with the contents of the Clipboard
Esc	Cancels the edits made to a cell

Formatting a Cell, Row, or Column

After your data has been entered into a cell, row, or column, you still might need to format it. The Works Spreadsheet gives you a healthy selection of formatting possibilities. In this section, I discuss each one.

Choosing a number format

Number formatting determines how a cell displays a number, such as a dollar amount, a percent, or a date. (Actually, the number format also controls the appearance of numbers used as text values in certain cases, like when you use Text and True/False.) Characters and formatting rules like decimal places, commas, and dollar/percentage notation are included in number formatting.

To specify a number format, follow these steps:

1. **Select the cell(s), row(s), or column(s) that you want to format.**

2. **Choose Format⇨Number.**

   Alternatively, you can right-click the selected cell(s), row(s), or column(s) and then click Format from the pop-up menu that appears. Works Spreadsheet displays the Format Cells dialog box that you see in Figure 3-2.

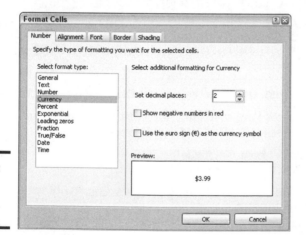

Figure 3-2:
Format numbers here.

3. **Click the type of formatting that you want to apply.**

   The program displays the settings for that type; each type of formatting includes different options. You also see a sample window that shows you how the selected formatting will look within the selected cells. The default number formatting is the General format.

4. **Click OK to apply the formatting.**

Changing cell alignment

You can also change the horizontal and vertical alignment of text and numbers in the selected cells. (The default alignment for text is flush left; the default alignment for numbers is flush right.) Follow these steps:

1. **Select the cell(s), row(s), or column(s) that you want to format.**

2. **Choose Format⇨Alignment to display the Alignment tab of the Format Cells dialog box.**

3. **Click the desired horizontal position and vertical position.**

4. **To prevent Works Spreadsheet from wrapping text values that don't fit on a single line, click the Wrap Text within a Cell check box to disable it.**

5. **Click OK to apply the formatting.**

Changing the text formatting

Need to set apart the contents of some cells? For example, you might need to create text headings for some columns and rows or to highlight the totals in a spreadsheet. Follow these steps to change the formatting of the text displayed within selected cells:

1. **Select the cell(s), row(s), or column(s) that you want to format.**

2. **Choose Format⇨Font to display the Font tab of the Format Cells dialog box.**

3. **From the Select Font list, click the font that you want to use and then click the style that you want to apply.**

    You can also apply the **bold**, *italic*, or <u>underline</u> attributes to selected cells from the toolbar.

4. **Click the desired size (in points) in the list or click in the Size box and type the desired size.**

    A point is approximately ½ inch on the printed page.

5. **Choose a font color or leave the field set to Automatic, which tells the program to change it as necessary.**

6. **If you need underlining or strikethrough formatting, enable the corresponding check box.**

7. **If you want to use this formatting scheme as your default formatting throughout the document, click the Set as Default button.**

8. **Click OK to apply the formatting.**

Formatting the borders

You can also add special formatting to the borders surrounding a cell, a row, or a column; again, this is a great trick to use when something needs to stand out. To format the borders of cells, rows, or columns, follow these steps:

1. **Select the cell(s), row(s), or column(s) that you want to format.**

2. **Choose Format➪Border to display the Border tab of the Format Cells dialog box.**

3. **Click to select a border color from the scrolling list (or use Automatic to let Spreadsheet choose a contrasting color).**

4. **Click the desired Line Type.**

5. **Click the Border Location buttons to specify no border, a standard outline border, an inside grid, or a custom border.**

   The results are shown in the sample window. (A cell can contain two separate text areas.)

6. **Click OK to apply the formatting.**

Choosing shading options

Shading the contents of a cell, row, or column is helpful when your spreadsheet contains subtotals or logical divisions. Follow these steps to select the shading or pattern for the selected cells:

1. **Select the cell(s), row(s), or column(s) that you want to format.**

2. **Choose Format➪Shading to display the Shading tab of the Format Cells dialog box.**

3. **Click the desired shading color from the Select Color list (or use Automatic to have the program choose a contrasting color).**

4. **Click the desired color for any pattern that you want to apply (or use Automatic and let Spreadsheet do the work).**

5. **Click a pattern from the Pattern list and admire your handiwork in the Preview window.**

6. **When you've achieved the right effect, click OK to apply the formatting.**

TIP

To choose a predesigned formatting scheme for a range of cells equal to or less than 100 cells x 100 cells, select a range of cells and choose Format➪ AutoFormat to display the dialog box that you see in Figure 3-3. Choose the desired format from the list at the left and then specify whether the selected range contains column/row headers and column/row totals. (The Preview window displays the formatting scheme at work.) When you like what you see, click OK.

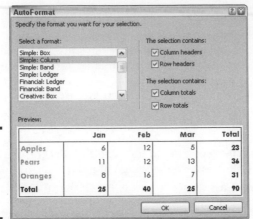

Figure 3-3:
Put
AutoFormat
to work for
you.

Inserting and Deleting Rows and Columns

What's that? You forgot to add a row, and now you're three pages into your data entry? No problem. It's easy to add or delete rows and columns. Really — it is! First, select the row or column that you want to delete or that you want to insert a row or column next to. (If you insert, the new row or column appears above the selected row or to the left of the selected column.) Right-click a selected row and then select either the Insert Row or the Delete Row from the pop-up menu that appears. Or you can right-click a selected column and then choose Insert Column or Delete Column from the pop-up menu that appears.

Remember, you can also take care of such business from the Insert menu. (Personally, I like to right-click.)

Using Easy Calc

Sorry, but it's time to talk about *formulas*. These equations calculate values based on the contents of cells that you specify in your spreadsheet. For example, if you designate cell A1 (the cell in column A at row 1) to hold your yearly salary and cell B1 to hold the number 12, you can divide the contents of cell A1 by cell B1 (to give you your monthly salary) by typing this formula into any other cell:

    =A1/B1

By the way, formulas in the Works Spreadsheet always start with an equal sign (=).

"So what's the big deal, Mark? Why not use a calculator?" Sure, but what if you wanted to calculate your weekly salary? Instead of grabbing a pencil and paper, you can simply change the contents of cell B1 to 52, and boom! The spreadsheet is updated to display your weekly salary.

That's a simple example, of course, but it demonstrates the basis of using formulas (and why spreadsheets are often used to predict trends and forecast budgets). However, building those formulas can be a real pain, and that's why Microsoft wisely chose to add a friendly wizard called Easy Calc to Works Spreadsheet. To use Easy Calc to generate a formula, follow these steps:

1. **Choose Tools⇨Easy Calc or click the Easy Calc button on the toolbar (it looks like a little calculator).**

   The first screen of the wizard appears, as shown in Figure 3-4.

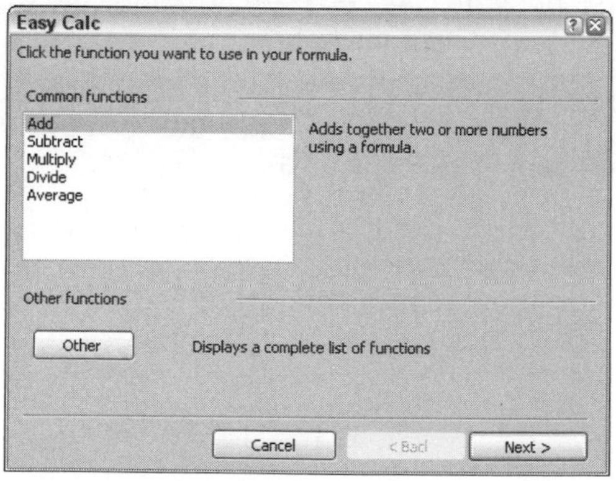

Figure 3-4:
Starting the Easy Calc wizard.

2. **Click the operation that you want to perform from the Common Functions list at the left side of the screen.**

   By default, Easy Calc shows only five of the most basic functions, but you can choose from a huge list of other functions (arranged by category) if you click the Other button. After you choose the function for the formula, click Next to continue.

3. **On the second wizard screen (see Figure 3-5), click the individual cells (or drag the mouse to highlight a group of cells) that will be used in the calculation and then click Next.**

   Alternatively, you can type the cell numbers in the Range box, separated by either commas or colons. Easy Calc displays the formula in the box at the bottom of the dialog box.

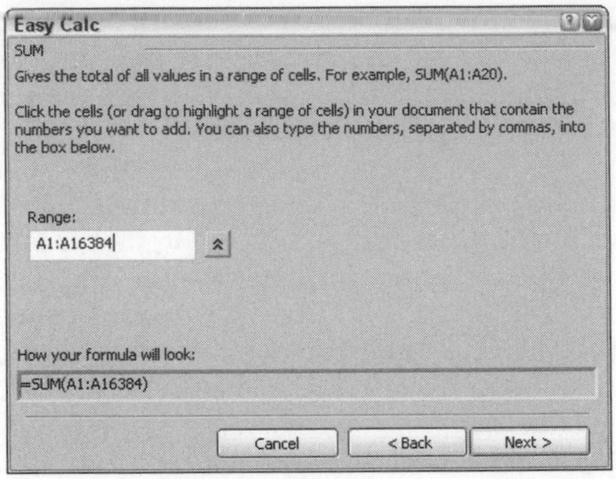

Figure 3-5:
Select the
cells to
use in the
calculation.

Note: The fields that you see here vary depending on the type of function that you select. For example, if you're adding numbers, you have only one Range box, but you have separate boxes for the Numerator and Denominator if you're dividing numbers.

4. **Click the cell in your spreadsheet or type the cell reference (like A1 or F3) into the Result At box to indicate where the result of the calculation will appear (as shown in Figure 3-6).**

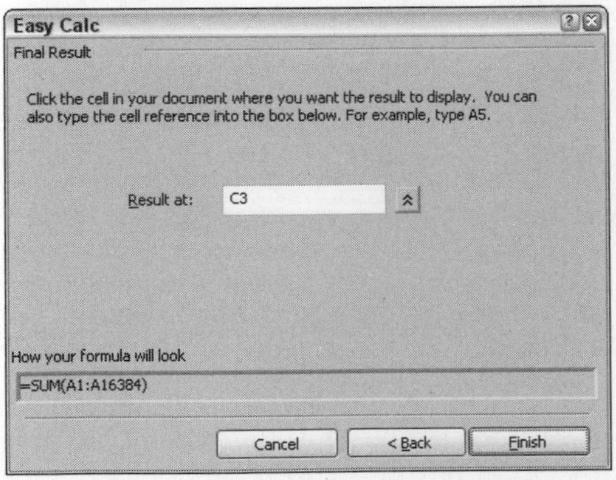

Figure 3-6:
Choose a
cell to
display the
result.

5. **Click Finish to create the formula and copy it to the result cell.**

Instead of displaying the formula, the cell that holds the formula displays the result of the calculation. If you want to edit or delete the formula, click the result cell, and the formula is displayed (and can be edited) from the toolbar.

Adding a Chart

Sometimes, you just have to see something to believe it — hence the ability to use the data that you add to a spreadsheet to generate a chart. Follow these steps to create a chart:

1. **Select the cells that you want to chart (including any column or row labels that you might have created).**

2. **Choose Tools⇨Create New Chart or click the New Chart button on the toolbar (it looks like a bar graph).**

   Spreadsheet displays the dialog box that you see in Figure 3-7.

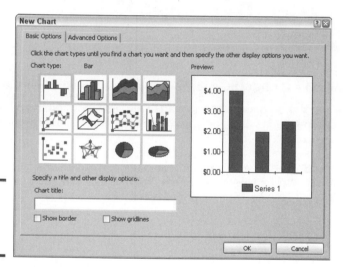

Figure 3-7:
Generating
a chart is
a snap.

3. **Click the thumbnail representing the type of chart that you want to create.**

   The Preview window is updated to illustrate how the finished chart will look.

4. **Type a new title for your chart in the Chart Title text box.**

5. **If you'd like to add a border, select the Show Border check box to enable it. To display gridlines on the finished chart, select the Show Gridlines check box to enable it.**

6. **To display the additional settings that many of the chart types have, click the Advanced Options tab (see Figure 3-8) and change them as necessary.**

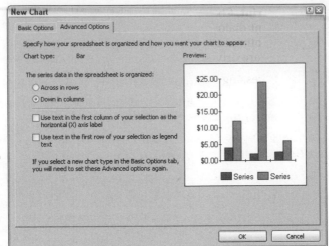

Figure 3-8:
Set
advanced
options for a
chart here.

7. **Ready to go? Click OK, and Works Spreadsheet displays the chart.**

   You can switch back to the spreadsheet view by choosing View➪
   Spreadsheet; likewise, you can display the chart again by choosing
   View➪Chart.

   Each Works Spreadsheet document can have several charts, and they're
   saved with the Spreadsheet document. To delete or rename a chart, choose
   Tools➪Delete Chart or Tools➪Rename Chart.

Printing Your Documents

It's time to put your spreadsheets on paper! But first, choose File➪Print
Preview (or click the Print Preview button on the toolbar) to see exactly how
your printed data will look. If you're not satisfied, you can click Close and
make any edits or formatting changes before you print.

You can use any of these methods to print a Works Spreadsheet document:

✦ **Click the Print button on the Standard toolbar.** If you don't need to
make any changes to your printer settings, click this toolbar button to
immediately print the entire document.

✦ **Click the Print button in the Print Preview window.** Clicking this
button also prints the document immediately with the current settings.

✦ **Choose File➪Print.** Choose this method if you want to change any settings on the Print dialog box, such as the number of copies. Click the Properties button to set printer options that are provided by the manufacturer's software driver.

✦ **Press Ctrl+P.** Pressing this keyboard shortcut also displays the Print dialog box.

Choose File➪Send to automatically create an e-mail message and attach the open Works Spreadsheet document to it. (This is a good timesaver if you mail your documents on a regular basis.)

Book IV
Chapter 3

Working with
Spreadsheets

Chapter 4: Using the Works Calendar

In This Chapter

✔ **Running the Works Calendar**

✔ **Introducing the Calendar window**

✔ **Selecting a view**

✔ **Adding and editing appointments**

✔ **Finding a specific appointment**

✔ **Filtering appointments and events**

✔ **Exporting appointments**

✔ **Printing your Calendar**

*I*s your daily schedule kept somewhere within a heap of sticky notes, napkins, and business cards? I used to be even worse — I tried to keep much of my busy schedule in my head, including both my personal and business appointments. That included everything from media interviews to soccer practice dates . . . and somewhere along the way, I was constantly forgetting something important. (Usually a birthday or a lunch date — you know, the so-called *secondary* events that seem to embarrass you so badly when you forget 'em.)

If you've begun to use the other applications in Microsoft Works 8, don't sell the Works Calendar short. If you take the time to enter your appointments, recurring events, and dates (such as anniversaries and birthdays), you'll be able to view, search through, and print your upcoming schedule on a monthly, weekly, or daily basis. It makes all the difference in the world!

In this chapter, I take you on an excursion through the Calendar, and you discover how to use it to organize — and finally master — your schedule.

Checking Out the Calendar

You can run the Works Calendar in either of two ways:

✦ Double-click the Works shortcut on your desktop to run the Task Launcher and then click the Open Calendar button on the Home screen.

✦ Choose Start (or press a Windows key) and then choose Programs⇨ Microsoft Works⇨Microsoft Works Calendar. (The Windows keys look like the waving Windows flag and are located on either side of the space-bar, if your keyboard is so equipped.)

Cast your eye upon Figure 4-1, and you'll see the Works Calendar in action.

The highlights of the window include

✦ **The menu:** See your old friend, the menu bar — somewhat shorter in this application but still as useful as ever.

✦ **The toolbar:** Calendar displays only one toolbar; clicking a toolbar button has the same effect as choosing the corresponding menu item from the menu system. To hide the toolbar and make more room for the editing window, choose View⇨Toolbar⇨Show Toolbar; you can also choose View⇨Toolbars⇨Large Icons to display a larger set of toolbar icons.

✦ **The editing window:** Works Calendar always has some type of calendar view visible in the editing window, allowing you to add, view, or edit appointments.

Menu   Toolbar

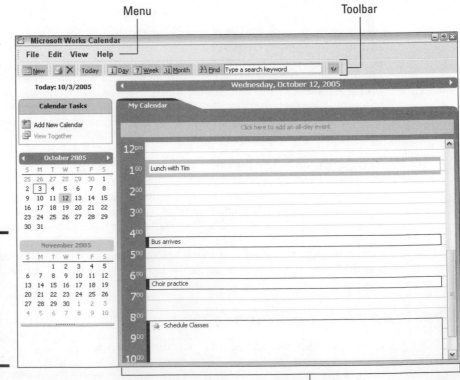

Figure 4-1: The Works Calendar main window, displaying the Day view.

Editing window

Selecting a Calendar View

The Calendar offers three different views. You can zero in on a single day (refer to Figure 4-1), display an entire week's appointments (as shown in Figure 4-2), or zoom out to view a month's calendar at a time (check it out in Figure 4-3).

To change the view, you can

✦ Click one of the three view buttons on the Calendar toolbar.

✦ Choose View and then choose Day or Week or Month.

✦ Press Alt+1 for the Day view, Alt+– (minus sign) for the Week view, or Alt+= (equal sign) for the Month view.

To move between days, weeks, or months, click the Previous and Next buttons on either side of the date display, and they change to match the view that you're using.

No matter where you wander in the past or future, you can always jump immediately to today's date. Just click the Go to Today button on the toolbar. It's the key to time travel.

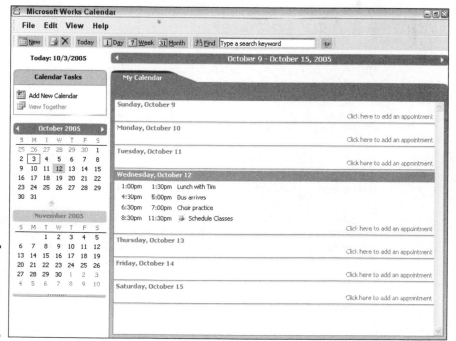

Figure 4-2:
It looks like a busy week in Works Calendar.

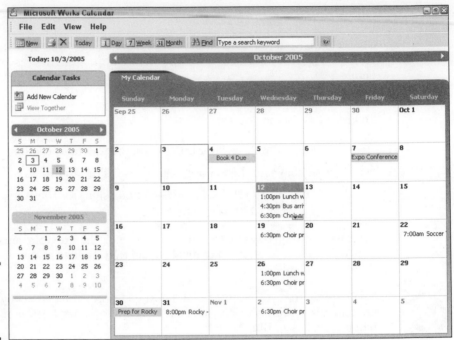

Figure 4-3:
How can a
month go by
so fast?

Creating a New Calendar

(Brace yourself, you're about to encounter the densest conglomeration of
the word *calendar* ever printed. Sorry, but *almanac, datebook,* and *agenda*
just don't seem to fit here!)

By default, Works Calendar opens with a blank calendar titled `My Calendar`.
This is fine if you're the only one using Works . . . but what if others in your
family need a calendar of their own? Luckily, you can add up to three additional calendars — each calendar you create is represented by a separate tab
in the Editing window. To switch between the different calendars, you need
only click on the desired calendar tab.

To add a new calendar, click the Add New Calendar link in the Calendar
Tasks list at the upper left of the Works Calendar window. The new tab
appears immediately — to rename the calendar to something more descriptive than "Calendar 1," click the calendar name in the tab to select it, then
click it again to open a familiar text editing box.

In the next section, you find out how to share appointments betwixt different
calendars.

Adding and Editing Appointments

Of course, the heart of the Works Calendar is the appointments that you set. After all, without appointments and events, you might as well stick with a paper calendar thumb-tacked to the wall of your cubicle!

To set up an appointment within the currently selected calendar, follow these steps:

1. **Double-click the date (or, in the Day view, the time) when the appointment will begin.**

   Alternatively, you can click to select a time or date and then click New Appointment on the toolbar, or choose File⇨New Appointment, or even press Ctrl+N.

   Calendar displays the New Appointment dialog box that you see in Figure 4-4.

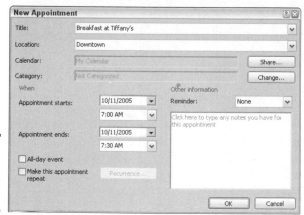

Figure 4-4: Add a new appointment here.

2. **Type a title for the appointment (or, if you've already entered appointments earlier in this Calendar session, click the drop-down list box to choose a previously entered title) and then press Tab.**

3. **Type a location (if necessary) or click the Location drop-down list box to choose a location that you've already used.**

4. **To share an appointment with another Works calendar (so that the event also appears in that calendar display), click the Share button and select one or more calendar check boxes to enable them. Click OK, and the calendars that share the appointment appear in the Calendar field.**

5. **If you want to add a category, click the Change button, select one or more category check boxes to enable them, and then click OK to save them.**

   Although choosing a category is not required, I show you later in this chapter how categories help you when searching through and viewing appointments.

6. **By default, the appointment starts at the time slot that you double-click (or select). However, you can click the Appointment Starts and Appointment Ends drop-down list boxes to set the time and date for the beginning and end of the appointment.**

   If you select the All-Day Event check box, the time list boxes disappear.

7. **For appointments that recur at the same time slot, select the Make This Appointment Repeat check box to enable it and then click the Recurrence button to display the Recurrence Options dialog box that you see in Figure 4-5.**

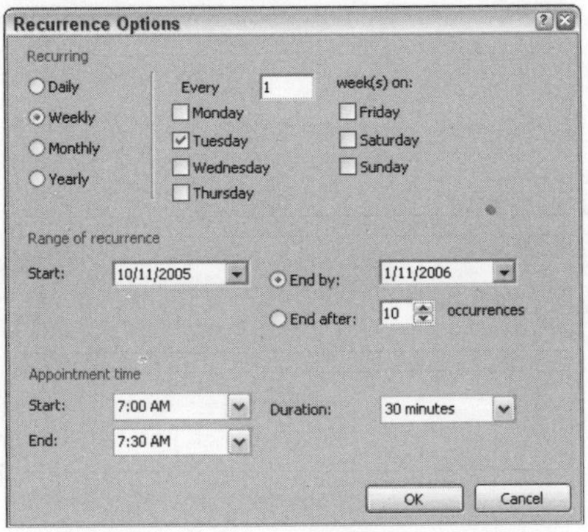

Figure 4-5:
Set options
for a
recurring
appointment
here.

8. **Set the date, range, and time options as needed and then click OK to return to the New Appointment dialog box.**

9. **To set a reminder that will alert you at a specified time before the appointment, click the Reminder drop-down list box and select the time that the reminder should appear before the appointment is scheduled.**

10. **You can jot down any notes about this appointment in the Reminder box; just click in the box and type your notes.**

11. **When all is set how you like, click OK to save the appointment, which now appears in your Calendar (as well as any calendars you marked to share it).**

Note that if a reminder has been set, the Calendar application displays a bell icon next to the appointment title.

You can easily edit an upcoming appointment. Just double-click the appointment title to display the Edit Appointment dialog box, which is exactly like the New Appointment dialog box (except for the dialog box title, of course). Anyway, make any changes to the appointment that you need and then click OK. If you've changed the day or date, the Works Calendar automatically moves it to its new position in your schedule.

To delete an appointment, right-click the appointment or event title and then choose Delete Item from the pop-up menu that appears.

Searching for Specific Appointments

Need to know precisely when you last attended a meeting or to locate a certain reminder or note that you made to yourself? No problem — Works Calendar allows you to find appointments based on three criteria:

✦ A keyword in the title or notes

✦ The time that the appointment begins or ends

✦ The category that you assigned to your appointments

Follow these steps to find specific appointments:

1. **Click the Find button on the toolbar (look for the little binoculars) or choose Edit⇨Find.**

   You can also press Ctrl+F. Calendar displays the Find dialog box that you see in Figure 4-6.

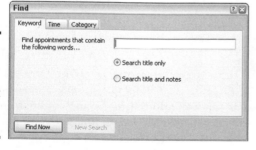

Figure 4-6: Searching for an appointment in a haystack.

2. **Click the desired tab to select the type of search.**

3. **Enter the specific criteria.**

For example, you can enter a word or phrase for a keyword search or you can select the appointment's beginning or end and the time period for a time search.

4. **Click the Find Now button.**

   Calendar displays any matching appointments in a list at the bottom (see the results in Figure 4-7).

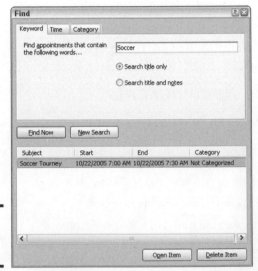

Figure 4-7: Eureka! I've found it!

You can double-click any of the matching appointments to edit them, or you can delete an appointment by selecting it from the list and then clicking the Delete Item button.

5. **To begin a new search, click the New Search button. Or, if you've found what you need, click the Close button of the Find dialog box to return to the Calendar main window.**

Filtering Appointments

The appointment categories that you select in Calendar can help you selectively *filter* (or hide) some types of appointments and events from view. This comes in especially handy if you've added both business and personal appointments and you want to concentrate on one or the other, or if you'd like to hide recurring events such as birthdays and anniversaries. (But *don't* forget to turn that particular filter off . . . take it from someone with a bad memory for birthdays.)

To filter one or more categories from view, choose View⇨Category Filter⇨ Customize. To clear them, select the check boxes of any appointment categories that you don't want to see, and the appointments and events that were assigned to those categories will be hidden.

To close the Category Filter dialog box until you need it again, click OK.

Exporting Appointments

After you take the trouble to organize your Calendar, that data can become pretty doggone important to you. This is yet another reason to back up your PC on a regular basis, but I cover that elsewhere in the book. (And I tend to nag readers about backups. Like you haven't noticed.)

Works Calendar gives you the ability to *export* your calendar information for use in other programs or for transfer to your Palm or Pocket PC personal digital assistant (PDA). Of course, this only creates a copy of that data; the original data remains safely where you want it, in your Works Calendar data file.

To export data, follow these steps:

1. **Choose File⇨Export and then choose one of the four types of export data. The four types are**

   • **vCalendar:** *vCalendar* files use a standard file format recognized by most personal information manager (PIM) programs (like Microsoft Outlook) and many PDA calendar programs. You can select the starting and ending date for your calendar data, and you can also choose to include only filtered appointments or all appointments and events. By using vCalendar files, you can easily "trade and collect" appointment schedules with co-workers. After all, knowing when your boss is attending that meeting with your presentation is A Good Thing.

   You might have already used the equivalent business-card data file, called a *vCard,* to transfer contact information between programs or computers. vCalendar files use the .vcs extension. From within Microsoft Outlook, you can choose File⇨Import and Export to export them from your Works Calendar.

   • **iCalendar:** Like vCalendar, *iCalendar* files offer another standard format for importing and exporting calendar data among different applications (and different types of computers as well). Again, you can select the starting and ending date for your calendar data, and you include only the currently filtered appointments or all appointments. These files end with the .ics extension.

- **HTML:** Awesome! Choose this option to create a HyperText Markup Language (HTML) file in one of three formats: a Day list, a Week list, or a Month list (see Figure 4-8). You can specify the start date and time as well as the ending date and time. Calendar also allows you to include only your current appointments (as displayed by using the Category Filter) or all appointments. You can optionally add details of the appointment; otherwise, Calendar includes only the appointment title. After you export your calendar as an HTML file, you can add it as a separate page to your company intranet or even to your public Web site. This is a great trick if you maintain a club or organization's Web site . . . post an up-to-date calendar of club events!

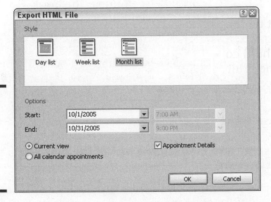

Figure 4-8: Create a Web page from your Calendar data.

- **Tab-Delimited:** As old programmer curmudgeons like myself always say, "If you can't beat 'em, use tab-delimited." This option creates a simple text file with your appointment data arranged in tabbed format. It's a pain to import (because you have to manually specify what information is in what column before it can be imported), but tab-delimited data is practically a universally recognized standard (even in other types of programs, like Excel). Bottom line: If the destination application or computer doesn't support vCalendar or iCalendar, you'll have to use tab-delimited. On the bright side, you can select the starting and ending date for your Calendar data, and you can choose to include only filtered appointments or all appointments and events.

2. **Enter the desired settings for the file format you chose (as I mention earlier) and then click OK.**

   After a bit o' churning, Works displays a standard Windows Save As dialog box.

3. **In the Save As dialog box, navigate to the location where you want to store the file, type a descriptive name in the File Name text box, and then click Save to create the file.**

To tackle the other side of the coin — that is, to import vCalendar data from another program — choose File➪Import.

Printing Appointments

What would a PC-based calendar be without the ability to print your appointments and events? Would you use it to organize your schedule? (I can guarantee you that I wouldn't touch it with the proverbial ten-foot, pole-like object.)

With Works Calendar, you can choose any of these methods to print your calendar:

✦ **Click the Print toolbar button on the Standard toolbar.** This displays the Print dialog box, as shown in Figure 4-9, from which you can choose which style of hard copy you need, the time and date range to include, and whether the printed document should cover all your appointments and events or only those currently displayed in the Category Filter.

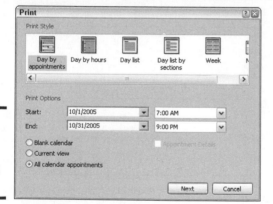

Figure 4-9: The Works Calendar Print dialog box.

✦ **Choose File➪Print.** Again, this displays the Print dialog box.

✦ **Press Ctrl+P.** You get one guess. . . .

Unlike other Works applications, Works Calendar doesn't include a Print Preview function, and you can't specify multiple copies or change any printer-specific options.

Chapter 5: Having Fun with Works Database

In This Chapter

✔ **Running Works Database**

✔ **Creating and opening a database**

✔ **Entering new data**

✔ **Editing a database**

✔ **Sorting or searching your database**

✔ **Building reports**

✔ **Printing database documents**

1 have fun with Works Database all the time. No, really!

Mind you, not the straight-laced, business-oriented, ho-hum inventory database or the dry customer database of a home business — although those *are* great examples of the versatility and value of a well-maintained database in the business world. (Think of a *database* as a collection of different pieces of information that you can search and arrange as you like.) No, my databases are very personal: I use them to track my audio CD collection, and they help me keep tabs on my stacks of DVD movies. I even have a database that's dedicated to all three seasons of *Batman* TV episodes! (For a look at my Bat-fanaticism, check out The Original BatCave at `http://batcave. mlcbooks.com` — it's a hoot.)

Even if Bat-Databases (Zowie!) aren't your thing, in this chapter, I show you how to put Works Database to work for you — handling whatever type of data you need to store, search, edit, and display. You discover how to generate reports, how to search and sort your data records, and how to edit an existing record to update or correct it. Create your own data warehouse. And if you value your data, you'll have fun (when it's all typed in, that is).

Getting Started with Works Database

Works allows you two methods of starting the Works Database application:

◆ Double-click the Works shortcut on your desktop to run the Task Launcher and then click the Works Database entry in the Quick Launch bar.

◆ Click Start (or press a Windows key) and then choose Programs⇨ Microsoft Works⇨Microsoft Works Database. (The two Windows keys, if your keyboard is so blessed, look like the waving Windows flag and are located on the same row as the spacebar.)

Whoops! What's this dialog box mean?

Hey, wait a second! Unlike the other applications in the Works suite, the Database doesn't open its main window when you first run the program. That's because the Works Database really doesn't have a single main window! Instead, the starting point for a Database session is the dialog box that you see in Figure 5-1, which has only three options:

Figure 5-1:
Shall we run, pass, or kick?

◆ **Blank Database:** Select this radio button if you want to create a brand new database by defining each field . . . in other words, you're building things from the ground up. If you choose a blank database, you'll be ushered into the Database window that I discuss in the next section.

◆ **Template:** When you choose this option, the Works Task Launcher is loaded (if it's not already running), and you see a list of the predesigned Database task templates, like Home Inventory worksheets and recipe books. Click a task in the list on the left and then click Start This Task. (You can either use the database as is or tweak it by editing it later.)

◆ **Open an Existing Database:** If you've already built a database and you want to edit the data that it contains, add new records, or print it, choose this option. The Database application displays a standard Open dialog box that you can use to locate and load your database file. (By the way, a Works Database file ends with the extension .wdb.)

In database-speak, a *field* is a value — such as your last name, age, or your blood type. A *record,* on the other hand, is a complete group of fields that describe one person, place, or thing. Thus, your record might contain your last name, age, blood type, and telephone number. The next person in the database has a unique record as well, composed of the same fields as your record.

Elements of the Works Database window

Although Works Database doesn't really have a single main window, it does have a window that you'll use when creating a new database, editing existing data, or entering new data. Figure 5-2 illustrates this Database window.

Database Record check boxes   Menu   Toolbar

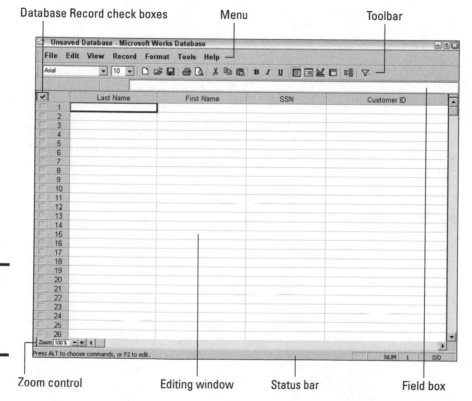

Figure 5-2:
The Database List view window.

Zoom control   Editing window   Status bar   Field box

The controls on this window include

✦ **The menu:** Here lies the standard Works menu system, with a new menu family — the Record menu — added for good measure. (More on this menu in a bit.)

✦ **The toolbar:** Like Works Calendar, Database has only one toolbar, and you can click a toolbar button to perform the same action as the corresponding menu item on the menu system. Choose View➪Toolbar to hide the toolbar and expand the editing window; choose this menu item again to display the toolbar. You can customize the buttons on the Database toolbar by choosing Tools⇨Customize Toolbar.

✦ **The editing window:** In Works Database, the editing window displays the data values within each record and allows you to edit them.

✦ **The records:** This list of records in the database appears only in List view (choose View⇨List or click the List View button on the toolbar). (Find this button to the immediate right of the Underline button.) Each row represents a single record.

✦ **The Zoom control:** Like the Zoom control in the Works Spreadsheet, you can click the plus or minus Zoom buttons (far-bottom left) to magnify or shrink the view. I often zoom out with the minus button to 75%, which allows me to pack more records on the screen without losing too much legibility.

✦ **The status bar:** The status bar provides context-sensitive help and also displays the status of your Num Lock and Caps Lock keys; it also shows information while you're in different modes (like the word EDIT when you're editing data in a record).

You can also toggle off the Spreadsheet-style gridlines in List view. If they offend your eye, choose View⇨Gridlines to toggle them off.

Creating a Database and Entering Data

If you elect to start a new blank database, you're met at the door with the Create Database wizard dialog box that you see in Figure 5-3.

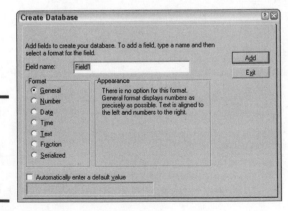

Figure 5-3:
Works
Database
starts
asking
questions.

Follow these steps to create your new datahouse:

1. **Type a name in the Field Name box.**

   I always use something descriptive, such as *Last Name* or *Salvos Fired* (for that database that I created to keep track of my Battleship winnings).

2. **Select the radio button for the format that you prefer.**

   Works Database uses your choice to format a data value and might also use it for basic error checking (like if you try to type the letter *A* into a Date field).

3. **Select the proper appearance of the data format from the Appearance list.**

   This is how you want your data to display onscreen and when it's printed out. For example, if you select the Time format, you can choose to display either hour:minutes or hour:minutes:seconds, or you can go completely hog-wild and choose military (24-hour) time. (***Note:*** Some formats offer fewer options . . . or, in the case of the General format, you see no options at all.)

4. **If the data field should have a default value, select the Automatically Enter a Default Value check box and enter the default value in the accompanying text box.**

   If the user types in nothing, Works Database will automatically use any value that you enter in this box. For my Battleship database, for example, I might have a Win/Loss column, and the default value could be *Win* — if I play a mean game of Battleship. Or, if I'm making a recipe database, the number of servings might default to 6 if there are 6 people in the family.

5. **When everything is done, click the Add button.**

   The program adds a column for the field that you created — in Figure 5-4, it's `LastName` — and clears the Create Database dialog box for your next value (which now reads `Field2`).

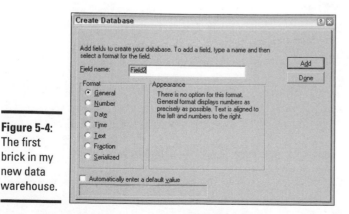

Figure 5-4:
The first brick in my new data warehouse.

6. Repeat Steps 1 through 5 for each field that you want to add to your database — or, if you're done with adding fields, click Done.

After you create your database, the program provides two methods of entering your data:

✦ **By using List view:** You can enter data in the same List view that you used to create your database. (Click the List View button on the toolbar.)

✦ **By using Form view:** Form view, as shown in Figure 5-5, displays a single record at a time in a user-friendly format for data entry, just like the blanks in a printed form. Click the Form View button on the toolbar to switch to Form view.

Entering data is the same within both views: Simply click your mouse pointer in the desired field and then type. When you're done entering data, you can press Tab to move to the next field or press Shift+Tab to move to the previous field.

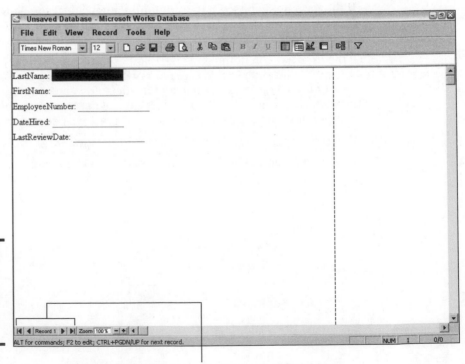

Figure 5-5:
Entering a record in Form view looks like this.

Use these buttons to move among records in Form view.

In List view, all the records in your database are shown within the Database window, and you can use your old friends — the scroll bars, Page Up/Page Down keys, and pressing Ctrl+Home/Ctrl+End — to leap about. Within Form view, however, you need some sort of a control to move between records. That control is the Record box at the lower left of the form, right above the status bar. The Record box always displays the current record number, but don't forget the four navigation buttons surrounding it:

✦ Click the arrow pointing to the bar at the left to move to the first record in the database.

✦ Click the arrow pointing to the left to move to the previous record.

✦ Click the arrow pointing to the right to move to the next completed record.

✦ Click the arrow pointing to the bar at the right to move to the last completed record in the database.

Editing a Database

After you enter your data and you're able to keep track of your customer information, what do you do if the data in a field is incorrect? That's part of the beauty of a database: Your information is easy to modify and update. You can use either List view or Form view to make your changes (whichever you find easier to use).

To change the contents of any field, follow these steps:

1. **Navigate to the record that you want to change.**

   In List view, use your scroll bars. In Form view, either use the Record box (see the preceding section) or search for the record (as I describe in the next section).

2. **To select it, click the field that you need to change and then press F2.**

   The program switches to Edit mode.

   Note that you can also enter the field value in the Field box on the toolbar.

3. **Type the new data value.**

   Depending on the data format, you might need to select the original value with your mouse (or use the Shift+arrow keys) first.

4. **Press Enter to save your changes and update the field.**

By the way, you're not locked in to a particular database design when you've entered data. To insert new fields before or after a selected field in your database, choose Record⇨Insert Field. You can also delete the selected field from your database. (These commands are a great way to fine-tune a database that you originally created from a Works Database template.) You can also insert or delete selected records from the Record menu.

Sorting and Searching for Specific Records

Works Database allows you to organize and search through the records in your database:

✦ **By sorting your records:** Choose Record⇨Sort Records; the program displays the Sort Records dialog box that you see in Figure 5-6. Click the Sort By drop-down list box to specify a primary sort field. If necessary, you can select a second- and third-level sort by clicking the Then By drop-down list boxes to choose additional fields. (You can also choose whether the sort will be in ascending or descending order.) Click OK to sort your database. For example, this feature comes in handy when you want to organize your DVD movie database by the year that each film was released; if you know that a particular movie hit the theaters in 1979, this might help you track it down.

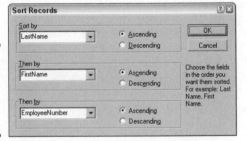

Figure 5-6: Preparing to sort my database by last name.

✦ **By searching for a specific record:** Choose Edit⇨Find or click the Find button on the toolbar. (From the keyboard, press Ctrl+F.) The Database opens the Find dialog box as shown in Figure 5-7. In the Find What box, type the text that you want to find and then select either the Next Record or the All Records radio button to determine which record(s) will be matched. Then click OK.

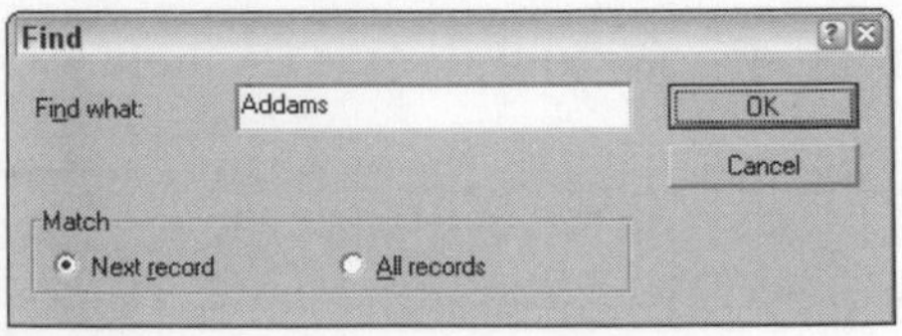

Figure 5-7: Look for a specific text string here.

Building Reports

In addition to storing your data (and displaying it when you need it), Works Database can produce another valuable product: a database report. To create a report, follow these steps:

1. **Choose Tools⇨ReportCreator to bring up the first screen of the ReportCreator.**

2. **Type a name for your new report and then click OK to continue.**

   The program displays the ReportCreator dialog box that you see in Figure 5-8.

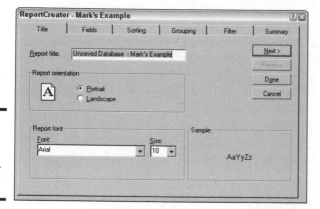

Figure 5-8: Choose an orientation and font for the report.

3. **On the Title tab, select the appropriate radio button to specify whether the report should be displayed in Portrait or Landscape mode and then click Next to continue to the Fields tab.**

   Landscape is generally a better pick if your records contain a large number of fields.

4. **On the ReportCreator Fields tab (as shown in Figure 5-9), you can add the fields that you want included in the report by selecting them from the Fields Available list and then clicking the Add button. (Or to add all fields at once, click the Add All button.)**

   By default, ReportCreator adds the field names, but you can toggle field names off (by enabling the Show Field Names at Top of Each Page check box), or you can specify that the database records should be summarized and totaled but not listed in detail (by enabling the Show Summary Information Only check box).

5. **Click Next to continue to the Sorting tab.**

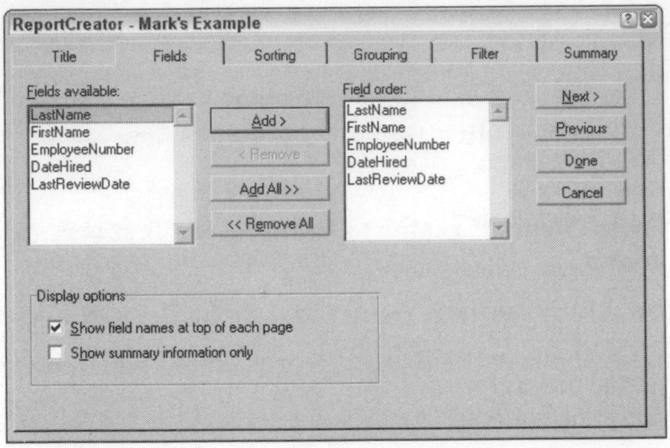

Figure 5-9:
Select the
fields to add
to your
report.

6. **On the Sorting tab: Set the primary, second-level, and third-level sort fields as necessary; choose ascending or descending sort order; and then click Next to continue to the Grouping tab.**

   The Sorting tab is essentially a duplicate of the Sort Records dialog box discussed in the "Sorting and Searching for Specific Records" section, earlier in this chapter.

7. **If you specified any sorting on the Sorting tab, you can arrange your records together in groups based on when the sorted field changes, as shown in Figure 5-10. Click Next to continue to the Filter tab.**

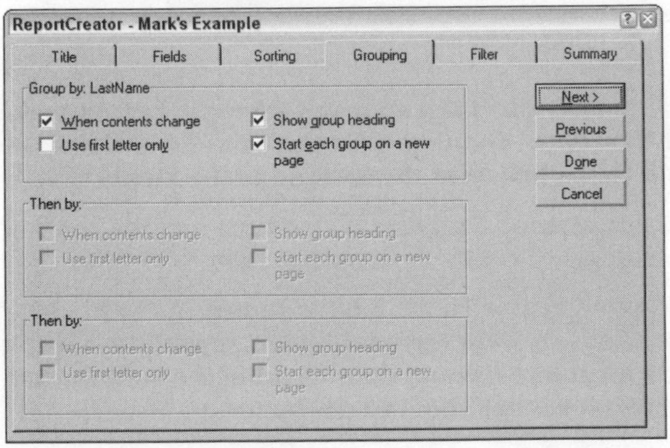

Figure 5-10:
Group
records in
the report
by their
sorted last
name.

For example, if you're sorting on *LastName,* each identical last name is grouped together in a separate section of the report (even on a separate page, if you like).

Optionally, you can group according to the first letter, as in grouping by all last names beginning with *C.* If you specify a second-level or third-level sort, you can also group by those criteria.

8. **If you've set up a filter and you want to apply it to this report, click it in the list at the left; to build a new filter for this report, click Create New Filter. Click Next to continue to the Summary tab.**

A filter hides records that match the filter criteria.

For more information on filters, refer to your Works documentation and the Works Database Help file.

9. **On the final ReportCreator panel, you can apply specific summaries to fields in your report (such as adding together all the goals scored by your soccer team over a season or averaging the goals per game).**

This summary information can be displayed at the end of each group or at the end of the report.

10. **Click Done to generate the report.**

Works Database switches to Report view to display your report. You can show the report again at any time by clicking the Report View button on the toolbar. (If you have multiple reports, you're prompted for the name of the report to display.)

Reports can be renamed, duplicated, or deleted, and you can change the sorting, groups, or filtering on an existing report. All these functions are available from the Tools menu when you're in Report view.

Printing Database Documents

Works Database can print out lists of records, or records as forms — or you can print a report that you've generated. Whatever you decide, I highly recommend that you use the File➪Print Preview command to double-check your document before you print it.

When you're ready, you can use any of these methods to print:

✦ **Click the Print toolbar button on the Standard toolbar.** This immediately prints a Database document with the current printer settings. (Or, if you haven't changed any Print settings earlier in this session, Database uses the default settings.)

✦ **Click the Print button on the Print Preview toolbar.** This also prints the document immediately by using the current (or default) Print settings.

✦ **Choose File➪Print.** Database displays the Print dialog box, from which you can specify which type of document you want as well as the number of copies and any restrictions on what should be printed.

✦ **Press Ctrl+P.** Press Ctrl+P to display the Print dialog box.

Book V

Office 2003

The 5th Wave   By Rich Tennant

WIRED HOME OF THE FUTURE

©RICHTENNANT

"I'm setting preferences–do you want Turkish or Persian carpets in the living room?"

Contents at a Glance

Chapter 1: Introducing Office 2003

In This Chapter

✔ Working with Word

✔ Using Excel

✔ Creating with PowerPoint

✔ Keeping track of data with Access

✔ Managing information with Outlook

✔ Working with the Office Clipboard

✔ Collaborating with others on shared documents

✔ Using the Office Help system

Introducing Microsoft Office 2003 is a little like introducing Beethoven's *Fifth Symphony*. We're all familiar with it, we all think that it's a true work of art, and we all wish that we had the royalties (or, in Bill's case, the mound of cash generated by licensing).

That familiarity might be your ticket to skipping this chapter. For instance, most PC power users need no overview of Office; they know what it can do, what the different applications are for, and how to access the Office Help system. Heck, chances are good that you're already using at least Word or Excel every day or that you already rely on Outlook to handle your e-mail and personal contacts.

But, just like the intricacies of Beethoven's masterpiece, there's a ton of substance to absorb within Office 2003. Perhaps you've only used Word and you'd like to know what the rest of the stuff that you've paid for can do. Or maybe you're brand new to the PC scene and you just bought Office 2003. For those folks who need a formal introduction to the rest of this mini-book, I present to you this chapter — it provides a little information on each of the separate Office applications so that you can pursue the more in-depth information in the later chapters.

The Components of Office 2003

I first mention the idea behind a productivity suite in the previous mini-book. Like Works, Office 2003 is designed to produce a wide range of documents, covering most of the tasks that you need to accomplish in a home or office environment. However, Office 2003 is far more powerful than Works, including features and functionality that Works doesn't have. (In some configurations, Microsoft ships Works with Windows XP Home Edition and ships Office 2003 with Windows XP Professional Edition.)

In this section, I describe each of the Office 2003 applications and provide you with an idea of what you can accomplish.

Word 2003

Microsoft Word, the world's best-selling word processor for Windows, is an institution these days. (You want to know just how ancient I really am? Your author remembers using the first DOS-based version of Word.) Sold as a separate title, it forms the foundation of Office 2003. You can see a typical Word window in Figure 1-1. Word is suitable for creating any kind of document from a simple one-page letter to a book-length manuscript. It also includes features designed for creating scientific, academic, and technical documents as well as powerful collaborative tools for workgroups.

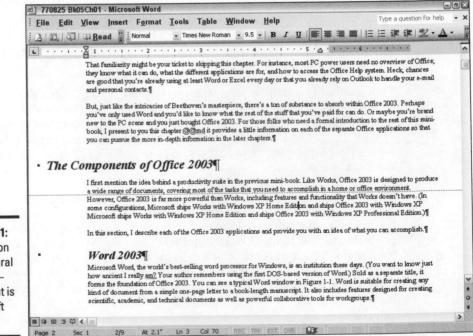

Figure 1-1:
Gaze upon the cultural phenom—enon that is Microsoft Word.

Other important features that set Word apart include

✦ **Complete control over all levels of document formatting:** This includes the appearance of everything in a Word document from the character level to the entire manuscript. (Believe me, it can handle a book this size without batting an eyelash.)

✦ **Sophisticated tables:** Gotta have 'em, and Word delivers . . . complete with a wide array of sorting, numbering, shading, and border options.

✦ **Collaboration tools:** If you share editing chores with others on documents, you'll welcome the ability to highlight or use revision marks. (This is a trick that enables Word to track any changes with colored text to show who did what and when. As a writer who works with editors, I can attest that the "why" factor can prove a bit more nebulous.) You can also compare two Word documents, add comments, and implement a basic version control system. Word documents can be write-protected as well (to keep unnecessary fingers away from your work).

✦ **Spell-checking:** Whether you use the default spelling dictionary or create your own custom dictionary, Word's spell-checking feature can be a lifesaver. And if you're looking for exactly the right word (utterance/ remark/exclamation), you'll flip over the thesaurus.

✦ **Artwork and graphic tools:** Sure, you can use clip art, but you can also draw your own graphics or even add all sorts of 3-D effects to titles, sidebars, and callouts.

✦ **Powerful macros:** Why type the same stuff or format the same text over and over? With Word's macro feature, you can automate all sorts of repetitive tasks . . . and it's easy to record a macro, too.

✦ **Printing:** Word can zoom or scale your printed pages and even collate longer documents. With plug-ins like Adobe Acrobat, you can also produce PDF files from within Word.

✦ **Advanced search and replace:** You can find and replace just about anything in a Word document. There's even an option to search phonetically, or you can search according to specific formatting. ("Hey, Earl, how can we find every italicized word in this 50-page list?")

For a more complete overview of Word, skip to the next chapter of this mini-book.

Excel

Microsoft Excel (see an example window in Figure 1-2) is much more than just a spreadsheet application. It's a regular jack-of-all-trades in the Office 2003 lineup, handling everything from a simple family budget to complex statistical and financial forecasting. Like Word, Excel is also sold separately, but it really comes into its own when a worksheet is linked with data in other Office documents.

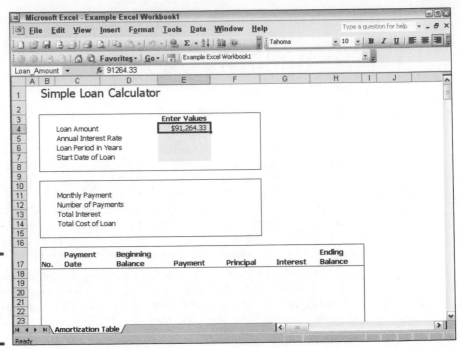

Figure 1-2:
If it's a
worksheet,
it must be
Excel.

Excel offers support for

✦ **Lists:** Excel can generate (and automatically update) lists as you need them, or you can use the complete set of list tools to build your own from scratch.

✦ **Smart tags:** These are used to embed and link to all sorts of external data from within your worksheet — contacts, stock quotes, e-mail messages, and more.

✦ **Charts and reports:** If your data needs to be charted or you need to generate reports to your exact specifications, look no farther than Excel!

✦ **Forms:** Offices all around the world rely on Excel for building customized forms. You can print them or complete them onscreen and save the worksheet for later use.

✦ **Formulas:** Excel provides task-based examples for common formulas and even includes an error-checking option that checks for potential problems with the formulas that you create.

✦ **Functions:** You can use the predefined functions provided by Excel or use the recommendations provided by the Function Wizard. Excel even pops up the arguments for a function when you enter it!

Read through Book V, Chapter 3 for more on this handy application.

PowerPoint

Slide-based and PC-based presentations used to be a business-only proposition, but now many schools are teaching kids how to create their own presentations as part of their classwork. PowerPoint, illustrated in Figure 1-3, is the king of the PC presentation application, with dozens of predesigned templates and styles to help you deliver professional results. Plus, you'll find that it's easy to build either a standalone, self-running presentation or a manual presentation under your control.

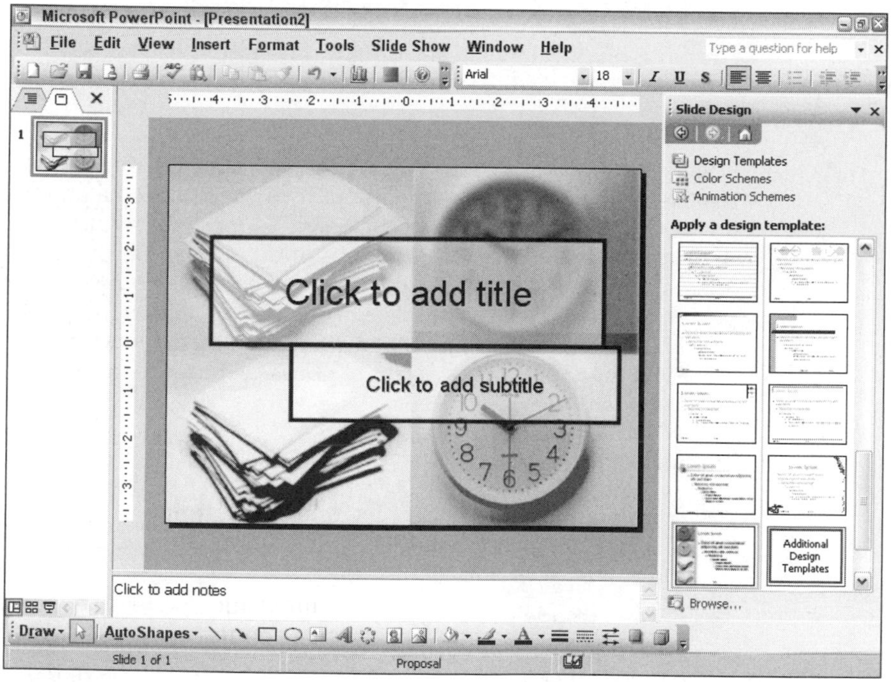

Figure 1-3:
Creating
a class
presentation
with
PowerPoint.

Highlights of PowerPoint include

✦ **Easy-to-use design tools:** No graphic design experience is necessary when using PowerPoint. Even a normal human being can handle the placement of elements. Master slides make it easy to apply global changes across your entire presentation, too.

✦ **Presentation print preview:** Check out your entire presentation before you print a single slide. And you can check out different layouts for notes pages and handouts as well.

✦ **Notes and handouts:** Use PowerPoint to easily produce notes for your reference or handouts that you can print for members of your audience.

✦ **Support for multiple screens:** With multiple monitors, you can display a special Presenter's view during your presentations. This separate display allows you easier control over the sequence of your slides and makes it easy to track the elapsed time.

✦ **Animation and transition effects:** Keep your audience interested in your message with animation on your slides and transitions between major sections.

✦ **Graphics control:** You can rotate or flip images, use the automatic layout feature to adjust the design when you insert objects, and display a grid when aligning elements on your slides.

For more on PowerPoint, see Book V, Chapter 4.

Access

I think that Access (as shown in Figure 1-4) is the unsung hero of Office 2003 — that is, if it's included in your edition. (I've encountered a number of experienced Office users who have never even *heard* of the application, since they've never used the Professional edition of Office.) However, when you tell folks what they can do with Access, they quickly become its most fervent supporter. You can create a database in just a few minutes, complete with reports, charts, and even Web pages that display data on demand. It's a great way to store whatever data is important to you — without requiring a degree in software engineering.

Top features of Access include

✦ **Sophisticated error checking and validation:** Let Access double-check the data that's entered. You'll cut down on human error and help ensure the accuracy of your database.

✦ **Connection with SQL servers:** If your business uses large-scale, corporate-level Structured Query Language (SQL) database applications, you can use Access to pull that information into your own database projects.

✦ **Database encryption:** If you need to keep your databases secure, Access can encrypt the entire file automatically each time that you use it.

✦ **Customized queries and reports:** What's the use of keeping a database if you can't view that data intelligently? Define relationships that help define trends or predict problems.

✦ **Web reports and database access:** Offer data from your Access files to others on your office intranet (or to anyone who connects to your Web site).

✦ **Forms:** Build professional-looking data entry and special input dialog boxes that can collect information and act on that data automatically. (Hey, you're a database programmer now!)

Hone your database magic skills with Access in Book V, Chapter 5.

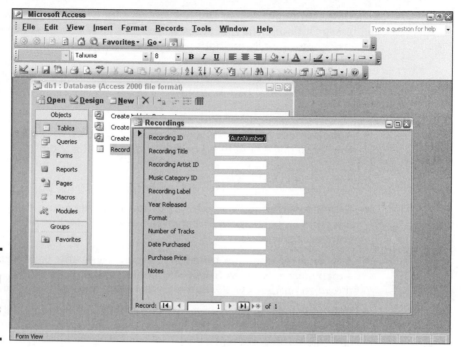

Figure 1-4:
Take control
of your data
with Access
2003.

Outlook

Ah, Outlook — no other single application has done so much for so many. (I know it's sure done a lot for my organization.) Outlook 2003 is a combination of an e-mail manager and a PIM (a rather ridiculous acronym that stands for *personal information manager*), which keeps track of your contacts and your

---

Dig that crazy Office shortcut bar

The Office shortcut bar is the launch pad for everything that's Office. From this toolbar, you can create a new Office document, open an existing Office document, and run any Office application.

I won't go into detail about the Office shortcut bar in this book because it's an optional element — and because I show you how to run each of these programs within the chapters of this minibook. (Plus, you probably already know how to use the File➪New and the File➪Open commands.) However, if you're not using the Office shortcut bar (and you installed it), try it out by choosing Start➪All Programs➪Microsoft Office Tools➪Microsoft Office Shortcut Bar.

schedule. Although you get Outlook Express for free with Windows XP, the full-blown Outlook 2003 that ships with Office 2003 is a far superior program because it additionally includes features like

✦ **Contact tracking,** which ties together all the Office documents and e-mail associated with a contact.

✦ **An event calendar.**

✦ **Appointment reminders,** which appear onscreen at the time that you specify to make sure that you don't miss The Big Date.

Some of the top Outlook features include

✦ **Group scheduling:** Not only can Outlook handle your personal calendar, but you can participate in a shared common schedule with others in your workgroup.

✦ **A truly awesome Find function:** Imagine being able to search all your e-mail messages, all your appointments, and all your scheduled tasks for the word *pickle* — well, whatever *you* want, naturally.

✦ **Calendar coloring:** Mom always said, "If it's color coded, it's easier and faster to use." Evidently, the folks in Redmond agree because you can assign colors to appointments.

✦ **Support for Hotmail accounts:** If you use Microsoft's Hotmail Web-based e-mail service, Outlook can retrieve those messages for you.

✦ **Mailbox cleanup options:** It's a messy job, but you've got to do it . . . or do you? Outlook can automatically archive older messages, or you can manually clean your Inbox according to the message date or size.

✦ **Onscreen reminders:** Let Outlook prompt you to attend that meeting or make that phone call. You can set reminders with an audible alarm or keep things quiet with an onscreen notification dialog box.

Discover how to stay in touch (and organized) with Outlook in Book V, Chapter 6.

Putting the Office Clipboard to Work

The *Office Clipboard* (shown in Figure 1-5 as it appears in Word) is essentially a supercharged version of the standard Windows XP Clipboard. It's specially designed to hold, display, and paste multiple items from one or more Office documents. For example, you can copy an amount from an Excel spreadsheet, a contact name from Outlook, and even a company logo graphic from PowerPoint — and then copy all those items into a Word document.

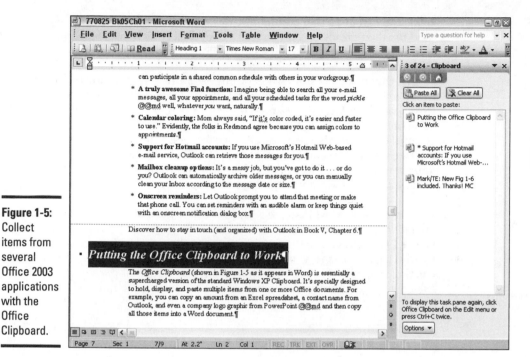

Figure 1-5:
Collect
items from
several
Office 2003
applications
with the
Office
Clipboard.

You can display the Office Clipboard task pane at any time by choosing Edit⇨ Office Clipboard or by pressing Ctrl+C twice.

When you display the Office Clipboard, anything that you copy from the Edit menu (or with the Ctrl+C shortcut) is added to it instead of to the XP Clipboard. After it's on the Office Clipboard, you can right-click items to selectively paste or delete them (which you can't do from the system Clipboard). To paste all the items at once, click the Paste All button in the task pane; to clear everything in one fell swoop, click the Clear All button.

Note that any items that you add to the Office Clipboard stay there until you exit all Office applications, and they aren't affected by the single item stored on the Windows XP Clipboard. Now *that*, my friends, is handy.

Sharing Well with Others

Do you collaborate often with the other PC users in your home or office — perhaps working on the same PowerPoint presentation for an upcoming board meeting, or making tweaks to a shared family budget worksheet? If so, you'll appreciate the collaboration and file-sharing tools built in to Office

2003. You can even add comments, or allow others to revise a document (and nix those revisions if you don't like 'em). I show you how to share your stuff — and protect it as well — in the chapters that follow.

In fact, Office 2003 contains a very important new feature for those collaborative spirits who share documents: shared workspaces. Consider a shared workspace as a Web site where you, your documents, and your colleagues hang out — but that site is available right from within your Office 2003 applications! (You can also use a shared workspace from anywhere with an Internet connection and Internet Explorer, like when you're on the road with your laptop.) Members can share documents right from the workspace library, assign tasks, and exchange messages.

To create a shared workspace within an Office 2003 application, click Tools⇨ Shared Workspace to display the Shared Workspace task pane that you see in Figure 1-6. Since you're the administrator of the new workspace, you can specify who gets access to your library and lists. Naturally, if you want to join an existing shared workspace set up by someone else, that person will have to assign you member privileges before you can join in the fun.

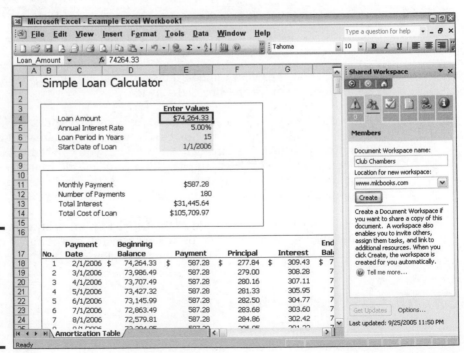

Figure 1-6: Creating Club Chambers — a shared workspace hangout.

Using the Office Help System

No introduction to Microsoft Office 2003 would be complete without information on the excellent Office Help system, as shown in Figure 1-7. Believe me, the Help system is *especially* helpful in Excel and Access. For example, it can save your derrière when you need assistance with a complex formula or function in Excel!

Displaying the Help system

You can display the Office Help system for the Office application you're using by

✦ Clicking the question mark icon in the Standard toolbar

✦ Pressing F1

✦ Pressing Alt+H to display the Help menu and then clicking the application Help menu item

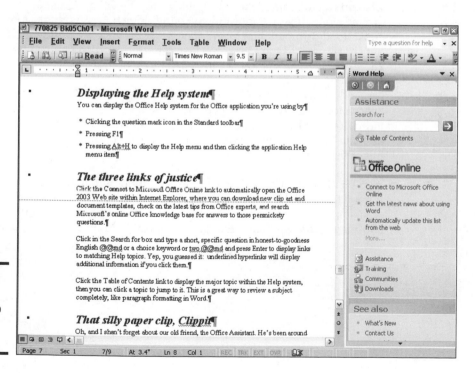

Figure 1-7:
Putting
Office Help
to work in
Excel.

The three links of justice

Click the Connect to Microsoft Office Online link to automatically open the Office 2003 Web site within Internet Explorer, where you can download new clip art and document templates, check on the latest tips from Office experts, and search Microsoft's online Office knowledge base for answers to those persnickety questions.

Click in the Search For box and type a short, specific question in honest-to-goodness English — or a choice keyword or two — and press Enter to display links to matching Help topics. Yep, you guessed it: underlined hyperlinks will display additional information if you click them.

Click the Table of Contents link to display the major topic within the Help system, then you can click a topic to jump to it. This is a great way to review a subject completely, like paragraph formatting in Word.

That silly paper clip, Clippit

Oh, and I shan't forget about our old friend, the Office Assistant. He's been around since the Big Bang, and you either love him or hate his guts. (Microsoft considered dropping him from Office XP, but a sudden, unexpected outpouring of user support saved him at the last minute — and so he remains in Office 2003. However, he's no longer installed by default.)

Actually, this animated Help gadget is simply a friendlier version of the Search for box, but some Office users swear by his occasional random antics. (When he's turned on, the Office Assistant keeps track of your work and can actually appear on his own if the application perceives that you might be having trouble!)

If you find the Office Assistant to be too much of a distraction, you can turn him off from the Help menu. (You can also assign him a different look — the Assistant can become a bouncing ball, a cat, Merlin the Magician, or even a soothing animated Planet Earth. No, I'm not kidding.)

Chapter 2: Using Word

In This Chapter

- Starting Word
- Changing views in Word
- Typing and editing text
- Using Find and Replace
- Creating tables
- Setting tabs and margins
- Formatting your document
- Printing in Word
- Building Web pages in Word

*I*t's time to dive into Word 2003 — probably one of the top five most-used applications on the face of this planet. I first used Word as a character-based DOS program — yes, it's that old. And even then, it was easy to use and produced flawless printed pages . . . which, in my opinion, are the two all-important requirements for any word processor.

Today, Word is the cornerstone of most PC-based word processing; it's versatile enough to perform equally well for everything from a kid's homework to the most professional-looking yearly report. Therefore, this chapter starts with the basics — key shortcuts and the different views that you can use in Word — and ends up delving into more advanced topics, such as collaborative features and Web page creation. Enjoy!

One note about this chapter (and the others in this Office mini-book) — as Popeye might say, "It ain't quite completes." A casual walk through any computer bookstore will convince you that there are a dozen 400-page books that *completely* concentrate on Word (or Excel, or PowerPoint, or Access), so you won't find tons o' advanced features or tons o' complex tips in these 30-or-so pages. However, what you *will* find is good, solid coverage of the most commonly used Word features, and that's enough to take care of the vast majority of common documents that you might require.

Running Word

Enough talk! To start Word, use one of the following methods:

✦ Double-click the Word shortcut on your desktop.

✦ Choose Start (or press a Windows key)⇨All Programs⇨Microsoft Word.

✦ If you're using the Office shortcut bar, click the Word icon.

✦ Double-click a Word document within the Explorer window or on your desktop.

✦ Are you ready for a really fast trick? If you have a keyboard with the Windows keys (they look like the Windows waving flag), press Win+R (hold down the Windows key and then press R), type **winword**, and then press Enter. This opens the Run dialog box, and *winword* is the actual executable name for Word. Whoosh!

As an author, I use Word more than any other application on the planet . . . except, perhaps, for World of Warcraft. Anyway, if you use Word every hour of your business day, add it to your *Quick Launch bar* like I did. As you can read earlier in the book, that's the left part of the taskbar that rests snugly against the Start button. Choose Start⇨All Programs and then right-click and drag the Word icon to the Quick Launch bar. When the plus sign cursor appears, release the mouse button and then choose Copy from the pop-up menu that appears. Voilà! Now you can summon Word with a single click from the taskbar.

The Elements of Word

After Word has churned its way onto the screen, you'll see the program's window, which should look something like Figure 2-1. (I say *something like* because I've customized my Word toolbars to my taste, which appears not to match the prevailing thought in Redmond. The default screen looks somewhat different.)

Although you probably know most of the guests invited to the party, here's a quick rundown of who showed up:

✦ **The menu:** No surprise here. However, Word does turn on what I call the "shortified" menus by default, so you see only what you've been using recently. (To see the rest, you have to click the down button at the bottom of the menu.) This drives me up the wall, so I force the display of the full menu. To do this, choose Tools⇨Customize, click the Options tab, select the Always Show Full Menus check box to enable it, and then click Close to save the change.

✦ **The toolbars:** And geez, what toolbars they are! Clicking a button on one of these toolbars does the same job as the corresponding menu commands. If you see a small double-arrow icon pointing to the right at the end of a toolbar, you can click it to display additional icons that didn't fit at the current window size. To select which toolbars you want to see within Word, choose View⇨Toolbars and then click a specific toolbar in the pop-up menu to toggle it off or on.

Hey, did you ever notice those little icons next to the items in Word's menu system? For example, open the File menu, and you'll notice a tiny printer next to the Print menu item. Well, bucko, those aren't there by accident — in fact, those icons match the button icons used on Word's toolbars! Peruse the menu system and take a moment to match the menu item that you're using with its corresponding toolbar button — if that particular toolbar is displayed, of course. After you learn the different toolbar buttons by heart, the convenience of clicking kicks in, and you'll never use that menu item again!

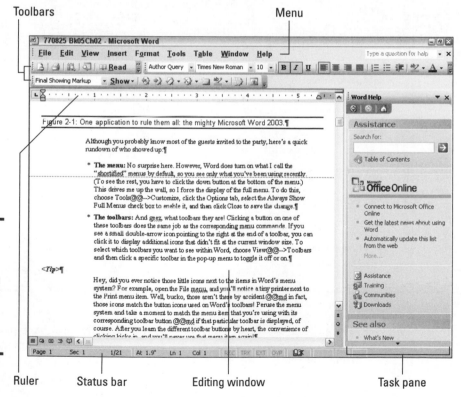

Figure 2-1:
One application to rule them all: the mighty Microsoft Word 2003.

Toolbar is not a dirty word

Let's talk toolbar customizing for a moment. Move your mouse pointer to either end of a toolbar, and you'll note that it turns into a funky, four-direction cursor. This indicates that you can now click and drag to relocate the toolbar to any side of the screen. Or, if you drag the toolbar to the middle of the window, it magically turns into a floating toolbar that can be repositioned like any other window.

Also, you can add or remove buttons by clicking the down-arrow button at the end of a toolbar; choose Add or Remove Buttons and then mark the name of the toolbar from the pop-up window that appears. Mark the check boxes next to an individual button name to toggle the display of that button on or off, as shown in this figure.

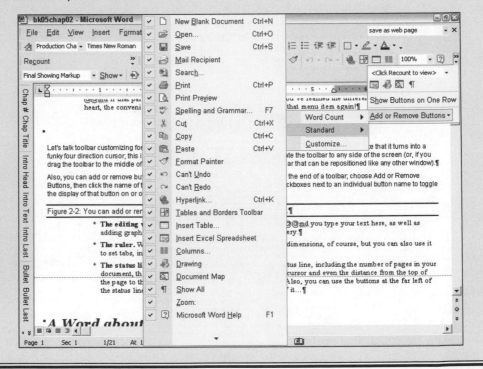

✦ **The editing window:** This is where all the real work takes place. Type your text here and add graphics, tables, and all sorts of specialized tomfoolery.

✦ **The task pane:** Word uses this resizable piece of window real estate to display all sorts of information, and also provides you with clickable links for common functions — for example, you can open a file you've recently created or edited from here, instead of that "antique" File menu. The task pane is available from the View menu. Using the task pane, you can display the Word 2003 Help system, choose a piece of clip art, pick from the contents of the Office Clipboard, or switch to a new style and paragraph formatting. (To switch between the different functions of the task pane, click the down arrow icon next to the pane's Close button.)

✦ **The ruler:** Word's ruler can be used to keep track of page dimensions, of course, but you can also use it to set tabs and margins. (More on this in the later section "Adjusting Tabs and Margins.")

✦ **The status bar:** You'll find all sorts of statistics on the status bar, including the number of pages in your document, the current line and column position of the text cursor, and even the distance from the top of the page to the text cursor. (Currently, it's at 7.6 inches.) Also, you can use the buttons at the far left of the status bar to change your view mode. Come to think of it. . . .

A Word about the Views

Speaking of views, Word can display your document in more than just one mundane way. You can switch between views by clicking the View menu and then clicking the desired view (each appears as a separate menu item), or you can click the view buttons at the bottom-left corner of the editing window, right above the status bar. Take a gander at this selection of views.

Normal view

Normal view is your plain vanilla, default viewing mode (as shown earlier in Figure 2-1). However, I've always found Normal view to be the quickest to use when I'm typing or when I'm editing an existing document. ***Remember:*** What you see in Normal view might definitely *not* be what you get when you print, so switch to Web Layout or Page Layout views to edit the appearance of a document. And use Print Preview (click the Standard toolbar icon that looks like a document with a magnifying glass) to check on the appearance of the printed pages before you send 'em to the Monster of Toner. The first button at the lower left selects Normal view.

Outline view

In Outline view (check it out in Figure 2-2), the structure of your document is the important thing, much like the outlining that you learned in grade school. Word's Outline view allows you to change and rearrange the sections of your entire document. (Except that this time, you get to use a click of the mouse instead of that doggone eraser.) Within Outline view, you can click the symbol next to any heading and drag it to a new spot — just release the button to drop the section at the insertion point. Headings and sections of body text can also be reassigned to different levels by clicking the symbol next to the heading and dragging it to the left (to promote it) or to the right (to demote it). You can select Outline view by clicking the fourth button at the bottom-left corner of the editing window.

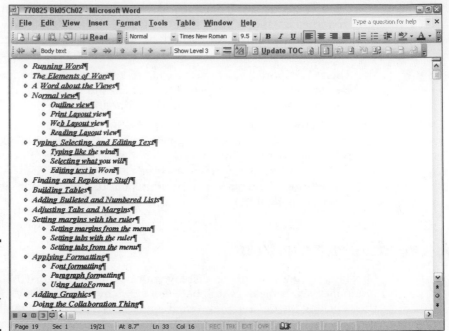

Figure 2-2:
Hey, an outline that I really *like* for a change!

Print Layout view

I recommend switching to Print Layout view when you need to design the look of your page because you can easily work with page elements such as columns and graphics by clicking and dragging them from place to place. (You can also click most elements and drag their borders to new locations.) If you're familiar with desktop publishing programs like Adobe PageMaker or FrameMaker, you'll feel right at home in Print Layout view. Click the third tiny button at the left of the status bar to switch to Print Layout view.

Web Layout view

Of course, there's the Internet side of things. In Web Layout view, Word adds any background that you specify, places images where they will appear in a Web browser, and wraps the text to fit the window size. You can use this view to design a document that will be saved later as a Web page. Click the second button at the lower left of the Word editing window to use Web Layout view.

If you're building Web pages within Word, don't forget the Web Page Preview feature, which operates just like Print Preview — you'll see exactly what your page will look like in Internet Explorer. (Probably because Word automatically runs your Web browser and automatically loads the document!) To use the Web Page Preview, choose File➪Web Page Preview.

Reading Layout view

The latest edition of Word adds the new Reading Layout view, which is specially designed to make your document easy to read onscreen. (Call this view the E-Book Special if you like.) Pages appear one at a time, like a book, and the page is automatically sized to fit virtually all of the application window. (Note that the page will *not* appear this way if printed!) Word also turns on Microsoft's ClearType font-smoothing feature to help make the text easier on the eyes — and personally, I think it works. Since the Reviewing toolbar is still active in Reading Layout view, it's easier to use Word's revision and markup tools, too. Click the last button at the lower left of the Word editing window, which looks like an open book, to use Reading Layout view; to return to the previous view, press Esc.

And don't forget Document Map. It's a great convenience when moving quickly through large documents. Just choose View⇨Document Map, and Word opens a separate pane at the left side of the editing window (as shown in Figure 2-3). To close Document Map, just choose View⇨Document Map again. You can move immediately to any heading within your document by clicking it within Document Map.

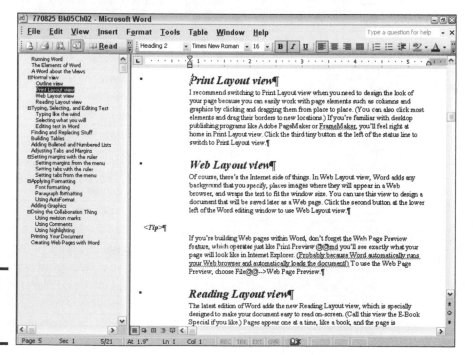

Figure 2-3:
Go,
Document
Map, go!

Typing, Selecting, and Editing Text

Ready to start your first foray into the editing window? In this section, I discuss the three all-important things that you'll be doing most often during your Word session: typing new text, selecting existing text, and editing existing text.

Typing like the wind

Okay, I know this seems like a no-brainer — and typing in Word is indeed pretty simple. First, locate the insertion cursor (which looks like a blinking bar) where you want in the editing window (by clicking the mouse pointer, which looks like a tiny I-beam, or by using the movement keyboard shortcuts listed in Table 2-1). Tickle the ivories to enter your text.

You can press Insert to enter *Overwrite mode,* in which the new characters that you type overwrite any existing text; to return to *Insert mode,* in which new characters are inserted at the cursor point, press the Insert key again.

Table 2-1	Movement Shortcut Keys in Word
Key	*Movement*
Left arrow (←)	Moves the cursor one character to the left
Right arrow (→)	Moves the cursor one character to the right
Up arrow (↑)	Moves the cursor to the preceding line
Down arrow (↓)	Moves the cursor to the next line
Ctrl+←	Moves the cursor one word to the left
Ctrl+→	Moves the cursor one word to the right
Ctrl+↑	Moves the cursor one paragraph up
Ctrl+↓	Moves the cursor one paragraph down
Page Up	Moves the cursor up one screen
Page Down	Moves the cursor down one screen
End	Moves the cursor to the end of the current line
Home	Moves the cursor to the beginning of the current line
Ctrl+Page Up	Moves the cursor to the top of the previous page
Ctrl+Page Down	Moves the cursor to the top of the next page
Ctrl+Home	Moves the cursor to the beginning of the document
Ctrl+End	Moves the cursor to the end of the document

Selecting what you will

My father always used to say, "Nothing is perfect the first time around" — and a Word document is no exception. However, don't break out the Liquid Paper for your screen! Instead, use the mouse to select text or graphics by clicking and dragging the I-beam cursor across the text that you want to change or format or use the selection keyboard shortcuts provided so conveniently by Table 2-2.

To select a word, just double-click it — to select a graphic, click it once. To select several pages of text, click to place the insertion cursor at the start of the text that you want to highlight and then hold down Shift while you click at the end of the text.

Table 2-2	Selection Shortcut Keys in Word
Key	*Selection*
Shift+←	Selects one character to the left of the cursor
Shift+→	Selects one character to the right of the cursor
Shift+↑	Selects characters to the previous line
Shift+↓	Selects characters to the next line
Shift+End	Selects characters to the end of the current line
Shift+Home	Selects characters to the beginning of the current line
Shift+Page Down	Selects characters to the next screen
Shift+Page Up	Selects characters to the previous screen
Ctrl+Shift+←	Selects characters to the beginning of the word
Ctrl+Shift+→	Selects characters to the end of the word
Ctrl+Shift+↑	Selects characters to the beginning of the current paragraph
Ctrl+Shift+↓	Selects characters to the end of the current paragraph
Ctrl+Shift+Home	Selects characters to the beginning of the document
Ctrl+Shift+End	Selects characters to the end of the document

Editing text in Word

After you select the text and graphics that you want to change, you can then pick an action (either from the toolbars or the menu system) or use one of the editing keyboard shortcuts shown in Table 2-3.

Table 2-3	Editing Shortcut Keys in Word
Key	*Function*
Any character	Replaces the selected text
Delete	Deletes the selected text and graphics
Ctrl+X	Cuts the selection and adds it on the Clipboard (or the Office Clipboard, if it's displayed)
Ctrl+C	Copies the selection to the Clipboard (or the Office Clipboard, if it's displayed)
Ctrl+V	Replaces the selection with the contents of the Clipboard

Finding and Replacing Stuff

I don't know about you, but manually tracking down every single occurrence of the word *salacious* in my Word documents is not my idea of fun! (Okay, perhaps not *salacious* — substitute your own most common word there.) Anyway, Word provides you with all the Dynamic Duo of Find and Replace, which ensures that no word or phrase in your document can escape your all-seeing eye.

To perform a Find or Replace, follow these steps:

1. **Choose Edit⇨Replace or press Ctrl+H.**

   This displays the Find and Replace dialog box that you see in Figure 2-4. Actually, the Find command (choose Edit⇨Find or press Ctrl+F) displays the same dialog box, but you see the Find tab instead. You'll note that this dialog box floats above the Word window. And, unlike other active dialog boxes, you can continue to click, select, and type in the Word window while the Find and Replace dialog box is open.

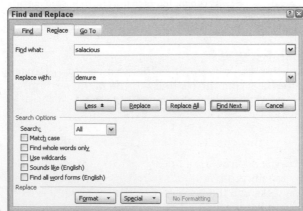

Figure 2-4: Substituting *salacious* with *demure* is child's play with Replace.

2. **Type the word or phrase that you need to locate or change in the Find What text field.**

   If you've already searched for the target string earlier, click the down arrow next to the box and select it from the drop-down list box.

3. **To replace any matches with something new, type the word or phrase that you want to substitute in the Replace With text field.**

   Again, if you've already used the new value to replace something earlier in this writing session, just click the down arrow and choose the desired value from the drop-down list box.

   Click the Special button to display a pop-up menu of special and non-printing characters that you can insert at the cursor position in the Find What or Replace With boxes. For instance, if you need to search for (or replace using) a graphic, a Tab character, or a caret character, you can pick it from the Special button menu.

4. **To find the next occurrence, click the Find Next button; to replace the next occurrence, click the Replace button.**

   You can also click the Replace All button to locate and replace all occurrences of the word or phrase. However, I recommend clicking Replace one time first just to make sure that you're indeed matching what you think! If the correct word or phrase is replaced, click Replace All to finish the job.

   Remember that you can immediately use Undo after any Word action goes awry. In this case, if you suddenly find that you've replaced every *the* in your document with *thee* by accident, choose Edit⇨Undo Replace or use the Ctrl+Z keyboard shortcut.

5. **If you used Find Next or Replace in the previous step, Word selects the next occurrence.**

   You can continue your Find or Replace activities, or you can click Cancel if you're done.

That's the mundane side of Find and Replace. However, if you click the More button at the bottom of the Find and Replace dialog box, as in Figure 2-4 (which switches the More button to Less), you'll see all sorts of interesting options that can help you fine-tune your search, including

✦ **Match Case:** By default, Find and Replace are case-insensitive toys — mark this check box to make capitalization matter.

✦ **Find Whole Words Only:** When this check box is disabled, Word matches portions of a word, which comes in handy when changing tenses, prefixes, or suffixes. To force Word to match only the exact string that you entered, select this check box to enable it.

✦ **Use Wildcards:** A throwback to the days of DOS, *wildcards* allow you to search for specific combinations of letters or numbers in your target string. Unix folks call this *pattern matching*. (Check the Word Help system for a complete list of wildcards.)

✦ **Sounds Like:** If you know what the target word sounds like but you can't spell it, enable the Sounds Like check box, and Word will locate matching words that sound the same. For example, *role* will match *roll*.

✦ **Find All Word Forms:** Enable this check box to locate all forms of the target noun or verb — tenses, plurals, and such. Trick indeed!

To perform a search based on any sort of formatting (such as character or paragraph formatting or a specific language within your document), click the Format button and then select the appropriate type of formatting from the pop-up menu that appears.

Building Tables

Tables are great for displaying . . . well . . . tabular information. (Stunning stuff, Mark.) But that information need not be uniform, and you can add all sorts of eye candy (like shading) and different types of borders.

Follow these steps to add a standard table to your Word document:

1. **Click within your document to place the insertion cursor in the desired spot for the table.**

2. **Choose Table⇨Insert⇨Table to display the Insert Table dialog box that you see in Figure 2-5.**

Figure 2-5:
Inserting a table into a Word document is easy.

3. **Click in the Number of Columns text box and type the number of columns that you need in the table.**

4. **Click in the Number of Rows text box and type the number of columns that you need in the table.**

5. **Select the AutoFit Behavior option that you prefer.**

   The default, Fixed Column Width, is fine if all the values that the table will hold will be uniform in length; however, I recommend that you choose AutoFit to Contents if you need to save space in your document, or if certain values are far longer than others. If you're creating a Web page, select AutoFit to Window.

6. **Click OK to create the basic table structure, as shown in Figure 2-6.**

7. **Click in each cell (in front of each of the markers, which I like to call Space Invaders) and type the value.**

   You can apply the same formatting attributes to the text in a table cell, too. For example, I select the top row of a table and then press Ctrl+B to create bold column headings. (More on how to display the Space Invaders — which, in actuality, are paragraph markers — later in the chapter.)

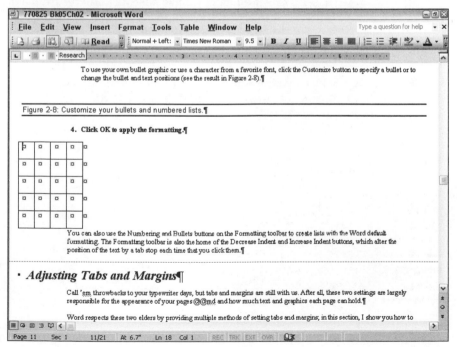

Figure 2-6:
A new table, ready for your values.

This provides you with a basic table. Right-click the table itself, choose Borders and Shading from the pop-up menu that appears, and be amazed at all the fun fashions that you can use to decorate that simple frame! You can change the type, width, and color of the border, for instance; or click the Shading tab and choose your own colors, shading, and patterns (either for the entire table or just for the cells that you select).

Adding Bulleted and Numbered Lists

Creating bullets and numbered lists automatically in Word is a cinch. Follow these steps:

1. **Click anywhere within the paragraph that you want to format.**

2. **Choose Format⇨Bullets and Numbering to display the dialog box that you see in Figure 2-7.**

3. **Click the type of bullet formatting that you want to apply to the paragraph, or click the Numbered or the Outline Numbered tabs to create a numbered list or outline (respectively).**

   To use your own bullet graphic or use a character from a favorite font, click the Customize button to specify a bullet or to change the bullet and text positions (see the result in Figure 2-8).

4. **Click OK to apply the formatting.**

You can also use the Numbering and Bullets buttons on the Formatting toolbar to create lists with the Word default formatting. The Formatting toolbar is also the home of the Decrease Indent and Increase Indent buttons, which alter the position of the text by a tab stop each time that you click them.

Figure 2-7: Select a bullet format from Word's impressive selection.

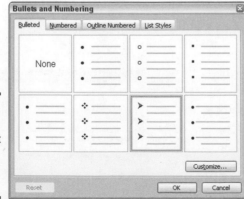

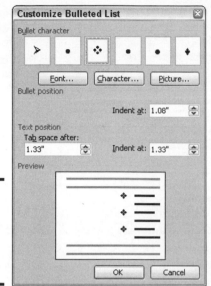

Figure 2-8:
Customize
your bullets
and
numbered
lists.

Adjusting Tabs and Margins

Call 'em throwbacks to your typewriter days, but tabs and margins are still with us. After all, these two settings are largely responsible for the appearance of your pages — and how much text and graphics each page can hold.

Word respects these two elders by providing multiple methods of setting tabs and margins; in this section, I show you how to configure tabs and margins by using both your mouse and your keyboard.

Setting margins with the ruler

Follow these steps to set up margins by using Word's horizontal and vertical rulers:

1. **Change to Print Layout view by clicking the Print Layout button at the left of the status bar.**

2. **Move your mouse cursor over the end of either of the shaded bars on the ruler.**

   These bars indicate the current margin, and the mouse pointer will turn into a twin-arrow cursor to indicate that the bar can be moved (as shown with the right margin in Figure 2-9).

3. **Click and drag the arrow cursor in the desired direction.**

4. **Release the mouse button to set the new margin value.**

The two-arrow cursor indicates that a margin can be moved.

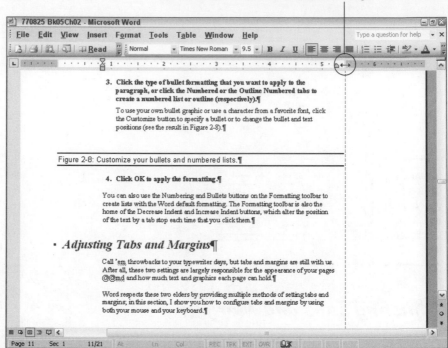

Figure 2-9:
Set margins
with the
ruler.

Setting margins from the menu

Follow these steps to set margins from the File menu:

1. **Choose File⇨Page Setup, which displays the Page Setup dialog box that you see in Figure 2-10.**

2. **Click in the appropriate Margins text box (for the margin that you want to change) and then type the desired value in inches.**

3. **Click the arrow of the Apply To drop-down list and then select Whole Document.**

   To apply margin changes to just a part of the document, select the desired text before opening the Page Setup dialog box and then choose Selected Text from the Apply To drop-down list. If you want the margin change to apply to the remainder of the document starting at the current position of the insertion cursor, choose This Point Forward instead.

4. **Click OK to save your changes and return to your document.**

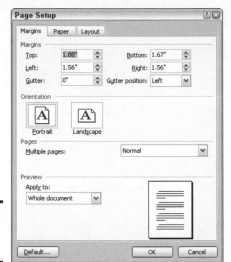

Figure 2-10:
Set margins
from here.

Setting tabs with the ruler

Word offers several different types of tabs, including left, center, right and decimal- or bar-aligned. To add a tab stop with the ruler, follow these steps:

1. **Click anywhere within the paragraph where you want to place the tab.**

2. **Click the Tab button at the upper-left corner of the editing window —
   it appears at the left side of the ruler — until you've selected the type
   of tab that you need.**

   To check the current tab type, just leave your mouse pointer hovering
   on top of the Tab button until the tooltip description appears.

3. **Click the desired spot on the ruler where you want to place the tab.**

To help you keep track of your tab, Word automatically adds a tab stop mark
(looks like the old-fashioned tab pointer on your trusty manual Olivet typewriter) on the ruler.

Setting tabs from the menu

Follow these steps to set a tab stop from the menu:

1. **Choose Format⊏⟩Tabs to open the Tabs dialog box as shown in
   Figure 2-11.**

2. **Click in the Tab Stop Position field and then type the position of the
   new tab stop in inches.**

3. **Select the desired Alignment option.**

4. To add a leader to the new tab stop, select one of the Leader selections.

A *leader* is a character that's used to fill the open space that normally appears when you press the Tab key. Leader characters are often used in a table of contents, telephone list, or restaurant menu.

Word sets your default tab stops to every half inch; to choose a new default value for tab stops, click in the Default Tab Stops field and type the new value (in inches).

5. Click the Set button to set the new tab.

6. To clear a tab stop, click the tab stop that you want to remove within the list on the left and then click Clear.

Or you can clear all the tab stops in one fell swoop by clicking the Clear All button.

7. Click OK to return to your document.

Applying Formatting

Word offers a number of different formatting commands. At the lowest level, you can manually format individual characters by changing their attributes. At the highest level, you can set Word to automatically format your document while you type! In this section, I describe how to fine-tune your formatting.

Font formatting

You probably already know the trio of attributes that I like to call The Big Three:

✦ **Bold:** Press Ctrl+B to add emphasis to the selected text.

✦ *Italic:* Press Ctrl+I to italicize the selected text.

✦ <u>Underline:</u> Press Ctrl+U to underline the selected text.

Of course, each of The Big Three is represented by a separate button on the Formatting toolbar (**B**, *I*, and <u>U</u>). But there's a heck of a lot more font formatting where that came from — you can also add these attributes to selected text:

✦ **The font family:** (No relation to the Addams Family.) Choose Format⇨ Font to display the Font dialog box that you see in Figure 2-12 and then click the font name that you want to use. (Alternatively, click the Font drop-down list box on the Formatting toolbar.)

✦ **The size:** Click the desired font size (in points) from the Size list or type the size that you want directly into the Size text box.

✦ **The color:** You can click the Font Color drop-down list to choose the latest fashion color for your text.

✦ **The standard effects:** Select check boxes in the Effects section to enable an effect, and Word automatically updates the Preview window with the results.

✦ **The spacing:** Click the Character Spacing tab and then choose the amount of space between characters, or you can raise and lower the characters by the amount that you specify. Word shows you the fruit of your labor in the Preview window.

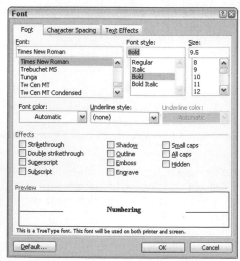

Figure 2-12:
The Font dialog box is a busy metropolitan location.

✦ **The text animations:** Click the Text Effects tab, and . . . wow! Check out the optional animation effects that you can add to any font! Again, Word updates the preview to show you what kind of exotic creature that you've created.

Note that you don't need to actually select text to use font formatting. If no text is specifically selected, Word simply applies your font changes to any new text that you type at the current location of the insertion cursor.

Paragraph formatting

Word is a consistent machine. And, as you might expect, formatting a paragraph is very similar to formatting individual characters. (Note, however, that not every separate text element on a page is actually a true American paragraph; in order to qualify, the text block must end with a paragraph mark, which is represented by that weird backwards *P* symbol.)

Because Word normally hides formatting marks, you probably won't see any paragraph marks in your document unless you specifically tell Word to display them. You can do this by choosing Tools⇨Options and enabling the Paragraph Marks check box on the View tab. Personally, I like to be able to see where my paragraphs come to a halt because I do quite a bit of formatting on manuscripts (and it makes a great difference whether you select a paragraph *with* or *without* the paragraph mark)!

Commonly used paragraph formatting attributes include

✦ **The alignment:** Choose Format⇨Paragraph to display the Paragraph dialog box (that you see in Figure 2-13) and then click the Alignment drop-down list box. Word can align text to the left or right margin or center the paragraph in the page. You can also choose to *justify* a paragraph, which adds extra spacing to stretch each full line in the paragraph from the left to the right margin.

✦ **The indentation:** As I show you in the earlier section "Adding Bulleted and Numbered Lists," you can automatically add bullets and line numbers to your text. From the Paragraph dialog box, you can specify the amount to indent the selected paragraph as well as what kind of indent to use.

✦ **The spacing:** Click the Line Spacing drop-down list box of the Paragraph dialog box to choose double spacing or to specify a precise line spacing of your own choosing. This is also the place where you can add extra space before or after a paragraph.

These commands are also conveniently located as buttons on the Formatting toolbar.

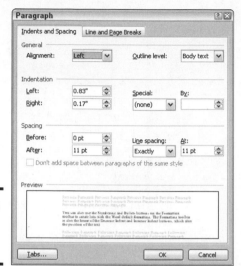

Figure 2-13:
Need to
format a
paragraph?

Using AutoFormat

Before I leave the fair shores of formatting, I'd like to mention another "either you love it or you hate it" feature. This one ranks right up there with the Office Assistant. I'm talking about Word's *AutoFormat* feature, which — true to its name — automatically recognizes what it feels should be formatted and then takes care of the task for you . . . whether you want it to or not. To illustrate: If you type an asterisk at the beginning of a line and press Enter at the end, AutoFormat figures, "Oh, that crazy human actually wants a bulleted list item" and thus formats the paragraph with an indent and a bullet character and then adds another bullet for your next item. The same thing happens with num-bered lists, too. Try typing **1.** at the beginning of the line and pressing Enter just to see the results.

Now don't get me wrong. If you're a newcomer to Word or you don't need precise control over the formatting in your document, AutoFormat can be a true timesaver and a big help. (Pause.) However, if you *do* need that precise formatting control, AutoFormat suddenly becomes a nightmare when you're forced to helplessly watch Word do what it thinks is right.

Therefore, here's how to disable AutoFormat — which is on by default — just in case you find it nerve-wracking instead of helpful:

1. **Choose Tools➪AutoCorrect Options and then click the AutoFormat As You Type tab to display the settings shown in Figure 2-14.**

2. **To completely disable AutoFormatting while you type, disable all the check boxes and then click OK.**

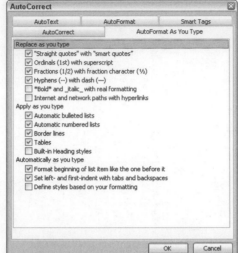

Figure 2-14:
No, Word!
Bad
AutoFormat!
No biscuit!

Note that you can still run AutoFormat on your entire document at once at any time — just choose Format➪AutoFormat.

3. Click OK to save your changes.

(And you can bet that I didn't use AutoFormat to create this numbered list, either. Harrumph.)

Adding Graphics

You have a number of different ways to add graphics to your Word document. After you click in the desired spot (which moves the insertion cursor to that point in your document), use one of the following methods:

✦ **Paste it from the Clipboard.** If you've copied a graphic to your Windows or Office Clipboard, you can paste it to the current cursor location (as shown in Figure 2-15).

✦ **Insert it from a file.** If the graphic is stored on your hard drive, choose Insert➪Picture➪From File. Word displays the familiar Insert Picture dialog box, from where you can navigate to the location of the image. Click once on the filename to select it and then click the Insert button.

✦ **Insert a clip art image.** Choose Insert➪Picture➪Clip Art to display the Insert Clip Art panel. Type a keyword in the Search text box, click the Search In drop-down list box, and then choose All Collections. Click the Search button to display thumbnail images of any matching clip art. As you can see in Figure 2-16, I'm not the only person who loves Halloween!

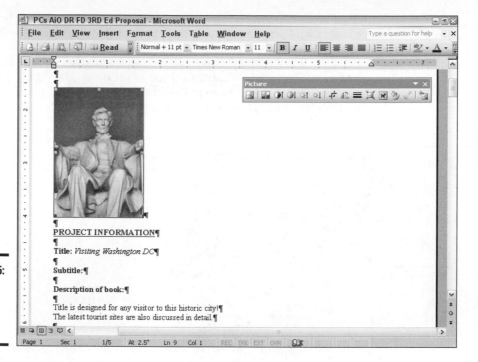

Figure 2-15:
Add a
graphic
from the
Clipboard.

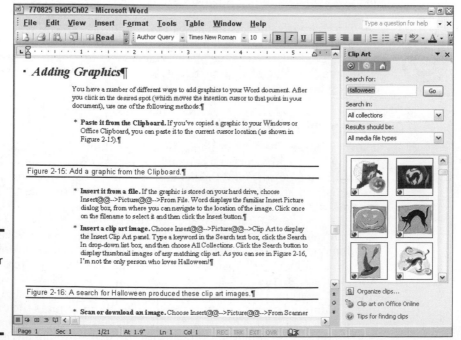

Figure 2-16:
A search for
Halloween
produced
these clip
art images.

✦ **Scan or download an image.** Choose Insert⇨Picture⇨From Scanner or Camera, and you can actually insert an image directly from either of these peripherals! What you see next depends on your scanner or camera's TWAIN (technology without an interesting name) driver. For instance, Figure 2-17 illustrates the dialog box displayed by my Web camera, so you might have to refer to the device manufacturer's user manual for more information on what does what.

Figure 2-17:
Insert an image into Word via your scanner or camera.

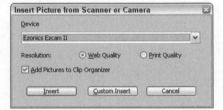

Doing the Collaboration Thing

Word includes several features for managing collaborative documents — keeping things straight about who revised what or perhaps adding comments and highlighting to indicate where changes are necessary.

Need to share the information in your Word document with data-mining or database applications? You'll be happy to learn that Word 2003 can save a document in XML (Extensible Markup Language) format using the standard File⇨Save As dialog box. Choose XML Document from the Save as type drop-down list box.

Using revision marks

If several editors have their hands in a single document, revision marks are the only way to go. Everyone can make changes (Word assigns different colors to each editor), and those changes can be reviewed and applied (or discarded) on an individual basis, or you can accept or revert all changes at once.

To use revision marks, choose Tools⇨Track Changes. (Alternatively, if you're a toolbar person, click the Track Changes button on the Reviewing toolbar. Show this toolbar by choosing View⇨Toolbars⇨Reviewing.) Now you've told Word to track anything that anyone does within the document. Nothing appears to happen . . . at least, that is, until you make any change to the document. Continue typing or editing as you like. Word formats the changes that you make with a unique color, underlining them to make things easier to see. Deleted text and graphics are shown with the strikethrough attribute.

When you're ready to review the revision marks in a document, display the Reviewing toolbar. I highly recommend that you work with revision marks using the toolbar because using the menu can get a little ponderous. Click the Next button on the toolbar to jump to the next revision and then click either the Accept Change or Reject Change button. (For just a second, you'll feel like you have the ol' Caesar thumb . . . you know, the one that Caesar gets to use in any gladiator movie.)

Just in case you don't quite have the power of Caesar, you can always save the revised document under another filename before you decide for or against the edits. (Even a Roman emperor could use a little insurance.)

To accept in one fell swoop all the changes made with revision marks, click the arrow next to the Accept Change button to display the drop-down list box and then click Accept All Changes in Document. To toss out all those silly edits, click the arrow next to the Reject Change button and then choose Reject All Changes in Document. The *nerve* of some people, tampering with perfection!

Using Comments

Next, take a look at *Comments,* which allow anyone to flag a document without directly changing its contents. To add a Comment, select the text that you want to comment on and then choose Insert⇨Comment (or click the New Comment button on that now-familiar Reviewing toolbar).

Word displays a color marker at the word or point where you made the Comment and opens the Comment window, which you see at the bottom of Figure 2-18. The insertion cursor is also automatically relocated in the Comment window, so you can type your Comment text, which is marked with the name, date, and time. When you're done, click anywhere in the editing window to continue or click the Reviewing Pane button in the Reviewing toolbar to toggle it off.

If you need more room to view the comments, click and drag the bar separating the Comment pane from the editing window to relocate it.

When you're ready to review comments, you can

✦ Review the comments in a document by using the Next and Previous buttons on the Reviewing toolbar.

✦ Hover your mouse pointer on top of the highlighted comment marker in the text.

✦ Double-click the shaded header in the Comment pane, which automatically switches Word into Print Layout view and displays the comment.

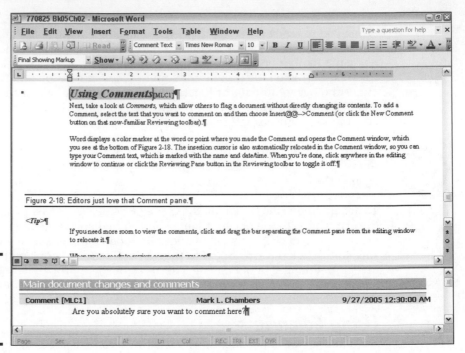

Figure 2-18: Editors just love that Comment pane.

Of course, you can't "apply" a comment, but you can delete those that offend. Just click anywhere in the commented text and then click the Delete Comment button on the Reviewing toolbar (or just right-click the Comment marker in the text and then choose Delete Comment from the pop-up menu that appears).

Circulating your document among the more unsavory members of your office? Luckily, Word 2003 introduces a new feature that allows you to restrict others from making certain types of edits! Choose Tools➪Protect Document to display the Protect Document task pane, where you can restrict others to leaving just comments, limit the formatting and editing others can perform, or even turn your document into a read-only master-piece that can be opened but not changed at all! (The read-only option is especially fun as a practical joke on my editors.)

Using highlighting

Ever wish that you could turn the editing clock back to paper and those classy neon yellow highlighter markers that you used in school? Fear not: Word can take you there as well. Follow these steps to highlight text in your documents:

1. **Display the Formatting toolbar (View➪Toolbars➪Formatting) and then click the Highlight button (it looks like a fat, smelly marker).**

a. **To select a color, click the down-arrow next to the Highlight button and then click the desired color.**

b. **To erase previous highlighting, click None.**

2. **Select the text to highlight.**

3. **When you're done highlighting, turn the feature off by clicking the Highlight button again.**

Alternatively, you can first select the text that you want to be highlighted, and then click the Highlight button on the Formatting toolbar.

Printing Your Document

Word offers you a number of different ways to print an open document:

✦ **Click the Print toolbar button on the Standard toolbar.** This immediately prints the entire document by using the printer's default settings.

✦ **Choose File⇨Print.** Although it takes longer, the Print dialog box that you see in Figure 2-19 gives you more control over what gets printed and what printer you use — including the number of copies and the option to print only part of the document. (To display the printer-specific options supported by the printer's Windows XP software driver, click the Properties button.)

✦ **Press Ctrl+P.** This method also displays the Print dialog box.

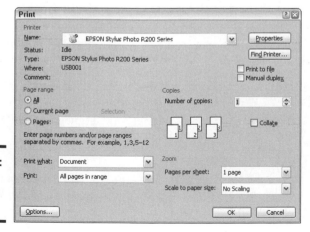

Figure 2-19:
The Word
Print dialog
box.

Creating Web Pages with Word

Although it's no FrontPage, Word can actually step in as a serviceable Web page creation tool! After you create a document, follow these steps to turn that document into a Web page:

1. **Choose File⇨Save As Web Page to display the special Save As dialog box that you see in Figure 2-20.**

2. **Click the Change Title button and then type a title for this page.**

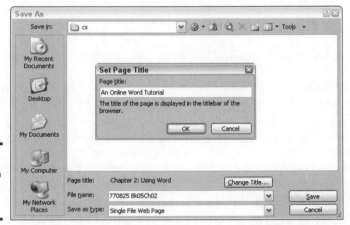

Figure 2-20: Preparing to save a Web page.

3. **After Internet Explorer displays this text in the browser's title bar, click OK.**

4. **Click the Save As drop-down list box and make sure that it's set to Web Page.**

5. **Navigate to the spot where you want to save the file and type a new filename for the page.**

   You don't need to add a HyperText Markup Language (HTML) extension because Word does that automatically.

6. **Click Save.**

   Word creates an HTML page and a separate folder that contains any graphics that are necessary to display the page; all you have to do is move both to your Web server.

Figure 2-21 illustrates one of my Web sites that I created completely in Word. Because some of the advanced formatting that you can use in Word doesn't translate at all to a Web page, the application does the best job that it can. But at least you can rely on Word to produce a Web page that will load in virtually every browser on the planet.

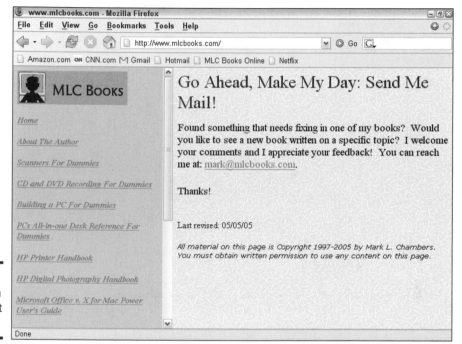

Figure 2-21:
A page from
a Word-built
Web site.

Chapter 3: Putting Excel to Work

In This Chapter

- ✔ Running Excel
- ✔ Presenting the Excel window
- ✔ Typing, selecting, and editing cell text
- ✔ Handling numbers and dates
- ✔ Manipulating rows and columns
- ✔ Formatting cells in Excel
- ✔ Understanding Excel formulas
- ✔ Inserting graphics
- ✔ Adding charts to your worksheets
- ✔ Linking cell values
- ✔ Adding headers and footers
- ✔ Printing worksheets

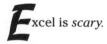 xcel is *scary.*

There, I said it. Most Office 2003 users know that Excel is one doggone power-ful and versatile tool, but It has a reputation for being difficult to learn. (Not to mention all those strange, foreign-looking formulas and functions . . . heck, I can barely remember my long division. And don't even get me started on my kid's math homework.)

In this chapter, however, I can help you with that common Excel-phobia that grips the novice who runs Excel for the first time. I show you the basics of selecting cells and entering cell values, manipulating rows and columns, for-matting numbers and dates, and adding graphics. And yes — believe it or not — I get you started on the road to understanding and using formulas to calculate the values that you need. After all, that's the real power behind Excel — plugging in values to see what happens.

As Thomas Edison, a personal hero of mine, never said, "After Excel formulas are your friends, the world is your oyster." (Then again, he certainly *could* have said it, and perhaps no one was around to write it down. Yeah, that's it.)

Running Excel

You can start the number-cruncher that is Excel in any of the following ways:

✦ Double-click the Excel shortcut on your desktop.

✦ Choose Start➪Microsoft Excel.

✦ If you're using the Office shortcut bar, click the Excel icon.

✦ Double-click an Excel document within Windows Explorer or on your desktop.

✦ If you've added an Excel icon to your Quick Launch bar, click it.

✦ Press Win+R, type **excel** in the Run dialog box that appears, and then press Enter. (That's assuming that your keyboard is equipped with Windows keys, which look like the waving Windows flags and are located on either side of the spacebar.)

Waltzing Around the Excel Window

The Excel main window (as shown in Figure 3-1) has one immediate drawback, and Microsoft has never really been able to address it: Excel simply looks complex from the moment that you start it! However, don't be intimidated by all those cells. When you take a second look, the familiar Office controls are still there.

Although you know most of the guests invited to the party, here's a quick rundown of who showed up:

✦ **The menu:** As expected, the Excel menu system shares a number of commands with other Office programs.

✦ **The toolbar:** This puppy is the very seat of convenience in Excel. Most of the menu commands are replicated on the toolbar, where a single click performs the same action. Note that the Excel toolbar includes a unique field called the Formula Bar, in which you can type in a formula for a cell or view a formula that's already associated with the selected cell. (More on formulas later in the chapter.) If there's not enough room to display all the icons on the toolbar at the current window size, Excel displays a small, double-arrow icon pointing to the right at the end of a toolbar; you can click it to display the additional icons.

To specify which toolbars are displayed, choose View➪Toolbars and then choose the toolbar that you want to toggle on or off.

✦ **The sheet tabs:** These nifty tabs allow you to jump among worksheets and charts in the Excel window. Just click a tab to switch to that worksheet.

✦ **The editing window:** Each individual square in the editing window is a cell, which can hold text, numbers, tables, and graphics.

Toolbars   Menu

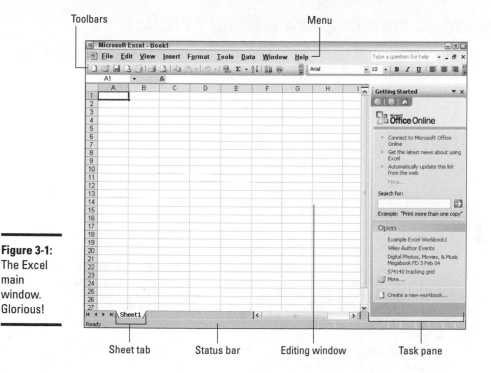

Figure 3-1:
The Excel
main
window.
Glorious!

Sheet tab   Status bar   Editing window   Task pane

✦ **The status bar:** The Excel status bar displays information about calculations and the contents of cells.

Before I launch into a discussion of cells, however, let me clear up a common misunderstanding among novice Excel users concerning the difference between a workbook and a worksheet:

✦ **Workbook:** A *workbook* acts just like a file folder in a filing cabinet, storing all the worksheets required for a single project. Because a workbook acts as the container for worksheets, it's the file that you're working with when you create a new project or when you load and save in Excel (and is featured in the task pane for that reason).

✦ **Worksheet:** A *worksheet* is what you actually use to enter data, graphics, and charts. You can create a new worksheet inside the current workbook at any time. To switch worksheets in the current workbook, use the sheet tabs.

Oh, and with Office 2003, you have to keep in mind that a *workspace* is another thing entirely, and isn't specific to Excel 2003. As I explained in the first chapter of this mini-book, you can collaborate and share your Excel projects on your shared workspace, which resides on a Web server. (Perhaps our friends at Microsoft should come up with a different prefix besides "work" for new features.)

Selecting, Entering, and Editing Cell Data

As I mention earlier, a *cell* is one individual block within a worksheet, and it can hold a number of things:

✦ Numeric values

✦ Text

✦ Graphics

✦ Formulas and functions (which are used to calculate new values)

In this section, I show you how to select one or more cells, enter data into a cell, and edit existing cell data.

Filling a cell to the top

To enter data in a cell, just click it and begin typing. The cell changes into a data entry box, as shown in Figure 3-2. After you're done entering data, press Enter (to move one cell down) or Tab (to move one cell to the right). See there . . . I told you it was easier than it looks, didn't I?

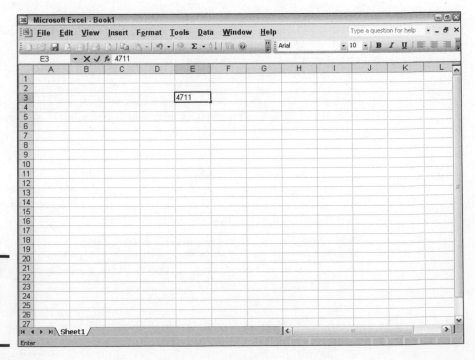

Figure 3-2: To enter data into a cell, just type.

Later in the chapter, I discuss the Formula Bar, which is another method of entering stuff — in this case, a formula — in a cell.

Moving around the worksheet

An Excel worksheet can grow to absolutely momentous proportions. And even at the highest screen resolutions, you're still limited to the same onscreen space as any other Office document. Therefore, your scroll bars are *very* important controls in Excel; use them often and in good health.

You can also use a number of keys and keyboard shortcuts to get to the right place in your worksheet, as shown in Table 3-1.

Table 3-1	Movement Shortcut Keys in Excel
Key	*Movement*
Left arrow (←)	Moves the cursor one cell to the left
Right arrow (→)	Moves the cursor one cell to the right
Up arrow (↑)	Moves the cursor one cell up
Down arrow (↓)	Moves the cursor one cell down
Home	Moves the cursor to the beginning of the current row
Ctrl+Home	Moves the cursor to the beginning of the active worksheet
Ctrl+End	Moves the cursor to the last cell in the worksheet with a value
Page Down	Moves down one screen
Page Up	Moves up one screen
Alt+Page Down	Moves one screen to the right
Alt+Page Up	Moves one screen to the left
Enter	Moves the cursor one cell down (also works within a selection)
Tab	Moves the cursor one cell to the right (also works within a selection)
Shift+Enter	Moves the cursor one cell up (also works within a selection)
Shift+Tab	Moves the cursor one cell to the left (also works within a selection)
Ctrl+arrow key	Moves the cursor to the corresponding edge of any range containing data

Selecting cells the easy way

The next topic is selecting one or more cells, which you'll do before performing an action on the entire group. You can use the following mouse actions to select cells in Excel:

◆ To select a *single* cell, just click it.

◆ To select a *range* of multiple adjacent cells, click a cell at any corner of the desired cells and then drag the mouse in the desired direction.

◆ To select *multiple nonadjacent* cells, hold down Ctrl while you click them.

◆ To select a *column* of cells, click the alphabetic heading button at the top of the column.

◆ To select a *row* of cells, click the numeric heading button at the left of the row, or press and hold Shift while pressing the arrow keys.

You can also select a graphic by clicking it once. Table 3-2 illustrates how to select cells from the keyboard.

Table 3-2	Cell Selection Shortcut Keys in Excel
Key	*Selection*
Ctrl+spacebar	Selects all cells in the current column
Shift+spacebar	Selects all cells in the current row
Ctrl+A	Selects all cells in a worksheet
Shift+←	Selects one cell or column to the left (depending on the current selection)
Shift+→	Selects one cell or column to the right (depending on the current selection)
Shift+↑	Selects one cell or row above (depending on the current selection)
Shift+↓	Selects one cell or row below (depending on the current selection)

Of course, you can also use your mouse or keyboard to select existing data in a cell:

◆ With your mouse, double-click the cell, and it again changes into a text-editing box. You can then click and drag to select characters for editing, just like you do in Word.

◆ From the keyboard, select a cell and then press F2. You can use the keys and shortcuts shown in Table 3-3 to select the contents for editing.

Editing cell contents

After you select the desired data, you can choose an action from the toolbars or the menu system or use one of the editing keyboard shortcuts (also shown in Table 3-3).

Table 3-3	Cell Editing Shortcut Keys in Excel
Key	*Selection*
Shift+←	Selects one character to the left of the cursor
Shift+→	Selects one character to the right of the cursor
Shift+End	Selects characters to the end of the text
Shift+Home	Selects characters to the beginning of the text
Any character	Replaces the selected text
Alt+Enter	Starts a new line within the same cell
Delete	Deletes the selected text or the character to the right of the insertion cursor
Ctrl+Delete	Deletes the text to the end of the line
Ctrl+X	Cuts the selection and adds it in the Clipboard (or the Office Clipboard, if it's displayed)
Ctrl+C	Copies the selection to the Clipboard (or the Office Clipboard, if it's displayed)
Ctrl+V	Replaces the selection with the contents of the Clipboard
Esc	Cancels the edits made to a cell

Working with Numbers and Dates

Excel includes the font formatting basics on the standard Office Formatting toolbar — which I cover in a bit — but you also need to familiarize yourself with a different type of formatting that's unique to spreadsheet, statistical, and financial applications. It's called number formatting, and it controls the appearance of all sorts of numbers, including

✦ Dollar amounts

✦ Dates

✦ Times

✦ Telephone numbers

✦ Zip codes

✦ Social Security numbers

The characteristics that specify a particular number format include

✦ The number of decimal places that appear

✦ The notation that represents negative numbers (a minus sign or parentheses)

✦ Whether a comma placeholder separator appears in the numbers

✦ Whether a number carries a dollar sign or a percent sign

Excel provides a whopping 11 different number-formatting categories. Or, if you like, you can go a little wild and create your own custom format that can be applied whenever necessary.

To specify a number format, follow these steps:

1. **Select the cells that you want to format.**

2. **Choose Format⇨Cells or press Ctrl+1 (the number one) to make Excel display the Format Cells dialog box that you see in Figure 3-3.**

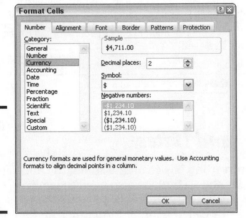

Figure 3-3: Apply number formats to selected cells here.

By default, Excel uses the General format for cells, which basically means they have no specialized number format at all.

3. **On the Number tab, click the formatting category that you need. For example, if you're working with dates, click Date.**

Excel displays the different format types for the category that you select as well as a sample of how the formatted numbers will appear.

4. **If you need number formatting for a specific geographic location, click the Locale drop-down list box and pick the right spot on the planet.**

This field might not appear for some format types.

5. **Click the type of formatting that you need from the Type list.**

Again, this field might not appear for some format types.

6. **Click OK to apply the formatting and return to your worksheet.**

By the way, the General number format often works for a simple whole number. Excel displays up to 11 digits, but a decimal counts as a digit; so, for example, the numeral *11.11* actually counts as five digits. Excel then uses scientific notation for values over 11 digits (or those too big to fit in the cell). I don't know about you, but my puny budget doesn't even *begin* to strain 11 digits.

Working with Rows and Columns

I won't lie to you; every Excel worksheet is a haven for rows and columns. (No big surprise there.) However, you're definitely not constrained to the default arrangement of cells, and you can even insert rows and columns in an existing worksheet if necessary. In this section, I show you how to take charge of your troops.

Resizing rows and columns

Changing the dimensions of any row or column is easy — and often a requirement when adding a longer line of text or when you need to display multiple lines of text in a cell.

To resize, follow these steps:

1. **Move the mouse pointer on top of either divider line at the desired row or column heading.**

   The mouse pointer turns into a bar with opposing arrows to indicate that you're in the right spot.

2. **Click and drag to reposition the dividing line (see how this looks in Figure 3-4).**

   To make the job easier, Excel displays a pop-up menu that tells you the new height (for rows) or width (for columns).

3. **Release the mouse button when the row or column is at the desired dimension.**

Inserting blank cells

You can plug new blank cells into a worksheet at any point. Follow these steps:

1. **Select a range of cells.**

   Note: You have to select the same number of cells that you want to insert. For example, if you want to insert two cells at a point in your worksheet, you should select two cells at that location.

2. **Choose Insert⇨Cells.**

   Excel displays the Insert dialog box, as shown in Figure 3-5.

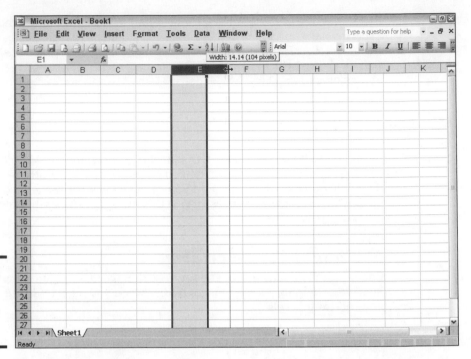

Figure 3-4:
Resizing
rows and
columns is
a cinch.

Figure 3-5:
Preparing
to insert
a passel
o' cells.

3. **Choose which direction the selected cells will move by selecting either the Shift Cells Right or the Shift Cells Down radio button.**

   Alternatively, select the Entire Row or the Entire Column radio button to shift the row or column, respectively, containing the selected cells.

4. **Click OK.**

Inserting cells from the Clipboard

You can also insert cells with what you've cut or copied from another spot. Follow these steps:

1. **Cut or copy the desired cells by using the keyboard shortcuts Ctrl+X or Ctrl+C, respectively.**

2. **Select the cell at the upper left of the desired location.**

3. **Choose Insert➪Cut Cells/Copied Cells.**

   These menu items appear immediately after you cut or copy cells.

   Excel displays the Insert Paste dialog box (see Figure 3-6).

Figure 3-6:
Inserting
cells that
I've copied.

4. **Select either the Shift Cells Right or the Shift Cells Down radio button to determine which direction Excel will move the adjoining cells.**

5. **Click OK.**

Inserting rows and columns

To insert one or more rows or columns in your worksheet, follow these steps:

1. **Click any cell in the row below (or the column to the right) of the desired spot.**

   Inserting multiple rows or columns works just like inserting multiple cells: You need to select the same number of rows or columns that you want to insert.

2. **To insert rows, choose Insert➪Rows.**

3. **To insert columns, choose Insert➪Columns.**

Formatting in Excel

Excel includes the standard font formatting that you expect from an Office application, but you'll also find that you can modify a number of unique attributes for cells, rows, and columns. In this section, I explore the basic formatting tricks that you can pull.

Font formatting

Like Word, you can easily apply the Big Three font attributes from either the toolbar or a keyboard shortcut:

✦ **Bold:** Press Ctrl+B to add emphasis to a selected cell's contents.

✦ *Italic:* Press Ctrl+I to italicize a selected cell's contents.

✦ <u>Underline:</u> Press Ctrl+U to underline a selected cell's contents.

To apply other font attributes to selected cells, choose Format➪Cells to display the Format Cells dialog box. Then click the Font tab to display the standard font settings that you see in Figure 3-7. They include the font family, size, color, and standard effects.

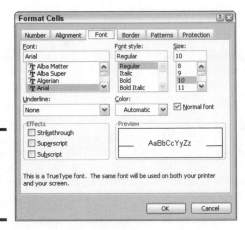

Figure 3-7:
Excel
provides
all sorts of
font fun.

Cell alignment

Click the Alignment tab on the Format Cells dialog box, and you see the settings in Figure 3-8. Here you can

✦ Change the horizontal and vertical alignment of the characters in selected cells.

✦ Specify the indent for the contents of a cell.

✦ Modify the orientation of cells — hey, dig those crazy angles!

✦ Choose to wrap text to fit cell dimensions or shrink the text to fit the size of the cell.

✦ Change the right-to-left/left-to-right direction of text in the cell.

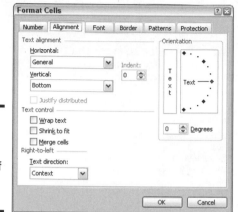

Figure 3-8:
Modify the
alignment
attributes of
selected
cells here.

Unless you specify otherwise, Excel always aligns numbers, dates, and times
to the right edge of a cell. Negative numbers are preceded by a minus sign or
are enclosed with parentheses; a single period is recognized as a decimal
point. By default, text is displayed as left aligned within a cell.

Changing borders and shading

Need to add a kick to certain cells to make them stand out, like a heading or
a total? Click the Border tab on the Format Cells dialog box to display the
settings shown in Figure 3-9. From this tab, you can

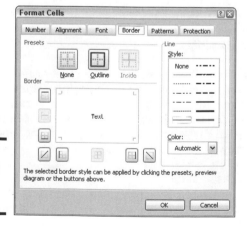

Figure 3-9:
Modify cell
borders
here.

✦ Choose a line style and color.

✦ Specify no border, a standard outline border, or an inside grid.

✦ Design a custom border by using the buttons. (Excel displays the effects of your work in the Border preview window.)

Click the Patterns tab to display the color selector that you see in Figure 3-10. You can choose just a color or combine a color with a pattern by clicking the Pattern drop-down list box. Excel displays a sample block to illustrate the effect that you create.

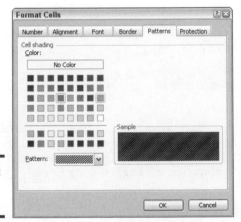

Figure 3-10:
Can I do
plaid?

The Basics of Excel Formulas

Okay, talking about spreadsheet formulas might give you the creeps. (I know that they're not a favorite topic around my dinner table.) However, it's important to understand how to enter formulas correctly in Excel, or you'll end up with a lot of cells stuffed full of data and nothing else.

A single cell in a worksheet can hold *constants* — like text or numbers that you type into a cell yourself — or *formulas,* which perform calculations based on the contents of specific cells and ranges of cells. Formulas in Excel start with an equal sign (=), so they're easy to spot. Also, a formula typically includes a cell reference, like F3 (which stands for the current value in the cell located at column F, row 3).

Examples of simple formulas include

✦ =A1–125: This instructs Excel to subtract 125 from the value in cell A1.

✦ =C9/B4: This instructs Excel to divide the value in cell C9 by the value in cell B4.

See? All that math that you studied was worth it! Formulas always include at least one operator as well, which in the previous examples are the minus sign (–) and the division sign (/).

Excel calculates formulas in sequence from left to right following the equal sign (just like you and I were taught in school). However, you might need to force a calculation to be performed out of order within a formula, and you can do it with parentheses. To illustrate, I expand on the original example:

    =50*(A1–125)

Without the parentheses, the contents of cell A1 would be multiplied by 50 first, and then 125 would be subtracted from that total. With the parentheses, however, Excel first subtracts 125 from the value in A1 and then multiplies that total by 50.

To insert a formula in a cell, follow these steps:

1. **Click in the cell that should hold the formula.**

   It will also display the calculated value, so this is usually the cell that will display a total or the final value.

2. **Type an equal sign (=) to alert Excel that you're going to enter a formula.**

3. **Type the remainder of the formula and then press Enter.**

You can also click your mouse pointer in the Formula Bar and enter the formula there. As you can see in Figure 3-11, the Formula Bar always displays any formula that you enter in the selected cell.

If you change a number in a cell that's used in a formula, the value of the cell containing the formula is automatically changed to reflect the new number. For example, suppose that I add the formula

    =A1+B1

in cell C1 of my trusty worksheet. If I put the number 1 in cell A1 and the number 5 in cell B1, cell C1 will show . . . anyone? Yes, you there . . . that's right! Cell C1 will contain the number 6. However, if I change the number in A1 to 3, C1 is automatically updated with the number 8 because the formula will now calculate 3 + 5 and return the number 8.

To enter the same formula into a range of cells, select the cells, type the formula, and then press Ctrl+Enter. (This is great for those repetitive worksheets that calculate the performance of players on a team or a salesman in a department.)

Formula Bar

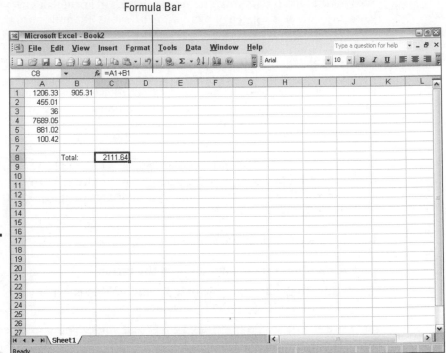

With just the simple basics that I outline in this section, you can build a home budget or a mortgage calculator. But then again, why not use the built-in templates provided by Excel? Click the <u>On my computer</u> link in the Templates section of the Excel task pane to open the panel that you see in Figure 3-12, and then double-click the desired template icon to create a new worksheet, complete with snappy formatting, predesigned formulas, and built-in instructions!

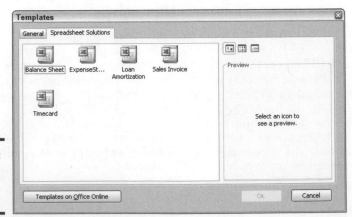

If you don't see a solution in the default Templates that are installed with Excel, click the <u>Templates on Office Online</u> link on the taskbar — you'll need an Internet connection, of course. Excel automatically loads the Template Gallery on the Office 2003 Web site, which contains dozens of templates for all sorts of Excel projects. They're all free, ready for your downloading pleasure.

For example, you'll find all sorts of task-oriented Excel templates that were specifically created to help with chores such as

✦ Remodeling your kitchen

✦ Maintaining a checkbook register

✦ Tracking stock values and quotes

✦ Billing clients and customers

✦ Keeping an allergy log

✦ Planning a baby shower

✦ Generating a grocery list

I told you that this program was versatile!

Excel also offers another important resource that you can use when pondering formulas: the Excel Help system. And it's but a click away of the question mark toolbar icon. To search for a specific need — such as calculating the days remaining before a date — type a short question or phrase into the Answer Wizard box, like **count down days before *xx***, and then press Enter. To see the list of commonly used formulas, type the word **formula** into the Answer Wizard box and then click Examples of Commonly Used Formulas in the topic list on the left.

Of course, formulas (and their siblings, *functions,* which are predefined formulas that use arguments taken from cell values) can get *very* hairy *very* quickly. (There's a lot more to do with a powerful spreadsheet than just add two numbers together.) Because I have limited elbow room here, I must move on. However, I can recommend the bestselling *Excel 2003 For Dummies,* by Greg Harvey, for a complete tour of everything Excel. It's by Wiley Publishing, Inc., naturally.

Working with Graphics in Excel

Your worksheets aren't limited to text. Like any other Office 2003 application, you can import pictures with aplomb. Click the cell at the upper-left corner of where the graphic should be located, and then

✦ **Paste it from the Clipboard.** After you copy an image into the Clipboard by pressing Ctrl+C, you can press Ctrl+V to paste the graphic into your worksheet from your Windows or Office Clipboard.

✦ **Insert it from a file.** To insert a graphic file from your hard drive, choose Insert⇨Picture⇨From File and then navigate to the location of the image. Click the filename once to select it and then click the Insert button.

✦ **Insert a clip art image.** Choose Insert⇨Picture⇨Clip Art to display the Clip Art panel. Type a keyword in the Search text box, click the Search In drop-down list box, and then choose All Collections. Click Search to display thumbnail images of any matching clip art. When you find the image that you're looking for, click it to insert it into your worksheet.

✦ **Scan or download an image.** Choose Insert⇨Picture⇨From Scanner or Camera to acquire an image directly from your scanner or camera. Your scanner or camera manual will include information on what settings are available when acquiring an image.

As you can see in Figure 3-13, Excel doesn't give a hoot about limiting an inserted graphic to specific cells, rows, or columns. Just use the resizing handles around the border of the image (also visible in Figure 3-13) to change the dimensions of the image. Click and drag a handle to expand or contract the image. To move the image, click in the middle of the image and drag it any which way.

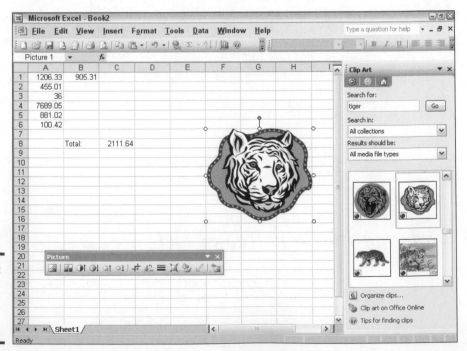

Figure 3-13:
No rows or columns can hold this tiger!

Adding a Chart

Another hit among the Excel crowd are *charts,* which can present your precious data in the easy-to-digest fashion that we all crave in our digi-frenetic, Internet-straddled, talking-head world. (Easy, Mark. Sorry about that.)

Social commentary aside, you have two choices for displaying charts:

✦ **A separate *chart sheet* within the current workbook:** Your chart gets its own fantabulous tab — pun gleefully intended, seeing as how I'm strung out on Diet Coke — and you can display it at any time, just like any other worksheet.

✦ **An *embedded object* within a worksheet:** The chart acts like a picture to be relocated and resized just like any other graphic.

No matter which type of chart you decide to use, your journey begins with the Excel Chart Wizard. Follow these steps to add a chart:

1. **Select the cells containing the data you want to include in the chart (with column and row labels, if you've created any).**

2. **Choose Insert➪Chart, which displays the first screen of the Chart Wizard, as shown in Figure 3-14.**

Figure 3-14:
The Chart Wizard is in the house.

3. **Click the desired chart type from the list on the left.**

   The wizard updates the sub-type thumbnails on the right. (No need to stick with the boring column, bar, or line chart . . . try a cone or pyramid or even a doughnut chart! Mmm . . . doughnuts.)

4. **Keep refining the chart or accept it as is.**

   • **Click Next to continue to the second wizard screen.**

   or

   • **Click Finish to use the default values, and the chart is created as an embedded graphic in your worksheet.**

To display a thumbnail preview of how your chart will look with the selected sub-type, click and hold the Press and Hold to View Sample button.

5. **Click Next on the second wizard screen.**

   Because I've already selected a range, Excel has filled in the data range.

6. **Add a title and label your axis on the third wizard screen or relocate the legend (as you can see in Figure 3-15) or hide it completely and add labels for specific values on the chart.**

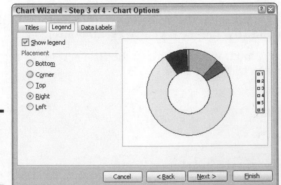

Figure 3-15:
Add legend filigree to your chart.

7. **Click Next to continue.**

8. **The final Chart Wizard screen (as shown in Figure 3-16) prompts you for the Big Decision: whether you want your chart created as a separate sheet (with the name that you specify) or whether you want it created as an embedded graphic in any current sheet in your workbook (which you can choose from the As Object In drop-down list box).**

Figure 3-16:
So which type of chart will it be?

9. **After you select the type of chart, click Finish, and the wizard will generate it for you.**

Figure 3-17 illustrates a chart sheet that I created within a workbook.

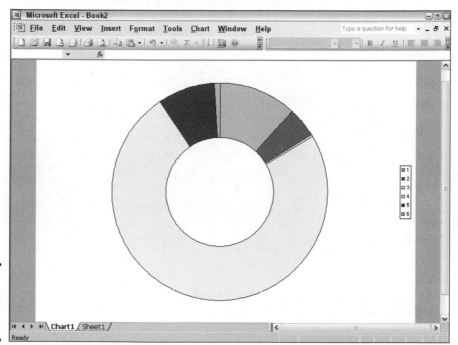

Figure 3-17:
A completed
chart in
sheet form.

Linking Cells

Another powerful feature that's a big favorite with Excel power users is the ability to *link* values. That is, when one value changes in one of the cells, it's automatically updated when you display the other cell! For example, if cell A1 is linked to cell E3 on the same worksheet, whatever value you place in cell A1 automatically appears in cell E3.

To create a link between cells on the same worksheet, follow these steps:

1. **Select the cell that contains the data that you want to link to another cell.**

2. **Press Ctrl+C or click the Copy button on the Standard toolbar.**

3. **Click the cell that you want to link to and then press Ctrl+V to paste the value.**

   Note that Excel displays a pop-up icon next to the cell when you press Ctrl+V.

4. **Click the pop-up icon to display the menu that you see in Figure 3-18 and then select the Link Cells radio button.**

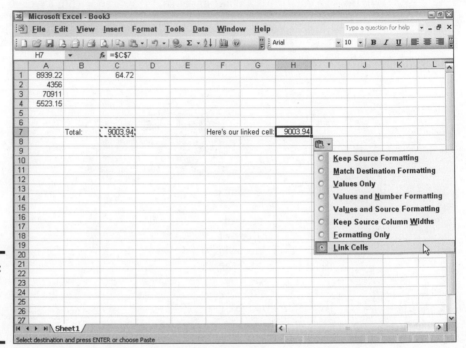

Figure 3-18: Link cells from the Paste pop-up menu.

Adding Headers and Footers

When printing a worksheet, headers and footers can contain quite a bit of valuable identifying information. And that's from someone who has waded through a year's supply of printed personnel worksheets from a mid-sized company.

To add headers and footers to the active worksheet, follow these steps:

1. **Choose View➪Header and Footer to display the Header/Footer pane of the Page Setup dialog box (see Figure 3-19).**

2. **Click the Header drop-down list box and choose a predesigned header.**

3. **Click the Footer drop-down list and choose a footer.**

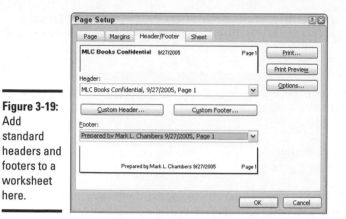

Figure 3-19:
Add
standard
headers and
footers to a
worksheet
here.

4. Click OK to save your changes and return to the worksheet.

Click the Custom Header or the Custom Footer button to get all artistic and
design your own header or footer format (check it out in Figure 3-20). Click to
place the insertion cursor in the proper section — the left, center, or right section of the design — and then click the template buttons to insert the prefor-
matted element(s) that you want to add, like the time or date. (You can also
type your own text instead of using a template.) When your header or footer is
set up as you like, click OK to return to the Page Setup dialog box.

Figure 3-20:
Create a
custom
header and
footer here.

Printing Your Worksheets

When you're ready to print the active worksheet (or worksheets, if you have
more than one workbook open) in Excel, take a moment to use the Print
Preview feature. Choose File⇨Print Preview or click the Print Preview button
on the Standard toolbar.

To print without the cell grid, choose File⇨Page Setup and then click the Sheet tab of the Page Setup dialog box. Clear the Gridlines check box to disable it. (You can also choose to turn off the row and column headings from this panel.)

To print the contents of certain cells in your worksheet, select the cells first before you open the Print dialog box and then enable the Selection radio button on the Print dialog box.

After you're satisfied that you'll get what you expect, use one of these methods to start the printing process:

✦ **Click the Print toolbar button on the Standard toolbar.** This immediately prints the entire active worksheet(s) from the printer's default settings.

✦ **Choose File⇨Print.** This displays the Print dialog box that you see in Figure 3-21. From here, you can select from multiple printers, print multiple copies, or print only specific pages from the worksheet. Click the Properties button to set any printer-specific options supported by the printer's Windows XP software driver. When you're ready, click the Print button.

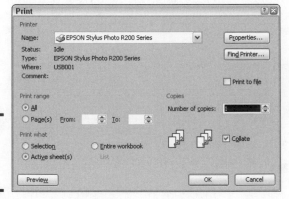

Figure 3-21: The Excel Print dialog box.

✦ **Press Ctrl+P.** This method also displays the Print dialog box.

✦ **Click the Print button of the Page Setup dialog box.** This displays the Print dialog box as well.

You can also print selected cells/rows/columns or the entire workbook at once. From the Print dialog box, select either the Selection or the Entire Workbook radio button.

Chapter 4: Performing with PowerPoint

In This Chapter

- ✔ Working with the PowerPoint window
- ✔ Changing views in PowerPoint
- ✔ Importing and inserting slides
- ✔ Adding text and graphics
- ✔ Using templates and schemes
- ✔ Adding movies and sound to slides
- ✔ Creating a slide show
- ✔ Choosing transitions between slides
- ✔ Using Package for CD
- ✔ Printing in PowerPoint

*N*eed a slide show? How about a set of professional-looking transparencies for that overhead projector? Have no fear; Microsoft PowerPoint 2003 is here! PowerPoint has always been easy to use — now you have even more graphically gorgeous templates to use, and the ability to add movies, and transitions, and CD-quality audio, and . . . whoops, I'm getting a little ahead of myself.

In this chapter, I provide you with the basics of PowerPoint — you find out how to accomplish the most common tasks. If you're brand-spanking new to the program, you see how to spice up that blank slide with text and graphics, and I also show you the power user keyboard shortcuts to use in PowerPoint. If you're already familiar with the PowerPoint window, you also find out how to create a Pack and Go package — no, I'm not kidding, that's what it's called — and add all sorts of spiffy transitions to your slide shows.

Get ready to find out why so many PC owners of all ages love PowerPoint!

Getting Your Bearings in PowerPoint

You can run PowerPoint in a number of different ways:

✦ Choose Start➪All Programs➪Microsoft PowerPoint.

✦ Double-click the PowerPoint shortcut on your desktop (or click the shortcut on your Quick Launch bar, if you've added an icon there).

✦ If you're using the Office shortcut bar, click the PowerPoint icon.

✦ Press Win+R, type **powerpnt** in the Run dialog box that appears, and then press Enter. (This assumes that your keyboard is equipped with Windows keys, which look like waving Windows flags and are located on either side of the space bar.)

When you first run PowerPoint, the application's main window looks remarkably simple (as shown in Figure 4-1), especially when you contrast it with the rather frightening appearance of Excel 2003. You'll quickly find, however, that this program is no pushover. The digital-and-silicon equivalent of a '69 Dodge Charger is lurking behind the curtain!

In lieu of formal introductions, here's a quick guide to what you see onscreen:

✦ **The menu:** Typical in every respect.

✦ **The toolbar:** Another familiar old friend. Clicking a toolbar button performs the same action as selecting the corresponding menu command. If a small double-arrow icon pointing to the right appears at the end of a toolbar, all the icons on the toolbar can't be displayed at the current window size; just click the arrows to display the additional icons. You can also choose which toolbars are displayed: Choose View➪Toolbars and then click the toolbar that you want to toggle on or off.

You can relocate toolbars just about anywhere in the PowerPoint window. Move your mouse pointer to either end of a toolbar and then click and drag when the pointer turns into a four-direction cursor. A nomadic toolbar can be relocated to any side of the screen, or you can pull it into the editing window to make it a floating toolbar. In Figure 4-1, for example, my Drawing toolbar is located at the bottom of the screen.

To customize a toolbar, click the down-arrow button at the toolbar's end, click Add or Remove Buttons, and then click the name of the toolbar. PowerPoint displays a pop-up menu with a list of all the buttons on that toolbar, and from there you can enable or disable the check box next to a button name to show it or hide it.

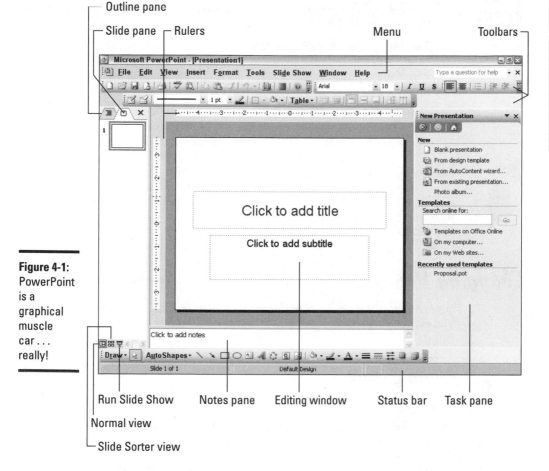

Figure 4-1:
PowerPoint
is a
graphical
muscle
car...
really!

✦ **The editing window:** You design your slides here, adding graphics and
text and moving slide elements around the layout guide. The editing
window also does double-duty in other view modes, which I discuss in
a bit.

✦ **The ruler:** Get a grip on dimensions. You can also use the ruler as a
guide when placing objects on your slides.

✦ **The Slide and Outline panes:** Click on either tab to switch between a
numbered thumbnail display of the slides in your presentation (the Slide
pane) or a display of the text on each slide in outline format (the Outline
pane). The Slide pane helps you navigate quickly — you can simply click
on a thumbnail to jump to that slide — and the Outline pane helps you
organize your presentation.

You can also click the vertical scroll bar in the editing window to move through the slides in your presentation.

✦ **The task pane:** Here, PowerPoint displays a selection of its most common tasks. You can hide the task pane to make more room within the editing window by choosing View⇨Task Pane. (Another click on the same menu item displays the task pane again.)

✦ **The status bar:** Like other Office applications, PowerPoint's got one of these, too. It displays information about your current view as well as information relating to the currently selected slide or pane.

Each of the panes within the PowerPoint window can be adjusted. For example, if you don't need the Slide pane at the moment, move the mouse pointer over the border between the Slide pane and the editing window until it turns into those nifty opposing arrows, and then click and drag to enlarge the editing window.

Changing Views

You can view the PowerPoint application window in a number of different views. In this section, I give you the details on the ones that you'll use most often.

Normal view

Normal view, which is the default in PowerPoint, is the best view for adding and editing text and graphic objects. You can display your slides in Normal view by choosing View⇨Normal or by clicking the Normal View button at the lower-left corner of the PowerPoint window (above the status bar). 'Nuff said.

Need to see what your elegant color slides will look like when printed on a monochrome laser printer? Choose View⇨Color/Grayscale and then choose Grayscale (With Shading) or stark Black and White. When you and Toto are done, return to the Land of Oz by choosing Color from the same menu.

Slide Sorter view

Figure 4-2 illustrates Slide Sorter view, where the slides in your presentation are arranged in a larger, easier-to-see format. It's not just the scenery that's important, however: You can also click and drag thumbnails to move them and reorder the flow of your presentation. You can also right-click a slide to delete it or to add a completely new slide (a great thing when you've forgotten to include something).

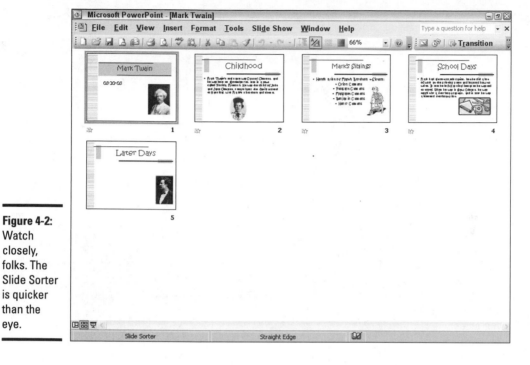

Figure 4-2:
Watch
closely,
folks. The
Slide Sorter
is quicker
than the
eye.

To switch to Slide Sorter view, choose View⇨Slide Sorter or click the Slide
Sorter View button at the lower-left corner of the PowerPoint window.

Notes Page view

Choose View⇨Notes Page to view a full-size layout for your Notes pages
(which I discuss later in the chapter), as shown in Figure 4-3. The top portion of the Notes page contains the corresponding slide from your presentation. From this view, you can edit the text in your Notes pages just like you
edit the text boxes in your slides (as opposed to the Notes pane, which is
somewhat cramped if you have a large number of notes to enter for a slide).

Slide Show view

Oh, no — this is not your Aunt Harriet's idea of a slide show. ("Enough with
the beach pictures, Harry!") Instead, this displays a PowerPoint slide show
using the slides from the open presentation. I cover slide shows later in the
section "Building and Running a Slide Show," so hang tight.

To activate the Slide Show view, choose View⇨Slide Show, press F5, or click
the Slide Show View button at the lower-left corner of the PowerPoint window.
(Note that this runs the show from the current slide, so you won't see any preceding slides.)

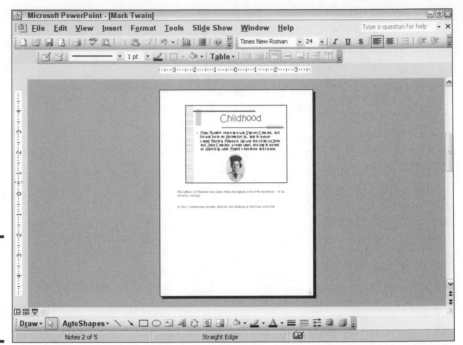

Figure 4-3:
Use Notes
Page view
to put the
spotlight on
your notes.

Creating Slides

As a personal favor to you, PowerPoint creates a new, blank first slide each
time that you start the program (or each time that you create a new presentation, by either using the Blank Presentation command in the task pane or
by clicking the New button on the Standard toolbar).

To add a new slide to a presentation, follow these steps:

**1. If you already have a number of slides in the presentation, click an
existing slide in the Slide pane.**

The new slide is inserted after the selected slide.

If you have only one slide, the new slide is appended at the end. Go
figure.

**2. Choose Insert➪New Slide or click the New Slide button on the
Formatting toolbar.**

Or, for a real treat, right-click the Slide pane and then choose New Slide
from the pop-up menu that appears. Or heck, you can even press Ctrl+M.
Geez, Microsoft, do you think we have enough options here?

PowerPoint adds the new slide to the Slide pane and displays it in the editing window.

Note: Each slide is given a sequential number as you add it, which comes in handy, such as when you want to print only certain slides.

Have you got existing slides in your presentation that you'd like to use as the model for new slides? No problem! Instead of creating blank slides from scratch, PowerPoint allows you to *duplicate* one or more existing slides as well. Click the slides that you want to duplicate in the Slide pane (hold down Ctrl while clicking to select multiple slides) and then choose Insert⇨Duplicate Slide menu item. After the new slide(s) appear, you can move them individually within the Outline or Slide panes by dragging them to their new home. (And when the slides are moved, they are automatically renumbered.)

If you need to ax a slide, right-click it in the Slide pane and then choose Delete Slide from the contextual menu that appears. It's a goner. Again, renumbering is automatic.

Inserting slides

If you have another PowerPoint presentation with slides that you need for your current project, you can insert them by following these steps:

1. **Click a slide in the Slide pane where the inserted slides should appear.**

   An inserted slide appears *after* the slide that you click in the Slide pane.

2. **Choose Insert⇨Slides from Files to display the Slide Finder dialog box that you see in Figure 4-4.**

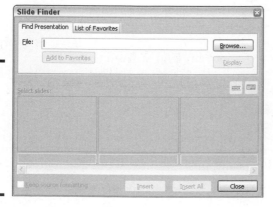

Figure 4-4:
You can easily import slides from another presentation.

3. **Click the Browse button.**

 PowerPoint displays a standard Windows Browse dialog box.

4. **Navigate to the folder containing the existing PowerPoint presentation, click the file to select it, and then click Open.**

5. **Click Insert All to insert all the slides in the file.**

6. **To pick one or more slides, click the thumbnail(s) representing the desired slides to select them (a gray border appears around selected slides) and then click the Insert button.**

7. **Click Close to return to your presentation.**

Inserting a document

You can also insert the contents of a Word document directly into your slides as an outline. This is a great option for those who need to pull the text for a presentation from an existing document, like a student who needs to provide both a written assignment and a PowerPoint presentation on the same material.

Follow these steps to insert a document:

1. **Click a slide in the Outline pane where the inserted text should appear.**

2. **Choose Insert⇨Slides from Outline.**

 PowerPoint displays the Insert Outline dialog box.

3. **Navigate to the location of the document and then click the filename to highlight it.**

4. **Click the Insert button.**

Naturally, you get the best results if the document that you're inserting is written in outline form, but I've found that PowerPoint does a surprisingly good job importing just about any kind of Word document.

Typing, Selecting, and Editing Text

After you create a blank slide — or insert slides from an existing PowerPoint presentation, or perhaps insert text from a Word document — you're ready to type and edit text. Luckily, this section is about exactly that.

Adding text

You've probably already noticed the huge `Click to add xx` prompts all over your slides. Reminds me a little of *Alice in Wonderland*, with little slides running around your feet bearing signs that read *Click Me!* Anyway, things couldn't get much easier. Just click the text, and PowerPoint erases it and displays an insertion cursor just like the one in Microsoft Word (see Figure 4-5).

While you type, the text is updated on the thumbnail in the Slide pane, and the text is also displayed in the Outline pane.

You can also edit text in a slide directly from the Outline pane. Just click and drag to select the text that you want to change and then type to replace it.

Moving within text fields

Table 4-1 provides the movement shortcuts that you can use while typing text in a PowerPoint field.

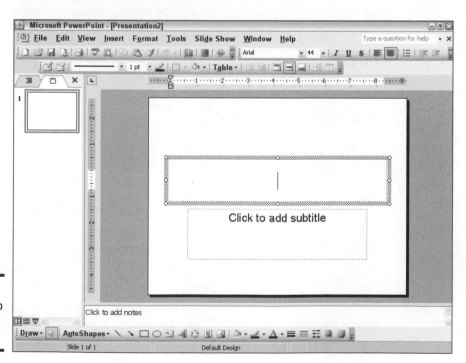

Figure 4-5:
Preparing to
type within
a text box.

Table 4-1	Text Field Movement Keys in PowerPoint
Key	*Movement*
Left arrow (←)	Moves the cursor one character to the left
Right arrow (→)	Moves the cursor one character to the right
Up arrow (↑)	Moves the cursor to the preceding line
Down arrow (↓)	Moves the cursor to the next line
End	Moves the cursor to the end of the current line
Home	Moves the cursor to the beginning of the current line
Ctrl+←	Moves the cursor one word to the left
Ctrl+→	Moves the cursor one word to the right
Ctrl+↑	Moves the cursor one paragraph up
Ctrl+↓	Moves the cursor one paragraph down
Ctrl+Home	Moves the cursor to the beginning of the text box
Ctrl+End	Moves the cursor to the end of the text box
Ctrl+Return	Moves to the next title or body text entry box

To switch between titles or body text entry boxes with your mouse, click once on the box that you want to edit. You can add a text box by choosing Insert➪Text Box.

Selecting text and objects

After you enter text-editing mode, you have a number of keyboard shortcuts at your disposal for selecting text that needs to be changed. Table 4-2 provides these selection keys as well as selection shortcuts for slide objects.

Table 4-2	Text Field and Object Selection Keys in PowerPoint
Key	*Selection*
Shift+←	Selects one character to the left of the cursor
Shift+→	Selects one character to the right of the cursor
Shift+↑	Selects characters to the previous line
Shift+↓	Selects characters to the next line
Ctrl+Shift+←	Selects characters to the beginning of the word
Ctrl+Shift+→	Selects characters to the end of the word
Tab	Selects the next object
Shift+Tab	Selects the previous object
Ctrl+A	Selects all objects, slides, or text (depending on your view)

You can also get the mouse into the selection act: Double-click a word in a text box to select it, and you can select multiple objects on a slide by holding down Shift and then clicking each object.

Editing text

From the keyboard, you can use the shortcuts shown in Table 4-3 to play Frankenstein with the contents of a text box.

Table 4-3	Text Field Selection Keys in PowerPoint
Key	*Function*
Any character	Replaces the selected text
Enter	Starts a new line
Delete	Deletes the selected text or object
Ctrl+X	Deletes the selection and adds it in the Clipboard (or the Office Clipboard, if it's displayed)
Ctrl+C	Copies the selection to the Clipboard (or the Office Clipboard, if it's displayed)
Ctrl+V	Replaces the selection with the contents of the Clipboard

You can choose Format➪Font to display the Font dialog box (as shown in Figure 4-6). And from there, you can add all sorts of attributes, change the font family or font size, and determine the color of the text. The Formatting toolbar provides many of these same commands in convenient mouse-click form.

Figure 4-6:
Change font
attributes in
PowerPoint
here.

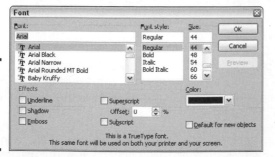

Moving slide elements

Naturally, the elements on your slide — text boxes and graphics — aren't embedded in cement. You can use your mouse or the keyboard to move these elements to a different location around the slide:

✦ **To move an element with the mouse:** Click the object to select it (you get that funky, four-direction cursor again) and then drag it to the desired spot. (For text boxes, click the frame. For graphics, click in the center of the image.)

✦ **To move an element with the keyboard:** Press the Tab key to cycle through the elements on the slide. After the desired item is selected, press the arrow keys to move it. This is great when you need fine control over the placement of an object, but remember *not* to click a text object. That puts you in edit mode, and as you can read in earlier parts of this section, the cursor keys have different uses when you're editing.

Installing Graphics in Your Slides

No good presentation is complete without a dog or a pony — don't ask me why, I just work here. Add graphics to your slides to capture (and securely hold) your audience's attention. From personal experience of watching many a boring presentation (thankfully, not my own), I can tell you that a pure-text presentation will have your audience heading for a restroom break in less than five minutes.

Follow these steps to add a graphic from your hard drive to a slide (or, if you're using Notes Page view, to your Notes page for the slide):

1. **Click the desired slide in the Slide pane.**

2. **Choose Insert⇨Picture⇨From File.**

   PowerPoint displays — you guessed it — the Insert Picture dialog box.

3. **Navigate to the folder where the image is stored and click that file to select it.**

4. **Click the Insert button.**

The image can be resized by clicking and dragging any of the circular handles arranged around the edges (check out the toast graphic in Figure 4-7), or you can drag the entire image by clicking in its center and dragging the graphic to its new home.

If you're inserting an image that might be updated later — for example, a graphic of your company's stock price — click the down-arrow next to the Insert button and then click Link to File instead, which will automatically reload the image from disk each time that you display the slide in PowerPoint.

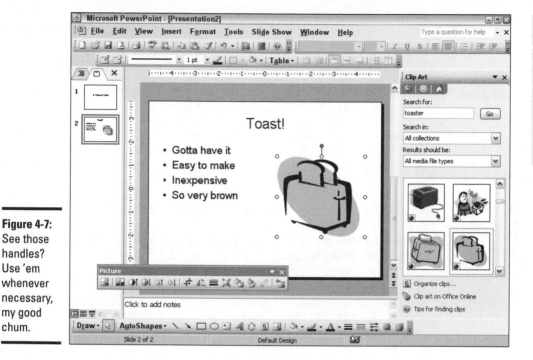

Figure 4-7:
See those handles? Use 'em whenever necessary, my good chum.

As always, an image can be pasted into your slide from either the Windows Clipboard or the Office Clipboard. And yes, our old friend, the Clip Art pane, is also available in PowerPoint! (Again, this is the beauty of an application suite.) To insert clip art, choose Insert⇨Picture⇨Clip Art, choose the graphic that you want, and then click the Insert button.

If your system has a scanner or digital camera connected to it, you can also acquire an image directly into PowerPoint. Choose Insert⇨Picture⇨From Scanner or Camera and adjust your scanner or camera's settings as necessary. When the image is ready, it's placed on the slide just as if you had loaded it from disk.

Applying Templates and Schemes

Repeat after me: "Templates in PowerPoint are *sassy* things." That's because a design template can change the entire appearance of your slides with just a click or two of the mouse. Templates can control

✦ The position of the objects on your slides

✦ The background design

✦ The fonts and formatting used in text objects

✦ Animation effects

✦ The color scheme

Plus, a design template can be used at any time — even when you've got an entire presentation's worth of slides already built!

A *scheme* is a little less powerful than a template, but that's on purpose. A scheme applies just one aspect of a template, so you can apply a design that you like and then change the colors in one fell swoop . . . or perhaps change just the animations used in a slide show.

To apply a design template or scheme, follow these steps:

1. **Click the Design button on the Formatting toolbar or choose Format⇨Slide Design.**

   PowerPoint opens the Slide Design pane that you see in Figure 4-8.

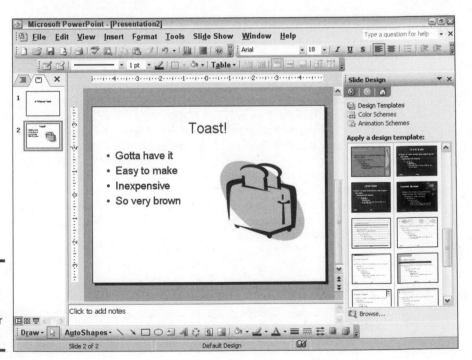

Figure 4-8: Select a design template for your slides.

2. **Choose the type of template or scheme that you want to apply from the three categories at the top of the Slide Design pane.**

You can select a design template, a color scheme for your current design, or an animation scheme for your slide show. (More on slide shows later in the chapter.)

3. **Apply the template or scheme.**

- **To apply the template or scheme to all the slides in your presentation, click the arrow next to the design thumbnail that you want to use and then click the Apply to All Slides button.**

- **To apply the template or scheme to only certain slides in your presentation, select them in the Slide pane, click the arrow next to the desired design thumbnail, and then click the Apply to Selected Slides button.**

If you're applying an animation scheme, click the Apply to All Slides button at the bottom of the pane.

PowerPoint immediately updates your presentation with the new design (like the spiffy one shown in Figure 4-9), so you can either approve or disapprove on the spot. Feel free to try on all sorts of new looks. Microsoft won't charge you for the privilege (at least for now).

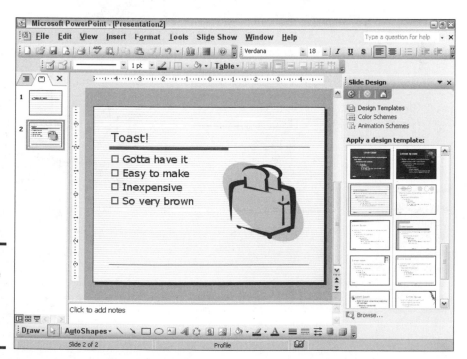

Figure 4-9: I must have gone to art school to produce this, right?

Entering Notes

Notes are a handy tool, allowing you to jot down reminders and information about a slide (without those notes actually appearing on the slide itself). Many folks also print the contents of the Notes pane as handouts — I show you how to print them later in the chapter.

Although PowerPoint has support for more formal handouts, I've found that the printed Notes pages (which, as I mention earlier, also boast the images of the slides in your presentation) work just fine for distribution to your audience.

To enter notes, just click in the Notes pane and begin typing (check out Figure 4-10), or you can paste text directly into the pane. If you like, you can also edit the notes for a slide from the Notes Page view, as I describe earlier in the chapter. To add graphics to your Notes page, you must use Notes Page view — and note that any graphics that you add in Notes Page view are not visible in Normal view. To enlarge the Notes pane as I have in Figure 4-10, click the divider at the top of the Notes pane and drag it upward.

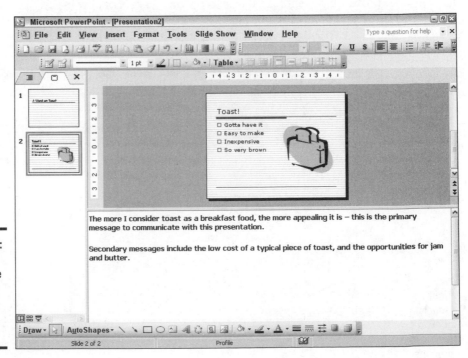

Figure 4-10:
Use the Notes pane to hold those last-minute reminders.

Using Movies and Sound

PowerPoint allows you to add video clips and audio to your slides. Naturally, these won't work too well with those presentations that use transparencies (no surprise there), but you'll like the effect if you use a laptop screen, monitor, or a liquid crystal display (LCD) projector!

To add multimedia to a slide, follow these steps:

1. **Click the desired slide in the Slide pane.**

2. **Choose Insert⇨Movies and Sounds⇨*xx* From File (where *xx* could be either *Movie* or *Sound*) to display the ubiquitous, all-knowing Insert Movie/Insert Sound dialog box.**

3. **Navigate to the folder where the image is stored and then click the file to select it.**

4. **Click the Insert button.**

   PowerPoint will prompt you to decide whether the movie clip or audio track should play automatically when the slide appears in a slide show or whether it should be activated when you click it (see the prompt in Figure 4-11).

Figure 4-11:
PowerPoint can play a clip or sound automatically or by your leave.

5. **To make the clip play automatically, click Automatically.**

Figure 4-12 illustrates both a movie and a sound clip inserted into a slide. To play the movie clip within the editing window, right-click the clip and choose Play Movie from the pop-up menu that appears. You can pause the clip by clicking; stop it altogether by right-clicking it.

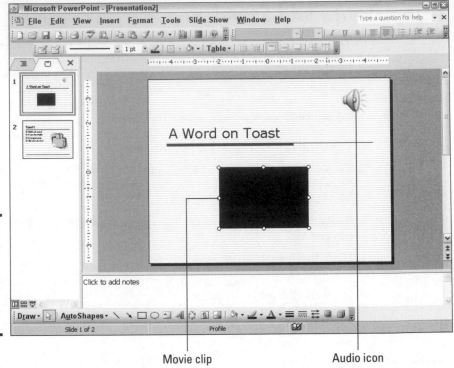

Figure 4-12:
A movie clip and a sound, hard at work in a PowerPoint slide.

Movie clip   Audio icon

The sound icon appears on your slide like any other object. If you've added a track from an audio CD (Insert➪Movies and Sounds➪Play CD Audio Track), the icon changes to a CD-ROM. To play the movie or sound clip within the editing window, right-click the clip and choose Play Movie or Sound from the pop-up menu that appears. You can pause the clip by clicking; stop it altogether by right-clicking it.

Although a movie object can be moved and resized just like a graphic, don't be surprised if expanding it by a large amount causes it to turn *jaggy* (rough-edged). Movie clips (and even images in JPEG, bitmap, or TIFF format) are created at a fixed dimension, and they might not look that good when stretched like taffy.

Building and Running a Slide Show

As I mention earlier in the chapter, you can choose to view your presentation as a slide show whenever you like. Follow these steps to run your own show:

1. **Click the Slide Show View button above the status bar, choose Slide Show⇨View Show, or press F5.**

   PowerPoint takes control, switches to a full-screen display, and shows the current slide in the presentation.

2. **Click the mouse button or press N (or Enter, or the right-arrow key) to move to the next slide.**

   To move backwards to the previous slide, press P (or Backspace, or the left-arrow key).

3. **Click the mouse button on the final screen in your presentation to return to the PowerPoint window or press Esc at any time to exit.**

That's the basic method of running a slide show. However, PowerPoint also allows you to build a self-running show that needs no intervention — and you can even choose to limit user input, which is a good feature in case strange fingers hit the keyboard.

To create a self-running show from the open presentation, follow these steps:

1. **Choose Slide Show⇨Set Up Show to display the Set Up Show dialog box that you see in Figure 4-13.**

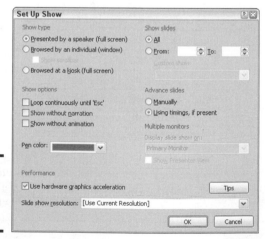

Figure 4-13: Preparing a self-running slide show.

TIP

2. **Select the Browsed at a Kiosk (Full Screen) radio button to enable it.**

   In *kiosk mode,* there are no controls or visible windows, and the slide show fills the entire screen.

3. **Choose the slides that you want to display.**

   • To show 'em all, select the All radio button.

- To show a selection of slides, select the From/To radio button and then enter the starting and ending slide numbers in the appropriate fields; you can type the numbers directly in the boxes or use the up and down buttons next to each box.

4. **Select the Using Timings, If Present radio button.**

   This sets the slide show to advance slides automatically. Your viewers can also click the mouse button to advance to the next slide, but everything else is disabled in kiosk mode except the Esc key, which exits the show.

5. **Select the Loop Continuously Until 'Esc' check box to enable it.**

   Your slide show will repeat endlessly until the Esc key is pressed.

6. **Click OK to save your changes.**

If your PC or laptop has a 3-D hardware-accelerated video card — and most PCs built since the turn of the century do have one — selecting the Use Hardware Graphics Acceleration check box is always a good idea. This can greatly improve the speed and smoothness of your presentation.

To run your show, choose Slide Show⇨View Show. I listed the basic slide show control keys that you can use during a presentation in Table 4-4.

Table 4-4	Slide Show Control Keys in PowerPoint
Key	*Function*
slide number+Enter	Jump to a specific slide
W	Toggle the display of a white screen
B	Toggle the display of a black screen
S	Stop or restart an automatic slide show
Shift+F10	Display a shortcut menu
Ctrl+Shift+B	Start the slide show from the current slide
Ctrl+U	Hide onscreen controls and pointer in 15 seconds
Ctrl+H	Hide onscreen controls and pointer immediately
F1	Display the slide show control list

Making a Transition 'twixt Slides

One way that you can add a little life to a long slide show is the inclusion of *transitions,* which are animated effects that occur in between slides. However, remember that a little goes a long way when it comes to transitions. You want your audience to pay attention to the content in your presentation and not gawk at the visual spectacle of your transitions.

To add transitions to your slide show, follow these steps:

1. **Switch to either the Normal or the Slide Sorter view.**

   I find this task much easier in Slide Sorter view.

2. **If you want to apply a transition to selected slides, highlight all the slides to be preceded by the same transition.**

3. **Choose Slide Show➪Slide Transition to display the Slide Transition pane that you see in Figure 4-14 (or click the Transition button on the Slide Sorter toolbar).**

4. **Click a transition in the Apply to Selected Slides list to check it out.**

   As long as the AutoPreview check box is enabled at the bottom of the Slide Transition pane, PowerPoint will give you a short, animated preview of the effect.

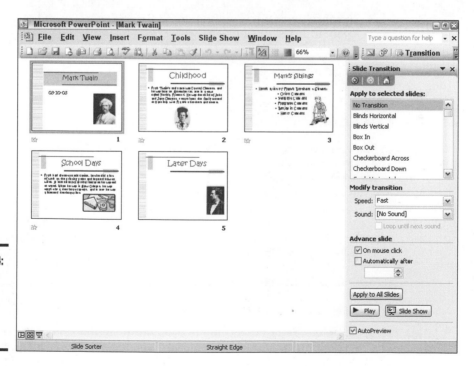

Figure 4-14:
Selecting
slide
transitions
is fun and
easy.

5. **Click the Speed drop-down list box to choose the speed of the effect (slow, medium, or fast) — and believe me, *fast* in this case means really, really *fast!***

   To see the effect again, click the Play button at the bottom of the Slide Transition pane.

6. **To add sound to the transition, click the Sound drop-down list to see your choices.**

   (I've gotta admit that the typewriter and the applause sounds are favorites of mine, but you have to address the audience . . . the CEO of your company might not approve.) To play the sound continuously until the next slide that has another sound is up, select the Loop Until Next Sound check box.

7. **Decide whether the slide should advance with a mouse click (the default) or whether it should advance automatically after a delay period that you set.**

   Enable both, and you get the best of both worlds: A click works; otherwise, the slide advances automatically.

8. **To apply the same transition to all the slides in your show, click the Apply to All Slides button.**

   Otherwise, you can close the Slide Transition pane when you're done assigning transitions.

Using Package for CD

I know, I know, that sounds *really* weird. (Even the professionals in Redmond can shrug their shoulders from time to time.) Anyway, you can use PowerPoint's *Package for CD* feature to package a PowerPoint presentation to run on another Windows PC.

"But what if my good friend doesn't have a copy of Microsoft PowerPoint installed?" Good question, and Microsoft has the answer: by default, a copy of the free PowerPoint Viewer is included in your packaged presentation!

To create a Package for CD, follow these steps:

1. **Open the presentation file that you want to package.**

2. **If you want to save the file to removable media (like a floppy disk or a Zip disk) instead of to a folder on your system, load the media into the drive.**

3. **Choose File⇨Package for CD to display the dialog you see in Figure 4-15.**

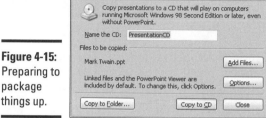

Figure 4-15:
Preparing to
package
things up.

4. **Type a descriptive name into the Name the CD field.**

5. **If you need to add multiple presentations to a single CD, click the Add Files button.**

   This opens an Open dialog box, allowing you to locate and select the other presentations.

6. **If you've included any even slightly unusual fonts in your package, click Options and select the Embedded TrueType fonts check box to include them in your package.**

   I mention linked graphics earlier in the section "Installing Graphics in Your Slides." If you package a presentation that displays linked graphics, those images will either have to be on the destination PC (and in the same exact folder structure), or you have to include them in your package file. Otherwise, the graphics won't show up in those slides.

   Take it from someone who's done a lot of work with service bureaus: Assume nothing, and *always* include linked files! (That's why the Include Linked Files check box is enabled by default.) However, you're also assuming that the destination PC has the same fonts. To make absolutely sure that your presentation can be viewed on any PC running Windows, I recommend that you also enable the Embed TrueType Fonts check box as well.

7. **Click Copy to Folder to specify the target location on your hard drive for the package, or click Copy to CD to burn the files to a CD-R or CD-RW disc.**

TIP

If you update your presentation, you must repeat this process again to repackage it. However, you can save it on the same CD-RW disc or in the same folder, and PowerPoint will prompt you for permission to overwrite the original package.

Printing Your Document

The final stop on the PowerPoint tour is the Print function. In addition to your slides, you can also print several other types of documents, including your Notes pages and any handouts that you've created.

REMEMBER

Don't forget that you can use Print Preview to verify how things look before you print. (On the Standard toolbar, look for the icon that bears a document with a magnifying glass.)

To print the slides from the entire presentation by using the default settings, you can simply click the Print button on the Standard toolbar. However, if you choose File⇨Print (or press Ctrl+P), PowerPoint offers you quite a bit of control over what gets printed and how it looks, as you can see in Figure 4-16. From this dialog box, you can choose

✦ The printer to use

✦ The number of copies

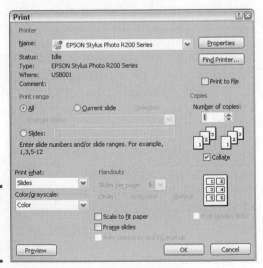

Figure 4-16:
Preparing
to print in
PowerPoint.

✦ The documents to print (from the Print What drop-down list box)

✦ Color or grayscale (from the Color/Grayscale drop-down list box)

✦ Whether to surround your slides, Notes pages, and handouts with a frame (the Frame Slides check box)

✦ Whether to print the entire presentation, specific pages, or a range of pages

As I mention in other Office chapters in this mini-book, your printer's software driver might offer additional settings. To display these settings, click the Properties button next to the Name drop-down list box.

Chapter 5: Doing Database Magic with Access

In This Chapter

- ✓ Starting Access
- ✓ Touring the Access window
- ✓ Creating tables
- ✓ Creating forms
- ✓ Building a query
- ✓ Printing your data
- ✓ Using templates in Access

*W*hat? You've never used Access? Don't sweat it: There's a good reason why Access 2003 isn't everyone's bag of potato chips. Much like Excel, Access can be more complex and harder than the average application for the novice to use. Hence, the relative obscurity of Access compared with Office applications like Word and PowerPoint. (Based on what I see in my appearances at user group meetings, even Works Database is better known!)

However, Microsoft has done its best to help bring Access to the home PC owner. Wizards abound, and the Access Help system is one of the most extensive in the Office 2003 suite. (It's no coincidence that the other stand-out in the Help system is Microsoft Excel.) I'm happy to report that you can now take care of basic Access chores — like building tables and forms — without requiring a degree in particle physics. In this chapter, I introduce you to those basics and show you how to keep track of really important data . . . like your collection of porcelain chicken planters.

If you're interested in taking the plunge and trying everything that Access has to offer, I can heartily recommend the more comprehensive book *Access 2003 For Dummies* by John Kaufeld, by Wiley Publishing, Inc. He has the elbowroom to cover Access from one end of the menu to the other. A good working knowledge of Visual Basic and VBScript is a great help, too.

Running Access

You can use any of the following methods to start Access:

✦ Double-click the Access shortcut on your desktop.

✦ Choose Start (or press a Windows key) and then choose All Programs⇨ Microsoft Access. (The Windows keys, if you're so blessed, lurk on either side of the Alt keys on your keyboard.)

✦ Double-click an Access database or project file.

✦ If you're using the Office shortcut bar, click the Access icon.

✦ Press and hold a Windows key on your keyboard while pressing R to bring up the Run dialog box. Type **msaccess** in the Open text box and then press Enter.

A Quick Tour of the Access Window

As you can see in Figure 5-1, the initial Access 2003 window looks somewhat empty when you start the application by itself (without a data file). That's because the idea behind Access is to accept, store, display, and edit information in a free-form manner — and you can create your own look-and-feel for the program.

Here's a quick rundown of the elements within the Access window:

✦ **The menu:** This offers many of your Office 2003 favorites, like the Office Clipboard on the Edit menu (which can hold any sort of Office data for use within the Office 2003 application suite).

✦ **The toolbars:** Access is somewhat lean on the toolbars — only three of 'em — but the toolbar buttons can save you a dozen mouse clicks per hour because they perform the same action as the corresponding menu commands. To toggle the display of each Access toolbar, choose View⇨ Toolbars and then choose the toolbar name to toggle it off or on.

To position a toolbar at a different area in the Access window, move your mouse pointer to either end of the toolbar until it turns into a four-direction cursor and then drag the toolbar to relocate it to any side of the screen. (You can even create a floating toolbar — which can be moved as an independent dialog box — by dragging the toolbar to the middle of the window.)

To add or remove buttons from a toolbar, click the down-arrow button at the end of the control and then choose Add or Remove Buttons. Click the toolbar name, and you can click next to individual buttons to toggle them on or off.

Toolbars   Menu

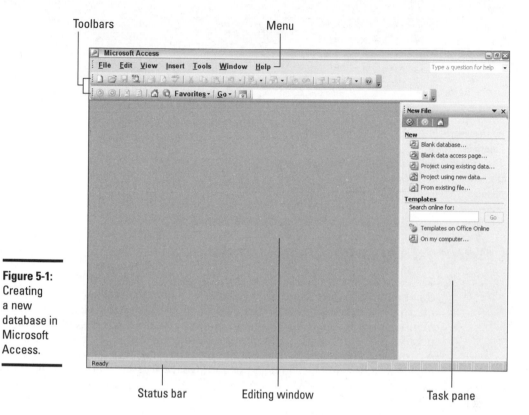

Figure 5-1:
Creating
a new
database in
Microsoft
Access.

Status bar   Editing window   Task pane

✦ **The editing window:** In Access, the editing window is more of a container
for the tables that you create as well as other windows and displays.
However, I've used that name already for Word, Excel, and PowerPoint,
and I'm not going to stop now.

✦ **The Database window:** One of the windows that you'll use most often,
the Database window allows you to create and edit database objects
(such as tables, queries, and forms, which I discuss in a bit). Figure 5-2,
which you can find in the following section, illustrates the Database
window.

✦ **The status bar:** In Access, the status bar displays the current status of
your Num Lock, Caps Lock, and Scroll Lock keys, and also provides
simple help messages and information about database fields. Not exciting stuff, but such is the life of a status bar.

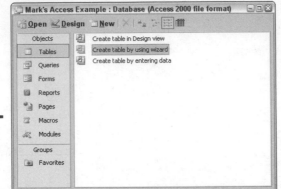

Figure 5-2:
The Access
Database
window.

Creating Tables with the Wizard

Tables in Access are interesting database beasties: They look like the tables that I discuss in the earlier Word chapter of this mini-book, but they store information as *fields* (or individual pieces of data, like your telephone number) within *records* (each record contains all the fields describing one person, place, or thing). Tables are the building blocks of an Access database. A name and address of a customer, for example, might make up a record; the customer's first and last name, street address, city, state, and ZIP code are all fields within that record.

A table uses the Datasheet view, which organizes fields as columns. Records appear as rows.

The easiest way to create a table is to use the Table Wizard. Follow these steps:

1. **Click the Blank Database item in the task pane at the right side of the window.**

   If the task pane is hidden, you can display it by choosing View⇨ Toolbars⇨Task Pane.

   Access opens the File New Database dialog box, which operates just like a standard Windows Save dialog box except that you're creating a blank database instead.

2. **Type a descriptive name for your database in the File Name field and then click the Create button.**

To open an existing database that you've recently been using, click the filename in the Open a File list in the task pane or choose File⇨Open. (From the keyboard, press Ctrl+O.) Access displays the Database window that appears in Figure 5-2.

3. **Click the Tables button at the left — if necessary — and then double-click the Create Table by Using Wizard entry in the list on the right.**

Now you're admiring the first screen of the Table Wizard, as shown in Figure 5-3. In the leftmost column, Access gives you a number of sample tables to choose from, arranged by either business or personal categories.

Figure 5-3: Invoking the hoary Table Wizard.

4. **Click a sample table that sounds similar to the table that you need, click each sample field in the center list that you want to add to your database, and then click the single right-arrow, which adds the selected fields to the Fields in My New Table list.**

Clicking the double right-arrow adds all the fields in the sample database. You can rename any field in the Fields in My New Table list by clicking it, clicking the Rename Field button, and then typing the new name in the dialog box that appears.

If you decide that you want to remove a field from your list in the right-most column, click the offending field name and then click the single left-arrow. Or click the double left-arrow to completely empty your field list and start all over again.

You can use fields from different sample tables to create your ideal table — just click each sample to browse its contents.

5. **After the list on the right has the fields that you need, click Next to continue.**

6. Type a descriptive name for your Access table (top-left of Figure 5-4).

You also have the option to pick your own primary key field to uniquely identify each record in your database. The *primary key* is a unique value (like a Social Security number) that can be used to identify each record in your database.

- Select Yes to allow Access to set the primary key for you.

- Select No if you want to set it yourself.

  If you choose No and you want to specify your own primary key, you get three choices in the extra wizard screen that appears (as shown in Figure 5-5).

7. Click Next to continue.

8. **(Optional) Click the What Field Will Hold Data That Is Unique for Each Record? drop-down list box and then choose a field with a unique value for each record.**

When I'm creating a database to store information about customers or clients, I usually pick a customer ID or Social Security number.

9. **(Optional) In this screen, you must also decide the following:**

   • Whether you want Access to generate a new number in the key field automatically (like a customer ID that automatically increments each time that you add a record)

   • Whether the primary key field will be a number

   • Whether the primary key field will be a combination of letters and numbers that you add yourself manually (like a Social Security number)

10. **Click Next to continue.**

   On the final Table Wizard screen (see Figure 5-6), you can choose to modify your table fields, begin typing data into the table immediately (see Figure 5-7), or have Access automatically create a *form* — an easy screen dialog box for entering data — for your new table.

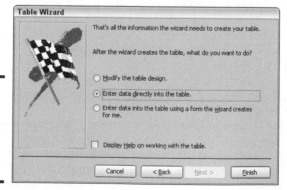

Figure 5-6: What's to follow after you complete your table?

11. **Choose what you fancy and then click Finish.**

The table that you created now shows up in the Database window when you click the Table button. (Check it out in Figure 5-7.) You can open it to enter additional records (or view or edit existing records) at any time by double-clicking it within the Database window.

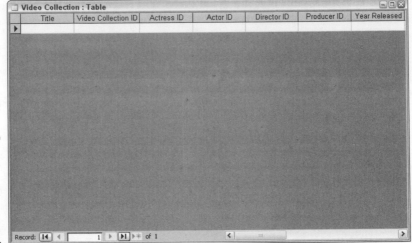

	Title	Video Collection ID	Actress ID	Actor ID	Director ID	Producer ID	Year Released

Record: |◄| ◄ | 1 | ► | ►| | ►* of 1

Figure 5-7:
A raw look at your table, which is ready to accept data.

To delete a table, just click it once (to highlight it in the Database window) and then press Delete. Access will prompt you for confirmation before trashing the file.

I describe how to enter data directly into a table a little later in the chapter. First, I'm going to delve into creating a form with the Form Wizard.

Creating a Form with the Wizard

Creating your own form is not a necessity — after all, the form that's automatically generated at the end of the table-creation process by the Table Wizard is just fine. Figure 5-8 illustrates the generic data entry form that the wizard produced for me automatically. By using forms, anyone can input data into your database, even if they're not familiar with the database creation process or if they've had little experience with Access.

By default, all forms are saved within the Forms category in the Database window with the same name as the corresponding table. You can enter data into a table by clicking the Forms button to display a list of your forms and then double-clicking the corresponding form to run it. Forms are also used to display existing data in a table. For example, if I just want to find out the length of the film *Alien,* I can just display the record for that film within the form.

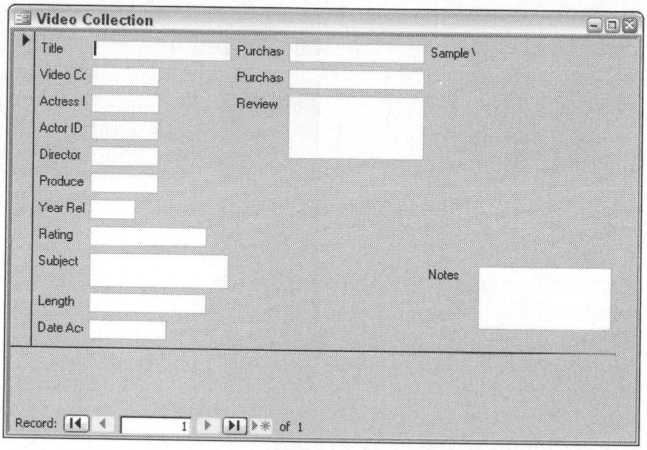

Figure 5-8:
Access
automatic-
ally
generates
simple
forms.

However, you're not stuck with the generic data entry form. You can create
a custom form for a database table by using the Form Wizard. Follow these
steps to build your own form from scratch:

1. **Click the Forms button at the left of the Database window and then
double-click the Create Form by Using Wizard entry in the list on the
right.**

   The first screen of the Form Wizard appears, as illustrated in Figure 5-9.

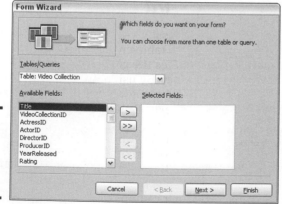

Figure 5-9:
You can
build a new
form from
scratch.

2. **From the Tables/Queries drop-down list box, choose the table that will
be linked to this form.**

To specify the fields that will appear in the form — not all of them need be included, of course — click each field in the Available Fields list that you want to include in the form and then click the single right-arrow. (Like with the Table Wizard, you can also click the double right-arrow to add all the fields in the table.) When you click each field, it is moved to the Selected Fields box.

3. **When the Selected Fields list on the right has the fields that you need, click Next to continue.**

To remove a field from the Selected Fields list, click the field name that you don't want and then click the single left-arrow; to completely empty your field list and start all over again, click the double left-arrow.

From the wizard screen shown in Figure 5-10, you can select from a number of predesigned formats, including the Datasheet layout (which looks very similar to Excel or Works Database) and the standard Columnar layout that Access uses when it generates a form automatically.

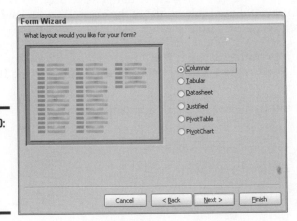

Figure 5-10:
Time to choose a layout for your new form.

4. **Select the layout that you need and then click Next to continue.**

5. **Select the style that will be used with your new form (see the list of choices in Figure 5-11).**

A form *style* includes a background pattern, color scheme, and font selection.

Access updates the Preview window with a sample of how things will look.

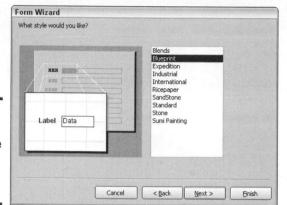

Figure 5-11:
A style can enhance the look of your Access form.

6. **When you've chosen the most fashionable look for your Access form, click Next to continue.**

   The final Form Wizard screen shown in Figure 5-12 prompts you for a descriptive title for your new form. You can choose to open the form immediately to add records or view existing records, or you can edit the design of the form.

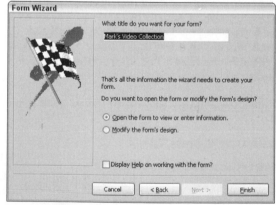

Figure 5-12:
You're nearly finished building your Access form.

7. **Click Finish to exit the Wizard.**

   Check out the custom form that I created for my video collection in Figure 5-13! "I'm so international and so very professional. . . ."

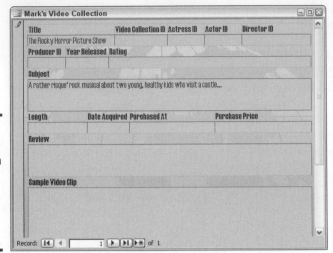

Figure 5-13:
Hey, I could be running a video store with a database like this one!

To delete a form that you no longer need, click it once to highlight it in the Database window and then press Delete. You'll be prompted for confirmation before the file is deleted. *Note:* Deleting a form will not delete any data from your tables.

So how do you use a form? Entering data is probably more intuitive within a form than any other method in Access because a form looks so doggone much like an online form that you'd encounter on a Web site. (If you're familiar with the Microsoft Works Database that I cover in the preceding minibook, you'll feel right at home here.) The instructions that you need to use a form are this simple:

1. To enter data, click your mouse pointer in the desired field and then type.

2. To move to the next field, press Tab.

3. To move to the previous field, press Shift+Tab.

4. To close the form and save your data, click the Close button at the top-right corner of the form.

If a field has the value (`AutoNumber`), it indicates that the field will be automatically incremented when you close the table. For example, if the previous record had a 5 in that field, the next record that you add will automatically use a value of 6 in the field.

The control for moving between records is also very similar to Works Database: It's the Record box at the lower-left of the form, which displays the current record number. To navigate between records, use the navigation buttons around the Record box:

✦ Click the arrow pointing to the bar at the left to move to the first record in the table.

✦ Click the arrow pointing to the left to move to the previous record.

✦ Click the arrow pointing to the right to move to the next completed record.

✦ Click the arrow pointing to the bar at the right to move to the last completed record in the table.

✦ Click the arrow pointing to the asterisk at the right to move to the end of the table and add a new record.

Entering and Editing Fields Manually

I'll admit, I get pretty enthusiastic about forms: They're easy for computer novices to use, and they look quite professional. However, you can view, enter, and edit your data directly from the table itself. Access calls this the *Datasheet view.* And because the table displays many records at once in rows, it's often faster than using a form.

Follow these steps to enter or edit a field value in a table:

1. **Select the record that you want to enter or change by either clicking it with the mouse or by using the Tab/Shift+Tab combination to move to it.**

2. **Type the new data value; depending on the data format, you might have to select the contents with your mouse (or the Shift+arrow keys) and the original value first.**

   Access displays a pencil icon at the far left of the record to indicate that you've made a change to the record (upper-left of Figure 5-14).

3. **If you're entering data in a new record, press Tab to move to the next field.**

4. **Click within any other record to save the new values.**

5. **To edit another record, begin again at Step 1.**

Each time that you enter a value in the empty record at the bottom of the window, Access automatically adds a new empty record; however, if you create a new record by mistake, just press Esc to cancel your edits.

This icon indicates a changed record.

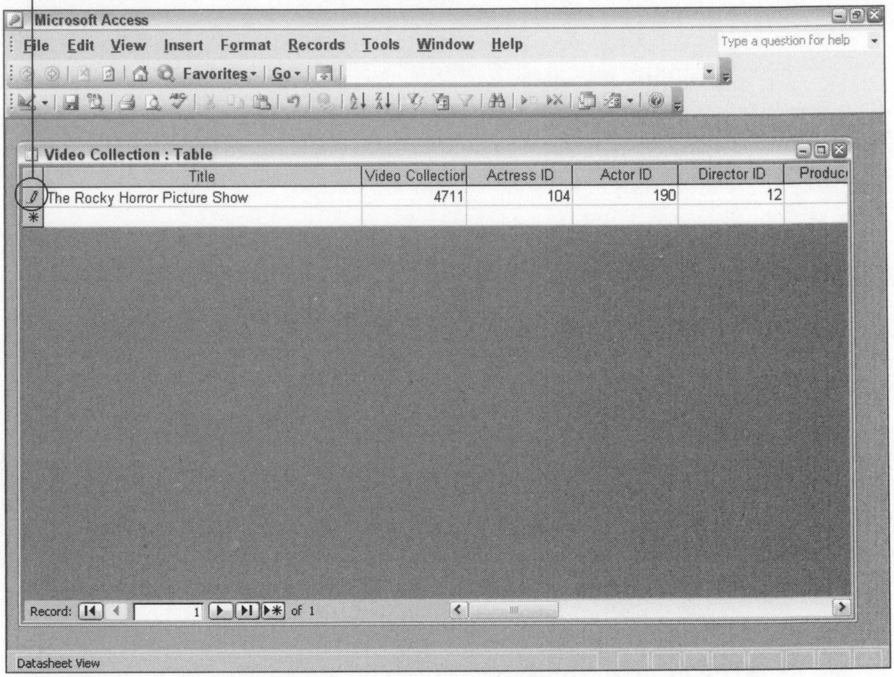

Figure 5-14:
Editing data
values in
Datasheet
view.

Using Queries

In Access-speak, a *query* is a method of viewing only selected data fields. For example, you might want to see just the customer ID, number of orders, and product ID so that you can tell what items in your store are selling well. Queries can help you analyze trends or perform a simple summary on one or two fields in your database. Naturally, there's a wizard to help you create a query, so that everyone can try it — even without suspenders, a beard, and a pocket protector.

Follow these steps to create a query:

1. **Click the Query button at the left of the Database window and then double-click the Create Query by Using Wizard entry in the list on the right.**

   Figure 5-15 illustrates the first screen of the Simple Query Wizard.

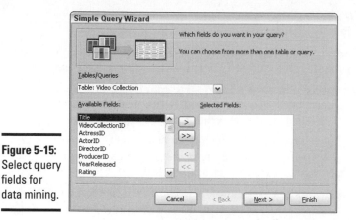

Figure 5-15:
Select query
fields for
data mining.

2. **Click the Tables/Queries drop-down list box to specify the table that will be linked to this query; then choose the fields that will appear in the query by clicking each desired field in the Available Fields list and then clicking the single right-arrow.**

   (Alternatively, click the double right-arrow to add all the fields in the table.) Like the Form Wizard, you can remove a field from the Selected Fields list by clicking the field name that you don't want and then clicking the single left-arrow. (Or you can send all the fields packing by clicking the double left-arrow.)

3. **When the Selected Fields box contains every field that you want in your query, click Next to continue.**

4. **In the next wizard screen that appears, choose either a detail or summary query (see the choices in Figure 5-16) and then click Next to continue.**

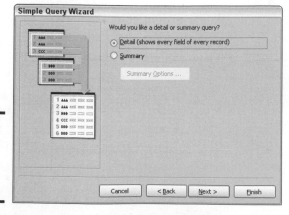

Figure 5-16:
Will that be
a summary
or detail
query?

- **A** *detail* **query** includes every field in each record that contains any of the specified fields.

- **A** *summary* **query** allows you to calculate the sum, average, minimum, or maximum of numeric fields, like a simple Excel function.

5. **Type a descriptive name for your query, specify whether you want to open the query immediately or modify the design created by the Simple Query Wizard, and then click Finish to generate the query.**

   The query returns your data in a standard Datasheet view so that you can enter new records or edit the fields displayed in your query, just as if you were looking at the entire record in a table or a form.

   Your new query appears in the Database window when you click the Query button, and you can open it to view or modify it by double-clicking it within the Database window.

You can delete a query by clicking it in the Database window and then pressing Delete. Access will prompt you for confirmation before deleting the file.

Using Access Templates

Although most folks tend to design their own databases for specific purposes, Access comes with both a number of built-in templates and a rather bodacious number of templates that are online at www.microsoft.com.

To use a general template, display the New File task pane, click On my computer, and then click the Databases tab to display the selection of templates that you see in Figure 5-17. Double-click a template icon to load it.

Figure 5-17: Access 2003 includes a good selection of starter templates.

You'll find dozens of high-quality, predesigned templates grouped by category on the Microsoft Web site. At the bottom of the Templates dialog box, click the Templates on Office Online button, which will load Internet Explorer and display the Microsoft Office Template Gallery.

Printing Your Data

Before you decide to put your data on paper, I always recommend that you use the Access Print Preview feature. Just choose File⇨Print Preview or click the Print Preview button on the Standard toolbar. Many times I've been thankful that I checked first to verify that what I expected to print was actually what was going to appear on the hard copy!

Access can print from just about any view, whether the active window is displaying a table, a form, or a query. When you're ready to print, choose one of these methods:

✦ **Click the Print button on the Standard toolbar.** The contents of the active window are immediately printed with the current settings.

✦ **Choose File⇨Print.** Use this method to print just selected pages (or the currently selected records in a datasheet window). You can also select from multiple printers or specify multiple copies from the Print dialog box. If you need to change any printer-specific options supported by the printer's Windows XP software driver, click the Properties button. When you're ready, click the Print button.

✦ **Press Ctrl+P.** This method also displays the Print dialog box.

Chapter 6: Staying in Touch with Outlook

In This Chapter

✔ **Running Outlook 2003**

✔ **Introducing the Outlook window**

✔ **Setting up your Outlook e-mail account**

✔ **Reading and replying to incoming mail**

✔ **Sending messages**

✔ **Adding file attachments to messages**

✔ **Entering contacts**

✔ **Creating appointments**

✔ **Using the Outlook Today screen**

✔ **Printing within Outlook**

*I*f you're not using Outlook 2003, *run* — do not dawdle — to your bookshelf and grab your Office 2003 CD-ROM. You see, you'll need it to install Outlook. It's that good, and using just about anything else — including that old workhorse, Works 8 Calendar — is strictly second best. (No offense to those other applications; it's just that Outlook can organize just about everything in your life better than any other program that I've ever used — without becoming confusing or complex.)

In this chapter, I provide you with the basics that you need to use Outlook as your comprehensive e-mail, address book, and calendar application. You'll be attaching files, reading messages, making appointments, and sending blind carbon copies in no time at all. I also mention a number of tips that I've found helpful in my experience with Outlook.

For a complete discussion of everything that Outlook 2003 can do and store, you'll obviously need more than just a single chapter. And I can't recommend a better book than the bestselling *Outlook 2003 For Dummies* by Bill Dyszel (by Wiley Publishing, Inc.). My copy has become quite dog-eared since I bought it, and I fear that I've put several cracks in the book's spine from constant use . . . always a first-rate indicator of a good book.

Running Outlook

You can start Outlook by using any of the following methods:

✦ Double-click the Microsoft Outlook icon on your desktop.

✦ Choose Start➪All Programs➪Microsoft Outlook.

✦ If you're using the Office shortcut bar, click the Outlook icon.

✦ Press a Windows key while holding down R (Win+R) to bring up the Run dialog box; type **outlook** in the Open text box and then press Enter.

Look for the two Windows keys on your keyboard; they reside in the same stratosphere as your spacebar and Alt keys. If ya got 'em (and you probably do), they bear the waving Windows flag.

Elements of the Outlook Window

Figure 6-1 illustrates the Outlook window in all its glory.

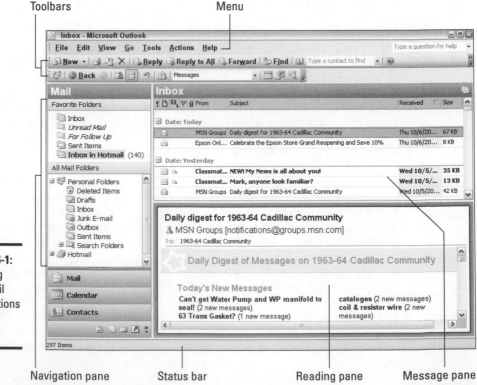

Figure 6-1: The king of e-mail applications is in the house.

Here's a quick rundown of the elements within the Outlook window:

✦ **The menu:** Standard fare on any Office 2003 application.

✦ **The toolbars:** Outlook can display up to three toolbars. A click of each toolbar button performs the same action as the corresponding menu command. To make additional room on the (somewhat) crowded Outlook window, choose View➪Toolbars and then click the toolbar name to toggle it off or on. The Outlook toolbars can also be relocated within the program window: Move your mouse pointer to either end of the toolbar until it turns into a four-direction cursor and then drag to relocate the toolbar. (It "sticks" to the sides like glue.) To create a *floating* toolbar (which can be moved like an independent dialog box), drag the toolbar to the middle of the window.

You can easily add or remove buttons from a toolbar: Click the down-arrow button at the end of the control and then choose Add or Remove Buttons. Click the toolbar name on the menu that appears and then click next to individual buttons to toggle them on or off.

✦ **The Navigation pane:** The top of this pane includes a tree display, where you can select an Outlook folder. Just click the desired folder, and the contents are displayed in the Message pane. You can use the buttons at the bottom of the Navigation pane to jump between the different views and functions within Outlook. For example, you can immediately switch to your Outlook Calendar view, or you can click the Contacts button to check a telephone number from your Address Book.

✦ **The Message pane:** This pane's primary job is displaying the messages in the current folder; however, in other views (like the Contacts or Tasks view), the contents change to match the data that you're displaying.

✦ **The Reading pane:** If you click a message in the Message pane, the contents are displayed in the Reading pane. This is a neat way to see what's contained in the message without actually opening the message in a separate window.

Virtually any pane can be resized in Outlook. Move your mouse pointer over the divider bar until it turns into opposing arrows and then drag to relocate the bar.

✦ **The status bar:** Outlook's status bar typically displays the total number of messages in a folder or the total number of contacts in your Contacts list — you get the idea. (Don't get me wrong; I do appreciate the totals. The status bar is a good soldier in the fight to hold down RIE, or *Runaway Inbox Expansion* — but that's about it.)

Configuring Your Mail Account

First things first. In order to use Outlook, you need to set up a mail account. Adding a mail account within Outlook involves — surprise! — a wizard. (I think that someone got the message in Redmond that wizards are A Good Thing.) Follow these steps to add an Internet e-mail account within Outlook:

1. **Choose Tools⇨E-mail Accounts to display the wizard screen you see in Figure 6-2, select the Add a New E-Mail Account radio button, and then click Next.**

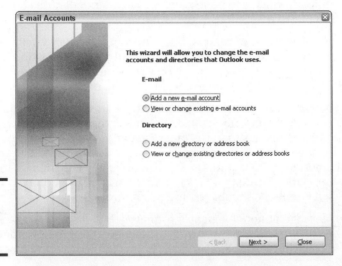

Figure 6-2: The E-mail Accounts Wizard.

Note you can also use this wizard to modify an existing account.

2. **Select the type of e-mail server that you'll be using (see the choices in Figure 6-3) and then click Next to continue.**

For virtually all home PC owners, that'll be a POP3 server, which is the common choice with most dialup and digital subscriber line (DSL)/cable Internet service providers (ISPs). (Enough abbreviations for one sentence?)

You can also set up a separate account for a Web-based HyperText Transfer Protocol (HTTP) server (like Hotmail). If you're connecting to an office e-mail server, check with your network administrator to determine what you need to select on this screen.

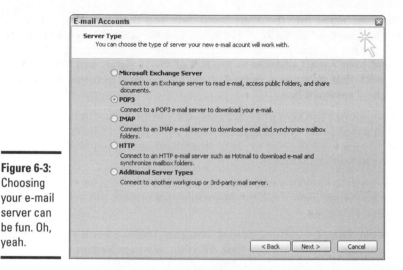

Figure 6-3:
Choosing
your e-mail
server can
be fun. Oh,
yeah.

Figure 6-4 illustrates the E-mail Settings screen for a POP3 server. Make
sure that you have any instructions or account information from your
ISP handy when you enter each value because your ISP will have to
supply 'em. (Guessing will do no good.) If security isn't a problem at
your location, mark the Remember Password check box to enable it. (If
you don't enter a password, Outlook will prompt you each time that you
connect to the server to send or receive mail.)

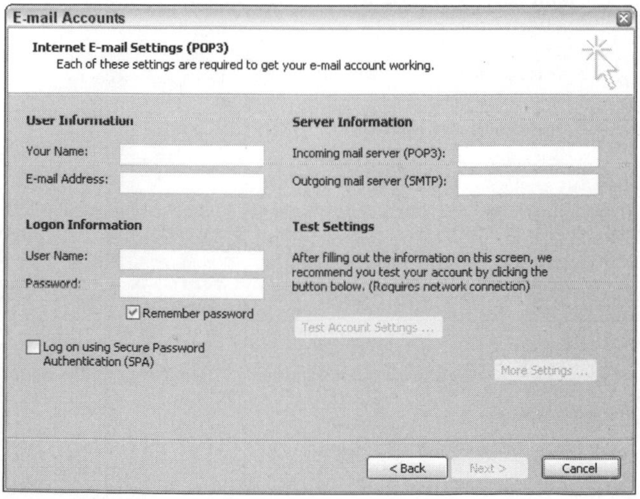

Figure 6-4:
Time to type
in all those
settings that
your ISP
gave you.

3. **Type your name into the Your Name box and then type the e-mail address supplied by your ISP into the E-mail Address box. Your Logon Information is actually your e-mail account username (probably the part of your e-mail address to the left of the @ sign), and Outlook fills it in with that string as a default; type your e-mail account password into the Password box.**

Did you notice the similarity between User Information and Logon Information? Good eye; mistaking these two easily confused combinations for each other often leads to frustrated and irate calls to your ISP's technical support number.

If you need to specify a name for the account or add your company's name to the account, click the More Settings button and enter them on the General panel.

4. **After you complete all the boxes, you can double-check your account information by clicking the Test Account Settings button.**

Outlook attempts to connect to the specified server and download a sample message.

Any errors are reported within a separate window. Click Next when you're ready to move on.

5. **Click Finish to exit the wizard.**

To remove an account or to specify a new account as the default, run the wizard again. On the first screen that appears, select the View or Change Existing E-Mail Accounts radio button. From the resulting window, as shown in Figure 6-5, make the appropriate changes.

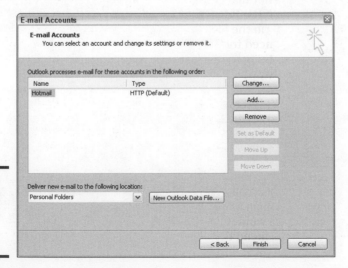

Figure 6-5: Remove or change an account here.

If you rely heavily on Outlook to store all your important information, I beseech you — even more than usual — to ***back up your doggone hard drive!*** You might be able to re-create most of your résumé, but how about every single telephone number that you've ever stored in Contacts or every single e-mail message that you've ever received? Do it. **Back up. Do it!**

When you create a mail account, Outlook creates a folder that contains the data that you store in your Personal Folders as well as all the messages that you've created. As you can imagine, this jewel of a folder is a prime candidate for backup. By default, you'll find these folders in the Documents and Settings folder under your Windows XP user account name, but they're buried deep; look in the `\Local Settings\Application Data\Microsoft\Outlook` folder.

Reading and Replying to E-Mail

Naturally, receiving and reading your incoming mail is the primary thrust behind Outlook, and it's easy to check all your accounts at once. From the menu system, choose Tools➪Send/Receive or click the Send/Receive button on the Standard toolbar — or press F9. (To send and receive from just a specific account, choose Tools➪Send/Receive and then choose the desired account from the resulting pop-up menu.)

Oh, joy! "You've got mail" — and it's not a chunk of worthless spam that you want to immediately delete. (More on eradicating spam later in this chapter.) New messages appear as bolded entries in the Message pane; double-click the message to open it in a message window (as shown in Figure 6-6). If you'd rather scan your mail, click the message once, and it will be shown in the Reading pane. (If the Preview pane is missing, choose View➪Reading Pane to toggle it on (in the location of your choice) or click the Reading Pane button on the Advanced toolbar. If you're not interested in previewing your mail, this is a good thing to toggle off because you'll see much more of the Message pane that way.)

If you'd rather read your messages in a Usenet/newsgroup format — where the messages are arranged in a conversational style instead of by the date you received them — click View➪Arrange by➪Conversation. (This style of display is also called *threading,* where a message is followed by all of its replies in a linear order.)

To add the author of an incoming message to your Contacts list, just right-click the person's e-mail address in the From field (while the message is displayed in a message window) and then choose Add to Outlook Contacts from the contextual menu that appears. (More about adding contacts later in the chapter.)

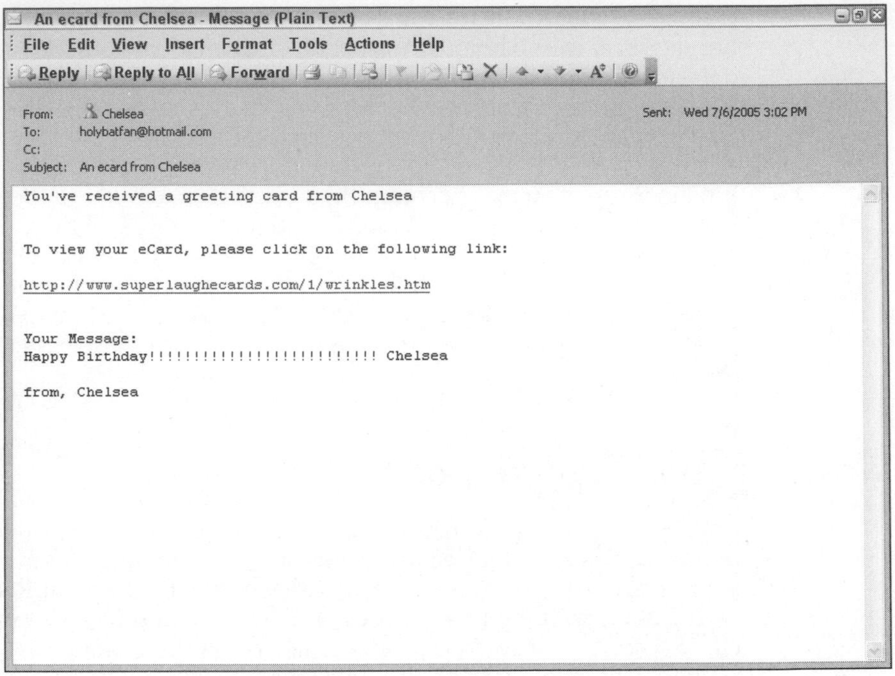

An ecard from Chelsea - Message (Plain Text)

File   Edit   View   Insert   Format   Tools   Actions   Help

Reply | Reply to All | Forward |

From: Chelsea   Sent: Wed 7/6/2005 3:02 PM
To: holybatfan@hotmail.com
Cc:
Subject: An ecard from Chelsea

```
You've received a greeting card from Chelsea

To view your eCard, please click on the following link:

http://www.superlaughecards.com/1/wrinkles.htm


Your Message:
Happy Birthday!!!!!!!!!!!!!!!!!!!!!!!!!! Chelsea

from, Chelsea
```

Figure 6-6:
Reading a
message in
its own
window.

Does one of your incoming messages deserve a pithy reply? (Otherwise called "returning a piece of flaming e-mail" — all in fun, of course.) If so, follow these steps to reply to it:

1. **Click the desired message in the Message pane list to select it and then click the Reply button on the toolbar.**

   If the message is currently open in its own window, you can also click the Reply button within the message window.

   Was the original message addressed to additional folks besides yourself? If so, you can send your reply to everyone who received a carbon copy of the original message by clicking the Reply to All button on the toolbar instead of Reply.

   Outlook opens the Reply window that you see in Figure 6-7, with the insertion cursor already hanging out at the top of the message. Outlook includes the text of the original message, too — just look underneath the header ----Original Message---- to see the original message. The To field is already completed, filled with the name of the person who sent the original e-mail.

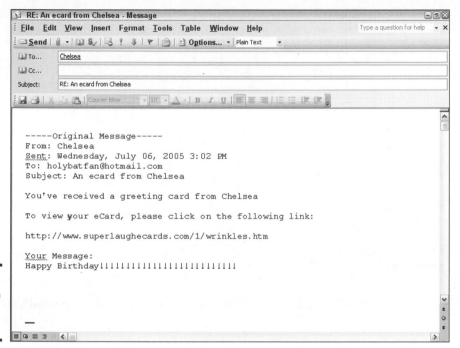

Figure 6-7:
Preparing to
reply to a
message.

You'll notice that Outlook automatically adds the prefix RE: to the
beginning of the original subject line, but feel free to click in the Subject
box and type a new subject if you like.

2. **(Optional) To send carbon copies of the reply to other individuals,
   click once in the Cc box and enter addresses manually (separated by
   semicolons) or click the Cc button to select names from your Outlook
   Contacts list (see Figure 6-8).**

Don't forget that the text of the original message is included. If necessary, you can delete it manually to preserve that all-important privacy.

"Hey, can't I send *blind* carbon copies too?" (That's where the recipients
of carbon copies don't see the others who have also received a copy.)
You surely can . . . but for some strange reason, Outlook hides the Bcc
field in the reply header unless there's already a Bcc recipient. To add
a Bcc recipient, click the To or Cc button to display the Select Names
dialog, and type one or more a Bcc addresses directly into the Bcc box.

3. **Go ahead — type like the wind! After you enter the text of your
   message (and format it, if you like, by using the familiar formatting
   controls on the toolbar), you can add attachments.**

I cover attachments later in this chapter, in the section wittily titled,
"Using File Attachments."

Figure 6-8:
Selecting
names from
my Contacts
list for
carbon
copies.

4. **When all is in readiness, click the Send button to send your message immediately.**

To save a draft of the message without sending it immediately, click the Save icon in the toolbar and then close the window. The message appears in your Drafts folder; to send it later, double-click the Drafts folder to open it, double-click the message to open it, and then click Send.

You can also choose to forward a message, allowing you to add a comment to the body of the original message before you send it to the new recipient. To forward a message, click the Forward button instead of the Reply button. Then sally forth, following the instructions that I detail within this section.

Could you use some help prioritizing the messages that need replies? That's where the Outlook Quick Flag feature comes in handy. You'll notice a separate column at the far right of the Message pane that contains a ghostly outline of a pennant — right-click the Flag column for a particular message, and you can assign any one of six different colors to indicate the importance of a timely reply. When you need to prioritize your Inbox, click View⇨Arrange by⇨Flag, or just click on the Flag column heading button. Once you're done with a message, you can right-click the Flag column again and choose Clear Flag from the pop-up menu. *Sublime!*

Composing and Sending Messages

Sometimes a reply just isn't enough; instead, you need to stir up trouble by initiating the e-mail conversation. To compose and send a new message, follow these steps:

1. **Click the New toolbar button in the Standard toolbar or press Ctrl+N.**

   Outlook displays the new message window that you see in Figure 6-9.

2. **Address your message.**

   • If the recipient for this message isn't in your Contacts list: Click in the To box and type the e-mail address.

   • If you do have the recipient for this message in your Contacts list: Click the To button and then choose the person from the Select Names dialog box that appears. You can also add carbon copies and blind carbon copies from this dialog box.

   Click OK to return to the new message window.

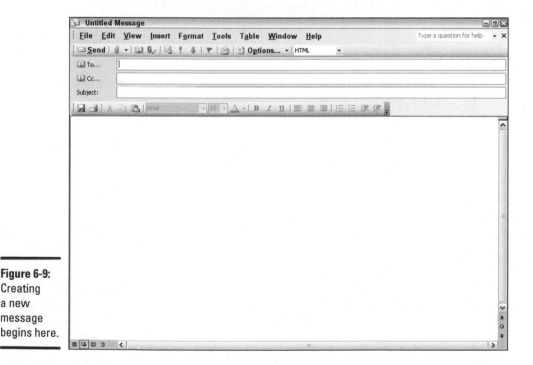

Figure 6-9:
Creating
a new
message
begins here.

3. **Click in the Subject field, type the subject for this message, and then press Tab to move to the message editing box.**

4. **Type the text of your message and apply any desired formatting to the text.**

5. **Add any attachments.**

   Use the procedure that I show you in the next section.

6. **Send the message.**

   • **Now:** Click the Send button to send it immediately.

   • **Later:** Alternatively, you can click the Save button on the toolbar to save the message in your Drafts folder, as I explain earlier in the preceding section.

   The ability to save your e-mail messages is a really neat feature, especially if you're composing messages offline on your laptop without an Internet connection. You can turn that idle time spent waiting in the airport into productive time. When you get back to your home or office and your Internet connection, send each message as I describe earlier.

Using File Attachments

Next, turn your attention to file attachments — you can include all sorts of files with your e-mail messages, such as

✦ Office documents

✦ Pictures, sound clips, and *short* video clips (no message should have more than 2MB of total attached files)

✦ Programs and data files

If the recipient of your message is using Outlook (or another popular e-mail application), she should be able to save and use the files that you send just as if they had been stored on a floppy disk or a CD-ROM.

Attaching files and sending them to your friends with Macintosh and Linux computers is a great way to swap documents that can be read on multiple platforms (like a Word document, for example).

ISPs place a maximum ceiling on the size of an individual message — and that includes any attachments. How much is too much? The typical limit is under 2MB for a single message, but the exact limit is determined by both your Internet e-mail server and the recipient's e-mail server. With this in mind, another Mark's Maxim appears:

Never send a 300MB video clip to your best friend and expect it to arrive in one piece.™

You'll know that you've exceeded the maximum message size if you receive an error message from either server that declares your original e-mail to be undeliverable. The *noive* of some people!

Here's how to send an attachment:

1. **Reply to a message or compose a new message.**

2. **Click the Insert File button on the Standard toolbar or choose Insert⇨File.**

   Outlook displays the Insert File dialog box.

3. **Navigate to the location of the file(s) that you want to attach and then click each one.**

   For multiple files, hold down Ctrl while you click.

4. **Click the down-arrow next to the Insert button and then click Insert to add the files to the message.**

   Attached files appear in the Attach header area of the message dialog box (see Figure 6-10).

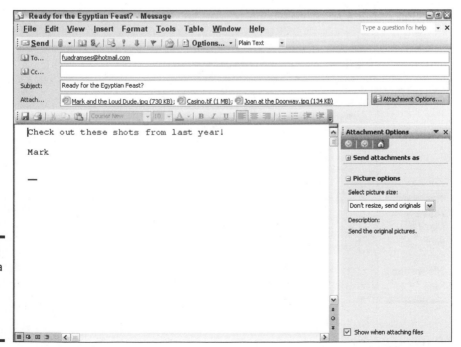

Figure 6-10: I've added a number of pictures to this e-mail message.

If someone sends you an attached file, right-click the file attachment in the header and choose Save As from the pop-up menu that appears; then browse to select a spot on your system where the file will be stored.

Repeat after me: "Mark, I promise never to run an attached file unless I've manually scanned it — or unless my scanning software has already scanned it automatically!" E-mail viruses and malicious macros are widespread these days, and running any attachment (even one from someone that you know) without protection is just asking for trouble.

Keeping Track of Your Contacts

Enough with the e-mail! Outlook can also take care of your contacts, like any other good Personal Information Manager (PIM). To display your contacts, click the Contacts button on the Navigation pane or press Ctrl+3. The Contacts window appears, as shown in Figure 6-11.

To jump directly to a specific first letter of a contact's last name, click the desired letter on the button strip down the right side of the Contacts screen.

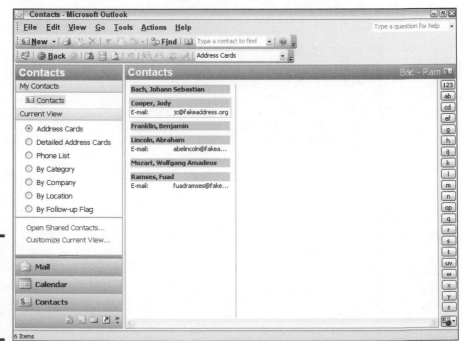

Figure 6-11:
Maintain
your
Contacts
information
here.

So what can one do with a contact? Of course, half the value of the Contacts window is the ability to simply store your Address Book entries in an organized central location, but you can also

✦ Create a new e-mail message to that contact.

✦ Set up an appointment or a meeting request with that contact.

✦ Set a new task or journal entry for that contact.

All these sundry actions are available when you right-click any contact entry displayed in the Contacts window.

Entering a contact

To enter a new contact from the Contacts window, follow these steps:

1. Press Ctrl+N or choose File⇨New⇨Contact.

Outlook displays the Contact window that you see in Figure 6-12.

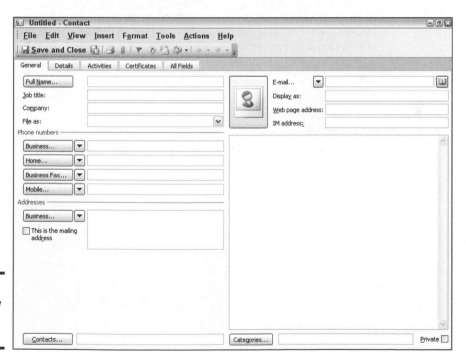

Figure 6-12:
Enter a new contact here.

2. **Click in the appropriate field to enter information such as the person's telephone number(s), job title, home address, and Web page address.**

   Entry is completely free-form; the only fields that you should always enter are the person's name and his e-mail address.

   If a field has a down-arrow button next to it, you can click the button to display additional fields of the same type. For example, click the down-arrow next to the business phone field, and you can click to display the person's pager or home fax machine number.

3. **To display additional fields, click the Details tab (see Figure 6-13); from this panel, you can enter the person's birthday and anniversary, their spouse's name, and other such data.**

4. **When you've entered all the data for a contact, click the Save and Close button on the toolbar.**

Editing a contact

It's easy to add new information to an existing contact or even edit the data that you've already entered. Just double-click a contact entry in the Contacts window. Outlook opens the same window that you used to enter the contact information — of course, the data that you've already added to the contact is still there, but everything can be edited if necessary, and you can add new data.

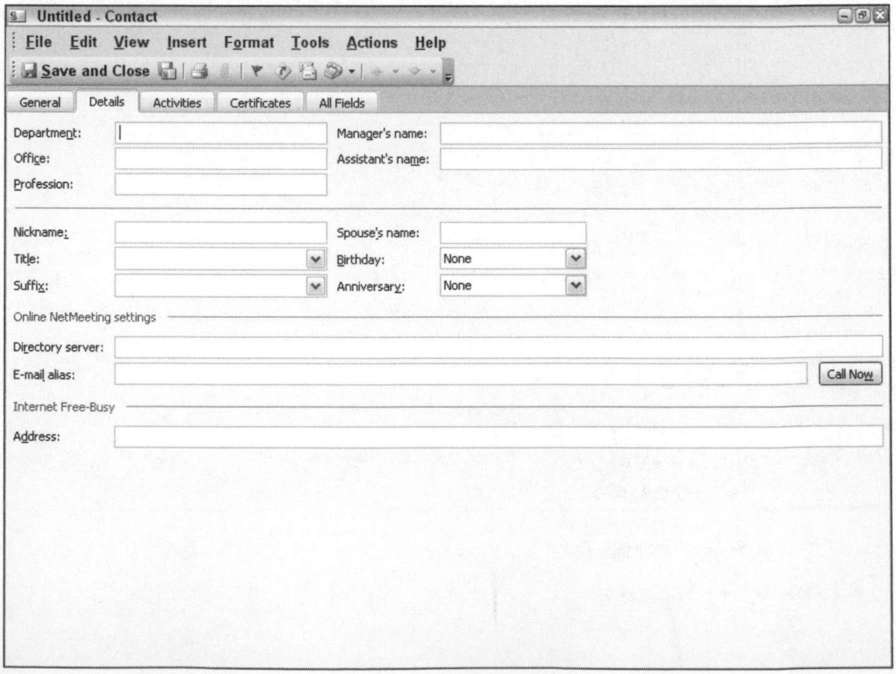

Figure 6-13:
You can enter additional contact data on the Details panel.

Untitled - Contact	

File   Edit   View   Insert   Format   Tools   Actions   Help

Save and Close

General | Details | Activities | Certificates | All Fields

Department: _____   Manager's name: _____
Office: _____   Assistant's name: _____
Profession: _____

Nickname: _____   Spouse's name: _____
Title: _____   Birthday: None
Suffix: _____   Anniversary: None

Online NetMeeting settings

Directory server: _____
E-mail alias: _____   Call Now

Internet Free-Busy

Address: _____

To close the window and save the updated information, click the Save and Close button again.

Using the Outlook Calendar

If I told you that Outlook is also a full-featured calendar program, would you believe me? Yep, this program is a regular Swiss Army knife! To display the Calendar, click the Calendar button on the Navigation pane or press Ctrl+2. Figure 6-14 illustrates the Calendar window.

Click the appropriate button in the Standard toolbar to display the different Calendar periods, which are highlighted within the Calendar window:

✦ Day (a single day)

✦ Work Week (a five-day work week)

✦ Week (a full, seven-day week, beginning on Sunday and ending on Saturday)

✦ Month (an entire month)

From these views, you can set appointments that will appear on your Calendar.

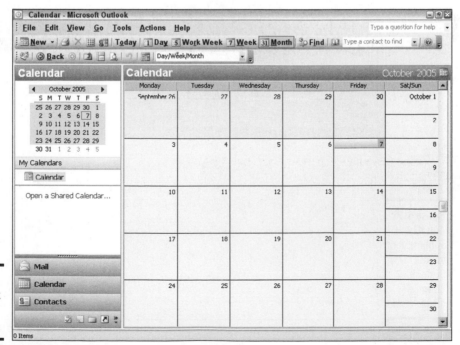

Figure 6-14:
The Outlook Calendar window.

Creating an appointment

To create a new appointment for your Calendar from the Calendar window,
follow these steps:

1. **Press Ctrl+N or choose File➪New➪Appointment.**

   Outlook displays the Appointment window that you see in Figure 6-15.

2. **Type a descriptive subject for the appointment, press Tab, and then
   type the location for the meeting.**

   To use a location that you've used previously, click the Location drop-
   down list box and select it from the list.

3. **Set the start and end times for the meeting.**

   a. **Start:** Click the Start Time drop-down list, choose the date for the
      appointment, and then click the start time.

   b. **End:** Likewise, click the End Time drop-down list boxes and set the
      ending date and time for the appointment.

   c. **All Day:** If the appointment will last all day, select the All Day Event
      check box to enable it, and Outlook will disable the End Date and
      Time fields.

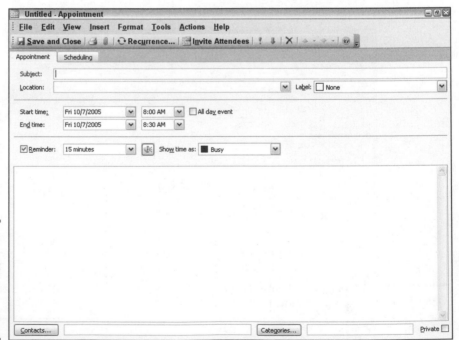

Figure 6-15:
Add a new
appointment
to your
Outlook
Calendar
here.

4. **(Optional) If you need a reminder from Outlook before the appointment, mark the Reminder check box and choose the period of time that you need to reach your appointment after the reminder appears.**

   You can click the Reminder Sound button to choose an alarm sound to play as a little added "encouragement."

5. **From the Show Time As list, choose a status for the appointment.**

   The appointment status will show up in your Calendar as a shaded or colored block.

   By default, Outlook uses Busy as the status for a new appointment.

6. **Click in the notes box at the bottom half of the Appointment window and type any free-form comments or notes that you want to associate with this meeting.**

7. **Click the Categories button at the bottom of the Appointment window to assign a category to this appointment.**

   The program displays the Categories dialog box, as shown in Figure 6-16.

Figure 6-16:
Categories help you organize your appointments.

You can group your appointments into categories such as VIP, Suppliers, or Personal. Note that you can assign multiple categories to an appointment.

8. **After everything's set, click the Save and Close button to add the appointment to your Calendar.**

Displaying appointments in Outlook Today

To view your daily appointments and summarize your entire existence each morning — pretty cool when you think about it — click the Personal Folders entry in the Navigation pane folder tree. Outlook displays the screen that you see in Figure 6-17, with everything that's happening today arranged on a single screen. This, folks, is a neat trick, and I use Outlook Today throughout my workday.

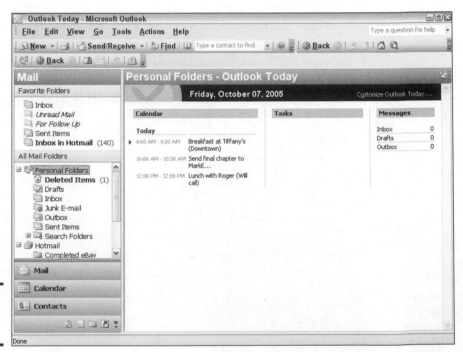

Figure 6-17: Hey, there's my day!

To display the specifics about an appointment or task, double-click the item.

Printing within Outlook

Believe it or not, you can print just about any data from Outlook in its native form — and considering the wide variety of information stored within Outlook's copious environs, that's quite a feat. Depending on the current view and the selected item(s), you can print anything from the contents of an e-mail message to your appointment schedule and your Contacts list.

Like with the other Office 2003 applications, I strongly recommend that you pause long enough to use the Print Preview feature. (Figure 6-18 illustrates a Print Preview from an e-mail message.) When you're displaying the view that you need within Outlook and you've selected any specific items, choose File⇨Print Preview (or click the Print Preview button on the Standard toolbar) to view how things will look.

Remember how I just finished crowing about how great the Outlook Today view is? And here we are talking about printing. Hmmm . . . what better way to print a reminder of what you need to do during the day than by printing the Outlook Today screen? It's your entire day on one sheet of paper.

When you're satisfied with the preview, use one of these methods to print:

✦ **Click the Print toolbar button on the Standard toolbar.** Outlook immediately prints the screen or selection with the printer's current (or default) settings.

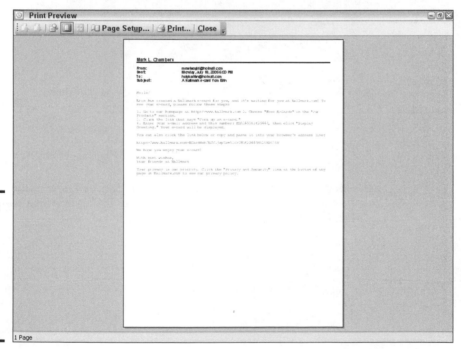

Figure 6-18:
Always use Print Preview — it's the secret to Office 2003 printing happiness!

✦ **Choose File⇨Print.** Outlook displays the Print dialog box that you see in Figure 6-19. *Note:* The specific settings on the Print dialog box will change depending on your current view or the items that you select to print. The Print dialog box allows you to set the page style, print multiple copies, select the target printer (including network printers), and select a range of pages to print. To set any printer-specific options provided by your printer's driver, click the Properties button. After you set the printer options that you need, click Print.

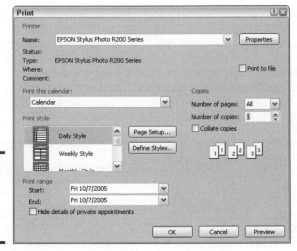

Figure 6-19:
Printing a
Calendar
page within
Outlook.

✦ **Press Ctrl+P.** The handy keyboard shortcut also displays the Print dialog box.

✦ **Click the Print button on the Print Preview or Page Setup dialog boxes.** Clicking the Print button on either dialog box also displays the Print dialog box.

Book VI

Fun with Movies, Music, and Photos

The 5th Wave   By Rich Tennant

"Well, well! Guess who just lost 9 pixels?"

Contents at a Glance

Chapter 1: Scanning with Gusto

In This Chapter

- ✔ Understanding scanner technology
- ✔ Shopping for a flatbed scanner
- ✔ Acquiring an image
- ✔ Rotating and cropping your scans
- ✔ Converting and saving scanned images
- ✔ Guidelines to follow while scanning
- ✔ Handling copyrighted material

A scanner might rank as one of the most versatile pieces of hardware that you can slap onto your PC. With an investment of anywhere from $75 U.S. to $400 U.S., you can add the ability to copy and fax printed documents (with a modem and printer, of course), create digital images from all sorts of materials, and even use optical character recognition (OCR) to read text from documents directly into your PC's word processing application.

What's inexpensive isn't always easy to use, however. You'll have to choose from different types of scanners that use different types of connections to your PC — and to produce the best results, you need at least an introduction to the basics of scanning. You also need the skinny on cleaning a scanner, deciding on an image format, and handling copyrighted material.

In this chapter, I provide you with an introduction to the basics of scanning. Consider these recommendations, tips, and tricks as a quick-start guide from my book *Scanners For Dummies*, Second Edition, by Wiley Publishing, Inc. If scanning catches your fancy and you decide to delve deeper, I'd naturally be honored if you would add that volume to your home or office library as well. (By the way, if you're planning to copy your face — or any other body part — you don't need to read this chapter. Just visit your local copy center or stay a little late at the office . . . oh, and be discreet.)

What Happens Inside a Scanner?

I can't say that it's Party Central inside your scanner; in fact, most popular scanners on the market today actually have very few moving parts, so the entire device is rather boring compared with a DVD recorder. Plus, you don't really have to know how your scanner does its job to use one, so you can skip to the next section with a clear conscience.

Still with me? Then read on to discover how this magic box can turn a printed document into a digital image. Check out Figure 1-1.

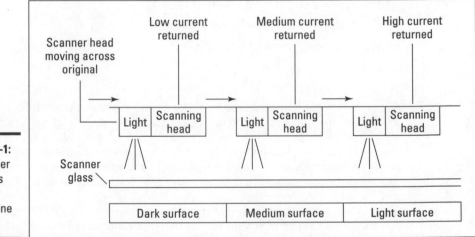

Figure 1-1: A scanner captures a digital image, line by line.

Here's how it works:

1. The scanner's sensor (an array of photosensitive cells) moves one line across the material that you're scanning. (In some scanners, the material actually moves past a fixed sensor; this gets important pretty soon.) The sensor is paired with a strong light source that illuminates whatever you're scanning.

2. As the sensor moves past the original, each cell sends a level of current corresponding to one dot (a pixel) of the reflected light from the material. For example, scanning the white part of a printed page results in a far different signal than scanning the black text on the same page.

3. Your scanner's electronic brain (tiny as it is) collects all the signals from each pixel, resulting in a digital picture of one line of the original.

4. The scanner sends the data from the scanned line to your PC.

5. The sensor (or the material) advances one line, and the entire process begins again at Step 1.

I often compare this process with taking a digital photograph of each line of your document and then laboriously pasting those separate images together in an image-editing program. Luckily, you don't have to do the hard work: Your PC collects each line sent by the scanner and builds the document for you, usually while you watch. Technology is grand that way.

Your Friend, the Flatbed

Presenting the Mark's Maxim for this page:

Buy a *flatbed* scanner.™

Figure 1-2 illustrates a flatbed scanner preparing to do its duty; note that the top lifts up, just like a copy machine. The sensor head moves in a flatbed scanner while the material that you're scanning remains motionless on top of the scanning glass. (In a second, you'll discover why a motionless original is A Good Thing.)

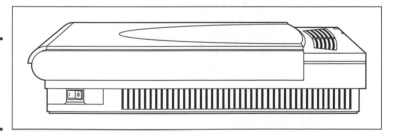

Figure 1-2:
Nothing pleases like a flatbed scanner.

Comparatively, with a sheet-fed scanner, the material that you're scanning moves through a system of rollers while the sensor remains stationary. Printer manufacturers typically use sheet-fed scanning hardware in all-in-one or *multifunction devices,* which combine the functionality of a printer, a scanner, a fax machine, and a copy machine in one svelte case. Gotta be honest, though; I don't recommend sheet-fed scanners. And before all you owners of sheet-fed scanners out there in PC Land begin reaching critical mass and flooding my e-mail inbox, let me attest to the one major advantage to sheet-fed scanners like the one that you see in Figure 1-3: They do take up far less space. (I know this from personal experience because I have both sheet-fed and flatbed scanners in my office.)

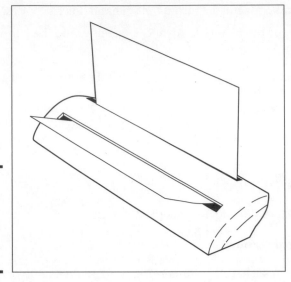

Figure 1-3:
A sheet-fed scanner looks much like a fax machine.

"Okay, Mark, I'll byte: If I can save valuable desktop space with a sheet-fed scanner, why are you such a die-hard supporter of flatbed models?" Dear reader, here are the top three reasons why you should pick a flatbed:

✦ **They deliver a better quality scan.** Because the original material remains fixed in a flatbed (compared with the moving original in a sheet-fed), you have less chance of shifting, allowing a flatbed to deliver a better scan with more detail.

✦ **They're versatile:** If an original can fit on top of the flatbed's glass, you can scan it — pages from a book, very small items such as business cards, or even items such as clothing. With a sheet-fed scanner, you're limited to paper documents, and you have to use a clear plastic sleeve to hold those business cards. (Many sheet-fed scanners won't accept small items at all.)

Sheet-fed owners: Keep those documents as pristine as possible — meaning no torn edges, no staples, and no antique documents that could suddenly decide to decompose inside the hard-to-reach areas of your all-in-one unit.

✦ **They have fewer moving parts:** Sheet-fed scanners can easily jam if the original document doesn't feed correctly — and I've found them less reliable over the long run than flatbed models because sheet-fed scanners require more cleaning and adjustment.

If you've already invested in a sheet-fed model, don't despair; there's no reason to scrap your hardware. However, you'll have to limit yourself somewhat in your material . . . unless, of course, you don't mind tearing pages from books and magazines to scan them.

Here are other specialized types of scanners:

✦ **Negative scanners:** These expensive models are especially designed to produce the best possible scans from film negatives. They do nothing else, so versatility isn't their claim to fame.

✦ **Business card scanners:** Again, the name says it all. These portable scanners capture images and information from standard-size business cards. They're often used in conjunction with laptop computers or palmtop computers.

✦ **Pen:** A pen scanner captures only a single line of text at once, but they're easy to carry around and can be used with a laptop computer and OCR software to read text from documents into a word processing application.

Popular Scanner Features

Here's a list of the minimum features that I typically recommend for home or home office use when you're shopping for a flatbed scanner:

✦ **An optical resolution of at least 600 x 1200:** Without delving too deeply into the details of scanner *resolution* — the number of pixels that your scanner can capture — you should reject any scanner that offers less than 600 x 1200 dots per inch (dpi). Note that you should be checking the *optical* (also often called *raw*) resolution and not any resolution figure that's *enhanced* or *interpolated.* Those are just fancy words that indicate that the scanner's software is adding extra dots in the image. I call 'em *faux pixels* because they aren't actually read from the original. Just ignore any enhanced or interpolated resolution figures when shopping for a scanner.

✦ **Single-pass operation:** If a scanner can capture all the color data that it needs in one pass, it takes less time (and introduces less room for registration error) than a scanner that must make three passes across the same original. 'Nuff said.

✦ **One-button operation:** Most of today's scanners offer one or more buttons that can automatically take care of common tasks. For example, one button might scan the original and create an e-mail message with the scanned image as an attachment, and another might scan the original and automatically print a copy on your system printer. I'm all about convenience.

✦ **A minimum of 36-bit color:** The higher the bit value, the more colors that your scanner can capture. Ignore any scanner that can't produce at least 36-bit color; most of today's scanners can produce up to 42-bit color.

✦ **A transparency adapter:** Whether it's optional or included with the scanner, the ability to add a transparency adapter allows you to scan film negatives and slides with much better results.

✦ **USB or FireWire connection:** Although a number of the most inexpensive scanners still offer parallel port connections (which share the parallel port with your printer), steer clear of them. Instead, I strongly recommend that you choose a scanner that uses either a Universal Serial Bus (USB) connection (good) or a FireWire connection (much better). Of course, your PC will need the prerequisite ports, as I explain in Book I, Chapter 3. These Plug and Play ports are much faster than a parallel connection.

Basic Scanning with Paint Shop Pro

Scanner manufacturers ship a bewildering number of different capture (or *acquisition*) programs with their hardware, so there's no one proper way to scan an original. However, scanners that comply with the TWAIN standard can be controlled from within popular image editors such as Photoshop or Paint Shop Pro. *TWAIN,* for you acronym nuts, is not actually an acronym — it refers to the line "and never the twain shall meet" from that Kipling guy. (Many folks think that TWAIN means *t*echnology *w*ithout *a*n *i*nteresting *n*ame. It don't.)

Now that you've been properly introduced, here's the important part you'll be tested on: devices that are TWAIN compatible are operating system-independent, meaning that these devices are interchangeable between Windows and Macintosh. Any TWAIN-compatible hardware device can work with any TWAIN-compatible image editor or software application . . . pretty *sassy,* no?

Acquiring the image

In this section, I demonstrate how to use a typical USB Hewlett-Packard scanner within Paint Shop Pro, which is my favorite image editor. If you follow along with this procedure, you'll end up with an image that you can edit within Paint Shop Pro, convert to another format, or simply save to your hard drive. (I can heartily recommend Paint Shop Pro for its Big Three features: It's much, much cheaper than Photoshop, almost as powerful, and much easier to use!)

Assuming that you have Paint Shop Pro loaded on your computer, follow these steps:

1. **Double-click the Paint Shop Pro icon on your desktop or choose Start⇨Programs⇨Jasc Software⇨Paint Shop Pro.**

   The main program window shown in Figure 1-4 appears.

2. **Choose File⇨Import⇨TWAIN.**

3. **From the pop-up menu that appears, choose Select Source to select which TWAIN source you're using to capture the image.**

   The Select Source dialog box that you see in Figure 1-5 appears.

**Book VI
Chapter 1**

**Scanning with
Gusto**

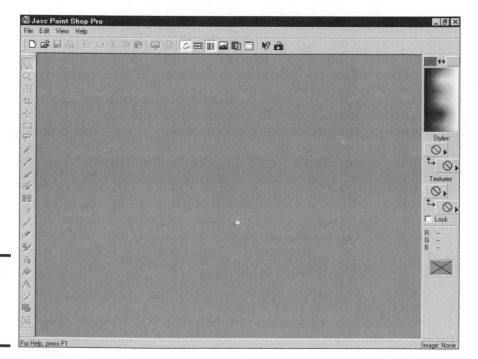

Figure 1-4:
The Paint
Shop Pro
main
window.

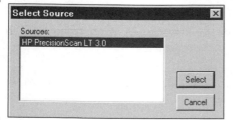

Figure 1-5:
Select your
scanner
from the
Select
Source
dialog box.

4. **Highlight the TWAIN entry for your scanner and then click the Select button.**

5. **Choose File again, choose Import and TWAIN, and then choose Acquire from the pop-up menu that appears.**

   At this point, Paint Shop Pro invokes the scanner's TWAIN driver, so if you're using another brand of scanner, the resulting dialog box will look different; however, the same controls should be available if you explore a bit. Figure 1-6 shows the Acquire dialog box for an HP scanner.

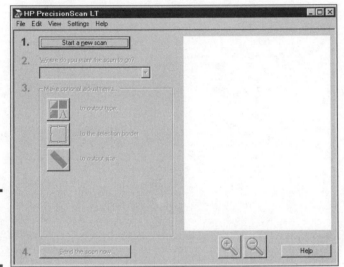

Figure 1-6:
My scanner
is ready
to go.

6. **Click the Start a New Scan button.**

   Your scanner should rumble to life, and eventually the Acquire dialog will produce a thumbnail image of the original, as shown in Figure 1-7. (That's me in Alaska, making friends with the local wildlife. Eat your heart out, Sir Edmund Hillary.)

7. **If you're satisfied with the dimensions of the image and the automatic settings chosen by your scanning software, click the Send the Scan Now button.**

   The result appears as a new image within Paint Shop Pro, as shown in Figure 1-8, ready for you to edit and experiment to your heart's content.

Figure 1-7:
Use the thumbnail image to resize the capture area.

Figure 1-8:
The finished scan appears in Paint Shop Pro.

However, if you need to fine-tune the image before sending it to Paint Shop Pro in Step 7, here are the common settings that you can change in most scanner drivers, along with what you'll accomplish. (With my scanner driver, you click the icon buttons under Step 3.)

✦ **Output type:** This setting controls what type of image file that the scan will produce. Typically, you'll want a color photograph in 24-bit (or 16.7 million) colors, but other choices might include a Web image at 256 colors, a grayscale image, a black-and-white drawing, or simple text (that's been optimized for reading with an OCR program).

✦ **Image boundaries:** Use this feature to click and drag the boundaries of the scanned image. For example, I recommend moving the scanned image border inside any extraneous material on the edges of the original, such as text that surrounds a picture that you want from a magazine page. By reducing the size of the actual scan, your image file is smaller, and the scanner takes less time to do its job — plus, you'll eliminate the need to crop that extraneous part of the image later within Paint Shop Pro.

✦ **Image scale:** Figure 1-9 illustrates the scale options for my HP scanner. Note that I can use the original image size, or I can scale the scanned image by a specified percentage. Also, I can set the width or height of the scanned image in inches, and the software automatically calculates the proper proportion change for the other dimension.

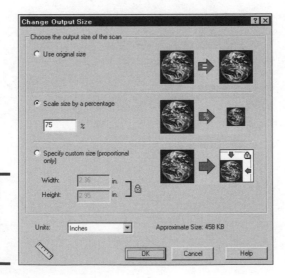

Figure 1-9: Adjust the size of the scanned image.

✦ **dpi (or resolution):** A setting of 150 dpi is usually fine for scanning photographs or documents, but if you're planning on enlarging an image with a lot of detail, you might want to specify a higher resolution. However, this will significantly increase the size of the finished image file.

Rotating and cropping images

After the scanned image is safely in Paint Shop Pro or Photoshop, you're free to have fun — fixing problems big and small, removing portions of the image that you don't want, or even zooming in to view and change individual pixels.

Although a complete discussion of image editing is far too in-depth of a subject for this chapter — in fact, you can find dozens of books on Paint Shop Pro and Photoshop on the shelves, including the step-by-step coverage of image editing in *Scanners For Dummies* — I'd like to cover the two most common procedures that are required for most scanned images:

✦ **Rotation:** An image that's literally standing on end or displays upside-down needs to be *rotated* (turned).

✦ **Cropping:** An image with too much extraneous background needs to be *cropped* (trimmed). Cropping an image can significantly cut down its file size.

To rotate an image that you've scanned so that it displays in the proper orientation, follow these steps:

1. **Scan an image into Paint Shop Pro.**

   Read how in the previous section.

2. **Choose Image⇨Rotate⇨Free Rotate to display the Rotate dialog box (as shown in Figure 1-10).**

Figure 1-10:
Rotate an image from here.

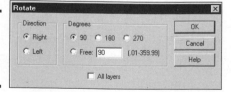

3. **Select either the Left or the Right radio button to specify the direction of rotation.**

4. **Select a Degrees radio button to rotate the image (usually either 90 or 180 degrees) or select the Free radio button and then enter a specific amount of rotation in its accompanying text field.**

5. **Click OK to rotate the image.**

To crop a scanned image, follow these steps:

1. **Click the geometric selection tool — it looks like a dotted rectangle — on the left toolbar.**

2. **Click in the top-left corner of the image area that you want to keep; then, while holding the mouse down, drag the selection rectangle to the lower-right corner of the desired area.**

3. **Release the mouse button to select the area.**

   Paint Shop Pro indicates the area you've selected with an animated dotted line, as shown in Figure 1-11.

4. **Choose Image and then choose Crop to Selection to remove everything outside the selection box; see the results in Figure 1-12.**

The geometric selection tool

Figure 1-11:
Select an
area of an
image
before
cropping it.

Figure 1-12:
The image is
cropped.

If you make a mistake, you can always click the Edit menu and choose Undo to cancel the last action that you performed.

Converting and saving the image

When you're finished editing your image, your new work of art is ready to be saved to disk. That takes me to discussing another feature of Paint Shop Pro: the ability to convert the existing image format into a format that might be more suited to your needs.

Think of a format as the structure of the image file — which, after all, is a data file just like the programs that you run and the documents that you save. The format is the method that the image data is organized within the file. I'm not going to go into a huge discussion of the different formats in this section; rather, I just indicate which formats are better for certain applications and which ones you should avoid for those same applications.

You want to consider converting an image that you've scanned because

✦ **Some formats can save space.** The winner in this first category is definitely the JPEG (or JPG) image format, which is a file compression format that can save you several megabytes over image formats such as Windows bitmap (BMP) and uncompressed TIFF.

✦ **Some formats maintain image quality.** The reason why JPEG images are so small is that they use a form of compression (rather like that used in Zip files) to crunch the file size down to a minimum. Unfortunately, that compression can result in degradation of the image over time; each time that you open and edit a JPEG file, it can lose a tiny bit of detail. If archival image quality is your aim, throw file size limitations to the wind and use BMP or uncompressed TIFF; they're huge in size, but they preserve image quality no matter how often you open them.

✦ **Some operating systems prefer certain formats.** Naturally, those folks on the Mac and Linux side of the fence might have problems loading and using an image in Windows (BMP) format. For compatibility reasons, consider saving your image in TIFF format, which is well supported on just about every computer in use today.

✦ **Some formats are better suited for the Web.** Virtually all Web pages use JPEG and GIF images, which are the common formats recognized by all browsers. GIF images are well suited for smaller graphics such as buttons and animated banners, but JPEG images are better for inline graphics and full-size images that are designed to be downloaded.

Okay, now that you know whether your image needs converting, follow these steps to save (and optionally convert) your image within Paint Shop Pro:

1. **Choose File➪Save As to display the dialog box shown in Figure 1-13.**

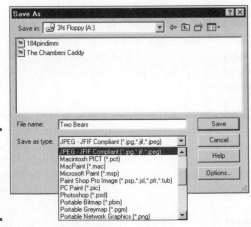

Figure 1-13:
Convert the format of a scanned image here.

2. **To convert the image to another format, click the Save as Type drop-down list and then highlight the desired format.**

3. **Type a filename in the File Name field.**

4. **Some formats allow you to choose additional settings — click the Options button to display them.**

   For example, Figure 1-14 shows the settings that you can change for JPEG images within Paint Shop Pro. Generally, I recommend sticking with the defaults, but if you need these advanced options, make your changes and then click OK, which will return you to the Save As dialog box.

Figure 1-14:
Change the advanced settings for a JPEG image here.

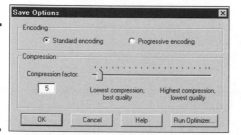

5. **Click the Save button.**

Scanning Do's and Don'ts

Today's scanning software helps to make the scanning process easier than it was just three or four years ago, but here are a number of tried-and-true guidelines that you should follow for the best results from your hardware. Here's a cheat sheet of rules that every scanner owner should follow:

+ **Don't place heavy objects on your scanner's glass.** Believe it or not, I've heard horror stories of people trying to scan bricks and rocks — usually trying to capture a particular color or pattern for an e-mail attachment or a Web graphic. Besides the possibility of a cracked or a broken scanner glass, rough or pointed objects can cause scratches that will show up in your images.

   Don't forget that paper clips and staples are public enemy number one for your scanner. Please remove them before you place your original!

+ **Do work with the largest possible original.** The larger the original, the better quality image that you're likely to get. (Sure, you can scan a postage stamp, but use a higher dpi setting so that you have enough pixels to enlarge the image later.)

+ **Do clean your scanner glass with the right material.** Never spray glass cleaner directly on the glass: Too much liquid on the glass can leak under the surface, causing condensation later. Instead, use a soft photographer's lens cloth or a monitor wipe moistened with alcohol, which evaporates quickly. I clean my scanner glass at least once a week.

✦ **Do add as much memory to your PC as you can afford.** The more memory that you add, the easier and faster your PC can handle larger scans. Remember that some of those scanned images might end up being 40 or 50MB in size. Also, any image editor will perform much better with additional memory. If you're using Photoshop or Paint Shop Pro on a regular basis, I recommend a minimum of 256MB. Memory, my friend, is cheap.

✦ **Don't overwrite your original scan.** If you're experimenting with a scanned image — for example, if you're applying filters or changing the color balance for an artistic effect — keep the original as is and save a copy with your changes. After you've applied changes in an image editor and saved those changes, you usually can't backtrack to the quality of the original image.

✦ **Do keep your scanner drivers up to date.** Like other hardware devices that I mention throughout this book, check your scanner manufacturer's Web site often for updates to your scanning software and for Windows drivers.

✦ **Don't use outdated or specialized image formats.** PC owners should avoid Microsoft Paint (MSP) images. (I like to call these little-known and less-recognized formats by a single collective acronym — WIF, which stands for *Weird Image Format*.) My point is simple: By using one of the major image formats (TIFF, JPEG, BMP, or GIF), you give others a better chance to load and work with your scanned images.

Those Irritating (Or Invaluable) Copyrights

Of course, copyrights aren't so doggone irritating if you happen to be the creator of a work of digital art (whether it be a photograph, a painting, or a poem). As an author, I'm personally all for copyrights. However, as a scanner owner, you might find yourself walking a legal tightrope without a pole when you decide to include scanned material in your own documents.

Like I said, I'm an author — **not a lawyer!** (I do know some great lawyer jokes, but that's not the same as a law degree.) Therefore, before I describe some of the common myths about copyright law, let me say that you should *always* consult with a knowledgeable copyright lawyer. These guidelines are here to help, but they're not a substitute for bona fide legal advice.

With that well-worded disclaimer in mind, here is a selection of the most common fallacies concerning copyrighted material:

✦ **"I got it off the Internet, so it must be public domain."** Wrong. It doesn't matter where you got a creative work — from the Internet, a publication, or even off the wall of a subway tunnel. If you use anything that you didn't create completely by yourself, you need permission from the author.

✦ **"I added a line and some shading to this scanned image, so now it's mine."** Embellishing an original work does *not* make it yours. (After all, I can add an extra line of lyrics to any Beatles song that you can name, but that doesn't give me the copyright to "Eight Days a Week.")

✦ **"This photograph didn't carry a copyright mark, so the scan is my original work."** Nope. An original work, whether a document, a photograph, or a scribble on a napkin, doesn't need any mark (although a copyright mark does reinforce your copyright claim). In the legal world, a copyright is bestowed automatically in most cases as soon as the creator completes the work.

✦ **"This is a not-for-profit project, so I can include this artwork."** This might be true, but only if you're using a clip art collection or royalty-free photograph archive that gives you specific rights to use intellectual property in your work. Otherwise, it doesn't matter whether your work is for profit or nonprofit — a copyright applies to the original work in either case.

✦ **"Why, the very act of scanning this photograph gives me the copyright."** I don't hear this one often. Evidently, by creating a digital copy, these folks think that they can magically acquire the copyright. (Sound of palm slapping forehead.) Why didn't I think of that before? Oh, yes, now I remember — it's **not true.** Simply changing the form of a work doesn't release the creator's copyright.

✦ **"This artwork was drawn a hundred years ago — the copyright doesn't apply to me."** Before you assume that a copyright has expired on a work, check with a copyright lawyer. Descendants of the original copyright owner might now own the rights to the work.

**Book VI
Chapter 1**

Scanning with
Gusto

Adding a Copyright Line

If you'd like to add a copyright line to the work that you've scanned, Paint Shop Pro can help you out there as well. Run the program and follow these steps:

1. **Choose File⇨Open to display the familiar Windows Open dialog box.**

2. **Navigate to the location of the scanned image file, click it to highlight the file name, and then click the Open button.**

3. **Click the text icon on the left toolbar (it looks like a capital letter A).**

4. **Click the cursor in the area of the image where you want the mark to appear.**

   Paint Shop Pro displays the Text Entry dialog box as shown in Figure 1-15.

5. **To select a new font, click the Name drop-down list.**

   From the Text Entry dialog box, you can also change the size of the text as well as its color and characteristics (such as bold, italics, and under-lining).

6. **After the font in the Sample Text display appears as you want, click within the Enter Text Here box and type the text of your copyright line.**

   A typical copyright mark reads like this: **Copyright (c) *[year]* by *[name]*, All Rights Reserved.** (Naturally, you'll want to substitute the current year and your name where I've indicated.) Figure 1-16 illustrates an image with a copyright line added.

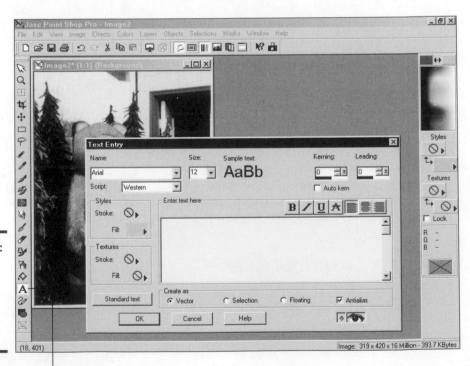

Figure 1-15: Select the font characteristics for a copyright line.

Text tool

Figure 1-16: My image sports a copyright mark.

7. **Save the new image under a new filename by choosing File⇨Save As and entering a filename in the Save As dialog box that appears.**

Chapter 2: Dude, MP3 Rocks!

In This Chapter

✏ **Understanding the MP3 format**

✏ **Ripping MP3 files from an audio CD**

✏ **Playing MP3 files**

✏ **Downloading MP3 music to your MP3 player**

✏ **Comparing other audio formats with MP3**

✏ **Burning audio CDs from MP3 files**

Can you name one or two truly revolutionary technologies that have
arrived in the last ten years? Perhaps CD-ROMs and DVD-ROMs, mobile
telephones, or the *Jerry Springer Show?* (Okay, that last one was a deliberate
attempt at humor.) Anyway, historians often claim that no person can accurately point to a world-changing technology in his or her lifetime because we
just don't have the perspective to recognize its importance when it happens.

Well, guess what? MP3 is here in your lifetime; it absolutely rocks, and, my
friend, it is *indeed* one of those revolutionary technologies. You can quote
me on this, with a Mark's Maxim that will make me a visionary (who wears
glasses):

> **The creation and distribution of digital music will permanently
> change everything in the recording industry, including the career of
> every musician on the planet.™**

To be honest, that's not really such an earth-shattering prediction . . . in fact,
it's already happening! In this chapter, I tell you what's so incredibly cool
about MP3 digital music, how you can create your own MP3s, and — here's
the spoiler — why the recording industry would love to stop you from using
MP3 files altogether.

(Yes, MP3 is legal when used correctly. Sorry, Big Brother Music.)

An MP3 Primer

First off, what is a furshlugginer MP3, anyway? Things can get real technical real fast here, and that's not what this book is about — therefore, here's my definition of the MP3 process for Normal Human Beings:

> When you create (or *rip*) an MP3 (short for MPEG-1 Layer 3) file, you're capturing (or *sampling*) an analog sound recording and saving that audio in digital form.

Clear as mud? Here's another way to think of it: MP3 files store music and audio in the same fashion that music is stored on an audio CD — as a string of *binary* characters. It's all zeroes and ones, but your PC — and Macs, and MP3 players, and even many personal electronic devices, such as personal digital assistants (PDAs) and portable stereos — can decode that binary information and re-create it as the original analog signal.

Note that just about any CD-ROM drive — including the read-only variety — can rip tracks, so you don't need a CD or DVD recorder to do the job. The process is technically called *digital audio extraction,* but you and I call it *ripping*.

Here are more parallels between audio CDs and MP3 files:

✦ A typical MP3 file corresponds to a single track on an audio CD (which makes sense because virtually all MP3s are ripped directly from audio CDs).

✦ MP3 files offer the same — or even better — audio quality than audio CDs.

✦ Like the tracks on an audio CD, MP3 files can contain information about the song title and artist.

✦ Like the music on an audio CD, the quality of an MP3 recording stays pristine no matter how many copies of that MP3 file you make. Because it's digital, there's no degradation when you make additional copies of an MP3.

✦ A series of MP3 files can be recorded (or burned) onto a blank CD-R, creating a new audio CD. You can even burn MP3 files from many different CDs to produce your own compilation discs.

Because an MP3 file is just another data file to your PC, you can do many of the same things with an MP3 file that you can do with other digital media files (such as an image from your digital camera). For example, you can

✦ **Send 'em:** Send smaller MP3s as e-mail attachments.

✦ **Download 'em:** Allow MP3 files to be downloaded from your Web site or File Transfer Protocol (FTP) server.

✦ **Save 'em:** Save MP3 files to removable media such as Zip disks, CDs and DVDs, and Universal Serial Bus (USB) Flash drives.

Of course, this very portability is a double-edged sword because it makes MP3 music easy to copy — which, under copyright law, is a synonym for *steal.* I discuss what you can and can't legally do with your MP3 files in a sidebar toward the end of the chapter.

The audio quality of an MP3 file is determined by the *bit rate* at which it is sampled. The higher the bit rate, the better the sound file (and the larger the size of the physical MP3 file itself, which makes sense). Table 2-1 lists some of the common bit rates for different types of MP3 files — anything over 128 Kbps is actually better than the quality of audio CD tracks.

Table 2-1	Bit Rates for MP3 Files
Quality Level	*Bit Rate*
Audio books	48 Kbps
FM stereo	64 Kbps
Near CD	96 Kbps
Audio CD	128 Kbps
Audiophile	160/192/256/320 Kbps

Ripping Your Own MP3 Files

To demonstrate just how easy it is to rip MP3 files from an existing audio CD, I'll choose an audio CD from my collection at random — hmmm, how about jazz legend Count Basie and his classic 1957 album *Count Basie at Newport* — and then extract a set of MP3 files that I can listen to with my Apple iPod MP3 player.

For this demonstration, I use a popular program for ripping MP3 files on the PC: Musicmatch Jukebox 10, from Musicmatch (www.musicmatch.com). You can download the basic version of Jukebox for free from the company's Web site or upgrade to the Plus version for a mere $20 U.S.

Here's the first inkling of the copyright controversy, which I wade into at the end of this chapter: You can legally rip MP3 files only from audio CDs that you've bought for yourself! By ripping songs from a friend's CD — or even an audio CD that you borrowed from the public library — you're violating copyright law. (In this case, I own this audio CD, so I can legally create MP3 files from it for my own personal use. However, I can't give those MP3 files to anyone else, or I'm in violation of copyright law.)

Now that Perry Mason has had his say, follow these steps to create your own MP3 files from an audio CD:

1. **Choose Start➪All Programs➪Musicmatch➪Musicmatch Jukebox to run the program, which displays the main window that you see in Figure 2-1.**

Figure 2-1:
The familiar curvaceous lines of Musicmatch Jukebox.

2. **Load the audio CD into your drive.**

   Jukebox displays the track names in the playlist pane, shown at the right in Figure 2-2, and begins to play the CD. Because I don't want to listen to the disc right now, I click the Stop button (the square) on the program's control panel.

3. **Before you extract any tracks, you must configure the MP3 settings within Jukebox.**

   a. **Click the Options menu.**

   b. **Choose Recorder.**

   c. **Click Settings to display the Settings dialog box shown in Figure 2-3.**

      In this case, I want my MP3 tracks for my iPod player, so I want CD-quality music. Typically, this will be your best choice as well, unless you need the smallest possible MP3 file sizes (use 8 Kbps) or you're ripping something like an audio book.

Figure 2-2:
Jukebox can automatic-ally play an audio CD.

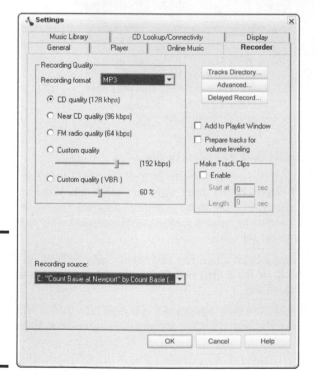

Figure 2-3:
Always configure (or check) your MP3 settings before you rip.

4. **Click the Recording Format drop-down list and choose MP3; then select the CD Quality (128 Kbps) radio button.**

If you want to listen to the tracks while you rip 'em, clear the Mute While Recording check box. Click OK to save any changes that you've made and return to Jukebox.

TIP

If you have more than one CD or DVD-ROM drive in your PC, check to ensure that the Recording Source is set to the proper drive before you leave the Settings dialog box.

5. **To start the actual ripping process, press Ctrl+R to display the Recorder pane, which is proudly displayed in Figure 2-4.**

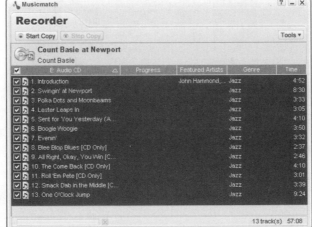

Figure 2-4:
The
Recorder
pane
appears
when you're
ready to rip.

6. **Mark the tracks that you want to rip.**

   By default, Jukebox automatically rips all the tracks on the disc, so they're all checked. If you don't want to rip a track, just clear the check box next to the track title. Note that you can click the None button to remove all the checks, which makes it easier to rip only one or two tracks from an entire CD.

7. **Let the ripping begin! Click the red Start Copy button on the Recorder pane and then sit back and watch the progress for each track, as shown in Figure 2-5.**

   The completed MP3 files are placed in a separate folder within your My Music folder, complete with the artist name and album title.

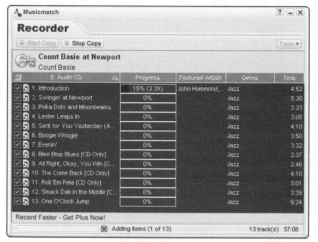

Figure 2-5:
Keep an eye
on the
progress of
your rip.

Listening to Your Stuff

After you're riding the digital wave of the future and you've ripped a number
of MP3 files, you're ready to enjoy them. Here are a number of different ways
to listen to MP3s on your PC, using both Musicmatch Jukebox and the built-
in MP3 support in Windows XP:

✦ **Double-click an MP3 file in Explorer.** Double-clicking an MP3 file loads
the program associated with MP3 audio on your system. By default, this
is Windows Media Player, but if you've installed another MP3 player —
such as Jukebox or Apple's great free digital audio player, iTunes (www.
apple.com/itunes, shown in Figure 2-6) — Windows plays the file
with that program instead.

✦ **Right-click an MP3 file and choose Play from the menu that appears.**

✦ **Run an MP3 player application such as Musicmatch Jukebox.**

If Windows XP is using the wrong application to play MP3 files — for example, if you want Windows Media Player to run when you double-click an MP3
file — it's time to change the association for the file. Right-click the MP3 file
and choose Open With from the menu that appears; then click Choose
Program to display the Open With dialog box that you see in Figure 2-7. Click
the application with which you want to play your MP3 files, make sure that
the Always Use the Selected Program to Open This Kind of File check box is
enabled, and then click OK.

Internet radio arrives

But wait, there's more! Digital audio players like Musicmatch Jukebox, Windows Media Player, and iTunes can now open up an entirely new world of music: broadcasts of Internet radio stations! Computer techno-music jocks call this method of delivery *Internet audio streaming*.

You can tune in to an Internet radio station from a sponsoring Web site (like my favorite, SHOUTcast, at www.shoutcast.com) or by typing an Internet radio address directly into your MP3 player. In fact, both iTunes and Musicmatch Jukebox come with an impressive list of stations, ready to listen.

Just like everything else on the Internet, you'll enjoy better-quality stations and have less trouble if you have a broadband DSL or cable connection, but even dialup Internet users can take advantage of Internet radio. To try out a station, visit my Web site at www.mlcbooks.com and follow the instructions you find there to connect to *MLC Radio* — we specialize in classic hits from 1969 to 1979, delivered commercial-free (and in CD-quality stereo, if you have a broadband connection).

Figure 2-6: Another MP3 favorite, iTunes from Apple, hard at work.

If you're using Jukebox, follow these steps to listen to one or more MP3 files:

1. **Choose Start⇨All Programs⇨Musicmatch⇨Musicmatch Jukebox to run the program.**

2. **Click and drag the desired MP3 files from an Explorer window and drop them in the Jukebox playlist pane.**

3. **To skip to the previous and next tracks, click the Previous and Next buttons on the Jukebox control panel — huge surprise there, right?**

   MP3s are easy to pause while you're retrieving your toaster pastry from the toaster. Just click the Pause button to pause the audio and click it again to restart the playback.

Jukebox remembers the songs that you added to your playlist, so if you want to start over with a clean slate, click the Clear button at the bottom of the playlist. Also note that you can repeat the playlist by clicking the Repeat button. To save a playlist for future use, click the Options menu, choose Playlist, and then click Save Playlist — you can open the playlist file later by pressing Ctrl+O.

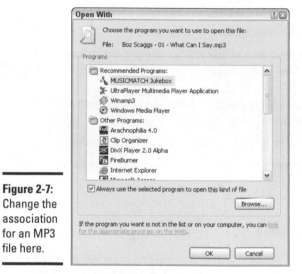

Figure 2-7:
Change the
association
for an MP3
file here.

Downloading to an MP3 Player

Here's yet another significantly cool thing that your PC can do for you: It can download MP3 files to your personal MP3 player for your portable listening pleasure. For example, I use my iPod, which has 15GB of storage, a built-in 12-hour battery, and a very fast FireWire connection. (Although PC owners might not like it, the iPod is another masterpiece of design from our friends at Apple Computer, www.apple.com. Luckily, it works on the PC as well when using Apple's iTunes player.) I heartily recommend the iPod sweet machine as the best MP3 player on the market today. In fact, iTunes automatically downloads and synchronizes your music on both your PC and your iPod, so there's really not much else to say.

But wait . . . what if you don't have an iPod? If you're using one of the many MP3 player models supported within Musicmatch Jukebox, you're still in good shape! However, you must first download the proper device plug-in from the Musicmatch Web site. This process is easy because Jukebox takes care of it automatically. After the plug-in is in place, follow the steps in the previous section to add MP3 tracks to your playlist (or to load an existing playlist).

To download the songs in your current Musicmatch Jukebox playlist to your MP3 player, follow these steps:

1. **Plug your MP3 player into the USB or FireWire port.**

   Windows should automatically recognize that you've plugged the device in.

2. **Choose File⇨Send Current Playlist to Portable Device.**

   The Portable Device Manager window appears.

3. **If you want to rearrange any of the tracks before downloading them, click the track title that you want to move and then drag it to its new location in the window.**

   You can also click the Add Tracks button to add extra MP3 files that weren't originally included in the playlist.

4. **Click the Sync button to copy the songs to your MP3 player.**

5. **After the copying process is complete, click the Eject button, unplug your player, and jam!**

Using Other Sound Formats

I would be remiss if I didn't mention some of the other sampled sound formats out there on the Internet (and sometimes swapped between PC owners). However, the MP3 format is now so popular for music that these other formats have been reduced to storing Windows sound effects and such. Some sound editors can convert audio between different formats, but if you're working with music, you can't lose with MP3.

WAV format

Microsoft's Windows Audio/Video (WAV) audio format is the standard format used by Windows for playing sound effects, and it's also used in games and on the Web. Your browser should recognize and play WAV audio files like a familiar old friend. Although WAV files can be recorded at audio CD quality — and therefore can be used to record music — MP3 files offer the same (or better) quality and are much smaller (I mean megabytes smaller) in comparison. All current versions of Windows include a simple sound recorder that can capture WAV files by using a microphone plugged into your PC.

WMA format

Not to be outdone by MP3, Microsoft has recently been pushing the WMA format (short for *Windows Media Audio*) as a real contender for the Best Digital Audio Format crown. Indeed, WMA files are as high in quality as MP3 files, and WMA audio can be recorded in multichannel 5.1 surround sound. However, I don't see the challenger from Redmond usurping MP3 anytime soon. For once, I think that the open standard is stronger than any proprietary standard that Microsoft will attempt to enforce. For example, many current MP3 players won't recognize or support WMA tracks — and portable MP3 players sure don't need Surround sound. Plus, the built-in DRM protection (short for *Digital Rights Management*) severely limits what you can do with your WMA tracks — you may not be able to burn an audio CD with your WMA-format music, for example, or play that track on another PC.

AAC format

Apple's entry into the digital audio format wars is a little less restrictive than WMA when it comes to DRM protection, but you're still limited to a total of five Macs and PCs that can play an AAC track. (On the positive side, you can use iTunes to burn your AAC tracks to an audio CD with no problem.) AAC files are higher in quality and smaller in size than MP3 files, so they make a good choice for squeezing the largest number of songs into your audio player (as long as it supports AAC, like the iPod). Any music that you download from the iTunes Music Store will be in AAC format.

AU format

The Audio Unix (AU) format was introduced by Sun Microsystems, so (as you would expect) it's a popular standard for systems running Unix and Linux. AU audio files are typically of lower quality than MP3 files, but they're even smaller in size, making them popular on many Web sites. Luckily, both Internet Explorer and Netscape Navigator can play AU files with ease.

AIFF format

Apple once used the Audio Interchange File Format (AIFF) as standard equipment within its operating systems, including music files. However, these days, the Cupertino Crew has switched wholeheartedly and completely to AAC, so AIFF has already started down the road once taken by the dinosaurs. (Mac OS 9 and Mac OS X still recognize AIFF files for sound effects, but that's about it.) Although AIFF files can be recorded at CD quality, they're simply huge, so don't expect to find them on the Web or on your personal MP3 player.

MIDI format

Musical Instrument Digital Interface (MIDI) files aren't actually digital audio but instead are directions on how to play a song — kind of like how a program is a set of directions that tells your computer how to accomplish a task. Your PC or a MIDI instrument (like a MIDI keyboard) can read a MIDI file and play the song back. As you might guess, however, MIDI music really doesn't sound like the digitally sampled sound that you'll get from an MP3 or WMA file. I discuss MIDI support when I cover upgrading your sound card in Book VII, Chapter 6.

Burning Audio CDs from MP3 Files

Return with me to the multitalented Musicmatch Jukebox so that I can demonstrate how to burn your own audio CDs from your MP3 collection. The resulting disc is a perfect match for any home or car CD player and can also be played in your PC's CD or DVD drive. (Both the free version and the Plus version of Jukebox can burn CDs, but here I describe how to record a disc by using the Plus version.)

To record an audio CD from MP3 files, follow these steps:

1. **Build your playlist within Jukebox as you normally would.**

2. **When you've added all the tracks that you want to record, click the Burn button at the bottom of the Playlist pane.**

   Jukebox displays the Burner Plus window that you see in Figure 2-8.

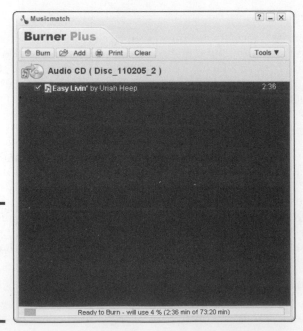

Figure 2-8:
Arrange
MP3 tracks
before
burning
them to an
audio CD.

3. **Like the Portable Device Manager window that I describe earlier (see "Downloading to an MP3 Player"), you can rearrange the order of the tracks on your audio CD by clicking the desired track title and then dragging it to its new location in the window.**

   To add more songs, click the Add button; to remove a track from the disc layout, right-click the track name and click Remove Files. This does not delete the offending MP3 file from your hard drive.

   The Burner Plus window keeps track of the percentage of space that you've used with the current playlist as well as the remaining time left on the disc layout (measured in seconds). You can use these totals to determine how many additional tracks you can squeeze onto your CD.

4. **Load a blank CD-R into your recorder.**

   Only certain audio CD players can read a CD-RW (rewriteable disc), so always use write-once CD-R media for true compatibility with all audio CD players.

5. **Click the Burn button on the Burner Plus window, sit back, and relax while your new disc is recorded.**

**Book VI
Chapter 2**

Dude, MP3 Rocks!

I got the music in me — illegally?

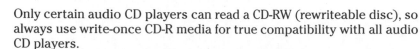

"Okay Mark, everything that I've read in this chapter is cool beyond belief — now, what's this you're telling me? My MP3 (or WMA, or AAC) collection might be *illegal?*" It's possible . . . it all depends on where you obtained the original audio CDs! Here's the rule: If you didn't buy the audio CD and you don't own it, you can't legally rip any audio. **Period**.

The reasoning behind this copyright law is similar to the law governing the duplication of computer programs, where only the owner is generally allowed to copy a piece of commercial software. By law, any copy of a program that you make is to be used for backup purposes; you can't give that copy to anyone else, and it can't be loaded on anyone else's PC.

Likewise, you can create all the MP3 files from your own audio CDs that you like, and you can listen to them with your personal MP3 player — but you can't give those MP3 files to anyone else. You also can't distribute them over the Web or Internet newsgroups, and you can't give one of your *Best of Slim Whitman* compilation CDs to your friend.

Music publishers are considering a number of different copy protection schemes that can help safeguard audio CDs from wanton ripping; as I mentioned earlier, the WMA and AAC formats include copy protection. Only the future will determine just how successful these schemes will be. You know how tricky those hackers can be, and it's likely that any copy protection will be broken sooner or later.

Of course, not everyone follows these rules to the letter. As a matter of fact, I don't know any folks who spend their nights tossing and turning because they ripped tracks from *Johnny Cash at Folsom Prison*. However, it's my duty to make sure that you know the legal ramifications of The Rip Thing. End of story.

Chapter 3: Making Movies with Your PC

In This Chapter

✓ **Importing video clips**

✓ **Assembling a movie**

✓ **Adding transitions**

✓ **Using titles**

✓ **Using special effects**

✓ **Adding a soundtrack**

✓ **Previewing your movie**

✓ **Saving and recording the finished film**

*H*ave you long harbored the urge to make your own film? You pick the subject — from your kid's kindergarten graduation to a science fiction action flick worthy of Arnold himself. You edit your footage, add professional-looking transitions and special effects, and even set the mood with a custom soundtrack recorded on your aunt's antique Hammond organ. Ladies and gentlemen, this is the definition of *sweet* — and it's all made possible by your PC. (For the full effect, buy a canvas director's chair and a megaphone.)

In this chapter, I demonstrate how you can use footage from your digital video (DV) camcorder — or, with the right equipment, even the footage that you've recorded on tape — to produce your own film. Your finished work of visual art can be saved to a recordable DVD or stored on your hard drive for use on your Web pages.

Getting the Lowdown on ArcSoft's ShowBiz DVD 2

My filmmaking tool of choice is ShowBiz DVD 2, which is a popular, entry-level $99 U.S. video editor from ArcSoft (www.arcsoft.com), as shown in Figure 3-1. ShowBiz DVD 2 has far more features than Windows Movie Maker (which ships with XP Home and Professional Editions), and I find it easier to use. The program runs on Windows 98 SE/Me/2000, too.

Media library   Player

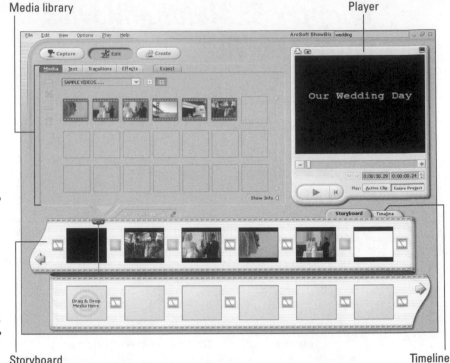

Figure 3-1:
ArcSoft
ShowBiz
makes it
easy to
edit and
enhance
your movies.

Storyboard   Timeline

After you install ShowBiz, you can run it from the Start menu by choosing
Start➪All Programs➪ArcSoft ShowBiz DVD 2➪ShowBiz DVD 2.

Take a moment to examine the ShowBiz DVD 2 main window, and you'll see
the four major controls that you'll be using:

✦ **Media library:** Consider this collection your treasure chest of things that
you can add to your film. Movies can contain any mix of items from these
four categories: media (includes video clips, still images, and audio), text,
transitions, (effects that occur between the clips and images) and special
effects (which you apply to the clips and images themselves).

✦ **Player window:** It sounds self-explanatory, and (for a change) it actually
is. The Player window allows you to play back and view your movie
within ShowBiz while you're working on it.

✦ **Storyboard strip:** If you're familiar with the concept of *storyboarding* in
cinematography — where sketches of scenes are arranged to create a
paper mock-up of the film — you've probably already guessed that you
use this strip to add items from the Media library list. And you'd be
right. These media clips, audio clips, and effects are the building blocks
of your finished movie.

✦ **Timeline strip:** Click the Timeline tab at the top of the Storyboard strip, and voilà! — you switch to the Timeline strip, where you can trim or expand the length of effects and transitions. The Timeline strip is also the control that you use to add and edit the soundtrack for your movie.

Rounding Up Clips and Images

A video editor like ShowBiz DVD 2 allows you to use raw footage, or video *clips,* transferred to your hard drive from a DV camcorder (or downloaded from the Web, or taken from a royalty-free video clip collection). You can also import digital photographs and use them anywhere you like within your movie — even directly from your scanner or your digital camera.

However, throwing together a hodgepodge of unorganized clips is (to say the least) not particularly creative or satisfying. (Imagine trying to build *Star Wars* by using clips from *Gone With the Wind,* and you'll see what I mean.) Before you build your first work of cinematic art, you must import your own video and still images into one or more *albums,* which is the name that ShowBiz gives to each of those tabbed sections within your Media library. Each item in an album is actually a link to a file on your hard drive.

To import video clips or images that are saved to your hard drive, follow these steps:

1. **Click the Media tab at the top of the Media library.**

2. **Click < New Album > in the drop-down list to create a new empty media album (named Untitled_1).**

   You can create a new album — ShowBiz won't allow you to add items to the *Sample albums,* which contain preloaded ShowBiz media — or add the item to an existing album you created.

3. **Click the Click Here to Add Media button that appears under the list.**

   For subsequent media, click the file folder button that appears to the left of the drop-down list to display the Open dialog.

4. **From the Open dialog box that appears, navigate to the location of the video, photograph, or sound effect that you want to add, click the file name to select it, and then click the Open button.**

   ShowBiz displays the new album (if you created one) or adds the item to the existing album that you chose.

To change the size of the album thumbnails, click the Album view mode button next to the drop-down list. To rename an album, click the album name to select it, type a new name in the drop-down list box, and then press Enter.

Never the TWAIN shall meet

TWAIN. You're probably saying to yourself, "Self, that's the most ridiculous acronym yet." Well, it sounds silly — many folks think that the acronym stands for *technology without an interesting name.* However, in this case TWAIN is actually not an acronym at all; it refers to the famous poem by Kipling, *"The Ballad of East and West,"* which includes the line "and never the twain shall meet." It makes sense, considering that the TWAIN standard helps make sure that your scanner and software like ShowBiz DVD 2 can work together. Never let it be said that techno-types don't have occasional flashes of wry literary humor!

By the way, if you're not completely acronym-happy by now, visit VERA — the *Virtual Entity of Relevant Acronyms,* no less — on the Web at `http://cgi.snafu.de/ohei/user-cgi-bin/veramain-e.cgi`, and you can discover the true meaning of computer-related acronyms to your heart's content.

ShowBiz DVD 2 allows you to sort an album in many different ways, such as by size or date. Just click the Sort button (which sports a capital *A* and *Z* conjoined with the numbers *1-2-3*), choose the desired sort order, and then click OK. Sorting makes it easier to locate a specific item in an overstuffed album.

Besides the method I describe earlier, here are three other easy ways to import items:

✦ **By downloading them:** ArcSoft offers registered users the opportunity to download new media items from the ArcSoft Web site. These freebies include new transitions, still images, audio clips, and sample video clips.

✦ **By capturing video and audio:** If you have a video capture board or a FireWire port on your PC, you can capture video from your VCR, DVD player, or camcorder. Hook up your video source, click the Capture button at the top of the ShowBiz DVD 2 window, and then click the Record button (the button with the red dot) to save the video (or just the audio component) to a new album within the library. (For information on connecting your video hardware, refer to the user manual for your video capture card and camcorder.)

✦ **By acquiring images from your scanner or camera:** If your scanner or digital camera is TWAIN compatible — and just about every decent model is — connect your hardware and then click the Acquire button (which bears a tiny digital camera and scanner) to import items directly. ShowBiz DVD 2 will prompt you to select the image source from the available TWAIN-compatible hardware devices. Again, the process varies according to the hardware that you're using, but if you're experienced with scanning or downloading images, you'll be in familiar waters.

Building Your First Movie

You import all the pieces of your new film — video, photographs, and audio effects — and you arrange them into orderly albums, ready for use in ShowBiz DVD 2. Now it's time to grab your megaphone and start creating. You'll start by adding items on the linear Storyboard strip, which you use to literally assemble your movie, moving from left to right on the strip.

I recommend mapping out the general flow of my film on paper — even as a simple list of scenes, titles, and images — before I start creating it. However, ShowBiz DVD 2 makes editing so easy that many folks can simply build a film on the fly, following their inspiration where it takes them. Go figure.

**Book VI
Chapter 3**

Anyway, when you're ready for the real work, follow these steps:

1. **Start ShowBiz DVD 2 by choosing Start➪All Programs➪ArcSoft ShowBiz DVD 2➪ShowBiz DVD 2. Or, if you're already using the program, click the New Project button (under the File menu).**

2. **To add either a video clip or an image, click the Media tab in the library to view the corresponding type of items; if you've built multiple albums, you can switch between them by clicking the drop-down list arrow next to the album name.**

If you need help identifying an item, view any item in the Player window before you add it to the strip by clicking on the element in the Media list. You can also hide and display information about the selected item by clicking the Hide Info/Show Info button at the bottom right corner of the Media library.

3. **To include an item, add it to the strip in either of two ways:**

   - Click and drag the item from the library directly to the storyboard.

     or

   - Click the item in the library to select it and then click the triangular Add Media button at the bottom of the library.

   ShowBiz DVD 2 adds the item to the next open media square on the strip. Figure 3-2 illustrates a video clip that I added as the first scene in my film.

   When you have multiple items on the storyboard, you can change the order in which they appear on the strip by clicking and dragging an item from one media square to the desired media square.

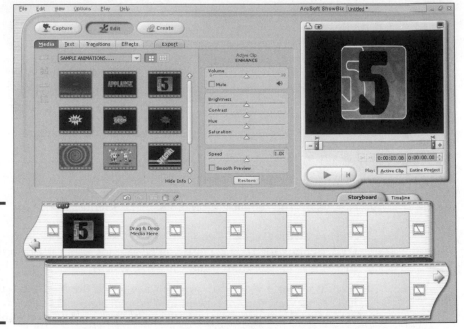

Figure 3-2:
I've added
a video clip
to the
beginning
of the
storyboard.

4. **Delete any item that you've added to the strip by right-clicking the item on the strip and then choosing Delete from the pop-up menu that appears, as shown in Figure 3-3.**

   Decided that you don't need that (somewhat disturbing) image of Uncle Milton feeding the family dog? No problem! I wholeheartedly agree.

5. **To trash all the media that you've added to the strip and start over, right-click any item on the strip and then choose Delete All Video Track Content from the pop-up menu that appears.**

   Remember: All Hollywood directors occasionally throw tantrums.

To display the properties of an item on the Storyboard strip — for example, the format of a video clip or its location on your hard drive — right-click the item in the strip and choose Properties from the pop-up menu that appears. Figure 3-4 illustrates the file information for a video clip on my storyboard.

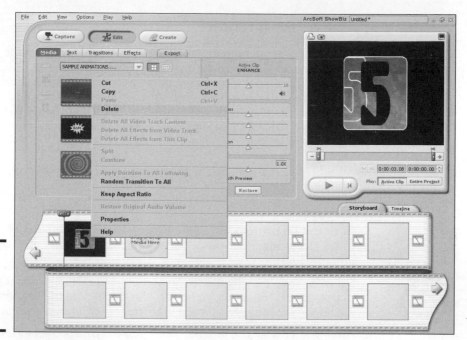

Figure 3-3:
Delete an
item (or the
whole
enchilada).

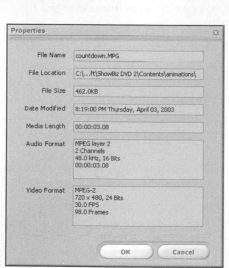

Figure 3-4:
Check
properties
for a video
clip here.

Adding Transitions without Breaking a Sweat

Imagine a film that cuts directly from scene-to-scene with no fade-ins, fade-outs, dissolves, or wipes. These are all types of *transitions* — and without transitions, your movie will end up moving at a frantic pace. (I call it *jarring the audience;* most horror films are shot with few transitions.) Of course, this might be your intention with some projects, but it's not likely to be your goal with most films that you make. In this section, I demonstrate how to add transitions to your film.

Transitions can be placed on the Storyboard strip only after you've added at least one video clip or still image. After the strip contains at least one item, follow these steps:

1. **Click the Transitions tab in the library to display the list of transitions. (Click the album drop-down list to select a different category of transition effects.)**

   ShowBiz has a cool feature to help you decide which transition you want to use: click a transition in the list, and the item actually animates in the Player window to demonstrate how the transition will appear onscreen.

2. **After you choose the perfect transition for this point in your film, double-click the item to copy the transition into the next open transition square on the strip.**

   The effect is placed in front of the clip.

   Note: Transition squares are smaller than media squares, and they're marked with a filmstrip icon with a diagonal cut. Figure 3-5 illustrates the list of wipe transitions in the library list.

3. **To delete a transition that you've added to the strip, right-click the transition square on the strip and then choose Delete from the pop-up menu that appears.**

   Or, to get really radical, choose Delete All Transitions — from the same pop-up menu — to remove all the transitions in your film with one fell swoop.

   To add the same transition throughout your movie, right-click any transition square on the strip and choose Apply Transition to All. (You can even add a different transition between all the items by right-clicking and choosing Random Transition to All. However, I personally don't use this feature because I think it generates a very haphazard film. Think *Monty Python's Flying Circus* . . . without the humor.)

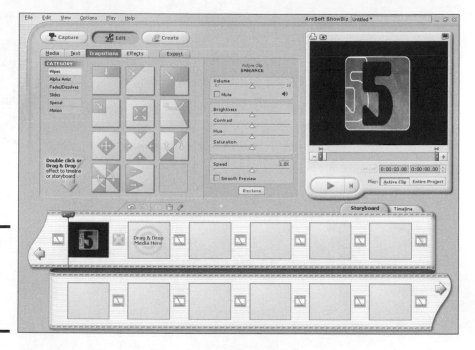

Figure 3-5:
Add
transitions
to tie your
clips
together.

As you experiment with transitions, you'll begin to understand where your
movie needs them to link scenes and still images together, as well as where
you can simply cut from one item to the next. Remember, one of the cardinal
rules of filmmaking is to maintain the focus of your audience on your message: Too many transitions are distracting.

Adding Special Effects without Paying George Lucas

I haven't mentioned the Timeline strip yet because the first step of movie
making is to edit the clips and still images in your movie and add transitions
(all of which is taken care of on the Storyboard strip). After you finish these
tasks, click the Timeline tab to switch to the display that you see in Figure 3-6.
From here, you can add special effects, incorporate a soundtrack and text
titles, and then modify the starting and ending points for each.

Note that the Timeline strip also has two smaller mini-strips (bottom-left of
Figure 3-6). Audio 1 and Audio 2 allow you to edit the two audio tracks you
can add to your movie. (I discuss each of these in the sections to come.)

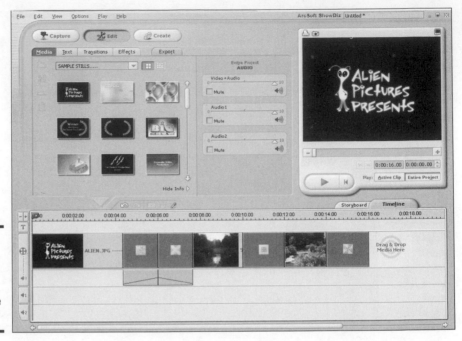

Figure 3-6:
Add the bells and whistles in the Timeline strip.

To refresh your memory on what's happening in your film at any point on the timeline, rest your mouse pointer over the desired spot for a moment, and ShowBiz DVD 2 displays a pop-up that tells you the name of the transition, clip, or still image that you added previously on the Storyboard strip.

When most of us think about special effects in the movies, *Star Wars* and *Harry Potter* come to mind: light-sabers, flying brooms, and invisibility cloaks. (I really, *really* want one of those.) However, in the world of video editing, an *effect* is a special visual appearance that you add to the video. For example, ShowBiz DVD 2 allows you to

✦ Flip your movie's alignment (horizontally or vertically).

✦ Add virtual raindrops or flames.

✦ Display your movie on the side of a blimp.

✦ Turn a video clip into a neon sign.

Maybe these effects aren't appropriate for your sister's wedding video, but when the subject of your movie is fun and games or when you want to create a new film *noir* masterpiece in stark black-and-white, effects are just the ticket. (Horrible pun intended.)

Because ShowBiz DVD 2 is an entry-level (and hence relatively "low-powered") video editor, you can have only one effect active at a time, but you can place multiple consecutive effects throughout your movie.

To experiment with effects, follow these steps:

1. **Switch to the Timeline strip display and click the Effects tab in the library to check out the available effects.**

   Again, you can choose another album of effects by clicking the album drop-down list box.

2. **Click the desired effect in the list to highlight it.**

3. **Drag the effect thumbnail to the desired clip in the Timeline.**

   The effect appears superimposed on the clip (see Figure 3-7).

4. **To determine where your new effect will start and end during the movie, hover your mouse pointer over the beginning or ending edge of an effect block and then click and drag the edge.**

   To move the entire effect to another spot, simply click and drag the effect block up or down the row to the desired spot.

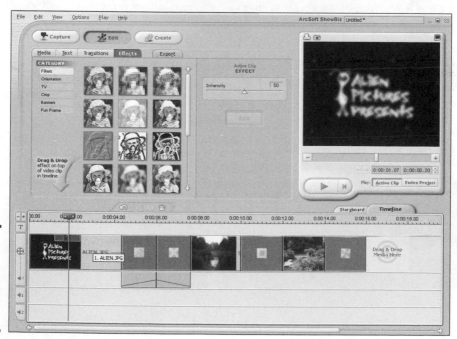

Figure 3-7:
Things are suddenly blurry — oh, wait, it's just an effect.

Naturally, you can toggle back and forth between the Storyboard strip and the Timeline strip as you work. In fact, one of the things that I enjoy most about video editing is the freedom to try new things. With just a few clicks of the mouse, you can add and delete clips, tinker with the effects, and just generally monkey around with timings and placement until you get precisely the film you want. How about them apples, Mr. Hitchcock?

Adding Sound

What movie is complete without a stirring soundtrack? For example, would the zombies in *Return of the Living Dead* have been anywhere near as scary without that punk rock playing in the background? Or how about the signature scary chord every time you saw any body part from the monster in *Creature from the Black Lagoon*?

With ShowBiz DVD 2, you can add two audio tracks to your film; typically, I use one for the soundtrack and a second one for any additional narration or sound effects that weren't recorded with the video clips.

If a video clip already contains audio, you don't have to add anything. (In fact, most of the sample video clips provided with ShowBiz already have their own audio.) However, you can still overlay — or, as videoheads call it, *dub* — extra music or sound effects, which will play along with the audio from the clip.

In addition to the sample audio provided with ShowBiz DVD 2, the program also accepts audio in MP3, AIFF, and Microsoft WAV formats, and you can add your audio tracks to the library in the same manner as video clips and still photographs.

To add a soundtrack, follow these steps:

1. **Switch to the Timeline strip display, click the Media tab in the library, and then choose either the Sample Audio album or an album of audio that you've added yourself.**

   Click the album drop-down list box to choose another album.

2. **Click the desired audio entry in the list to select it.**

3. **Drag the audio item to the desired audio row.**

   Remember, the Audio 1 and Audio 2 rows appear below the Timeline strip.

   Just like when adding an effect, each audio clip appears as a block.

4. **To move an audio block to another point within your film, click and drag the block to where you want it.**

   Unlike an effect, however, you can't adjust the beginning and ending points for an audio clip.

You've Just Gotta Have Titles!

In movie jargon, *titles* can be anything from the opening titles of your film to the ending credits. With ShowBiz DVD 2, you can open your film with impressive titles that fill the screen, or you can thank your brother for being Best Boy, Grip, or Gaffer. (I have no earthly idea what those exalted individuals do, but they must be pretty important.)

To add titles, you can use either of two methods (or mix both methods in one film):

**Book VI
Chapter 3**

**Making Movies
with Your PC**

✦ **Add a text item from the library:** With the built-in animated text formatting provided by ShowBiz DVD 2, you can impress your audience with your powerful message. (This is the easier method, but you're restricted to the text formats provided by the application.)

✦ **Insert a still image that you've created from the Media library:** If you need a specific title to match your exact specifications — for example, something incorporating a company logo — create a digital image with Photoshop CS or another image-editing program and then add the still image to your library. A title that you build yourself outside of ShowBiz DVD 2 is added to a media square just like a video clip, so follow the steps in the earlier section "Building Your First Movie."

To create and add a text item, follow these steps:

1. **Click the Text tab in the library.**

   Feel free to switch between simple and fancy styles, using the buttons at the left side of the library.

2. **Drag the desired style thumbnail in the album list to the desired spot in the Timeline.**

   ShowBiz DVD 2 will display a Text Editor dialog like the one illustrated in Figure 3-8. In addition to typing the text for the effect, you'll typically be able to choose a font type, the size and color of the letters, and even niceties such as shadows and blurring.

Figure 3-8:
Would you give your film anything less than 36-point titles? I think not.

3. **Drag a text effect thumbnail on top of the text style block you just added.**

   Note that your text title effects resemble transitions — you can switch between different categories of text effects by clicking on the category buttons at the left side of the library.

4. **After you set the style, typed the text and set the text effect, click any other block on the Timeline strip to return to your work.**

Text blocks can be adjusted and moved just like the visual effects: Simply click and drag the beginning and ending edges of the text block, or click the block and drag it to a new location.

Previewing Your Oscar-Winning Work

Okay, I know you're itching to see what your next masterpiece looks like. Lucky for you, ShowBiz DVD 2 allows you to preview your work any time. Of course, your Storyboard strip must contain at least one video clip or still image, or you'll have nothing to preview. These are the two different Preview modes:

✦ **Preview the current clip:** To see how a single clip or image will look, click the desired media square on the Storyboard strip to select it and then click the Active Clip button (which appears under the Player window). Click the familiar Play control — the right-pointing triangle — to start the preview.

✦ **Preview the complete movie:** To view the entire film from beginning to end, click the Entire Project button under the Player window and then click the Play button. Like most other video editors, ShowBiz must apply the effects that you've selected before the film can be shown. This process is *rendering,* and it can lead to a considerable wait on older PCs. (This is the reason that professional video editors crave the most powerful personal computers on the market . . . otherwise, they tend to keel over from sheer boredom while the rendering drags on.)

ShowBiz DVD 2 generally has to render your effects any time that you preview a film if you've changed anything. Therefore, I advise that you save a full-length preview until you've finished as much of your effects work as possible.

When you click Play, ShowBiz DVD 2 displays a yellow line (commonly called a *scrubber bar*) across the Timeline or Storyboard strip to show you the current point in the film, which comes in handy when you need to check the synchronization of different elements in your film with one another, such as effects, titles, or audio. The program also displays the total duration of the selected clip (or the entire movie) as well as the elapsed time.

The other controls under the Player window operate much like they do in Microsoft's Windows Media Player. To stop the preview, click the Stop button (it's the button with the yellow square); to pause the film at the current point, click the Play button again. You can also reposition the preview at any point within your film by clicking and dragging the slider underneath the Player window.

For a larger preview, toggle the Player window into full-screen mode with the View button at the top-right corner of the Player window.

Saving and Burning Before Traveling to Cannes

I think that Cannes is somewhere in France . . . or perhaps Belgium. Anyway, it's a big thing among filmmaking legends like you and me, so you'll want at least one copy of your finished masterwork to carry along with you. Luckily, ShowBiz DVD 2 allows you to save your films or even record them to a disc — both of which I cover in this last section.

You can always save your work in progress. To save a project that you're working on to your hard drive for later, click the File menu and choose Save. Windows opens the familiar Save As dialog box, where you can specify a location and a filename.

After your project is completed, here are two methods that you can use to produce a finished movie.

Creating a digital video file on your hard drive

If you simply want to watch your film on your PC monitor — without necessarily burning it to a CD or DVD — this is the best option. Just don't forget that it can take several hundred megabytes or more of space to store a single movie. Follow these steps:

1. **Click Export (located at the top of the Media library).**

   ShowBiz displays the Export settings that you see in Figure 3-9.

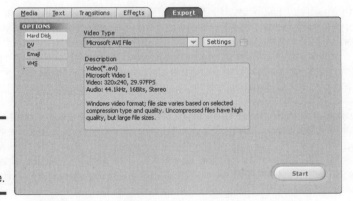

Figure 3-9: Save your master-pieces here.

2. **Click the Video Type drop-down list box to choose the format (MPEG, QuickTime MOV, or Windows AVI format).**

   I usually choose either MPEG (which is the most common format and can be readily viewed on Mac OS and Linux) or Windows AVI (which is limited to PCs, but any machine running Windows 98 or later can view your movie).

3. **Click the Settings button to specify advanced options such as the frame size and audio quality.**

   The Format dialog box opens.

Check out the settings for a Microsoft AVI movie in Figure 3-10. Naturally, your movie's file size will grow if you choose larger frame sizes, higher frame rates, and the better audio and video quality settings.

Figure 3-10:
Specify
settings for
a digital
video file
here.

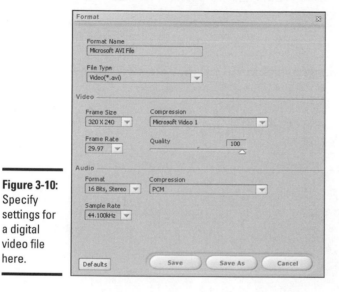

After these settings are correct, click Save to return to the Export pane.

4. Click the Start button.

If you haven't saved your project, ShowBiz DVD 2 automatically prompts you with a Save As dialog box (as I describe earlier).

5. Type a filename and click the Browse button to specify a location where the video file will be stored.

If you enable the Add to Album check box, your movie becomes a clip that you can use in future projects; just click the Album drop-down list box to specify the destination album. (Why re-edit that chariot race over and over? Turn it into stock footage!)

6. Click Save to create the DV file.

ShowBiz DVD 2 also allows you to save your film as a video e-mail file, which is small enough to attach to an c-mail message and send to anyone running Windows. This is guaranteed to amaze and delight your Dad, who will think you've been hobnobbing with Bill Gates.

Recording your own DVD

For me, this is the neatest option of all. You can walk up to that smug know-it-all at your local video store and boast that you have the world's only DVD copy of *My Family Reunion Bloopers 2006!* (Heck, tell him you'll be happy to burn him a copy for a small fee.)

To record your movie on a CD or DVD, follow these steps:

1. **Click the Create button at the top of the ShowBiz DVD 2 window, and then click the Write Disc tab.**

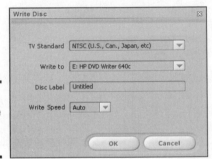

Figure 3-11:
Houston, we are go to burn!

2. **Click Start.**

   ShowBiz snaps to attention and displays the disc details that you see in Figure 3-11.

3. **Click the default text in the Disc Label box and type an appropriate label for your new DVD.**

   The defaults on this dialog are typically fine as-is, but if you're burning a disc for folks in Europe or China, you'll probably want to pick the PAL TV standard. Also, if your PC has more than one recorder, you can choose which drive will do the burning deed from the Write to drop-down list box.

4. **Click OK.**

   ShowBiz automatically begins burning the disc.

Chapter 4: I Can Make My Own DVDs?

In This Chapter

✔ Creating a menu

✔ Selecting a style

✔ Previewing your DVD menu

✔ Recording a finished DVD video

✔ Recording a DVD disc image

As a PC owner — and as a dedicated movie fan with my own digital video (DV) camcorder — I honestly can't think of a current technology in the world of personal computers that's more exciting than burning my own DVD videos! That's why I chose the title for this chapter: DVD recording is still new enough and sounds so much like rocket science that even many PC power users don't know much about it. (Another large cross section of PC owners knows that recording DVDs is possible on a PC but thinks that it's too complex or far too expensive.)

With the drop in the price of DVD recorders — and the availability of easy-to-use DVD authoring software like MyDVD Studio 6 — recording your own DVD videos is now kid's stuff. Trust me: You *can* do this, and it won't cost you an arm and a leg. Your DVD videos will have professional-looking menus, and they'll run on standard DVD players. But instead of watching Arnold Schwarzenegger, you'll be watching your family at Walt Disney World. (And unlike those VHS tapes, your DVD home movies will never wear out!)

MyDVD Studio 6 can also create video CDs, which means that the program even accommodates those of us limited to "antique" CD-RW drives. Note, though, that a video CD has much less storage space than a DVD, so your movies must be much shorter (usually about an hour). Also, the video quality of a video CD is nowhere near as good as that of a DVD. Therefore, I eschew video CDs in this chapter and concentrate on recording DVDs by using existing video clips and multimedia files from your hard drive.

Welcome to MyDVD

As you can tell, I'm a big fan of MyDVD Studio 6, from Sonic Solutions (www.sonic.com); for about $70 U.S., you can produce truly professional-looking DVD movies on your own PC. To begin your foray into the world of *Digital Versatile Discs* (or whatever the heck *DVD* means — check out the nearby sidebar), either double-click the MyDVD icon on your desktop or choose Start➪All Programs➪Sonic➪MyDVD Studio. The program displays the combination welcome screen and wizard that you see in Figure 4-1.

From the opening wizard, you can choose to

✦ **Create a new MyDVD project or edit an existing project.**

✦ **Transfer video Direct-to-DVD.**

✦ **Edit an existing DVD and then re-record it.**

✦ **Watch a DVD by using Sonic's CinePlayer software DVD program.**

Speaking of the MyDVD main window, click Create Project. The wizard displays all of the different types of discs you can create — in this chapter, I cover the genuine DVD article, so click the DVD item. Figure 4-2 illustrates the program's main window that appears.

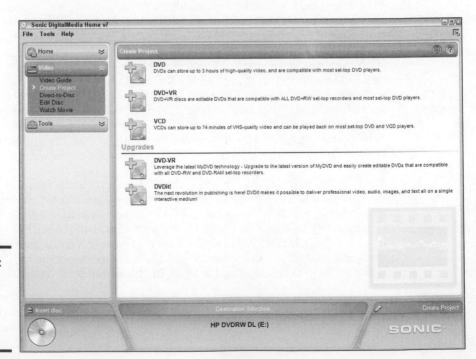

Figure 4-1: The Sonic Digital-Media wizard screen.

I *should* know what DVD stands for . . .

. . . and the rest of the civilized world is still scratching its head as well. Normally, I'm pretty sure about what an abbreviation stands for, but in this case, I have two choices!

When the DVD standards were being developed, everyone agreed that the recordable version of the new disc would be useful for all sorts of neat things — not just for storing video, but for backups, data, superior audio, and anything else that a PC owner could think of with 4.7GB of free space handy. Therefore, everyone proudly agreed that the new standard should be called DVD, short for *Digital Versatile Disc.* Everyone went home and celebrated.

However, it took three or four years for recordable DVD technology to arrive at a price point that regular folks could afford. And by that time, *DVD* had become firmly entrenched in people's minds as a video storage medium. (After all,

DVD movies caught on like wildfire — there was none of that VHS-versus-Beta waffling that the 40-something crowd remembers.)

During that same time, everyone without a DVD standards book handy took one look at the abbreviation and exclaimed, "That's got to mean *Digital Video Disc,* right?" Now, even most computer books and Web sites claim that Digital Video Disc is the original meaning!

That leaves us with one of the most interesting acronyms this side of TWAIN, which is commonly considered to mean Technology Without an Interesting Name, but actually *doesn't* (in fact, it's not an acronym at all). And whether you side with the original translation or the popular meaning, everyone still agrees that DVD technology is the cat's meow. (You can still celebrate if you like.)

Of the slew of different DVD formats out there, only one is compatible with virtually all DVD players: That's *DVD-R,* the record-once version of the DVD-RW (rewriteable disc). If you burn a DVD project on a DVD-RW, DVD+R, or DVD+RW, it might not run on an older DVD player. Or, even worse, it might run fine on yours but be completely useless on your Aunt Betty's machine. *+R/RW* and *-R/RW* are different formats, too, and they're not compatible! I do believe that a Mark's Maxim is in order:

> **The only way to be completely sure that a DVD format produced by your recorder will work on a particular DVD player is to actually try it!**™

Content window   Toolbar

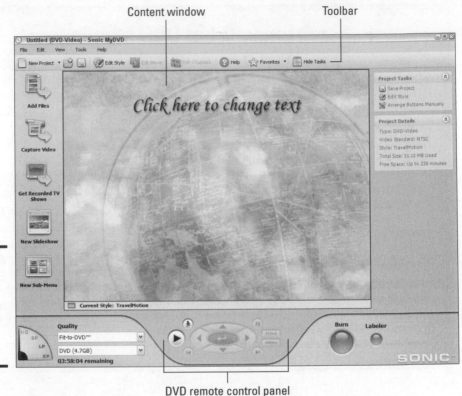

Figure 4-2:
Your DVD
wonder-
land — the
MyDVD
main
window.

DVD remote control panel

Menus 'R Easy!

DVD authoring programs allow you to build a menu system that can be controlled by a DVD player's remote control; the person viewing your disc will press buttons to select from the menu choices that you've laid out. After you build the menu framework, you essentially connect your video clips to the menu system. MyDVD also enables you to add screens with still photos from your digital camera or scanner. I always think of an art gallery, where the walls provide a backdrop for the paintings (and where those silly little rope fences are supposed to guide you to the proper place). (Personally, I jump right over the fences — which is why I'm barred from visiting any art galleries in my town.)

In the past, DVD authoring software was a confusing nest of weird-looking arrows, funky technical terms, and configuration settings that would give a Mensa member a splitting headache — but applications like MyDVD (and iDVD in the Mac world) have revolutionized how you construct a DVD video.

The default style used in MyDVD is TravelMotion, which has an Old World feel to it. A MyDVD *style* is a combination of a menu background, a button appearance, and a font format. (More on this in the next section.)

In this example, I show you how to build a menu system with a video clip, a submenu, and a still image slideshow. Run MyDVD and follow these steps:

1. **First, change the menu title to something more appropriate than** `Click here to change text` **(refer to Figure 4-2).**

   Okay, it's catchy and instructive, but I doubt Uncle Milton would be impressed.

   a. **Click the title to open a text editing box (see Figure 4-3).**

   b. **Type the new title for your disc menu and then press Enter to save it.**

2. **Add your first video clip to your menu.**

   a. **Click the Add Files button in the toolbar at the left of the window (or press Ctrl+G).**

   MyDVD displays a standard Open dialog box.

Book VI
Chapter 4

I Can Make My
Own DVDs?

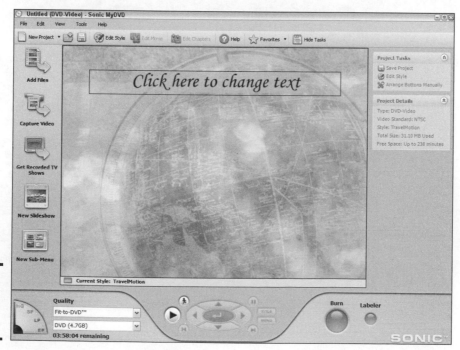

Figure 4-3: Change the title for your menu.

b. **Navigate to a specific clip on your hard drive and double-click it to load it.**

This displays your first menu button, as shown in Figure 4-4, with the clip filename as the default button label.

MyDVD can accept all three of the Big Three digital video formats: AVI, MOV, and MPEG (or DV). Therefore, you don't have to convert your video clips from one format to another before you use them in your projects.

3. **If you wish, change the title on the button to something more appealing.**

a. **Click the text under the clip button.**

MyDVD opens a text editing box.

b. **Type the new label for the button and then press Enter to save it.**

You just created your first menu! (A little rudimentary, of course, but you could actually save the project and record it at this point.)

Figure 4-4:
Add video clips to your menu.

If you're going to record your project onto a dual-layer DVD or DVD-RAM disc, click the drop-down list next to the disc graph to switch between different DVD format capacities. Keep an eye on the disc-shaped graph in the lower-left corner of the MyDVD window. When you add menus, photos, and video clips, it's updated to show how much space is available on a disc (and how much space remains on the DVD format you picked).

By default, MyDVD uses a system called Fit-to-DVD, where the video and images you add to your project are automatically compressed to fit a standard 4.7GB recordable DVD. This way, you don't have to worry about fitting all of your content on a DVD, but the more content you add, the lower the quality of your video. Instead of a space-remaining graph, you see a video quality display — the more you add (past 4.7GB), the lower the quality of the video. The display ranges from HQ (for High Quality) to EP (Extended Play, which is the same as lower-quality VHS recording).

You can now add a submenu to your DVD menu. A *submenu* is a branch command that takes you to another menu level under the top-level menu. I use submenus for organizing different clips and images by date or subject. For example, you could create a single DVD with clips from an entire year and then add submenus for vacation video clips, Christmas videos, and school clips.

To create a submenu, just follow this yellow brick road:

1. **Click the New Sub-menu button on the left toolbar to create the Untitled Menu button that you see in Figure 4-5.**

   Note: The default icon for the submenu is different from a video clip button, which uses a frame from the clip itself.

2. **To change the label on the submenu button to something appropriate, click the text under the submenu button, type the new label for the button, and then press Enter to save it.**

   Look at the structure of the submenu screen. Double-click the submenu button to display it (see the results in Figure 4-6). MyDVD always adds two new navigation buttons to the bottom of the new screen:

   • **Home:** Clicking this takes you back to the main Title screen of the menu.

   • **Previous:** Clicking this takes you back to the previous menu screen, which is handy for when a submenu appears within another submenu.

These buttons also work while you're creating the menu; just double-click a navigation button to use it. (After all, you need a way to move between menu screens.)

**Book VI
Chapter 4**

**I Can Make My
Own DVDs?**

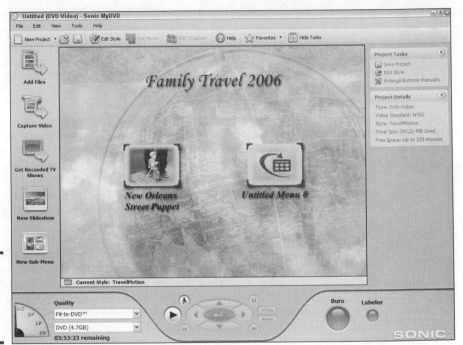

Figure 4-5:
A submenu
button in its
natural
habitat.

Other than the Home and Previous buttons, a submenu works just like the
top-level Title menu. You can add another video clip by clicking the Add Files
button (as I demonstrate earlier) or the New Slideshow button or even add
another menu level with another submenu. However, note this one thing that
you can do with a submenu that you can't do to the Title menu screen: *A submenu can be deleted.* (This makes sense because your project always needs a
Title menu.) To delete a submenu, display it, right-click the menu background,
and then choose Delete Menu from the pop-up menu that appears.

Deleting a submenu also deletes any buttons (and the corresponding content) that might still be on the submenu. For this reason, MyDVD prompts
you for deletion confirmation. To verify that you want to delete everything
on the current menu from your project, click OK. (Note, however, that deleting a submenu doesn't permanently delete any video clips that were on it
from your hard drive. That would be the very definition of A Bad Thing.)

Speaking of deleting items, you can also delete any button that you've added
to a menu by right-clicking it and then choosing Delete Button from the pop-
up menu that appears. Again, deleting a button is like deleting a menu: You
remove everything that was linked to the button — so MyDVD again
prompts you for confirmation, just to make sure.

Home   Previous

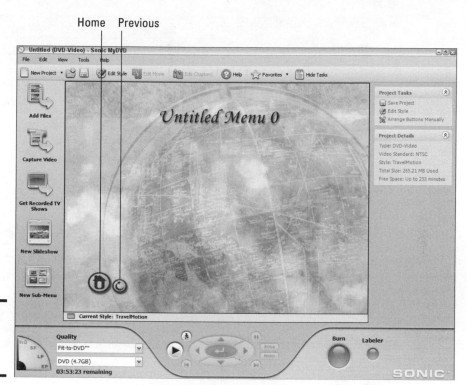

Figure 4-6:
An empty
submenu
screen.

Onward. To add a slideshow to your submenu, walk this way.

1. **Click the New Slideshow button (left side of the main screen).**

   MyDVD opens the Create Slideshow dialog box that you see in Figure 4-7.

2. **Click the Add Files button (left side) to display the Open dialog box. There, select one or more pictures from your hard drive for your slideshow and then click the Open button, which displays the images in the filmstrip.**

   At the bottom of this screen, check out how MyDVD keeps track of how much space the show takes on the DVD as well as the length of the show.

3. **To choose a specific picture as the slideshow button image, click the desired image in the filmstrip and then click the Set Button Image button on the left toolbar.**

4. **To control the delay for each image and choose an audio soundtrack (in MP3 or WAV format), click the Options button, which displays the Slideshow Settings dialog box, shown in Figure 4-8.**

Figure 4-7:
Choose
photos
for your
slideshow.

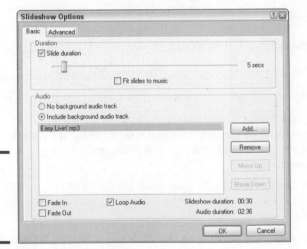

Figure 4-8:
Set your
slideshow
options
here.

5. **Click the Advanced tab to choose an optional transition that will appear between slides; then click OK to return to the Create Slideshow dialog box.**

6. **After you add all the photos that you want to your slideshow filmstrip, click OK to save your changes and return to the submenu screen.**

   Figure 4-9 shows the slideshow button (Untitled Slideshow) on the sub-menu. (You'll probably want to change the label on the slideshow button as well. Just click the text, type in a new name, and then press Enter.)

You've finished your menu system — in a minimum of short steps, no less! Press Ctrl+S to save the project, enter a filename when MyDVD prompts you, and then click Save to store your masterwork on your hard drive.

Book VI Chapter 4

I Can Make My Own DVDs?

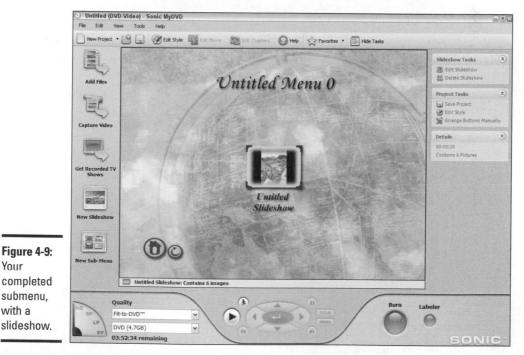

Figure 4-9: Your completed submenu, with a slideshow.

Changing the Look of Your Menus

At this point, you might be satisfied with the results of your work. If so, you're ready to move to the next section. However, what if your video clips and photo slideshow have nothing to do with travel? At this point, it's time to dump TravelMotion (no offense) and choose a menu style more fitting for the content of your disc. MyDVD includes special styles for holidays and all sorts of events as well as themes based on colors.

You can switch styles at any time during the development of your DVD menu. Generally, I wait until the end because I can see the entire effect with the fonts, colors, and button borders on the different elements in my project.

To choose a new style, follow these steps:

1. **Click the Edit Style button in the top toolbar.**

   This displays the Edit Style dialog box that you see in Figure 4-10. Here, you can choose from two different types of menu styles. By default, MyDVD uses animated graphics.

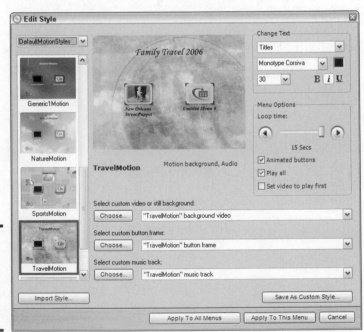

Figure 4-10: Change the style to fit the mood of your DVD content.

2. **To use an animated style, choose DefaultMotionStyles from the drop-down list at the upper-left of the Edit Style dialog box.**

   Other animated styles carry the tag (`Animated`) after the name, while non-animated styles carry the tag (`Still`).

3. **Click the style that you want from the scrolling list at the left of the dialog box.**

   The preview window is automatically updated with the new style.

To use the new style as it is, click OK. Figure 4-11 illustrates the menu system that uses the SportsMotion style. You can also use the options on the Edit Style dialog box to choose a favorite background picture, button frame, or background music track for your style. And, in turn, if you want to use it for future MyDVD projects, you can click the Save as Custom Style button to create a new style under the name you provide. (For instance, I create new styles with my own background pictures and save them for later.)

To pick a photo (or a video clip) of your own as a background, click the Choose button next to the Select Custom Video or Still Background drop-down list in the Edit Style dialog box (refer to Figure 4-10) and then select the item from the standard Open dialog box that appears.

Figure 4-11: Now you're ready for that soccer footage.

Time to Preview

Would a Hollywood studio release a movie these days without editing it thoroughly first? Not very likely . . . and MyDVD allows you to preview your disc before you burn it, so that you can edit and fix the occasional goof. I'm all for avoiding the possibility of wasting a recordable DVD because something was wrong with my videos or my menu system. In Preview mode, MyDVD displays your project just as it will appear in a DVD player. You even get a virtual remote control that you can use to test out your menu system.

To enter Preview mode at any time, click the Preview button at the bottom of the screen (or press Ctrl+P). Your menu system appears exactly as it will onscreen, and the remote control pad (which is normally disabled) is ready to use, as shown in Figure 4-12. Click any button to simulate the press of that button on your DVD player's remote control.

Click the Title button to display the Title menu and click the Menu button to display the last menu that you used.

After you've checked each button and function on your menu, click the Stop button on the remote control to exit Preview mode. You can then make any changes that you need to make to your menu, or you can burn your project to disc.

Figure 4-12: Preview your work before you record the disc.

Dig that crazy safe zone!

Did you know that your TV has a safe zone? Well, at least it does to a video editor. The *safe zone* refers to the actual height and width dimensions of the TV signal that's displayed by an NTSC television (that's the video standard in North America). An NTSC signal is somewhat larger than the television screen. That additional border helps prevent you from seeing any distortion at the edges of your picture, but it also means that you could conceivably chop off part of the background or a video clip.

To verify that your movies look good in the safe zone before you record them, use MyDVD's safe zone border. The program displays a rectangle that marks the boundary of the safe zone. To turn on the safe zone border, choose View➪Show TV Safe Zone. To turn it off, choose the menu item again.

Now if they could only invent a gadget to edit out that reality-TV trash that they show these days.

Burning Your DVD and Celebrating Afterward

Here it is — the moment that you've been waiting for with such anticipation! But before you decide to spend a disc on your project, I should mention that MyDVD can actually create three different types of DVD videos:

✦ **A standard DVD video:** This is a physical DVD disc that can be loaded in a DVD player.

✦ **A standard DVD disc image:** This is a single file (with an `.iso` extension) that you can use to record a DVD disc later, using any DVD recording application. For example, if you're creating a DVD on the road with your laptop and it doesn't have a DVD recorder, you'd normally be out of luck. However, with this feature, you can create a disc image and copy that to your desktop PC for recording when you return.

✦ **A DVD folder:** If you select this method of recording a DVD, the files aren't actually burned to a disc, and they're not used to create a DVD disc image. Instead, MyDVD records them to a separate folder on your hard drive, where you can either record them later or view them with a software DVD player like Sonic's CinePlayer, as shown in Figure 4-13. (This is a great option if you know you won't need to burn the disc at all in the future — for example, if you're creating a slideshow for a one-time corporate presentation, and you'll run the slideshow from your hard drive using CinePlayer.)

Figure 4-13:
You can watch the contents of a DVD folder by using Sonic's CinePlayer viewer.

To burn a DVD video from your project, follow these steps:

1. **Load a blank disc into your recorder.**

2. **Click the Burn button on the remote control pad on the bottom of the MyDVD window (or press Ctrl+D).**

   MyDVD prompts you to save the project.

3. **Click Yes, type a filename, and then click Save.**

   The program displays the Disc Recorder Information dialog box that you see in Figure 4-14.

4. **If you have more than one recorder on your system, click the Device drop-down list to choose which drive will be used.**

5. **Click in the Copies box and type the number of copies that you want to make.**

   I recommend leaving the Write Speed setting at Auto; that way, your DVD recorder can record at a slower speed if the DVD media that you're using doesn't support full-speed burning.

6. **Click OK and sit back to watch your recorder do the work.**

Figure 4-14:
Preparing
to burn a
DVD video.

To save a DVD folder, follow these steps:

1. Choose File⇨Save As DVD Folder.

MyDVD displays the Browse for Folder dialog box that you see in
Figure 4-15.

Figure 4-15:
Selecting a
location for
a DVD
folder.

2. Click the location where the DVD folder should be stored.

3. Click OK to begin creating the DVD folder.

To save a DVD disc image, follow these steps:

1. Choose File⇨Save As Disc Image.

MyDVD displays the Burn Disc Image to File dialog box that you see in
Figure 4-16.

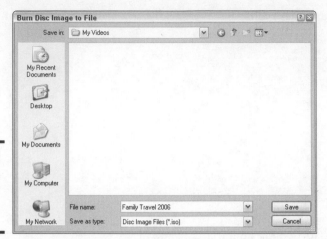

Figure 4-16:
Selecting a
location for
a DVD disc
image.

2. **Navigate to the desired location on your hard drive and type a file-name (or use the default filename provided by MyDVD).**

3. **Click Save to create the** `.iso` **image file.**

Chapter 5: I'm Okay, You're a Digital Camera

In This Chapter

✔ Understanding digital camera technology

✔ Evaluating the advantages of digital photography

✔ Buying extras (besides your camera)

✔ Composing photographs for better results

✔ Organizing your images

✔ Downloading your images

I'll be the first to assure you that I'm no Ansel Adams, yet I've been capturing moments and memories on film for most of my life, and I've slowly worked my way into what most folks would deem semiprofessional photography. (That means I can shoot a decent portrait, I take on a commission from time to time, and I have a reasonably well-stuffed camera bag.)

Does that mean I'm loaded down with expensive 35mm cameras and a dozen different varieties of film? Definitely not! I've never been darkroom material, and film photography no longer excites me. These days, I work entirely with *digital* cameras, which don't use traditional film at all. Why digital? My entire portfolio of digital photos — which would easily fill up a dozen traditional bound photo albums — fits comfortably on a 700MB CD-ROM. I can display those photographs on practically any PC or print hard copies that are almost impossible to tell from film prints. I don't spend a dime on film processing, either — and when you take 10 to 20 images a day, that savings really adds up.

I spend this chapter introducing you to the world of digital photography. You discover how a digital camera works, why it's better in many respects than a film camera, and how to move images that you've taken from your camera to your PC. If you're interested in shooting better pictures, I also cover a number of well-worn basic rules used by professional photographers all over the world. You also discover how to download your images from your digital camera (by using the features that are built into Windows XP) and how to catalog your photographs (thus making it easier to locate a specific image).

One more thing before I get started: I should mention that I'm the author of the *HP Digital Photography Handbook,* by Wiley Publishing, Inc. If you're hungry for a much more comprehensive, in-depth look at digital photography (after you finish this appetizer of a chapter), you'll find it a valuable guide. Plus, it's a full-color book — the pictures look much better!

How Does a Digital Camera Work?

A common misconception surrounds today's digital cameras: Because they don't use film and because they produce pictures as data files, many folks think that digital cameras must use a radically different method of capturing an image. Actually, your family film camera and that power-hungry, battery-munching digital camera that you got for Christmas are remarkably similar in most respects.

As you see in Figure 5-1, a film camera has a shutter that opens for a set amount of time (usually a fraction of a second), admitting light into the body of the camera through at least one lens. (Of course, that lens can be adjusted to bring other objects at other distances into focus, or different lenses can be tacked on.) Figure 5-2 illustrates (up to this point, anyway) that your film camera and its digital brethren work exactly the same.

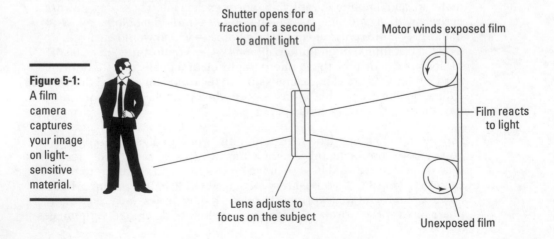

Figure 5-1: A film camera captures your image on light-sensitive material.

Shutter opens for a fraction of a second to admit light

Motor winds exposed film

Film reacts to light

Lens adjusts to focus on the subject

Unexposed film

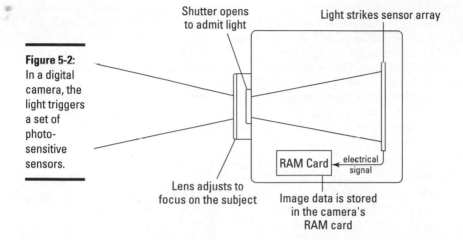

Figure 5-2:
In a digital camera, the light triggers a set of photo-sensitive sensors.

Shutter opens to admit light

Light strikes sensor array

RAM Card ← electrical signal

Lens adjusts to focus on the subject

Image data is stored in the camera's RAM card

The big difference is the method that each of these two types of cameras uses to record that incoming light. To wit:

✦ A **film camera** uses a strip of light-sensitive celluloid coated with silver halide, which retains the image. The film must later be developed, and the negatives/positives that are produced can be used (reproduced, usually on photographic paper) to make copies of the photograph.

✦ A **digital camera**, on the other hand, uses a grid (or *array*) of photosensors to record the incoming pattern of light. Each sensor returns an electrical current when it's struck by the incoming light. Because the amount of current returned varies with the amount of light, your camera's electronic innards can combine the different current levels into a composite pattern of data that represents the incoming light — in other words, an image in the form of a binary file.

If you've read some of my other books on CD/DVD recording and scanning, you already know about *binary,* which is the common language shared by all computers. Although your eye can't see any image in the midst of all those ones and zeroes, your computer can display them as a photograph — and print the image, if you like, or send it to your Aunt Harriet in Boise as an e-mail attachment.

"Wait a second, Mark. How does the image file get to my computer?" That's a very good question; naturally, no one wants to carry a PC around just to shoot a photograph. Your digital camera stores the image file until you can *transfer* (download) it to your computer. Different types of cameras use different methods of storing the image files:

✦ **RAM cards:** *Random access memory (RAM) cards* (the most common storage method) are removable memory cards that function much like the memory modules used by your computer. In fact, some cards are actually interchangeable with personal digital assistants (PDAs) and palmtop PCs. The most popular types of media include CompactFlash (www.sandisk.com), SmartMedia (www.microtech.com), and Memory Stick (www.sony.com) cards, generally ranging from 8MB to 2GB of storage. When the card is full of images, you either download the images from the card to free up space, or you can eject it and put in a spare empty card.

✦ **Hard drives:** Yep, you read right; some cameras have their own onboard hard drives, and others use tiny removable hard drives that are roughly the same size as a RAM card. Naturally, these little beauties can easily store gigabytes of your images. (Geez, I'm old enough to remember when a full-sized computer hard drive couldn't store that much.)

✦ **Floppy drives:** Okay, I know that I rant on and on throughout this book about how unreliable floppies can be and how I use them only as a last resort, yet some digital cameras use floppies to store photos. (Guess what? I don't like those cameras. Go figure.) If your camera uses floppies, make doggone sure that you get your images backed up to your computer's hard drive as soon as possible. Because of the larger image sizes produced by today's higher-resolution cameras, floppy-based digital cameras are rapidly disappearing from the market.

✦ **CD-RW drives:** Here's the ultimate: a camera that can burn your digital photographs directly onto a CD-R or CD-RW! Although these cameras can be a little bulkier than models that use RAM cards, this just plain *rocks*. As you might expect, you pay a premium price for one of these jewels.

If you're wondering approximately how many images you can fit onto a specific RAM card, remember that most of today's 3- to 5-megapixel cameras produce images of about 200–500 kilobytes (K) at their highest-quality mode.

The Pros and Cons of Digital Photography

I mention earlier in this chapter that I've switched completely from my 35mm single lens reflex (SLR) cameras to a (rapidly expanding) collection of digital cameras. However, there's a lot more to like about the digital revolution than just cutting the expenses of film and processing. Other advantages include the following:

✦ **Digital prints are versatile.** The digital photographs that you take can be enclosed in e-mail messages, burned as CD or DVD slide shows, or displayed as your PC's Windows desktop and screensaver. Of course, you can also print them; and with today's special inkjet papers, your images can end up on things like greeting cards and T-shirt transfers.

If you're interested in producing prints from your digital photographs in the shortest time possible, check out one of the latest inkjet printers that can directly accept memory cards from your digital camera. Heck, with one of these inkjet marvels, you don't need a PC. Some of these printers can even rotate and resize images as well.

✦ **Look, Ma, no developing!** With a digital camera, you have practically instant access to your photographs. Save yourself the trip to the photo store — even a one-hour photo lab can't match the five minutes that it takes to connect your camera to your PC (with a Universal Serial Bus [USB] or FireWire cable) and download your images to your hard drive. (And you'll also avoid the ravages of a misaligned development machine or a clumsy operator.)

✦ **Editing is easy with your PC.** Imagine everything that can go wrong with a picture: a bad exposure, a case of red eye, or perhaps a tree sprouting from someone's head. With a digital photograph, you can reduce or eliminate these problems altogether; with the proper editing, a bad picture becomes mediocre, and a good picture can become a work of art. ***Bonus:*** After the images are on your PC, you can edit or print them immediately.

✦ **You can manage your photographs on location.** Imagine being able to review a shot as soon as it's taken. With a traditional film camera, you're stuck with what you've taken, and you won't see the results until that roll of film has been developed. A digital camera, however, gives you the freedom to actually manage your images. For example, you can view each image on a memory card and delete the ones that you don't need to free up space. Using the camera's liquid crystal diode (LCD) screen also allows you to review a photograph as soon as you've taken it. Don't like the way a particular photograph turned out? If you review each shot as soon as you've snapped it — which I always do — you can try to retake most pictures immediately! (Of course, this feature won't help you if the UFO has already zipped over the horizon, but it's darned handy on vacation.)

Many digital cameras on the market these days can also do double-duty as simple video camcorders — at least for anywhere from 30 to 240 seconds — using a feature called *movie mode*. Some cameras can even record audio along with the video; the amount of time that you can record depends on the amount of storage available, so a digital camera with a 128MB memory card can capture many more seconds of video than a camera with only a 16MB memory card.

However, all is not perfect in the digital world . . . not yet, at least. Film cameras aren't doomed to share the fate of the dinosaurs because traditional film photography still has these advantages over digital photography:

✦ **Film cameras are still less expensive.** Although digital cameras have dropped considerably in price over the last few years, film cameras still provide better resolution and image quality for a lower initial price. In fact, at the time of this writing, any film camera under $50 U.S. can still take a better photograph than most digital cameras selling for under $300 U.S. Of course, if you're willing to spend more, you'll narrow the quality gap . . . but not for long. While digital camera prices continue to drop, an average digital camera will eventually be able to take a shot that's as good as a film camera.

How can you tell which digital cameras produce better images? While shopping for a digital camera, keep the camera's *megapixel rating* in mind — that's the number of *pixels* (or individual dots) in an image that the camera can capture. Here's another Mark's Maxim to keep handy:

The higher the megapixel value, the better the image quality, the more expensive the camera, and the larger the photographs that you can print.™

As a rule, a 2- to 3-megapixel camera is suitable for most casual photography, but amateur photographers will prefer at least a 4-megapixel camera. Cameras in the 4- to 5-megapixel range can match a typical 35mm camera in quality.

✦ **Film cameras are better at capturing motion.** Most consumer digital cameras in the 2- and 3-megapixel range still have trouble taking shots of subjects in motion, such as at sporting events. (This is because of the longer delay required for those photosensitive sensors to capture the image.) Today's more expensive, higher-megapixel cameras are much better at *motion* (stop action) photography.

✦ **Man, do those digital cameras use the juice!** Unlike a film camera, a digital camera relies on battery power for *everything,* including that power-hungry LCD display. If you're in the middle of shooting a wedding and you haven't packed a spare set of batteries, you have my condolences. A film camera is far less demanding on its batteries.

✦ **You need those ports.** If your PC doesn't have USB ports (or, for a more expensive camera, FireWire ports) handy, you'll have to add an adapter card that provides the correct type of port for your camera.

As you might have already guessed, many photographers have chosen to carry both traditional film and digital cameras, which allows them to use whatever best fits the circumstances (depending on the subject and the level of control that they need on location). For me, the long-term savings and convenience of my digital cameras — and the ability to review my photographs as soon as they're taken — makes them the better choice.

So what can you do with digital photographs? A heck of a lot more than a film print, that's for sure (at least on your PC and in the online world)! Common fun that you can have with digital images includes

✦ **Printing 'em:** Today's inkjet printers can produce a hard copy on all sorts of media (everything from plain paper to blank business cards and CD/DVD labels), but naturally you'll get the best results on those expensive sheets of glossy photo paper.

✦ **Using them on your personal or business Web site:** Jazz up your Web pages with images from your camera.

✦ **Sending them as e-mail attachments:** I get a big kick out of sending photos through e-mail! As long as you add a total of less than 2MB of images to an e-mail message, the recipient should receive them with no problem. (And then the attached files can be viewed, printed, or saved to the recipient's hard drive.)

✦ **Creating slide shows:** Check your camera's software documentation to see whether you can create a slide show on your hard drive (or on a CD/DVD disc) to show off your digital photographs.

✦ **Using them in craft projects:** Plaster your digital photographs on T-shirt transfers, buttons, greeting cards, and all sorts of crafts.

Digital Camera Extras to Covet

No one gets a pizza with just sauce, and the extras are important in photography, too. If you'll be taking a large number of photographs or you're interested in producing the best results from your camera, consider adding these extras to your camera bag.

External card readers

As I mention earlier, the majority of modern digital cameras connect to your computer via a USB cable to transfer pictures. The downside to this is that you can't take more shots until the downloading process is complete. If you're in a hurry or if convenience is important, buy an external card reader that takes care of the downloading chores for you. Simply pop the card into the reader (which in turn connects to your PC's USB port), load a backup memory card into your camera, and you're ready to return to the action.

External card readers are also the best solution if you have an older digital camera that connects to your PC's serial port. Because a serial connection is as slow as watching paint dry, you can speed things up considerably by ejecting the memory card from your camera and pushing those pictures to your PC through a much faster USB connection. An external reader is cheap, too, usually running less than $50 U.S.

Rechargeable batteries

Gotta have 'em. I'm not kidding. You'll literally end up declaring bankruptcy if you use your digital camera often with single-use batteries. For example, one of my older 2.1-megapixel cameras can totally exhaust four AA alkaline batteries after one session of 20 photographs.

Here are the three major types of rechargeable batteries to choose from:

✦ **Nickel-cadmium (NiCad):** *NiCad* batteries are the cheapest and are available in standard sizes, but they drain quickly and take longer to recharge.

✦ **Nickel-metal-hydride (NiMH):** NiMH rechargeable batteries provide the middle of the road between higher cost and longer life; they take less time to recharge than NiCad batteries, and they last longer, but they're not as expensive as LIon batteries.

✦ **Lithium-ion (LIon):** These are the best batteries available. They provide more sustained power over a longer period than either of the other types, but they're the most expensive, and they're hard to find in standard sizes. Your camera might need an adapter to use them.

Just as I recommend an extra memory card, I also recommend carrying a spare set of charged batteries in your camera bag. The Boy Scouts are right on this one: Be Prepared.

Lenses

Like their film brethren, most medium-priced and higher-end digital cameras can use external (add-on) lenses. Although your digital camera is likely to have several zoom levels (both digital and optical), photographers use a number of specialized lenses in specific situations. For example, consider these common extra lenses:

✦ **Telephoto:** Using a *telephoto* lens provides you with tremendous, long-distance magnification, but you don't have to be James Bond or a tabloid *paparazzo* to use one. For example, wildlife and sports photographers use telephoto lenses to capture subjects from a distance. (Referees tend to get surly when you stray on the field just to photograph the quarterback.)

- ✦ **Macro:** These lenses are especially designed for extreme close-up work; with a *macro* lens, you can capture images at a distance of a few inches. (They're great for making your fiancée's engagement ring look much, much bigger.)

- ✦ **Wide-angle:** A *wide-angle* lens can capture a larger area — what photographers call the *field of view* — at the expense of detail. These lenses are often used for scenic or architectural photographs.

 Don't forget a decent lens cap and a photographer's lens-cleaning cloth to help prevent scratches on those expensive lenses!

Tripods

When most people think of tripods, they think of unwieldy, 5-foot-tall gantries suitable for launching the Saturn V. Yes, some tripods do meet those requirements, but they're absolutely required for low-light, time-lapse, and professional portrait photography.

My camera bag also stows two other platforms that are much smaller:

- ✦ **Mini-tripod:** My Ambico mini-tripod can hold my cameras anywhere from 2 inches to 4 inches above the table. I use it in concert with my macro lens for shooting my scale models from a realistic perspective.

- ✦ **Monopod:** My collapsible monopod (which looks just like a walking stick) can hold the camera steady for quick shots on just about any surface. It also works great when you trip over exposed roots in the forest . . . but you didn't hear me admit to that.

Although a tripod isn't a requirement for the casual photographer, you'll find yourself wishing for one quickly if you move to more serious amateur photography. They sell tripods at Wal-Mart for a reason.

The Lazy-Man's Guide to Composing Photographs

If you'd like to remain firmly in the point-and-shoot casual photography crowd, you can comfortably skip any discussion of *composition* — that's the process (most call it an art) of aligning your subject and compensating for the available light at your location. Composition isn't a requirement for simple snapshots, but if you're going to create true visual art, you need the time to prepare your subject, your viewing angle, and your lighting.

In fact, what if I told you that composing a shot can result in less cropping and editing time on your computer — and that you'll end up taking better photographs? If you follow the tips that I provide in this section, I can just about guarantee that you'll discover at least one FRP in every set of images that you download! (*FRP,* coined by a favorite instructor that I had in journalism at LSU, means First Rate Photo — the kind of photograph that you'll be proud to display on your wall.) The example photographs in this chapter are taken from my personal FRP collection.

And despite what you might have heard about composing photographs, it only takes a few seconds before each shot to make a difference. Take it from me — with practice, you'll compose your shots automatically.

The Rule of Thirds

The *Rule of Thirds* is the foundation of good composition for most photographers. Applying this guideline helps draw the eye toward multiple subjects or to the focus of interest while maintaining balance within the frame. To use the Rule of Thirds, simply split the frame in your viewfinder into nine equal areas, as shown in Figure 5-3, "Time Tunnel." Align your subject(s) and the surroundings (where possible) along either

✦ A line crossing the frame

✦ One of the intersections where two lines meet

Figure 5-3: Divide your photograph by the Rule of Thirds.

The Rule of Thirds works exceptionally well when taking photographs of landscapes or architecture, as you can see in Figure 5-4. This photograph, "View from Hoover Dam," uses the rule to draw the viewer's eye along the river until it disappears around the bend. (Bet you never knew that Mother Nature was a shutterbug, right?)

Figure 5-4:
The movement of water flows closely along one line and ends at an intersection.

That's all there is to it. If you take a moment to examine the composition of the photographs in your favorite magazines, you'll see this time-tested classic rule followed over and over.

The Rule of Asymmetry

The second rule of composition often used in photography, the *Rule of Asymmetry,* presents the subject against a number of minor subjects as well as the background. Asymmetrical composition revolves around a relationship that you build between the major subject and either one or more minor subjects or the background itself. Following this rule, you merge different combinations of the three basic shapes — the square, the circle, and the triangle — to form a new outline or contour.

To illustrate, take the still life in Figure 5-5, "Cultures." Here, I mix a light circular shape (the instrument) with strong rectangles (the skis). I find that an asymmetrical composition works better when you feature a sharp contrast level between light and dark elements or between strong color patterns and shadows.

Figure 5-5:
Add interest with a classic asymmetrical composition.

TIP

I always make it a point to experiment with different camera angles — for instance, moving to the side or below the subject, as in "Warbird" (see Figure 5-6). Of course, sometimes you won't have the luxury of extra time to try something different, but I think that you'll like the results. (And remember, you're not wasting any film.)

Using lighting creatively

Before I finish this quick tour through photo composition, turn your attention to lighting. Virtually every digital camera made these days has an automatic flash feature, and this is usually a good thing to use. However, if your camera allows you to disable the flash, you'll take better photographs in many different situations.

Here's a list of exposure do's and don'ts for those who want to compose with light:

✦ **Do** make use of existing light when possible, if you can disable your camera's flash. Natural lighting can really make the photo.

✦ **Don't** attempt to photograph your subject through a sheet of glass or plastic if you're using a flash. Also don't pose your subject against a reflective background — you'll create *hotspots* or flash reflections.

✦ **Do** use a tripod (or brace your camera if possible) when taking photographs without flash (which requires a longer exposure time to capture the image).

✦ **Don't** use a flash if your subject is illuminated internally or with spotlights, such as a neon sign or a statue at night.

✦ **Do** use your PC's image editor — such as Photoshop or Paint Shop Pro — to enhance the contrast for underexposed shots. You can also change the hue and saturation levels for the colors in a photograph with your image editor. In Chapter 1 of this mini-book, I cover some of the basics within Paint Shop Pro (like cropping and rotating images, converting images to different formats, and saving them to disk).

Shadows can add a tremendous visual impact, as shown in a favorite FRP of mine, "French Quarter Staircase," in Figure 5-7. In this case, I needed no additional light, but I'm not above using an isolated spot *flood* (light source) to cast the shadow effect that I want. Even a flashlight can do the job in a pinch.

Figure 5-6:
Experiment with unusual camera angles.

Figure 5-7:
Remember that shadows can be your friend.

Organizing Your Pictures

If you'd rather not stare at a meaningless collection of filenames, here are some tricks that you can use to help you locate a photograph that you stored on your hard drive or a CD-ROM full of images. First, organize your photos into folders based on the date, location, or subject of your photographs. Also, use the long filename support in Windows XP to better describe your photograph. After all, it's easier to visualize `Goats Grazing Outside Nepalese Village.jpg` than `nepgoats.jpg`.

To take your organization a step further, use an image-cataloging program, such as Photo Album 6 from Corel (`www.corel.com`). The contents of your photo collection are shown as *thumbnails* (small images), making it easier to spot the photograph that you're looking for. Plus, Photo Album 6 can create a collage from your images, back up your images easily to CD-ROM, and even perform simple image editing. At $45 U.S. for the downloadable version, Photo Album 6 is an invaluable tool for any amateur photographer.

Downloading Your Images

Before you launch into the downloading process, make sure you've taken care of those dull prerequisites:

✦ Make sure that you've installed any software that came with your digital camera or card reader; this ensures that any USB or FireWire drivers are installed before you connect.

✦ Connect the cable that came with your camera (or your external card reader) to the corresponding port on your PC . . . which is very likely your PC's USB port. If you're using a card reader, eject the memory card from your camera and load it into the slot in the card reader (as shown in the card reader's documentation). For more details on ports, visit Book I, Chapter 3.

✦ If you're connecting your digital camera directly to your PC and it has an AC adapter, make sure that you plug the camera in to the AC adapter first; this can save you an hour of recharge time!

Although most digital cameras come with their own software, Windows XP has its own built-in wizard for downloading images. (If your camera comes with its own downloading software, it's a better idea to use that program instead, but at least XP can likely do the job alone in a pinch.) If your camera or card reader is supported within Windows XP (check the manufacturer's Web site or the specifications on the side of the box) and you're not using your camera or card reader's software, you'll see the Scanner and Camera Wizard screen (as shown in Figure 5-8) when you plug in the USB cable from your camera.

**Book VI
Chapter 5**

I'm Okay, You're a
Digital Camera

Figure 5-8:
Let
Windows
XP help you
download
images
from your
camera.

To complete the download process using the wizard, follow these steps:

1. **In the Welcome wizard screen, click Next to advance to the second screen, illustrated in Figure 5-9.**

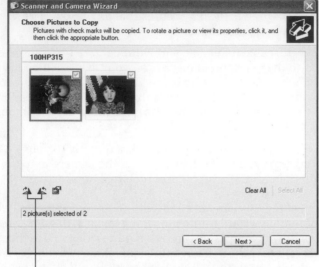

Figure 5-9:
Select and rotate images before they're even transferred!

Rotate your image by clicking either of these buttons.

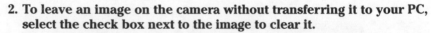

By default, the wizard copies all the images from your camera.

2. **To leave an image on the camera without transferring it to your PC, select the check box next to the image to clear it.**

   Click the Clear All button to deselect all the images, which comes in handy when you just want to select one or two pictures to download.

3. **To rotate an image, click the desired photograph to highlight it and then click either of the rotation buttons below the thumbnails.**

4. **After you select the images that you want to transfer and you rotate any shots that need attention, click Next to continue.**

5. **In the next wizard window (see Figure 5-10), type a descriptive name and then choose a destination folder or drive where the images will be saved.**

   • **Name:** Windows XP uses this name as the basis for the image. In this example, the filenames will be `Fun Photos 001.jpg`, `Fun Photos 002.jpg`, and so on.

   • **Destination:** If you want to use a location that you've used before, click the drop-down list, and the wizard displays it. To choose a new location, click the Browse button, navigate to the desired spot on your system, and then click OK.

6. **To delete the images from your camera after they've been successfully transferred to your PC, select the Delete Pictures from My Device After Copying Them check box.**

7. **Click Next to begin the transfer.**

   The wizard displays the progress window that you see in Figure 5-11.

**Book VI
Chapter 5**

I'm Okay, You're a
Digital Camera

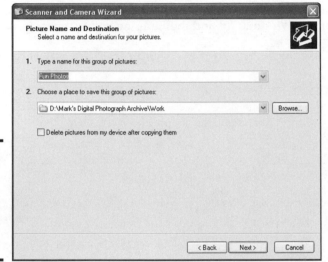

Figure 5-10:
Choose a
name and
destination
folder for
your photo-
graphs.

Figure 5-11:
Watch the
progress of
your photo-
graphs from
camera to
PC.

As soon as the transfer is complete, the next wizard screen appears.

8. **After the images have been transferred, you can choose to publish them to a Web site that you choose or to order prints of your photographs from a photo printing Web site. If you simply wanted to transfer the photographs, select the Nothing radio button.**

9. **After you make this choice, click Next.**

10. **In the final wizard screen that appears, click the Finish button to return to Windows XP and then unplug your camera from your PC.**

Book VII

Upgrading and Supercharging

The 5th Wave   By Rich Tennant

"Can't I just give you riches or something?"

Contents at a Glance

Chapter 1: Determining What to Upgrade

In This Chapter

- Knowing when to upgrade your CPU and motherboard
- Figuring out whether you need additional memory
- Determining whether you need extra ports
- Considering a hard drive upgrade
- Evaluating a CD/DVD recorder or a tape backup drive
- Deciding on audio and video improvements

My father always said, "Son, never take a long trip without a road map handy." This is why our old family Plymouth had six metric tons of paper maps for every state in the Union stuffed into the glove compartment, ready to be pulled out just in case we went astray. (Now I just visit Yahoo! and use the Maps service — progress marches on.)

Consider this introductory chapter a road map to upgrading your PC: what you can do, what you should add or replace, and what your benefits will be after the dust has cleared. After you read this PC upgrade primer, you'll be able to easily determine what you need to upgrade, and you can jump to the proper chapter within this mini-book to find the specifics.

One note before you jump in: Upgrading your PC is not a difficult job! All it requires is

- ✦ The courage to remove your computer's case. (Believe me, you'll get used to it.)
- ✦ The ability to follow step-by-step instructions.
- ✦ Basic skills with a screwdriver.

With that in mind, read on to determine what you need to turn your PC back into a hot rod.

Making Performance Upgrades: CPU, Motherboard, and Memory

I've cordoned off these first upgrades into a separate category that I call *performance upgrades;* that is, they give your PC an overall performance boost that affects all the programs that you run, including Windows XP.

Upgrading your CPU and motherboard

A *central processing unit* (CPU) is the brain of your PC. A significant upgrade to your CPU usually results in more than just replacing the CPU chip itself. For example, if you decide to upgrade from an older Pentium 4 computer to a Pentium Extreme Edition, your PC's motherboard will probably need to be replaced as well. The *motherboard* is the largest circuit board in your computer's case — it holds the CPU, memory, and all the rest of the electronics — so this is probably one of the most technically demanding upgrades that you can make.

Naturally, replacing your computer's brain with the next generation of chip will result in faster performance. How much faster depends on the speed of the chip — which is usually specified in megahertz (MHz) or gigahertz (GHz) and whether you're skipping a generation. For example:

✦ Upgrading from a Pentium 4 2.0 GHz processor to a Pentium 4 3.0 GHz processor will result in a speed increase. And because the chip generation may remain the same, you'll probably be able to use your current motherboard. However, the performance increase might not actually be significant enough to be noticeable in many of your programs . . . you're not really advancing very far.

✦ On the other hand, upgrading from an 800 MHz Pentium III processor to that same Pentium 4 3.0 GHz will change your plodding plowhorse into Shadowfax (the uber-stallion from Tolkien's *The Lord of the Rings*). Not only are you installing a CPU that's much faster, but you're also upgrading from Pentium III technology to Pentium 4 technology — and the tasks that you perform now will finish in a fraction of the time.

Hence this Mark's Maxim:

> **Upgrade your CPU and motherboard only when you're either moving to a new generation of processor or when you're at least doubling the speed of your current CPU.**™

Anything less is a waste of time and effort (unless the CPU fairy dropped a new chip on your pillow for free).

Adding memory

I'll be honest — adding memory (random access memory, or RAM) is my favorite performance upgrade, and I recommend adding memory far more often than I recommend upgrading a CPU/motherboard combo. Here's why:

✦ **Memory packs performance punch.** Any PC tech will tell you that dollar for dollar, adding additional memory results in a far more significant performance boost than simply upgrading your processor by a few megahertz. Windows will use every *bit* of that additional memory (bad techno-nerd pun intended there), and everything that your PC does will be faster.

✦ **Memory is cheap.** I'm talkin' really, *really* cheap. Most folks can now afford to max out their memory capacity. (The total that you can add is dependent upon your motherboard, so check with the PC manufacturer or the specifications for your motherboard to determine the maximum amount of memory that you can add.)

✦ **Memory is easy to install.** Compared with upgrading a motherboard and CPU, adding memory is one of the simplest upgrade tasks that you can perform in the bowels of your machine.

Here's Mark's Maxim for memory:

> **Add additional memory to your PC before embarking on a CPU and motherboard upgrade.™**

'Nuff said.

Expansion Upgrades: USB 2.0 and FireWire

Consider adding ports onto an older PC — what I call *expansion upgrades.* Although adding or upgrading ports won't speed up your computer, you'll be able to connect a wider range of external devices — and those devices are likely to run faster, transferring data to and from your PC at many times the rate of your pokey old serial and parallel ports.

Like the RAM upgrade that I discuss earlier in this chapter, adding Universal Serial Bus (USB 2.0) or FireWire ports to your PC is a relatively easy upgrade. All this involves is removing the cover from your PC and adding an adapter card to one of the open slots on your motherboard. Remember, this is how that original cadre of IBM engineers — the ones who designed the architecture of the first PCs and sat in those squeaky nerd-chairs — intended for you to add functionality to your computer, so it's practically a walk in the park.

**Book VII
Chapter 1**

**Determining What
to Upgrade**

Because I discuss USB 2.0 and FireWire ports earlier (see Book I, Chapter 3), here I just reiterate the major differences and what each type of port will do for you:

+ **USB 2.0:** This is the faster version of the USB port, with blazing speed and the ability to connect to older USB 1.*x* hardware. Unless you're using an external FireWire drive, digital camera, or digital video (DV) camcorder, USB 2.0 is the best choice for adding state-of-the-art, modern portage (ports for scanners, external hard drives, CD/DVD recorders, fax machines, printers, and the like) to your PC.

+ **FireWire:** If you'd like to upgrade your PC for use with your DV camcorder — or if you're interested in adding a fast external hard drive or DVD recorder — FireWire is your port of choice. Also, FireWire peripherals are usually easy to share with Mac owners because every modern Mac made within the last two or three years has at least one FireWire port.

If you already have USB or FireWire ports on your PC and you've simply run out of connections — for example, you have two USB ports, and you're using one for your printer and one for your Web cam — you don't need to add yet another set of ports. Instead, you just need a nifty little device called a USB or FireWire *hub,* which plugs into one of those ports and turns it into four or eight additional ports! (Think of the familiar AC extension cord, which plugs into one of your wall power sockets and allows you to plug three or four cords.)

Making Storage Upgrades: Internal and External Drives

Why limit yourself to that sorry patch of digital real estate that originally shipped with your PC? I'm talking about your hard drive, a tape backup unit, or perhaps a slower, older CD recorder. Upgrading these devices is a *storage upgrade* because you use these devices to permanently store (or record) data for later use.

Hard drives and CD/DVD recorders are both constantly dropping in price (and adding extra capacity and features), which is fortuitous because today's operating systems and applications tend to take up more and more hard drive space. Therefore, it's only natural that most serious PC users will eventually decide to add a second drive (or replace their existing drive with a new unit).

Adding a hard drive

The vast majority of today's PCs use Integrated Drive Electronics (IDE, sometimes called PATA) hard drives, which can be mounted *internally* (within your PC's case) or *externally* (by connecting to a USB or FireWire port). You'll also encounter Serial ATA (or SATA) hard drives, which are becoming more popular every day — they're a little faster than IDE drives and easier to configure. Finally, some high-performance machines still use internal SCSI hard drives (read more about SCSI in the sidebar titled, "Just let external SCSI hardware fade away . . .")

Here's how to tell which type of drive you should choose:

✦ **Internal:** Choose an internal drive if you don't mind opening up your PC's case and installing a new drive. (I show you how later, in Chapter 4 within this very mini-book.) Internal drives are significantly cheaper than external drives, and they're somewhat faster than even an external FireWire or USB 2.0 drive. Finally, you won't use any more of your precious desktop space.

✦ **External:** Choose an external drive if you'd rather not open your computer or if you have no available hard drive bays left in your computer's case. (Don't laugh — techno-types can fill up even the largest tower case with all sorts of devices.) External hard drives can be shared among computers that have the same ports, and you can simply unplug an external drive and carry it with you. (How's that for security?)

Adding a recorder or a tape drive

CD/DVD recorders and backup tape drives have been around for years now, but only with the advent of USB and FireWire have they become attractive to the PC power user as external devices. That's because in years past, hardware manufacturers had to depend on the PC's parallel port to connect these peripherals. (If you had *real* money, you could get an external Small Computer System Interface [SCSI] drive, but I recommend avoiding SCSI altogether unless you need the absolute fastest performance; read why when I describe SCSI hardware in the sidebar "Just let external SCSI hardware fade away . . ." elsewhere in this chapter.) The PC's parallel port was never designed for high-speed data transfer, so parallel port drives were as slow as your Aunt Harriet in her '53 Pontiac.

However, today's FireWire and USB 2.0 drives are almost as blazing fast as their internal brethren! Therefore, as long as you have a USB or FireWire port, you now have the same choice that I describe with hard drives: Either stick it in your machine or leave it outside. It'll work like a charm either way.

One final word about today's tape backup drives: They're beginning to disappear from the PC landscape because today's recordable DVD formats can hold 4.7GB (or 8.5GB for a dual-layer drive) on a single disc — and DVD recorders are faster and more reliable than most tape drives. Therefore, before you invest in a hideously expensive Digital Audio Tape (DAT) backup drive, consider buying a (comparatively) inexpensive rewriteable DVD drive instead and use that for your backups.

Just let external SCSI hardware fade away . . .

Officially, the acronym *SCSI* stands for *Small Computer Systems Interface,* but for most PC owners, it used to stand for *waking nightmare.* Before the arrival of FireWire and USB, a SCSI adapter card was the only way that you could add fast external devices to your PC. In fact, you can add multiple SCSI peripherals to the same card, like a SCSI scanner and a SCSI CD recorder — and, to be honest, SCSI internal hard drives are still the fastest performers for today's PCs. (That's why you still encounter them in server computers, as well as PCs dedicated to gaming and digital video editing.)

Unfortunately, SCSI hardware has always been more expensive. SCSI devices were also once notoriously difficult to configure, and even

today's SCSI implementation — which offers more automated setup features — is nowhere near as reliable and easy to install as either FireWire or USB 2.0. (Forget Plug and Play — the running gag is that SCSI is *Run and Hide* or *Plug and Pray.*)

Both FireWire and USB 2.0 ports can handle more external devices than a SCSI port, and they can transfer data at speeds that are fast enough to allow external SCSI hardware to fade into the archaic computing past. Take the word of a graying techno-Gandalf here: You're better off without SCSI for an external drive, good buddy. (As for internal SCSI hardware, if you need that kind of performance, you're willing to put up with the hassle and the extra cash involved.)

Making Sound and Video Upgrades: Sound and Video Cards

To finish my road map of PC upgrades, consider the hottest video and audio cards on the market today. There are more reasons than just gaming to add or upgrade your PC's eyes and ears: For example, maybe you'd like to move up to a sound card with Dolby Surround sound support or perhaps a video card with video capture capability. Like the addition of USB and FireWire ports, these upgrades are pretty simple: Just take the case off your PC, remove your current sound or video adapter card, and plug the replacement card in its place.

Before I jump in to a discussion of these cards, I should note that some of today's motherboards have their sound (and/or video) hardware on the motherboard instead of on separate adapter cards. If you have a motherboard with either a built-in video card or sound card, you should be able to disable the onboard hardware so that you can add your upgrade card. Typically, you must either display your PC's Basic Input/Output System (BIOS) and disable the onboard hardware from there, or you need to move a jumper on the motherboard. Read your motherboard user manual to discover which avenue to take.

Sound cards on parade

A number of specialized sound cards are available for the discriminating audio connoisseur — which, no doubt, you are. Consider these gems:

✦ **An MP3 card:** If you're an MP3 wizard with a hard drive's worth of MP3 digital audio files, you'll appreciate one of these specialized audio cards. An MP3 card contains a hardware encoder/decoder, which speeds up your PC's *ripping* (another name for the process of creating MP3 digital audio files from existing audio CDs) and MP3 playing performance. With one of these cards (which typically run about $50–$100 U.S.), you can listen to (or rip) the Talking Heads while using Photoshop CS2, and the sound quality stays just as good.

✦ **A 24-bit card:** For the absolute best in audio reproduction, a card such as the Audigy 4 from Creative Labs can produce 24-bit audio (that's 192 KHz for you audioheads), which is far superior to the sound produced by virtually all audio CD players. The fact that these cards can also support DVD audio, feature front-panel controls that fit in an open drive bay, and carry a built-in FireWire port is just the whipped cream and cherry on the sundae. Expect to pay a prime price for one of these cards, usually in the $200 U.S. range.

✦ **A Surround sound card:** These cards are specifically designed for 3-D environmental audio within games as well as full support for Dolby Surround sound as you watch DVD movies on your PC. Naturally, you'll need more than two mundane speakers from Wal-Mart to enjoy the full effect — which is why a premium set of speakers is usually included with these cards. Look for these cards to set you back around $100 U.S.

Deciding which video card is right for you

When you think about upgrading a video card, please do not — I repeat, *do not* — just think "gamers only." A number of specialized video cards on the market have nothing to do with games. (Okay, I admit it . . . gamers like myself do indeed love video cards.) Here's a cross section of what's available:

✦ **A gamer's card:** The latest 3-D video cards (equipped with GeForce 7 and Radeon X850 chipsets, from NVIDIA and ATI, respectively) simply kick serious tail no matter whether your favorite games involve mowing down Nazis, building a civilization one stone at a time, or matching wits with your computer over a chess board. If you haven't seen the realistic 3-D figures that these cards can produce, visit the Maze o' Wires store at your local mall (okay, maybe it's not exactly called *Maze o' Wires,* but you know what I mean) and ask a salesperson to crank up the latest game. Of course, Windows will display ho-hum applications faster with one of these cards as well. Many 3-D gaming cards also offer dual monitor support so that you can run two monitors side-by-side for a really big desktop.

**Book VII
Chapter 1**

Determining What
to Upgrade

These high-end, 3-D cards run tremendously hot — after all, they're practically separate computers — so they usually have a fan already installed on the card. However, if you're planning on installing the card in an older PC, I recommend having at least two fans installed in your case — that's one for the power supply (which is standard equipment) and at least one auxiliary fan (to help circulate air to all those hot components).

✦ **An MPEG card:** These cards are specifically designed for encoding and decoding Motion Picture Experts Group (MPEG) digital video (usually from a DVD, but hardware MPEG support is also very useful for doing serious video editing on your PC). Like the MP3 card that I describe in the previous section on audio cards, the idea is simple: Let the card do the video grunt work instead of your PC's processor, and everyone is happier. High-end video cards especially designed for digital video editing are significantly more expensive than video cards meant for home and gamer machines.

✦ **A capture card:** This popular video upgrade card allows you to capture an incoming analog video signal and convert it to digital video. For example, you can connect your VCR or older analog VHS-C camcorder into the card, convert the signal to digital video, and then record CD or DVD backups of your home movies. I've even seen these cards used to capture footage from Xbox games — if you can display it on your TV, you should be able to capture it with one of these toys.

Chapter 2: Adding RAM to Your Hot Rod

In This Chapter

✔ Determining what type of memory you need

✔ Understanding the myth behind "minimum RAM"

✔ Installing additional memory

*W*hat's not to like about a memory upgrade? As I discuss in the previous chapter, the *dinero* required for extra random access memory (RAM) is a mere pittance compared with a new CPU (or CPU and motherboard combination). Plus, RAM is easy to install, requiring only that you remove your PC's case and plug in the modules. Your PC should recognize additional RAM immediately, with no silly drivers required. Also, additional RAM will make everything run faster in Windows . . . both the applications that you run and the operating system itself.

"Mark," you say, "there's *got* to be a hitch *somewhere*." True: The problem is that you have so many different types of RAM modules to choose from. Therefore, read through this chapter before you buy your RAM modules and keep these pages handy when you upgrade.

Figuring Out What Type of Memory You Need

To begin a primer on memory, review the different types of RAM available for PCs made within the last five years or so.

One tip before I begin: If you're considering installing a new motherboard and CPU on an older PC, you might want to double-check to make sure that the new motherboard will still use the same RAM type and speed as your current motherboard. (To check, visit the manufacturers' Web sites to compare the specifications for your existing motherboard and the new toy, or you can refer to the documentation for both motherboards.) If not, the RAM that you add now won't do you any good when you upgrade your motherboard. If you have your eye on a significant motherboard/CPU swap in the near future, I definitely recommend that you upgrade the motherboard, CPU, *and* RAM all at the same time. For example, the memory modules that work with your older Pentium III PC aren't likely to work with a fast Pentium

4 motherboard. In cases like this, I recommend simply ordering a *populated* motherboard, which comes complete with a preinstalled CPU and the amount of RAM that you specify.

DDR

Double Data Rate (DDR) modules are the standard 168-pin Dual Inline Memory Modules (DIMM) available at the time of this writing; they're commonly used on today's Pentium and Athlon computers that run Windows XP. The *double* in the DDR name is significant because a DDR module effectively doubles the speed of the module (compared with older synchronous DRAM [SDRAM] memory). Also, DDR memory is assigned a speed rating as part of the name, so it's commonly listed as DDR266 or PC2100 (for the 133 MHz speed versions) and DDR333 or PC2700 (for the 166 MHz version). As you might guess, the faster the access speed, the better the performance. The speed rating that you should choose is determined by the memory speeds that your motherboard supports. DDR memory modules have one notch on the connector and two notches on the each side of the module.

DDR2

Here's a good question — what's the new memory specification that will eventually replace DDR? "Gee, Mark, *could* it be DDR2?" That's right — the latest DDR2 modules double the data transfer rate between your RAM and your motherboard, providing the best performance around, but they basically look the same. DDR2 is still the new kid on the block, so these modules are significantly more expensive than their older DDR brethren.

RDRAM

Rambus dynamic random access memory (RDRAM) modules are much faster (and also more expensive) than standard DDR modules — in fact, until the arrival of DDR2 memory, RDRAM was the memory standard of choice for high-speed PCs. Today, DDR2 has crept up from behind and taken that coveted title of First Place Performer, and RDRAM is slowly disappearing from the market. If your PC uses RDRAM, it's really cooking already, so you're likely preparing to add more memory to your existing RDRAM motherboard.

SDRAM

SDRAM (sometimes called *SyncDRAM*) takes the form of standard 168-pin DIMMs. These modules are standard equipment for most Pentium III and some older Pentium 4 machines. SyncDRAM runs at an access speed of 133 MHz, which is too doggone slow for today's fast processors. SDRAM memory modules have two notches in the bottom and only one notch on each side.

EDO

Older Pentium motherboards used Extended Data Output (EDO) memory in the form of 72-pin Single Inline Memory Modules (SIMMs). Typically, you must add SIMM memory in pairs.

If you're planning on adding memory to a motherboard that uses EDO modules, I strongly urge you to instead upgrade the Big Three — motherboard, CPU, and memory. (I don't intend to offend, but I'll be blunt: Your PC is so far behind the performance of today's models that it just isn't worth adding EDO memory to your older motherboard. Plus, EDO memory is now much harder to find and is actually getting more expensive over time. Just chalk that up to the price of running antique hardware.)

Here are two methods to determine what type of memory modules your current motherboard requires and what memory speeds it can handle:

+ **Check the specifications:** Refer to the motherboard manual. Or, if you purchased your PC from a manufacturer, check the documentation that accompanied the computer. If you didn't get any manuals with a used PC, visit the company's Web site for memory compatibility information or specifications. This is definitely the preferred method because you won't have to open your PC's case until you're ready to install the new RAM modules.

+ **Check the existing modules:** If you can't find any documentation, specifications, or data on the Web concerning your PC's RAM modules, it's time to remove the case from your computer. (For more details on removing the cover, see the step-by-step procedure at the end of this chapter.) Look for the memory slots on your motherboard; DDR and DDR2 modules look like Figure 2-1. (*Note:* You might have more than one module already installed on your PC.) Your RAM modules might have a descriptive label (which will allow you to read the specifics without actually taking anything out); however, it's more likely that you'll have to remove one and take it to your local computer shop. Use the instructions later in this chapter to remove a module; then protect the module in an empty CD-ROM jewel case when you take it for identification. The good techs should be able to tell you what type and speed of memory you're using when presented with the module.

Figure 2-1: A DDR/ DDR2 DIMM, caught in the open.

Deciding How Much RAM Is Enough

Every motherboard has a maximum amount of memory that it can support. You can install the maximum amount by filling up all the motherboard's memory banks (sockets) with modules of the right type.

Time for another one of Mark's Maxims:

> **Whenever possible, buy RAM modules of the same brand at the same time from the same dealer.** ™

This will ensure that you are spared any compatibility problems when you install the modules. (Theoretically, any RAM module of the same type and speed should work with any other brand of RAM, but I date back to the earlier days of PCs when using memory chips from different manufacturers would result in errors and a locked computer.) In fact, I still hear tales of compatibility problems, even in our new, improved, fresher-smelling world.

However, not everyone can afford to take their PC's memory to the max — even with today's prices, buying half a gigabyte of RAM modules can set you back. Therefore, the following table illustrates my recommendations for the minimum amount of RAM that you'll need to run the different versions of the Windows operating system comfortably on your PC. (By *comfortably,* I mean my opinion of decent performance, perhaps with a copy of Microsoft Word running. Of course, memory-hungry applications such as Adobe Photoshop will only run their best with plenty of memory elbow room to spare, so I'd consider this the *absolute* bare minimum.)

Windows 98	*Windows NT*	*Windows Me*	*Windows 2000*	*Windows XP*
64MB	64MB	64MB	128MB	256MB

You might notice that my recommendations sometimes don't jibe with Brother Bill's — that's because the folks in Redmond literally mean *the least you can get away with* when mentioning minimum memory requirements. With 24MB of RAM, Windows 98 is slower to awaken than my kids on a school day. Personally, I actually like to *use* my computer and not wait half an hour for a scanned image to load.

Installing Extra RAM

Ready to install your new RAM upgrade? Follow these steps to install a typical SDRAM or DDR/DDR2 module:

1. **Cover your work surface with several sheets of newspaper (to protect your case).**

2. **Unplug your PC and place it on top of the newspaper.**

3. **Remove the PC's case.**

Most PC cases are held on with two or three screws; just remove the screws and slide the case off. (Don't forget to stash those screws in a safe place.) Other cases are hinged, often with a lock. If you're unsure how to remove your PC's case, check the manual that accompanied your computer.

4. **Touch the metal chassis of your case to dissipate any static electricity on your body.**

An electrical charge can send your new RAM modules to Frisco . . . permanently.

5. **Locate the DIMM slots.**

Check the motherboard manual, which should have a schematic that will help you locate the slots. Typically, the RAM modules are found close to the CPU, in the center or one corner of the motherboard.

6. **Turn your PC's chassis so that the DIMM slots are facing you (as shown in Figure 2-2) and make sure that the two levers on the side of the socket are extended.**

Figure 2-2:
Align a
DDR/DDR2
module with
its socket.

Note that the notches cut into the connectors on the bottom of the memory module match the spacers in the sockets themselves, so you can't install your modules the wrong way. (Smart thinking there.)

7. **Align the connector on the bottom of the module with the socket and push down with a light pressure to seat the module.**

8. **While you push down, the two levers at each side of the socket should move toward the center, as shown in Figure 2-3, until they click in place.**

Figure 2-3:
Hey, those
levers just
clicked into
place!

After you correctly install the module, the two levers should be tightly
flush against the sides of the memory module to hold it securely.

9. **Slide the cover back on your PC and secure it.**

10. **Move your PC back to its place of honor and plug it in.**

11. **Restart your computer and prepare to enjoy a faster PC!**

Chapter 3: Scotty, I Need More Power!

Upgrading your central processing unit (CPU)/motherboard — the Big One — is the most costly and the most complex upgrade that you can make to your PC. In this chapter, I discuss what you should look for in a CPU and a motherboard . . . and the very real possibility that you shouldn't upgrade this combo at all. (Hey, I'm always open minded, upfront, and cutting edge.)

If you do decide to upgrade, take heart. You'll find the proper step-by-step procedure in this chapter.

Hey, Do I Need to Do This?

Before you read another sentence of this chapter, take note of yet another Mark's Maxim:

> **Postpone a CPU/motherboard upgrade as long as possible.™**

I know that sounds a little silly, considering that there are several pages of perfectly good tips and procedures remaining in this chapter, but I stand by my maxim. Here are four good reasons:

✦ **A CPU/motherboard combo is one of the most expensive upgrades that you can make to your computer.** First consider upgrading random access memory (RAM) and your video card. Adding RAM and a faster video card is (usually) cheaper than upgrading a CPU/motherboard combo. And depending on the types of applications that you run, the RAM/video card upgrade might actually provide a better performance boost than using a new CPU and motherboard. (**Side benefit:** The longer that you postpone a CPU/motherboard upgrade, the more of a performance jump that you'll get when you finally do take the plunge.)

Which is better: Intel or AMD?

Chip choice time. Intel and AMD are the two leading processor manufacturers. I can honestly say that both today's Pentium series from Intel (Pentium 4, Pentium D, and Extreme Edition) and the Athlon 64 series from AMD are great processors, so let price and the chip speed be your guide. Just make sure that you get the right CPU for your motherboard because every motherboard is specifically designed for one brand of CPU. In general, AMD processors are less expensive than Intel processors of the same performance level.

You might see three relatively recent features advertised whilst shopping for your PC's cranium, and all three are distinct advantages. I won't get too technical here — if I did, we'd both likely need a vacation after a page of engineer-squawk — but you should be familiar with these designations:

✔ **Dual-core processor:** In effect, a dual-core processor is "two, two, two CPUs in one!" (Boy howdy, I'm getting old.) Anyway, these processors essentially embody the inner guts of two processors, even though there's only one physical chip. A dual-core processor is much better at multitasking and juggling more than one running program at a time, or both "virtual" processors can work on the same task. Very sexy — in a computer hardware sort of way, naturally.

✔ **64-bit processing:** 32-bit processors like the Athlon XP and the Pentium 4 are slated to turn antique soon, because a 64-bit processor can input and output much more data (and work with a whopping larger amount of RAM). If you've invested in a 64-bit version of a CPU, you're investing in the future, since neither Windows XP Home nor Professional makes use of all that extra bandwidth and memory capacity.... However, Windows XP Professional x64 Edition and the upcoming Windows Vista are 64-bit systems.

✔ **Hyper–Threading:** Geez, what a moniker . . . just think of a Hyper–Threading processor as much more efficient and significantly better at handling multiple programs at the same time than a processor of the same speed without Hyper–Threading. (Who thinks up these names? The Marketing guys?)

✦ **A CPU/motherboard combo is one of the most difficult upgrades to install.** To facilitate this upgrade, you're going to have to take out every adapter card and unhook every wire and possibly even disassemble parts of your case — then do it all again in reverse. (That's what we techies call "putting it back together." My Dad used to tell me I'd have to eat anything left over after fixing the family car, so I got very careful very quickly about assembly.)

✦ **A CPU/motherboard combo has dependencies.** Hmm . . . strange term here, so let me explain. You see, no matter how fast your new motherboard and CPU combo might be, it will still depend on your existing adapter cards — including video, sound, modem, and port cards — to take care of putting video on your monitor, sound in your speakers, and Internet data in your browser (respectively). Therefore, if you upgrade to a blazing fast CPU/motherboard combination but you're still using a five-year-old video card, your 3-D games might still end up as slow as Aunt Harriet in her Plymouth Volare.

✦ **You might have to scrap your existing memory modules and power supply.** Along the lines of the previous reason, using a new CPU/motherboard combo might force you to dump all the memory modules that you've been collecting over the last few years as well as that low-rated power supply. You can sell 'em on eBay, of course, but don't expect a whopping amount back.

With these reasons in mind, I recommend that you upgrade your motherboard and CPU only when you've exhausted the other possibilities — upgrading RAM or your video card, for example. I'm not saying that you shouldn't eventually put a new heart and brain in your PC. Just don't resort to major surgery until it's really necessary.

Selecting a New Motherboard

Keep these guidelines in mind while shopping for a new motherboard to match your CPU of choice:

✦ **Determine what type of motherboard fits in your PC's case.** Virtually all PCs manufactured in the last few years use ATX cases and ATX motherboards, but it never hurts to make sure. Older cases might use AT or Baby AT motherboards. If you need help with classifying your case, take it to your local computer shop and have a technician tell you.

✦ **FSB means Front Side Bus.** The higher the bus speed on your new motherboard, the better the performance — and the more expensive the RAM modules. (At higher bus speeds, more data is sent to the CPU at one time, and the data arrives there faster; from an efficiency and performance standpoint, this is A Good Thing.) Most CPUs will work with a range of bus speeds.

✦ **Shop for the best controllers.** Today's motherboards have onboard hard drive controllers that vary widely in performance — for example, my current motherboard has both SATA and EIDE controllers onboard, and SATA hardware is significantly faster than EIDE. Therefore, make sure that you compare the motherboard controller's rated speeds and supported hard drives when shopping for a motherboard.

✦ **Consider onboard FireWire, Universal Serial Bus (USB) 2.0, sound and network hardware.** Why force yourself to add a separate adapter card later when you can buy a motherboard with networking, FireWire, Dolby Surround sound, and USB 2.0 ports built in?

✦ **RAM capacity is important.** Check what type of RAM is supported and the maximum amount of RAM that the motherboard can accept. (For more information about the RAM types on the market today, check the previous chapter.)

I *highly* recommend that you buy one of the package deals — a CPU already installed on the motherboard of your choice — offered by many PC Web stores. This will simplify both your shopping (you're guaranteed to buy a motherboard and CPU that work together well) and your installation. Trust me! (I've been recommending J&N Computer Services to my friends and family for years now for CPU/Motherboard/RAM bundles. Visit www.jncs.com to see why.)

Installing a Motherboard and CPU

Before you decide to launch into a motherboard/CPU swap, carefully read over the following procedure and then visit the nearest bathroom. (No, I don't expect you to be sick; I want you to stand in front of the mirror.) Look yourself in the eye and ask yourself honestly, "Can I do this? If I can do this, do I really *want* to do this?"

If your answer is a confident "Yes," by all means continue with your upgrade, and may you have the wind always at your back.

If, however, your answer is an uncomfortable "Maybe," don't forget that you can always take your PC to a local computer shop and have the techs there install your new hardware for you. This is the only spot in this entire mini-book where I even consider the option of professional installation. Of course, anything in this mini-book can be professionally installed, but a CPU/motherboard combo is often more difficult and more of a hassle for the typical PC owner than any other upgrade.

With that said — and if you're still reading on — then get to work!

Installing an Athlon 64 or Pentium 4 CPU

If you didn't buy a combo motherboard with the CPU already installed, follow these steps to install your processor before you install the motherboard:

1. **Touch a metal surface.**

   Static is bad. You know the drill.

2. **Locate the CPU socket on your motherboard — it's the largest socket on the planet, with several dozen pins.**

   Check the motherboard manual if you have a problem finding it.

The CPU socket is also called a ZIF (short for *zero-insertion force*) socket, which means that you can quickly install and remove the CPU without undue pressure on the chip (and with as little danger of bending the CPU pins as possible). The little lever clamps the CPU firmly to the motherboard, as you will see.

Pay close attention to the markings on your new CPU. "What markings, Mark?" Well, cast your eyes on Figure 3-1, which illustrates different types of markings on both CPUs and sockets. Look for a stubby corner, a tiny groove, or a dot or triangle on one corner of the chip — that marked corner will match up with the socket's marked corner. If you can't locate the marked corner, your motherboard and CPU manuals will identify them for you.

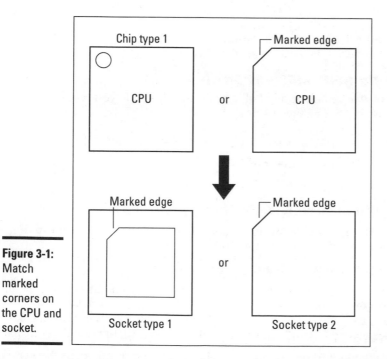

Figure 3-1: Match marked corners on the CPU and socket.

3. **Raise the ZIF lever on the side of the socket to unlock the socket.**

4. **Align the CPU chip on top of the socket, matching marked corners and double-checking your pin placement from the side of the chip.**

5. **Use your fingertips to gently press down evenly on the edges of the chip.**

   The chip should settle in until the pins aren't visible from the side.

Do not force your CPU! If it doesn't comfortably settle into place, put it down and retreat to the comfort of your motherboard and CPU manuals. Breaking the pins on your CPU will turn it into an extremely expensive, nonfunctioning brooch.

6. **Lower the ZIF lever on the side of the socket to lock the CPU in place.**

7. **Clamp the fan on top of the processor.**

    Note: You might need to apply a special glue or compound between the fan plate and the processor before you install the fan.

8. **If your CPU fan has a separate power cable, plug it into the proper connector on the motherboard.**

    The location of the CPU fan plug will be listed in your motherboard manual.

Relax. Breathe deeply. Congratulations!

Installing your motherboard

Time to put that granddaddy of all circuit boards inside your case. Grab your screwdriver and follow these steps:

1. **Unplug your PC and move it onto your work surface.**

2. **Remove the cover from the case.**

    Keep the screws handy, naturally.

3. **Work that anti-static magic by touching your PC's metal chassis.**

4. **Unscrew and remove all the adapter cards, placing them on top of a handy sheet of nearby newspaper.**

5. **Unplug all cables leading to your motherboard.**

    Note: You might also have to remove sections of your case as well as all internal devices such as hard drives, CD/DVD drives, and your floppy drive. (I told you this was going to be a bear, didn't I?) Because all cases are designed differently, this might take a little investigation on your part.

6. **After the motherboard is completely uncovered, remove all the screws and nonconductive washers holding down the motherboard and put them in a bowl, keeping them separate from any other screws.**

Carefully note the location of the screw holes and any plastic spacers securing the old motherboard to the case before you remove them. This will save time later. If necessary, grab a piece of paper and a pencil and sketch a quick drawing of which holes you should use when installing the new motherboard.

7. **Reach into your PC's case and gently work the old motherboard free.**

   Take the time to make sure that you don't scratch the surface of your motherboard on exposed metal or sharp edges. A deep-enough scratch can ruin the delicate circuitry etched into the surface of the board.

8. **After the old motherboard is clear, put it in the anti-static pouch that protected your new board, and start wondering who will buy it. (If any plastic spacers were attached, remove them and put them with your motherboard screws.)**

9. **Holding the motherboard by the edges, carefully place it inside the case to align it. Keep the memory modules and CPU side facing up and toward you, ensuring that the adapter card slots line up with the slots in your case (see Figure 3-2).**

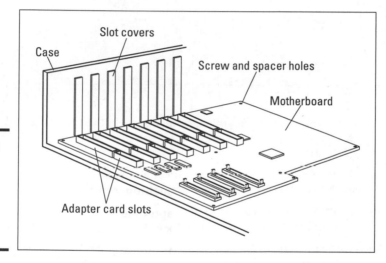

Figure 3-2: Check the alignment of your new mother-board.

Slot covers

Case

Screw and spacer holes

Motherboard

Adapter card slots

10. **Check to determine which screw holes in your motherboard line up with which screw holes in your case.**

    Note that your case will likely use three or four screws to actually hold the board, but other spots on the board might need to be supported by those plastic spacers; the spacers slide under metal grooves in the case.

11. **If you need to add spacers, remove the new motherboard from the case and push the spacers through the holes from the bottom of the board until they snap into place (as shown in Figure 3-3).**

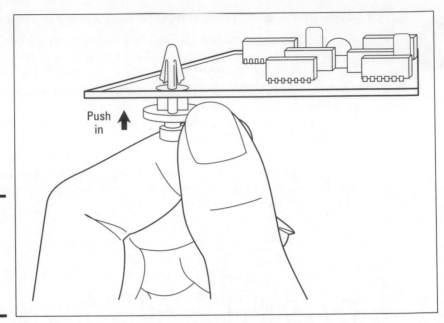

Push
in

Figure 3-3:
Add
spacers,
if needed,
to the new
mother-
board.

12. **If you had to remove your motherboard in Step 11, slide it back into the case (making sure that all the plastic spacers are correctly positioned).**

13. **Check each corner of the motherboard to make sure that it's separated from the metal of the case and doesn't wobble.**

14. **Secure the motherboard with the screws and washers from Step 6, being careful not to overtighten them.**

15. **Plug the power cables, hard drive, floppy cables, and case control cables back into the new motherboard.**

    Because every motherboard is different, you'll have to rely on your motherboard manual to locate what goes where. (This is why I've never tossed a motherboard manual in the trash.)

16. **Reinstall any drives or case chassis parts that you had to remove in Step 5.**

17. **Reinstall your adapter cards, connecting any cables that you had to remove back to their original location.**

18. **After you double-check every connection, replace the cover on your case.**

19. **Plug your PC back in and boogie.**

It is now appropriate to book a vacation to Disneyland.

Chapter 4: Adding Hard Drive Territory to Your System

In This Chapter

✔ Understanding virtual memory

✔ Selecting the proper drive

✔ Choosing an internal or external drive

✔ Adding a second internal drive

Here is what I call the *Elbowroom Hypothesis:* Both mankind and his computer tools will expand to fill whatever room they're given. If you're bent on becoming a PC power user, I can assure you — in fact, I can downright *guarantee* you — that the largest hard drive that you can buy today will eventually be filled in the future. As you discover in this chapter, even Windows XP demands a chunk of hard drive territory . . . both when you install it and when it's running.

Hence the explosion in hard drive capacities over the last five years or so. I'm old enough to remember when a 1GB drive was an unheard-of dream. Heck, I still have the first hard drive that I ever owned: a huge RadioShack 15MB (yes, you read right, *fifteen megabyte*) Disk System that I used with my TRS-80 Model IV. (Oh, did I mention that those 15 megabytes of storage cost me over $1,000 U.S. in 1983 and that the drive is about the size of a typical modern PC case?) I use it as a combination monitor stand, conversation piece, and possible proof of past visits by extraterrestrials.

Luckily, you can upgrade your PC's hard drive with ease either by connecting an external drive or by upgrading your current internal hard drive. Alternatively, you can simply cast yourself to the four winds with abandon and keep your current internal drive and add a second drive. This chapter is your road map.

The Tale of Virtual Memory

"Wait a furshlugginer minute here, Mark — you cover memory upgrades in Chapter 2 of this very mini-book. Why bring it up now?" Good question, and the answer lies in the fact that the pseudo-RAM called *virtual memory* actually exists on your hard drive rather than as memory modules on your motherboard.

Now that you're totally confused, here's the explanation: Today's modern operating systems (meaning Windows XP and 2000, Mac OS X, UNIX, and Linux) all use a trick called *virtual memory* to feed your applications the memory that they need. Suppose that your PC has only 64MB of random access memory (RAM) installed, but you've just run Photoshop CS2 and demanded that it load a 30MB high-resolution digital image. If Windows XP were limited to using only your computer's *physical* RAM (the memory modules that you've installed on your PC's motherboard), you'd be up a creek because Windows XP requires a minimum of around 24MB of memory itself, and Photoshop CS2 takes a significant chunk of memory to run. And on top of all that, you're loading 30MB of data, too! With the size of today's documents and the amount of RAM needed by memory-hungry mega-applications, your 64MB PC literally can't do its job. And don't forget, you're probably running more than one application at once. What's a computer to do?

As you can see in Figure 4-1, Windows turns to your hard drive for help. It uses a portion of the empty space on your hard drive to temporarily hold the data that would otherwise be held in your computer's memory. In this case, our hardworking silicon warrior uses 64MB of hard drive space, so the total memory available within Windows (using both 64MB of physical memory and 64MB of virtual memory) is now 128MB, providing more elbowroom to work with. Your programs actually don't know that they're using virtual memory — Windows takes care of everything behind the scenes, so Photoshop CS2 thinks that you have 128MB of physical memory.

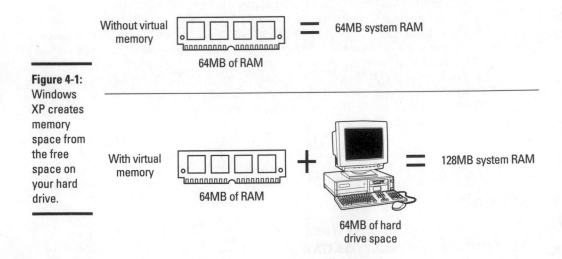

Figure 4-1: Windows XP creates memory space from the free space on your hard drive.

Now that you understand how virtual memory works, commit this Mark's Maxim to heart:

Always leave enough empty hard drive space for Windows to use as virtual memory!™

How much is enough? I try to leave at least 1 or 2GB free on the C: drive at all times on my Windows XP machines. A PC that runs out of hard drive space is a terrible thing to see; applications will start to lock up, you might lose any changes that you've made to open files, and Windows will begin displaying pitiful error messages begging you to close some of your open application windows (or even restart).

Also, note that virtual memory is always — and I mean *always* — slower than true physical memory. After all, that data has to be written to and read from your hard drive instead of super-fast memory modules. This is why I'm such a proponent of adding as much RAM to your PC as possible; the more memory that you add, the less likely that Windows XP will need to resort to virtual memory.

PC techs call your computer's use of virtual memory *drive thrashing* because Windows must constantly write to, read from, and erase data from your hard drive. When you run out of physical memory, the hard drive activity light never seems to go out. And yes, if you're wondering, all that activity will shorten the life of your hard drive.

Recognizing a Well-Dressed Hard Drive

When you decide to take the plunge and add storage space, reading this section helps you shop by separating the good specifications from the gobbledygook.

Today's PCs use Enhanced Integrated Drive Electronics (EIDE) or Serial ATA (SATA) hard drives. Although a PC can use an internal Small Computer Systems Interface (SCSI) hard drive, anyone using expensive and complex SCSI hardware is already a PC power user and can probably skip this chapter without a second glance.

Size definitely does matter

Virtually all EIDE and SATA drives on the market today are 3 ½" format, meaning that they can fit within a typical floppy drive/hard drive combo bay within your computer's case. Unfortunately, some mini-tower cases have only one or two of these 3 ½" bays.

Therefore, if you're planning on parking that 3 ½" drive within a much larger 5 ¼" bay — the kind used with CD- and DVD-ROM drives — you'll need a metal framework called a *drive cage kit.* In effect, the hard drive is mounted into the drive cage, which in turn is mounted in the PC's 5 ¼" bay. Most drives don't come with a drive cage kit, so you'll need to buy one at your computer shop. (They usually run about $10 U.S.)

How fast is your access?

When you see a drive's *access* (or *seek*) time listed, that's the amount of time (in milliseconds; ms) that it takes the drive to read or write data. Naturally, a lower access time is desirable — and usually somewhat more expensive. Drives with access times below 10 ms are usually at the top of their price range, especially when the drive in question has a higher revolutions-per-minute (rpm) rating.

What does rpm have to do with hard drives?

In the world of personal computers, just like in the world of the Indy 500, the abbreviation *rpm* means *revolutions per minute.* (However, I'm counting the revolutions that the magnetic disk platter turns inside the drive.) And, with a refreshing constancy, a higher rpm hard drive means better performance, just like a beefier engine's rpm means greater speed in auto racing.

Most of today's EIDE and SATA drives fall into one of two rpm ranges:

+ **5,400 rpm:** These drives are standard equipment on most older PCs and can also be found on low-cost Pentium and Athlon computers. As reliable as vanilla ice cream, one of these drives will get the job done . . . but don't expect whipped cream and a cherry.

+ **7,200 rpm:** 7,200 rpm drives used to be 10–20 percent more expensive than their slower brethren, but lately, the cost on these faster drives has dropped to about the same price point.

+ **10,000 rpm:** Lucky dog! These "sports car" hard drives are found on today's high-performance PCs. You'll pay a bit more, but a 10,000 rpm SATA drive can really speed up your disk-intensive applications (as well as Windows XP itself).

I heartily recommend that you select a 7,200 rpm or 10,000 rpm drive when upgrading any Athlon or Pentium 4 computer. The significantly faster read/write performance on one of these drives will pep up your entire system.

Internal versus External Storage

I address the idea of internal and external peripherals in a number of places elsewhere in the book, so I won't go into a crazy amount of detail here. Suffice it to say that I recommend using an internal hard drive whenever

✦ You don't need to share the drive among multiple computers or take it with you while traveling.

✦ Your PC has an additional open drive bay, or you're willing to upgrade the existing drive.

✦ You want to save money.

As you might expect, with those criteria, I usually push internal hard drives on both my unsuspecting consulting customers and myself as well. Figure 4-2 shows the curvaceous rear end of a typical modern hard drive. (Well, at least it *looks* curvaceous to a techno-nerd like me.)

**Book VII
Chapter 4**

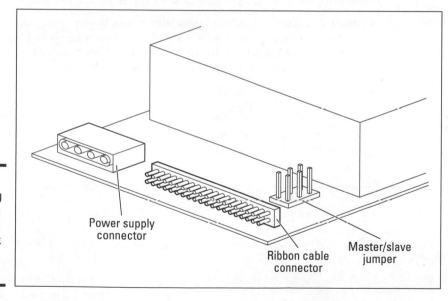

Figure 4-2:
A sweeping vista — the connectors on the back of an EIDE hard drive.

Power supply connector

Ribbon cable connector

Master/slave jumper

Adding Hard Drive Territory to Your System

Don't get me wrong — external drives are neat toys. However, they cost significantly more than their internal counterparts, and you'll lose some of your precious desk space accommodating them. Most external drives also have their own power cord, meaning that you have to pull yet another AC wall socket out of your magician's hat. If you really do need an external drive and you want to save yourself the hassle, consider a drive that's powered over a Universal Serial Bus (USB) or FireWire connection, which means no additional power cable worries.

TIP

If someone tries to give you a USB 1.*x* hard drive — or, heaven forbid, if you're thinking of buying a used USB 1.*x* hard drive — I beg you *not* to do it! The first generation of USB drives was ridiculously slow. In other words, your kids are likely to graduate from college before you finish transferring a single gigabyte's worth of data from that drive to your PC. Keep a safe distance from that tired drive and call your local antique hardware shelter.

Adding a Second Internal Hard Drive

For most current PC owners, the easiest method of adding more hard drive space is to add a second hard drive to your system. I cite three very good reasons for this:

✦ **No backup is required.** Of course, *you should be backing up your current hard drive anyway.* (If not, shut this book immediately and back up your drive!) Adding a second drive eliminates the setup that you'd have to perform if you upgraded your current drive because you won't have to restore the current contents of your old drive to the new drive.

✦ **Most PCs have at least one open drive bay.** Unless your computer is already stuffed to the gills, you should have enough room to add a second hard drive. If it *is* stuffed to the gills, you'll either have to upgrade the current drive or add an external FireWire or USB 2.0 drive.

✦ **It's like . . . well . . . more for less.** Rather than replace your existing 30GB drive with a 60GB drive — and end up with only 30GB more room — I always find it more attractive to leave the original drive as is and add that second drive, resulting in the full 60GB that you paid for. (*Remember:* You *will* eventually use that space. Trust me.)

Serial ATA is in the house . . .

Although EIDE is still the most popular hard drive interface for today's PCs, serial ATA is rapidly catching up. That's because a SATA connection allows significantly faster data transfer rates — in English, SATA is faster than EIDE — and there are no jumpers for a SATA drive. The installation of the physical drive is the same as I outline here for an EIDE drive . . . then, simply plug in the data cable from your motherboard (it only goes on one way) and the power cable from your PC's power supply, and the drive is ready for action.

In fact, virtually all of the latest motherboards on the market today have both EIDE (sometimes called PATA, short for Parallel ATA) and SATA connectors onboard. You can mix-and-match and use both, or work only with the faster SATA connections.

Are you girded and ready for battle? Then follow this procedure to add a second internal EIDE hard drive to your current system:

1. **Cover your work surface with several sheets of newspaper.**

2. **Unplug your PC and place it on top of the newspaper.**

3. **Remove the case screws and slide the case off, putting the screws aside in a bowl or cup.**

   If you're unsure how to remove your PC's case, check the manual that accompanied your computer.

4. **Touch the metal chassis of the computer to dissipate any static electricity.**

5. **Verify the jumper settings on the back of your original drive, as shown in Figure 4-3. If necessary, change the existing drive to *multiple drives, master unit* (or just *master*) by moving the jumper to the indicated pins.**

Figure 4-3: Change jumper settings on an EIDE hard drive when installing a second drive.

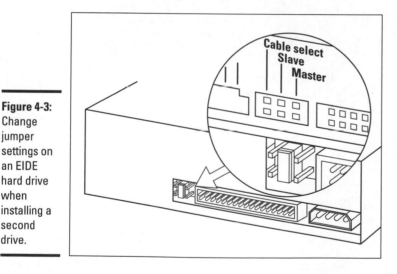

If you haven't encountered *jumpers* yet, they're the tiny plastic and metal shunts that you use to configure hard drives and CD/DVD drives.

Your jumper configuration will probably be different than Figure 4-3. Most hard drive manufacturers now print the jumper settings on the top of a hard drive. If the settings aren't printed on the drive, you can refer to the drive's manual or visit the manufacturer's Web site and look up the settings there. If all this seems a little exotic, the terms are really not risqué; *master* means *primary* (and if you have at least one drive, there must be a master device), and *slave* means *secondary*. Other than that, the devices are treated the same way by your PC.

6. Set the jumpers on the back of the new drive for *multiple drives, slave unit* (often listed as just *slave unit*).

7. If your new drive needs a drive cage to fit into the desired bay, use the screws supplied by the drive manufacturer to attach the cage rails onto both sides of your drive.

   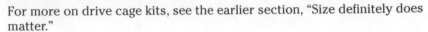

   For more on drive cage kits, see the earlier section, "Size definitely does matter."

8. Slide the drive into the selected bay from the front of the case, making sure that the end with the connectors goes in first and that the exposed circuitry of the drive is on the bottom.

9. Slide the hard drive back and forth in the drive bay until the screw holes in the side of the bay are aligned with the screw holes on the side of the drive (or the drive cage rails).

10. Tighten the drive down to the side of the bay with the screws that came with the drive (or your cage kit), as illustrated in Figure 4-4.

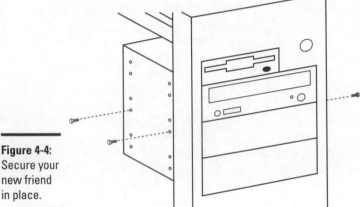

Figure 4-4:
Secure your
new friend
in place.

11. Choose an unused power connector and plug it in, making sure that the connector is firmly seated (see Figure 4-5).

   Joyfully, there's only one way to connect a power cable to a hard drive: the right way.

12. Plug the other connector from the hard drive cable into the back of the drive and make sure that the cable is firmly seated.

   Note that both hard drives will use the same cable, so you might need to unplug the original drive from the cable and switch connectors. Don't worry: It doesn't matter which connector goes to which drive as long as the jumpers are correctly set.

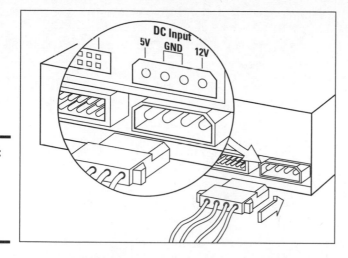

Figure 4-5:
A drive
without
power is
a paper-
weight.

Check for a blocked hole in the cable connector, which should align with a missing pin on the drive's connector. This alignment trick, called *keying*, helps ensure that you're installing the cable right-side up. However, don't panic if the cable isn't keyed: Remember that the wire with the red or black marking on the cable is always Wire 1 and that it should align with Pin 1 on the drive's connector (see Figure 4-6).

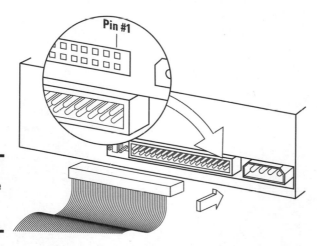

Figure 4-6:
Connect the
drive to the
data cable.

13. **Replace the cover on your PC and tighten its screws.**

14. **Plug your PC back in and turn it on.**

15. **Run the drive formatting utility that accompanied your new drive to prepare it for use.**

Chapter 5: Partying with USB, FireWire, and Hubs

In This Chapter

✔ **Comparing USB 1.x with USB 2.0**

✔ **Using FireWire for high-end fun**

✔ **Extending your system with a hub**

✔ **Adding a USB or FireWire card**

*I*n the days of the early IBM PCs, practically every device that you added was *internal* (located within the computer's case). Because so few peripherals existed that you could add to your system, this really wasn't a problem. Naturally, the parallel port took care of the printer (if you could afford one), and as the modem grew in importance, it took up residence with the serial port.

Today, however, PC cases are shrinking. When it comes to size, I can't tell the difference between many new desktops and my kid's PlayStation. Less internal room means more need for external stuff. Also, because of the huge increase in the number of portable devices that you can add to your computer, those toys are naturally designed to be external, such as digital cameras, MP3 players, and the like. The days of the PC as a monolith are over.

So what's a poor CPU to do? Enter the two star ports of the digital age: Universal Serial Bus (USB) and FireWire. Talk about *sassy:* They're fast, offer plug-and-play convenience, and won't hassle you with arcane errors or strange settings. Plus, you can use them to connect practically everything but the kitchen sink to your computer simultaneously.

In this section, I share the joy as we party with these two ports together.

Comparing USB Ports

You might think that all USB ports are the same, but they're not. In the beginning, only USB 1.*x* was available. Sure, USB 1.*x* was a fine little port (easy to use and requiring no configuration) but only a few times faster than an old-fashioned serial connection. To be honest, a FireWire device will wipe the floor with the first generation of USB devices when it comes to speed. Two or three years ago, the list of peripherals that really required 400 Mbps of transfer speed was limited to digital video (DV) camcorders and external audio/visual (AV) hard drives used by video professionals. Today, that list has expanded.

To illustrate:

✦ **Digital cameras** that produce images with bigger file sizes.

✦ **High-resolution scanners** that need to churn out images with 200MB of pixels.

✦ **External high-speed CD and DVD recorders;** USB 1.*x* external CD recorders are limited to about 4X speed — and don't even dream of recording a DVD over a USB 1.*x* connection.

✦ **MP3 players** — including my favorite, Apple's iPod, which was the first MP3 player to use a FireWire connection.

Check out Table 5-1 to see just what a dramatic lead FireWire offered in connection speed.

Table 5-1	Comparing Speeds of Popular PC Ports	
Port	*Year Appeared on PCs*	*Transfer Speed (in Megabits/ Second)*
PC serial	1981	Less than 1 Mbps
PC parallel	1981	1 Mbps
USB (version 1.1)	1996	12 Mbps
FireWire 400 (version A)	1996	400 Mbps
USB (version 2.0)	2001	480 Mbps
FireWire 800 (version B)	2003	800 Mbps

Enter USB 2.0, the current specification. This new generation of port ups the ante, delivering 480 Mbps, which handily tops the original FireWire specification, version A. It's backward compatible with older 1.1 devices, so you won't have to start all over with your USB hardware, but naturally, only those peripherals that support the USB 2.0 standard can take advantage of the warp speed increase.

Not to be outdone, a new FireWire 800 version B specification — which can pump an unbelievable 800 Mbps between your PC and an external device — began showing up on Macs in the first months of 2003. This new port now appears on a select few power-user PCs — if yours doesn't have one and you need that kind of performance, you can add a FireWire 800 port to your current machine with a port adapter card. The new version of FireWire is also backward compatible, but the connector is different; to connect a FireWire 400 device to a FireWire 800 port, you need an inexpensive go-between adapter.

1 Vote for FireWire

Even with the faster 2.0 USB specification, I'm still a FireWire kinda guy, and not just because it has a cooler name. Here's why:

✦ **Device support:** FireWire has been around since 1996 on most DV equipment, so it's a well-recognized standard. On the other hand, USB 2.0 has only been around since 2001, so don't expect to see a high-speed USB port on an older DV camcorder.

✦ **Control over connection:** Ignore the engineer-speak. Basically, this feature allows you to control your FireWire device from your PC. For example, if you have a DV camcorder with a FireWire (or *IEEE 1394,* which is the techie name for FireWire) port, you can control your camcorder from your keyboard. Just click Play within your editing software, and your camera jumps into action just as if you had pressed the Play button on the DV camcorder itself. Although USB can send a basic signal or two to the device (for instance, a command to erase an image from your digital camera), it's nowhere near as sophisticated as the control over connection possible with a FireWire connection.

✦ **Mac and PC compatibility:** Macs that are more than a couple of years old don't have USB 2.0 ports; you get USB 1.1 ports on these older Apple machines. However, every single Mac leaving Cupertino (or wherever they're manufactured) has come equipped with at least one FireWire port for four or five years now. This compatibility allows me to pull my DVD recorder from my PC and plug it right into my Mac. (I prefer life without hassles.)

"Hey, Gladys, the external USB drive isn't getting any power. And I've got it plugged in and everything!" Of course, that drive might not be plugged in to the wall socket for AC power — an easy troubleshooting task — but if you're using a USB device that's powered through the USB port itself, the problem might be more insidious. Some USB ports don't provide the full power support called for by the USB standard because they're designed only for connecting mice, keyboards, and joysticks. Therefore, try plugging that USB drive into another PC's USB port to see whether it wakes up.

Or Do You Just Need a Hub?

A technician friend of mine has a great T-shirt with the logo *Got Ports?* If your PC already has FireWire or USB ports but they're already all taken, you don't need to install an adapter card to provide your computer with additional portage. (Of course, you could eject one of those devices and unplug it each time when you want to connect your digital camera, but that probably involves turning your PC around and navigating through the nest of cables on the back.)

PC power users eschew such hassles. Instead, buy a *hub,* which is a splitter box that turns one USB or FireWire port into multiple ports. (Don't get a USB/FireWire hub confused with a network hub, which is an entirely different beast altogether.) Although using a hub fills a port, you'll gain four, six, or eight ports in the bargain (depending on the hub), and everything stays as convenient and plug-and-play as before. (Engineering that's both simple and *sassy.*)

Don't forget to check whether some of your USB/FireWire devices have daisy-chaining ports on the back that will allow you to connect another device. You can tell that a device is designed for daisy-chaining by checking whether it sports two of the same type of port (like a scanner that has two USB ports). If so, you should be able to daisy-chain additional devices. A series of daisy-chained devices will likely help you avoid buying a USB or FireWire hub because everything is still linked to one physical USB or FireWire port on the back of your PC.

By using these methods, you can theoretically plug 63 devices into one FireWire port and 127 devices into one USB port. Heck, not even James Bond can stack gadgets that high!

Installing a Port Card

Here's where the original modular design of the IBM PC (all those many, many moons ago) comes in handy. If your computer didn't come with USB 2.0 or FireWire ports, you'll find that adding new ports to your PC is as simple as plugging in an adapter card into a slot at the back of your motherboard. A typical FireWire 400/USB 2.0 combo card costs around $100 U.S. and gives you two USB and two FireWire ports. Follow these steps to do it once the right way:

1. **Cover your work surface with several sheets of newspaper.**

2. **Unplug your PC and place it on top of the newspaper.**

3. **Remove the case screws and slide the case off, putting the screws aside in a bowl or cup.**

   If you're unsure how to remove your PC's case, check the manual that accompanied your computer.

4. **To dissipate any static electricity, touch a metal surface before you handle your new adapter card or touch any circuitry inside the case.**

   Yes, I know I keep haranguing you about static electricity — but it's important. I typically touch the metal chassis of the computer.

5. **Locate an adapter card slot of the proper length at the back of your computer case.**

This should be a Peripheral Component Interconnect (PCI) slot, which is the standard adapter card connector in today's PCs.

6. **Remove the screw and the metal slot cover at the back of the case, as shown in Figure 5-1.**

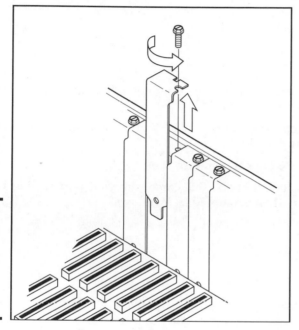

Figure 5-1: Remove the slot cover and screw before installing a new card.

Because you won't need them again, put these in your spare parts box.

7. **Pick up your port card by the top corners and line up the connector on the bottom of the card with the slot on the motherboard.**

The card's metal bracket should align with the open area created when you remove the slot cover from the back of your PC.

Never try to force a connector into a slot designed for another type of card! AGP video cards and PCI-Express video cards have different types of connectors, and they won't accept a PCI card. If you need help determining the location of your PCI card slots, check your motherboard manual.

8. **After the connector is aligned correctly (as shown in Figure 5-2), apply even pressure to the top of the card and push it down into the slot until the bracket is resting against the case.**

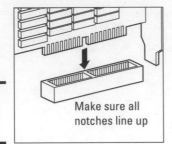

Make sure all
notches line up

Figure 5-2:
Alignment!
Alignment!

9. Place the screw in the corresponding hole in the bracket and tighten it down.

10. Place the cover back on your PC and replace the screws that you saved from Step 3.

11. Plug your PC back in and turn it on.

12. Run the installation disc that came with your port card or load the driver disc when prompted by Windows.

Chapter 6: Pumping Up Your Sound and Video

In This Chapter

✔ Selecting a sound card

✔ Upgrading your video card

✔ Installing your new toys

Technology has advanced so much that at last we've reached the point where the personal computer lives up to all that personal entertainment hoopla. You know, the idea that your PC is at the center of your gaming, audio, and TV environment. Or, as I've been putting it for the last couple of years (yet another one of Mark's Maxims):

One box to rule them all and in the den to find them.™

(Man, I love that one. That's T-shirt material.)

However, putting your PC at the center of your digital lifestyle is a bit difficult if you're still stuck with a subpar sound card, or if your computer's video card is more than a year or two old. Look at what you're missing out on: Closing your eyes and enjoying Dolby Surround sound with better-than-CD quality audio, watching TV with TiVo-style control on your PC's crystal-clear monitor, and playing games where you can behead a super-realistic, 3-D orc with extreme prejudice. This, ladies and gentlemen, is a good time to be alive!

If your system needs an audio/visual upgrade, you'll find what you need to know right here.

Sound Card Features to Covet

The first stop on your audio-visual upgrade tour is your PC's sound card (naturally). Shoppers, in this section, I show you what to look for when comparing sound cards.

3-D spatial imaging

Most PC owners think of 3-D sound as a pure gamer's feature, but nothing could be further from the truth. Sure, today's games are even more fun when you can use your ears as well as your eyes to locate your enemy, but 3-D sound comes in handy when you're listening to audio CDs or playing digital audio files from your hard drive. With audio files and music, 3-D spatial imaging can add an auditorium or concert hall effect, where the stereo separation is enhanced.

Surround sound support

With a Dolby Surround sound card and the right speakers, your PC can deliver Dolby Surround sound while you're listening to audio CDs or watching DVD movies on your PC. (For me, the biggest hassle wasn't the extra cost or upgrading my PC's sound card: It was finding the space for all five speakers around my already crowded computer desk!)

High-end Surround sound cards such as the Sound Blaster Audigy 4 from Creative Labs can deliver Dolby Digital 6.1 Surround sound, 24-bit/192 KHz audio playback (which is far superior in quality than even a commercial audio CD), and 3-D imaging for your games — and all for about $250 U.S. from most Web stores. In fact, this card even has a front panel control that you can add to an empty drive bay, so you don't have to move your PC to plug in all your speakers and other external sound hardware. Life is truly good.

Figure 6-1 illustrates an old friend to any PC audiophile: A *subwoofer* not only adds realistic, deep subsonic bass to your music but to your games as well. Whether you're experiencing the grinding of tank treads or launching a Hellfire missile, a subwoofer provides the necessary sonic punch. Most subwoofers should be placed on the floor where the vibration isn't a factor.

MP3 encoding support

Although I discuss MP3 files in detail in Book VI, Chapter 2, I want to mention them again here because anyone who's heavily into MP3 digital audio will really appreciate a sound card with built-in MP3 encoding and digital effects. That MP3 hardware feature relieves your PC's processor from the job of ripping and playing MP3 files so that you can rip music while you edit a digital photograph in Photoshop with nary a drop in performance. No stuttering audio or long delays, especially on older PCs.

Many hardware MP3 sound cards also allow you to introduce the same concert hall environmental effect that I mention earlier to the MP3 files that you create . . . now your garage band can claim to have played Carnegie Hall.

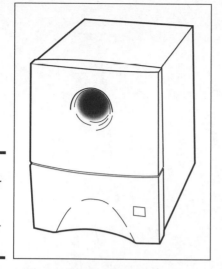

Figure 6-1:
All hail your subwoofer, King of the PC Speaker System.

Game and FireWire ports

Many sound cards are equipped with a little something extra: a FireWire port or a joystick/gamepad port like the one shown in Figure 6-2, which was once a dear friend of any PC game player (because it used to be the only way to hook up most joysticks and external game controllers). Lately, most PC controllers have switched to the Universal Serial Bus (USB) port, but it's still a plus for a sound card to include a game port. Older game peripherals — like many joysticks and flight throttles — won't work with USB, so it's a legacy thing. (Chapter 5 of this mini-book delivers the goods on FireWire.)

MIDI ports

Before I move on, I have to address musicians and their Musical Instrument Digital Interface (MIDI) ports. A sound card with standard MIDI ports allows you to connect synthesizers and many different electronic musical instruments, such as drums and keyboards, to your computer. With a MIDI instrument connected, your computer can play MIDI music files on the instrument, or you can play the instrument and record the music as a MIDI file on your computer.

Note, however, that most of today's sound cards can play MIDI music files without attaching an instrument, so it's not necessary to buy a card with built-in MIDI ports just to play MIDI music files.

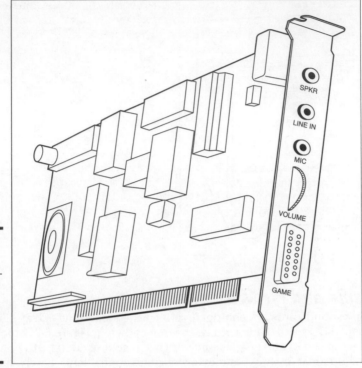

Figure 6-2: Gamers, take note — you get a free game port with most sound cards.

Shopping for a Monster Graphics Card

Having a terrific graphics card isn't all about blasting aliens to kingdom come. A fast 3-D video card can speed up the display of digital video and even Windows XP (and the upcoming Windows Vista to boot). In this section, I clue you in on what to look for when considering a video card upgrade.

Pray, what slot do you need?

Although today's video cards look like any other typical adapter cards, they actually fit in either of two types of motherboard slots:

✦ **Accelerated Graphics Port (AGP):** AGP cards for today's Athlon and Pentium computers use a dedicated AGP slot; no other adapter cards will fit into this slot. (Refer to your motherboard or PC manual to make sure that you have an AGP slot before you buy an AGP video card.) AGP video cards provide excellent performance, but they're slowly being replaced in the marketplace by PCI-Express cards.

✦ **PCI-Express:** Again, PCI-Express video cards can fit only into a dedicated PCI-Express video card slot, so check your motherboard or PC manual to make sure that your machine will accept a PCI-Express video card. However, once you install a PCI-Express video card, you'll enjoy the fastest possible video performance: if you're a hard-core gamer, I strongly recommend that any new machine you build or buy be equipped with a PCI-Express video slot!

Rate the performance of a particular card while you're shopping by checking on the box or the manufacturer's Web site for benchmark results that you can use to compare with other cards. Try the popular benchmark program 3DMark05 Pro ($20 U.S., from www.futuremark.com). You can also run Half-Life 2, Doom 3 or Unreal Tournament 2004 and compare the maximum frames-per-second that the card can display (the higher the frame rate, the better). You can also find up-to-date reviews of the latest cards and video chipsets at Tom's Hardware on the Web at www.tomshardware.com.

Exploring the differences between chipsets

Short trip. There really aren't any differences among *chipsets,* which are the separate Graphics Processing Unit (GPU) "brain" that powers today's top 3-D video cards. Allow me to explain. The two major players in the PC video card chipset battle are

✦ **NVIDIA:** The cutting-edge crew at NVIDIA (www.nvidia.com) has produced some of the fastest video cards for the PC in recent years, including the classics RIVA TNT and TNT2 as well as the GeForce series. The latest NVIDIA chipset, the NVIDIA GeForce 7, is just plain awesome. In fact, very few games or 3-D applications on today's software market can actually push a GeForce 7 series card to its limit.

✦ **ATI:** ATI Technologies (www.ati.com) has been producing popular video chipsets for a decade now, including its Rage line. Typically, ATI video cards are somewhat cheaper than NVIDIA cards, and many motherboard manufacturers build ATI video hardware directly onto their products. Lately, ATI's new Radeon X850-series chipset has been a big winner with performance that even tops the latest GeForce 7 cards.

And here's the payoff for you, the consumer — the latest offerings from *either* of these companies will deliver more performance than PC gamers are likely to need for at least a year. In fact, I've been told recently by my friends at NVIDIA that they're appealing directly to the PC game development community, attempting to help develop games that actually use all the hardware power featured on the cards. (Ahh, for once . . . hardware that doesn't suddenly turn outdated in six months. *Sassy.*)

Other video card features that you'll want

Naturally, you can evaluate more than just chipsets and connectors when comparing video cards. Keep an eye out for these features and specifications while you shop.

✦ **Onboard random access memory (RAM):** Like your motherboard, your video card carries its own supply of memory. Today's cards typically include anywhere from 64–512MB of memory. Again, the general rule is to buy a card with as much onboard RAM as possible. More RAM equals higher resolutions with more colors onscreen.

✦ **Driver and standards support:** Any PC video card should fully support the Microsoft DirectX video standards — currently at DirectX 9.0. Gamers will also appreciate robust *OpenGL* support (an open video standard that's becoming very popular in 3-D action games). Support for these standards should be listed on the box.

✦ **Maximum resolution:** The higher the resolution that a card can produce, the more that your monitor can display at once — and not just in games, but documents, digital photographs, and your Windows desktop. For example, I like to write manuscripts at a resolution of 1152 x 864 instead of 1024 x 768 because I can see more of the page in Microsoft Word without scrolling. Today's cards can reach truly epic resolutions, such as 2048 x 1536; personally, however, I don't work at such stratospheric resolutions often because a few hours of work usually leaves me with eyestrain (and possibly a headache as well).

The maximum resolution that you can display on your system is also dependent upon the monitor that you're using. Therefore, if you upgrade to the latest video card but you're still using an old clunker of a monitor with a maximum resolution of 1024 x 768, you're stuck there. (Time to invest in a new display.) For more about your monitor, see Book I, Chapter 1.

✦ **Video capture and TV output:** A card with these features can create digital video footage from an analog TV signal (that's the *video capture* part) and transfer the image that you see on your monitor to a TV, VCR, or camcorder (that's the *TV output* part). If you need to produce a VHS tape with images from your PC, or if you want to create video CDs or DVDs from your home movies on VHS tape, spend a little extra on a video capture/TV output card.

✦ **TV tuner:** A card with a built-in TV tuner can actually turn your PC into a TV set, including the ability to pause and replay programs on the fly (like how a TiVo unit works with a regular TV). You can use a traditional antenna or connect the card to your cable or satellite system. Just don't let your boss know that the new video card that the company bought gives you the ability to watch your favorite soaps in a window on your desktop . . . you're supposed to be working.

✦ **Multiple monitor support:** Many of today's video cards allow you to connect two monitors to one card. You can either choose to see two separate desktops, or you can opt to make the two monitors into a seamless desktop. Imagine the size of your Windows workspace when it's spread across two displays!

✦ **MPEG hardware support:** Finally, I come to digital video — which, as you can read about in earlier chapters of this book, is typically stored in MPEG, AVI, or MOV formats, with the most popular being the MPEG format. Without the *compression* that these video formats offer (which shrinks the digital video file in size), you'd never get a full-length movie on a single DVD. Although your PC can use software to *encode* (create a compressed MPEG file) and *decode* (read a compressed MPEG file) MPEG files on your hard drive or a DVD, a video card with built-in encoding and decoding features can really speed up the process. This hardware support is particularly valuable if you're going to do serious video editing on your PC because you'll cut down the amount of time required to save your movies to disk.

Installing Sound and Video Cards

Installing a sound card or video card is much like adding any other adapter card to your PC. If you're installing a sound card, make sure that you connect the audio cable from your CD-ROM/DVD-ROM drive (Step 5); if you're installing a video card, make sure that you pick the right AGP or PCI-Express slot (Step 7).

Follow these steps:

1. **Cover your work surface with several sheets of newspaper.**

2. **Unplug your PC and place it on top of the newspaper.**

3. **Remove the screws on the back of the case and slide the case off, saving the screws for later.**

4. **To dissipate static electricity, touch a metal surface before handling any cards or touching your PC's motherboard.**

   For example, touch the PC's metal chassis — I shudder to think of what I'll do if anyone develops a fiberglass computer.

5. **If you're installing a new sound card, check for a thin audio cable connected from your old sound card to your CD-ROM or DVD-ROM drive; if so, disconnect the cable from the old sound card.**

6. **Remove the screw holding the adapter card that you're upgrading and pull upward to remove it.**

Don't forget to put the screw in your spare parts box and put the old adapter card in an anti-static bag for safekeeping. (I use the bag left behind by the new card.)

Some AGP card slots have plastic tabs that act as a locking mechanism. Just bend the tab gently with your finger, and you should be able to remove the existing AGP card.

7. **Locate the adapter card slot that matches the card that you're installing.**

An AGP video card can fit only in a dedicated AGP slot — likewise, a PCI-Express video adapter requires a dedicated PCI-Express 16 slot. On the other hand, a standard PCI sound card should fit in any open PCI slot. Naturally, if the upgrade card uses the same type of slot as the card that it's replacing, use the empty slot that you've just opened up.

8. **Pick up the adapter card by the top corners and line up the bottom connector on the card with the slot on the motherboard, making sure that the card's metal bracket aligns properly with the opening in the back of the PC.**

9. **After the card is aligned, apply even pressure to the top of the card and push it down into the slot.**

10. **Place the screw in the corresponding hole in the bracket and tighten it down.**

11. **If you're installing a sound card and you disconnected a CD-ROM/ DVD-ROM audio cable from the old card, reconnect the cable from your drive to the new card.**

Check the manual for the card to determine where the CD/DVD audio connector is located; this is a standard connector, so it should be easy to track down.

12. **Place the cover back on your PC and replace the screws that you saved from Step 3.**

13. **Plug your PC back in and turn it on.**

14. **Run the installation disc that came with your upgrade card or load the driver disc when prompted by Windows.**

Book VIII

Home Networking

"Quick Kids! Your mother's flaming someone on the Internet!"

Contents at a Glance

Chapter 1: Do I Really Need a Network?

In This Chapter

✔ Evaluating the advantages of a network

✔ Connecting to other computers and devices

✔ Selecting networking hardware and software that you might need

Networking is neat stuff: The ability to copy or edit a document that's on another computer halfway down the hall is invaluable, whether that hallway is in a business or your own home. (Even a home office like mine, where six computers are constantly vying for my attention in the same room, benefits from a network. Although they're only a few feet apart, moving 4GB worth of data between them would be no small feat without a common network connection.)

However, not everyone with multiple computers actually *needs* a network — and that's what this introductory chapter will help you determine. Here, I cover what a network can do for you, what hardware and software you'll need, and how much work will be involved. Later chapters in this mini-book will fill in the blanks, but after you read this introduction, you'll know whether a network is worth your effort.

Discovering the Advantages of a Network

If you've never used a network to link multiple computers, you might not realize what applications are network ready. Here's a quick list of the most common uses for a network.

File transfer

There's no faster method of moving files between computers than a network connection. And network file transfers are *transparent* to the person making the transfer, meaning that you don't have to do anything special to transfer files between computers on a network. You can just drag and drop files as usual or use your favorite file management application to copy or move files between computers on the network, and Windows acts like you'd expect. I like the Total Commander file management tool, as shown in Figure 1-1. To try out this great piece of shareware, visit www.ghisler.com. With Total Commander, it's a cinch to compare the contents of two different drives or folders, and the list display format can pack the maximum number of file names possible onto your monitor. Copying or moving files 'twixt the panes is as simple as selecting and clicking a button.

However, you certainly don't want just *anyone* transferring files to and from your PC — or, for that matter, even accessing your PC over the network at all. To help preserve security, Windows XP makes certain that only the users and PCs with the proper rights can transfer files over your network.

Sharing that there Internet

Another popular networking advantage is the ability for one computer to share a single Internet connection with all the other computers on a network. Typically, this works best with a broadband connection technology like a digital subscriber line (DSL) or cable, but it's possible with a dialup connection as well.

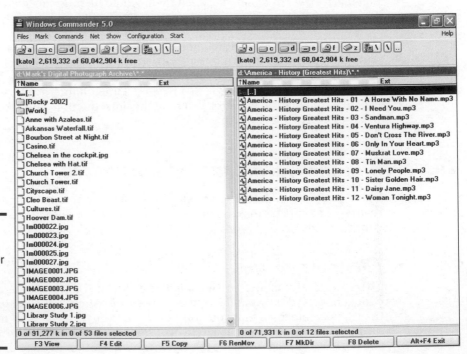

Figure 1-1:
I use Total Commander to quickly and easily manage files on my network.

The two methods of sharing a connection are

✦ **Through software:** You can use the built-in Internet Sharing within Windows XP.

✦ **Through hardware:** You can add an Internet sharing device (such as a network hub or switch), which usually comes with other features such as a built-in firewall.

I cover both of these methods later in Chapter 4 of this mini-book.

One word: Games!

What's that you're saying, bunkie? You're tired of predictable computer opponents in your favorite games? Hordes of zombies in Half-Life 2 that you can handle in your sleep? How about timid enemy monsters that won't attack you or ambush your character in Microsoft's Impossible Creatures (as shown in Figure 1-2)?

Figure 1-2: A favorite multiplayer network game of mine, Impossible Creatures.

Well, forget those lazy tactics because in network *multiplayer mode,* you'll be fighting real human beings — the treacherous, backstabbing kind (which, oddly enough, usually turn out to be your best friends). I try to attend *LAN parties* whenever possible — that's the term for a get-together where multiplayer games are the featured attraction. Your host might have all the PCs and network hardware necessary for 8 or 16 people, but I usually bring my desktop or laptop computer so that I can sit down and plug in with a minimum of effort.

Shared documents and applications

Of course, a document that's handed from person to person on a floppy disk is technically shared, but is that really a convenient method of working on a document together? (To this day, PC hardware technicians and software developers call this kind of floppy-based transfer a *sneakernet.*) Anyway, forget wearing out your shoe leather just to hand off a document for the next person's comments — today's office workgroup relies on the company network to share documents and common applications, the *right* way!

After you network your computers, any PC on your network can copy or open a document on another computer *if* the owner of the PC being accessed has been granted the proper rights to that file or to the folder where it's stored. For example, if you have a Word document that others need to edit but you'd like to keep it on your hard drive, you can move that document to a shared folder. Others on the network can open the document within Word from their computers, just as if it were on their local machine.

And if that's not *sassy* enough, consider the fact that Bob over in accounting (or your daughter in her bedroom) might be using an application that you don't have. If that application has been written for network use, you can run it on your computer remotely over the network! Such a program is a *shared application,* and I think that they're the neatest things since sliced cheese.

Read the details on both shared documents and shared applications in the next chapter of this mini-book.

What Can I Connect To?

A surprising number of objects on the planet have network ports or wireless network cards. Here's a list of the network-savvy stuff that I've used in the past:

✦ **Other PCs:** The most common connection on a Windows network is to other PCs — some of which are standard desktop and notebook PCs, and others are specialized network *servers* that perform only one task (like a *file server,* which is used like a mega-hard drive that everyone on the network can access).

✦ **Macintosh and Linux computers:** Your network need not be a snobby Windows-only country club; invite the neighbors to join in! Macs running Mac OS X Tiger or later can plug right in, as can those Linux folks with the beards and suspenders. Of course, you won't be able to run a Mac program on a PC, but — and this is a winner — many applications are available in versions for both operating systems, and they can share the same document! The best example is Microsoft Office, which is available in both Mac and PC versions. Word and Excel on both operating systems can open and edit the same Office documents.

Speaking of Mac OS X Tiger, I'm also the proud father of the *Mac OS X Tiger All-in-One Desk Reference For Dummies* (by Wiley Publishing, Inc.). And, yes, I really do own both PCs and Macs, and I take advantage of what both operating systems have to offer on my same office network. Anyway, if you find this tome helpful and you know a Mac owner who's using Tiger, please drop 'em a line and recommend the MOSXTAIODRFD! (Now how's *that* for an abbreviation?)

✦ **Personal digital assistants (PDAs):** With the right adapter, your Palm Pilot or Pocket PC can join in the fun.

✦ **Shared network hardware:** Some shared hardware actually resides within a PC on the network (like an internal hard drive or CD-ROM drive that you've selected to be "visible" and accessible on the network), and other network hardware works as standalone units (like an Internet sharing device, which is a box by itself).

✦ **Network printers:** Finally, a shared network printer can be connected to a PC on the network. Or, if you have enough pocket change, you can buy a standalone network printer that actually has its own network card.

Of course, this list is incomplete because it's constantly growing, but suffice it to say that a network usually includes more than just a smattering of desktop and laptop PCs.

What Hardware Do I Need?

The hardware basics that you'll need for a simple network include

✦ **A network adapter card or PC card:** Each computer on your network will require either a network adapter card (for desktops) or a PC card (for a laptop). These cards can accept either a wired connection or a

**Book VIII
Chapter 1**

**Do I Really Need a
Network?**

wireless connection. Naturally, if your desktop or laptop has wired and/ or wireless hardware built-in, you don't need to add a card — instead, smile quietly to yourself in a contented and smug manner.

✦ **A network hub or switch:** I describe these black boxes in depth in the next chapter of this mini-book. For now, I'll just say that they allow you to connect multiple computers onto the same network. Some hubs and switches are wireless, so no cables are necessary.

✦ **Cabling:** If you're not going the wireless route, you need an Ethernet cable for each computer that you add to the network. Again, more on this in the next chapter of this mini-book.

The hardware that I list here would be used in a standard Ethernet network, but remember that other types of network technologies might use your home's AC wiring or telephone jacks (which I cover in Chapter 3 of this mini-book). You can also network two computers by using special Universal Serial Bus (USB) and FireWire cables, but these are no substitute for the convenience and compatibility of an Ethernet network; they're simply for transferring files in a single session.

You might be able to pick up all these hardware toys in a single box — *a network kit* — which is a great choice for a home or small office network with four or fewer PCs. (Plus the documentation is typically pretty well written.)

What Software Do 1 Need?

Actually, if each of your PCs will be running any version of Windows 98 or later, you have all the operating system software that you need for a home network. (Thanks, Microsoft!) However, you might also need

✦ **Drivers for your network adapter card or PC card:** The manufacturer of your network card will provide you with the drivers that Windows will need during installation, but don't forget to check the manufacturer's Web site for updated drivers.

✦ **Network management software:** Although not necessary for a simple network, the administrator of a larger network (I consider a network of ten or more computers to be a larger network) will likely buy extra software to monitor network traffic and optimize network hardware.

✦ **Network-ready applications:** As I mention earlier in this chapter, network applications might include productivity suites (such as Office), fax software, and workgroup applications (such as Lotus Notes) that provide a common calendar and e-mail system.

To Network or Not to Network . . .

So that's the scoop. If you have more than one desktop within your home or office and you need to share files, applications, and an Internet connection between them on a regular basis, you can buy a network kit for $75 U.S. to $100 U.S. that comes complete with everything that you need.

If, on the other hand, you have only two computers and you don't exchange information very often between them (or if you don't need to share an Internet connection), you might consider a simple USB or FireWire transfer cable.

(I think you know which course of action I usually recommend. After all, look at the rest of this mini-book!)

**Book VIII
Chapter 1**

**Do I Really Need a
Network?**

Chapter 2: Ethernet to the Rescue

In This Chapter

- ✔ Understanding how Ethernet works
- ✔ Gathering the various pieces o' hardware
- ✔ Configuring XP for your network
- ✔ Putting shared folders to work
- ✔ Configuring a network printer
- ✔ Connecting a switch to the Internet
- ✔ Troubleshooting your network

This is it, my friend: the chapter with the bravado and the chutzpah to actually show you how to set up a home or small office network in Windows XP! Setting up a network gives you many advantages, including saving money by sharing resources (such as printers and an Internet connection) and the added convenience of file sharing.

You'll find that a *working* network — note that I stress the word *working* — quickly becomes as essential as Tabasco sauce (or insert name of your favorite condiment here). By the way, if you find that word *working* to be more elusive than you first expected, I include a section at the end of this chapter that highlights common problems experienced by folks running their own network . . . as well as several possible solutions for each, of course.

After your network is purring as smoothly as the proverbial kitten, you'll walk proudly to the closest person on the planet and proclaim proudly, "I am . . . a *network administrator!*" (Feel free to throw confetti or have a T-shirt made. If you like, send me an e-mail message at mark@mlcbooks.com — use the subject line "Ohmygoodnessitworks" — and we can celebrate together.)

A Quickie Ethernet Primer

No, don't close the book! Of all the supposed techno-wizard technologies connected with PCs, Ethernet networking is the easiest to master. Windows XP has come a long way in taming the home networking beast. Sure, you used to need a gold medal in the Tech Olympics to install a small home network, but that was in the days of DOS and Windows 3.1. We've come a long way, baby.

In fact, Ethernet has been around since the days of stone-tipped spears. As the first widely used network structure, it's still the most popular structure for homes and offices with around 25 PCs or less. Sure, faster networking designs exist these days, but old faithful Ethernet is also the cheapest to set up and maintain, and it's directly supported within all flavors of Windows.

So how does Ethernet work? Surprisingly, it's much like ham radio. A PC that wants to share data (as in moving or copying a file, or sending and receiving stuff from the Internet) actually broadcasts that data across the network cabling in discrete bursts called *packets*. Each packet is marked with an address — much like how an e-mail message always has a To address — of the receiving computer.

When the PC with the matching address receives the packet across the network (along with tons of other packets bound for other locations), it processes it; other computers simply ignore any packets that aren't addressed to them. Figure 2-1 represents an Ethernet network at its best.

Figure 2-1: The basics of an Ethernet network.

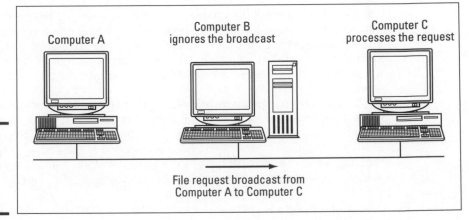

Computer A

Computer B
ignores the broadcast

Computer C
processes the request

File request broadcast from
Computer A to Computer C

This sounds just nifty, but here's the catch: If two computers on your network try to broadcast packets at the same time, a network *collision* occurs, and everything stops until one computer successfully gets its data across the network. Collisions slow down the transfer of data, and that's why Ethernet networks are slower than other types of networks. (Of course, you'll see far fewer conflicts with fewer machines, so if you have only four PCs on your network, you'll typically get great performance. It's only when 25 PCs are all trying to talk to each other at once that conflicts start slowing things down dramatically.)

The first step when installing a small network is to create a chart that lists which computers need to be connected and where they are, plus the approximate distances between all the players. Because of the limitations on the size of this chapter, I can't provide you with a complete discussion of how to plan the cabling for your network — that's a book in itself. In fact, that book is *Home Networking For Dummies,* written by Kathy Ivens and published by Wiley Publishing, Inc., which expands on all the basics that I mention in this chapter.

Hardware That You'll Need

Another advantage of Ethernet networks is their simplicity. You won't need a degree in Advanced Thakamology to install your network, and you can put four PCs in a simple Ethernet network for under $75 U.S. if you buy a kit.

In this section, I discuss the basic hardware requirements of any small Ethernet network.

Cables

In books that I've written that cover Ethernet networking, I discuss two different kinds of cabling that connect computer to computer (or connect a computer to a network device):

✦ **Coaxial (coax) cable:** This is the same type of cable used to connect your TV to your cable box. Coax is thick stuff and not easily routed or hidden. Also, each end of a coax Ethernet network must have a terminator to mark the end of the network circuit, which is a hassle (a small one, granted, but a hassle nonetheless).

✦ **Twisted pair cable:** Twisted pair cable looks almost exactly like telephone wire or the cable that runs between your PC's dialup modem and the telephone wall jack. It's easier to hide and much easier to route. (Figure 2-2 illustrates the connector — an RJ-45 connector — for a twisted pair cable.) The one downside to using a twisted pair Ethernet network is that you need a device called a *hub* (or its improved sibling, a *switch*) which acts as a central connection point. (See how it's used in Figure 2-3.) However, switches are cheap these days, and twisted pair cabling is much cheaper overall than coaxial cable.

**Book VIII
Chapter 2**

**Ethernet to the
Rescue**

Figure 2-2:
Most
network
techs think
this RJ-45
connector
is rather
attractive.

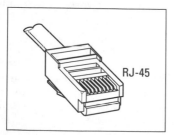

RJ-45

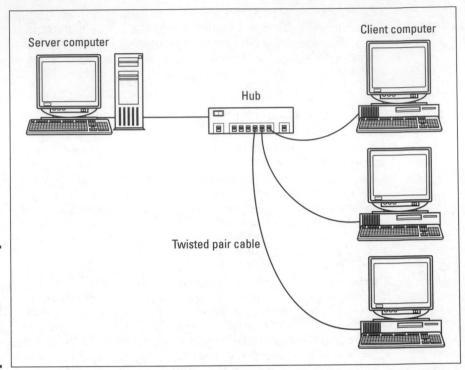

Client computer

Server computer

Hub

Twisted pair cable

Figure 2-3:
The hands-
down
favorite — a
twisted pair
Ethernet
network.

I used to cover coax cabling, but in this book, I cover only twisted pair cabling. It's by far the cheapest and the easiest to install, which makes it the most popular standard . . . and that explains why Ethernet networks that use coaxial cabling are rapidly disappearing from the face of the globe. In fact, you'll have to go out of your way to find a late-model network interface card (NIC) that has a coax connector on it. (As the MCP said so eloquently in the classic movie *Tron,* "End of line.")

If you'd rather eschew cables altogether — well, almost altogether — consider a wireless network. Although it's a bit slower, you'll have freedom of movement undreamed of by the wired crowd. (Plus, alternate wired networks can use your home or office's existing telephone or AC power lines. No, really!) I cover all these marvels of wireless (or almost wireless) networking in Chapter 3 of this mini-book.

Hubs

As I mention earlier, a *hub* is essentially just an overgrown connection box, linking (via cabling) each computer on your network to all the other network computers and peripherals (like a printer). However, you need at least a hub for a twisted pair network.

Hubs have been virtually replaced these days by switches. (Think of a switch as an improved hub that allows for faster and more efficient network transfers... there, you're an expert.) I'll delve into switches a little more in a page or two, but I thought I'd mention a hub in case you run across one whilst scavenging, or encounter one on eBay.

NICs

You need a *network interface card* (NIC) for each computer on your network. If your desktop or laptop PC doesn't have a built-in NIC, an internal adapter card is probably the best choice, but installing a NIC doesn't necessarily have to involve opening your PCs case. You can get a Personal Computer Memory Card International Association (PCMCIA; or PC Card) NIC for your laptop, and other network adapters can be connected through a Universal Serial Bus (USB) port. However, you probably won't actually need to buy a separate NIC for your PC because most PCs now include a built-in network connector. (Check your PC's manual or look for a port labeled *Ethernet 10/100* or *Network* on the back of the computer.)

NICs are rated by the speed of the network. Most home networks will use a *10/100 NIC* (meaning that your network can operate at either 10 Mbps or 100 Mbps), which will set you back about $30 to $40 U.S. The third speed, called *Gigabit Ethernet,* runs at a whopping 1000 Mbps, but you probably won't need such throughput. (Gigabit hardware is also as expensive as a meeting with a good lawyer, which is another reason why it's not a big hit with the home networking crowd.)

When shopping for your card, check the manufacturer's Web site and verify what drivers that the card uses. The card should support Windows 98, NT, 2000, and XP. (For me, the value of a NIC is in direct proportion to its compatibility.) Also, check how often those drivers are updated; two-year-old drivers are not a good sign. In general, most manufacturers display certification statements (both on the box and on the company's Web site) that guarantee that a NIC will work with specific operating systems.

Switches

A *switch* is kind of like a super-hub. In fact, a switch looks like a slightly bigger hub, but it's about as visually interesting as a shoebox. (There's not much need to include a picture of a hub in this chapter. Imagine the most boring, nondescript box that you can, add a few lights and several RJ-45 jacks, and you've got a switch.) On the inside, however, a switch is a mighty leap in performance because a switch prevents those dastardly collisions that I discuss earlier in this chapter. In effect, a switch narrows the broadcast of a packet to only the PC that needs it, so it's much more intelligent than a simple hub.

A switch now costs the same as a hub once did, meaning they're relatively cheap — how much you'll pay depends upon how many ports that the switch provides, ranging from about $50 to about $300 U.S.

Doing the Cable Dance

You have far fewer hassles when installing a twisted pair network as opposed to a coaxial network, as I mention earlier in this chapter. But even considering that the cables are easier to handle, I still have a number of time-tested recommendations that I can make from experience:

✦ **Always draft someone to help.** If you're wiring a small office, enlist the help of a steadfast friend (as a gopher, general cable handyperson, and sympathetic ear).

✦ **Always buy pre-made cables!** Building a cable yourself is like cutting a diamond yourself — it can be done, but you'd better be experienced or you'll ruin a perfectly good . . . well . . . length of cable. Plus, first-timers can very easily create a cable that appears to be correct but doesn't work or that introduces all sorts of spurious problems later on that will be practically impossible to track down. (Can you say *electrical short?* I knew you could.) Instead, do what I do (and everyone else who's already built one or two small networks does as well). Walk into your local computer store or online Web shop and buy pre-made cables in the lengths that you need.

✦ **Always buy extra cables.** Having a few spares never hurts. Hey, they're cheap. And buying cables that are at least a foot or two longer than what you think you're going to need is a wise idea.

✦ **Always test a cable before installing it.** Of course, you can buy a twisted pair cable tester (usually called a *remote cable tester*), but for those with a life other than networking, simply connect the cable between your switch and a laptop to check it.

✦ **Always consider pets!** Does Fluffy spend time in your home office unattended? Then prepare for the likelihood of chewed network cabling. (This can *really* test the relationship between pet and person.) To avoid such moments, use cable ties and anchors to run your Ethernet cabling underneath desktops and above the floor level whenever possible.

✦ **Always avoid exposed cable.** Make sure that your cables are well out of reach of clumsy feet. Also, never cover a cable with tape or a rug where it can become a victim of foot traffic. The stress on the connectors and the wear from contact will destroy even the best cable over time and will likely result in eventual network errors.

Don't forget that your switch is a powered device, so it needs to be located close to an AC outlet.

Configuring Windows XP for Your Network

After the NICs have been installed, the cabling is in place, and everything's plugged in, you're ready to flip that big Frankenstein-style leaf switch and start networking — and that's done from within Windows XP. In this section, I discuss what every home "network administrator" should know.

Ah, sweet DHCP

You know, very few acronyms in the computer world make me genuinely smile every time that I see them. There's BBS *(Bulletin Board System)*, of course. TWAIN (which most people think means *technology without an interesting name*) isn't actually an acronym at all! It refers to a poem by Kipling . . . you know, "and never the twain shall meet." (It's not often that I get to quote Kipling.) But in networking, folks hold a fond spot in their hearts for DHCP, which stands for *Dynamic Host Configuration Protocol.*

What's so uplifting about a networking standard? It's the *Dynamic* part. You see, DHCP was developed to automatically assign Internet Protocol (IP) addresses to the computers on your network. A computer's *IP address* is that address that I mention at the beginning of the chapter: It's a unique number that identifies that particular PC on the network.

In days of yore, whoever set up a network had to keep track of which IP addresses were assigned to which computers. If a number were assigned twice, all hell broke loose (at least on those two machines). A device with DHCP — such as an Internet sharing device or a PC that's acting as an Internet connection server — automatically assigns a number whenever needed.

If you're already using an Internet sharing device (such as a cable modem or digital subscriber line [DSL] Internet router that has DHCP built in) or a switch with DHCP built in and a connection port for your modem, you need to follow the steps provided in that device's manual. That's because you don't need a PC to act as the DHCP host for your network. I cover Internet connection sharing in Chapter 4 of this mini-book.

Setting up the host

To set up a network under Windows XP by using DHCP and a shared Internet connection — where your dialup modem or DSL/cable modem connects directly to the PC — you need to run the Network Setup Wizard on that PC. (That lucky computer becomes your Internet host, providing the DHCP functionality for your network.)

Remember: If your host PC is currently using a NIC to connect to a DSL or cable modem (as most do) and the switch *won't* accept a direct connection to your modem, **you need a second NIC installed in that computer** so that

**Book VIII
Chapter 2**

Ethernet to the Rescue

you can connect it to the switch! (Take a break and read the section titled, "Using a Standard Switch with a Cable or DSL Modem" toward the end of this chapter before you proceed any farther. Things get explained there.)

Ready to go? Follow these steps:

1. **Choose Start⇨All Programs⇨Accessories⇨Communications⇨Network Setup Wizard, which displays the wizard welcome screen.**

2. **Take a moment to connect to the Internet (if you're not using a broadband always-on connection) and then click Next to continue.**

   The wizard displays a checklist screen to make sure that all hardware has been installed, connected, and turned on. ("Now, Rochester, have you installed the network hardware like I asked?")

3. **Click Next to get with the program.**

   The next wizard screen (as shown in Figure 2-4) prompts you for the configuration that you're using to connect to the Internet.

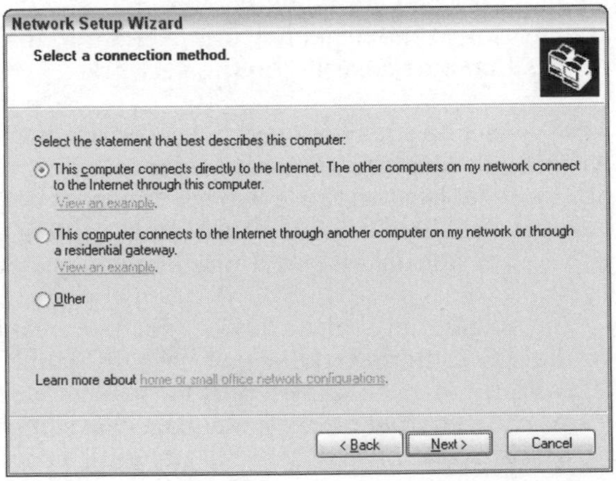

Figure 2-4: Select your Internet connection configuration here.

4. **In this case, you should select the This Computer Connects Directly to the Internet radio button and then click Next to continue.**

5. **The wizard prompts you to select the network adapter that's supporting your Internet connection (or, if you're using a dialup modem, the modem itself) — and the program takes the best shot at what it thinks is the likely choice (see Figure 2-5). After you make your choice, click Next to continue.**

   Note that if your PC has FireWire (IEEE 1394) ports, these are also listed because you can set up a FireWire network with the right hardware and cabling.

Figure 2-5:
Choose your
connection,
pardner!

6. **Type a description and name for the host PC (as shown in Figure 2-6) and then click Next to continue.**

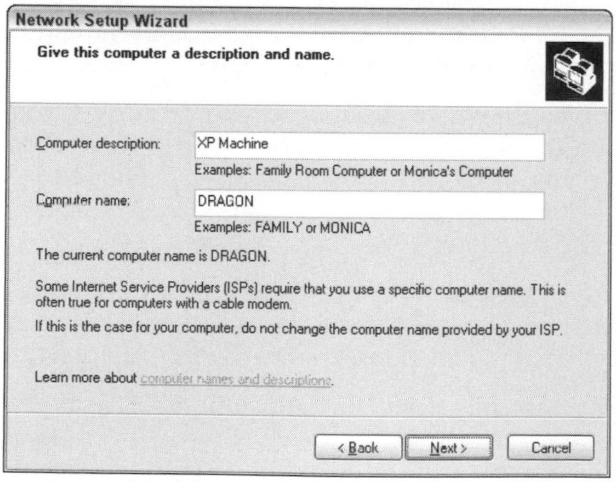

Figure 2-6:
Your new
network
host needs
a name.

If your Internet service provider (ISP) requires a specific computer name, use that here. Check your ISP's documentation to make sure.

7. **Name your network (or, in Microsoft-speak, your *workgroup*) and then click Next to continue.**

I recommend that you enter something unique. Jot down this name because it will be important later on.

Let's do this! The wizard displays a screen with your settings so that you can verify the proceedings.

8. **Click Next and sit back while Windows XP works its magic.**

9. **As a final step, the wizard offers you the chance to create a network setup disk (suitable for client PCs that aren't running XP).**

   a. **If you choose to create the disk, you need a single, blank floppy disk handy, and then select Create a Network Setup Disk.**

   b. **Otherwise, just select the Just Finish the Wizard option and then click Next to continue.**

10. **Click Finish to exit the wizard.**

Setting up the clients

After the host has been configured, it's ready to accept connections from the other computers on your network. However, you also have to configure each of those PCs as network clients. Yep, that's where the buzzphrase *client/server* comes from. The good news is that you'll be using your friend the Network Setup Wizard again, and the process is pretty similar.

Again, make sure that the host computer is connected to the Internet and then follow these steps on each PC running Windows XP that needs to join the network crowd:

1. **Choose Start⇨All Programs⇨Accessories⇨Communications⇨Network Setup Wizard to start the wizard and then click Next to continue.**

   If the client PC is running an older version of Windows, you can load the Network Setup Disk that you created on the host PC at the end of the previous procedure. Open Windows Explorer, navigate to the floppy disk, double-click NETSETUP.EXE to start things going, and then follow the onscreen instructions.

   You're graced with the same doggone Before You Continue screen, warning you of dire consequences if you haven't connected everything, turned everything on, and connected to the Internet via the host PC.

2. **Because you've already done all that, smile quietly to yourself and then click Next.**

3. **Select the network adapter that's going to connect this client PC to your network and then click Next to continue.**

   Because most client PCs have only one Ethernet adapter, this should be a cinch, and the wizard should already have the correct choice selected.

4. **Time to choose a network description and name for this client PC, like you did for the host. When you're done, click Next to continue.**

5. **Here's where you need to enter the workgroup name that you chose for the host PC (see Step 7 in the previous section). Make sure that it's spelled exactly the same and then click Next to continue.**

   The wizard again displays the settings verification screen.

6. **Click Next to make XP configure your client machine.**

7. **Select the Just Finish the Wizard option and then click Next to continue.**

8. **Click Finish to exit the wizard and have Windows XP reboot your client PC.**

   When it completes the boot process, the added client PC should be a member of your network family.

Browsing the neighborhood

After you set up your network, you can easily see which other PCs are available. Windows XP power users call this activity *browsing* your network, where you saunter around, admiring what's connected. Choose Start➪My Network Places and then click View Workgroup Computers to display each of the PCs in your networked surroundings (as shown in Figure 2-7).

Whoops! I can hear all sorts of irate Windows XP faithful growling in irritation. "What's that in your My Network Places window? Is that a . . . (gasp) *Macintosh* that I see there?" That's right. As long as other computers conform to standard Ethernet protocols and they've been recognized by the host PC (or DHCP device), they'll show up as well. (This includes PCs running Linux, Macs running Mac OS 9 or Mac OS X, and UNIX machines.)

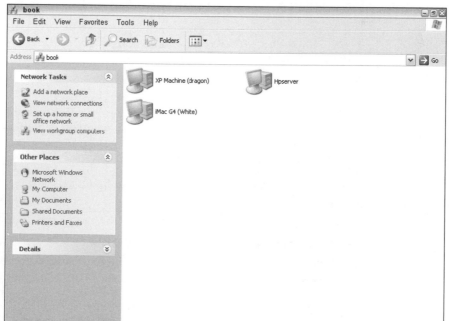

Figure 2-7: The Windows XP My Network Places window.

"Wait! Where's Boopsie?" Well, if the client PC that you named *Boopsie* has been turned on *after* you opened the My Network Places window, it won't show up. To see it, choose View⇨Refresh, which will rescan the network and update the window's contents. (And whatever moved you to name a PC *Boopsie,* anyway?)

To display which folders and devices are available on each computer, simply double-click the computer icon to open it up. Note that you might be greeted by a login dialog box, like the one that you see in Figure 2-8; I get this because I've set up my iMac as a secure system, and I have to supply my username and password to my Mac OS X account. (If you set up your clients with the procedure above, you shouldn't require a login to access their stuff . . . unless, of course, that computer's user has specifically configured Windows XP to require a login.)

Figure 2-8:
A closed
system
requires a
password.

Windows XP automatically adds shared folders and printers and displays them in the My Network Places window. However, you can also manually add a new location to your My Network Places window. Display the taskbar (if necessary) and click Add a Network Place to run the Network Place Wizard, which will guide you through the steps. Or, you can simply create a shortcut by dragging a network folder or URL address to the My Network Places window.

Sharing folders and documents

"So, Mark, what, precisely, controls what I can and can't see when browsing the network?" Now you've entered The Sharing Zone, where time and space have no meaning. What *does* matter are the shared files and folders that you've set up on each computer in your network.

Sharing something across the network allows other computers to see it when browsing. (Note that network sharing is very different from sharing a local file among users of the same PC, which I cover in Book II, Chapter 4.)

By default, Windows XP takes the safe and conservative approach: Nothing is shared across a network until specifically set. (To be honest, I like it that way instead of defaulting to a completely open machine.) However, you can share a folder and all its contents by following these steps:

1. **Double-click My Computer (the icon on your desktop) to open the Explorer window; then navigate to the folder's location.**

2. **Right-click the folder and then choose Sharing and Security from the pop-up menu that appears to display the settings that you see in Figure 2-9.**

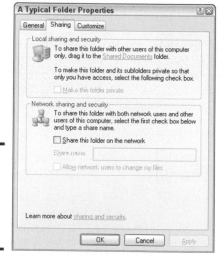

Figure 2-9:
Mark a folder as a shared network folder here.

3. **Select the Share This Folder on the Network check box to enable it.**

   Windows XP provides a default share name based on the folder name, but you can type a new name if you like (less than 24 characters, please). I usually add the PC's network name so that I know which Really Important Cool Stuff folder I'm actually looking at. The share name must be 12 characters or less for PCs running Windows 98/Me/NT that need to access the folder. Also, periods and exclamation points are allowed in the share name.

4. **Decide whether you want anyone on the network to be able to edit, delete, or rename the files in this folder.**

If so, mark the Allow Network Users to Change My Files check box to enable it. If this check box remains disabled, others can open any documents or files in this folder, but they can't make changes. (To do that, they must copy the file to their own computer and edit their local copy.)

5. **Click OK to close the dialog box.**

You'll note that the icon for a shared folder is different from a standard folder. Windows tacks on an open hand, so it's easy to tell which folders on your system are shared.

You can also share a drive in the same fashion, but Windows XP cautions against it — and so do I. It's much better to assign just one shared folder on your drive.

When you share a folder, you place everything in that folder on the network. Therefore, if there's even one item (either a document or a subfolder) that you don't want to distribute with others inside a folder, **do not share that folder!**

After a folder is share enabled, its contents can be opened, moved, or copied either from Windows Explorer or from the File Open/Save/Browse dialog boxes that are common throughout XP and your applications. (This assumes that the client user has the proper access level, as you can discover in the previous procedure.) That's the neat thing: Everything works normally across the network by using the same functionality that I cover in Book II.

Printing across the Network

Although sharing an Internet connection is one of the prime advantages of using a network these days, one other resource has been shared across networks now for decades: the network printer. (Read all about Internet connection sharing in Chapter 4 of this mini-book.) And any printer connected to any PC on your network can be used by any other PC, which is a real boon when your office has only one large-format inkjet and only one color laser printer.

You can follow one of four avenues for network printing:

✦ **Hook up the printer to a PC so that it acts as a printer server.** As long as the printer only receives moderate use and it's in an open area, this option can work. (If the PC is in a private office, don't even think about it. You'll drive the occupant smackers.)

✦ **Set up a separate PC as a simple print server.** This is the traditional solution for high-traffic printers that need a central location. The client PC is basically just a doorman, existing only to queue print jobs for the connected printer. Expensive, but efficient.

✦ **Buy a network printer box.** These standalone devices are essentially Ethernet cards with a slightly more intelligent brain, and they provide the same functionality as a print server.

✦ **Buy a printer with onboard Ethernet network support.** Sure, they're more expensive, but a network-ready printer is the most elegant solution of all.

If you choose one of the latter two — either a network printer box or a network-ready printer — you'll have to follow the manufacturer's specific instructions to set things up. However, if you decide to use a client PC to provide printing services, you can follow these steps to set things up in Windows XP:

1. **Set up the printer normally under Windows XP and make sure that it's working properly.**

2. **Choose Start⇨Printers and Faxes to display the Printers and Faxes window that you see in Figure 2-10.**

3. **Right-click the printer that you want to share and then choose Sharing from the pop-up menu that appears to display the Properties dialog box with the Sharing tab active (see Figure 2-11).**

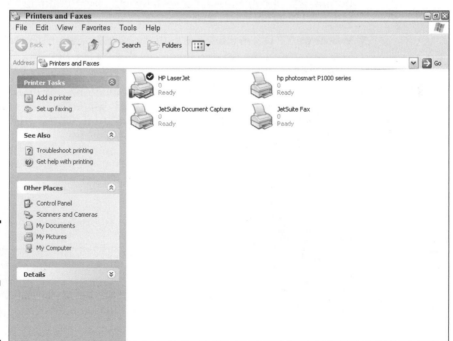

Figure 2-10: Enable printer sharing from the Printer and Faxes window.

Figure 2-11:
Sharing my
HP inkjet
printer, for
the good
of all.

4. **Select the Share This Printer radio button.**

   Windows XP creates a default share name for the printer, but it might not be descriptive enough (especially in a larger building with many identical printers). Feel free to edit it.

5. **Windows XP offers a feature called *shared printer drivers*, in which you can install the drivers for other PCs on the network that might be using different versions of Windows besides Windows XP.**

   a. **If you want to make printer drivers available for these folks (which, believe me, will make things easier for both you and them), click the Additional Drivers button, which displays the dialog box that you see in Figure 2-12.**

Figure 2-12:
With shared
printer
drivers,
everyone
can join in
the fun.

b. **Mark (to enable) the check boxes next to the other operating systems that might access this printer and then click OK.**

You'll need the manufacturer's driver CD-ROM when prompted by Windows XP. Or, if you're really hot stuff, you can download the latest drivers to your hard drive, expand (or unzip them), and browse to that location instead.

By the way, don't mark the IA64/Windows XP check box unless someone on your network is running a computer that an Intel's 64-bit chip. This environment is not required for regular PCs running standard Windows XP. That's taken care of by the Intel/Windows 2000 or XP check box, which is enabled by default.

6. **Click OK to close the dialog box.**

The icon for a shared printer (like a shared folder) is different; look for the open palm icon, as shown in Figure 2-10. (A reminder to cross it with additional funds, perhaps?)

Now any computer on the network can connect to the shared printer, but of course, it has to be added to each client first. You can do this by running the Add a Printer Wizard (which appears in the task pane on PCs running Windows XP when you open the Printers and Faxes window). When prompted, make sure that you choose to install a network printer and then use the Browse function to allow Windows XP to locate the printer on the network for you.

Using a Standard Switch with a Cable or DSL Modem

I discuss Internet sharing devices earlier in this chapter, and they're covered in detail in Chapter 4 of this mini-book. Most have built-in switches, virtually all of them have DHCP support, and they have ports that allow a direct connection to your cable or DSL modem. That's great: In fact, as I mention earlier, you won't even need a host PC in that case. Feel free to prance about.

But what if your switch *doesn't* have a connection point (typically called a wide area network [WAN] port, or an uplink port) for your DSL or cable modem? That's the situation that I mention earlier, where your host PC will need two NICs, and you will have to set it up as a host PC.

To do this, connect your hardware and cables so that

✦ The cable or DSL modem is connected to one of the NICs on the host PC. (It should already be configured this way, so no big deal.)

✦ The other NIC on the host PC is connected to one of the ports on the switch.

✦ The client PCs on the network are connected to the switch.

Book VIII Chapter 2

Ethernet to the Rescue

Now follow the procedure that I provide earlier for setting up the host PC and the client PCs, and all should function like butter.

Troubleshooting Your Network

I sure hope you're reading this section for fun . . . or because you thirst for knowledge, or just to be thorough. Why? Well, unfortunately, a misbehaving network can leave even the best techs with a four-bell headache. Your network is a mass of differing hardware, software, and data, all of which must work well in concert before you can send or receive a single packet.

Windows XP does the best job that it can to automate the process; and if you've bought a networking kit, you can pretty much assume that everything will be compatible. But if you have one bad cable or one faulty NIC driver, your state-of-the-art network becomes a family of dead cables and a little box with no lights. (Sounds like my last attempt at outdoor Christmas decorations.)

In this section, I provide the most common solutions to the most common problems.

Windows XP doesn't recognize my NIC

Man, talk about starting with a problem from step one! That's my kind of luck as well. Anyway, here are the possible problems and fixes:

✦ **An incompatible driver:** NIC drivers are legendary for their fickle behavior. Unlike some printers that allow you to use the same driver for both Windows 98 and 2000, or for Windows 2000 and XP, a network interface card simply demands the proper driver, or it won't work. Period. Reinstall the driver from the manufacturer's media (making sure that you select the right operating system version). If that doesn't work (and you still have access to the Internet on another computer), download the manufacturer's latest driver for your operating system from the company's Web site. (To download a driver, you will need to have access to another, working PC, and you might need a formatted floppy to install them.) And oh, by the way: You might actually have to uninstall the NIC and reinstall it to reload the driver. Such fun.

✦ **A faulty NIC:** This is a definite possibility. If you have a NIC that you know is working, replace the misbehaving card (along with its drivers) to see whether the problem is solved.

✦ **A hardware conflict:** This is quite rare under Windows XP, but it can still happen (and if your client PCs are running Windows 98 or Me, conflicts can crop up much more often). Use Device Manager to check whether Windows is having problems getting everyone to play nicely together; I demonstrate how to do this in Book II, Chapter 5.

No lights show up on my network card(s) or switch

This is classic stuff. Not the most comforting thing to hear, but then again, it's good to know that others have been here before you. (To be precise, me. I used to handle network problem calls at a major hospital.) Anyway, a lack of lights indicates that you're not getting a signal, which suggests a number of possible hardware problems:

✦ **Your cable is faulty.** An improperly made cable can short, causing everything to come to a crashing halt. This is a likely cause if all the other client PCs have illuminated signal lights, and the switch's lights are lit as well. (If the computer store sold you a special type of cable called a *crossover* cable, march right back and demand a standard twisted pair cable; crossover cables are meant to hook two computers together directly via their network ports. Unfortunately, it's hard to tell the difference with just your eye unless you see the word *crossover* printed on the cable.)

✦ **Your NIC or switch is faulty.** If either has gone off the deep end, they need to be replaced. If other client PCs are working, you can remove a working NIC from one of them and use it to test your switch.

✦ **Your switch isn't powered on.** (Whoops . . . no need for embarrassment.) A switch needs AC power to operate.

✦ **You're using the WAN/uplink port.** This is a special port on your switch, as I explain in the previous section; it won't work for a client PC connection.

Nothing shows up when I browse

Just plain nasty. If everything seemed to go well when you set up your host PC and your client PCs, but you still come up empty when you browse, here are the possibilities (and my recommended troubleshooting tips):

✦ **Client PCs are powered down.** Simple, but effective. Boot up a client PC and then refresh the My Network Places window by choosing View⇨ Refresh. **The client should now be visible.**

✦ **A piece of hardware is faulty.** I use this term because any piece of your networking hardware might be experiencing problems, and you wouldn't be able to browse. See what I mean about the four-bell headache? Anyway, make sure that all your NICs and your switch have lighted activity/signal lights.

✦ **No network resources are shared.** Remember, Windows XP doesn't share diddly by default, so when you first browse your My Network Places window, it's likely to be absolutely blank. However, click the View Workgroup Computers link in the window's taskbar to see whether the client PCs don't show up.

✦ **Workgroup names are mismatched.** As I declare earlier, if you don't assign the exact same workgroup name to the host PC and every client PC on the network, those network packets are "walking around in different neighborhoods," as an old boss of mine used to say. Check to make sure that everyone has joined the same party.

I can't connect (or print) to a shared printer

I saved the best for last because this problem is usually much easier to solve (apart from the obvious, such as running out of paper, ink, or toner). Try these stress relievers:

✦ **The printer is powered down.** I wish I had a dime for every time that someone complained that they couldn't connect to Fred's printer, only to find that Fred was out of the office . . . and (ahem) his PC (and the specific printer in question) was turned off. (Sound of hand slapping forehead.)

✦ **The printer isn't actually shared.** Yep, you guessed it; this is the other hot potato. Make sure that the shared printer hasn't been disabled (either by accident or on purpose).

✦ **You have faulty NIC or cables.** Again, check the NIC for the PC that's connected to the printer. The easiest thing to do is to see whether you can browse or work with shared files on that PC. If not, there's a good chance that either the NIC or the twisted pair cable is giving you problems.

✦ **The printer has been placed offline.** Some older laser printers have an Online/Offline button. If a printer like this is offline, the printer goes comatose and won't respond.

Chapter 3: Going Wireless

In This Chapter

✔ **Comparing wireless and wired networks**

✔ **Comparing wireless standards**

✔ **Using existing telephone and AC wiring**

✔ **Making a wireless connection under Windows XP**

Welcome to the future: A world where network cables are on display in museums, and your PCs can wirelessly access your home or office network from 100 feet away. Fast, convenient, and (most of all) as secure as a wired network, the wireless network of years to come will even bring other types of devices under its umbrella, such as cellular phones, palmtop PCs, and personal digital assistants (PDAs), just to name a few.

Hang on a second . . . now that I think about it, all that stuff is available now! Wireless networks are rapidly overtaking traditional wired networks in homes and small offices. Even companies with extensive wired networks have added access points (APs) for the laptop crowd, just to be hip.

In this chapter, I show you how wireless networking works, what's available, and how you can set up a wireless network under Windows XP.

Understanding Wireless Networking

In a sense, wireless networking isn't as revolutionary as you might think. In fact, it operates in the same manner as the standard wired Ethernet configuration that I discuss in the preceding chapter of this mini-book, complete with packets, collisions, and all the hoo-hah that accompanies networking. Of course, the method of transmitting and receiving packets is different when you're using wireless networking; instead of being sent over a wire, the packets are broadcasted through the air like a radio signal.

(However, you can't use your wireless network hardware to run a pirate radio station. Sorry about that, matey. Arrgh.)

How does wireless compare with wired?

Other than the transmission method, here are the only three major differences between a wired network and its wireless sibling:

✦ **Wireless connections are slower.** This is the big 'un as well as the big reason why most, larger networks still depend on wired Ethernet for the bulk of their connections. Even the fastest current wireless technology can only pump data at 54 Mbps, but any run-of-the-mill wired network can easily deliver 100 Mbps; heck, the fastest wired networks can hit gigabit (1000 Mbps) speeds! In fact, they can use fiber optic cabling instead of plain copper wire cabling to hit their top speeds; recently, a group of researchers used fiber optic connections to transfer the same amount of data stored in 2 DVD movies in less than 60 seconds.

✦ **Wireless hardware is more expensive.** Depending on the standard supported by your wireless hardware — more on standards in the next section — you'll pay significantly more for wireless hardware as you would for 10/100 Mbps wired hardware.

✦ **Wireless networks require no hubs or switches.** Most wireless base stations and APs can provide connections for up to 253 simultaneous users, so a larger wireless network (with 50 PCs or more) requires far less hardware and upkeep than a wired network that can handle the same number of computers.

Would you like to impress your network administrator? Of course . . . don't we all? (If you run your own home or small office network, you can impress a hardware-savvy friend instead.) Use the techno-nerd buzzwords for network transmission technologies and refer to your wireless network as an *unguided* network — as opposed to a *guided,* or wired, network.

Naturally, you can add a *wireless access point* — or, as it's commonly called, a *WAP* — to your wired network, which will give you the best of both worlds. Figure 3-1 illustrates a typical WAP device, which brings 802.11g wireless connectivity to an existing wired network; this baby runs about $75 U.S. Most WAP units actually require two physical connections: one to your wired Ethernet network (naturally) and a Universal Serial Bus (USB) connection to the computer that will control it. You can also share your Internet connection with a dual router, which has both wired and wireless hardware built in (as I discuss in the next chapter of this mini-book).

The standards involved

Like any other evolving PC technology, wireless networking suffers from competition between different standards — some are compatible with others, and some are not. Readers of my other books are already acquainted with my overwhelming love for strange names and obfuscating acronyms in the PC world . . . **not.** Unfortunately, wireless networking has a handful of the most confusing names in the entire PC world, so make sure that you have a bottle of aspirin handy.

Here, in one easy-to-consume section, is the lowdown on the different wireless standards as well as which you should consider and which you should eschew.

Figure 3-1:
A typical WAP for your LAN. (Try to keep a straight face when you say that.)

The original standard: 802.11b

Commonly called *Wi-Fi* (short for Wireless Fidelity), the first 802.11b wireless base station (named the AirPort) was introduced by Apple Computer in 1999 — a fact that the good folks at Cupertino have been gloating over ever since. Wi-Fi supports a maximum transfer rate of 11 Mbps, which is just a little faster than the slowest 10 Mbps wired Ethernet standard in common use.

A word about USB wireless connections

You can connect a desktop PC to a wireless network without using any internal adapter card at all. Just use a *USB wireless adapter,* which uses a USB connection to your PC as a path for wireless network data packets. Hey, that USB is really amazing, isn't it? (Note that this toy isn't the same as a simple USB cable network, which allows PCs to share files and printers over USB cabling.) The remote PC gets all the benefits of a wireless Ethernet connection.

As you can read in Book VII, Chapter 5, USB 1.1 ports can transfer a maximum of 12 Mbps, so they work just fine with 802.11b hardware. However, you'd have to turn to a FireWire or USB 2.0 wireless adapter to deliver the 54 Mbps

top speed of an 802.11a or 802.11g connection. (Personally, I think that both FireWire and USB 2.0 are examples of tremendous overkill in this scenario. After all, you're moving 54 Mbps over a cable that can reach as high as 480 Mbps! However, USB 1.1 won't cut it at 54 Mbps, so what's a poor PC owner to do?)

Anyway, an external USB wireless adapter is a great way to add "temporary wireless" to a PC in your home or office. Many of these external adapters can also be used to make a printer a standalone wireless device, so you can place your printer in a central location that's convenient to everyone.

Distance is important in the wireless world, of course. It's one thing to be able to use your laptop on your network from across the room and another thing entirely to use it in your backyard. 802.11b devices are rated at a maximum distance of 300 feet from the base station, but that figure is about as realistic as an African wildebeest wearing a hula skirt appearing in your living room. This idea of "theoretical top speed" also applies to high-speed dialup modems, which practically never deliver the top speed that the manufacturer lists on the box. By experience, I can tell you that you can count on 150 feet — and even less if a number of intervening walls stand between you and your network, or if you're a victim of interference.

Oh, didn't I mention the interference? 802.11b networking uses the 2.4 GHz broadcasting spectrum, which unfortunately is now being used by a regular horde of devices, including cellular phones, cordless phones, Bluetooth devices (which I cover in a bit), and even microwave ovens. Therefore, 802.11b wireless networks can slow down significantly because of interference from other devices. It's not likely that your entire wireless network will shut down completely, but you will *definitely* be able to tell when your teenage daughter is using your cordless phone.

The misfit: 802.11a

Why is 802.11a such a misfit, and why did I list it after 802.11b? Well, you're going to love this:

+ **The numbering is wrong.** Believe it or not, 802.11a is a more recent standard. (Can someone please explain to me why this select group of engineers decided to number successive standards in *reverse* order?)

+ **It has a shorter range.** Although it's officially rated at 150 feet under perfect conditions, in the real world, 802.11a can only reach a distance of 60–70 feet — your wireless world shrinks even further.

+ **It doesn't play well with others.** 802.11a is completely incompatible with both 802.11b and 802.11g, so you're effectively limited to 802.11a equipment. (And there's not all that much out there.)

So why did folks develop 802.11a, anyway? It has two advantages:

+ **It's speedy.** 802.11a was the first speed demon in wireless networking, delivering up to 54 Mbps (over five times as fast as 802.11b).

+ **It uses a different broadcasting spectrum.** 802.11a uses the 5 GHz spectrum, which prevents it from working in the 2.4 GHz range needed by 802.11b (hence the incompatibility). Because there's a lot less activity around most homes and offices in the 5 GHz spectrum, you get less interference and a better chance of achieving the best reception.

Here's a bit of trivia that no person should be without: 802.11b networking uses a modulation scheme called *Direct Sequence Spread Spectrum* (DSSS). On the other hand, 802.11a networks use the *Orthogonal Frequency Division Multiplexing* scheme (OFDM). Why the heck is this important? Well, DSSS uses less power than OFDM, so — yes, there's actually a point — 802.11b networking hardware uses less power than 802.11a hardware, and that translates into longer battery life for your laptop if you use an 802.11b Wi-Fi card while you're traveling.

The darling child: 802.11g

I know you're probably thinking to yourself, "Self, I sure wish someone would get off their duff and produce a standard that's both compatible with 802.11b and provides speeds as fast as 802.11a." Good news: Your wish has been heard! Today's 802.11g wireless standard does precisely that, combining the best of both worlds. If you (or your company) have already invested in 802.11b wireless hardware, you can continue to use it on an 802.11g network. Naturally, you won't get 54 Mbps, but at least it'll work at 11 Mbps. New 802.11g hardware will transfer packets at that magic 54 Mbps.

The downside? Aw, geez, we're back to the 2.4 GHz spectrum again, so once again, your buddy in the next cubical who loves microwave popcorn is going to introduce interference. It just goes to show that nothing's perfect . . . except, perhaps, a 1964 Cadillac two-door coupe. (See the first photo in the book, on my About the Author page.)

The strangely named: Bluetooth

Okay, now here's a wireless standard name that sounds like some scriptwriter or concept artist in Hollywood was working overtime . . . but at least it does break the 802.11x mold. Unlike the other three standards, Bluetooth is not designed for full-scale wireless Ethernet networking. Instead, it was developed in 1995 as a specialized wireless technology for short distances to be used with cellphones, PDAs, laptops, palmtops, printers, and other external devices. The maximum distance for a Bluetooth network is about 30 feet.

The Bluetooth wave is even supposed to reach household appliances, like your TV and your stereo system. I'm sure there's a Bluetooth toaster out there. If you've seen it, drop me a line at mark@mlcbooks.com and tell me all about it.

Anyway, unlike the other standards that I discuss here, Bluetooth requires very little power to use (befitting its design, which concentrates on battery-operated devices). It's also painfully slow compared with 802.11b — only about 1 Mbps — but that's not supposed to affect the small fry as much as it would your desktop PC. No base station is required for Bluetooth communications between devices. For example, after your laptop gets within 30 feet of your cellphone, they can update each other's telephone number directories. Eerie.

Oh, and Bluetooth also uses the — you guessed it — 2.4 GHz spectrum, so it will actually conflict with existing 802.11b and 802.11g networks! (The airwaves are getting so overpopulated that tin cans and string start to look attractive again.)

Table 3-1 sums up each of the four wireless networking standards.

Table 3-1	Wireless Standards on Parade		
Standard	*Transfer Speed*	*Maximum Distance*	*Compatibility*
802.11b	11 Mbps	300 feet	802.11g
802.11a	54 Mbps	150 feet	None
802.11g	54 Mbps	150 feet	802.11b
Bluetooth	1 Mbps	30 feet	None

I should note here that you can buy an external wireless antenna for your base station or WAP. An 802.11g directional antenna is typically about $40 or $50 U.S., and it can boost your existing signal quality as well as extend the range of your wireless network into every nook and cranny of your home or office. Check your station/WAP to see whether it can accept an external antenna.

AC and phone line networking

Although wireless hardware has become very popular over the last four years, here's another alternative to a traditional wired network: You can also build a network by using either the existing AC power wiring (a *powerline* network) or the telephone wiring (a *phoneline* network) in your home.

If running packets across your AC power lines sounds a little dangerous, let me put your fears to rest: Both of these alternative wired networks have been around for several years now — longer, in fact, than 802.11b — and they're perfectly safe. (If you're wondering, you can continue to use your telephone or your AC appliances with no changes.) The advantages of an alternative wired network over a wired or wireless network are clear:

✦ **No wires — at least, no Cat 5 cables:** Your home or office is already set up with all the "cabling" you need, and you likely have "ports" in every room.

✦ **Better security than a wireless network:** Although a wireless network can be made quite secure — I cover how to do this in the next section — you're still beaming a signal that might be picked up outside in the street. On the other hand, the network packets transferred over a phoneline or an AC network stay within the building and are practically impossible for anyone outside to intercept.

✦ **Very easy to install:** A wireless network might be the easiest to install, but a phoneline or an AC network is still much easier to set up than a traditional wired network.

So why aren't phoneline and powerline networks more popular? Unfortunately, compared with wireless, both of these network solutions leave much to be desired:

✦ **They're slower than wireless.** Both the latest phoneline standard (from HomePNA, at www.homepna.org) and the HomePlug powerline standard (www.homeplug.org) deliver approximately 10 Mbps. An 802.11g network will wipe the floor with either alternative wired network when it comes to raw file transfer speed.

✦ **They're less convenient than wireless.** Even though you don't have to string Ethernet cabling all over your office, your networked PCs and peripherals are still tied down to certain areas (either around your telephone jacks or your AC power sockets). A wireless connection works wherever you are as long as you're in range.

✦ **You can connect fewer computers.** A wireless network can accept twice as many users (or standalone network devices) as either a phoneline or powerline network.

When readers ask me to recommend a network solution for their home or small office, I almost always recommend either a traditional wired (Cat 5) network (for the fastest speeds and the best security) or a wireless network (which offers convenience and easy installation). The drawbacks of phoneline and powerline networks (along with the explosive popularity of wireless hardware) will likely doom them to gradual extinction.

Using Wireless Hardware in Windows XP

After you install your wireless base station or WAP, you're ready to configure your PC for use on your network.

Book VIII
Chapter 3

Going Wireless

Preparing to install

Before you begin the installation of an internal adapter card, make sure that

✦ **You've read the manual.** Even if you've already installed an adapter card in your PC, take a few minutes to check the documentation that shipped with the card. A Mark's Maxim to live by:

It's better to know about a "gotcha" before you install.™

✦ **You've gathered the Big Four.** That means a Phillips screwdriver, a plastic bowl to hold any spare parts, a good light source, and some sort of static-free cover for your work surface. (Newspaper always works well if I'm away from my workbench.)

✦ **You've grounded yourself.** After you've removed the cover from your PC, I highly recommend touching the metal chassis of your computer to dissipate any static electricity that's stowing away on your body before it can cause damage to the card.

Installation tricks

All manufacturers of wireless adapter cards (for desktops) and wireless PC Cards (for laptops) include their own installation and setup programs — which, under XP, also create the necessary wireless connection automatically — so I won't go into the gory details here. However, here are some suggestions that I can give you that will help with the installation, no matter what type of card you're using:

✦ **Choose between ad hoc and infrastructure.** You might be prompted to choose between ad hoc and infrastructure mode. In most cases, you want to choose *infrastructure* mode (where your laptop and PC workstations connect by using a base station or wireless access point) instead of *ad hoc* (where the devices actually talk directly to each other on a specific channel number that you determine, just like the CB radio days of old, without a base station or WAP). Note: If you're trying to connect your wireless device to your existing wired network, you must use infrastructure mode.

✦ **Check your WEP encryption.** When prompted for WEP information, use the highest level that the PC card supports. WEP is designed to automatically fall back to the encryption level used by your base station or WAP.

✦ **Check your SSID.** You need an SSID that matches the SSID used by your base station or WAP. *Remember:* Change it to the unique value that you used on your base station or WAP. For the best security, **don't** use the default SSID!

✦ **Keep your drivers current.** I sound like a broken record, but check for the latest drivers from the manufacturer's Web site every time that you install new hardware . . . and that includes wireless networking hardware.

Making the connection

You have two methods of connecting to your wireless network in infrastructure mode: the easy way (where your base station or WAP broadcasts its SSID for public use) and the harder way (where you've turned off the SSID broadcast feature for greater security, which I mention earlier in this chapter).

The easy way? Just plug your wireless network card into your laptop, and XP will automatically search for and connect to your network. If you're using a desktop PC with a wireless card, this same process occurs when you first log in to Windows XP. (See? I told you it was easy.) XP displays a notification icon in the taskbar letting you know that the connection has been made as well as how strong the signal is.

If you're smart and keep your SSID close to the chest, follow these steps to do things the slightly harder way:

1. **Choose Start⇨Connect To, right-click the Wireless Network Connection icon, and then choose View Available Wireless Networks from the pop-up menu that appears.**

   XP displays the Connect to Wireless Network dialog box.

2. **Click the Advanced button.**

   The Properties dialog box opens.

3. **Click the Add button on the Properties dialog box.**

4. **Type the matching SSID value from your base station or WAP in the Network Name (SSID) text box and then select the Data Encryption (WEP Enabled) check box to enable it (if necessary).**

   If you've set your own WEP key, select the This Key is Provided for Me Automatically check box to disable it and then type the key in the Network Key text box. Click the Key Length drop-down list box and choose the proper key length. (It's okay to use an automatically generated key, but your base station or WAP is likely to choose a shorter key than you can assign manually.)

5. **Make sure that the This Is a Computer-to-Computer (Ad Hoc) Network check box is disabled.**

6. **Click OK to close the dialog box.**

   This adds the network to your Preferred networks list.

7. **Click OK again to return to your XP desktop, which should initiate the connection.**

Chapter 4: Sharing Your Internet Connection

In This Chapter

✔ **Understanding the advantages of connection sharing**

✔ **Sharing your connection using Windows XP**

✔ **Using a wired hardware sharing device**

✔ **Using a wireless hardware sharing device**

A high-speed Internet connection is a thing of beauty, especially when it's shared with everyone in your home or office over your network. After your network is set up and running smoothly, consider whether you want to share that connection through hardware or software as well as what sort of security that you'll need to protect everyone on your network.

In this chapter, I discuss all the possibilities and show you how to set up Internet connection sharing within Windows XP.

Why Share Your Internet Connection?

"Don't I need a separate Internet connection for each PC on my network?" Actually, you've just answered your own question: That network that you've installed allows for all sorts of data communications between PCs, including the ability to plug in to a shared connection.

I should note here that it is indeed technically possible to share a dialup Internet connection by using the software connection-sharing feature in Windows XP. However, I don't think that you'll be satisfied with the results. (Sorry, that won't provide enough horsepower to adequately handle more than one computer.) Therefore, I'm going to assume for the rest of this chapter that you're already using either a digital subscriber line (DSL), a cable modem Internet connection, or a satellite connection.

Here's a list of advantages that help explain why Internet connection sharing — whether through a program or a dedicated hardware device — is so doggone popular these days:

✦ **It's cheap.** As long as your Internet service provider (ISP) allows you to share your broadband connection, you'll save a bundle over the cost of adding completely separate connections for multiple machines in your home or office. (Naturally, this is the major advantage.)

✦ **It's convenient.** With a shared Internet connection, other PCs on your network are easy to configure, and each is content as a sleeping cat. Each PC on your network operates just as if it was directly connected to the Internet, and all computers on the network can all do their own thing on the Internet at once.

✦ **It offers centralized security.** With a *firewall* in place — either running on the PC (if you're sharing through software) or on the device itself (if you're sharing through hardware) — you can protect the Internet activity on all the PCs on your network at one time.

✦ **It's efficient.** Most folks whom I talk to are surprised that a shared Internet connection is so fast — even when multiple computers on your network are charging down the Information Superhighway at the same time.

A connection shared through a dedicated hardware device, however, will always be faster than a connection shared through software. Keep that in mind.

Speaking of convenience and efficiency, I should also mention that many hardware sharing devices also double as Ethernet hubs or switches. This allows you to build your entire home or office network around one central piece of hardware rather than using a separate hub or switch and a PC running a software sharing program.

Sharing through Software in Windows XP

If you decide to use the built-in Internet connection sharing (ICS) feature of Windows XP, first double-check that you already have everything in this list:

✦ **A working Ethernet network.**

✦ **A working broadband Internet connection to one of the PCs on your network.** Okay, you can use ICS with a dialup connection as well, but everything will be much faster with a DSL, cable, or satellite connection.

✦ **An installed copy of Windows XP on the PC that's connected to the Internet.** This PC will also need two network cards installed — one that leads to the network hub or switch, and one that leads to the cable or DSL modem. Because many flavors of network cards exist (using many different connections, like USB, PC card, and the more traditional internal adapter card), follow the installation instructions provided by the card manufacturer to add both cards to your PC.

Everything shipshape? Good. Follow these steps to share that existing Internet connection with the other computers on your network:

1. **Choose Start⇨Connect To, right-click the connection that you want to share, and then choose Properties.**

   The An Example ISP Properties window appears.

2. **Click the Advanced tab to display the settings that you see in Figure 4-1.**

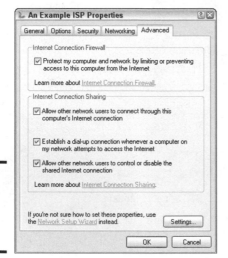

Figure 4-1: Set up ICS within Windows XP.

3. **Select the Allow Other Network Users to Connect through This Computer's Internet Connection check box to enable it.**

   - If you are sharing a dialup connection, I recommend enabling automatically dialing. If necessary, select the Establish a Dial-up Connection Whenever a Computer on My Network Attempts to Access the Internet check box to enable it. (Keep in mind, however, that this can wreak havoc on a voice call.)

   - To allow other network users to control the shared connection — as in disconnecting it — clear the Allow Other Network Users to Control or Disable the Shared Internet Connection check box.

4. **Click OK to save your changes and return to the XP desktop.**

   Windows XP indicates that a connection is shared by adding a friendly looking cupped hand under the connection icon.

Figure 4-2 illustrates how things will work after you're done. Of course, your IP addresses will be different from those in the figure, but it should help you understand how everything will fly.

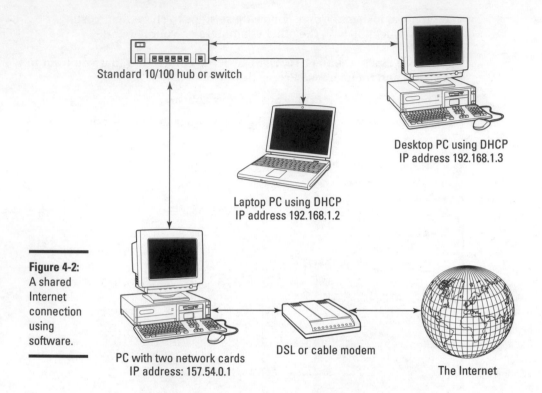

Standard 10/100 hub or switch

Desktop PC using DHCP
IP address 192.168.1.3

Laptop PC using DHCP
IP address 192.168.1.2

Figure 4-2:
A shared
Internet
connection
using
software.

PC with two network cards
IP address: 157.54.0.1

DSL or cable modem

The Internet

Sharing through Hardware

As I mention earlier, I personally think that a hardware sharing device is somewhat preferable to sharing a connection through software. For example, with a software solution,

✦ You end up with at least one PC on your network that must always remain on if anyone wants to use the Internet.

✦ You'll notice a significant slowdown on the sharing PC when several other PCs are using the Internet.

✦ You still need a hub, switch, or wireless base station.

With a hardware device, all the PCs on your network can concentrate on their own work, eliminating the need to leave a PC running constantly as an "Internet server." (After all, a PC that's capable of running Windows XP at a decent clip is an expensive resource compared with an investment of $50–$100 U.S. on a hardware sharing device.)

In this section, I familiarize you with the two different types of hardware sharing devices.

Wired sharing devices

For those PC owners who either already have a traditional wired Ethernet network — or those who are considering building one — a device like the combination switch-firewall-DHCP-server-sharing-thing that you see in Figure 4-3 is the perfect solution to Internet connection sharing. (*Dynamic Host Configuration Protocol,* or DHCP, is a feature that allows your hardware sharing device to automatically configure IP addresses on your network. If all that sounds like an alien language, visit Chapter 2 of this mini-book, where I wax enthusiastic about DHCP.)

Figure 4-3:
An Internet
connection
router.

Perhaps I should be a little more specific in my description. (Not even Google will return much if you search for *switch-firewall-DHCP-server-sharing-thing.* The illustrated device is actually a cable/DSL router with a four-port switch.

For an idea of why hardware sharing is so popular, look at what you get — in one small tidy box — selling online for a mere $50 U.S:

✦ A built-in, four-port Ethernet 10/100 switch into which you can plug four PCs (to start with) directly into the router for an instant Ethernet network. (For more information about network speeds, see Chapter 2 of this mini-book.)

✦ A direct-connect port for your DSL or cable modem, which can also be used as a wide area network (WAN) connection to hook the device to an existing external network.

✦ A DHCP server, providing near-automatic network configuration for the PCs hooked into the device.

✦ The ability to block certain Internet traffic (both coming in and going out) as well as the ability to lock out individual PCs from Internet access.

✦ An easy-to-use, Web-based configuration screen, which can be used on any PC connected to the router. Figure 4-4 illustrates the Web configuration screen from my router.

✦ Built-in NAT functionality. (I dive into NAT in the next chapter.)

Pretty neat, eh? Remember, this device is used in tandem with your existing cable or DSL modem, which is typically included by your ISP as part of your Internet subscription (but you might be paying more because you're renting the modem).

I should also note that you can get a similar device with all these features *and* a built-in DSL or cable modem. Because you won't be charged a monthly rental for a modem, you can thumb your nose at your ISP and save money in the long run. (Please avoid mentioning my name when you gleefully return your modem to your ISP.)

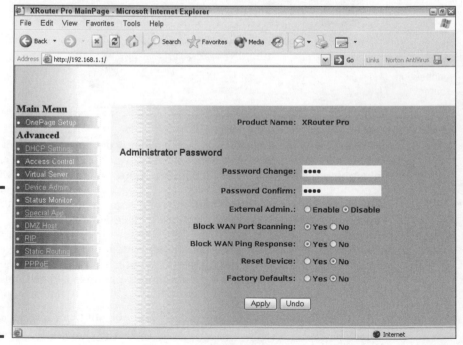

Figure 4-4: Most Internet sharing devices can be configured with a Web browser.

Naturally, the setup procedure for each device on the market is different, but here's a sample of what's in store when you take your new Internet sharing router out of the box:

1. **If you're currently running a typical standalone network switch or hub, you can either unplug all the existing computers and put them on the new box, or you can connect the WAN port from the existing hub into one of the ports on the Internet sharing device.**

   The device manual will tell you how to take care of the latter method.

   If you're setting up a new network, naturally, you'll just connect each Ethernet cable directly to the sharing device.

2. **Plug the power supply from the sharing device to your AC socket.**

3. **Configure one of the PCs on your new network with the default network settings provided by the device manufacturer.**

4. **Run Internet Explorer on the PC that you configured in the last step and use the Web-based configuration utility to finish configuring the device.**

That's it! If you're running a typical home or home office network, you'll likely keep the default settings for everything. For an idea of just what kind of power you can wield over your network as you share your Internet connection, take a gander at the sidebar titled, "What the Sam Hill does *that* mean?" in Chapter 5 of this mini-book. Luckily, you probably won't have to use any of those optional settings, but it's good to know that they're there.

Wireless sharing devices

Most folks think that sharing an Internet connection over a wireless network must be harder to set up than a traditional wired network — and that it's likely to be a tremendous security risk as well. I'm happy to tell you that both preconceptions are wrong. Wireless connection sharing with a hardware device is as simple to set up as the wired device that I discuss in the preceding section. And, with the settings that I discuss in Chapter 5 of this mini-book, you'll make it very difficult (if not impossible) for someone to hack his way to your network or your Internet connection.

As an example of a truly versatile all-in-one Internet sharing device, check out the device shown in Figure 4-5. It's got the antenna that marks it as a wireless switch, but what you don't see is that it also sports four 10/100 Ethernet ports on the back for your old-fashioned wired network. Yep, you guessed it, this is just plain neat: It can accommodate multiple 802.11g wireless connections *and* four wired connections, all at the same time! (The somewhat spaghetti-fied world of wireless networking is covered in depth in Chapter 3 of this mini-book.)

Figure 4-5:
Is it wired?
Is it
wireless?
This sharing
device is
both!

As you might expect, the cost on this puppy (about $150 U.S. online) is much higher than the wired-only device (see the preceding section). Another factor is the speed of the wireless connection; as you can read in Chapter 3 of this mini-book, 802.11b devices are rapidly disappearing from the market, so costs are dropping fast on 802.11g hardware. (And yes, if you've decided to opt for a wireless-only network, you can find a cheaper wireless sharing device that doesn't include any of those silly "antique" wired ports.) Wireless adapter cards (including the USB and PC Card varieties) are much more expensive than standard wired adapter cards, too.

As I mention in Chapter 5 of this mini-book, don't forget to demand a wireless sharing device that offers 128-bit Wired Equivalent Privacy (WEP) private encryption. Anything less, and your wireless network will be much easier for outsiders to hack.

Chapter 5: Securing Your Home Network

In This Chapter

✓ Keeping your wired network secure

✓ Ensuring security on your wireless network

✓ Working with shared folders

✓ Understanding NAT security

✓ Setting up Virtual Private Networking (VPN) in Windows XP

*I*t's probably Question Number One in my Outlook Inbox these days — readers are constantly asking me about home network security. "Am I opening my files to everyone on my block?" ranks right up there with "Am I sharing my Internet connection with the seedy teenager next door?" (A frightening thought indeed.)

Wireless folks will find a discussion of security tips and tricks in this chapter as well. Naturally, a wired Ethernet network is easier to secure, but I've got good news for the wireless network crowd: You can indeed keep the private stuff private, even while sharing the stuff you want to disseminate amongst others on your network (using shared folders).

In this chapter, I'll delve deeper into the world of Ethernet network security, providing tips and tricks you can apply to your network to help keep it safe from outside interference. If you're always on the move, I'll also introduce you to Windows XP's whiz-bang Virtual Private Networking (VPN) feature, which will allow you to reach your network securely using any Internet connection!

Common Sense Tips for Wired Networks

Folks with wired home networks are often pretty doggone smug about their computer security — and there's some reason for that, because a connection to your network can occur only over a wired port or over the Internet. (In other words, you don't have to worry about broadcasting your Address Book across the street.)

What the Sam Hill does that mean?

When you're shopping for a wired or wireless Internet sharing device, you'll find that the side of the box mentions a number of nifty security features that seem to have been named by a very depressed engineer (who didn't speak English either). Allow me to translate for you:

Static routing: This is a feature that enables you to set up a preset network path between the device and an Internet host, which is likely to be an external network. Without static routing, you might not be able to use virtual private networking (VPN), which I discuss at the end of this chapter.

Dynamic routing: Basically, this is the reverse of static routing — and it's a great feature for those who are constantly yanking PCs, servers, and network hardware off the network and plugging stuff back in at other locations. With dynamic routing, the sharing device automatically compensates and adjusts for changes made to the *topology* (whoops, I meant *layout*) of your network.

Port forwarding: If you're running an e-mail, Web, or File Transfer Protocol (FTP) server on your network, you can set the router to automatically divert any incoming traffic of that type — HyperText Transfer Protocol (HTTP) for the Web server, for example — directly to the server PC.

IP filtering: This is the feature that allows you to block certain users or PCs from Internet access. It's also a good feature to have when you're using VPN.

WAN blocking: This sounds like something that happens in a nuclear reactor, doesn't it? Luckily, this feature just prevents other PCs on the Internet from *pinging* (scanning) for your network, so it's a good idea to leave this one on. Another Mark's Maxim is in order: **It's generally a good thing to be invisible to other computers on the Internet.™** (More on this in Book III, Chapter 3.)

Demilitarized Zone (DMZ) host: Finally, here's a feature that's designed just for us Internet gamers: You can set up your router with a special set of "holes" to "reveal" your PC to others on the Internet when you're connecting to an Internet game server (or if you're hosting your own server). Without a DMZ, your router's NAT firewall would likely block your PC from communicating with others (as I explain later in this chapter), and you wouldn't be able to join or create an Internet gaming battleground. Anyone for a fragfest in Half-Life 2?

First, the good news: If you've followed my advice in earlier chapters about using the Windows XP firewall on each of your network PCs — or if you've installed a third-party firewall application on each PC — you can be reasonably sure that your Internet connection is secure from The Bad Guys.

However, it is still possible to be a little *too* complacent about your wired network's security: don't forget, that seedy teenager next door might end up dating your kid, and spending time within the comfortable confines of your own home. Yep, it's Maxim time again:

Unless you can be absolutely certain that no one else has access to your wired network, it still pays to practice good network security policy!™

With that Ultimate Truth in mind, here's a common-sense checklist you can follow to help keep your wired network as secure as possible:

✦ **Use the armed guards supplied with Windows XP.** The moment you leave your PC unattended, you're opening the door for anyone else to step up and use it. For this reason, I recommend that you use a screen saver with the password feature enabled. Also, if security is an issue for your network, set Windows XP to require a password login. (You can set this from the Windows XP Control Panel. Click Start⇨Control Panel⇨ User Accounts to display the User Accounts dialog, then click on the Change the way users log on or off link. Disable the Use the Welcome Screen check box, then click Apply Options. From now on, Windows XP will use the classic logon prompt, which is far more secure!)

✦ **Don't share passwords.** In the same vein, do you regularly swap your credit card numbers with friends and relatives? I'm betting that you don't — and you should keep your login and screen saver passwords just as private.

✦ **Monitor your connections.** Are you using an Internet router or Internet sharing device? If so, that device likely has a feature that allows you to see who's connected to your network (typically as part of the DHCP commands). Figure 5-1 illustrates my Internet router's DHCP connection table. Use this feature once a week or so, just to verify that the connections you see listed are the connections you *expected* to see.

✦ **Unplug unnecessary computers.** If a PC doesn't need a connection to your network, why keep it connected at all? Your wired network will run faster with fewer machines, and you've opened a port on your switch or router for future use. (And need I mention that another possible opening to your network has been closed?)

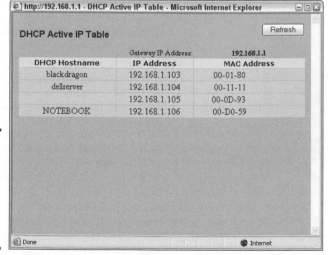

Figure 5-1: Monitoring the machines on my wired Ethernet network.

Ensuring Security on Your Wireless Network

If you're adding a wireless network to your home or office, security should be your first consideration before you send a single packet over the airwaves. First, for those who are currently shopping for wireless hardware, let me list the standards that you should look for:

✦ **Do the WEP.** WEP is blissfully short for *Wired Equivalency Privacy*. It's a form of encryption that acts as your main defense against outside intrusion, as shown in Figure 5-2. Without the proper *key* (or, in human jargon, the proper *password*), a hacker is faced with a decoding job. That's not a hard job because hacker applications are available that will help the bad guys decode WEP, but at least it's a first level of defense. WEP is supported in wireless hardware at several different levels, ranging from 40-bit encryption (a rather weak implementation that might as well be called Diet Protection) to 256-bit (Armor Plated Protection). The 128-bit WEP standard is the most common these days, and it does a creditable job of keeping your data secure. Choose hardware that supports the 128-bit WEP standard whenever possible, and **make sure that WEP is enabled.**

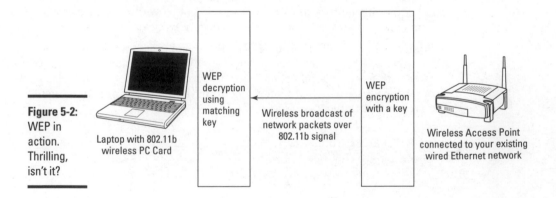

Figure 5-2: WEP in action. Thrilling, isn't it?

Laptop with 802.11b wireless PC Card

WEP decryption using matching key

Wireless broadcast of network packets over 802.11b signal

WEP encryption with a key

Wireless Access Point connected to your existing wired Ethernet network

Make your WEP key as long as allowed by your hardware and also use the same common sense that you use when choosing your Internet passwords. Keys should be completely random. Don't use your middle name or your Social Security number, and remember to mix both letters and numbers together.

✦ **LEAP for security.** Man, these acronyms are such a delight. (If you need an aspirin, I'll understand.) *Lightweight Extensible Authentication Protocol* (LEAP) is also an encryption protocol, but unlike WEP, the key is automatically changed periodically while you're connected, which turns a hacking job from a difficult proposition into a nearly impossible feat. You can specify the time delay before the key changes . . . five minutes ought to do it. (Big grin.) Hardware that offers LEAP is much more expensive than the run-of-the-mill WEP hardware, but for those who need the best possible wireless security, it's the best that you can get.

After you configure your wireless network, here are the security guidelines I recommend that you should follow:

✦ **Use Virtual Private Networking (VPN) for extra security.** As you can read in this chapter, VPN is a hard nut for an outsider to crack. When security is all important, set up a VPN session.

✦ **Secure your SSID.** I know that sounds weird, but your *SSID* is your *Service Set Identifier* — essentially, the name for your WAP or base station. Change your SSID immediately when you install your wireless base station or access point, making sure that you've configured your system so that your SSID is not broadcast to the outside world. (This means that you have to configure your wireless connections manually — your WAP or base station won't show up automatically when your PC is in range.) Determining your SSID is the first step in hacking your wireless network. I guarantee that it'll be practically impossible for an outsider to guess that your SSID is *Bullwinkle007* (or something similar).

✦ **Change your access point/base station password.** Naturally, you also don't want anyone to be able to guess the password that secures your wireless access point or base station, so change that hardware password to something unique.

If anyone asks you to jump in his vehicle for a bit of *war driving,* you'll understand why wireless security is so important. The term refers to hackers who rig up their cars with a laptop PC, equipped with a wireless network card and a cheap omnidirectional antenna, and then drive around neighborhoods in their town looking for unsecured wireless networks. When such an example of easy pickings is found, the hacker can use any broadband connection that's hooked up to that network (read that as *free Internet connection*), or — much worse — haul away copies of the shared files and documents found on that network.

Using Shared Folders (The Right Way)

In Chapter 4 of Book II, I mentioned the Shared Documents folder — any file you store in the Shared Documents folder is immediately available to everyone else using your PC. You can always access your Shared Documents folder from the Windows Explorer task pane.

The contents of your My Documents folder are private — no one else but you can access it, and the files in your My Documents folder are not shared with other PCs across your network. Likewise, the contents of the Shared Documents folder aren't shared across your network, either . . . only among the user accounts on that one PC.

For multiple users sharing only one PC, the Shared Documents folder is the bee's knees: It's already set up as soon as you install Windows XP. But what if you need to share the contents of a folder across the network with other PCs? That's where *shared network folders* come in handy.

I show you how to create a shared network folder in Chapter 2 of this mini-book, so I won't go into the specifics here. Instead, I want to remind you of these three important security guidelines you should follow when using shared folders:

✦ **Never, never, *never* share a folder unless it's necessary!** Remember that Windows XP doesn't differentiate who gets to open what documents when you share a folder — the contents are available to everyone using your network. Perhaps that updated copy of your resume should be withheld from prying eyes. . . .

✦ **Leave the Allow Network Users To Change My Files check box disabled.** By default, this check box is disabled when you create a shared folder . . . and with good reason. Think carefully before you turn this feature on because others will have the ability to edit (or even delete) files in your shared directory. If you'd rather keep these files pristine, leave this check box disabled; that way, other network users will be able to open and print the documents in the folder, but not edit or delete them.

✦ **Use descriptive names for your shared folders.** It just makes good sense — you've got up to 23 characters, so use 'em. I generally create only one shared folder for each PC on a network, and that folder name reflects the PC's network name (like *Shared Folder – Den* or *Shared Folder – Rm 321*), which help you keep track of which shared resources are on which PC.

Why You Need NAT

Okay, you may have heard of NAT (short for *Network Address Translation*). You know that it's probably important, but what does it actually *do?* Well, check out Figure 5-3. If your Internet sharing device (or your Internet sharing software) supports NAT, a number of different PCs — each with a different Internet Protocol (IP) address — are masked behind the single IP address that your ISP assigned to your cable or DSL modem. No one can tell what individual IP addresses are used behind your NAT device.

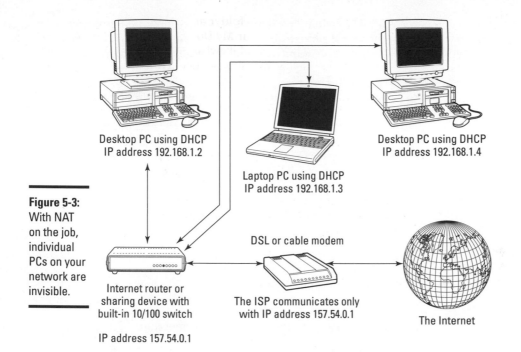

Figure 5-3:
With NAT on the job, individual PCs on your network are invisible.

Desktop PC using DHCP
IP address 192.168.1.2

Laptop PC using DHCP
IP address 192.168.1.3

Desktop PC using DHCP
IP address 192.168.1.4

DSL or cable modem

Internet router or sharing device with built-in 10/100 switch

IP address 157.54.0.1

The ISP communicates only with IP address 157.54.0.1

The Internet

In order to hack a PC on your system, someone on the outside (meaning elsewhere on the Internet) has to know the IP address of an individual computer on your system, and NAT prevents the intruder from learning just that. Instead, the only IP address that's visible is the modem/Internet-sharing device itself. Plus, a NAT blocks the most common weapon in the hacker arsenal: probing "port sniffers" that hunt for open, unprotected ports across the Internet.

Note that NAT isn't a complete firewall. But when your connection-sharing hardware or software uses NAT in conjunction with a commercial firewall program such as Norton Personal Firewall (www.symantec.com), you've effectively shut the door on Internet intruders!

By the way, the built-in XP firewall (which I discuss in Book III, Chapter 3) has NAT built in, naturally.

The Magic of Virtual Private Networking

Imagine if you could take your networking one step farther. Instead of wires or even a wireless network, what if you could create a secure network connection over the Internet into your private network? You'd be able to enjoy the benefits of using your private office network anywhere in the world . . . as long as an Internet connection was handy.

Such is the reality of Virtual Private Networking — and the emphasis, of course, is on the words *private* and *secure*. (It's one thing to have access to your files from across the country, but giving that same access to an interested hacker is another thing entirely.) Your data is protected by encryption when it passes over the Internet; so for all intents and purposes, your connection is as well protected as a correctly configured wireless network.

VPN places you squarely back into the realm of client/server networking, where the VPN *client* is the PC that you're using remotely and the VPN *server* is the machine on the network that you're connecting to. (If you're unsure whether your office network is set up for VPN, ask that dashing system administrator.)

In this section, I demonstrate how to set up your laptop PC (or a remote desktop) as a VPN client under Windows XP, with the following assumptions (based upon how VPN is used most often in real-world situations):

✦ You're using either

• A broadband connection to the Internet

or

• Another company's network Internet connection.

✦ VPN over a dialup connection is the definition of the word *frustrating*, and I don't recommend it.

✦ Your network administrator has provided you the IP address of the VPN server.

✦ You'll use your regular network username and password to log in.

Follow these steps to create and use a VPN connection:

1. **Choose Start⇨All Programs⇨Accessories⇨Communications⇨New Connection Wizard and then click Next on the first wizard screen.**

   The wizard displays the options shown in Figure 5-4.

2. **Select the Connect to the Network at My Workplace radio button and then click Next to continue.**

3. **Select the Virtual Private Network Connection radio button and then click Next to continue.**

4. **Type a descriptive name that will help you keep track of the connection, such as** MLC Books VPN Client, **and then click Next.**

5. **On the wizard screen that you see in Figure 5-5, type the VPN server address provided by your network administrator (such as 157.54.0.1) and then click Next to continue.**

   Note that this can also be in the form of a host name in good ol' English (like *mlcbooks.com*).

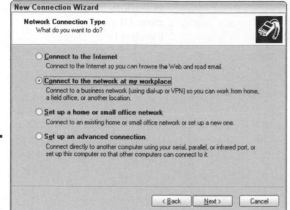

Figure 5-4:
Build a VPN client the wizard way.

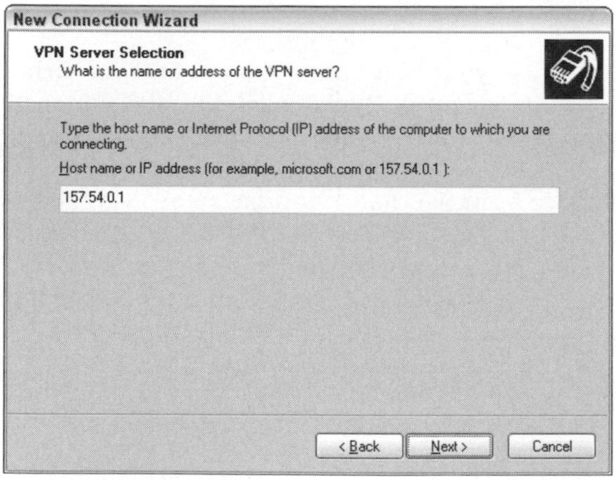

Figure 5-5:
Enter the IP address or host name for a VPN server

6. **If you'd like to add a desktop shortcut for your new VPN connection, select the Add a Shortcut to This Connection to My Desktop check box to enable it.**

7. **Click Finish.**

   XP creates the connection.

If you need to make changes to your VPN connection properties — for example, if your network administrator gets all high and mighty and changes the IP address of the VPN server — choose Start⇨Connect To. From the pop-up menu that appears, right-click your VPN connection and then choose Properties, which will display the VPN Client Properties dialog box that you see in Figure 5-6. From here, you can make any necessary changes.

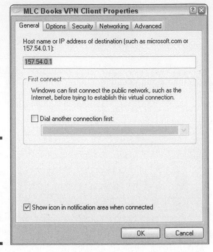

Figure 5-6:
It's easy to
change the
properties
of a VPN
connection.

When you're ready to use your VPN connection — and you're hooked up to
the Internet during your travels — double-click the VPN connection shortcut
on your desktop or choose Start⇨Connect To and then choose the VPN entry.

XP will prompt you for your username and password via the Connect VPN
Client dialog box that you see in Figure 5-7. As always, I'm a bit paranoid
about enabling the Save This User Name and Password for the Following
Users check box because anyone using your (unattended) computer could
simply log on as you. Click the Connect button to begin your VPN session,
and you'll find that you can now access all the network resources that you're
accustomed to on your office PC.

Figure 5-7:
Making
the VPN
connection.

Now tell me that technology ain't grand!

Index

B

G

H

1

S

#

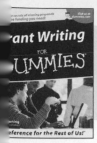

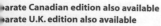

SPORTS, FITNESS, PARENTING, RELIGION & SPIRITUALITY

0-7645-5146-9

0-7645-5418-2

Also available:
- Adoption For Dummies
  0-7645-5488-3
- Basketball For Dummies
  0-7645-5248-1
- The Bible For Dummies
  0-7645-5296-1
- Buddhism For Dummies
  0-7645-5359-3
- Catholicism For Dummies
  0-7645-5391-7
- Hockey For Dummies
  0-7645-5228-7

- Judaism For Dummies
  0-7645-5299-6
- Martial Arts For Dummies
  0-7645-5358-5
- Pilates For Dummies
  0-7645-5397-6
- Religion For Dummies
  0-7645-5264-3
- Teaching Kids to Read For Dumm
  0-7645-4043-2
- Weight Training For Dummies
  0-7645-5168-X
- Yoga For Dummies
  0-7645-5117-5

TRAVEL

0-7645-5438-7

0-7645-5453-0

Also available:
- Alaska For Dummies
  0-7645-1761-9
- Arizona For Dummies
  0-7645-6938-4
- Cancún and the Yucatán For Dummies
  0-7645-2437-2
- Cruise Vacations For Dummies
  0-7645-6941-4
- Europe For Dummies
  0-7645-5456-5
- Ireland For Dummies
  0-7645-5455-7

- Las Vegas For Dummies
  0-7645-5448-4
- London For Dummies
  0-7645-4277-X
- New York City For Dummies
  0-7645-6945-7
- Paris For Dummies
  0-7645-5494-8
- RV Vacations For Dummies
  0-7645-5443-3
- Walt Disney World & Orlando For Dum
  0-7645-6943-0

GRAPHICS, DESIGN & WEB DEVELOPMENT

0-7645-4345-8

0-7645-5589-8

Also available:
- Adobe Acrobat 6 PDF For Dummies
  0-7645-3760-1
- Building a Web Site For Dummies
  0-7645-7144-3
- Dreamweaver MX 2004 For Dummies
  0-7645-4342-3
- FrontPage 2003 For Dummies
  0-7645-3882-9
- HTML 4 For Dummies
  0-7645-1995-6
- Illustrator CS For Dummies
  0-7645-4084-X

- Macromedia Flash MX 2004 For Dum
  0-7645-4358-X
- Photoshop 7 All-in-One Desk
  Reference For Dummies
  0-7645-1667-1
- Photoshop CS Timesaving Techniqu
  For Dummies
  0-7645-6782-9
- PHP 5 For Dummies
  0-7645-4166-8
- PowerPoint 2003 For Dummies
  0-7645-3908-6
- QuarkXPress 6 For Dummies
  0-7645-2593-X

NETWORKING, SECURITY, PROGRAMMING & DATABASES

0-7645-6852-3

0-7645-5784-X

Also available:
- A+ Certification For Dummies
  0-7645-4187-0
- Access 2003 All-in-One Desk
  Reference For Dummies
  0-7645-3988-4
- Beginning Programming For Dummies
  0-7645-4997-9
- C For Dummies
  0-7645-7068-4
- Firewalls For Dummies
  0-7645-4048-3
- Home Networking For Dummies
  0-7645-42796

- Network Security For Dummies
  0-7645-1679-5
- Networking For Dummies
  0-7645-1677-9
- TCP/IP For Dummies
  0-7645-1760-0
- VBA For Dummies
  0-7645-3989-2
- Wireless All In-One Desk Reference
  For Dummies
  0-7645-7496-5
- Wireless Home Networking For Dumm
  0-7645-3910-8